For Carol Ann Corrody
—D.G.I.

To Gina Masucci MacKenzie,
whose dedication
to the life of the mind
continues to inspire me
—D.O.

Henry James Against the Aesthetic Movement

Essays on the Middle and Late Fiction

EDITED BY DAVID GARRETT IZZO
AND DANIEL T. O'HARA

McFarland & Company, Inc., Publishers
Jefferson, North Carolina, and London

Editorial assistance by
Ganina Lagodsky

LIBRARY OF CONGRESS CATALOGUING-IN-PUBLICATION DATA

Henry James against the aesthetic movement : essays on the middle
and late fiction / edited by David Garrett Izzo and Daniel T.
O'Hara.
    p.   cm.
Includes bibliographical references and index.

ISBN-13: 978-0-7864-2578-5
ISBN-10: 0-7864-2578-4 (softcover : 50# alkaline paper) ∞

1. James, Henry, 1843–1916—Criticism and interpretation.
I. Izzo, David Garrett.   II. O'Hara, Daniel T., 1948–
PS2124H436   2006
813'.4—dc22   2006009588

British Library cataloguing data are available

Cover photograph: Henry James, c.1894 (Library of Congress)

Manufactured in the United States of America

McFarland & Company, Inc., Publishers
  Box 611, Jefferson, North Carolina 28640
  www.mcfarlandpub.com

Acknowledgments

David Garrett Izzo: Carol Ann Corrody, Martin Blank, and Dan O'Hara, who treated me like a colleague even before I was one.

Dan O'Hara: There are many people I could thank, but two in particular deserve special mention here: David Garrett Izzo, for his friendship, good humor, and passionate expertise in modern literature; and Gina Masucci MacKenzie, also for these things, and something else that I have come to know well from working with her over several years now—her critical courage.

Table of Contents

IV. Issues of Representation: Art and Fiction

V. Decadence, Identity, and Homosexuality

Introduction

DANIEL T. O'HARA

When I began rereading Henry James's 1902 novel *The Wings of the Dove* for the introduction to this collection of essays, a friend of mine, Gina MacKenzie, reminded me of one of the features of his late style that I tend to forget, which is the confusion over pronoun references. In one of his long sentences, or even longer paragraphs, the antecedents of pronouns often get lost, as the syntactic unit moves quickly yet *fully* on. James's late style, of course, is notorious for its weight, not to say its occasional ponderousness, but its embedded subordinations, elaborate subjunctive conjectures, and involved twists and turns are usually rendered, surprisingly enough, in a speedy, almost breathless manner, moving in a virtual rush, as if the narrator were carrying a large trunk in his arms and had to finish his say before he dropped the trunk. Often, too, the reader is not sure where the narrator may be going with his, and now the reader's, shared (and headlong) burden.

James's late style also is often said to have resulted, in part, from his having to switch from direct composition to dictation due to his increasingly arthritic wrist on his writing hand. Whatever the reason for its adoption by James, the late style, it is clear, does make for confusions of the sort just mentioned, as well as for greater impressions of obscurity, because of the nature of the metaphors and other figures James uses to distinguish and connect his characters. These figures are most like metaphysical conceits that are at times bizarrely original but at others, like corny jokes, deliberately pathetic (and so comically if self-consciously "lame") elaborations of dead metaphors or other nearly invisible "poetical" sayings. Since *The Wings of the Dove* is the first of the big last completed novels to be published, we can catch the late style as if in the act of being born. I will look

1

closely at a passage from it to analyze this style's characteristic features. First, however, I will offer an admittedly speculative theoretical framework for trying to understand James's late style as a whole, which is representative of the aesthetic decadence.

I begin with a passage from Sigmund Freud's *Totem and Taboo* (1913), in which he explains the confluence of feelings attached to the rituals of primitive forms of religion:

> Satisfaction over the triumph [over the primal father via his murder by the sons] led to the institution of the memorial festival of the totem meal, in which the *restrictions* of deferred obedience no longer held. Thus it became a duty to *repeat* the crime of parricide again and again in the *sacrifice* of the totem animal, whenever, as a result of the changing conditions of life, the cherished fruit of the crime—appropriations of the paternal attributes—threatened to disappear. We shall not be surprised to find that *the element of filial rebelliousness* also emerges, in the later products of religions, often in the strangest disguises and transformations [145 (emphasis added)].

We see condensed into a single paragraph Freud's entire theory of the origins of religion and culture. Admittedly, it is a fabulous tale, and Freud himself, in *Group Psychology and the Analysis of the Ego* (1922), refers to it as his "scientific myth of the primal father" (136).

Once upon a time, the sons of the primal human horde's tyrannical father rose up together against him for his monopolizing of all the women and thus reducing the sons to occasional homosexuality and permanent adolescence. They murdered him and ate him, attempting thereby to assimilate those qualities of his with which they had strongly if ambivalently identified. Thereafter, in times of crisis, in the war of each against all and all against each that necessarily followed, the estranged brothers longed for the father's return, for under his often cruelly self-regarding rule, there had at least been a comparative, albeit frustrating, peace. Eventually, however, when the father did not return, and no brother was strong enough to permanently assume his father's role, the brothers established the reign of totemism. They would agree to share the women, and promote exogamy for their posterity, so that their sons would leave the horde to set up their own families elsewhere with the women they brought or found there. A memorial sacrifice of the totem animal representing the father would mark this agreement.

After this, as other difficulties arose, the longing for the father returned in even greater strength, and both the act of his overcoming and the brothers' deferred obedience to his imperatives would be struggling to return. By establishing the sacrifice of the totem animal and the totem meal in common as a festival, however, the brothers thereby commemorated the father's death and his spiritual return, and so could relieve the terrible stresses of their chronic anxieties. The real father may be dead, but the symbolic father's power now was more alive then ever before. This founding symbolic pact of the commemorative festival, with its inherent logic of sacrifice, guilt and expiation, then became the ironic, not to say often tragic, basis of human civilization.

Julia Kristeva, in *The Sense and Non-Sense of Revolt* (2000), uses Freud's theory of cultural origins to elaborate upon her earlier use of what in *The Ego and the Id* (1923) Freud terms "the imaginary father of individual prehistory" (13). Kristeva argues that behind the scrim of the primal horde and father, of the subsequent ironically celebratory expiation of the brotherhood, lies, for the individual and the collective life alike, the real and imagined experience of the child with the mother (*SN*, 21). Basing herself upon Melanie Klein's work in "Envy and Gratitude" (1947), Kristeva points to an original emotional response characteristic of this formative relationship between mother and child that the commemorative festival of the brothers would recapture (*SN*, 81). Although Kristeva does not identify this emotion, Klein (as I was again reminded by Gina MacKenzie) does, and Klein refers to it as the mother and child's "mutual reverie" (*EG*, 57). I would like to tweak this formulation just a bit, by introducing one word between mother and child that captures more precisely the tone characteristic of such a state, and that word is: "excited." I do so because Klein's term is referring to the creative play of signs of love, acts of care, and reciprocal vocalizations that mother and child engage in as the child learns to daydream, and so to imagine *with the other*, not in a condition of isolated desire and ultimate disappointment when the hallucinated fulfillment is not forthcoming, but in a state of serene and generative contentment, from which a generous jubilation may spread like the rings in a pool after even the tiniest of leaves falls and touches its shimmering surface.

"Mutual excited reverie," then, is the fundamental distinctive feeling encompassing mother and child and underlying the commemorative festival informing the productions and institutions of culture. It is this feeling that the brothers wish to get back to, and it is both a sign of their continuing oedipal condition, at least in fantasy, and their longed-for childlike relationship to the father and with each other, what (thanks to Eve Kosofsky Sedgwick's *Between Men: English Literature and Homosocial Desire* [1993]) can be seen as their culturally productive homosociality. This feeling of "mutually excited reverie" is the aesthetic basis of socially symbolic acts that go beyond, or are apparently different from, festivals, ancient or modern. These acts are textual or creative acts in the broadest sense and, in literature especially, style and form are keys to appreciating and understanding them. "Mutual excited reverie," in other words, is the affect of original creation, and the founding basis of art and aesthetics, which operates most obviously in the symbolic pacts and commemorative rites of culture, but it is also the imaginative, affective substratum of the artwork.

Besides the risk of overgeneralization, this formulation runs the risk of forgetting something important, the most nagging question that naturally arises at this point: "What mutuality can exist in the spectator's or reader's response to a work?" Here is where a rather figurative extension of an aesthetic concept of "mutually excited reverie" is required. Once again, Gina MacKenzie has suggested an important idea: that in the artist's relationship to the work—in its creative conception, often hard gestation, and subsequent careful revision—we may find the initial imaginative recapturing of the experience of "mutual excited reverie." I do not think it is too farfetched to see in the writer's experience with the formation of the text the fundamental example of what Jacques Lacan in his late work on James Joyce calls "the sinthome," by which Lacan means, according to Roberto Harari's reading of the final Lacan in *How James Joyce Made His Name*, the artistically transformed and now aesthetically enjoyed symptomatic behavior of the writer that imaginatively supplements the faulty structure of the writer's psyche and so avoids any psychotic breaks with reality. This initial experience of imaginative mutuality between writer and text is then repeated between, and imaginatively produced and sustained by, the reciprocal performances of writer and reader in the unfolding of the text between them. Insofar as an emotional intuition or knowledge is transferred between these poles of the reading experience of literature, then the power of "mutually excited reverie" can be realized in the equally creative processes of composition and reading. Writer and reader, then, can become for each other their own imaginary fathers and mothers, brothers and sisters in an imaginative community of emotionally (as well as cognitively) informed literary subjects whose deliberative critical reflections are necessarily imbued with potential social import. Unlike the modern neurotic personality who, Freud claims, lives in total alienation and isolation and so must symptomatically reproduce in and through his own body all the affective experiences of social institutions or the very reality from which he is taking flight by becoming ill, the sublimating artist and his audience may enjoy to the fullest, even under the constraints of modernity, the surprising prodigy of this mutually creative imagination, a prodigy we may best name "Eros" (*GPAE*, 142).

Admittedly, this is a highly romantic and idealistic notion, reminding me of such passages (among many others) as Wordsworth's from the preface to the *Lyrical Ballads* (second edition, 1800) where he claims that "the poet always brings with him relationship and love," especially when he does not at first find it in society, and so must habitually create it. Thus, "poetry" is ever, Wordsworth also declares, "the finer spirit," the smiling "face" of modern science and knowledge (*PLB*, 425). Perhaps so.

Henry James's late style, that characteristic style of the Victorian aesthetic decadence, is, in fact, as all the essays in this collection demonstrate in their different ways, the creative imagination of "mutual excited reverie," a propitious renewal of the spirit of modernity, and not simply a powerful sign of its possibly interminable ending.

The following passage comes from, as promised, *The Wings of the Dove*. The plot of this novel is melodramatic, to be sure. Kate Croy and her secret lover, Merton Densher, do not have enough money to get married. Kate's Aunt Maud, however, is wealthy but wants Kate to marry up—specifically, to Lord Mark, the aunt's noble hanger-on. Susan Shepherd Stringham, Aunt Maud's old school friend, introduces into this set her discovery, Milly Theale, a rich American heiress who, we learn, is dying from a mysterious unnamed disease. Kate conceives a perfect design: she will let her lover woo the dying maiden with the aim of her shortly leaving him most, if not all, of her money.

This melodramatic plot supports three kinds of points of view and appropriately matched sets of generic conventions, so that Kate's perspective appears in the reductive discourse of naturalism, Milly's in the symbolic discourse of romance, and Merton's, the least formed of these three protagonists, in the latest, impressionistic discourse of James's modern consciousness. It is as if James lends Densher his own creative and critical consciousness in the sense that Densher, like James, comes to see Milly and Kate as two sides of the same coin of femininity, the hard London girl, and the self-consciously odd yet still spontaneously generous American princess. Moreover, like James's impressionistic narrative style, Densher's consciousness, even as it gains a conscience about his role in Kate's plot, acts like the fiery ambience in which this coin of femininity, with its two sides of the head of Milly and the tail of Kate, is being forged. Additionally, the production and proliferation of extended and innovative conceits and motifs form the skein that attempts to tie, not always successfully, all of these elements together into a single coherent text.

The passage comes from the first chapter of Book Four of the novel's Volume One. The two volumes are like the novel's symbolic embodiment of the enfolding wings of its dove Milly. This passage deals with Milly and Susan Shepherd Stringham's first, generally romantic and symbolic impressions of Kate Croy:

> While, for this first week that followed their dinner, she drank deep at Lancaster Gate, her companion was no less happily, appeared to be indeed on the whole quite as romantically, provided for. The handsome English girl from the heavy English house had been as a figure in a picture stepping by magic out of its frame: it was a case in truth for which Mrs. Stringham presently found the perfect image. She had lost none of her grasp, but quite the contrary, of that other conceit in virtue of which Milly was the wandering princess: so what could be more in harmony now than to see the princess waited upon at the city gate by the worthiest maiden, the chosen daughter of the burgesses? It was the real again, evidently, the amusement of the meeting for the princess too; princesses living for the most part in such an appeased way, on the plane of mere elegant representation. That was why they pounced, at city gates, on deputed flower-strewing damsels; that was why, after effigies, processions, and other stately games, frank human company was pleasant to them. Kate Croy really presented herself to Milly—the latter abounded for Mrs. Stringham in accounts of it—as the wondrous London girl in person (by what she had conceived, from far back, of the London girl; conceived from the tales of travelers and the anecdotes of New York, from old porings over *Punch* and a liberal acquaintance with the fiction of the day). The only thing was that she was nicer, since the creature in question had rather been, to our young woman, an image of dread. She had thought her, at her best, as handsome just as Kate was, with turns of head and tones of voice, felicities of stature and attitude, things "put on" and, for that matter, put off, all the marks of the product of a packet society who should be at the same time the heroine of a strong story. She placed this striking young person from the first in a story, saw her, by a necessity of the imagination, for a heroine, felt it the only character in which she wouldn't be wasted; and this in spite of the heroine's pleasant abruptness, her forbearance from gush, her umbrellas and jackets and shoes—as these things sketched themselves to Milly—and something rather of a breezy boy in the carriage of her arms and the occasional freedom of her slang [164–165].

Gina MacKenzie is certainly on target about the confusion of pronoun references! On a first and quick reading, can anyone follow the references correctly? But the reason for this initial confusion is more important to explore than it might at first appear because it highlights how the narrative perspective in this paragraph flits from Milly—although even looking back at the previous paragraph (not reproduced) does not immediately help to determine definitively the consciousness we are first tasting—to Susan to Milly to Susan again, and finally back, with more certainty, to Milly in the end. Similarly, the object of their "mutual excited reverie," Kate Croy, receives a series of identifications, all of which fit the symbolic discourse of romance, but which also blur Kate's sharper features, so much so that from Milly's (and presumably Susan's) point of view Kate, like Milly herself, must be a heroine in a "strong story," otherwise she would be wasted. (Whether this "strong story" would also be as romantic as the fairy tale she and Susan feel they live in, or otherwise, is not clear.) Finally, and most significantly, this "mutual excited reverie" shared by Susan and Milly, over Kate, and presumably their narrator-author and, in James's intention, also the reader, desexualizes Kate; or rather, as the quick albeit weighty spurts of the narrative perspective turns Kate from "the handsome girl" into the more neutral "person," it also transforms her, perhaps with some of her female attributes still intact and thanks to the unique "carriage of her arms and the occasional freedom of her slang," into "something rather of a breezy boy." The logic of sacrifice underlying any "mutual excited reverie" or, rather, the path to such an aesthetic resurgence of the archaic feelings underlying civilization, requires the sacrifice of Kate's given gender identity so as to make her first into a neutral "person" and then into "a breezy boy," with or without any of her female gender traits trailing the clouds of gloriously crimson ribbons.

I think we can draw a tentative conclusion from this passage, which foregrounds James's late style so well, viz, that the hallmark of the aesthetic decadence, indeed of the aesthetic experience itself, may be best conceived as the creative resurgence of the archaic dimension, both in individual and cultural terms.

The essays herein will discuss James's style and his various reactions to the new British Aestheticism (and decadence) of the late Victorian period. James interpreted the English upper class and their—to him—decadent morality and attitude through his writings.

In a critical context, coeditor **David Garrett Izzo** leads off with "The Henry James Revival of the 1930s." He considers the fact—surprising, in light of James's present stature—that James once fell so low in the esteem of scholars that only by concerted effort in the 1930s was his reputation redeemed. Why did he go out of favor, and why did he come back in?

A selective overview of men and women follows with two Italian scholars (James has his fervent following in Italian academia)—first **Maurizio Ascari** with a study of three of James's male aesthetes. Although James's attitude to the aesthetic movement was extremely cautious, his novels and stories include various portraits of aesthetes, such as Gilbert Osmond in *The Portrait of a Lady*, Mark Ambient in "The Author of 'Beltraffio'" and Gabriel Nash in *The Tragic Muse*. After briefly analyzing the early stages of the aesthetic adventure, the essay goes on to deal with these three characters, who subvert the concepts of cultural, national and gender identity. Due to his tendency to turn human beings into items to add to the collection of objects that frame his elusive identity, the Italianate Osmond enabled James to explore the dark side of the aesthetic movement. On the other hand, by means of Ambient and Nash—who draw their flair for art from a dynamic intermediate space between cultures—James called the identity of the English gentleman into question, exploring the borderline between gentlemanliness and genius (Ambient) and creating the epitome of the itinerant aesthete (Nash).

Women are next in **Donatella Izzo**'s "Killing Mothers: Decadent Women in James's Literary Tales." James's stories of writers have been mostly read in terms of male-male relations, whether in the form of an exclusive dedication to art (coded as a male profession) or of a homoaesthetic and homoerotic desire. Women are thus doubly rejected, both as objects of desire and as representatives of the bourgeois world that the artist needs to repudiate if he is to be true to his aesthetic calling. This essay attempts to probe the function of women as characters and readers in the complex nexus created by aestheticism and homoeroticism. An analysis of the textual representation of the two women characters in "The Author of 'Beltraffio'" attempts to show that James's story represents women as, in fact, deeply involved in the aesthetic sphere on several levels. By self-consciously foregrounding the operation of women's rejection from the world of art, the story undermines the dichotomous gender arrangement that regulates both the social and the aesthetic sphere.

Contemporaneous connections start with **Ascari**'s second essay. Max Beerbohm's celebrated parody of Henry James's manner—"The Mote in the Middle Distance"—is far from being his only act of homage to the Master. Thanks to his versatile talent, Beerbohm celebrated James also through several caricatures and poems, as well as some delightfully unreliable biographical anecdotes like "The Guerdon" and "An Incident." Moreover, in an essay titled "Books within Books," he dared to intimate that the Master himself was not exempt from the sin of forgery, although of a peculiar kind. For James's stories of artists and writers are often focused on brilliant pictorial and literary works of art which can be regarded as pieces of illusionism. James did not go so far as to try thematic forgery or to lament the decay of lying, as Wilde did, but stopped on the brink of this attitude, mingling truth and its alternatives, thus achieving—mainly through irony—a peculiar balance between nineteenth century realism and fin de siècle aestheticism.

Solveig C. Robinson's "'At All Times Conspicuous as Art': Henry James, Margaret Oliphant, and Resistance to Decadence" notes that, although they are seldom discussed in relation to one another, Henry James's and Margaret Oliphant's professional careers and critical stances share striking parallels. Despite her greater conservatism, Oliphant (1828–1897) serves as a useful gloss on James's resistance to Victorian Decadence. Oliphant's critical personae during the late 1880s to mid–1890s were masculine and urbane, aligning her with aestheticism even as she critiqued it. Her efforts to champion naturalness in artistic expression support and illuminate key themes in James's criticism of the same period.

Issues of representation in art and fiction follow with four essays: **Sheila Teahan**'s "The Face of Decadence in *The Sacred Fount*" is an allegory of figuration, especially prosopopoeia and anastomosis. Prosopopoeia, which entails the attribution of a face to an inanimate object, is explored in an important passage whose description of a painting constitutes a *mise en abyme* of the novel. Anastomosis, a hydraulic trope that undoes the distinctions between inside and outside, container and contained, corresponds to the narrator's controlling metaphor of the fount. Focusing on the theme of portraiture, the essay considers *The Sacred Fount*'s relation to the aesthetic topos of the encounter of the self with the work of art.

Andrea Cabus-Coldwell sees the title character in *The Princess Casamassima* through the refracted prism of Walter Pater's *Renaissance* essays in "Figuring the Princess: *The Princess Casamassima* and Pater's Mona Lisa." Critics of his work are quick to point out James's struggles throughout his career with the Paterian aesthetic. James ultimately attempted to strike a compromise between his approval of Pater's ideas as an artistic way of perceiving life and reading people and his dissatisfaction with their implications if used as a guide to leading one's life in place of traditional morality. Regardless of his final evaluation, however, James's attempt to come to terms with aestheticism is visible throughout his work, most clearly through the various characters who profess aspects of aesthetic theory.

Mark Conroy's essay, "On Not Representing Milly Theale: Sacrificing for Art in *The Wings of the Dove*," engages how James takes the projects of the novel's three central characters—Milly Theale, Kate Croy, and

Merton Densher—as embodying the relation of economic and aesthetic spheres. Milly makes use of her wealth to overcome her pressing mortality by transmogrifying herself into a beautiful image; whereas Kate, from the opposite angle, uses her talent for appearance (her own beauty and her lover Densher's ability to make love to the dying Milly) to accrue money. It is, however, Densher's ultimate aesthetic project that raises the essay's other thesis: that Constance Fenimore Woolson is at least as critical to the probable inspiration for novel as that favorite of conventional wisdom, James's cousin Minnie Temple.

Our third Italian scholar is **Vittoria Intonti**, in whose essay "The Figure in the Carpet" is read as a representation not so much of an objective reality outside the text, (or not only that) as of the communicative situation of literary discourse itself, with its three main actants: the author, the reader and the message to be interpreted. The essay illustrates how, once the very existence of a "figure" to be found in the carpet/text is put into question by the first-person narrator himself, the ambiguity or double-binding of the story forces the reader to question his own role as interpreter at textual and metatexual levels.

The next section covers decadence, identity, and homosexuality. **James Fisher**'s essay examines images of decadence and questions of morality in Henry James's *Washington Square* and Oscar Wilde's *An Ideal Husband*. The characters of James's novels and Wilde's plays might not at first seem comparable or compatible; certainly the tone of their works is markedly dissimilar, even if the whiff of social satire, the central paradigm of Wilde's comedy, is also present in James's writing. Moral decay, and perhaps its inevitability, is a central conception that connects them. James and Wilde display aspects of Victorian literary decadence in their individual representations of privileged young men of means (or in search of means) maintaining a façade of social propriety masking calculated amorality.

For **Robert Combs** it seems part of Henry James's fate to be haunted by Oscar Wilde. From the time of their first meeting in Washington, D.C., in 1882, when Wilde piqued James by responding to his solicitous sincerity ("I am very homesick for London") with an aphorism ("Realism? You care for places? The World is my home"), James repeatedly experienced Wilde's flamboyance, his notoriety, his success in the theatre—perhaps even his very existence—as potentially overwhelming. Surely a deeply personal— though perhaps we could add a deeply philosophical—anxiety underlay James's overreaction to the triumphs and tragedies of Oscar Wilde.

Stephen da Silva, in "Papa, Postcards, Perfume, Phallic Keys: James,

Symonds, and Late–Victorian Fictions of Homosexuality," reads "The Author of 'Beltraffio,'" and beyond that tale itself, to see the limited but complex and ambivalent relationship between James and the late–Victorian homosexual apologist John Addington Symonds, who is represented as the writer Mark Ambient in the tale.

David Garrett Izzo will round out the collection with a pair of afterwords: "The Disappearing Act of Gabriel Nash, or How His 'Wilde-ness' Got the Better of Him," and "Walter Pater: From *Renaissance* to Mysticism in *Marius the Epicurean*."

The Henry James Revival of the 1930s

DAVID GARRETT IZZO

Without exception ... the characters in Henry James are concerned with moral choices; they may choose evil, but we are left in no doubt about the importance of choosing it.

W. H. Auden

Considering the stature of Henry James in the canon of American and English literature today, one might find it difficult to imagine that he ever had less than a stellar position in the hierarchy of writers. Yet, at one time, James was not only less than exalted but nearly in eclipse to the degree that in the mid 1930s he required a concerted effort to mount a revival for his literary reputation. Even as recently as 1993, Hilton Kramer felt the need to write in the *New Criterion* that, indeed, the revival had been a success: "This is a happy fate for a writer who, in the last years of his long literary labors, when his market had dwindled and a new generation of writers had taken to ridiculing his style, had ample reason to wonder if his work would enjoy any posterity at all." By 2003, his posterity is a given and no one is debating James's rank in the canon even if some disagree with the placement. (Kramer: "Thus, even James's enemies pay him the homage of wishing to distort his achievement. That, too, is immortality of a kind" [online]). In 1934, however, placement was not an issue, as he almost had no place. Yes, in the 1920s there were stubborn holdouts who would not let him be eviscerated completely—among them Eliot and Pound—but the voices were too few. To James's rescue came upstart writers and critics who were, if one can even imagine this, outré rebels for taking up James's cause.

Leon Edel wrote his first book on James in 1931 but was not yet *The* James critic and influence he would become in later decades. Instead, the initial charge was led by future New York dance impresario Lincoln Kirstein and by Briton Stephen Spender. With the former's literary magazine *The Hound & Horn* and the latter's book *The Destructive Element* (1935) as mediums, a revival of a champion was championed. One must account for the reasons for James's temporary banishment, and chronicle the surge of the rebels for his reinstatement.

James died in 1916 and few noticed, especially in America. To a large degree this was personal, as James, in his last year, became a British subject, thus substantiating what many felt was his rejection of America, from which he had removed himself for most of his adult life. A second substantial factor was the emergence in the 1910s and 1920s of Dreiser, Lewis, Hemingway, Fitzgerald, and their many contemporaries, with their more direct prose and portrayals of a variety of American types rather than only the moneyed socialites of Wharton and James. One of the most respected and well-read critics of the 1920s, Van Wyck Brooks, himself now eclipsed, wrote *The Pilgrimage of Henry James* (1925), with the title a deliberate stab at James's antipathy toward the land of his birth, and in which he declared that James was not an American writer at all but, in effect, a snob, whose later books were "Magnificent pretensions, petty performances!—the fruits of an irresponsible imagination, of a deranged sense of values, of a mind working in a void, uncorrected by any clear consciousness of human cause and effect" (134).

Damning—yet, in retrospect, tinged with the personal vitriol of one who resents a family member who seemed to turn against his family while the other family members (Dreiser, et al.) were doing very well, thank you, writing about family doings. Moreover, the 1930s leftist and proletarian inclinations also worked against James, who seemed to have written only about the faults of the bourgeois, thus proving that the bourgeois needed to go and James along with them.

Nonetheless, there were still some James supporters. A number of them were in England either as native Britons or expatriates and they, as could be expected, did not view James in the same manner as Brooks, etc. James, in fact, had chosen to be one of them, which must have seemed to them, in contrast to American critics, a sign of intelligence.

Kramer's essay gives credit to the emergence of the New Criticism that could be read in *The Hound & Horn* as an impetus for a James reappraisal, in part; but one could also argue that the admiration of James by the leaders of the Auden Generation—Auden, Spender, and Christopher Isherwood—

HOUND & HORN

Henry James

APRIL : JUNE 1934   ONE DOLLAR

The literary magazine *Hound & Horn* helped start a Henry James revival.

who praised James in the early 1930s—also helped James. This meant mainly Spender and Auden, who were both, however, deeply influenced by Isherwood, their elder by five and three years respectively. Isherwood was much influenced by the author and family friend, Ethel Colburn Mayne, whom he calls "Venus" in his biography of his parents, *Kathleen and Frank* (1967).

(When Isherwood wrote *Kathleen and Frank* he considered it a Jamesian period piece.)

Isherwood said of her in 1954: "Ethel Mayne came to London from Ireland in the 'nineties. Her first publications (under a pseudonym) were in the volumes of *The Yellow Book* for '95 and '96; daintily breathless tales spiced with bits of French and with words put between quotation marks to indicate some exquisite shade of meaning utterly beyond the reach of the barbarous English tongue. She became skilled at writing the fashionable, neo–[Henry] Jamesian kind of dialogue that resembled championship tennis: two participants exchanging shots of impossibly oblique repartee throughout a rally of half a dozen pages" (249). Mayne was Isherwood's first mentor and he read James at her urging and continued to admire him thereafter. (In a 1955 *Diary* entry Isherwood is quite pleased to record that a hotel he stayed at in Venice was the very same James occupied during his frequent visits there, and Isherwood's very dear friend Dodie Smith [Beesley] loved James and wrote her 1949 play *Letter from Paris* as adapted from James's novella *The Reverberator*.)

Auden, the first of the trio to become famous, also admired James. Auden always said that his prose poem "Caliban to the Audience," his late James imitation from *The Sea and the Mirror*, was his favorite effort in any genre, whether verse, drama, or essay. James also makes an important appearance in "New Year Letter" (1940) and Auden critic and executor Edward Mendelson writes, "Henry James, the American who in Auden's version of literary history first portrayed a world in which all acts that matter are invisible inward ones, begins to rise to the heroic stature he maintained in Auden's thought for the next half decade" (232). The poem "At the Grave of Henry James" (1941) is another sympathetic parody, as was "Caliban to the Audience," portraying James as a secular saint from whom an artist can learn. Even with Auden and Isherwood's admiration, however, it was Spender who initially took action in the James revival.

Spender's first books of poems, stories, and criticism would not be published until 1933 and 1935 respectively. They were, however, written from 1927 forward while he was befriending Isherwood and Auden. Before his art was published, Spender was writing book reviews. One of his earliest, written in 1932, is a review of Desmond MacCarthy's *Portraits*, which was MacCarthy's recollections of public figures he had known, one of whom was James. Spender quotes MacCarthy, who "knew James personally." The choice of the quotation tells as much about Spender as it does of Henry James:

> It occurred after a luncheon party of which he had been, as they say, "the life." We happened to be drinking our coffee together while the rest of the party had moved on to the verandah. [James said] "What a charming picture they make...." In his attitude ... I divined such a complete detachment, that I was startled into speaking out of myself: "I can't bear to look at life like that.... I want to be in everything. Perhaps that is why I cannot *write* [fiction], it makes me feel absolutely alone." The effect of this confession on him was surprising.... "Yes, it is solitude. If it runs after you and catches you, well and good. But for heaven's sake, don't run after *it*. It is absolute solitude" [554–57].

MacCarthy's sense of a "complete detachment" in James sounds like the cypher-witness approach to writing that Spender, Isherwood, and Auden practiced in their early work, which is one of passive observation to be undertaken in an "absolute solitude." This does not mean physical solitude, but rather a solitude that reflects the inner detachment of the private sphere in order to observe the public chaos. More importantly, while the writer observes outwardly from within this sanctuary of inner solitude, he understands that each person observed in a public role also has an inner life that is separate from his outer life. From this perspective Spender regarded James as the first modern novelist. (As regards the solitary observation of another's duality, James cited Hawthorne as the first modern writer.)

Spender began corresponding with Kirstein in the early 1930s and would do reviews for *The Hound & Horn*. In the letters, the cause of James is an issue. When Spender's first volume of verse, *Poems* (1933), was well received and made him a new voice to be reckoned with, one of his first undertakings was to give James his due in a critical study he began in 1933 but that would not be published until 1935, or shortly after *The Hound & Horn* Henry James issue. Hence, Spender's essay in the James issue was a segment of a greater consideration that would follow. Yet there is no question that the initial bell for the first round of the James revival was sounded by *The Hound & Horn*, which in previous issues had contributors such as James Joyce, T. S. Eliot, and Paul Valéry. In fact, when Kirstein started *The Hound & Horn* he set out to emulate Eliot's *Criterion*.

The contributors to this issue were all well-known at the time and many are still renowned today: Marianne Moore, Edmund Wilson, Spender, R. P. Blackmur, John Wheelwright, Newton Arvin, Glenway Wescott, Lawrence Leighton, Francis Fergusson, Edna Kenton, H. R. Hays, and Robert Cantwell. Kramer writes of these revivalists, "It was in the name of art ... that the James revival was initiated by writers who, upon rediscovering this native master for themselves, felt an acute sense of loss at his rejection by philistine opinion. Clearly, their own literary aspirations were felt to be implicated in the rehabilitation of a writer who, in the reach of his aesthetic ambition and his remarkable consistency in realizing it, might serve as a model of future achievement" (online). Rebelliousness was not a small aspect of this revolt against the philistines as the new wave (in the manner of new waves before and since) rejected their immediate precursors by rejecting what these antecedents had accepted and—in James's case—accepting what they rejected.

The Hound & Horn (title from a line in Pound's poem "The White Stag")[1] began in 1927 while founding editor Lincoln Kirstein was at Harvard. He was joined by coeditors Varian Fry and Bernard Bandler.[2] In 1930, the magazine moved from Boston to New York and took on a national identity. The magazine began with a literary intent but over time found that literature could not be separated from the rampant politics of the period and it was, according to Kirstein, in his foreword to The Hound & Horn Letters, the politics, in which he had little interest, that prompted the demise of his venture, although he made sure the James issue was published. The brief editorial that precedes this issue was titled "Homage to Henry James 1843–1916."

> In expressing its admiration for Henry James, The Hound & Horn does itself and its contributors great honor, for there is no American artist who can serve as such an admirable point of departure for an inquest into the present condition of our literature. An attempt has been made to illuminate the several facets of his genius as they have attracted individual writers who have felt the pressure of his influence. As a whole this tribute comes from a younger generation who, as yet, have not expressed their gratitude to the novelist [xi].

The intent is to praise, which at the time, for these writers, was to buck against the tide and smack their recent elders. Here is the table of contents: "James as a Characteristic American" (Moore); "Armor Against Time" (Leighton); "The Ambiguity of Henry James" (Wilson); "Drama and The Golden Bowl" (Fergusson); "The School of Experience in the Early Novels" (Spender); "James and the Almighty Dollar" (Arvin);"The Critical Prefaces" (Blackmur); "Henry James and Stanford White" (Wheelwright); "A Little Reality" (Cantwell); "Henry James in the World" (Kenton); "James as a Satirist" (Hays); and "A Sentimental Contribution" (Wescott). Lastly was "The Ambassadors, Project of a Novel," by James, and edited with commentary by Kenton, of a "manifesto" sent to Harper's in September 1900. (All of the quotes from James below were quoted by each writer in the essays.)

Marianne Moore's essay is first and its title, "James as a Characteristic American," rebuts Brooks, etc., who said James was *not* an American. She begins: "To say that 'the superlative American' and the characteristic American are not the same thing perhaps defrauds anticipation yet one must admit that it is not in the accepted sense that Henry James was a big man and did things in a big way" (364). Moore writes, "His respectful humility toward emotion is socially brave..." (365); a criticism of James was his "lightness." Moore counters that James, in his art and letters, was "reverent" in his feelings and that his emotions were quietly and deeply felt rather than histrionic: "Things for Henry James glow, flush, glimmer, vibrate, shine, hum, bristle, reverberate. Joy, bliss, ecstasies, intoxication, a sense of trembling in every limb..." (365). Moore goes on to quote James in instances when his joy extended to American scenes, and says Henry James's warmth is clearly of our doting native variety. James writes: "Europe had been romantic years before, because she was different from America; wherefore America would now be romantic because she was different from Europe" (368). Moore credits James for being both "nationally and internationally the sensitive citizen" and says that his relation to America was strongly tied to his childhood and youth when he would meet Emerson and later write of him—"He was an apparition sinuously and elegantly slim ... commanding a tone alien to any we heard round about..." (368). Moore credits James with fond memories of an America already seen and claims that his shift of scene to Europe was to avail himself of new scenes, as the older, American scenes were ingrained in those younger memories and could not be matched and, in fact, might be subject to an altering disappointment if seen in the present. She writes that James's photos convey a "terrible truthfulness" and "naturalness," which were traits also found in his letters. "If good-nature and reciprocity are an American trait, Henry James was a characteristic American..." (369). In the letters to family and friends—especially family, "Love is written about more than anything else, and in the mistaken sense of greed. Henry James seems to have been haunted by awareness that rapacity destroys what it is successful in securing. He feels a need 'to see the other side as well as his own, to feel what his adversary feels'; to be an American is not for him 'just to glow belligerently with one's country'" (371).

> Some complain of his transferred citizenship as a loss; but when we consider the trend of his fiction and his uncomplacent denouements, we have no tremor about proving him to have been an American. What we scarcely dare ask is, how many Americans are there who can be included with him in his Americanism. Family affection

is the fire that burned within him and America was the hearth on
which it burned. He thinks of the American as "intrinsically and
actively ample ... reaching westward, southward, anywhere, everywhere," with a mind "incapable of the shut door in any direction"
[372].

Moore's conviction of James's "family affection" as his tether to America
is also a factor in the following essay.

    Lawrence Leighton's "Armor Against Time" also rebuts the notion of
James being anti–American and considers that James wrote letters vigorously to his family and friends that held a fondness for his American past
but less appreciation for the America that was becoming modern too rapidly and too voraciously for James's more conservative and traditional
biases. Leighton writes, "Stability was desirable, was necessary, hence
change—and here James was at his weakest—was in itself bad" (375). Yet,
James was not at all enamored of Europe's own road to modernism.
Leighton: "His letters are clear that the English were vulgar, superficial, rot-
ten, hypocritical; by sojourning among them, he wrote Miss Norton, 'I am
losing ... my standard of wit, of grace, of good manners, of vivacity, of
urbanity, of intelligence'" (377). Hence, the armor against time that James
wears, according to Leighton, is his shield from behind which James wished
to preserve both his courtly manner and his place as one who seeks to be
the "perfect artist" despite the encroachment of the philistines on both sides
of the Atlantic. Consequently, Van Wyck Brooks is wrong in *The Pilgrimage of Henry James*, when he writes that, for James, "Europe had been a fairy-
tale to the end" (170).

    Yet James stayed in Europe despite his misgivings, and Leighton,
through quotes from James's letters, seeks to explain why. James: "'I find
myself a good deal more of a cosmopolitan (thanks to that combination
of the continent and the U.S.A. which has formed my lot) than the aver-
age Briton of culture; and to be a cosmopolitan is of necessity to be a good
deal alone.' Eleven years later in a letter to his brother this ideal had received
a literary form: 'I aspire to write in such a way that it would be impossible
to an outsider to say whether I am at a given moment an American writing in England or an Englishman writing about America (dealing as I do
with both countries), and so far of being ashamed of such ambiguity I
should be exceedingly proud of it, for it would be highly civilized.' The cosmopolitan was armed against the treachery of the provincial, the mark of
which showed itself everywhere.... James was seeking the international style
which would free him from the accidents of time" (378).

    Leighton offers a second reason for James remaining in England, one in which James, in his "consecration as an artist" (380) blames his own artistic limitations. "James, the artist, could not work in America.... But it was rather that Europe did the work for one. 'Here a certain part of the work of discrimination and selection and primary clearing of ground is already done for one, in a manner that enables one to begin, for one's self, further on or higher up; from my own experience, often beginning so "low down," just in the way of sifting and selecting that all one's time went to it'" (381). James credits Hawthorne as a greater artist who could delve into the mind's depths and find stories that did not depend on, Leighton writes, "an old civilization to set a novelist in motion" (382). James would write to William Dean Howells in 1880, "It is on the manners, customs, usages, habits, forms, upon all these things matured and established that a novelist lives—they are the very stuff his work is made of." In an earlier letter of 1871 James states of America, "the face of the nature and civilization in this country is to a certain point a very sufficient literary field. But will yield its secrets only to a really grasping imagination. To write well and worthily of American things one needs more than elsewhere to be a master. But unfortunately one is less" (382). Leighton: "James knew his own limitations.... No major novelist of the nineteenth century was so narrow in his superficial range of subject, there was none whose novels are so much of a piece. But he was artist enough to make his limitations a strength" (382).

For Leighton, James did not hate America—far from it, as his letters demonstrate; but he didn't know what to do with the America that was no longer that of his youth and which he no longer understood. Leighton concludes: "...it is not possible to reduce James's problem [lack of appreciation] to an opposition between America and England. His traveling and his expatriation are the marks of a larger problem, that of a man fundamentally out of sympathy with his modern time. The terms of his problem are the same today for many. His answer was his self-devotion as an artist, as extraneous and factitious aid towards this solution, Europe was of some use" (384).

James refers to "ambiguity" as a virtue, not a fault, and Edmund Wilson takes this as his subject for the next essay, "The Ambiguity of Henry James." Wilson sees James's ambiguity differently, starting with *The Turn of the Screw*. "It is neither completely a virtue nor completely a fault" (398)—rather, it is a mystery that hinges on James's personal ambiguity regarding sex. "How then did James's ambiguity come to blur the whole effect of his work? He was squeamish about matters of sex, it is true—and the people he wrote about were squeamish ... much of his contact with life was affected, not at close quarters, but through long infinitely sensitive antennae. Yet why, in a given story, should he leave us in doubt as to the facts, as to what kind of people we should think the actors?" (398).

Wilson's assertions and resulting questions come after he has begun by identifying his own era of the "new" psychoanalysis as one that allows for explanations that were not acceptable prior to Freud and could not have been written about explicitly by James in his own time—nor would his conservative nature have wanted to do so even if he could have. Wilson credits fellow critic Edna Kenton for first pointing out an undercurrent of sex in *The Turn of the Screw*. "According to this interpretation, the young governess who tells the story is a neurotic case of sex repression, and the ghosts are not real ghosts at all but merely the governess's hallucinations.... It is made clear that the young woman has become thoroughly infatuated with her employer" (385–86). As for clues, Wilson writes, "Observe, also from the Freudian point of view, the significance of the governess's interest in the little girl's pieces of wood and of the fact that the male apparition first appears on a tower and the female apparition on a lake" (387). One may note that in 1934—as compared with today—even Wilson himself somewhat tacitly connotes his meaning through the phrase a "Freudian point of view" rather than explicitly refer to the clues as phallic symbols. Wilson continues to analyze the story as a sex parable, concluding, "'The Turn of the Screw,' then, on this theory, would be a masterpiece—not as a ghost story ... but as a study in morbid psychology" (390). "Morbid psychology" might also mean sexual psychology, but in James's time one simply could not say.

It is in the "not saying" that Wilson finds ambiguity in the work that follows *The Turn of the Screw*, and also sees in this later work a more pronounced ambiguity that began even before, and that *Screw* is simply a variation of one of James's familiar themes: the frustrated Anglo-Saxon spinster; and we remember that he presents other cases of women who deceive themselves and others about the sources and characters of their emotions. They are not always emotionally perverted. Sometimes they are emotionally apathetic (391–2). Apathy (depression) is the converse of strong will (manic) but both signify an ambiguity to the real cause—sexual frustration. Now Wilson turns to men.

"James's men are not precisely neurotic; but they are the masculine counterparts of his women. They have a way of missing out on emotional experience, either through timidity and caution or through heroic renunciation" (393). Wilson notes that these "heroes" are sometimes sympathetic, sometimes ironic, but all are ambiguous to some degree and sometimes to a large degree. Did James do this deliberately, knowing his men—such as the "hero" of "The Aspern Papers"—would be unsympathetic? (The Auden Generation would indeed see James's conflicted and confused heroes as the new hero—the anti-hero.) Wilson quotes Rebecca West on the "hero" of *The Sacred Fount* as "a week-end visitor [who] spends more intellectual force than Kant can have used ... in an unsuccessful attempt to discover whether there exists between certain of his fellow-guests a relationship...." (394). The visitor turns out to be amazingly wrong. What is one to conclude of James's men and women, who seem to expend a good deal of energy (even ennui requires a perverse energy) being hysterically or ironically or obsessively or manipulatively ambiguous?

"What has been kept out of sight ... in so much of James's other late work, and what becomes more sinister and obscene the more exquisitely it is suppressed, is the simple existence of sex..." (396). One could argue that as James got older he became more constipated, as well as more repressed (Freud again?). Wilson writes, "Ambiguity ... passes all bounds in those scenes in his later novels.... What had happened to Henry James to make his stories become so confusing?" (397). "He was squeamish about matters of sex ... and the people he wrote about were squeamish" (398). Wilson blames the milieu of the cultivated bourgeois for the squeamishness. "The men ... bring to it the bourgeois qualities of timidity, prudence, primness, the habits of mind of a narrow morality which, even when they wish to be open-minded, cause them to be easily shocked.... The women have the corresponding qualities: they are innocent, conventional and rather cold" (398–99).

Wilson observes that the central characters undergo a "strange diminution" (403) in which they observe from the outside looking in—they are cypher witnesses (later, an Auden-Isherwood device), or, in a word that Wilson infers—voyeurs. Wilson considers these works of the later middle period as prelude to the late period of *The Ambassadors*, *The Wings of the Dove*, and *The Golden Bowl* where "the psychological atmosphere thickens.... The characters though ... are seen dimly through a phantasmagoria of dream-like metaphors and similes..." (404). Moreover, Wilson notes that it is the Americans in the late work that come off better than the Europeans— another case for James's Americanism despite his expatriation. Finally, Wilson concludes that James "was one of the most cool-headed of novelists, one of the least capable of faking. And the very phases of ambiguity I have noted, blurring, the focus of a mind of the first order, avow the dilemmas by which it is taxed, the maladies of which they are symptoms" (406). Certainly, then, in his "blurring" James became, as Spender would say, the first modern novelist.

Francis Fergusson's essay, "The Drama in *The Golden Bowl*," begins, "Henry James was wont to call himself a writer of romances. The romantic seems to have represented for him originally a rejection of the United States he knew just after the Civil War, a society by all accounts engrossed in demagoguery and money-getting, but permitting to its women that gentle loop-hole of 'Romance' through which James was able to make his escape" (407). Fergusson, however, believes James dealt with "romance on his own terms," and quotes his preface to *The American*: "The real represents to my perception the things one cannot possibly *not* know, sooner or later, in one way or another; it being but one of the accidents of our hampered state, and one of the incidents of their quality and number, that particular instances have not yet come our way. The Romantic stands on the other hand, for the things that, with all the facilities in the world, all the wealth and all the wit and all the courage and all the adventure, we never *can* directly know; the things that can reach us only through the beautiful circuit and subterfuge of our thought and desire" (407–8). Fergusson adds, "The final stage of this development was reached when he wrote that novelists give us release from the actual by means of 'another actual.'" Fergusson: "It appears that the Romantic idea has here been broken up into two or three distinct ideas: Art, in the sense of craftsmanship; the work of art, and perhaps also the 'other actual': which the work of art imitates" (408).

Fergusson sees in James's sense of romance and art that his later novels became "drama," with Europe as the stage and certain characters as outsiders on that stage who by their interactions upon the stage grow in awareness, as do readers. James: "It is the art of drama ... that is above all the art of preparations, that is true only to a less extent of the art of the novel, and true exactly in the degree in which the art of the particular novel comes near that of drama. The first half of a fiction insists ever on figuring to me as the stage or theatre for the second half" (409). For Fergusson, *The Golden Bowl* sets the stage as that of "empire, with the connotations of rule and loot," and compares this " vast and jumbled empire" (409) to *Antony and Cleopatra*. This empire could be anywhere but happens to be in a "visible London," which, for Fergusson, in part explains why (in 1934) "it is so hard to read him in this country" (410). This is yet another defense of James's expatriation, which is ameliorated by James putting Americans in a setting that is London only by name but which can be any empire by metaphor.

James's characters are called onto the stage and their later significance prefigured, as James writes, "subject to fine intensification and enlargement" (410). Fergusson: "The spectator in fact will finally see the characters hierarchized according to their awareness of the metaphysical 'setting,' and as the possibilities of this setting are explored the spectator is kept just far enough ahead of the actors to feel their discoveries as dramatic: surprising and right at once ... the audience knows how to watch and what to look for" (411).

Fergusson then points out that James's massive attention to detail with its consequent "verbosity" and the bourgeois world he described is not in vogue in 1934. "It is a class which no one accepts now in just the way he did.... We must simply admit ... that James saw things in his own way, and perhaps saw things which nobody else had seen" (412–13). She concludes by quoting James: "Tell me what the artist is, and I will tell you of what he has *been* conscious. Thereby I shall express to you at once his boundless freedom and his moral reference" (413).

The next essay is Stephen Spender's on "The School of Experience in the Early Novels." Spender believes that an artist early in his career first absorbs experiences and from them creates his art, with more of his details provided by those experiences to give his setting and characterizations details from life. Later, an artist who has over the years absorbed in his consciousness an inventory of past experiences can derive settings inspired by them, no longer as imitation but as the "custom" settings of a mature imagination. Nonetheless, the later art cannot exist without the accumulated experiences depicted in the earlier efforts. Spender was twenty-five when he wrote this essay, and his praised first volume of poems had come out the year before. In it, he was much inspired by his observations—and imitation—of the ideas and art of Isherwood and Auden.

Spender then compares *Roderick Hudson*, James's first novel, with the later work. "The relationship between Roland and Roderick ... is ... the relationship of protector and protégé which recurs often in James, and it is also the relationship between a person who is an artist in his work and the person who is an artist in his life. If we view Roland and Roderick as a split personality [a dominant theme of the Auden Generation], we have indeed a portrait of an aspect of James himself: because James combined in himself the person who, like Rowland, was the spectator at the edge of life, always refusing to enter into it: and the sculptural artist who Roderick might have been" (420). Overall, Spender believes that in all of James's work, "The personal conflict to be detected ... is a conflict between the desire to plunge too deeply into experience, and the prudent resolution (leading eventually to a certain prudishness), to remain a spectator..." (421). Another conflict Spender considers, as did Wilson, is James's attitude toward sex. He says James has an element of "vulgarity" that comes out in "its expression of violence," first begun in *Roderick Hudson*, and that the classic example of such vulgarity is [Wilde's] *The Picture of Dorian Gray*" (423). Spender does not refer so much to physical violence as to a violence that castigates shallow bourgeois mores, and he quotes from James's letters that disparage this milieu.

Ultimately, however, "The vulgarity of Henry James is not explained by his superficial snobbishness or by any fundamental failing of his political or social sense. The key to it is the attitude to the body and to the sexual act.... The vulgarity consists in the sexual act being referred to only as the merest formality" (425). Spender will point to James's earliest work as being highly melodramatic and violent, with purple prose that is not only a condition of the younger writer but a symptom of sublimated (homosexual) feelings given vent through histrionic posturing in other matters.

The American marks a new maturity, with its melodrama more "Elizabethan" than penny-dreadful; indeed, the melodrama of Christopher Newman's burning the telltale paper, and the otherwise ineffectualness of the other characters seem to derive from an avoidance of the sexual possibilities or yearnings that would seem natural, and to avoid them could only become artificial. The relationships between men are much better drawn than those between men and women, which was likely due to James's predilection for men, which allowed him to depict them more realistically. James's women are more idealized.

Spender next moves forward to more life and death and his most direct connection between *Hudson* and a later work. "Christina Light of *Roderick Hudson* marries a prince and becomes Princess Casamassima in the book which is named after her. She continues her career of charm and destruction and in this book the person whom she becomes involved in destroying is a young man called Hyacinth, who is the illegitimate son of an Earl by a prostitute, and who is brought up by a seamstress.... James explains in his introduction how he came to write this book partly because he was not satisfied with his treatment of Christina in the earlier novel, and partly as the result of 'the habit and interest of walking the streets' in London" (431). The result was a depiction of London as James came to see it as the backdrop of a bourgeois decay that permeated all levels of society. James presents all types—rich and poor, not just bourgeois—yet, Spender writes, "But when we meet Lady Aurora, the delightfully typical socialist aristocrat who devotes her life to working, in a crazy way, amongst the poor, and then the Prince and Princess, we realize that we are only looking at the same aristocratic setting from behind the wings.... The theme of *The Princess Casamassima* is essentially the same as that of *The American* and

Roderick Hudson. It is the death of a society which ... is ... implicitly decadent" (433).

Spender concludes, "In these novels of James's first period, we see him at work observing European society and we are able to read into his conclusions. After this period, the retreat of his work into a world of inner experience, expressed in the objective imagery derived from the first novels, begins" (433).

Newton Arvin writes about "James and the Almighty Dollar," although the title is somewhat misleading as it implies a greed fixed in America when the essay truly talks about James's distaste for bourgeois money-grubbing on both sides of the Atlantic. Arvin carries on the theme in previous essays that James did not leave America because he thought Europe better; indeed, for Arvin, James attacks Europe for its greater bourgeois vileness that runs deeper than any to be found in America. Europe's banality-turned-to-vulgar-decadence had been festering much longer and was on the eve of going the way of the French Revolution. In effect, one could say, James stayed in Europe *because* the corruption was much thicker—and thus richer—in the material it would provide him as an artist in his middle to later work that is consumed with portraying this decay.

Arvin also deflects the James critics who labeled him as merely depicting a "pretty" world now foreign to the hard times of 1934. His world may be well-dressed but it is hardly attractive:

> Henry James's world, especially the world of his later fiction, is far from being a pretty one; that, on the contrary, it is morally as ugly as any in the English novel, up to that point, and that a tiny handful of decent people wander through it, bravely or timidly as the case may be, like men astray in a land of condors and boas. I do not know whether it has been noted that some of our later disillusionists have been quite definitely anticipated by the older writer—that most of Aldous Huxley, for example, is already latent in *The Awkward Age* (remember Mitchy, who according to Nanda "thinks nothing matters," and who "says we've all come to a pass that's the end of everything") and *The Ivory Tower* (in which Davy Bradham observes that "we're all unspeakably corrupt").... James had intuitively taken a critical view not only of American but of European society, and that this view exposed both societies to him, at their most vulnerable spot—their gross preoccupation with money [437–38].

Arvin notes in a very early story, "A Landscape Painter," that a wealthy young man "has broken off his engagement with a girl owing to 'overwhelming proof of the most mercenary spirit' on her part: the irony of the tale is that Locksley proceeds to fall victim of the equally mercenary Esther Blunt [who] is the first of a longish line which reaches to Kate Croy in *The Wings of a Dove* and Charlotte Stant in *The Golden Bowl*. If these women are not good mathematicians—I had almost said good bookkeepers—they are nothing" (439). Arvin does not restrict the greed to young women but also blames their parents or their men, or men who are not already attached to women and are determined to start an attachment with one who has money. "'I won't pretend,' says Osmond to Isabel Archer [in *The Portrait of a Lady*] 'that I am sorry you are rich'" (441).

Arvin concludes that, if it had been finished, "*The Ivory Tower* represents not only a remarkable return to the American scene ... but a director [sic] grappling than James elsewhere attempted with the theme of money-making, of acquisition on a vast piratical scale, and of what follows, humanly and morally, in the wake of these activities" (442). If one looks at most of James's work, money and its corruption are pervasive.

A key essay—and the longest—follows as R. P. Blackmur writes about "The Critical Prefaces." James wrote these for the New York edition of his collected works, which was a dismal failure, leaving these important essays read by the very few. This essay in *The Hound & Horn* let James explain through his prefaces the why and how of his art. Blackmur: "The prefaces of Henry James were composed at the height of his age.... The purpose was high, the reference wide, and the terms of discourse had to be conceived and defined.... He had to elucidate and to appropriate for the critical intellect the substance and principle of his career as an artist ... with a consistency of part with part that amounted almost to the consistency of a mathematical equation, so that, as in the *Poetics*, if his premises were accepted his conclusions must be taken as inevitable. Criticism has never been more ambitious, nor more useful.... In short, James felt that his prefaces represented or demonstrated an artist's consciousness and the character of his work in some detail, and made an essay in general criticism which had an interest and being aside from any connection with his own work, and that finally, they added up to a fairly exhaustive reference book on the technical aspects of the art of fiction" (444–45).

Next Blackmur offers a defense of James's style, especially late James, which was much criticized as a symptom of his expatriation, seeming to his critics evidence of a cultural and intellectual snobbery: "His style grew elaborate in the degree that he rendered shades and refinements of meaning and feeling not usually rendered at all.... His intention ... was to represent dramatically intelligence at its most difficult, its most lucid, its most beautiful point. This is the sum of his idiosyncrasy; and the reader had better make sure he knows what it is before he rejects it. The act of rejection will deprive him of all knowledge of it" (450–51). In essence, Blackmur forcefully challenges James's critics by, in effect, saying that if they don't get it, it is because they are not smart enough to get it.

In Part II of his essay, Blackmur breaks down major and ancillary themes in the prefaces and comments on each. Major are, in order of importance, and pervading all of the prefaces, "*The Relation of Art and Artist, The Relation of Art and Life, Art, Life, and the Ideal, Art and Morals, Art as Salvation for Its Characters*" (452). Art, then, is the locus and focus of James's existence, from which all ideas and methods derive. Next Blackmur proceeds to a lexicon of sub-themes that also pervade the prefaces.

> *The Finding of Subjects and the Growth of Subjects* (453). *The Finding of Subjects and the Growth of Subjects* (453).
> *Art and Difficulty* (453–54).
> *Looseness* (454).
> *The Plea for Attention and Appreciation* (454).
> *The Necessity for Amusement* (454–55).
> *The Indirect Approach and the Dramatic Scene* (455).
> *The Plea for a Fine Central Intelligence* (456).

Blackmur follows here with additional ancillary themes that are featured in certain prefaces, but not all, as are the above themes. Some of the themes are sufficient in their titles alone. All of the themes will be followed, as Blackmur originally noted, with the volume numbers in which prefaces concerned with the topic appeared in the New York edition.

The International Theme XII, XIV, XVIII (457); *The Literary Life as a Theme* XV and *The Artist as a Theme* XII (457); *The Use of the Eminent or Great* VII, XII, XV, XVI and *The Use of Historical Characters* XII, XV; "*The Dead as a Theme* XVII (458); *On Wonder, Ghosts, and the Supernatural* XII, XVII and *How to Produce Evil* XII (458–59); *On the Use of Wonder to Animate a Theme* XI (459); *Romanticism and Reality* (II); "why is one picture of life called romantic and another real" (459); *The Time Question* I (461); *Geographical Representation* I: James felt exactness should be avoided and that a type of community would suffice rather than an actual one; *The Commanding Centre as a Principle of Composition* I, II, VII, X, XI, XIX, XXI, XXIII: James believed that the art of fiction was an organic form with a strong center (461); *The Proportion of Intelligence and Bewilderment* V (462); *The Necessity of Fools* V, X, XI and *The Use of Muddlement* XI, XIX (462); *Intelligence as Receptive Lucidity* XI, XXI: A character learns as the vehicle through which readers also infer certain ideas; *The Dramatic Scene* III, VII, IX, XIX, XXI (463); *On Revision* I, XXIII; *On Illustrations in Fiction* XXIII (464); *The Nouvelle as a Form* XV, XVI, XVIII, James's favorite form (464); *On Rendering Material by its Appearances Alone* V; *On Development and Continuity* I (465); *On Antithesis of Characters* X; *On The Emergence of Characters* X; *On Misplaced Middles* XII, XIX; *On Improvisation* XII (466); *The Anecdote and the Developmental* XV, XVI (466); *On Operative Irony* (XV): *James:* "It implies and projects the possible other case, the case rich and edifying where the actuality is pretentious and vain" (467). *On Foreshortening* VII, XV, XVII, XVIII: This is when an idea of possible novel length is artfully compacted to achieve greater force; *On Narrative in the First Person* XXI (468): James did not prefer it; *On Ficelles* XXI: "...characters who belong less to the subject than to the treatment of it" (468); *On Characters as Disponibles* II: passive characters who allow the author to "find for them their right relations and build their right fate" (468).

In Part III Blackmur elaborates on the preface to *The Ambassadors* because it is "the book James spoke of most endearingly" (469). Blackmur's purpose is to demonstrate that his own elucidation of James's themes in the prefaces can be applied to an individual work of James as a method of literary analysis in conjunction with the actual preface to *The Ambassadors* itself. Blackmur's intent is to show future critics how to approach James with the prefaces as a guide, and that this will prove James's value and validate those who advocate for his value.

Part IV is Blackmur's summary conclusion: "Henry James scrupled relentlessly as to the minor aspects of his art but of its major purpose and essential character his knowledge was calm, full, and ordered. One answer to almost every relevant question will be found, given always in specific terms and flowing from illustrative example, somewhere among his prefaces.... He wanted the truth about the important aspects of life as it was experienced, and he wanted to represent that truth with the greatest possible lucidity, beauty, and fineness, not abstractly or in mere statement, but vividly, imposing on it the form of imagination, the acutest relevant sensibility, which felt it.... It is because such sentiments rose out of him like prayers that for James art was enough" (476–477).

"Henry James and Stanford White," by John Wheelwright, focuses on James's visits to New York "between the panics of 1903 and 1907. It was the zenith of our archaeological architecture [that James observed] with his faculties as sensitized as the filed fingers of a picklock.... James paralleled Thorstein Veblen's discovery of the law of conspicuous waste and anticipated the theology of the mysticism of money.... James gave out the theme developed in Lewis Mumford's most valuable articles, that it is impossible to build a decent city upon an unworkable plan, by the mere accumulation of decent objects" (480). Wheelwright quotes extensively from James's *The American Scene*, in which "No criticism of New York has been less sentimental.... In *The American Scene*, his defeated archaeological nostalgia struggles with the growing aesthetic analysis of the machine age. The critic who hankered after feudal society anticipates the aesthetic of rationalized capitalism" (481). "The charm ... may lie in its reactionary wanderings from conclusive surrender to the fact of American society" (484).

Wheelwright quotes extensively from *The American Scene* to point out that James's criticism of society—whether in America or Europe—was equally about the increasing encroachment of "the mysticism of money" that was crowding out the world of his youthful nostalgia, and better manners for a new world of vulgar ostentation, and crasser behavior as exemplified in some of the new architecture and some of the new fashions. *James:* "Boots and shoes, he observed everywhere in American crowds, indicated a feeling for cult, elaborate and mature, the more remarkable in contrast to the barbarous hats, the savage golden teeth" (487). In 1934, James's disdain for conspicuous consumption by the bourgeois was no doubt meant by Wheelwright to align him with the leftist sympathies of the era and, perhaps, refute the charges against James of snobbery and instead see his expatriation as a frustration with the coming America that in 1934 was being repudiated for its greed just as James had written years before.

Robert Cantwell's "A Little Reality" begins as a book review of *The Early Development of Henry James* by Cornelia Pulsifer Kelley. Cantwell praises the book as an effort to revive James at a time when it was not a popular strategy to do so: "Miss Kelley's book is essential for an understanding of James. It revises drastically a picture of the early years built up out of a reading of the autobiographical volumes, the biographies of [Van Wyck] Brooks and Rebecca West and of several of the early short stories—'A Light Man' (1869), 'Master Eustace' (1871), those collected in the volumes *A Passionate Pilgrim* (1871) and *Traveling Companions* (1871). The new factors are largely James's early start, his independence and his intensity of purpose, and the significance of his sharp vacillations between romantic and realistic fiction" (496–97). Nonetheless, Cantwell finds fault for the book's reliance on analysis through James's printed words alone without considering that other *au courant* form of examination—psychoanalysis. This is the "little reality" that Cantwell then deals with. He faults Kelley and Brooks for not "visualizing clearly the conflict before and during and after the Civil War.... The trips abroad ... appear only as cultural searching parties; neither seems to understand that the air in the United States at that time must have been about as hard to breathe as Vienna is now" (496). Cantwell does give credit to Kelley for featuring James's early book reviews but goes further by seeing them as both reviews and insights into James's early ideas about writing that would later be enacted in his fiction, and he admires that James took unequivocal positions and was not deferential to a Dickens or a Trollope. Indeed, according to Kelley and Cantwell, James's own admonitions to other writers might have also applied to himself, as the works of James written in his early twenties are "mannered and melodramatic, and above all, unreal" (498). It would seem that the reviews were a process of thinking out loud about his own defects. "James ... wanted to be a realist and he wanted writing to be realistic; his enthusiasms were for Balzac and George Eliot, and when he stormed against sentimental novelists it was for their perversions of actuality.... What he learned was that his own class, its common concerns and catastrophes, was simply not good enough for his art ... and even he could not purify it" (499–500).

Cantwell sees James's criticism, letter writing, and fiction writing as evolving from this point from sharply blunt evaluations to more subtle, ironic, and often left-handed commentaries-disguised-as-compliments on the good and bad halves of his class: "Except for that first brief adventure in forthrightness he always wrote as if he were trying to get around a censor and yet could not determine, from the answers he received, if his messages were being properly interpreted.... As he grew polite and sly in his criticism, he ranged between realism and romanticism in his fiction—or rather between the romantic tale and a weird kind of melodrama he evidently considered an accurate mirror of reality" (502). Yet, for Cantwell, "There was not even a *place* in America sufficiently decorated with common associations to be recognizable to readers. Balzac, of course, made the places he wrote about; it was because of the efforts of Balzac and others that there were places which other writers could use without bothering about elementary stage directions. But when James tried to perform a similar service for his own country's future, he gagged at its reality" (502–03). James then, in his early work, realized that he could not adapt reality wholesale and depict it if it was in reality too shallow to sustain a story, but that he needed to take the merest "germ" or just "a little reality" and from it shape from his imagination a tale that would be more palatable. "When he wrote those first stories in his early youth he had not learned that he could only write of the bourgeoisie if he shut his eyes and closed his ears to most of its activities; he had not learned that the only way to rework that world was to take it in small doses, to fight off the people who tried to give it to him as it really was" (505).

In the last essay, "Henry James in His World," Edna Kenton asks why the question of James's leave-taking of America "has in recent years been played with and worried over by more than one intensely American-minded critic" (506). She responds that the answers are often an overzealous response by Americans resenting criticism of America, "which is so typically American," and that in this zeal James "is the most unrepresented and misrepresented figure in letters ... and he is victim to the modern thesis ... that James was a failure because he was an expatriate.... This ... elaboration is founded on what are ... false premises: the first one, 'All expatriates are failures'! But are they? The second, 'Henry James was an expatriate'! But was he?" (506–07). Kenton argues that James was not really an expatriate until the last months of his life after he became a British citizen and that he had only done so because the Great War had made traveling difficult for non–Britons.

Rather, she describes James's leave-taking with his own word—"*dispatriation*" (as used in his 1898 essay, "The Story-Teller at Large: Mr. Henry Harland")—and that James "subtly defines it as a kind of detachment in viewpoint of, not severance of interest in, the birthland.... A dispatriated point of view takes its place alongside that kind of curiosity he held so essential for appreciation, curiosity supremely *disinterested*, disentangled from personal bias, and so at white heat, intent only on arriving at the truth of a particular case, whatever the truth might be" (508). While one may now refute those early critics of James of whom Kenton speaks, her own explanation seems a bit of an overzealous stretch in his defense. So is her choice of James's words from the same essay that the "globe is fast shrinking, for the imagination, to the size of an orange that can be played with" (508–09). The intent of James and Kenton would seem to be that the world was not divided any longer and that he could be an American anywhere if he took his Americanism with him. Indeed, Kenton says that, "Without his 'American subject' James would have been ... nowhere at all; on it his long career opened and closed." Yet, unlike Hawthorne, who could create his "American subject within his American world alone, "Since James's American subject was an integral part of his general one his projected treatment of it could not be Hawthorne's close, confined, local kind.... James's treatment demanded dispatriation as a *sine qua non*; disattachment from any single measure of values; the Spartan virtue, constantly practiced for disinterested curiosity's sake, of triumph over distaste. It demanded—nothing less—the elimination of provincialism not only in attitude but in expression"

(510–11). Kenton notes that James's letters to America display an affection rather than disaffection: "I know what I am about, and I always have my eye on my native land." Thus, James was away but never absent.

With this landmark issue, Henry James was rediscovered, reappraised, and entered into the high place he has held since.

Notes

1. From Ezra Pound's poem "The White Stag" as quoted in Hamovitz (8).
> "'Tis the white stag, Fame, we're a-hunting,
> Bid the world's hounds come to horn!'"

2. Fry, in the late 1930s, risked his life by going to Germany to help artists leave. A film, *Varian's War*, with William Hurt as Fry, premiered on Showtime in 2000 and is available on video and DVD. Bandler loved James and took the lead in organizing the special volume; he later became a highly regarded psychiatrist.

Works Cited

Brooks, Van Wyck. *The Pilgrimage of Henry James.* New York: E. P. Dutton, 1925.

Hamovitch, Mitzi. "Introduction." *The Hound and Horn Letters.* Edited by Hamovitch. Athens, GA: University of Georgia Press, 1982.

The Hound & Horn: Henry James Issue, April-June, 1934.

Isherwood, Christopher. *Diaries: 1939–1960.* San Francisco: Harper, 1996.

_____, ed. "Ethel Colburn Mayne." In *Great English Short Stories.* New York: Dell, 1957.

Kramer, Hilton. "Henry James and the Life of Art." *The New Criterion* 11, no. 8. April, 1993. http://www.newcriterion.com/archive/11/apr93/Kramer.html (accessed 27 March 2005).

Mendelson, Edward. *Later Auden.* New York: Farrar, Strauss, Giroux, 1999.

Spender, Stephen. "Review of *Portraits* by Desmond McCarthy." *Criterion* 11 (April 1932): 554–57.

_____. *The Destructive Element.* London: Jonathan Cape, 1935.

Three Aesthetes in Profile: Gilbert Osmond, Mark Ambient, and Gabriel Nash

Maurizio Ascari

It was in the late 1870s that aestheticism attracted the attention of the public as a vogue at the intersection of art and social life, acquiring that visibility—perhaps that primacy—that would culminate in the apotheosis of the *Yellow Nineties*, when Max Beerbohm consecrated the *annus mirabilis* of the movement by devoting an essay to it entitled "1880." In that year, Henry James was thirty-seven, and had definitely settled in London after his stay in Paris in 1875–76. James's attitude to aestheticism did not answer to any simplistic description, for the author was both deeply sensitive to the new cultural currents and constitutionally cautious. This is proved not only by his critical and theoretical essays, but also by his fiction, as is apparent from works such as *The Portrait of a Lady* (1880–81), "The Author of 'Beltraffio'" (1884) and *The Tragic Muse* (1899–90).

These three texts represent a multifaceted literary rendering of the 1880s and may be regarded as James's answer to various phases of the "aesthetic: adventure." In the 1870s, in fact, the impact of the new aesthetic sensibility was mainly felt in painting and poetry, thanks to James Whistler's chromatic experiments, his interest in Japanese blue china, and Algernon Swinburne's pagan inspiration, which was linked by the public to the sensuous medievalism of the Pre-Raphaelites, stigmatized as the "Fleshly School of poetry."[1] It was around 1880 that aestheticism became a sophisticated trend, as Beerbohm remarks, "When lie describes the vogue 'Beauty began,

This essay originally appeared in RSA Journal 7 (1996): 39–62.

to enjoy' in furnishing and fashion: Dados arose upon every wall, sunflowers and the feathers of peacocks Curved in every corner, tea grew quite cold while the guests were praising the Willow pattern of its cup," every ball-room women dressed "in sinuous draperies and unheard-of greens," as well as "half a score of ragamuffins in velveteen, murmuring sonnets, postur-ing, waving their hands" (38–39). In 1880, however, Wilde was only twenty-six, and his works consisted mainly of uncollected poems. His American lecture, his plays, his novel, his tales, his revolutionary essays—the quin-tessence of aesthetic theory—were still to come, although Walter Pater's invi-tation to burn with a "hard, gem-like flame" (Water 153) had produced a lasting echo.

Against this colorful and ever-changing backcloth, each Jamesian aes-thete plays a highly individual role. Gilbert Osmond (whose sinister charm has been recently flavored with a distinct propensity to lust and sadism by John Malkovich's interpretation in Jane Campion's provocative film) embodies the cynical apologist of the *objet d'art*; Mark Ambient is qualified as the first great aesthetic novelist thanks to his *Beltraffio*; finally, the unflinching individuality of Gabriel Nash deconstructs the stereotypes that promptly crystallized around the aesthetic *coterie*.

In order to understand James's characters better, it may be useful to notice that each of them subverts in his own way the concepts of *cultural, national*, and *gender* identity, according to a pattern that is typical of the *art-for-art's-sake* decades. Although it represents an English phenomenon, aestheticism is rooted in Italian culture, as Pater's *The Renaissance* (1873) shows. The scholar is attracted by the Italian *Quattrocento* on account of its intellectual and artistic achievements, as well as its "general spirit and character" and its "ethical qualities" (Pater xxxii). The space and time coor-dinates of the Renaissance embody an ideal of art and life that fin de siècle British artists, following the example of the Pre-Raphaelites, translated into renewed creative impetus, what Wilde calls "The English Renaissance of Arts," to quote the title of one of his lectures. Moreover, one should not forget the debt aestheticism owes to the *art pour l'art* movement, whose apostle, Theophile Gautier, advocates the search for a format that eschews any form of utility.[2] Another important French forerunner is Charles Baudelaire, whose *Fleurs du Mal* (1857), is an exquisite hymn to evil, malaise, and malady, and whose translations reveal him to be the inheritor of a great explorer of hallucinatory states and subtle sensations—Edgar Allan Poe.[3]

These foreign influences combined with the powerful attraction Roman Catholicism had for the Oxford circles. No better example exists than the conversions of Henry Newman and Henry Edward Manning, who were both made cardinals in the 1870s, or the case of Gerald Manley Hopkins, who was ordained as a Jesuit priest in 1877. A similar tendency pervades Pater's *Marius the Epicurean* (1885, see appendix) and Wilde's early poetry.[4] In his sonnet "On Approaching Italy" Wilde proclaims his adoration for the land "for which my life had yearned," but ends his eulogy with an attack on the Italian government, guilty of annexing Rome to the new state, thereby forcing the Pope to live in the Vatican as an exile:

> But when I knew that far away at Rome
> in evil bonds a second Peter lay,
> I wept to see the land so very fair [725].

Forces as far apart as Hellenism (in its classical and Renaissance version), French spirit, and Roman Catholicism conspired to undermine the cultural and national identity of Britain, and was superseded by a cosmopolitan artistic professionalism. The aesthete's adopted countries are in fact Bohemia, Utopia, the past, and "elsewhere."

In the course of the nineteenth century, gender categories were likewise eroded. As early as 1835, Gautier's *Mademoiselle de Maupin* revived the myth of the androgyne. The process of blurring the traditional male/female opposition was accelerated both by the dandy and by the emancipation of women. A caricature by Grandville (from *Un Autre Monde 1844*) shows gentlemen wearing fur muffs and shawls, while their ladies smoke a cigar or a pipe, swinging an imposing cane or walking with hands in their pockets (311). Feminism was on the rise, and forty years later, while planning *The Bostonians* (1885–86), James described "the situation of women, the decline of the sentiment of sex, the agitation on their behalf" (*Notebooks*, 47), as the most salient feature of American society in the 1870s and 1880s. In the meantime, an analogous desire for "male" freedoms prompted European writers such as Aurore Dupin and Mary Ann Evans to choose the pseudonyms George Sand and George Eliot, just like the script of a modern *As You Like It*. James pokes fun at these mechanisms of reversal in "The Death of the Lion" (1894), where he introduces Guy Walsingham, the "authoress" of *Obsessions*, and Dora Forbes, the mustachioed "author" of *The Other Way Round*, and the narrator of the story cannot help but recognize that "in the age we live we get lost among the genders and the pronouns" (119).

As regards the aesthete—the Saint Sebastian of publicity, the pleased martyr of scandal, who walked the streets of London chaperoned by a lily or a sunflower—Sinfield remarks that this stereotype has an effeminate connotation, not necessarily a homosexual one. With reference to *Patience, or,*

Bunthorne's Bride (1881), the popular comic opera by Gilbert and Sullivan where aesthetes are surrounded by adoring women, Sinfield concludes that "the manifest image of the aesthetic poet is that of lady-killer: he desires ... and is desired by women" (92). Conscious of the ambiguities inherent in the aesthete, who shuns the canons of cultural, national, and gender identity, we may now approach James's characters.

Gilbert Osmond, the Aesthete of Immobility

Serialized in 1880–81, *The Portrait of a Lady* coincided with a climax in the aesthetic vogue, which was literally in the limelight in those years, being the subject of various plays (among them *Patience*) and of George du Maurier's popular caricatures in *Punch*. According to Freedman, who sees Gilbert Osmond as a product of the satiric aura that surrounded aestheticism, the character sums up the aesthete's upward mobility: the will to break class barriers thanks to his taste, his brilliant and cultivated conversation, his genius for art and social occasions. The aesthetic side of *The Portrait of a Lady*, however, is far richer, since, as Freedman claims, in the novel "aestheticism is understood as being an endemic—indeed epidemic— contagion." A symptom of this disease is a "reifying vision" (153), that is to say, the tendency to regard others as *objets d'art*, as emblems of one's taste, and the consequent desire to place them in one's collection. What differentiates Osmond from Isabel and Ralph is not so much his attitude as his motive since he is selfish and cynical, while the others are disinterested and disingenuous. In the novel, human relations have been imprisoned in a vicious circle that is broken by the author when he chooses an open ending, since by abstaining from depicting Isabel Archer's destiny after her return to Italy James refuses to close the frame that surrounds her portrait.[5]

The profile of Gilbert Osmond is defined in negative terms right from the words Madame Merle uses to present him: "He's Mr. Osmond who lives *tout bêtement* in Italy. No career, no name, no position, no fortune, no past, no future. No anything" (*Portrait*, 281). Far from expressing Osmond's nature, this absence of relations is a mask that happens to correspond to Isabel's romantic aspirations. When Merle explains to the young lady that all human beings have their "shell, made up of one's house, one's furniture, one's garments, the books one reads, the company one keeps," Isabel refuses to be defined by external attributes. Giving voice to the Emersonian spirit, which privileges the individual over concomitant circumstances, the girl asserts, "Nothing that belongs to me is any measure of me; everything's on the contrary a limit, a barrier" (288).

The contrast between Isabel's naive presumption (prompting her to cherish an ideal of life that seems satisfying only insofar as it is vague) and Osmond's ambition (causing him to regard the absence of social attributes as a symptom of privation, not of liberty) pivots on the concept of identity. Due to his exorbitant egotism, Osmond believes he is "the first gentleman in Europe" (197). It is this model of sublime fineness that sets the tone of his Florentine abode—"a seat of ease, indeed of luxury, telling of arrangements subtly studied and refinements frankly proclaimed"—housing a rich collection of "chests and cabinets of carved and time-polished oak," "angular specimens of pictorial art in frames as pedantically primitive," and "perverse-looking relics of mediaeval brass and pottery" (326–27). Osmond's attitude is redolent of Bunthorne's medievalism, which is dismissed in *Patience* as an affectation," born of a morbid love of admiration" (Gilbert 164). As the female characters in the comedy, being prey to an aesthetic fever, reject the Dragoon Guards and contend for the poet's favors, so Isabel turns from two traditional patterns of male identity—Caspar Goodwood, the athletic American industrialist, and Lord Warburton, the supreme ornament of the British aristocracy—in order to privilege Osmond, whose charm is greatly enhanced by his *objets d'art*.[6]

And yet, although his interest in "primitive" works is typical of aestheticism, Osmond is above the poses stigmatized by satirists in those years. It is Ned Rosier and Madame Merle, rather, who are devoted to old china, Spanish altar lace, and Venetian leather, while Osmond's taste is more complex and refined. In this respect, James's treatment of his character reminds one of the canonic texts of decadence, from Huysmans's *A Rebours* (1884) to D'Annunzio's *Il Piacere* (1889)[7] and Wilde's *The Picture of Dorian Gray* (1891), with their attention to objects and rituals.

The great adventure around which the first part of *A Rebours* is centered is, after all, the *aménagement* of Des Esseintes's house in Fontenay, where the Parisian takes refuge to perform solipsistic sensorial experiments, according to the Baudelairian motto *Anywhere out of the world* (Huysmans 45). Likewise, in *Il Piacere*, the furnishings of Palazzo Zuccari reflect Andrea Sperelli's nature, which is described by D'Annunzio with these words: "*E poiché egli ricercava con arte, come un estetico, traeva naturalmente dal mondo delle cose molta parte della sua ebrezza.*"[8] Andrea Sperelli, however, is an aesthete and a Latin lover at the same time, and his house represents "*un perfettissinio teatro*" where he may stage his love affairs, a backcloth whose seductive power ensnares Andrea together with his victims, "*a simiglianza d'un incantatore il qual fosse preso nel cerchio stesso del suo incantesimo"*[9] (20).

With decadent sensibility, the gilded moldings of the frame prevail over the painting, the opulent *décor* draws the attention away from the drama that is being acted out. This is what happens in *The Picture of Dorian Gray*, where Dorian's emotions are amplified by gestures and objects that become almost an end in themselves. With the aim of concealing his portrait, the young man theatrically envelops it in a piece of drapery once used as a pall: "a large purple satin coverlet heavily embroidered with gold, a splendid piece of late seventeenth-century Venetian work that his grandfather had found in a convent near Bologna" (Wilde, 96). This passage bears witness to Huysmans's influence on Wilde, a debt the author acknowledged by introducing into his novel a "yellow book" that becomes Dorian's guide to aesthetic excess; interpreting its spirit as literally as possible, Dorian buys it in nine copies and has them bound in various colors "so that they might suit his various moods" (102).

In the aesthetic set of values, objects have a primary role in shaping identity, which is "a form of representation," as Dryden points out (127), and identity that takes on the static quality of beauty becomes an object of art. A case in point is Dorian, whose face is immutable, while his portrait carries the traces of age. Another character in the novel, Lord Henry, remarks that the exercise of thought is sufficient to corrupt beauty, concluding with a witty paradox that, among successful men, only prelates maintain their looks, since "A bishop keeps on saying at the age of eighty what he was told to say when he was a boy of eighteen" (19).

The attitude of Wilde's characters does not substantially differ from Osmond's viewpoint, since the utmost desire of the Jamesian aesthete is to become an unalterable icon of ritual and power: "the Emperor of Russia," "the Sultan of Turkey," "the pope of Rome" (*Portrait*, 382). Similarly, after attracting Isabel's interest, Osmond feels like an "anonymous drawing on a museum wall," in which an enlightened critic has finally recognized the touch of a master (12). In other words, Osmond is ready to become an object of aesthetic fruition, inasmuch as Isabel is willing to "discover" him, thus sanctioning his value. The young lady, in turn, becomes worthy of figuring in his collection of "choice objects" (9) only after refusing the hand of a great nobleman, Lord Warburton. Not only does Osmond conform to the aesthetic injunction "to make one's life a work of art" (*Portrait* IV, 15), but he applies this principle to his wife Isabel and his daughter Pansy, whose innocence he regards as a "plastic" (84) quality. The rift between husband and wife is due to the fact that Isabel—unlike Pansy, who is docile and easily "moulded"—has an identity of her own, the main feature of which, moreover, is a claustrophobic fear of intellectual, emotional, and physical confinement.

While Osmond's profile tends toward the fixity of a portrait,[10] Isabel is afraid of "closure." By a tragic misunderstanding, she is drawn to the man because she finds it difficult to define him: "Her mind contained no class offering a natural place to Mr. Osmond—he was a specimen apart" (376), while Goodwood and Lord Warburton are all too predictable. What Isabel desires is an ever-changing self, a ready and enthusiastic acceptance of experience. That which she refuses is a predetermined role. This is apparent from the metaphors James attributes to the young woman, whose idea of happiness corresponds to a journey toward unknown lands: "A swift carriage, of a dark night, rattling with four horses over roads that one can't see" (235). This space with no limits—an adolescent dream that is destined to prove unrealistic[11]—turns into a nightmare when she marries Osmond: the "infinite vista of multiplied life" is now reduced to a "dark, narrow alley with a dead wall at the end" (189).

Isabel, a creature of the air, is imprisoned within the massive walls of Palazzo Roccanera, "the house of darkness, the house of dumbness, the house of suffocation" (196). Yet her eventual captivity was already implicit in her first visit to Osmond's villa, which "looked somehow as if, once you were in, you would need an act of energy to get out" (364). Osmond is a gravitational center, a sort of black hole, the master of enclosed spaces. His talent for furnishing enables him to create a perfect setting for exclusive social rituals aimed at magnifying his taste and status, thus satisfying his will to power. It is his ability and desire to dominate the domestic space that connects the refined Osmond with Gothic villains, turning him into a jailer whose coercive means are not violence and locks but a respect for conventions and appearances, which is as inflexible as it is cruel.

Osmond's attitude, in fact, may be described as the look of Medusa ("it was as if he had the evil eye" [188], Isabel meditates, because he reduces people and feelings to their "shell," depriving them of their vital core). This debased form of aestheticism deeply contrasts with the attitude of Ralph Touchett, Osmond's real antagonist, according to a nineteenth-century critic in whose opinion the book should have been entitled *The Portrait of Two Gentlemen*.[12] Ralph says to Isabel: "One ought to feel one's relation to things—to others. I don't think Mr. Osmond does that" (71), summing up what in Jamesian terms is a capital sin. Insensitive, egocentric, and manipulative, Osmond is a real villain among whose victims one may count his accomplice Merle. And yet a frustrated and disillusioned Isabel still defines the character as "the man with the best taste in the world" (193), unwittingly anticipating a comment that a few years later James was to refer in his own voice to another aesthete of doubtful morality: "ostensibly, transcendently, Signor D'Annunzio's is the most developed taste in the world" (James in "Gabriele," 268). According to a contemporary reviewer, in fact, "Isabel Archer is only Mr. James in kimono and Osmond is the sort of man to attract a female James,"[13] a judgment echoed by Edel when he describes Osmond and Isabel as "two sides of the same coin, two Studies in egotism—and a kind of egotism which belonged to their author" (Edel 1977, 1619).

To conclude that the novel reflects James's ambivalent attitude to aestheticism would be almost a truism. What is more significant is that the aesthete-villain (set against varieties of connoisseur, James draws with a more sympathetic pen, from Ralph Touchett to Ned Rosier) is marked by immobility, a concept embracing Osmond's indolence, his relationship with objects, and the paralyzing influence he exerts on his family ("I don't want to see you on your travels. I'd rather see you when they're over" (14), Osmond suggests to Isabel while courting her, thereby predicting the end of every material and imaginative journey) and the figurative language he uses.[14] The sphere of immobility is also reflected in Osmond's frequent association with confined spaces and with the choice to settle permanently in Italy, a country that in his eyes "had spoiled a great many people," since it makes one "idle and dilettantish and second-rate" (371). The coincidence between Anglo-Saxon identity (Osmond is of American origin) and the Italian dream decrees the failure of the Jamesian aesthete, a numbing of moral and intellectual faculties, a sense of exile from the latest currents of art and thought.

Thus, Osmond's mercenary marriage to Isabel may be seen as the last stage of a descending curve, mirrored by his paintings. When James first introduces his character, the reader's attention is drawn to a watercolor representing the Alps (347): when Osmond is last seen, he is intent on copying "the drawing of an antique coin" (352), whose artistic value scarcely conceals its commercial one. In the symbolic geography of the Jamesian novel, by abstaining from crossing the Alps Osmond refuses to bring aesthetic and ethical values together,[15] and by marrying Isabel he commodifies his life, which is his most precious artwork—by the author's standards— and twice fails in his aesthetic career.

Mark Ambient, the Aesthete of "Elsewhere"

A controversial and ambiguous story,[16] "The Author of 'Beltraffio'" (1884) has generated a wide range of imaginative critical interpretations, such as the case of Mary P. Freier, who sees in the death of Dolcino—the climax of the story—no more than a trick, albeit a rather unpleasant one, played on a "susceptible and egotistical narrator" (Freier 309). The dividing line between traditional and more innovative and recent readings is the attempt to bring James out of the "closet" where, according to the image coined by Eve Kosofsky Sedgwick, criticism kept him till the advent of gay studies, And yet, if an appreciation of James's work and life that takes into account the disavowed aspects of his personality commands our interest and respect, the self-assurance of certain misreadings induces caution.[17]

Labeling Mark Ambient as the aesthete of "elsewhere" means recognizing a hiatus between the man and the writer, for although Ambient imaginatively projects himself into the space and time of "elsewhere" (Renaissance Italy),[18] with which he identifies as an artist, he continues to live in all other respects as a perfect Englishman. It is this split that provides space for the narration to grow. Unlike Osmond, who has lost the marks of Anglo-Saxon identity,[19] taking on the hybrid tone of a cosmopolitan, Ambient is presented as at once an "English gentleman and a man of genius" ("Author," 7)[20] and at once dynamic (i.e., the coexistence of attributes not easily reconcilable), which represents the main feature of the character.

The same can be said of Ambient's house, described by the narrator with a curious play on words: "Mark Ambient called his house a cottage, and I saw afterwards he was right; for if it hadn't been a cottage it must have been a villa, and a villa, in England at least, was not a place in which one could fancy him at home." The image of the building evokes once more a tension—a coincidence that is hinted at and denied. Yet we should not underrate the presence of an observer behind this account, for the story is reported by a young American inclined to an aesthetic rewriting of reality. Thus, when readers are told that the garden walls, covered with creepers, looked as if "copied from a masterpiece of one of the Pre-Raphaelites," they are expected to detect in this remark not only the clue to an aesthetic genius loci, but the impression of an observer who tends to interpret reality in terms of artifice: "That was the way many things struck me at that time, in England—as reproductions of something that existed primarily in art or literature" (8). In the eyes of this Yankee of Wildean faith, Ambient's wife resembles a portrait by Joshua Reynolds or

Thomas Lawrence (26), while the writer's sister corresponds to the stereotype of the Pre-Raphaelite woman, whose aspect is studiously medieval. Her face is "pale and angular," her dark hair is "intertwined with golden fillets and curious clasps"; she wears a "faded velvet robe" cut "like the garments of old Italians. In short, she suggests a symbolic picture, something akin even to Durer's Melancholia" (24). As regards Ambient's son Dolcino, his Italian name reveals a dangerous affinity with his father's work, as the narrator acknowledges when he declares: "He's like some perfect work of art" (21).

Through the misdirected enthusiasm of their American guest, the "aesthetic temperature" (28) of the Ambients intensifies to paroxysm. As Brooke K. Horvath claims, "the master, as his greatest creation, produces the perfect protégé who in turn invents the masterfulness of his master" (102); but this reflexive mechanism has devastating effects in the story, since by inducing Mrs. Ambient to read her husband's "immoral" works, the clumsy admirer contributes to the death of little Dolcino, who is sacrificed to his mother's stern Calvinism. At the origin of this chain of events there is a fundamental mistake: the narrator's tendency to project the artist onto the man, breaking the basic law of the Jamesian ethic of reading: "The artist's life is his work and this is the place to observe him" ("Death...," 119). Mrs. Ambient's mistake does not differ from the narrator's, both in her former superstitious holding off from her husband's novels, and in her later purifying frenzy. It is the *at once* dynamic that proves first embarrassing then tragic, since the narrator and Mrs. Ambient both believe in the coincidence between the artist and the man, while in James's view they represent two distinct "beings," as is symbolically rendered in "The Private Life" (1892), where the writer Clare Vawdrey is made up of two parts: the literary genius (who is perpetually bent on working at his desk) and a social alter ego.

Ambient's duplicity, the conflict which divides him from his wife, the privileged relationship between the writer and his American disciple—all these elements provide the ground for Leland S. Person's reading, aimed at showing that "Where the boy evidences the creative power of heterosexual desire, Ambient's writing (at least to the adoring narrator) represents the creative or recreative potential of homoerotic desire" (191).[21] This interpretation, moreover, is in tune with the model who inspired Ambient, John Addington Symonds (the author of the *History of the Renaissance in Italy 1875–86*), who had abandoned his family to settle in Venice—with a gondolier.[22] While approaching the text, it is important to take these implications into account, without forgetting that they are present only as allusions, for the homoerotic tension the story seems to imply is latent, that is to say, directed towards an "elsewhere." Although in his *Notebooks* James claims he has never read any of Symonds' works, labeling them as "most *undesirable*," the mysterious *pruderie* of these words is followed by the project of a short story whose comparatively banal subject is the conflict between art and British Philistinism. The author, in fact, describes Dolcino's predicament with these words: "The father wishes to make him an artist—the mother wishes to draw him into the church"; and if the ecclesiastical ambitions Mrs. Ambient entertains for her son are aimed at expiating something, it is only the "godless ideas in the literary career of the father, who, however, is perfectly decent in life" (*Notebooks*, 57).

Ambient's more or less guiltless failure as a father and a husband is counterbalanced by his triumph as a writer, for his literary meditations repeatedly echo the tenets James proclaims in his critical and theoretical essays. This artistic achievement may be due to the distance that separates Ambient from his ideal, according to the process described by James in another artistic parable, "The Real Thing" (1892), where a painter paradoxically finds two low-class models more inspiring than two aristocrats corresponding in every detail to the subject of the picture he wants to paint. The real thing in art and literature may prove dangerously sterile, because it inhibits the imaginative tension that the artist translates into representation. James, in fact, conceives art as a personal view of reality, advocating a manner halfway between the mechanical adhesion to the real professed by naturalist writers and the visionary choice of Wilde's aestheticism.

Finally, "The Author of 'Beltraffio'" is not exempt from an autobiographical element, since Ambient is an aesthete in terms of taste, but a gentleman in life, embodying a compromise between eccentricity and convention that mirrors James's own attitude to art and life. Although this precarious balance will almost estrange Ambient from his wife, we know that James's writers can hope for very little understanding on the part of their spouses, whose only interest in their literary output is the amount of money they may get from it (we need only think of Mrs. St. George in "The Lesson of the Master," 1888). "The Author of 'Beltraffio'" may be therefore described as yet another parable in favor of the Jamesian religion of art, an ideal of celibacy not exempt from misogynistic and homoerotic nuances. With a final touch of tragedy (mingled with irony) James has Mrs. Ambient die at the end of the story, not before reading her husband's works, leaving Ambient defeated as a man, but certainly not as an artist.

Gabriel Nash, the Itinerant Aesthete

Centered on the conflict between art and the world, The Tragic Muse (1889–90) is the story of two young people, Miriam Rooth and Nick Dormer, asserting their respective vocations for the theatre and painting. The novel also features Peter Sherringham—a diplomatist who first helps Miriam become an actress, then tries to dissuade her from acting so that she might marry him—and Julia Dallow, who harbors the design to make a great politician of her beloved Nick. The tension is increased by Gabriel Nash, who persuades Nick to abandon Parliament and devote himself to art.

In a novel where conflicts and "parties" play a major role, the theme of identity is already highlighted in the opening scene, set at the annual Salon of Art in Paris, when the Dormers are described by an impersonal "foreign observer" (16)—an exquisitely Jamesian narrative ghost, who testifies to the author's obsession with the point of view as "striking products of an insular neighbourhood" (3). Whereas the Anglo-Saxon origin of the Dormer family is written in capital letters in their appearance and behavior, that is far from the case with Nash. Meeting him for the first time, Nick's sister Biddy judges him to be "a gentleman unlike any other gentleman she had ever seen" (22), adding that she would have taken him for a foreigner if his words had not "imposed themselves as a rare variety of English" (23). Once again, the aesthete's identity is elusive, for Nash combines the traits of the gentleman with a continental aura immediately denied by his perfect mastery of English, and when Biddy—after listening in silence for a little while—suspiciously asks: "Are you then an aesthete?" she obtains a negative answer whose scope is certainly wider than she thought: 'I've no profession, my dear young lady. I've no état civil.... Merely to be is such a métier to live such an art; to feel such a career!" (33).

Nash's words echo Pater's invitation to enjoy aesthetic impressions per se, apart from any artistic or theoretical elaboration: "Not the fruit of experience, but experience itself, is the end" (Pater, 152). To defend this philosophy of life against Nick's teasing accusations, Nash coins the following syllogism: "Being is doing, and if doing is duty, being is duty" (26). Unlike those people whose success depends on their achievements, he opts for detachment of a pagan ascetic whose target is the refinement of perception: "People's actions, I know, are for the most part the things they do— but mine are all the things I don't do.... All my behaviour consists of my feelings" (31). These words reveal an affinity between Nash and Osmond, who is himself devoted to a negative life, to indifference, to what he labels as "my studied, my willful renunciation" (*Portrait*, 381). Having chosen abstention as the guiding principle of their lives, the two characters pick a circumscribed identity; but while in Osmond this is a symptom of inner frigidity, and of inordinate self-esteem, in Nash it is a sign of an authentic aesthetic calling, which renders him indifferent to any social conditioning.

What is more, the uncompromising individuality of Nash marks even his relation to the aesthetic movement, as Nick explains while describing Lady Dormer's view of his friend:

> She has the darkest ideas about it—the wildest theories; I can't imagine where she gets them, partly I think from a general conviction that the 'aesthetic' is a horrible insidious foreign disease—is eating the healthy core out of English life (dear old English life!) and partly from the charming pictures, in *Punch* and the clever satirical articles pointing at mysterious depths of contamination in the weekly papers. She believes there's a coterie of uncannily artful and desperately refined people, who wear a kind of loose faded uniform and worship only beauty—which is a fearful thing that Nash has, introduced me to it, that I now spend all my time in it, and that for its sweet sake I've broken the most sacred Poor Nash, who so far as I can make out isn't in any sort of society, however bad! [212]

Although Nash replies to Nick's harangue with a mock confession: "I do worship beauty. I really think it's me the weekly papers mean" (212), James's solitary "merman" (169) is far from representing a malevolent caricature of the aesthete, or "the great piece of satire in the book" (Edel 1960, xv),[23] as Blackmur claims. The character is certainly not lacking in ambiguities; but he also gives voice—like Ambient—to artistic principles that frequently recur in James's work, as Edel recognizes when he writes that "behind his suavity and his epigrams, his Walter Paterism and his *dolce far niente*, Gabriel Nash talks undiluted Henry James."[24]

When Nash encourages Nick to accept his artistic calling, arguing that we must recognize the "instrument" that each of us "carries in his being," his definition of his own talent is both lucid and frank: "To speak to people just as I'm speaking to you" (27). In other words, Nash is depicted by James as a spokesman for the aesthetic conscience, a herald of beauty, who is endowed with a preternatural intuition that allows him, as Freedman remarks, "to give voice to that in Nick that Nick cannot accept" (Freedman 184). Gabriel Nash is an archangel of art sent to Philistine England to convert it, an ethereal being, a spirit perpetually burning with the sacred fire of aesthetics, or even a *jinn*, not unlike those we meet in *The Arabian Nights*. Nash's journeys, in fact, are directed to places associated with fairy tales rather than reality. From his first appearance, the aesthete claims *not* to live in the nineteenth century, and to stay in London only when he is not in Samarcand (25), while at the end of the story Nick imagines his absent friend "reclining on a bank of flowers in the vale of Cashmere" (419).

Whereas Osmond's immobility results in a paralyzing influence, Nash's volatile nature (a feature the character owes partly to Herbert Pratt, on whom he is modeled) does not prevent him from exerting a beneficial stimulus on Nick. Faithful to the slogan of the *itinerant aesthete*—"Where there's anything to feel I try to be there!" (27)—Nash repeatedly disappears to travel to exotic countries, but when his presence is needed he reappears as if by magic, confirming his commitment to the role of artistic mentor: "He emerged out of vagueness—his Sicily might have been the Sicily of *A Winter's Tale*, and would evidently be reabsorbed in it; but his presence was positive and pervasive enough" (22).

In spite of Nash's formative influence, however, his profile remains a puzzle even for Nick, as the young man realizes when he asks his friend to pose for a picture: "What was revealed was the difficulty—what he saw was not the measurable mask but the ambiguous meaning,"(409). This mercurial spirit does not agree to submit to the artistic vision, to be imprisoned by the fixity of a portrait. "He was so accustomed to living upon irony, in the interpretation of things that it was strange to him to be himself interpreted," Nick reflects, when he becomes aware of his friend's uneasiness, concluding, "From being outside of the universe he was suddenly brought into it" (410).

Although Nash has been the constant object of Nick's admiration (only vaguely tinged with suspicion), under close scrutiny his figure seems to diminish. Acting as an initiator, Nash is at the same time at a higher and a lower level than Nick and Miriam, for he is interested only in the theoretical aspects of art, while the two artists are more attentive to the technical and operative aspects, the "simplifications of practice" (395). Being the genius of aesthetic conscience implies not only indifference to his compromise with a Philistine society, but also with the concrete side of art. Therefore James prepares the apotheosis of hero and heroine by having Nash disappear without a trace, like "a personage in a fairy tale or a melodrama" (412). This sudden exit from the scene of the novel is caused by yet another confrontation on the theme of "doing." When Nick asks his friend how he will face old age, the prophet of "being" refuses that concept as a corollary of the prejudice that imposes action, but for him there'll be "no collapse, no transition, no clumsy readjustment of attitude for I shall only *be*, more and more, with all the accumulations of experience, the longer I live" (411).

After this disagreement, the influence of Nash on his friend weakens, and his portrait symbolically starts fading as if "the hand of time was rubbing it away little by little" (412). Nick arranges the portrait together with other canvasses, and when a few months later he picks it up, he realizes that every likeness is gone, reflecting that Nash himself "has melted back into the elements" (419). Just then, Biddy announces that Julia—the Muse of Politics—will come to Nick's studio to pose, and the young man betrays an expression which "denoted a foreboding that was not exactly a dread, yet was not exclusively a joy," turning the portrait of Nash to the wall with "unreasoning rancour" (422). At the end of the story, the itinerant aesthete looks defeated, but there are no real winners in this supposedly happy ending. The price Nick has to pay in order to reconcile Julia's hand with painting is compromise (that is, abjuring artistic perfection and its advocate, Nash). The same can be said of Miriam, whose theatrical success is based on her marriage to her impresario. Once again, James refuses to reduce his characters to the fixity of a one-dimensional destiny.

The Dynamics of Aestheticism

James's treatment of the aesthete has revealed the existence of an underlying dynamics of art, of the various combinations of elements such as *immobility* and *mobility, here* and *elsewhere,* the one corresponding to realism (*immobility, here* is out of the question in the works where James comes to terms with aestheticism). While realism traditionally implies the coincidence of the artist's creative drive with the surrounding reality ("They who made England, Italy or Greece venerable in the imagination, did so by sticking fast where they were" (Emerson, 54), James himself turns to an "elsewhere," insofar as he is an expatriate who has renounced depicting the American "real" in favor of portraying Americans in Europe, Europeans in America, Britons in Italy, and so on. Likewise, a journey to Italy, the Middle East, or North Africa rates among the formative influences in the lives of several nineteenth-century painters and literati—an experience linked to the colorful contaminations in Alma-Taderna's antiquarian pictures (where classical architecture is the backdrop to Victorian visages), Lord Leighton's mediaeval Italy or Eugène Delacroix's exotic scenes. Even Flaubert, the avatar of realism, after publishing *Madame Bovary* (1857), chose ancient Carthage as the setting for *Salammbo* (1862). In other words, along with realism, a form of art rooted in romanticism thrived in midcentury, combining *mobility* with *elsewhere.* We need only think of Bulwer-

Lytton's *The Last Days of Pompeii* (1834), Wilkie Collins's *Antonina; or, the Fall of Rome* (1850), or George Eliot's *Romola* (1863), set in fifteenth-century Florence. It is in this borderland between a Victorian frame of mind and a geographic/historical "elsewhere" that the germ of aestheticism develops. A case in point is Walter Pater, who sets the life of Marius the Epicurean during the reign of Emperor Marcus Aurelius, but conceives the story as a Victorian bildungsroman, with a rich autobiographical element (see appendix).

Returning to James's characters, by permanently settling in Italy abjuring his Anglo-Saxon origin, Gilbert Osmond betrays both his aesthetic calling (the combination between *immobility* and an Italian *elsewhere* seems fatal for James's artists, as is shown by Roderick Hudson's and Theobald's stories)[25] and James's ethical imperatives. After all, Italy is not only the country of Leonardo, but also of Machiavelli, the archfiend of the Renaissance.[26] On the other hand, Mark Ambient and Gabriel Nash derive their artistic vibrations from the interplay between Anglo-Saxon identity and foreign spirit linked to former times or exotic latitudes. This in-betweenness testifies to James's affinity with aestheticism, but the author, like Nash, is a "merman wandering free" (109). Although there is a little of James in Osmond, in Ambient or in Nash, the personality of their creator is too multifaceted to be reduced to the profile of an aesthete.

Notes

1. This label was coined by Robert Buchanan in *The Fleshly School of Poetry*, a pamphlet published in 1871.

2. "Il n'y a de vraiment beau que ce qui ne pent servir a rien" (Gautier, 23).

3. Poe's stories (which were illustrated by Aubrey Beardsley in the 1890s) represent an important antecedent of aestheticism because of their decadent aura as well as the author's interest in perceptions and objects. This latter element is also apparent in the essay entitled "The Philosophy of Furniture" (1840), which anticipates Wilde's American lectures on house decoration.

4. According to Chris Baldick, Pater develops "Arnold's tendency to jettison Christian theology in favor of its liturgical consolations." After quoting an essay where Arnold writes that the man of imagination and the philosopher "will always have a weakness for the Catholic Church," Baldick remarks that in *Marius the Epicurean* Pater extends this concession to ritualism "into a celebration of Pagan and Early Christian ceremony, looking forward to the 'aesthetic charm of the Catholic Church'" (Baldick, 51–2).

5. Fabi, however, argues that, "Isabel's enclosure occurs on a narrative level as well in that The *Portrait of a Lady* is framed by the initial and final absence of the lady and by the comments of others about her" (Fabi, 7).

6. This is apparent from Isabel's first visit to Osmond. Subsequently, the acute Mrs. Touchett remarks that her niece would be able to marry Osmond "for the beauty of his opinions or for his autograph of Michael Angelo" *(Portrait IV,* 396).

7. The relation between D'Annunzio and Anglo-Saxon culture was extensively analyzed during a conference held in Pescara in 1988. From the numerous essays that make up the proceedings of the conference (which have been published under the title *Gabriele D'Annunzio e la cultura inglese e americana),* I would like to mention Barbara Arnett Melchiori's "The Early D'Annunzio in England," Alberta Fabris Grube's "La fortuna americana di D'Annunzio" and Sergio Perosa's "Henry James on D'Annunzio."

8. "Since he was researching with art, like an aesthete, he derived from the world of things a great share of his intoxication.'

9. "like an enchanter who has been trapped in the circle of his own spell."

10. In a recent essay on the function of the portrait in nineteenth-century literature, Sergio Perosa argues that nineteenth-century art gradually abandoned its mimetic connotation and became a parallel world, a rival creation (think for example of the story told by Zola in *L'Oeuvre, 1886).* Thus, the uncanny, dangerous portraits described by Hawthorne, James, Stevenson and Wilde may be regarded as symbols of the anxiety generated by the conflict between an all-absorbing cult of art and the claims of life (Perosa, 106).

11. Isabel's revolt is actually founded on a rather conventional vision of society and gender identities, as Fabi proves by analyzing Isabel's attitude toward the opposite figures of Pansy and Henrietta Stackpole, "The female model Isabel upholds, at the same time that she believes herself exceptional enough to discard it temporarily, derives from the traditional, constrictive prototype of the pious, pure, submissive, domestic 'true woman that dominated the first part of the nineteenth century" (Fabi, 3).

12. Unsigned review from *Spectator,* November 1881, (Gard, 95).

13. H. A. Huntington from a review in *Dial,* January 1882, (Gard, 111).

14. I am referring to the oft-quoted passages where Osmond, conversing with Ned Rosier and Maclaine Merle, makes use of a refined *double entendre,* apparently talking about china, while actually referring to Isabel and Pansy. The two scenes are in Chapter XXXVII *(Portrait IV,* 104) and XLIX *(Portrait IV,* 337).

15. As Carl Maves points out, James "always insisted on judging England, France and America morally, as exponents of civilized values and wielders of power whether intellectual or political; Italy, in contrast, represented only aesthetic values" (Maves, 153).

16. In his essay, Guido Fink underlines the pervasive ambiguity of "The Author of 'Beltraffio,'" where most details may be interpreted in a variety of ways. The critic also successfully argues that this epistemological uncertainty reveals an underlying equivalence between the opposite poles of the story, since Mark Ambient's art and his wife's morality prove equally artificial and unnatural (Fink, 16–17).

17. Leland Person's reading of certain Jamesian metaphors in "James's Homo Aesthetics: Deploying Desire in the Tales of Writers and Artists" is a case in point. On the other hand, after writing the present essay I came across a brilliant article where Leland Monk analyzes "the mechanisms of homosexual panic at work in James's response to the British aesthetic movement" (Monk, 247), with particular reference to John Addington Symonds and "The Author of 'Beltraffio.'" Monk rec-

ognizes that there is an "ambivalent and finally deadly circuitry of homophilia and homophobia wiring the narrative of this lurid little tale about a specifically homo-erotic love of beauty" (Monk, 248), never losing sight of the interplay between desire and restraint that accounts for the ambiguous tone of the story.

18. "The time that was dear to him beyond all periods, the Italian cinque-cento" ("Author," 30).

19. "You would have been much at a loss to determine his original clime and country if he had English blood in his veins it had probably received some French or Italian commixture" (*Portrait*, 328–29).

20. In "The Lesson of the Master," Paul Overt meditates on the relationship between the gentleman and the artist, drawing this conclusion: "He noted that oftener than in France and in Germany his artist looked like a gentleman—that is like an English one—while, certainly outside a few exceptions, his gentleman didn't look like an artist" (*Lesson*, 14).

21. The homosexual undertone of the story was not lost on some turn-of-the-century readers. In 1914 Max Beerbohm remarked: "We are not told what exactly was the title of that second book which Ambient's wife so hated that she let her child die rather than that he should grow up under the influence of its author; but I have a queer conviction that it was THE DAISIES" (Beerbohm 1920, 109–10).

22. James had become interested in this Italianate aesthete through Edmund Gosse, who had told him about the estrangement of Symonds from his wife, perhaps leaving out the problem of the writer's sexual preferences, and imputing the failure of their marriage to a purely "ideological" conflict (see Edel, 11, 188–91, and Kaplan, 301–3).

23. "He falsified in the name of truth, degraded in the name of purity, made vivid sloth in the name of hard work, enslaved in the name of independence, he was the aesthete in the name of art" (Blackmur, 9).

24. Edel's judgment is echoed by Freedman, who regards Nash as "James's most expansive and sympathetic representation of the aesthete" (Freedman, 182).

25. See *Roderick Hudson* (1875) and "The Madonna of the Future" (1873).

26. The ambivalent attitude of nineteenth-century Anglo-Saxon travelers to Italy is highlighted by Cristina Giorcelli, who describes them as tightrope walkers perpetually oscillating between attraction and repulsion, admiration and diffidence (Giorcelli, 10). Likewise, according to Agostino Lombardo, "Italy is first and foremost, for James, a metaphor of art" (Lombardo, 231), but it is also "an experience of sorrow" (Lombardo, 235). Thus, in James's Italian works, "we can distinguish the double process by which through the representation of life, and beauty and joy we are led to the vision of death" (Lombardo, 238).

Works Cited

Baldick, Chris. *The Social Mission of English Criticism 1848–1932*. Oxford: Claren-don, 1983.

Beerbohm, Max. "1880." In *Works and More*. London: John Lane the Bodley Head, 1930.

_____. "Books Within Books." In *And Even Now*. Melbourne-London-Toronto: Heinemann, 1920.

Blackmur, Richard P. "Introduction." In *The Tragic Muse*, by Henry James. New York: Dell 1961.

D'Annunzio Gabriele. *Il Piacere*. Milano: Mondadori, 1928.

Dryden, Edgar A. *The Form of American Romance*. Baltimore: Johns Hopkins, 1988.

Edel, Leon. "Introduction." In *The Tragic Muse*, by Henry James. New York: Harper, 1960.

_____. *The Life of Henry James*. 2 vols. Harmondsworth: Penguin, 1977.

Ellmann, Richard. *Oscar Wilde*. Harmondsworth: Penguin, 1987.

Emerson, Ralph Waldo. "Self-Reliance." In *Essays: First and Second Series, English Traits, Representative Men, Addresses*. New York: Hearst, 1914.

Fabi, Maria Giulia. "The Reluctant Patriarch: A Study of *The Portrait of a Lady*, *The Bostonians*, and *The Awkward Age*." *The Henry James Review* 13, no. 1 (Winter 1992): 1–18.

Fink, Guido. "I Bambini Terribili di Henry James." *Paragone* 236 (October 1969): 4–28.

Freedman, Jonathan. *Professions of Taste: Henry James, British Aestheticism, and Commodity Culture*. Stanford: Stanford UP, 1990.

Freier, Mary P. "The Story of 'The Author of Beltraffio.'" *Studies in Short Fiction* 24, no. 3 (Summer 1987): 308–09.

Gard, Roger, ed. *Henry James: The Critical Heritage*. London: Routledge, 1968.

Gaunt, William. *The Aesthetic Adventure*. Harmondsworth: Penguin, 1975.

Gautier, Theophile. "Preface." In *A Mademoiselle de Maupin*, avec une introduction et des notes par Adolphe Boschot. Paris: Garnier, 1930.

Gilbert, W. S. *Patience, or, Bunthorne's Bride: The Savoy Operas*. Ware (Hertfordshire): Wordsworth, 1994.

Giorcelli, Cristina. *Henry James e l'Italia*. Roma: Edizioni di Storia e Letteratura, 1968.

Grandville, Jean-Ignace-Isidore. *Fantastic Illustrations of Grandville*. Introduction and commentary by Stanley Appelbaum. New York: Dover, 1974.

Horvath, Brooke K. "The Life of Art, the Art of Life, the Ascetic of Aesthetics: Defeat in James's Stories of Writers and Artists." *Modern Fiction Studies* 28, no.1 (1982): 93–107.

Huysmans, J. K. *A Rebours*. Vienne: Fasquelle, 1970.

James, Henry. *The Novels and Tales of Henry James*. Vol. 16, "The Author of 'Beltraffio.'" New York: Scribner's, 1907–9.

_____. *The Novels and Tales of Henry James*. Vol. 15, "The Death of the Lion." New York: Scribner's, 1907–9.

_____. "Gabriele D'Annunzio." In *Notes on Novelists, With Some Other Notes*. New York: Biblo, 1969.

_____. *The Novels and Tales of Henry James*. Vol. 15, "The Lesson of the Master." New York: Scribner's, 1907–9.

_____. *The Notebooks*. Edited by F. O. Matthiessen and Kenneth B. Murdock. New York: Oxford UP, 1961.

_____. *The Novels and Tales of Henry James*. Vols. 3–4, *The Portrait of a Lady*. New York: Scribner's, 1907–9.

_____. *The Novels and Tales of Henry James*. Vols. 7–8, *The Tragic Muse*. New York: Scribner's, 1907–9.

Kaplan, Fred. *Henry James: The Imagination of a Genius, A Biography*. London: Sceptre, 1993.

Lombardo, Agostino. "Italy and the Artist in Henry James." Edited by Agostino Lombardo and James W. Tuttleton. In *The Sweetest Impression of Life: The James Family and Italy*. New York: New York University Press, 1990.

Maves, Carl. *Sensuous Pessimism. Italy in the Work of Henry James*. Bloomington: Indiana University Press, 1973.

Monk, Leland. "A Terrible Beauty Is Born: Henry James, Aestheticism, and Homosexual Panic." In *Bodies of Writing, Bodies in Performance*. New York: New York University Press, 1996.

Nerozzi, Bellman Patrizia, ed. "Gabriele d'Annunzio e la cultura inglese e Americana. Atti del Convegno." *Pescara* 12–13 (December 1988). Pescara: Solfanelli, 1990.

Pater, Walter. *The Renaissance: Studies in Art and Poetry*. With an introduction by Adam Phillips. Oxford: Oxford University Press, 1986.

Perosa, Sergio. *L'isola la Donna il Ritratto: Quattro Variazioni*. Torino: Bollati Boringhieri, 1996.

Sedgwick, Eve Kosofsky. *The Epistemology of the Closet*. Los Angeles: University of California Press, 1990.

Sinfield, Alan. *The Wilde Century: Effeminacy, Oscar Wilde and the Queer Moment*. London: Cassell, 1994.

Wilde, Oscar. *The Complete Works of Oscar Wilde*. London: Collins, 1966.

Killing Mothers: Decadent Women in James's Literary Tales[1]

Donatella Izzo

But it is in the portrayal of female beauty that Aesthetic art is most peculiar, both in conception as to what constitutes female loveliness, and in the treatment of it.

Walter Hamilton, *The Aesthetic Movement in England* (1882)

He who fights monsters should be careful lest he thereby become a monster.
Nietzsche, *Beyond Good and Evil* (1886)

Setting aside the fact that I am a décadent, I am also its antithesis. My proof for this is, among other things, that I always instinctively choose the right means against wretched states: while the décadent as such always chooses means that are disadvantageous for him. As summa summarum I was healthy, as niche, as specialty I was a décadent.
Nietzsche, *Ecce Homo* (1889)

Genealogies

The stories of writers that Henry James wrote about between "The Author of 'Beltraffio'" (1884) and "The Real Right Thing" (1899) are in many ways the closest James ever came to the aesthetic movement.[2] While James depicted artists and aesthetes throughout his career and, as Jonathan Freedman has convincingly argued, produced with *The Wings of the Dove* and *The Golden Bowl* his own aestheticist novels, his stories of the 1880s and 1890s, taken together, are his most sustained and coherent narrative engagement with the writer's predicament under the new conditions dictated by mass culture, the professional status of the literary field, and the emergence of a definition of the aesthetic sphere as autonomous with regard to moral, religious, and economic demands. An analysis of this cluster of stories along the lines proposed by Pierre Bourdieu's *Les Règles de l'art* would be extremely rewarding, since they are as clear an illustration as any ever written of the phenomenology and the tensions accompanying the restructuring of the social space in forms that sharply oppose the artist to bourgeois society, and the consequent polarization of the literary field into "pure" and "commercial" artists, elite and mass products, refined and popular tastes. Just such unresolved tensions are at the core of aestheticism as a historically specific movement, keeping in fruitful suspension both its developments as commodity, and those avant-garde potentialities that modernism would claim as its own.

Parable-like in their quality, these short stories appear as explicit "moral fables for critics," quasi-allegorical in the clear equivalences they ostensibly establish between characters and situations on the one hand, and, on the other, the set of intellectual as well as practical questions that F. O. Matthiessen classically summarized as "the split between life and art" (2), noting that, however dated James's "monastic" solutions might seem, the questions themselves, cast in different terms, still confronted the writers of the post–World War II generation.[3] These tales seem to make criticism redundant, a mere repetition of what is transparently implied or, indeed, stated in each story. Not surprisingly, criticism has long exhibited a tendency toward tautology, restating in a variety of forms the self-evident truths each story rehearsed—first among these the inherent asceticism of the true follower of beauty and the incompatibility of a dedication to art with most activities comprising the sphere of ordinary social life.

Such a critical approach to James's tales of writers and artists, I would suggest, should be read as one chapter of the genealogical narrative of modernism: a narrative of alienation, disclaiming aestheticism as compromised with fashion and consumer society, and redefining art as the severe and demanding pursuit of the dedicated few—the high priests of high culture as a secular substitute for religion. These critical genealogies, as several scholars have shown, are gendered ones: starting with the late Victorian age and lasting well into the twentieth century, a "gendering of aesthetic categories" (Psomiades, 4) presided over the construction of the aesthetic sphere. Aestheticism first and modernism later coded art as masculine.[4]

With a radical break from the "great tradition" of the English novel from Jane Austen to George Eliot, women began to be systematically associated with the sphere of consumption rather than production of literary works, while women writers came to be consistently demoted from the sphere of high art to that of mass consumption (Showalter). Male aesthetes and 'serious' writers resented women's power both in the social sphere as consumers and in the literary field as rivals, and missed no opportunity to denounce it;[5] even Henry James, in spite of his frequent sympathetic attitude to women characters and women friends, offered some scorching portraits of popular women writers, both in some of his reviews and in such stories as "Greville Fane," "The Death of the Lion," and "The Next Time." This symbolic feminization of the disparaged sphere of successful popular culture (a process that, among other results, led to the erasure of women aestheticists and of women modernists from collective critical memory)[6] served the double purpose of simultaneously abjuring from the aesthetic sphere two polluting presences—women and the marketplace.

This gendered construction of the modernist aesthetic ideology might go some way toward accounting for the simplistic fashion James's critics long kept re-producing a face-value reading of the issues addressed in the tales of writers and artists, again and again sounding in their works the lesson of the master—namely, the incompatibility of a commitment to art with a commitment to woman and marriage—and upholding it as a general truth about art. Indeed, most readings of "The Lesson of the Master" have taken the content of the lesson for granted, only diverging in assessing St. George's motive and his degree of good faith. Never have they questioned the set of assumptions that ground the lesson, i.e., the equations life = love = woman = marriage = consumption = yielding to the market. In fact, each of these slippages is highly questionable, not just on an abstract theoretical level, but even in terms of James's work. Several women in the James canon (from Isabel Archer to Mona Montravers) give, and give generously, to their husbands: far from being inimical to it, they enable the men to lead the aesthetic life. The tales of writers feature "bad" wives (Mrs. Saltram in "The Coxon Fund") and "good" wives (Maud Limbert in "The Next Time") as well as "literary" wives (Gwendolen Erme in "The Figure in the Carpet" is the author of three novels; Marian Fancourt in "The Lesson of the Master" is a literary enthusiast). Even in "Collaboration," where women are spoken of by male artists as having "a mortal hatred of art" rooted as a "true, deep instinct" (*Complete Stories 1892–1898*, 244), Paule de Brindes's understanding of and yearning for the composer's music in the final scene belies the previous charge.

And then, does marriage exhaust all possibilities for "life," and are women the only possible object of a male writer's commitment? Even taking for granted that the "lesson of the master" is that an artist should abstain from marriage, that need not entail abstention from all sexual or emotional involvement. Thanks to the joint efforts of a number of critics and biographers bent on recovering and bringing to light the homoerotic subtext of James's work, we are now in a better position to assess the intense currents of male-male desire between artists and disciples in these tales. Instances range from Eric Savoy's reading of "The Figure in the Carpet" to Hugh Stevens's essay on "The Real Right Thing"; most recently, Eric Haralson has discussed "The Author of 'Beltraffio'" as James's engagement with homosexuality in the context of aestheticism, the historical watershed where alternative styles of masculinity were increasingly labelled as "deviant" and "perverse," and Leland S. Person has provided a brilliant rereading of four stories belonging to this corpus, focusing on James's "poetics of male desire—the deployment of male desire in acts of writing and reading between men" (125–126). While differing in emphasis and theoretical approach, these recent essays converge in their efforts: collectively, they question the traditional assumption of the inevitability of celibacy and ascetic sublimation for the truly dedicated writer, and recover alternative possibilities for the unfolding of an artist's desire and for his engagement with life in forms other than those prescribed by social proprieties. In fact, each tale enacts two different plots, one heteroerotic and one homoerotic, where rejection of woman as object of love frequently coincides with homoerotic attraction to man-as-artist.

What is it exactly, then, that is deemed incompatible with the pursuit of art? Is it "life," as in Matthiessen's well-known formula, or is it rather woman—and if so, why? In the critical tradition on these tales, "woman" has come to signify sex, love, family, the demands of social life, and a yielding to the marketplace, acting as the term epitomizing them all—an easy and culturally sanctioned slippage, simultaneously foreclosing all alternative possibilities. If the traditional reading of a story like "The Lesson of the Master" is a "fable for critics" of asceticism and renunciation, this construing of the artist as celibate priest of the religion of art is functional to the disclaiming of *both* the scandal of the artist's necessary reliance on the market *and* the scandal of homosexuality, consistently underlying the tales as a censored corollary of the rejection of women and an implied alternative to celibacy. It should be acknowledged, though, that while the ideology of modernism has tended to mystify the actual status of aestheticism as *both* high art and mass culture, Henry James very explicitly deals with the market in tale after tale. He depicts writers who constantly strive to be success-ful, repeatedly showing that the spheres of high art and of popular mass products constantly intersect, and the exquisite and the marketable are two sides of the same coin and operate according to the same mechanism. As for the issue of gender, James consistently, if more implicitly, addresses this through narrative situations as well as through his deeply suggestive use of language.[7]

What, then, does "woman" stand for? In the misogynistic and homo-phobic attitude of the critical tradition, she stands for everything that must be kept at a distance by the artist, and simultaneously acts as a screen pre-venting the emergence of homoeroticism—a scapegoating move effectively denying the possibility that the artist be a participant in social dynamics or a sexual being or a homosexual "pervert" rather than a temperate devo-tee of art. A question, though, remains to be asked: is this process enacted by James's critics, or is it inscribed in James's texts?

Triangles

Most of James's literary tales are constructed around triangles: an inti-mate relation grounded in shared aesthetic ideals exists between a writer and a disciple or friend or critic, who is also the narrator or the focus of narration;[8] a woman stands between them as either the object of conquest and desire (Marian Fancourt in "The Lesson of the Master"), the antago-nist (Beatrice Ambient in "The Author of 'Beltraffio'"), the helper (Fanny Hurter in "The Death of the Lion"), or an ambiguous mixture of such different roles, occasionally distributed between two distinct female char-acters. In the triangles of these tales, art is the term that unites men; woman is the term that divides them or the neutral term that sides with one of the male characters, figuring as his extension. What the tales collectively depict is a homosocial and homoaesthetic continuum, whose homoerotic potentialities are kept at bay by the presence of woman acting as both rup-ture within the continuum and screen for its unmentionable possibilities. As several critics have noted, aestheticism at the time was a code word for homosexuality, and Eric Savoy acutely connects the operation of allegory in these tales with the functioning of the closet: both share *occlusion* as their common ground ("Embarrassments," 229). The function of allegory, in Paul de Man's sense, is designating a distance in relation to its origin and establishing language in the void thus created. In this case, homosexual subjectivity as origin would be subject to a twofold occlusion, operating both in literary form (allegory as a "coded" genre) and at the level of plot, where a more conventional story of love, courtship, or marriage tends to coexist with the homoerotic attraction between literary men conveyed through suggestive situations and the use of a charged language and imagery. These stories, as Savoy writes, "conflat[e] hermeneutic and homoerotic desires" (230).

It comes as no surprise, then, that women stand within the triangle as both alluring and threatening, both invited and abjured, both accomplices and rivals: in the twofold dynamics of the text as overtly heterosexual and covertly homosexual, women are the switch that commutes the different currents of aesthetic and erotic identification and desire circulating within the narrated world. "Did he want hers as a supplement or as a substitute?" wonders the narrator of "John Delavoy" referring to the biographical sketch that Beston, the powerful editor of a journal, insistently demands of Miss Delavoy, the dead writer's sister (*Complete Stories 1898–1910*, 14). This alternative between supplement and substitute neatly sums up the shifting quality of this triangular relation, where the female character acts in turn (or simultaneously) as a substitute for, and alternative to, the pursuit of art ("The Lesson of the Master") or as the co-priestess worshiping at its temple ("The Death of the Lion," "John Delavoy"); that is, in terms of gender, as a heteronormative opponent or as a complicitous screen. Or else both, in the shifting alliances and intimacies making up each character's relation to (and desire for) one or the other member of the triangle. In the ambiguous overlapping of two scenarios—canonical-heteronormative and aestheticist-homoerotic—women act both as objects of desire in themselves and as figures allowing the expression of male-male desire by proxy, as shown by the revelatory scene in "The Lesson of the Master" where Paul Overt watches his admired master, Henry St. George, drive away in a carriage with the woman he intends to propose to, Marian Fancourt:

> An indefinite envy rose in Paul Overt's heart as he took his way on foot alone, and the singular part of it was that it was directed to each of the occupants of the hansom. How much he should like to rattle about London with such a girl! How much he should like to go and look at "types" with St. George! [*Complete Stories 1884–1891*, 575]

Similarly, shifts, exchanges, and superpositions of function characterize the triangular relation involving the dead writer Ashton Doyne, his widow, and the writer's close friend George Withermore in "The Real Right Thing." At first oppositional—husband and wife had been estranged in life; whereas Withermore was "'the one he liked most; oh, *much!*'" (*Complete Stories 1898–1910*, 122)—the two mourners become quite interchangeable, and the ghostly presence of the writer visits them in turn, alternately.[9] While the widow tries to reappropriate her estranged husband through Withermore (and perhaps appropriate Withermore through her deceased husband) by having him write Doyne's biography, Withermore feels that now she has "put him ... in the fullest possible possession" (125) of everything that had been Doyne's; "his master and he were really for the first time together" in "an intercourse closer than that of life" (124). A crescendo of puns and images of physical intimacy conveys the homoerotic implications of the man's relation with the ghost:

> What they were doing was what he wanted done, and they could go on, from step to step, without scruple or doubt. ... there were times of dipping deep into some of Doyne's secrets when it was particularly pleasant to be able to hold that Doyne desired him, as it were, to know them. He was learning many things that he had not suspected, drawing many curtains, forcing many doors, reading many riddles, going, in general, as they said, behind almost everything. It was at an occasional sharp turn of some of the duskier of these wanderings "behind" that he really, of a sudden, most felt himself, in the intimate, sensible way, face to face with his friend; so that he could scarcely have told, for the instant, if their meeting occurred in the narrow passage and tight squeeze of the past, or at the hour and in the place that actually held them.... Happily, at any rate, even in the vulgarest light publicity could ever shed, there would be the great fact of the way Doyne was "coming out." ... There were moments, for instance, when, as he bent over his papers, the light breath of his dead host was as distinctly in his hair as his own elbows were on the table before him.... the situation was ruled—that was but natural—by deep delicacies and fine timidities, the dread of too sudden or too rude an advance [126–127].

Simultaneously, though, the widow hovers behind the door at night alone in the house with Withermore, in a situation suggesting the possibility of further liaisons. See the following passage, coming shortly after the one just quoted, where Doyne's ghost has temporarily ceased to visit Withermore and the equivocal language used seems to mime sexual intercourse and the compulsory return to "normal" heterosexuality:

> They had taken kindly enough to what was of an order impossible to explain, perversely reserving their sharpest state for the return to the normal, the suppression of the false. They were remarkably beyond control when, one night, after resisting an hour or two, he simply edged out of the room. It had only now, for the first time,

> become impossible to him to remain there. Without design, but panting a little and positively as a man scared, he passed along his usual corridor and reached the top of the staircase. From this point he saw Mrs. Doyne looking up at him from the bottom quite as if she had known he would come; and the most singular thing of all was that, though he had been conscious of no notion to resort to her, had only been prompted to relieve himself by escape, the sight of her position made him recognize it as just, quickly feel it as a part of some monstrous oppression that was closing over both of them [129].

In the homoerotic and homoaesthetic relations connecting men in these stories, women are the element *in excess*, acting as channel, alternative, or obstacle to male-male desire, and taking their function or their multiple functions with reference to the relations between men they either mediate or hinder. This obviously makes for their abjuring and scapegoating, not just in the texts themselves but, what is more significant, in their recent critical reassessments, tuned as they are to the issues of a "queer" and "queering" masculinity. To Eric Savoy, "especially in James's early fiction, male friendship is both latently sexual and intensely gynophobic" (*"Hypocrite Lecteur,"* 29); elsewhere he argues (with reference to "The Figure in the Carpet") that James has a typical "gynophobic manner" of locating knowledge in women (in this case, Gwendolen Erme), who use it to "regulate the field of compulsory heterosexuality":

> If this narrative turn assures the inviolability of a closet that is always already compromised, it also excludes women from the homosocial game, however panicked, that unites authors and readers, textuality and sexuality, the phallus and the penis. Hence Vereker's assurance that, in some fundamental way, "a woman will never find out" ["Embarrassments," 235–6].

Indeed, these tales seem to exclude women from the deeper exchange of desire and identification ruling them. According to Leland Person, James always insists on "putting a woman in her place in order to re-establish the masculine identity she has put in jeopardy" (25). And most critics would seem to agree on the basically misogynistic quality of such male-male arrangements. Eve Kosofsky Sedgwick, for instance, maintains that "in any male-dominated society, there is a special relationship between male homosocial (*including* homosexual) desire and the structure for maintaining and transmitting patriarchal power: a relationship founded on an inherent and potentially active structural congruence" (*Between Men*, 25) that can take different forms, ranging from ideological homophobia to homosexuality, under different circumstances. And Elaine Showalter claims that the "rationalization of homosexual desire as aesthetic experience has as its subtext an escalating contempt for woman" (176).

Taken together, then, these tales, with their prevalent focus on male-male relations, would seem to belie my former contention that there is in James's stories a strong focus on femininity and its cultural representations, and a self-aware critical staging of and resistance to a fetishizing, aestheticizing cultural dynamic functioning along the male-female axis (Izzo). Hardly surprising, after all: in Henry James's multiverse, variety or even reversal of points of view is only to be expected. My former experience with stories focusing on women characters, however, makes me wish to suspend the question—if nothing else, to put my own arguments to a new and different test—and delay the apparently foregone conclusion that, at least in the literary tales, James is indeed embracing the misogynistic view and subjecting his women characters to a wholesale rejection, identifying them with the heteronormativity, the family sanctities, and the bourgeois proprieties that the protagonists of these stories repudiate and by which they are sometimes trapped.

Recent critical readings that have explored the gay and queer implications of these texts, and demonstrated the crucial significance of these implications to an understanding of their semantic and pragmatic dynamics, are both convincing and authoritative: I will, therefore, take them for granted here. These readings, though, still leave room for other questions. Leland Person has an extremely interesting point where he insists on the *readerly* quality of James's homoaestheticism, where the *reader's* desire constructs the writer's sexuality. How, then, does *a woman's* readerly desire come into play in these tales? Man as an object is doubly barred from her, since she is constructed as inimical to his integrity and since his own desire is directed elsewhere (be it at art or at another man) rather than reciprocating her own; the only identification open to her seems to be in cross-dressing as an artist, or in accepting the frustrating, ancillary role of the subordinate helper, or else the even more disagreeable one of the castrating wife. Person in his book programmatically explores the male-male relation as a writer-reader relation, positioning himself as a male reader and inviting the text to play out its "poetics of male desire." Let me, then, complement his act of reading by reading as a woman—by positioning myself as a female reader, and exploring a different set of questions: where *is* woman in these tales? Where does a woman stand in the homoerotic/homotextual network they create—where does the *story* place her, and where does the *text* place her? In other words, *what does a woman want* in, and from, these tales?

Reading Women

While displacing woman as the element in excess from their triangles and the element barring male artists from the aesthetic sphere and perhaps the enjoyment of their male-male relationships, these tales insistently position women as *readers*, at times sympathetic (like John Delavoy's sister, Gwendolen Erme, Marian Fancourt, or Miss Hurter in "The Death of the Lion"), at other times hostile, like Mrs. St. George in "The Lesson of the Master," who once made her husband burn one of his works because it was "a bad book"—whether morally, commercially, or artistically, we are not allowed to know, even though the narrator, taking for granted her lack of understanding, instantly convinces himself that "the burnt book (the way she alluded to it!) *was* one of her husband's finest things" (*Complete Stories 1884-1891*, 549). At least in one case, "The Author of 'Beltraffio,'" the whole dénouement hinges on an act of reading by a woman: Beatrice Ambient, the author of *Beltraffio*'s wife, who—even though she has never read them—opposes Mark Ambient's writings on moral grounds, and whose eventual reading of her husband's latest manuscript (prompted by the narrator, an American disciple and admirer of the writer) allegedly decides her to let their son Dolcino die of diphtheria rather than let him grow up to be contaminated by her husband's aestheticized corruption. In other words, however they relate to the various writings mentioned in the tales, these reading women seem to abide by the law stated above: they figure as either supplements—supporters, mere extensions of the male protagonist's or witness-narrator's aesthetic passion—or substitutes, opposing and trying to replace the primacy of the aesthetic with their own values (be they moral, or social, or both).

Should we take these characters as mirroring the implied position of the woman reader *of* the text, and read them as representations *en abyme* of the actual historical range of possibilities offered the woman reader when confronted with an "aesthetic" text? And if so, should we take them at face value as offering either an alliance tinged with subalternity or an irreducible enmity as the only options available? The rest of this paper will mainly focus on "The Author of 'Beltraffio,'" chronologically the first in this series of literary stories, and in many ways the most elusively complex one. Featuring as it does the one woman character in the corpus who is not just an "objective" hindrance for the artist *qua* wife to be responsibly supported, but explicitly and unreservedly fights against the male writer's aestheticism, even going to criminal lengths (as we are told) in her principled opposition, this story promises to be a particularly challenging test case for assessing James's representation of women's position vis-à-vis the aesthetic sphere, and for attempting to probe the function of women characters and of women readers in the complex nexus created by aestheticism and homo-eroticism.

Of all literary tales, "The Author of 'Beltraffio'" has been among the more systematically read in connection with aestheticism, not only by virtue of its subject matter, but also because of James's explicit mention of the marital trouble of John Addington Symonds, related by Edmund Gosse, as the germ of the plot in his note of 26 March 1884 (*Notebooks,* 57–8). To summarize an argument other critics have made much more extensively and in more detail, James had met Symonds in 1877, had sent him a copy of an essay on Venice accompanied by a fairly suggestive message in 1882, and was certainly aware of his homosexuality and of the private publication of his *A Problem in Greek Ethics* in 1883, although he probably did not read it until 1891.[10] It is true that he chose not to acknowledge that his depiction of Mark Ambient had homosexual overtones when Gosse complimented him on having divined and conveyed in his tale the secret reason for Symonds's domestic problems; however, there can be little doubt that this implication of what in his notebook entry he termed Symonds's "extreme and somewhat hysterical aestheticism" was clearly present to his mind (*Notebooks* 57). Whether or not we accept the notion advanced by Fred Kaplan that even before Wilde's trial, "hyper-aesthetic" was culturally synonymous with "homosexual" (302), the Paterian brand of aestheticism is clearly recognizable in Mark Ambient, and so are its homoerotic connotations. The narrator insists both on his being the uppermost representative of "the point of view of art for art" (*Complete Stories 1874-1884,* 865) and on the "scandal" (865, 882) accompanying his work; he mentions "the American poet" (866) to whom he owed his letter of introduction, "the other great man, the one in America" (867)—presumably an allusion to Whitman, who had in fact an epistolary correspondence with Symonds. Besides being modelled on Symonds, Ambient shares with Pater the inherent contradiction between the scandalous implications of his work and the scrupulous respectability of his public life.[11] He defines himself "a pagan" who, for his wife, is "no better than an ancient Greek," although he simply "care[s] too much for beauty" (892), thus aligning himself with the heroes of Pater's *Renaissance,* as well as with the implicit connotations of "Greek" as a widely used euphemism for male homosexuality. An association with both Pater's *Renaissance* and homosexual artistic cenacles is equally conveyed by the title *Beltraffio,* an alternative spelling of Boltraffio, a painter of Leonardo's circle. Finally, the use of religious language for art, consistently employed in the story from the narrator's first definition of Ambient's *Beltraffio* as "the most complete presentation that had yet been made of the gospel of art" (865), is typical of Pater, Wilde, Swinburne, and the artistic circles—*ambients?*—of the 1880s and 1890s. In other words, Mark Ambient is not just James's equivalent for Symonds, but a synthesis of the plights and paradoxes of the aestheticist artist, portrayed in his artistic, social, and gender dimensions. The latter, in particular, were very well present to the minds of James's contemporaries, be they supporters or critics; and this implicit awareness, coupled with the fact that the tale alludes to people who were still living, widely known, and easily recognizable, helps account for the fact that, compared with other tales of the literary life, the sexual and homosexual overtones of language here are extremely discreet, allusions being sufficiently conveyed by the situation.[12]

If Ambient is the bearer of the aesthetic gospel, though, one should not forget that his wife is his deuteragonist and his equal in prominence from the very ideational stage:

> It seemed to me *qu'il y avait là un drame—un drame intime*; the opposition between the narrow, cold, Calvinistic wife, a rigid moralist; and the husband, impregnated—even to morbidness—with the spirit of Italy, the love of beauty, of art, the aesthetic view of life, and aggravated, made extravagant and perverse, by the sense of his wife's disapproval [*Notebooks*, 57].

And she becomes the true protagonist by the projected end, when, in James's notes, she is the only subject of both thought and action: "She makes up her mind ... she determines ... she sits watching him sink" (58).

Whereas the notebook entry gave as Beatrice's motive her realization that Ambient lacked a faith in a life after death where he would rejoin his son—which makes the killing of Dolcino a matter primarily of fanatical religious belief, in keeping with the initial situation described as *donnée*—the actual story drops the religious emphasis and insists rather on aestheticism as in itself contaminating, and on Beatrice's fear of aesthetic corruption and, implicitly, sexual abuse for her son: "' She sacrificed him ... she determined to rescue him—to prevent him from ever being touched'" (909). Also, the actual tale to some extent obfuscates the wife's role in the ending, making it a matter of hypothesis rather than certainty: whereas in James's sketch the wife was to reveal the truth to the narrator "in her exaltation and excitement" (58), in the published story James has Ambient's sister Gwendolen present to the narrator her own imaginative reconstruction of the chain of events leading to the child's death, possibly with the intention of applying that "delicacy of touch" he felt was required to make such a "gruesome" and "unnatural" situation palatable for the public (*Note-books*, 58).

Whatever the intention, though, one effect is irrefutable: by having Beatrice Ambient's decision and gesture take place off stage and be related as partly observation, partly surmise, James makes her behavior and motives puzzling and open to interpretation—indeed, the main interpretative question as regards this tale. Is Gwendolen's reading of Dolcino's death correct? Is she just accusing a sister-in-law she hates in order to ostracize her from the family and replace her in her brother's affections? Is she trying her inventive powers at the expense of the credulous narrator, who had refused her advances and disparaged her aesthetic pretensions as "the inevitable imitation" (879) of her brother's attitude? And, provided we take it for granted that, following James's original sketch, Beatrice has actually killed her son, how are we to relate to her gesture—as proof of a deranged mind, evidence of the corrupting influence of morbid aestheticism, an extreme and perverse result of maternal fear, pity, and tenderness, of religious fanaticism, or rather of a stern and uncompromising morality?[13] Any interpretation of this disquieting tale finally revolves around our way of reading its two women characters and the implications of their acts of reading, Beatrice's of her husband's manuscript and Gwendolen's of her brother's wife's behavior. But strangely enough, most readings of this story have taken both women characters at face value and credited the narrator's assessment of them, dismissing Gwendolen as morbid but simultaneously trusting her interpretation of Dolcino's death, and sympathizing with Beatrice's moral standing while condemning its desperate excess. Critical attention has focused instead on the two male characters in the story, the artist and the narrator, producing a range of different assessments of their mutual relation and of their respective brands of aestheticism, and consequently of James's attitude to each. In thus concentrating on men as the exclusive representatives in the text of the aesthetic sphere (and, in more recent readings, of a related, exclusively male gender politics), critics have unwittingly reproduced the same ideological arrangement that ostensibly rules the narrative world of the story, namely, the polarity and irreconcilable opposition between men and women, the aesthetic and the domestic sphere. This opposition (in good deconstructive fashion) has operated as a hierarchy, foreclosing—despite several textual signals to the contrary—consideration of women's actual *involvement* in the aesthetic sphere. Rather than producing one more assessment of the characters' psychology and motives and of the plot's development, then, I will try to analyze the terms of women's representation, and the problematic ways in which these intersect with other major preoccupations of this tale to redefine both women and the aesthetic sphere.

Women's Fashions

Paradoxically, in view of their supposed foreignness to the domain of art, the women in literary tales are frequently marked as aestheticist characters. This is the first presentation of Marian Fancourt in "The Lesson of the Master": "Overt saw a tall girl, with magnificent red hair, in a dress of a pretty grey-green tint and of a limp silken texture, in which every modern effect had been avoided. It had therefore somehow the stamp of the latest thing, so that Overt quickly perceived she was eminently a contemporary young lady" (550). The red hair, immediately associating Miss Fancourt with Rossetti's models Elizabeth Siddall and Alexa Wilding; the subdued color and limp texture of the silk (a favorite style with women in Rossetti's paintings, as witness, for instance, "The Day Dream" of 1880, portraying a woman wearing exactly the same tint and make of dress); the sophisticated search for an effect of antiquity, all signal that Marian is the type of the woman aestheticist, even before Overt has mentally remarked on her "aesthetic drapery, which was conventionally unconventional, suggesting a tortuous spontaneity." However, in spite of the unmistakable resemblance between Marian Fancourt and the *Punch* parodies of aestheticist fashion, he convinces himself that "Miss Fancourt was really more candid than her costume," a reassuring fact since "though he was an artist to the essence, the modern reactionary nymph, with the brambles of the woodland caught in her folds and a look as if the satyrs had toyed with her hair, was apt to make him uncomfortable" (555). We go back to this "uncomfortable" feeling of male aesthetes toward female aesthetes, and to their aptness to fault aesthetic women for overdoing it: "The Lesson of the Master," with its two women characters respectively defined in aesthetic and in domestic terms, shares many interesting features with "The Author of 'Beltraffio.'" This attention to aestheticist women's fashion in James's tales of the 1880s extends well into the 1890s, recording the onset of its decadent variant, as witness the following description of Doyne's widow in "The Real Right Thing": "Her effect there—fantastic black, plumed and extravagant, upon deep pink—was that of some 'decadent' coloured print, some poster of the newest school" (129).

The arch-aestheticist among these women is of course Gwendolen in "The Author of 'Beltraffio'": Her laugh was modern—by which

I mean that it consisted of the vocal agitation which, between people who meet in drawing-rooms, serves as the solvent of social mysteries, the medium of transitions; but her appearance was—what shall I call it?—mediaeval. She was pale and angular, with a long, thin face inhabited by sad, dark eyes, and black hair intertwined with golden fillets and curious chains. She wore a faded velvet robe, which clung to her when she moved, fashioned, as to the neck and sleeves, like the garments of old Venetians and Florentines. She looked pictorial and melancholy, and was so perfect an image of a type which I—in my ignorance—supposed to be extinct, that while she rose before me I was almost as much startled as if I had seen a ghost [878].

The Rossetti effect is explicitly underscored a few paragraphs later: "she made up very well as a Rossetti" (879)—a remark suggesting as a further inspiration for the Ambients the relation between Dante Gabriel and Christina Rossetti.[14] Both "The Lesson of the Master" and "The Author of 'Beltraffio'" create a sharp contrast between the pairs of women characters inhabiting them: while Marian Fancourt's style is sharply at variance with Mrs. St. George's "aggressively Parisian dress" (548), Mark Ambient's wife is at the opposite extreme from his sister: "slim and fair, with a long neck and pretty eyes and an air of great refinement"; "a little cold, and a little shy" but "very sweet, and [with] a certain look of race, justified by my afterwards learning that she was 'connected' with two or three great families" (870); "delicate and proper and rather aristocratically dry" (875), "she was, physically speaking, a wonderfully cultivated human plant.... It was impossible to be more pencilled, more garden-like, more delicately tinted and petalled" (894). Were these physical and behavioral traits not enough, a pictorial simile definitely places her in relation to her sister in law: "she herself was not a Rossetti, but a Gainsborough or a Lawrence, and she had in her appearance no elements more romantic than a cold, ladylike candour, and a well-starched muslin dress" (880); "the beautiful mother and beautiful child, interlaced there against their background of roses, made a picture such as I perhaps should not soon see again.... the light hand of Sir Joshua might have painted Mark Ambient's wife and son" (898) .

This seemingly superficial classing of the two women characters according to their external appearance will bear some analysis. The pictorial similes define the two women not just in relation to each other but to the social and cultural ambiences they respectively embody. Beatrice Ambient's highly dignified, upper-class attitude points to the typically British continuum between the higher bourgeoisie and the landed gentry, in the common cultivation of a lifestyle based on decorum, restraint, and the careful improve ment of nature by culture to which Jane Austen's novels constantly bear witness. Like Reynolds's and Gainsborough's decorous family portraits set in parks—shorthand for both harmony with nature and the possession of a family estate—Beatrice Ambient's first appearance in the verdant and picturesque grounds of the Ambients' "old English demesne" (869), sitting in her white muslin in front of "a garden-table, on which a tea-service had been placed," with "her arm round the child's waist" and the child "leaning against her knee" (869), instantly evokes the highly ritualized quality of social life as depicted in the opening scene of *Portrait of a Lady*, as well as the inherent meanings of the "proper lady" as analyzed by Mary Poovey: propriety as instrumental to property, that is, the genealogical transmission of the estate that women's chastity ensures within a patriarchal arrangement.

Such an epitome of bourgeois propriety (and of the economic and social arrangements that underwrite it) is predictably enough the representative of a Philistine conception of art: "'Beatrice thinks a work of art ought to have a "purpose"'" (887); "'her conception of a novel ... is a thing so false that it makes me blush. It is a thing so hollow, so dishonest, so lying, in which life is so blinked and blinded, so dodged and disfigured, that it makes my ears burn.... There's a hatred of art—there's a hatred of literature!'" (893). Interestingly, the blushing face and burning ears—the traditional physical signs of shame at something immoral or disgraceful—are here elicited by the stern morality of the bourgeois requirements for art. This Philistinism is of course sharply contrasted with the Bohemian, artistic, antibourgeois milieu that Gwendolen, even more than Mark Ambient, embodies in the text. Curiously enough, whereas the artist looks like "at once an English gentleman and a man of genius" with "just a little of the Bohemian in his appearance" and the whole is described as "a happy combination" (867), Gwendolen is described in terms of disagreeable artifice and unpleasant excess:

> She was a singular, self-conscious, artificial creature, and I never, subsequently, more than half penetrated her motives and mysteries. Of one thing I am sure, however: that they were considerably less extraordinary than her appearance announced. Miss Ambient was a restless, yearning spinster, consumed with the love of Michael-Angelesque attitudes and mystical robes; but I am pretty sure she had not in her nature those depths of unutterable thought which, when you first knew her, seemed to look out from her eyes and to prompt her complicated gestures.... She had, I believe, the usual allowance of vulgar impulses; she wished to be looked at, she wished to be married, she wished to be thought original.... Putting aside the curious cast of her face, she had no real aptitude for an artis-

tic development—she had little real intelligence. But her affecta-
tions rubbed off on her brother's renown, and as there were plenty
of people who disapproved of him totally, they could easily point
to his sister as a person formed by his influence. It was quite possible to regard her as a warning, and she had done him but little
good with the world at large. He was the original, and she was the
inevitable imitation [878–9].

This uncharacteristically sharp reproof of a character so closely connected to the narrator's idol ("It costs me something to speak in this irrev-
erent manner of Mark Ambient's sister" [879]) should alert us to its deeper
significance in terms of both textual economy and contemporary culture.
A documented social phenomenon, the female aesthete dressing as if she
were a figure out of a painting is a regularly parodied character in the culture of the late 1870s and early 1880s; she makes her appearance in George
du Maurier's cartoons in *Punch* as well as in the Gilbert and Sullivan
operetta *Patience* (1882). Kathy Alexis Psomiades discusses at length the
implications of this contested figure, "the most widely distributed and recognized sign of aestheticist femininity," expressing the "misogynistic recoil
from the feminization of culture and a lower middle-class impatience with
a self-styled cultural elite" (136) experienced by the detractors of aestheticism. Even to the supporters of aestheticism, however, the woman aestheticist was something of a scandalous figure, exactly by virtue of her perfect
consumption and reproduction of an aesthetic aura that should be rightfully reserved for the artist and the work of art: "Through this ability to
signify both art and fashion, imaginary and 'real' femininity, the figure of
the woman aesthete poses and expresses significant challenges to aestheticism's conceptions of art and femininity. In her, the relation between
beauty's accessible surface and her invisible, inaccessible depths begins to
unravel as more and more the surface appears to be the place where art
resides" (Psomiades, 136). Paradoxically, Mark Ambient keeps art pure by
keeping his transgressive aestheticist identity separate from his bourgeois
gentleman's life, whereas Gwendolen, by acting out aestheticist ideas in
her daily life, contaminates and degrades them to the rank of fashion. He
is the artist-creator, in control of the separateness of the aesthetic sphere;
she is the copy-consumer, blurring the boundaries and reducing art to trav-
esty and commodity. The scapegoating mechanism is here operating at full
speed: by displacing on an aesthetic woman consumer the outer marks of
aestheticism that should rightfully belong to the aesthetic male author,
denying them all inner resonance, and amplifying them into parodic excess,
the narrator is able to blame on the female copy the public hostility toward
the male original. Much in the same way, as Schaffer and Psomiades have

argued, aestheticist women writers have been denied the status of independent and original artists, criticized as derivative, and erased from collective memory as a result of male writers' and critics' suspicion of and rivalry with them, in direct proportion to the self-aware challenge they posed to the construction of the aesthetic sphere as male, elitist, and separate.

Significantly, this misguided consumption and use of aesthetic signs is not just gendered as female, but explicitly related to that peculiar economic circuit that is the marriage market: "she wished to be looked at, she wished to be married." Third party and excluded middle in both the homosexual and the heterosexual circuits of desire, Gwendolen is frustratingly close to each and participant of neither, vicariously living the thrills of both. By reading Gwendolen's aesthetic trappings as a trap for prospective husbands, the narrator displays his gender politics and shows the limits of his own aestheticism: despite the aura of free sexuality accompanying the Pre-Raphaelite brotherhood[15] and the perverse desires characterizing aestheticism, what women want in his eyes (all the more if they are "spinsters" like Gwendolen) is, inevitably, to become wives (and by extension, mothers)—a stereotyping that will surface again in his platitudes about "'know[ing] the nature of mothers'" (883) and in his final exhortations to "'Trust a mother—a devoted mother, my dear friend!'" (908). In resorting to "nature" as the tautological explanation of women and to wifehood and motherhood as their true destiny, the narrator reinforces the gendered split separating the aesthetic and the domestic, the homosexual and the heterosexual sphere, but does not entirely account for the aesthetic woman's transgression of boundaries, her "artificial" look visibly disclaiming her allegiance to nature. Hence the narrator's repeated allusion to and simultaneous denial of her possible mystical depths, which by acknowledging a correspondence between her exterior and her interiority would reclassify her as the autonomous and original source of her appearance rather than the mere copy of a deeper original; hence his repeated puzzlement and avowed inability to understand her fully;[16] hence, finally, his confessed "grudge" (879), the sign of his discomfort at a figure that challenges his clear-cut separation of male and female, art and fashion, aesthetic and domestic, sexual and familial: "She was not so mystical as she looked, but she was a strange, indirect, uncomfortable, embarrassing woman" (879). A discomfort that will be echoed, as we have seen, by Paul Overt in "The Lesson of the Master."

However different their appearance and ways, then, the two women in this story share some crucial common traits: both are seen in terms of an inescapable feminine nature, which one woman mystifies and the other fully deploys; both are excluded from the domain of 'true' art, either as derivative imitators or as Philistine opposers; and both are aestheticized in the eyes of the narrator, who constantly reduces them to iconic embodiments of pictorial styles and fitting figures in a landscape perceived and represented through the filter of art:

> There was genius in his house, too; there was imagination in the carpets and curtains, in the pictures and books, in the garden behind it, where certain old brown walls were muffled in creepers that appeared to me to have been copied from a masterpiece of one of the pre–Raphaelites. That was the way many things struck me at that time, in England; as if they were reproductions of something that existed primarily in art or literature. It was not the picture, the poem, the fictive page, that seemed to me a copy; these things were the originals, and the life of happy and distinguished people was fashioned in their image [868].

Within the framework of this generalized inversion of life and art (closely echoing a well-known passage in Proust's *Contre Sainte-Beuve*), women are doubly copies, both as part of a world of nature reconceptualized as a copy of art, and as copies and consumers of art within that world. The apparent paradox of women's representation as at once natural and aestheticized is easily reconciled: here, as in numerous other James stories dealing with artistic representation, women relate to the aesthetic sphere as objects and muses, not as subjects and creators in their own right; even a Philistine like Beatrice Ambient can thus seamlessly figure as "worthy of the author of a work so distinguished as *Beltraffio*" (870) by virtue of her beauty, which equates her with the other objects of her husband's aesthetic passion.[17] Whether they are faulted for being too aesthetic or for not being aesthetic enough, what distinguishes women and connects them to each other despite their surface differences is their lack of agency and their abjection from the sphere of art. Contrasted with that in the narrator's discourse is their privileged status in the sphere of nature and consequently their authority as mothers and caregivers: "'Mrs. Ambient is probably right,' I said to him. 'Women know—women should be supreme in such a situation'" (908).

Decadent Women

What are we to make, then, of a woman and mother—an "angel of propriety" (894), a "perfect nurse" (904)—killing her exquisite only child? Isn't such an event totally unaccountable for in the narrator's ideological framework, and doesn't it refer to a troubling depth behind the polished surface of the Gainsborough family portrait?

Beatrice Ambient's gesture is usually read as the result of a fanatical morality—a worthy preoccupation pushed to an excess, and hence to some extent excusable.[18] In the framework of an art/morals opposition, it is seen as the last resort of an exaggerated moral scruple when confronted with the horror of moral (and sexual) contamination. And certainly the narrator's recurrent emphasis on the child's perfect beauty and on his seductiveness, as well as on his own desire to touch and hold him, authorize the reader to construct him as a "depraved young man" (898) and a threat of pederasty to the child's integrity. Still, the remedy chosen is so extreme as to create a breach in verisimilitude and Victorian decorum—a breach that demands to be read in semiotic rather than mimetic terms. This act— despite its respectable façade, is one of the most violent ever to take place in a James story—with reference not to religion and psychology, but to the dynamics of gender representation and its relation to the aesthetic sphere.

Note the ambivalence of Dolcino, less a character than a living symbol in the Hawthorne tradition, whose meaning, however, is unsettled by a textual policy that makes him an embodied deconstruction of the binaries ostensibly ruling the text. Endowed with a preternatural beauty, he represents at once the promising bloom of life and the shadowy threat of death: "the eyes, the hair, the more than mortal bloom, the smile of innocence. There was something touching, almost alarming, in his beauty, which seemed to be composed of elements too fine and pure for the breath of this world.... he was too charming to live.... there is a kind of charm which is like a death-warrant" (870–1). Although he has "the face of an angel" (870), he is mentally addressed by the narrator as "Poor little devil!" (871)— an expression conveying the narrator's sense of pity at what he perceives as his doom,[19] but also implying those darker possibilities that seem to surface, to the narrator's mind, in the complicity of mutual gaze the child seems to establish with him,[20] a complicity that elicits the narrator's desire to "hold Dolcino in [his] arms" (899) and that "gradually kindled the spark of [his] inspiration," prompting him to the lamentable "perversity" (900) of offering Ambient's manuscript to his wife. Consistent with his ambiguous status as regards the life/death, angel/devil, innocent/perverse binaries (a frequent ambiguity with James's children, as witness *The Turn of the Screw*), Dolcino is also simultaneously on both sides of the art/life divide: a flesh-and-blood child, he is nevertheless "'like a little work of art'" (877) in his beauty, and his status as an art object is reinforced by the miniature of him that hangs from a black velvet ribbon around his mother's neck (870), almost like a painting-within-the-painting. What is more significant, in his wordless dialogue with the narrator he describes himself as the product of a double filiation: "'I am my father's child, but I am also my mother's'" (900), thus pointing not just to the art/morals binary, but also to the two kinds of reproduction that wage battle in this story: the fleshly, sexed, heterosexual reproduction represented by "'[t]he mother that bore me and that presses me here to her bosom'" (900) and the aesthetic reproduction that his father expands on in his talks with the narrator, simultaneously intellectual and asexual *and* marked with homosexual overtones. In an economy of art as rivalling with life such as the one Ambient sketches—"'When I see the kind of things that Life does, I despair of ever catching her peculiar trick. She has an impudence, Life!'" (890)—Beatrice is his competitor and equal: they are both reproducers of life and both creators of works of art, be they in the flesh or of the mind.[21] Hence their enmity: as S. A. Smith writes, "A book and a son and a mother seem to be displaced by one another, suggesting ... that a male authorship and a female maternity cannot exist in the same space" (210).

Framed in this context, Beatrice Ambient's gesture becomes a terrible claim for the power of women as reproducers, set against both their rejection from the sphere of art as the only form of reproduction valued in the aesthetic ideology, and the aesthetic concealment to which the aestheticist credo would subject both woman and child: "I don't in the least consider that I am living in one of his books; I shouldn't care for that, at all" (874). Displaying the troubling potentialities of the platitude piously uttered by the narrator—"women should reign supreme in such a situation" (908)—Beatrice wields her power in the sphere that contemporary culture designates as her own (whether to uphold it as the Victorian repository of moral values or to reject it as inimical to the values of artistic creation), and claims for herself the prerogative of giving and taking life, not in the artistic but in a tragically literal sense. While acting as a maniac in her defense of purity at the cost of life, she is in fact symmetrically reversing the attitude of those artists (and critics) who would evacuate life from art to defend the latter's purity.

The point, however, is not just to pit sexual against artistic reproduction, and align Beatrice Ambient, through her crime, to that lineage of powerful women figures that, according to Nina Auerbach, haunted the Victorian imagination as the troubling underside of the "angel in the house." The subversive potential of Beatrice Ambient's gesture is best understood in the context of James's negotiation of the contemporary gendering of the aesthetic sphere and of women's historically unstable position as regards it.

One might argue that this story is a cautionary tale on the dangers of women readers and on the deadly effects of unsuitable reading on their weak minds and easily heated imaginations. Beatrice Ambient might be seen as a metaphor of "reading as a woman"—that is, as a philistine Victorian woman, applying strict moral standards that would kill art in its cradle and stifle the artist's imagination were they generally enforced.[22] In such a reading, the final catastrophe brought about by the narrator's misguided attempt to reconcile what should have been kept separate would confirm the necessary split between the philistine and the aesthetic public, emblematizing a radical divorce between the aesthetic sphere as it had historically come to be constituted in those years (i.e., professional, artistic, and masculine) and the domestic sphere, gendered as feminine and comprising most of the former reading public (the public of the three-deckers). However, the way women are represented in the tale complicates matters considerably.

In the passage from the Notebooks quoted above, James notes the "unnatural" quality of the catastrophe concluding his story, declaring nonetheless his intention to complete the tale as "full of interest and very typical of certain modern situations" (58). While the "modern" quality of the story suggests the topical character of the aesthetic ambience being addressed in it, "unnatural" is the operative word here. Under a single semantic field—the denial or perversion of "nature"—it connects Beatrice's deviance from a mother's expected behaviour to the other relevant and related transgressions evoked in the story—the aesthetic artist's choice of artifice over nature; the aesthete's perversion of sexual desire 'against nature.'[23] Normal/abnormal, natural/unnatural, healthy/perverse were the key terms of evaluation found in countless comments, reviews and parodies of aestheticism and aestheticist sexuality. Aestheticist women, in particular, were subject to criticism for their cultivation of an aesthetic surface seen as pertaining to the artificial rather than the natural—the result of a labor of self-fashioning, affirming the value of art over life in that most "natural" of fields, the individual's body (Psomiades, 163–164). On the other hand, decent bourgeois women, especially mothers, were the touchstone of woman's "natural" modesty and propriety and they are repeatedly and volubly set against the homoeroticism and homoaestheticism of males both in these tales and in their critical readings. It is somewhat surprising, therefore, to find one of these paradigms of the family as a moral and social value (as well as an economic unit of consumption) bundled in the same bunch and under the same label as the "scarcely edifying" (873) followers of the gospel of art. What becomes contested here is exactly the "nature" of woman, as well as its relation to an aesthetic sphere increasingly perceived as perverse, unnatural, and contaminating.

This effect, I would contend, is not occasioned exclusively by the lurid denouement of the story, but systematically built up in the tale. "The Author of 'Beltraffio'" features not one, but two decadent women: while portraying Gwendolen as an ostensible aestheticist icon through costume and attitude, James covertly constructs Beatrice as a proto-decadent character, by multiplying contradictory signals and allusions that undermine the narrator's simplistic definition of her as an "angel of propriety." Significantly enough, immediately after coming to this conclusion the narrator unwittingly evokes alternative possibilities: "She might have been, for there are guardian-spirits, I suppose, of all great principles—the angel of propriety. Mark Ambient, apparently, ten years before, had simply perceived that she was an angel, without asking himself of what" (894). Let us, then, try to ask this question.

Perceived as a pure, aristocratic, and ennobling (albeit stern) influence, Beatrice Ambient seems to be true to the Dantesque associations of her name. Tellingly, though, she is a Beatrice who, rather than converting her lover, is herself converted (as witness her reading of *Beltraffio* after the child's death). Her very Dantesque associations, furthermore, can be easily read along divergent lines: their Florentine overtones connect her to the Italian background of Ambient's work and of Pater's *Renaissance*, the sensual Italy that she opposes as an immoral influence. Dante's *Commedia* (itself keeping together heaven and hell) is a favorite subject with Pre-Raphaelite artists; Beatrice, in particular, under the guise of Rossetti's *Beata Beatrix*, is a veritable aestheticist icon and a highly suggestive one as regards this tale on account of its explicit association of purity and perfection with aestheticization and death. A quasi-mystical figure and an object of worship to Rossetti (who was obsessed with Dante and identified Beatrice with his adored wife Elizabeth Siddal), the Pre-Raphaelite version of Beatrice figured as both an object of scandal and a secular variant of the Virgin Mary. Indeed, even this most sacred and authoritative figure of motherhood is not devoid of ambiguous associations in this tale: Giovanni Antonio Boltraffio's famous painting in the National Gallery of a Madonna with child holds a book in her right hand, thus prefiguring the final scene of Beatrice reading at Dolcino's bedside. But then, even the Virgin Mary is not exempt from homicidal fantasies cultivated in a good cause, as witness this remark on a Botticelli Madonna in Palazzo Pitti found in James's "Florentine Notes" (1875): "Such a melancholy mother as this of Botticelli would have strangled her baby in its cradle to rescue it from the future" (287)—a remark not unrelated to what goes on in this story. But, going back to the associations of Beatrice's name, there are at least two more: Hawthorne's Beatrice Rappaccini, herself an unwitting poisoner, evoking a father-child relation that will prove fatal to the child, within the framework of an artful perversion of nature; and Beatrice Cenci, an archetype of the tragic murderess that is also central to another Hawthorne text, *The Marble Faun*.

An ambivalent angel at best, as the divergent connotations of her aptly chosen name show, Beatrice Ambient is a powerful figure in which opposite cultural stereotypes coalesce. Philistinic and puritanical but far from submissive, she displays her power through her mastery over the sphere of reproduction, much in the same way as Georgina Gressie in "Georgina's Reasons," another sensational James story collected in the same volume. What is more interesting, as a woman dealer of death, steeped in an atmosphere where disease and contamination figure prominently, she is a decadent *ante litteram*, a *femme fatale* inhabiting a world haunted by corruption. Thus, she displays features of all those decadent stereotypes of powerful and threatening femininity, mostly of Continental origin, that had been widely used in Gustave Moreau's paintings and were then just beginning to circulate in England, where they would especially thrive in the 1890s— the *Belle Dame sans Merci*, Salome, Circe, Morgan le Fay.[24] Prominent among these is of course Medea, the killing mother par excellence, poetically revived in Augusta Webster's *Portraits* in 1870 and represented in several renowned paintings (from Eugène Delacroix to Gustave Moreau to Anthony Frederick Sandys to Edward Burne-Jones) in the second half of the nineteenth century. The comparison with Medea is most revelatory: by letting Dolcino die, Beatrice Ambient is exacting a Medea-like revenge on her husband, acting—like her mythical prototype—out of *jealousy*. By killing her son, she is punishing her husband for yet another triangle—the adulterous, homoerotic, homoaesthetic triangle that, following the narrator's advent, threatens to disrupt the façade of domestic bliss and respectability. In a highly paradoxical gesture, she is simultaneously defending the heterosexual family and disrupting it, both by killing its outcome and by acknowledging its homoerotic alternative.

Indeed, the very construction of Beatrice in terms of a death-dealing femininity associates her with decadence. As Karl S. Guthke argues, the very phenomenon of the prevalent gendering of death as a woman was a new development connected with aestheticism, symbolism, and decadence: whereas earlier figures had been male or indifferently male or female, at this point the most influential representations "portray death as a woman, or rather, as two female figures, not always neatly distinguishable from each other: the angel of death and the seductress. (Hints of motherliness may be associated with either).... What all the forms have in common is the interchangeability of love and death, to the point where one may be mistaken for the other" (186–7). Building on Adorno and Beauvoir, Guthke interprets this decadent development as the return of the repressed—nature and biology—within the male-dominated, rationalistic dialectics of Enlightenment, and as an anxiety-ridden exorcism of the mortality of all living, blamed on women as mothers; that is, responsible for giving life and thus dooming their children to death. Hence the recurrence in fin-de-siècle culture of the iconology of the angel of death—a female angel, unlike the unequivocally male, sword-bearing angels in the Old Testament. In other words, in Beatrice Ambient the Victorian figuration of woman as "by nature" wife and mother, benignant and protective, shades into the decadent, self-awarely archaic and threatening one of the death-inflicting female avenger—an "unnatural" role grounded in the decadent fear and suspicion of woman as nature.

Another typical decadent topos enacted in James's story is the fin-de-siècle notion of the "fatal book," where—as Linda Dowling has written—the implications of decadent linguistic anxiety converge: "The fatal book *is* fatal ... not because of its power to kill outright, but because of its power decisively to change an individual life.... This power of linguistic autonomy becomes in a precise sense Decadent, however, only when portrayed as a poisonous or seducing power" (163–4).[25] By acting out the aesthetic topos of the fateful encounter between the self and what is explicitly termed as the "magical influence" (906) of the book, Beatrice Ambient qualifies as the forerunner of a number of better known aestheticist enactments of the same, ranging from "The Golden Book" in Pater's *Marius the Epicurean* (see appendix) to Gautier's *Mademoiselle de Maupin*, in George Moore's *Confessions of a Young Man*, to the book Lord Henry Wotton gives the hero in Wilde's *Dorian Gray*, or the guilty book mentioned in Rossetti's *Jenny*: "Like a rose shut in a book/In which pure women may not look/For its base pages claim control/To crush the flower within the soul" (vv. 253–6). As both Freedman and Wirth-Nesher note, by having her child die rather than be touched by his father's books, Beatrice Ambient confers on art an absolute shaping power that neither Mark nor Gwendolen claim for it (Freedman 145; Wirth-Nesher 120). This faith would already suffice to prove her the true decadent; what neither critic notes, however, is that Beatrice Ambient is herself an illustration of this topos, which perfectly applies to her own reading of Mark Ambient's manuscript.

This amounts to saying that Henry James is not just *representing* decadent topoi here; he is also *employing* them.[26] By conflating the fair Victorian lady and the decadent dark lady into a single character, he is revealing
the split *within* woman, rewriting both womanhood and the aesthetic experience in terms of complexity, as the mutual involvement of the alleged
binaries: art/life, art/morality, aesthetic/domestic.[27] By representing the
immoral male aesthete as a good bourgeois and a doting father, he is under-
scoring their mutual relation and interdependence, depicting the artist's
sexuality as not monolithic but ambiguously poised between conventional
masculinity—valued in terms of successful family, economic and social
life—and homosocial, homoerotic validation among confrères. By displacing aestheticist marks from the male artist to the female reader, and by a
self-aware *textual* extension of the sphere of decadence to include what is
allegedly outside of and opposed to it—women as mothers, the hearth as
reassuring seat of religion and social morality, the family as domestic readership—he is producing a paradox à la Wilde that undermines the
dichotomized gender arrangements regulating both the social and the aesthetic sphere. By playing on the more troubling potentialities of the culturally shared notion of women's "nature," and by doing so in terms that
are the highly artificial and exquisitely artistic ones of contemporary aestheticism and decadence (with all its suggestions of dark and perverse sexuality), he deconstructs the cultural split between the "natural"—healthy,
sane, edifying—and the "unnatural"—artificial, perverse, depraved—haunting contemporary culture. Significantly enough, the epithet of "queer"—a
telling word in James's use—earlier applied to Mark Ambient and to his
sister,[28] eventually comes to designate Beatrice as well: "I settled down to
my quarto again, with the reflection that Mrs. Ambient was a queer woman"
(903), says the narrator immediately after she has picked up the manuscript that will precipitate the tragic denouement.

Far from being a tale on the irreconcilable enmity between art and
life, the aesthetic and the domestic, artists and women, the homoerotic and
the heterosexual, the aesthetic and the moral, "The Author of 'Beltraffio'"
seems to me a tale on their puzzling, inevitable mutual implication, and a
relentless critique of their contemporary construction as sets of binaries.
This has also a bearing on the issue of readership. While James is certainly
depicting the contemporary gendering of readership and the historical
divide between different kinds of readers, he is also undermining its rigid
partitions. By contaminating the purity of the household and by rendering the angel in the house as an angel of death, James is also subverting
the representation of woman and of family values that grounded the Philis-

tine appeal to the woman reader as compulsory moral standard for a work of art. In that sense, the image of Beatrice sitting at her son's bedside, holding in her hand an aesthete's immoral work rather than an edifying Victorian book, is in itself a strikingly subversive one. By involving the guardian of morality in the decadent dynamics of the tale and by focusing on the dangerous interaction between the artwork and the woman reader— unleashing potentialities that are *already* hers and that explode conventional femininity, bringing out its darker side—the tale stages the *complicity* of the would-be detached, superior moral standing and the woman reader's involvement in that "unnatural" aesthetic world which she would reject, and from which she would be rejected in her turn.

According to Freedman, James's relation to aestheticism was "self-conscious, self-defining, and—ultimately—self-critical" (206): while recognizably sharing with aestheticism a number of crucial preoccupations, he seems to have simultaneously inscribed it in his texts and subjected it to what postmodernist lexicon would term a "complicitous critique." His unsettling representation of women in "The Author of 'Beltraffio'" provides a key to this complex gesture of simultaneous affiliation and disaffiliation.

Notes

1. I wish to thank Luisa Villa and Mario Corona for having, once again, shared my Jamesian readings and offered their suggestions, encouragements, and criticisms. To Mario Corona, in particular, I owe crucial insights regarding the gay subtext of this story—insights I hope he may be soon convinced to expand into a critical reading of his own.

2. "The Author of 'Beltraffio,'" 1884; "The Lesson of the Master," 1888; "Collaboration," 1892; "The Private Life," 1892; "The Middle Years," 1893; "Greville Fane," 1893; "The Death of the Lion," 1894 ; "The Coxon Fund," 1894; "The Next Time," 1895; "The Figure in the Carpet," 1896; "John Delavoy," 1898; "The Real Right Thing," 1899. Of these, three—"The Death of the Lion," "The Coxon Fund," and "The Next Time"—were published in *The Yellow Book*. Most of these tales were included, along with others, in Matthiessen's collection, *Stories of Writers and Artists* (1944), which provided a fundamental impulse toward their collective canonization.

3. It should be noted, though, that Matthiessen—a committed and militant scholar himself—clearly wished to rescue James from the image of an artist living in refined isolation from the general current of life. After introducing the tales in terms of the split between art and life, he goes on to examine the well known polemic between James and Wells, and finally claims that James really displayed more "[a]ttention, perception, sympathy" than his critic, and that his "scruples and renunciations" were not "sterile emptiness" but rather "the guides to a peculiarly poignant suffering and inner triumph" (17).

4. See Felski, Gilbert and Gubar.

5. This phenomenon applied both to British and to American culture: "The man of letters must make up his mind that in the United States the fate of a book is in the hands of the women," lamented Howells in "The Man of Letters as a Man of Business," *Scribner's Magazine*, XVI (July-December 1893), p.438.

6. For important contributions recovering this tradition and discussing the motives and modes of their erasure see Gagnier, Schaffer and Psomiades.

7. This issue has been widely explored over the last few years. For a particularly effective discussion, see Stevens, *Henry James and Sexuality*.

8. Savoy quotes Sedgwick's *Tendencies* on the "avunculate" as "a metonym for the whole range of older men who might form a relation to a younger man, offering a degree of *initiation* into gay cultures and identities" and consequently "not a persona or type but a *relation*, relying on a pederastic/pedagogical model of male filiation" (Sedgwick 59–60, quoted in Savoy, "Embarrassments," 233). This kind of relation is obviously privileged in these tales.

9. "And after a little, one of them said—it didn't matter which: 'It's here we're *with* him" (123); "Withermore gasped as it came to him why he had lost his friend. 'He has been with *you*?'" (129).

10. See Freedman 172; Haralson 62–6; Kaplan 301–3; Novick 369–70; Stevens "Resistance to Query" 261–2.

11. On discovering that the visiting neighbor he meets at Ambient's is the vicar's wife, the narrator remarks that "there was a certain surprise for me in seeing the author of *Beltraffio* even in such superficial communion with the Church of England" (871). Later, talking of Ambient, he adds that despite his uncompromising devotion to art, "at bottom the poor fellow ... had an extreme dread of scandal" (882).

12. Apart from a suggestive use of "gay" and "queer" at some points in the text, textual hints are Ambient's declaration that his wife thinks him "'immoral—that's the long and short of it'" (893); the narrator's explicit attraction to Dolcino—repeatedly described as seductive as well as beautiful—and his expectation that Ambient would be "an object of horror to vicars and their ladies" (871). The implication of haunting 'immorality,' however, is mainly conveyed through its effects on characters: Beatrice's horror at her husband and dislike for his followers ("She thought me an obtrusive and even depraved young man, whom a perverse Providence had dropped upon their quiet lawn to flatter her husband's worst tendencies" [898]), Gwendolen's unconventional attitude, and the narrator's own reactions to Ambient's credo; despite his self-definition as "a young American of an aesthetic turn" (867), he declares that his "youthful mind was considerably astonished at some of his speeches; he startled me and he made me wince" (882).

13. Recent critics, such as Scoggins, have frequently focused on the narrator's aesthetic irresponsibility as totally or partially to blame for Beatrice Ambient's gesture; Freier even suggests that the scene of Dolcino's death has been invented by Gwendolen. Most critical readings produced over the last few years, though, bring to the front the question of homosexuality rather than the interpretation of the story's ending: see for instance Bradley and Monk. For a history of criticism on "The Author of 'Beltraffio'" see Albers (44–71).

14. A further allusion to Pre-Raphaelitism is the narrator's later mention of Gwendolen as having "some of the qualities of the sibyl" (904), an allusion recalling countless paintings of sibyls by Pre-Raphaelites, from Rossetti's *Sibylla Palmifera* onward.

15. A hint of such an aura can be traced in the mention of nymphs and satyrs by the narrator of "The Lesson of the Master."

16. "I never, subsequently, more than half penetrated her motives and mysteries" (878); "I am bound to say that I feel I can only half account for her" (879).

17. "'Perhaps I care too much for beauty—I don't know; I delight in it, I adore it, I think of it continually, I try to produce it, to reproduce it. My wife holds that we shouldn't think too much about it. She's always afraid of that—always on her guard. I don't know what she has got on her back! And she's so pretty, too, herself! Don't you think she's lovely? She was, at any rate, when I married her. At that time I wasn't aware of that difference I speak of—I thought it all came to the same thing: in the end, as they say'" (892).

18. While most critics objected to the unpleasantness and immorality of the tale as a whole, the anonymous reviewer for *The Nation* (12 March 1885) suggested that most English-speaking people, in their deep-rooted demand for moral purity in art, would probably sympathize with the mother.

19. "I felt a sudden pity for him, as if he had been an orphan, or a changeling, or stamped with some social stigma" (871).

20. "I found myself looking perpetually at Dolcino, and Dolcino looked back at me, and that was enough to detain me. When he looked at me he smiled, and I felt it was an absolute impossibility to abandon a child who was smiling at one like that. His eyes never wandered; they attached themselves to mine, as if among all the small incipient things of his nature there was a desire to say something to me. If I could have taken him upon my own knee he perhaps would have managed to say it; but it would have been far too delicate a matter to ask his mother to give him up, and it has remained a constant regret for me that on that Sunday afternoon I did not, even for a moment, hold Dolcino in my arms" (898–9); "his exaggerated eyes, which had wandered, caught my own as I watched him. 'Do *you* think me agreeable?' he inquired, with the candour of his age and with a smile" (899).

21. Metaphors for artistic creation as pregnancy or fatherhood abound not just in the later Prefaces, but in such coeval stories as "The Death of the Lion," "The Coxon Fund," and "The Next Time."

22. A telling instance of this "double standard" is the dialogue between Ambient and the narrator, where Ambient plays on the notion of "bad," distinguishing what is "bad" for art from what is "bad" for children (892).

23. Interestingly enough, Dolcino is also perceived as looking "unnatural" (906) in his illness, while his mother is sitting at his bedside reading Ambient's manuscript—as if the diphtheria he has contracted and the aesthetic contagion that surrounds him were one and the same.

24. See Bernheimer; Dijkstra; Palacio.

25. Dowling devotes the whole of her chapter three, "The Fatal Book," to this topos, which is also examined in Praz's seminal *Romantic Agony*. Jonathan Freedman also agrees that "the transforming encounter between self and art object is a central—perhaps *the* central—topos of the aesthetic imagination in England" (211) in his reading of *The Wings of the Dove* as James's aestheticist novel.

26. Let me note in passing that James was himself perceived as a decadent by his American contemporaries on account of his association with British aestheticism and with *The Yellow Book* (Freedman, 177). The volume, taking its title from "The Author of 'Beltraffio,'" in particular was violently criticized by an anonymous reviewer in *Critic* (May 1885), defining the story "a painful and repulsive story, fol-

lowed by several others hardly less painful and repulsive," and going on to say that "Shine on putrescence as genius may, it cannot glorify it." After defining these stories as "*fleurs du mal*," the reviewer warns the author "not to patch his tunic with the cast-off purple patches of a fast-decaying Frenchy school, however great the temptation" (206–7). For a reading of the story in terms of decadence, see Geoffroy-Menoux.

27. Treitel also sees Beatrice as an embodiment of conflicting stereotypes. The conflation of dark and fair is also effected through the misleading signals pertaining to Gwendolen. On her first presentation we are told that her attitude of dejection and disillusionment could only be justified by her "having committed a crime for which she was consumed with remorse" (879), a false hint of something that will later apply to Beatrice. To complete the chiastic exchange of roles, the aestheticist sibyl ends up retiring to a Sisterhood, "deeply immured and quite lost to the world" (907). As Freedman notes, a similar process is also affected in *The Wings of the Dove* through James's fusion of the iconography of the innocent American girl and of the Dark Lady in Millie's presentation (Freedman 222–3).

28. "'Mark's ideas are—well, really—rather queer!' I reflected ... that none of them were probably quite so queer as his sister" (888).

Works Cited

Albers, Christina E. *A Reader's Guide to the Short Stories of Henry James.* New York: Hall, 1997.

Auerbach, Nina. *Woman and the Demon. The Life of a Victorian Myth.* Cambridge and London: Harvard University Press, 1982.

Bernheimer, Charles. *Decadent Subjects. The Idea of Decadence in Art, Literature, Philosophy, and Culture of the Fin de Siècle in Europe.* Edited by T. Jefferson Kline and Naomi Schor. Baltimore and London: The Johns Hopkins University Press, 2002.

Bourdieu *Les Règles de l'art. Genèse et Structure du Champ Littéraire.* Paris: Seuil, 1992.

Bradley, John R. *Henry James's Permanent Adolescence.* Houndmills, Palgrave, 2000.

Dijkstra, Bram. *Idols of Perversity : Fantasies of Feminine Evil in Fin-de-Siècle Culture.* Oxford and New York: Oxford University Press, 1986.

Dowling, Linda. *Language and Decadence in the Victorian Fin de Siècle.* Princeton: Princeton University Press, 1986.

Felski, Rita. *The Gender of Modernity.* Cambridge, MA: Harvard University Press, 1995.

Freedman, Jonathan. *Professions of Taste: Henry James, British Aestheticism, and Commodity Culture.* Stanford: Stanford University Press, 1990.

Freier, Mary P. "The Story of 'The Author of Beltraffio.'" *Studies in Short Fiction* 24, no. 3 (Summer 1987): 308–9.

Gagnier, Regenia. "Women in British Aestheticism and the Decadence." In *The New Woman in Fiction and Fact: Fin-de-Siècle Feminisms.* Edited by Angelique Richardson and Chris Willis. Houndmills: Palgrave, 2001.

Geoffroy-Menoux, Sophie. *Miroirs d'Outre-Monde: Henry James et la Création Fantastique.* Paris : L'Harmattan, 1996.

Gilbert, Sandra, and Susan Gubar. *No Man's Land: The Place of the Woman Writer in the Twentieth Century.* New Haven, CT.: Yale University Press, 1988–1994.

Guthke, Karl S. *The Gender of Death: A Cultural History in Art and Literature*. Cambridge: Cambridge University Press, 1999.

Haralson, Eric. *Henry James and Queer Modernity*. Cambridge: Cambridge University Press, 2003.

Izzo, Donatella. *Portraying the Lady. Technologies of Gender in the Short Stories of Henry James*. Lincoln and London: University of Nebraska Press, 2001.

James, Henry. *Complete Stories, 1874–1884*. Edited by William L. Vance. New York: The Library of America, 1999.

_____. *Complete Stories, 1884–1891*. Edited by Edward Said. New York: The Library of America, 1999.

_____. *Complete Stories, 1892–1898*. Edited by David Bromwich and John Hollander. New York: The Library of America, 1996.

_____. *Complete Stories, 1898–1910*. Edited by Denis Donoghue. New York: The Library of America, 1996.

_____. "Florentine Notes." In *Italian Hours*. New York: Grove Press, 1979.

_____. *The Notebooks*. Edited by F. O. Matthiessen and Kenneth B. Murdock. Chicago and London: The University of Chicago Press, 1981.

Kaplan, Fred. *Henry James: The Imagination of Genius, A Biography*. Baltimore and London: The Johns Hopkins University Press, 1992.

Matthiessen, Francis Otto. "Introduction: Henry James's Portrait of the Artist." In *Stories of Writers and Artists*, by Henry James. Norfolk, CT: New Directions, 1944.

Monk, Leland. "A Terrible Beauty Is Born: Henry James, Aestheticism, and Homosexual Panic." Edited by Thomas Foster, Carol Siegel, and Ellen E. Berry. In *Bodies of Writing, Bodies in Performance*. New York and London: New York University Press, 1996.

Novick, Sheldon M. *Henry James: The Young Master*. New York: Random House, 1996, Jean de. *Figures et Formes de la Décadence*. Paris: Séguier, 1994.

Palacio, Jean de. *Figures et Formes de la Décadence*. Paris: Séguier, 1994.

Person, Leland S. *Henry James and the Suspense of Masculinity*. Philadelphia: University of Pennsylvania Press, 2003.

Poovey, Mary. *The Proper Lady and the Woman Writer. Ideology as Style in the Works of Mary Wollstonecraft, Mary Shelley, and Jane Austen*. Chicago: University of Chicago Press, 1984.

Psomiades, Kathy Alexis. *Beauty's Body: Femininity and Representation in British Aestheticism*. Stanford: Stanford University Press, 1997.

Savoy, Eric. "*Hypocrite Lecteur*: Walter Pater, Henry James and Homotextual Politics." *Dalhousie Review* 72, no. 1 (1992): 12–36.

_____. "Embarrassments: Figure in the Closet." *The Henry James Review* 20, no. 3 (Fall 1999): 227–36.

Schaffer, Talia, and Kathy Alexis Psomiades, eds. *Women and British Aestheticism*. Charlottesville and London: University Press of Virginia, 1999.

Scoggins, James. "'The Author of *Beltraffio*': A Reapportionment of Guilt." *Texas Studies in Literature and Language* 5, no. 2 (Summer 1963): 265–70.

Sedgwick, Eve Kosofsky. *Between Men: English Literature and Male Homosocial Desire*. New York: Columbia University Press, 1985.

_____. *Tendencies*. London and New York: Routledge, 1994.

Showalter, Elaine. *Sexual Anarchy: Gender and Culture at the Fin de Siècle*. London: Virago, 1990.

Smith, Stephanie A. *Conceived by Liberty: Maternal Figures and Nineteenth-Century American Literature*. Ithaca and London: Cornell University Press, 1994.

Stevens, Hugh. *Henry James and Sexuality*. Cambridge: Cambridge University Press, 1998.

_____. "The Resistance to Queory: John Addington Symonds and 'The Real Right Thing.'"

The Henry James Review 20, no. 3 (Fall 1999): 255–64.

Treitel, Ilona. "Absence as Metaphor in Henry James's 'The Author of "Beltraffio."'" *Studies in Short Fiction* 34, no. 2 (Spring 1997): 171–82.

Wirth-Nesher, Hana. "The Thematics of Interpretation: James's Artist Tales." *The Henry*

James Review 5, no. 2 (Winter 1984): 117–27.

"The Master in the Middle Distance": Max Beerbohm, Henry James and Literary Forgery

MAURIZIO ASCARI

A disingenuous and provocative frivolity—a love for masks, makeup and artifice—pervades the works of Max Beerbohm. Suffice it to think of the subtle parable Beerbohm set in Regency times, *The Happy Hypocrite* (1897). In this tale the profligate George Hell is hopelessly in love with the young actress Jenny Mere, who refuses his advances because his face is "tarnished by the reflexion of this world's vanity" (22), but thanks to the help of a mask-maker George Hell becomes George Heaven. When his vengeful former mistress obliges him to reveal his true identity to Jenny, we discover that his pure love for the girl (or is it the mask?) has worked a miracle, for "his face was even as his mask had been. Line for line, feature for feature, it was the same. 'Twas a saint's face" (65).

This aesthetic parable—featuring a mask that can change the underlying face—is an apt symbol of Beerbohm's "creative criticism." Indeed Beerbohm's caricatures and parodies not only de-form his fellow writers so that we can see them better, perceiving their authentic nature, but also influenced their reception, ultimately changing their profile.[1] We can consider Beerbohm's parodies as a pure example of *art for art's sake*, a form that thrives on form, turning its back on life. Yet we also know that the brightest parodies are far from being mere exercises in style or instances of literary nostalgia. On the contrary, they are precious critical tools that enable the writer to pay homage to greatness while distancing himself from it. One of the most interesting instances of Beerbohm's critical attitude is the literary symbiosis, which linked him to Henry James through a whole range of forms—parody, caricature and satire.

Beerbohm's celebrated "The Mote in the Middle Distance" (1912) is described by Guido Almansi and Guido Fink as a literary time bomb. While other parodies do not survive a second reading, as the two critics mischievously remark, this text actually needs one; but with what result? To prove that "if we deprive James (or Beerbohm mimicking James) of his Jamesianism," as a result "we have nothing," simply a blank page (94). This experience reveals the deep and disconcerting idea that all literature is ultimately a mask—the mask that conceals the *story* behind the *discourse*—and that our appreciation as readers resides precisely in the aesthetic quality of that mask. With a final *coup de théâtre* Almansi and Fink also show that stories like "The Figure in the Carpet" and *The Turn of the Screw* are beset with formidable literary traps, enabling James to make fun of those professional readers who naively believe that their critical digging will lead them from the "falsity" of appearance to the "truth" of substance (84).

Conversely, one could claim that Beerbohm was interested in James precisely because of the writer's painstaking attention to the surface of language as well as his epistemological attitude, grounded on the impossibility of obtaining an objective knowledge of reality. Let us remember the emphasis with which Walter Pater—in his Conclusion to *The Renaissance* (1873)—described the "thick wall of personality through which no real voice has ever pierced on its way to us, or from us to that which we can only conjecture to be without" (51). While Pater (see appendix, *Marius the Epicurean*), was the apologist of "critical impressionism," James was a precursor of the "narrative impressionism" that marked the turn of the century, and a rather reckless experimenter, for he took this technique to the extreme consequences, offering his readers a rarefied vision of reality, mediated by virtually impenetrable layers of self-consciousness.

This is the subject of the critical sonnet "To Henry James," which was written alternatively, line by line, by Beerbohm and Edmund Gosse:

> Say, indefatigable alchemist
> Melts not the very moral of your scene,
> Curls it not off in vapour from between
> Those lips that labour with conspicuous twist?
> Your fine eyes, blurred like arc-lamps in a mist,
> Immensely glare, yet glimmerings intervene,
> So that your May-Be and your Might-Have-Been
> Leave us still plunging for your genuine gist.

How different from Sir Arthur Conan Doyle,
As clear as water and as smooth as oil,
And no jot knowing of what Maisie knew!
Flushed with the sunset air of roseate Rye
You stand, marmoreal darling of the Few,
Lord of the troubled speech and single Eye.

In this short poem—a casket full of critical treasures—James is presented as an alchemist of art who dematerializes reality, transforming it into an almost intangible form, a pure element that bears little trace of its former connection with life. The two writers also concentrate on James's omnivorous gaze, which characteristically recurs in many parodies, bringing us back to James's theory of the novel, notably to his well-known metaphor of the "house of fiction," behind whose innumerable windows an army of observers intensely stare at the horizon of life. Yet, the penetrating gaze of James clashes with the elusive character of reality and the complexity of every relation. The result of this confrontation is cognitive relativism, the ordeal of doubt that differentiates James from Conan Doyle, turning the former's novels into a refined dish that is destined for the happy few. Detection provided Beerbohm with a standard to underline the contrast of James's indirectness, and in one of his caricatures we are offered the nightmarish vision of James, who is called to testify as psychological expert in a *cause célèbre*, while a cross-examiner impatiently exclaims: "Come, Sir, I ask you a plain question, and I expect a plain answer!"

Not surprisingly, Beerbohm had a predilection for James's *late manner*, where reality is evoked through a halo of perceptions and inferences that translate into a stylistic maze. Incidentally, Keith and Eva Tantalus, the young heroes of "The Mote in the Middle Distance," are considered by critics as the ironic equivalents of Merton Densher and Kate Croy in the final scene of *The Wings of the Dove* (1902).[2] Beerbohm, however, did not seem to like James's act of self-travesty, the rewriting of himself he enacted when he revised his works for the New York edition. This disquieting internal conflict is the subject of a famous caricature by Beerbohm, where an old and corpulent James addresses a vehement accusation to his younger alter ego, who symmetrically reproaches him: "How badly you wrote!" / "How badly you write!"[3]

Various caricatures astutely capture the misty atmosphere of James's works. In "Mr. Henry James Revisiting America" (1905), an Indian chief welcomes him with these words, "Hail, great white novelist! Tuniyaba—the Spinner of fine cobwebs!" (94). Another image shows the writer wrapped in a dense fog—which is better described in the convoluted caption as "this to him so very congenial atmosphere"[4]—while James stares interrogatively at the hand he holds an inch or so from his eyes. On the cover of James's volume A Finer Grain, Beerbohm drew a sketch he entitled "A Memory" (1920), showing the Master in the act of shading his eyes from a vision that deeply unsettles him (Danson, 13).

James's famous reticence is also the subject of a caricature which was inspired by his essay on Gabriele D'Annunzio, where the Italian writer's vulgar treatment of passion is compared to "the boots and shoes that we see, in the corridors of promiscuous hotels, standing, often in double pairs, at the doors of rooms" (292). In Beerbohm's picture, James himself is kneeling beside the boots and shoes lined in front of a hotel room, staring at those incongruous objects, perhaps overhearing what is happening behind the door, as if to catch an echo of that great mystery (Davis, 83).

In addition to these revealing portraits, several of Beerbohm's biographical sketches rewrite James's life in the style of his novels.[5] In "An Incident"[6] Beerbohm related a curious episode that purportedly happened to him in 1906. The writer was going to his club to read a new story by James— "The Velvet Glove"—when he met the Master himself, who invited Beerbohm to accompany him to an exhibition. The man, however, would not fall into the trap the muse of writing had set for him that day and, feigning a previous engagement, went dutifully on to the Savile. Yet once at the club, Beerbohm found he could not fully concentrate on his book, which did not offer him "so intensely Jamesian a story as James would have founded on the theme of what had just been happening between us—the theme of a disciple loyally—or unloyally"—preferring the Master's work to the Master ("An Incident," 133).

James's stories of writers—such as "The Lesson of the Master" (1888), "The Private Life" (1892) or "The Death of the Lion" (1894)—abound in similar predicaments and play on the hiatus between the human being and the artist who happens to inhabit the same body, making it clear that "The artist's life's his work, and this is the place to observe him" (275). By reshaping his own relationship with James in the style of the latter's fiction, Beerbohm created a correspondence between those two planes, having life imitate art, according to Wilde's injunction. Biography is thus aestheticized—invention prevails over fact, a symbolic harmony supersedes the chaos of circumstances. Creatively rewriting the lives of the great, Beerbohm achieved a form akin to Pater's imaginary portraits, which are a hybrid of the essay and the short story, biography and autobiography.[7]

In crossing the boundaries between traditional genres, Beerbohm also anticipated Virginia Woolf's view of biography as a combination of truth and personality—granite and rainbow.[8] Moreover, the stories he collected in *Seven Men* (1919) can be likened to the playful modernist attitude that permeates *Orlando: A Biography* (1928). It is therefore not surprising that Woolf used precisely Pater and Beerbohm as aesthetic paragons in her meditations on essay writing, which went under the title "The Modern Essay" (1925). Here Beerbohm is described as "without doubt the prince of his profession" (221), by virtue of the gift he offered the public, the purest distillation of himself:

> He has brought personality into literature, not unconsciously and impurely, but so consciously and purely that we do not know whether there is any relation between Max the essayist and Mr. Beerbohm the man.... The triumph is the triumph of style. For it is only by knowing how to write that you can make use in literature of yourself; that self, which, while it is essential to literature, is also its most dangerous antagonist [220–21].

Through his essays and stories Beerbohm managed to accomplish a notable aesthetic feat, i.e., to turn himself into a literary character. As we know, Max is the seventh man Beerbohm portrayed in his gallery of imaginary portraits. Likewise, in the first of these portraits the unfortunate poet Enoch Soames, after selling his soul to the devil to travel into the future and see the signs of his posthumous fame, makes the disheartening discovery that he will be recorded in the British Library only as an imaginary character invented by Max Beerbohm (*Seven Men*, 33). These are only a few of the several short-circuits between art and life that make Beerbohm's work so fascinating a display of intelligence, so charming a piece of *trompe l'oeil*.

Given his love for masks and illusionism, it is not surprising that Beerbohm also analyzed the illusionistic element in James's works, paving the way for a critical appraisal of James's texts in relation to aestheticism. A case in point is "Books within Books" (1914), an eccentric essay Beerbohm devoted to those nonexisting books which are authored by literary characters. With his usual levity of tone, actually based on a deep theoretical awareness, Beerbohm focused his critical attention on what he deemed a literary theme par excellence, due to its auto-referential character. Yet the major British novelists had hypocritically eschewed this topic, with the notable exception of James, who thanks to his cosmopolitan status had found the courage and faith to devise stories that hinge on the works of imaginary writers.[9]

In his essay Beerbohm recounts the story of books such as Mark Ambient's *Beltraffio*, subtly playing on its implicit sexual ambiguity: "We are not told what exactly was the title of that second book which Ambient's wife so hated that she let her child die rather than that he should grow up under the influence of its author; but I have a queer conviction that it was The Daisies" ("Books," 109–10). Although "The Author of 'Beltraffio'" dates back to 1884, Beerbohm's essay was published in 1914. It is therefore difficult to imagine that while rereading the story Beerbohm did not happen to regard it as an indirect forewarning of the scandal that had befallen Wilde in the nineties.

As his tales of writers and artists show, James ironically courted masks and lies in art, without, however, taking a clear-cut position in the conflict that opposed the conventional Victorian thinkers to the prophets of aestheticism. As we know, the relationship James had with the aesthetes is contradictory. On the one hand, he shared their interest in subjectivity and the interaction between the arts, stopping short of the cult of art for art's sake, but he also wished to dissociate himself from the aesthetes, partly because he was aware of the homoerotic undertones of that literary milieu. In this respect, James's tales of writers can be regarded as a laboratory where James experimented with the various identities a fin de siècle writer could take on, using gender itself as a mask. This is what happens in "The Death of the Lion," where—in Beerbohm's words—"we make incidental acquaintance with Guy Walsingham, the young lady who wrote Obsessions, and with Dora Forbes, the burly man with a red moustache who wrote The Other Way Round" ("Books," 110).

Walsingham and Forbes, however, are novelists of dubious worth, who are merely seeking publicity, while James—following a traditional path— usually tended to associate the essence of art with truth rather than the contrary. In another famous short story, "The Liar" (1888), Colonel Capadose's flair for lying is described by the narrator as a form of aestheticism: "'He is the liar platonic,' he said to himself; 'he is disinterested, he doesn't operate with a hope of gain or with a desire to injure. It is art for art and he is prompted by the love of beauty.'" At first the narrator, who is a painter, goes so far as to acknowledge Capadose as a fellow artist—"'He paints, as it were, and so do I!'" (346). Yet the portrait that unmistakably reveals Capadose's ambiguous talent for alternative realities is surreptitiously destroyed by him and his wife, an ending that anticipates Dorian Gray's suicidal act and stigmatizes the art of lying as ultimately (self-) destructive.[10]

The contrast between truth and lies (inevitably in the plural) recurs in The Aspern Papers (1888), where Miss Tina describes the discoveries of literary critics as "mostly lies" and the narrator self-deceptively replies, "'The lies are what they sometimes discover.... They often lay bare the truth'" (85). James's dislike of biographers is proverbial and this is only one of the various parables he wrote to denounce their prying into the private lives of authors. Instead of focusing on the poetry of Aspern, the narrator of the story has developed a morbid curiosity about his life and, embodying a typical Victorian prejudice, intends to use it as a standard with which to measure the value of his work. The biographer's interest in Aspern's miniature is an emblem of his misguided attitude, and reminds one, by contrast, of the fake miniature that features in Wilde's "The Portrait of Mr. W. H." (1889). Aspern's portrait, which at first enables the narrator to experience a mystical communion with the poet, ironically turns against him, alternatively revealing mockery and compassion, when Juliana exacts the narrator's marriage with Tina as the price to be paid for Aspern's letters. The narrator's unconscious attempt to rewrite and purify the life of the poet so that it suits the high aesthetic status of his work proves a disastrous failure, for the past strikes back, threatening to rewrite the life of the biographer as a parody of Aspern's Venetian love story.

The opposition between truth and lies is also at the heart of "The Birthplace" (1903), the story James devoted to Shakespeare's house in Stratford. For the want of any positive traces of the great poet's actual life, a disappointed and tormented guide reverts to the creative power of his imagination, thereby remaining faithful—on an artistic, not factual, plane— to the genius who is revered in the house. Morris Gedge is conscious of *overdoing* his performances and his wife is worried that he will lose his job on this account,

> "Don't they want then *any* truth? None even for the mere look of it?"
> "The look of it," said Morris Gedge, "is what I give!" [156].[11]

At this stage in the story, truth is reduced to a mask, a semblance of coherence and plausibility, but when in the climactic scene of the story Gedge realizes that his technique is a success because bigger and bigger crowds flock to the shrine, he also finds his lies morally justifiable since truth is to be found elsewhere:

> "The receipts, it appears, speak."
> He was nursing his effect; Isabel intently watched on him, and the others hung on his lips. "Yes, speak—?"
> "Well, volumes. They tell the truth."
> At this Mr. Hayes laughed again. "Oh, *they* at least do?" [160].

With this play on words James created a subtle ambiguity. On the one hand, you have the prosaic truth of money, for the Bard's Birthplace is first and foremost a commercial enterprise; on the other, there is the truth of art, but it is by lying that Gedge is able at the same time to keep up the show and to fulfil his inner calling, renewing the public interest in the work.

James did not go so far as to turn forgery into a theme and to lament the decay of lying, as Oscar Wilde did, but stopped on the brink of this attitude, mingling truth with its alternatives, thus achieving—mainly through irony—a peculiar balance between nineteenth-century realism and fin-de-siècle aestheticism. In view of these facts, Beerbohm's choice to celebrate James through various kinds of forgery—as Ford Madox Ford did a few years later in the delightfully unreliable *Mightier than the Sword* (1938)— seems particularly apt. After all, since the Master repeatedly asserted that an artist's life is his work, what better homage could the modernists offer him than transforming it into a work of art?

Notes

1. Meditating on the ambivalent and paradoxical status of this literary genre, which implies at the same time authority and transgression, Linda Hutcheon wrote: "Overtly imitating art more than life, parody self-consciously and self-critically points us to its own nature." Linda Hutcheon, *A Theory of Parody: The Teachings of Twentieth-Century Art Forms* (1985), New York: Routledge, 1991, p. 69

2. See Lawrence Danson, *Max Beerbohm and the Act of Writing*, Oxford, Clarendon Press, 1989, pp. 151–52. Cfr. also John Felstiner, *The Lies of Art: Max Beerbohm's Parody and Caricature*, London, Victor Gollancz, 1973, p. 143

3. "Old Self and Young Self" (1936), in Lawrence Danson, *Max Beerbohm and the Act of Writing*, cit., plate 14. Henry James is also presented as double in "Henry James meets his other self" (1908), an image based on "The Jolly Corner" (1908) where the novelist meets the person he would be had he stayed in the United States instead of expatriating. Cfr. Rupert Hart Davis (ed.), *A Catalogue of the Caricatures of Max Beerbohm*, cit., p. 205

4. "London in November, and Mr Henry James in London" (1907), in *Ibid.*

5. Due to its negligible critical value, I will gloss over "The Guerdon" (1916), which describes in Jamesian style the circumstances in which the writer, after naturalizing as a British citizen, was awarded the Order of Merit in 1916, although according to this apocryphal version of the event, neither the king nor his secretary had the least idea of precisely what his merits were. For the same reason, I will not take into consideration Beerbohm's specimen chapter of the imaginary book *Half Hours with the Dialects of England*, including an excerpt from the sonnet sequence Miss Alice Peploe, a Rye dressmaker, addressed to James, who had predictably proved impervious to her courtship.

6. This anecdote was included in the enlarged 1958 edition of *Mainly on the Air.* See Lawrence Danson, *Max Beerbohm and the Act of Writing*, cit., pp. 138–40 and S. N. Behrman, *Conversation with Max*, London, Hamish Hamilton, 1960, p. 203

7. Although most of Pater's imaginary portraits pivot on fictional character, "A

Prince of Court Painters" (1885) relates in fictive terms the life of a real person, Antoine Watteau.

8. See Virginia Woolf, "The New Biography" (1927), in *The Essays of Virginia Woolf*, Vol. IV (1925–28), Andrew McNeillie, ed., (London, The Hogarth Press, 1994), p. 473

9. "It is fortunate for us (jarring though it is to our patriotic sense) that Mr. Henry James was not born an Englishman, that he was born of a race of specialists ... And it is fortunate for us that in Paris, and in the straightest literary sect, there, his method began to form itself, and the art of prose fiction became to him a religion." Max Beerbohm, "Books within Books," in *And Even Now*, Melbourne, Heinemann, 1920, p. 109.

10. While in the first part of the story Capadose's lies are harmless and inventive variations on the theme of his life, in the end they are tinged with malice. Indeed both the colonel and his wife claim that the painting was probably destroyed by a rejected model who had already visited the studio while Capadose was sitting for his portrait. By falsely asserting that they saw the woman roaming around the house on the day when the portrait was slashed, the couple lay the blame on an innocent. The dark side of the colonel's mind is thus revealed.

11. Henry James, "The Birthplace," in *The Jolly Corner and Other Tales*, Roger Gard, ed., (Harmondsworth: Penguin, 1990), p. 156

Works Cited

Works by Max Beerbohm

"Books within Books" (1914). In *And Even Now*. Melbourne: Heinemann, 1920.

"Enoch Soames." In *Seven Men and Two Others* (1919). Harmondsworth: Penguin, 1954.

"The Guerdon" (1916). In *A Variety of Things*. New York: Alfred A. Knopf, 1928.

The Happy Hypocrite (1897). London: John Lane The Bodley Head, 1936.

"An Incident" (1958). In *Mainly on the Air*. New York: Alfred A. Knopf, 1958.

"The Mote in the Middle Distance" (1912). In *A Christmas Garland*. London: Heinemann, 1912.

"A Nightmare. Mr. Henry James subpoenaed, as psychological expert, in a *cause célèbre*" (1908). In *A Catalogue of the Caricatures of Max Beerbohm*, edited by Rupert Hart Davis. London: Macmillan, 1972.

"To Henry James" and "Specimen Chapter of Forthcoming Work *Half Hours with the Dialects of England*" (1895–1910); "On the Uniform Edition of the Works of Henry James" (1910–15). In *Max in Verse: Rhymes and Parodies by Max Beerbohm*, edited by J. G. Riewald, 19, 20–25, 56. London: Heinemann, 1964.

Works by Henry James

"The Aspern Papers" (1888). In *Complete Stories, 1884–1891*. New York: Library Classics of the United States, 1999.

"The Birthplace" (1903). In *The Jolly Corner and Other Tales*, edited by Roger Gard. Harmondsworth: Penguin, 1990.

"The Death of the Lion" (1894). In *The Figure in the Carpet and Other Stories*, edited by Frank Kermode. Harmondsworth: Penguin, 1986.

"Gabriele D'Annunzio" (1902). In *Notes on Novelists, With some Other Notes* (1914). New York: Biblo and Tannen, 1969.

"The Liar" (1888). In *Complete Stories, 1884–1891*. New York: Library Classics of the United States, 1999.

Other Works

Almansi, Guido, and Guido Fink. *Quasi come* (1976). Milano: Bompiani, 1991.

Behrman, S. N. *Conversation with Max*. London: Hamish Hamilton, 1960.

Danson, Lawrence. *Max Beerbohm and the Act of Writing*. Oxford: Clarendon Press, 1989.

Felstiner, John. *The Lies of Art: Max Beerbohm's Parody and Caricature*. London: Victor Gollancz, 1973.

Ford, Ford Madox. *Mightier than the Sword: Memories and Criticisms*. London: George Allen & Unwin, 1938.

Hart-Davis, Rupert, ed. *A Catalogue of the Caricatures of Max Beerbohm*. London: Macmillan, 1972.

Hutcheon, Linda. *A Theory of Parody: The Teachings of Twentieth-Century Art Forms* (1985). New York: Routledge, 1991.

Pater, Walter. *The Renaissance: Studies in Art and Poetry* (1873). Edited by Adam Phillips. Oxford: Oxford University Press, 1986.

Woolf, Virginia. *The Essays of Virginia Woolf*. Edited by Andrew McNeillie. Vol. 4 (1925–28), "The Modern Essay" (1925); "The New Biography" (1927). London: The Hogarth Press, 1994.

"At All Times Conspicuous as Art": Henry James, Margaret Oliphant, and Resistance to Decadence

SOLVEIG C. ROBINSON

At first glance, the coupling of these two names may seem anomalous. Henry James's reputation in nineteenth-century Anglo-American literature, especially within the late-century aesthetic movement, remains secure, and the wave of recent reevaluations of his life and work, culminating in new editions, scholarship, biographies, and film adaptations (not to mention novels in which he is a character) has helped ensure that his star continues to rise. Margaret Oliphant, despite having been one of the most widely read British novelists of the nineteenth century, is little known today outside Victorian studies. However, James's and Oliphant's professional careers and their critical stances, particularly in relation to aestheticism and its most extreme expression, Decadence, share striking parallels. Despite her greater conservatism, Oliphant can serve as a useful gloss on James's critique of, and resistance to, Victorian Decadence.

To begin with, it may be helpful to lay out the biographical parallels that underpin their similar critical approaches. To the popular imagination, James (1843–1916) is the aesthete who inhabits the pages of many of his novels, but numerous studies have drawn a more complex picture. Jonathan Freedman's 1990 *Professions of Taste* is especially helpful in setting out James's relation to the aesthetic movement, and particularly in analyzing James's efforts to distance himself from the Decadent branch represented by Swinburne, Dowson, Beardsley, Symons, and Wilde. While Fred Kaplan (1992) and others have argued that James feared being associated with the Decadents' more open homosexuality, Freedman emphasizes aesthetic reasons over psychological ones. Freedman notes that James, through his work, came to demonstrate "how the aestheticist privileging of intense experience in general and of art in particular as the most efficient avenue toward such experience ... could be normalized" (252). By contrast, the Decadents valued an intentionally artificial mode of rendering "intense experience." In his 1908 essay on Aubrey Beardsley, Arthur Symons wrote that the model for the Decadent artists was Pierrot: "exquisitely false, dreading above all things that 'one touch of nature' which would ruffle his disguise, and leave him defenceless. Simplicity ... being the most laughable thing in the world, he becomes learned, perverse, intellectualising his pleasure, brutalising his intellect" (97). James rejected falseness, however "exquisite," and he sought ways of rendering intense experience and emotion that retained that "one touch of nature." Furthermore, far from being "perverse," the Jamesian version of aestheticism maintained a strong underpinning of morality (Roberts 62–63).

Unlike James, Oliphant (1828–1897) might be considered almost the antithesis of the aesthete. In her *Autobiography* she describes herself as a "fat, little, commonplace woman" who could never muster the "kind of self-denial" that would have enabled her to "pursue the higher objects of art, instead of the mere necessities of living" (53,183). Oliphant and her contemporaries generally agreed that, while her novels were good reads, they were not highly polished; musing on George Eliot's work and reputation, Oliphant wondered if she would have fared better "if I had been kept, like her, in a mental greenhouse and taken care of" (50). Besides the problem of the aesthetics of her fiction, there is also the problem of her criticism. Oliphant's reputation as critic rests largely on one oft-cited article entitled "The Anti-Marriage League." Her 1896 review of Hardy's *Jude the Obscure* and Grant Allen's *The Woman Who Did*, one of the very few essays in *Blackwood's Edinburgh Magazine* that Oliphant signed (with her initials, "M.O.W.O."), this scathing review has been credited with helping persuade Hardy to stop writing fiction, and the continuing furor over this piece may account for James's oft-quoted valedictory on Oliphant, that "no woman had ever, for half a century, had her personal 'say' so publicly and irresponsibly" ("London Notes," [Aug. 1897], 1412). However, a more comprehensive look at Oliphant's writing reveals a much more sophisticated range of critical work, and the articles she wrote in the late 1880s to mid–1890s, at the height of the aesthetic movement, are of particular interest in relation to James and Decadence. Oliphant's critical alter egos during this period were masculine and urbane, personae that aligned her with aestheticism even as she critiqued it.[1] Her efforts to expose falseness and champion naturalness in artistic expression support key themes in James's criticism.

That James and Oliphant shared some critical perspectives should not be surprising, as their half-century careers shared many features. Both authors published their first fiction at age twenty-one, began regular reviewing in their mid-twenties, and established their literary reputations by their mid-thirties—Oliphant with the *Chronicles of Carlingford* series (1862–1876) and James with the quick succession of *Daisy Miller, Washington Square,* and *Portrait of a Lady* (1878–1881). Both also experienced a falling-off of their literary capital shortly thereafter and reestablished their reputations in their mid- to late-fifties, with the publication of their mature work. In addition to fiction, both James and Oliphant published extensive and significant bodies of nonfiction prose, especially art and literary criticism, much of which appeared in the periodical press. Oliphant wrote mainly for the Tory monthly *Blackwood's Edinburgh Magazine,* while James most often (especially early on) wrote for the *Atlantic,* the *North American Review,* and the *Nation,* three American periodicals that shared some essential editorial and critical perspectives with *Blackwood's;*[2] significantly, none of these periodicals were ever associated with the avant-garde, and critics writing in their pages would have found themselves very out of step if they had supported Decadence. Both James and Oliphant were also strongly influenced by contemporary European authors, especially the French realists, and a substantial part of their critical *oeuvres* consisted of reviews of foreign fiction for Anglophone audiences. James's essays on French authors alone fill 900 pages of his collected criticism, and there are casual references to Continental literature in many of his other essays; Oliphant served as the editor for Blackwood's Foreign Classics series (1877–1890), and she also wrote significant articles on a number of Continental, especially French, writers. Perhaps understandably, given the venues in which they were reviewing, both James and Oliphant were markedly more open-minded in their own reading than in their recommendations for others.[3]

In addition, both Oliphant and James were intimately involved with the art world. James's many friendships with artists are well documented by Kaplan, and there has been some scholarship on his art criticism (see, for example, Eimers and Graham). Oliphant's husband, Francis, was an artist, and she retained a lifelong interest in painting and architecture; her art criticism has also begun to receive attention (see Onslow). These influences can be seen in the very knowledgeable way in which both writers employed the vocabulary of the visual arts in their analyses of literary works, thereby engaging in one of the defining aspects of the aesthetic movement, that "turn within Victorian culture toward valorizing art in general and visual art in particular as a means of provoking intense experience" (Freedman, "Introduction," 2). And finally, both Oliphant and James felt themselves to be somewhat at the margins of the world of English letters, Oliphant because of her gender and her Scottish identity, and James because of his sexuality and expatriate status. This sense of being outsiders may have sharpened their critical faculties, as it enforced upon each of them a degree of distance as they commented on contemporary art and society.

However, Oliphant's and James's lives did not simply run on parallel tracks: they also intersected in some crucial ways. The two authors corresponded, and on at least one occasion quite literally traveled in the same circles. James was among those who met Oliphant when she arrived in Venice in April 1881 for a research trip and holiday (*Autobiography* [1899 edition], 295), and he was also among those asked to purchase an annuity for Oliphant in 1896, when her health began to fail (Colby and Colby, 234). Perhaps most importantly, both James and Oliphant read and admired one another's work—although not without reservations—and each publicly commented on the other's fiction and criticism, Oliphant in *Blackwood's*, and James most fully in the last of his "London Notes" for *Harper's Weekly*.

James's *Partial Portraits* (1888) serves as a logical starting point for discussing James's and Oliphant's approaches to aestheticism. Not only does the book contain some of James's wittiest nonfiction satire of Victorian middlebrow attitudes toward art, but it also prompted a review by Oliphant that sounds the keynote of her resistance to aestheticism. In his essay on George du Maurier, James discusses du Maurier's *Punch* caricatures of the English who "dabble" in the aesthetic movement (*Partial Portraits*, 366). Despite claiming that in the wake of Pater's *Studies in the History of the Renaissance* (1873), "The love of Botticelli has actually remoulded the features of several persons," James notes that Pater's ideals have not really taken hold: the evidence "would fail to convince certain observant and sceptical strangers that the English are an aesthetic people" (369, 370). The English lack "a spontaneous artistic life," James continues:

> Their taste is a matter of conscience, reflection, duty, and the writer who in our time has appealed to them most eloquently on behalf of art has rested his plea on moral standards—has talked exclusively of right and wrong.... the artistic point of view is the last that they

naturally take.... They carry on their broad back a nameless mountain of conventions and prejudices, a dusky cloud of inaptitudes and fears, which casts a shadow upon the frank and confident practice of art. The consequence of all this is that their revivals of taste are even stranger than the abuses they are meant to correct. They are violent, voluntary, mechanical; wanting in grace, in tact, in the sense of humour and of proportion [370–71].

James follows up on this analysis in "The Art of Fiction," the final essay in *Partial Portraits*, where he satirizes the Victorian middlebrow readers' conflation of "good" with "moral" and their preference for plots crowded with incident and ending happily. According to some readers, he reports, "Literature should be either instructive or amusing, and there is in many minds an impression that these artistic preoccupations, the search for form, contribute to neither end, interfere indeed with both" (48).

James is concerned to redeem aesthetics both from Victorian moral suspicions and from a kind of formulaic, "mechanical" approach to art. He urges his contemporaries to stop approaching art dualistically, and instead to approach it holistically. Using a surprisingly homely metaphor, James states that "The story and the novel, the idea and the form, are the needle and thread" (60)—both are essential to the actualization of the literary work. While some critics of James have maintained that he "values artistic form to the exclusion of other sorts of meaning" (Hale 80), James explicitly states in "The Art of Fiction" that form is secondary: "The form, it seems to me, is to be appreciated after the fact: then the author's choice has been made, his standard has been indicated, then we can follow lines and directions and compare tones and resemblances" (50). The form, the style, should emerge organically from the artist's approach to the subject. Thus, James urges writers to reject advice that would "shut you up into corners ... and tell you that it is only here and there that art inhabits"; instead they should "try and catch the colour of life itself.... Remember that your first duty is to be as complete as possible—to make as perfect a work. Be generous and delicate and pursue the prize" (64–65).

Oliphant's review of *Partial Portraits* expands on many of James's points. Like James, she wishes to correct the notion that literature can be approached "mechanically," either by the reader or by the author. Naturalness is an important quality for Oliphant: as Elisabeth Jay notes, it was a crucial part of Oliphant's self-definition as a writer:

Literally she had always worked in the heart of domestic activity, taking her "share in the conversation" and never "shut up in a separate room, or hedged off"; economically her work and the care of her family had been inextricably linked and emotionally she knew both the family and the writing to be necessary to her. "I have written because it gave me pleasure, because it came natural to me, because it was like talking or breathing, besides the big fact that it was necessary for me to work for my children" [29].

This notion that writing should come "like talking or breathing" (and should *appear* to have done so), underlies Oliphant's hostility to the intentional artificiality of so many writers associated with aestheticism. What Arthur Symons, in *Studies in Two Literatures*, described as Decadence's "ingenious deformation of the language" (102) was anathema to her—as artificial as the writing exercises advocated by Walter Besant in his 1884 *Art of Fiction*, the inspiration for James's essay by the same name. In fact, Oliphant's primary target in her review of *Partial Portraits* is Besant rather than James. While James demurs about Besant's suggestion that novel-writing can be aided by learning a set of rules and then practicing them— "the laws of harmony, perspective, and proportion are suggestive, they are even inspiring, but they are not exact," he replies to Besant ("Art of Fiction," 51)—Oliphant simply rejects the proposal. Besant's "note-book system," she declares, "will produce but a humdrum, dull, and trivial impersonation of life, and the artist will rather be lowered than elevated by these portentous exercises of curiosity" ("Old Saloon," [June 1888], 841). To write well, novelists require more than "study [or] conscious observation of your neighbour's follies or peculiarities": they require inspiration. Oliphant vividly describes how such inspiration occurs: "A trifle here and there catches the creative eye—broken lights from this and that, gleams of comprehension, a sudden sight of how minds are working, of how feelings arise." "Anything more than this," she concludes, "definite and formal studies, are very unproductive" (841). Oliphant's approach is essentially Wordsworthian: nature plays providentially on a receptive mind. James himself, Oliphant notes, has a mind particularly susceptible to the impressions that can be rendered into art. "To see only the dull and commonplace is the attribute of observers who are commonplace and dull," she writes, but James has an "exceedingly rare and fine" degree of insight, a "width of sympathy which few critics or portrait-painters could surpass ... every shade of being is interesting to those who can see, and the more difficult it is to penetrate the soul and catch the secret of the dumb existence, the more interesting that secret becomes, and the more exquisite the art which finds it out" (838–39).

How to render those insights into art so as to make them palpable to readers or viewers is one of the central concerns of aestheticism. Oliphant suggests that the truly "exquisite art" is in the perceiving, a notion that James at least partially embraces in "The Science of Criticism." Writing of the critic's "sacrificial" relation to the artist, James emphasizes the necessity of intensely empathic sympathy:

> To lend himself, to project himself and steep himself, to feel and feel till he understands, and to understand so well that he can say, to have perception at the pitch of passion and expression as embracing as the air, to be infinitely curious and incorrigibly patient, and yet plastic and inflammable and determinable, stooping to conquer and serving to direct—these are fine chances for an active mind, chances to add the idea of independent beauty to the conception of success [98].

Deep understanding is the prerequisite here for "saying," as it is for Oliphant. Where James and Oliphant differ, however, is in their approach to refining what is said.

Oliphant, with her ideal of natural expression, is very suspicious of what she refers to as the "manipulation of words" ("Old Saloon," [Jan. 1890], 141). In her reviews of authors associated with aestheticism (particularly Walter Pater, but also James himself) and Decadence (particularly Swinburne), Oliphant repeatedly draws attention to their infatuation with words for words' sake. One of her strongest denunciations of this tendency comes in her review of Pater's *Appreciations* (1890). Much of the review is taken up by her refutation of Pater's remark that he "fears to miss the least promising composition" in the works of Wordsworth, "lest some precious morsel should be lying hidden within—the few perfect lines, the phrase, the single word, perhaps, to which he often works up mechanically through a poem almost the whole of which may be tame enough." Oliphant thinks this is "as nearly pure nonsense as it is possible for any assertion given forth *ex cathedra* and with a bland consciousness of authority, to be." "To what single word could Wordsworth, or any other poet, work up mechanically, so as to move us to rapture at the end when the effect was attained?" she asks. "Could it be Helvellyn? (a beautiful word), or Skiddaw? (not so fine), or—what?" ("Old Saloon," [Jan. 1890], 141) The key word in this passage is *mechanically*, which Oliphant echoes from Pater: she rejects the notion that poetry is "mechanically" worked up. This resistance to laboring over expression also extends to prose, as one of her sharper critiques of James makes clear. Toward the end of her review of *A London Life* (1889), Oliphant comments:

> The art of the American cosmopolitan is at all times conspicuous as art. It is impossible to lose sight of the skill with which he whips

up the very light materials at his command, and makes a graceful
something out of nothing, nor the perfection with which he bal-
ances the flow of conversation, flinging the foamy wave of words
from one vessel to another, as in one of the most delicate operations of the kitchen ["Old Saloon," [June 1889], 830].

This cookery metaphor is witty but deflating, a way of shooting down what
she sees as a misguided tendency in James's writing. "His pleasure in these
processes manifestly surpasses his pleasure in either the characters or the
story," she continues, indicating where she thinks his focus ought to be.
Reading his work becomes a matter of appreciating the craft, rather than
the content: "the delicate game is equally absorbing to the spectator from
the evident difficulty of the composition" (830).

While she is willing to indulge James's "delicate game" because the
results are so "graceful," Oliphant is much more severe with others who
seem to value style over substance. Pater draws fierce fire. Citing Pater's comments about the "eclecticism" of Tennyson's use of language—"How illustrative of monosyllabic effect, of sonorus [sic] Latin, of the phraseology of
science, of metaphysic, of colloquialism"—Oliphant sharply brings things
down to earth: "We should have been disposed to say without so many
phrases that Tennyson, like other great poets and masters of style, seized
his words where he found them, without pausing to think whether they
were monosyllabic or metaphysic, or 'savoursome' Latin, so long as they
run well into his music" ("Old Saloon," [Jan. 1890], 143). But Pater is just
one "*Precieuse*" or "disciple of Euphues" (142, 145) with whom Oliphant
takes issue. She brushes away Grant Allen in the same review that takes
Pater to task, and in 1895 she dismisses Coventry Patmore's suggestion of
Alice Meynell for poet laureate, noting that her own preference would have
been the recently deceased Christina Rossetti, whose poetry was less ornate
and thus, she claims, more powerful than Meynell's. "We have ourselves
got a little tired," she writes, "of words. The Looker-on stands by and sees
them pour out of the press in shallow rivers and floods till he is almost
carried away by the stream. Style is a beautiful thing in its proper place....
But when it is words, and not much more, the soul soon begins to sicken
of it" ("Looker-on," [Dec. 1895], 908–9). Max Beerbohm is mocked for
using such strange language that the printer queried one of the words she
had used in an extract from Beerbohm's work ("Looker-on," [Jan. 1895],
165). Oliphant also mentions Swinburne a number of times in her denun-
ciation of verbal excesses. In 1895 she writes of him that "Men will presently
forget, and women also, that the use of words is to say something" ("Looker-
on," [Dec. 1895], 909), and in an earlier critique, Oliphant tartly remarks

that Swinburne has achieved "all the music that can be put into verse—all the music, but perhaps less than the due amount of meaning" ("Old Saloon," [June 1887], 744).

Music without meaning may be the point at which James steps back from aestheticism and aligns himself with Oliphant's more conservative critical tastes. Leon Chai uses music to distinguish James's aestheticism from Pater's: for Pater, he claims, "all art aspires to the condition of music—i.e., to the purest embodiment of form," while for James "nothing surpasses the drama of human suffering and emotion" as a means to yielding "the most intense impressions" (114). Freedman similarly notes that at the heart of James's critique of Decadence is a concern for recovering "the aestheticist valorizing of *aesthesis*, of the heightening or perfection of sense experience" (*Professions of Taste*, 136). For James, then, the failure of Decadence involves losing touch with that original "sense experience" that moved the artists to expression. Form is no longer linked to and dependent upon its subject like needle and thread.

James's review of Flaubert's *Temptation of Saint Anthony* (1874) provides clues to what James sees as the ideal relationship of form and subject, as well as how to express "the most intense impressions." While James doesn't particularly care for the subject of Flaubert's novel, he is very impressed by Flaubert's execution. Flaubert, he claims, has a "peculiar talent" for description that translates to success "in making an image, in finding and combining just the words in which the *look* of his object resides" (90–91). This is an almost transparent rendering of experience: Flaubert's use of language evokes the thing itself. James notes admiringly that Flaubert even manages to describe St. Anthony's visions, usually "things of ambiguous shapes and misty edges," so vividly that they appear like "a gallery of photographs, executed with the aid of the latest improvements in the art" (90–91). The photography metaphor here is significant. Still a fairly new medium, photography appeared to recreate life more accurately than had been previously possible. But James emphasizes the "latest improvements in the art," reasserting the importance of craft in rendering life and experience so vividly that they can move the reader or viewer.

In her review of Pater's *Appreciations*, Oliphant declares sourly that "Nothing but a slowly growing climax of intellectual overproduction, and the artificiality of art could have brought him into being" ("Old Saloon," [Jan. 1890], 145). Her response was to turn her back on the "artificiality of art," a rejection that not only harmed her reputation but probably harmed her own work. In his last "London Note," written shortly after Oliphant's death, James sympathetically notes that Oliphant was "one of those difficult cases for criticism, an energy of which the spirit and the form, straggling apart, never join hands with that effect of union which in literature more than anywhere else is its strength" (1411). Allowing form and subject to "straggle apart"—indeed, by neglecting style, almost encouraging them to do so—is what James sees as the weakness of one of Oliphant's last novels, *Kirsteen*. "The complexion of a talent that could care to handle a thing to the tune of so many pages and yet not care more to 'do' it" baffles James, much as Oliphant was baffled by his (to her mind) over-attention to "doing" it in *A London Life*. "There is a fascination," James continues, "in the mere spectacle of so serene an instinct for the middle-way, so visible a conviction that to reflect is to be lost" (1413).

James's response to aestheticism—rejecting only its Decadence—obviously proved more fruitful than Oliphant's. In "The Future of the Novel," he reflects on the genre at the fin de siècle and seeks a balance between the contending criticisms. Those concerned about the direction of fiction, he writes, "see the whole business too divorced on the one side from observation and perception, and on the other from the art and taste. They get too little of the first-hand impression, the effort to penetrate—that effort for which the French have the admirable expression to *fouiller*—and still less, if possible, of any science of composition, any architecture, distribution, proportion" (110). James's solution is in fact encompassed in this summary of the problems: to redeem the novel, writers must combine insight with architecture, impression with proportion. Too little of either will never achieve that crucial "effect of union."

Notes

1. For a fuller discussion of Oliphant's late criticism and its place in her career, see my article "Expanding a 'Limited Orbit,'" forthcoming in *Victorian Periodicals Review*.

2. Sarah Daugherty notes that all three of the American periodicals James wrote for had been "founded by Eastern critics who hoped to raise American intellectual standards" (25).

3. The difference between their "private" reading and their "public" reading comes out in some characteristic comments in review-related writing. James, writing to William Dean Howells about his meetings in Paris with the French realist *coterie*, warned that "as editor of the austere *Atlantic* it would startle you to hear some of their projected subjects" (3 Feb. [1876]; *Letters* 2:23); despite reading rather a lot of it, especially when she was abroad, Oliphant nevertheless, in one of her "Old Saloon" columns, described French naturalist fiction as that in which "the realist is the literary *chiffonnier*, always grubbing in the dust-holes" ([Sept. 1888]: 420).

Works Cited

Chai, Leon. *Aestheticism: The Religion of Art in Post-Romantic Literature.* New York: Columbia University Press, 1990.

Colby, Vineta, and Robert A. Colby. *The Equivocal Virtue: Mrs. Oliphant and the Victorian Literary Market Place.* Hamden, CT: Archon Books, 1966.

Eimers, Jennifer. "'No greater work of art': Henry James and Pictorial Art." *Henry James Review* 23 (2002): 72–84.

Freedman, Jonathan. "Introduction: The Moment of Henry James." In *The Cambridge Companion to Henry James.* Edited by Jonathan Freedman. Cambridge: Cambridge University Press, 1998.

_____. *Professions of Taste: Henry James, British Aestheticism, and Commodity Culture.* Stanford: Stanford University Press, 1990.

Graham, Wendy. "Henry James and British Aestheticism." *Henry James Review* 20 (1999): 265–74.

Hale, Dorothy J. "Henry James and the Invention of Novel Theory." In *The Cambridge Companion to Henry James.* Edited by Jonathan Freedman. Cambridge: Cambridge University Press, 1998.

James, Henry. "The Art of Fiction." *Longman's Magazine* (September 1884). Reprinted in *Partial Portraits* (1888) and *Literary Criticism* 1:44–65. All page references are from *Literary Criticism.*

_____. "*Essays in Criticism* by Matthew Arnold." *North American Review.* July 1865. Reprinted in *Literary Criticism* 1:711–19.

_____. *The International Library of Famous Literature,* edited by Richard Garnett. Vol. 14, "The Future of the Novel." London: The Standard 1899. Reprinted in *Literary Criticism* 1:100–110.

_____. "Gustave Flaubert." *Macmillan's Magazine* (March 1893). Reprinted in *Literary Criticism* 2:295–314.

_____. *Letters.* 4 vols. Edited by Leon Edel. Cambridge: Belknap Press, 1974–1984.

_____. *Literary Criticism.* 2 vols. Edited by Leon Edel. Library of America, 1984.

_____. "London Notes." *Harper's Weekly* (February 6, February 20, March 27, July 31, 1897). Reprinted in *Literary Criticism* 1:1387–1413.

_____. *Partial Portraits.* London: Macmillan, 1888.

_____. "The Present Literary Situation in France." *North American Review* (October 1899). Reprinted in *Literary Criticism* 1:111–23.

_____. "The Science of Criticism." *New Review* (May 1891). Reprinted in *Literary Criticism* 1:95–99.

_____. "The Temptation of Saint Anthony." *The Nation* (June 4, 1874). Reprinted in *Literary Criticism* 2:289–94.

Jay, Elisabeth. *Mrs. Oliphant: "A Fiction to Herself."* Oxford: Clarendon Press, 1995.

Kaplan, Fred. *Henry James: The Imagination of Genius, A Biography.* New York: Morrow, 1992.

Oliphant, [Margaret]. "The Anti-Marriage League." *Blackwood's Edinburgh Magazine* 183 (January 1896): 135–49.

_____. *The Autobiography and Letters.* 1899. Edited by Mrs. Harry Coghill. Leicester: Leicester University Press, 1974. Unless otherwise noted, all quotes from the *Autobiography* itself are from the complete text edition, edited by Elisabeth Jay (Peterborough, Ontario: Broadview Press, 2002).

_____. "The Looker-on." *Blackwood's Edinburgh Magazine* 157 (January 1895): 148–70; (December 1895): 905–27; 160 (October 1896): 481–507.

_____. "The Old Saloon." *Blackwood's Edinburgh Magazine* 142 (June 1887): 831–52, (November 1887): 698–714; 144 (June 1889): 809–34; 147 (January 1890): 131–51.

Onslow, Barbara. *Women of the Press in Nineteenth-Century Britain.* New York: St. Martin's Press, 2000.

Roberts, Morris. *Henry James's Criticism.* New York: Octagon, 1970.

Robinson, Solveig C. "Expanding a 'Limited Orbit': Margaret Oliphant, *Blackwood's Edinburgh Magazine*, and the Development of a Critical Voice." *Victorian Periodicals Review*, forthcoming.

Symons, Arthur. "Aubrey Beardsley." 1908. Reprinted in *Collected Works, Vol. 9: Studies in Seven Arts.* London: Martin Secker, 1924.

_____. *Studies in Two Literatures.* Vol. 8 of *Collected Works.* London: Martin Secker, 1924.

The Face of Decadence in *The Sacred Fount*

SHEILA TEAHAN

Henry James's 1901 novel *The Sacred Fount*, often read as a self-reflexive parody of Jamesian hermeneutics at their most opaque, engages in rich dialogue with two major Victorian decadent intertexts: *The Picture of Dorian Gray* (1891) and *Dracula* (1897). The novel's nameless first-person narrator, whose sanity is in question throughout the text and who thus recalls the similarly "unreliable" narrators of *The Aspern Papers* (1888) and *The Turn of the Screw* (1898), attends a weekend house party at which he encounters the Brissendens, a couple who have undergone a disconcerting reversal since he last saw them: Mrs. "Briss," who is some dozen years her husband's senior, appears magically rejuvenated, whereas Brissenden himself has suddenly and hyperbolically aged. (His emasculation is reflected in the castrating apocope that truncates "Brissenden" throughout the text to "Briss.") When the narrator then perceives that the previously dull-witted Gilbert Long has become inexplicably sharp, he concludes that some principle of "exchange" is at work, and he determines to seek out the source of Long's and Brissenden's respective transformations. The narrator's metaphor for the theory of sexual vampirism that develops from his ruminations is that of the "sacred fount," and his increasingly feverish and convoluted speculations develop and rationalize "this master trope" (James 1953, 29, 47, 198).

Several critics have situated *The Sacred Fount* in the aestheticist and decadent contexts and conventions addressed in this volume. William Bysshe Stein discerns in the novel "a subtle parody of the British aestheticism and decadence of the fin de siècle," and Jonathan Freedman finds it to be "a decadent novel par excellence: in its equation between the acts of narration and sexual obsession and madness; in its imaging of human relations as a form of vampirism; even in the art that 'its characters gaze upon'" (Stein, 161; Freedman, 203).

For John Carlos Rowe, the novel is proto-modernist in its questioning of "claims to distinction and authority," and in his narrator James "seems indirectly to indict symbolist aestheticism or the 'pure poetry' of early modernism" (Rowe, 169).

Kathryn Humphreys observes that in *The Picture of Dorian Gray* "the magic picture that exchanges attributes with its subject also facilitates an exchange between characters, an exchange that provides the premise for James's *Sacred Fount* a decade later" (Humphreys, 524).

And most recently, John Paul Riquelme has explored the connections between modernism, aestheticism, and the Gothic, specifically aligning James with Wilde and Stoker and arguing that *The Picture of Dorian Gray*, *Dracula*, and *The Turn of the Screw* are "seminal texts" that illustrate the "development of Gothic writing as a discourse of modernity that influences the formation of literary modernism in 1890s' Britain" (Riquelme, "Toward a History of Gothic and Modernism," 587).

In the novel's thematics of vampirism and its recurring images of consumption, James is clearly troping on *Dracula*. Mrs. Brissenden "extracts" her "new blood" from her husband, who "pay[s] to his last drop" (James 1953, 29, 30), and *The Picture of Dorian Gray* is a key precursor for *The Sacred Fount*'s preoccupation with portraits and portraiture. Riquelme's observation that in Gothic fiction marriage or social relations are typically "threatened or abrogated" (Riquelme, 585) underscores the troubling implications of the parasitic sexual and interpersonal economy James's narrator labors to expose or, undecidably, to construct. In what follows, *The Sacred Fount* is an allegory of figuration in which the narrator's metaphoric strategies—the hydraulic trope of the fount (repeatedly activated by etymological play on "influence" (James 1953, 32), the synecdochic substitution of part for whole, the meta-metaphors of "transfer" and "exchange," and the trope of anastomosis—both speak to the novel's decadent context and adumbrate a theory of the relation between interpersonal relations and figurative language.

The narrator's interpretive strategy rests in part on a synecdochic logic of part and whole: he inveterately pieces things together, reconstructs putative wholes from perceived fragments, and speculates about the abstract relations that are inferable from perceived elements. The explanatory "law" of interpersonal exchange he seeks is produced by hyperbolic extrapolation from "delicate phenomena": "A part of the amusement they yielded came, I daresay, from my exaggerating them, grouping them into a larger mystery (and thereby a larger 'law') than the facts, as observed, yet warranted" (James 1953, 23). In conversation later in the novel with the painter Ford Obert, the narrator similarly ponders: "The next moment I was in all but full enjoyment of the piece and wanted to make all my other pieces right because of that special beauty in my scheme through which the whole depended so on each part and each part so guaranteed the whole" (James 1953, 223). As Paul Armstrong has observed, this formulation sounds a lot like the hermeneutic circle, in which understanding proceeds by means of a dialectical and synecdochic interchange between "part and whole" (Armstrong, 33–34).

It is no accident that the narrator employs the trope of the circle to figure the system of interpersonal relations he studies (James 1953, 89, 244). But synecdoche is only one of several competing metaphorical models at play in *The Sacred Fount.* Another is the hydraulic trope of the fount itself: the narrator seeks the "source of the flow of 'intellect'" (James 1953, 15) that has transformed Long. As when he identifies the aptly named Server, the putative sacrificial fount of Long's newfound wit, as "the controlling image, for me, the real principle of composition, in this affluence of fine things" (James 1953, 167), the narrator sounds like a New Critic endorsing the principle of organic unity. Referring to "the full-blown flower of my theory" (James 1953, 169), he compares his theory to an organic object, anticipating New Critical figurations of the poetic text as an organic system whose elements create a unified whole. However, the trope of the sacred fount as emblem of origins and plenitude threatens constantly to devolve into the not-so-sacred "font" of dissemination and non-self-identity. As Rowe comments: "The narrator longs to discover in a sacred fount an origin for his social being. James's fount is variant of the printer's font, from which the dissemination of writing issues" (Rowe, 188). This slippage from the would-be totalizing transcendental signified of the fount to the destabilizing font of difference is reflected in the ever-proliferating chain of metaphors by means of which the narrator endeavors to master the relationships he scrutinizes at Newmarch. None of these metaphors possesses the totalizing power he seeks; they neither progress logically nor add up to a coherent whole. As he acknowledges late in the text in a choice instance of litotes, "the interpretation of my tropes and figures isn't 'ever' perfectly simple" (James 1953, 284).

That metaphor itself is a central preoccupation of *The Sacred Fount* is suggested by James's notebook entries, which refer to "the little concetto

... of the young man who marries an old woman and becomes old while she becomes young" (James 1987, 176). Both in this vampiristic relation between the Brissendens and in the possible transfer of properties of "cleverness and stupidity" between Gilbert Long and May Server, James observes that the "liaison ... betrays itself by the transfer of qualities to be determined—from one to the other of the parties to it" (James 1987, 88, 176). Even without his explicit identification of the novel's originary germ as a conceit (concetto), we can see that James's formulation about a transfer of qualities comes close to a definition of metaphor, which is an etymological transfer or carrying over of properties from one entity to another. Since metaphor is structured around a constitutive tension between sameness and difference, one should not be surprised that this figure of transfer wreaks havoc with the narrator's determination to account for the exchanges he believes to have detected at Newmarch. The hydraulic trope of the fount predicates a closed economy in which a fixed volume of a given property or entity is transferred from one being to another. James's narrator is determined to verify a "complete exchange" between Server and Long (James 1953, 57). But his analysis is haunted by the possibility that the process of transfer and the "new combinations" it entails might alter the entities being transferred, effecting not only an exchange but a "conversion" (James 1953, 170, James 1987, 88). Of Long's suddenly manifested "gift of talk," he observes: "It put before me the question of whether, in these strange relations that I believed I had thus got my glimpse of, the action of the person 'sacrificed' mightn't be quite out of proportion to the resources of that person. It was as if these elements might really multiply in the transfer made of them" (James 1953, 52, 53). As with metaphor itself, the mechanism of exchange posited by the trope of the fount threatens to leave behind an unaccountable and undecidable residue that compromises the "ideal symmetry" of the narrator's formal system (James 1953, 169). Further, there is no confirming or disconfirming the results of the narrator's unwieldy tropological analysis of an interpersonal dynamic that he understands as itself being structured around a metaphorical transfer. There is no getting outside the tropological system he seeks to analyze by way of tropes.

Despite its prominent affiliations to both metaphor and synecdoche, the rhetorical figure that most closely corresponds to the narrator's privileged metaphor of the fount is the trope of anastomosis. Anastomosis, which derives from a Greek verb (astomuein) meaning to furnish with a mouth or outlet, is defined by the Oxford English Dictionary (OED) as follows: "Intercommunication between two vessels, channels, or distinct branches of any kind, by a connecting cross branch. Applied originally to the cross communications between the arteries and veins, or other canals in the animal body; whence to similar cross connexions in the sap-vessels of plants, and between rivers and their branches; and now to any cross connexions between the separate lines of any branching system, as the branches of trees, the veins of leaves, or the wings of insects" (OED, 1). As the image of a line joining two vessels or enclosures, anastomosis could be said to be the organizing concetto of *The Sacred Fount*. As J. Hillis Miller has shown, anastomosis is a privileged figure for interpersonal relations in fiction. In Miller's formulation, anastomosis is "a figure for the way the self becomes itself, maintains itself, or grounds itself in the other" (Miller 1992, 157).

Even critical discourse that seems implicitly to posit the autonomy of "solid, given selves" in fiction tends to assume in practice that "each self only completes or fulfills itself in its relation to another" (Miller 1992, 153). Insofar as its characters' relations are defined by vampiristic depletion rather than mutual completion or fulfillment, *The Sacred Fount* conspicuously ironizes this last element of anastomosis. It colorfully allegorizes Miller's assertion that in anastomosis the "self is always outside the self" and makes explicit, through the theme of sexual vampirism, his suggestion that the topic of interpersonal relations tends to contain a latent sexual component even when "the ostensible subject is the more spiritual question of the I-thou relation, or the question of other minds" (Miller 1992, 160, 152). *The Sacred Fount* dramatizes interpersonal relations in terms of figurative exchanges between part and whole or between container and contained, although it would be equally valid to say that it dramatizes the operations of figurative language in terms of interpersonal relations. Each of these is a figure for the other, although it would be impossible to determine which is the figure and which is ground. This problem of the relation between figure and ground is not limited to the reader: James's narrator laments that he "had at no moment since the day before made so poor a figure on my own ground" (James 1953, 240).

The Sacred Fount employs extensively the linear images of paths, channels, branches, vessels and so on associated with the trope of anastomosis. The novel's topography is one in which chambers and similar enclosed spaces are joined by terraces, staircases, and corridors, and in which human figures are glimpsed at the end of long vistas or alleys. The narrator refers to "branches" and "branch[ing]" staircases, "chains" of rooms and chambers, "channels," "currents," "branches," and "vessels" (James 1953, 20, 256, 195, 242, 100, 13, 245). The place-name "Newmarch" is itself suggestive of a linear path or "march," figured also in the "march" of conversation between the narrator and his interlocutors that organizes the narrative (James 1953, 27). He imagines his interpretive process as a linear sequence or "train," and the novel opens with a train journey from Paddington station that narrativizes this linear imagery. The narrator makes this figure explicit in his later reflection that "I hadn't missed a feature of the road I had thus been beguiled to travel"; note also his observation that "I followed many trains and put together many pieces" (James 1953, 127, 167). The trope of anastomosis is further salient to a rhetorical analysis of *The Sacred Fount* for its inherent double contradiction. As Miller explains, anastomosis can be thought of either as "an external link between two vessels or channels, or as entering into the vessel it opens" (Miller 1992, 155). It therefore destabilizes the distinction between outside and inside, or between container and contained. This destabilization is reflected in the Greek root *stoma*, meaning mouth, whose metonymic displacement from the orifice to the organ inside gives us the word "stomach." More, the double antithetical prefix ana-, which means "up, back, again, anew," signifies "both reaffirmation and reversal": "If the stomach is thought of as a container, as anastomosis makes an anastomach, an opening or mouth in it, reversing its enclosure" (Miller 1992, 155). On the score of the double antithetical prefix "ana-" that flags the contradiction analyzed by Miller, it is no accident that "sacer," the root of sacred, is one of Freud's "antithetical primal words" reflective of the tendency toward reversal in dreams and other psychic phenomena (Freud, 48). The "sacred" fount is undecidably either blessed or cursed. Riquelme's study of the interrelations between the Gothic, modernity, and aestheticism points to "a potential for dark doubling and reversal within aestheticism itself" (Riquelme, "Oscar Wilde's Aesthetic Gothic," 609).

The susceptibility of anastomosis to reversals between inside and outside or container and contained speaks to a larger dynamic of chiasmic reversal in *The Sacred Fount*, one that is enacted at the levels of plot, characterization, and syntax. Much like the binary oppositions aligned with the trope of anastomosis, the properties of age and youth or intelligence and stupidity prove susceptible to chiasmic reversal. In the most authoritative study of chiasmus in James, Ralf Norrman attributes his extensive use of "chiastic inversion" (along with the related devices of antithesis and oxymoron) to James's "characteristic mental habits," notably "his tendency to think in opposites and parallels" (Norrman, 141).

As in the following passages, chiastic inversion at the "thematic macrolevel" is matched syntactically at the "stylistic microlevel" (Norrman, 152):

"'Ah, well,'" he laughed, but as if his interest had quickly dropped, "'youth is comparatively speaking beauty.'"
"Oh, not always. Look at poor Briss himself."
"Well if you like it better, beauty is youth" [James 1953, 26].

"But where he comes she does, and where she comes he does" [James 1953, 41].

"She's all in it," he insisted. "Or it's all in her. It comes to the same thing" [James 1953, 68].

Shlomith Rimmon observes: "When used in an unnatural grammatical construction, chiasmus can intimate the fallacy of taking symmetry for granted ... like almost everything else in the novel, chiasmus is used both to pose ... and to undermine that which it describes."

If vulnerability to chiastic inversion (which would also seem to undo the distinction between "natural" and "unnatural"; after all, what would a "natural" grammatical construction look like?) is the rhetorical and conceptual foundation of the narrator's hermeneutic adventure, it occasionally hints at potentially fallacious logic, as in the dialectical and tautological interdependence of "knowing" and "seeing" in the following: "I was sufficiently aware even then that if one hadn't known it one might have seen nothing; but I was not less aware that one couldn't know anything without seeing all" (James 1953, 169). So, too, figure and concept are chiastically interdependent, indeed indistinguishable: the narrator's analogy of the "torch in the darkness" easily becomes "the torch of my analogy" (James 1953, 66, 64). Norrman suggests that, as reflected in James's predilection for chiasmus and antithesis, his fiction becomes a "world of pseudo-binarity, pseudo-choices, quasi-opposition, seeming dichotomies and false dualities" that ultimately "come to the same thing": "In James there is always a possibility that the ostensibly different is actually the same" (Norrman, 177, 160). But it is equally true that the ostensibly self-identical, for instance, the sacred fount understood as unambiguously either blessed or cursed, either positively or negatively valorized, may turn out to be either non-self-identical (both blessed and cursed) or strictly undecidable on the basis of textual evidence.

Especially for the purpose of considering *The Sacred Fount* in relation to the defining topoi of British aestheticism, the novel's most important mode of chiasmic inversion involves a recurring figurative exchange between the human and inanimate that suggests an unmooring of the ontological distinction between people and objects. The narrator refers to Gilbert Long as "a fine piece of human furniture," and finds Lady John's self-presentation "as strong as a coat of furniture-polish" (James 1953, 2, 17). If the principals

at Newmarch resemble ornamental pieces, the house at Newmarch recipro-
cally "reared a brave front" (James 1953, 108). The narrator conceives of Lady
John's sentiment for Long as "fitt[ing] so completely to the other pieces in
my collection" (James 1953, 104), and this troping of people as ornamental
objects culminates in his mental arrangement of Long, Lady John, Brissenden, and Server into a harmonious aesthetic composition:

> These opposed couples balanced like bronze groups at the two ends
> of a chimney-piece, and the most I could say to myself in lucid dep-
> recation of my thought was that I mustn't take them equally for
> granted merely because they were balanced. Things in the real had
> a way of not balancing; it was all an affair, this fine symmetry, of
> artificial proportion. Yet even while I kept my eyes away from Mrs.
> Briss and Long it was vivid to me that, "composing" there beauti-
> fully, they could scarce help playing a part in my exhibition [James
> 1953, 182–83].

As reflected by the self-conscious quotes, the narrator reads this little
tableau as a kind of materialization of his equally symmetrical theory of
vampiristic exchange, although the couples in question here are not those
implicated in his theory. In fact, this tableau recalls a passage at the novel's
center in which Server and the narrator come across a similar spatializa-
tion of his theory, this time in the pastoral setting of a "verdurous circle"
that gives material form to the hermeneutic circle of his interpretive efforts:

> Oh, it was quite sufficiently the castle of enchantment, and when
> I noticed four old stone seats, massive and mossy and symmetri-
> cally placed, I recognised not only the influence, in my grand adven-
> ture, of the grand style, but the familiar identity of this consecrated
> nook, which as so much of the type of all the bemused and remem-
> bered. We were in a beautiful old picture, we were in a beautiful
> old tale, and it wouldn't be the fault of Newmarch if some other
> green carrefour, not far off, didn't balance with this one and offer
> the alternative of niches, in the greenness, occupied by weather-
> stained statues on florid pedestals [James 1953, 130].

James places at the novel's own carrefours, or narrative crossroads, this
node or "nook" whose four benches stand in for the two couples implicated in the "mystic circle" of the narrator's theory (note the recurrence
here of the hydraulic trope of "influence"). He experiences this image of
the crossroads as "familiar" or already read as if, in violation of the commonsensical ontological order of representation, this pastoral scene is temporally secondary to its own representation in a "beautiful old picture" or
"beautiful old tale." His sense of the status of this image as a supplementary repetition of its own pictorial or narrative representation is itself

repeated when, as May Server comes into view at the end of the vista and "with the massed wood on either side of her," she strikes him as being "like the reminiscence of a picture or the refrain of a ballad" (James 1953, 131). In keeping with its unsettling of ontological distinctions, the passage concludes by "literally" blurring the distinction between the human and the ornamental, the natural and the artificial, as the narrator contemplates the "gilded tree-tops," "painted sky," and May's own countenance, which he perceives "as blurred as a bit of brushwork in water-colour spoiled by the upsetting of the artist's glass" (James 1953, 133).

The narrator's contemplation of the two couples "composed" like bronze groups participates in a long line of Jamesian aestheticizing objectifications, from Christopher Newman's attempted purchase of "the best article in the market" in the way of a wife to Maggie's objectifying gaze at Adam and Charlotte, who by the end of *The Golden Bowl* has been assimilated (in an echo of *The Sacred Fount*) to the "human furniture" of Adam's collection.

As a large body of scholarship has demonstrated, the relation between subjects and objects is central to the concerns of nineteenth-century realism. In a recent essay that challenges the longstanding Jamesian critical tradition positing "a chronologically progressive dematerialization in his aesthetic practice," Victoria Coulson argues that earlier James texts exhibit a "clear distinction between the object-world (the world of the signifier) and the sphere of novelistic meanings (the realm of the signified)"; objects in late James "symptomatize an increasing, and increasingly specific, imbrication of subject and object."

Works of art, to include what Coulson brilliantly analyzes as the Jamesian "grammar of furniture" (Coulson, 116), offer particularly rich sites for the exploration of this imbrication of the subjective and the objective. Coulson notes that "art objects that bear meaning, that have become signs, remain simultaneously and intrinsically material objects, because there can be no aesthetic expression purified of physical form"(Coulson, 121). As a representation of the human countenance, the portrait lends itself to the exploration of this mutual chiastic imbrication of people and things. Richard Stein has identified as a major topos of British aestheticism the transformative encounter between the self and a work of art, an encounter that can effect "a fundamental reorientation of the self."

I have written elsewhere about James's ironic treatment of this topos in *The Outcry* (1911), a novel about art collectors (and his last completed novel). In *The Outcry*, interpersonal relations are organized around the portraits whose sale and ownership drive the plot, and to which the characters are ontologically assimilated in a recurring tropological exchange between people and paintings.

This ontological confusion between people and portraits is also at play in *The Sacred Fount*, as when the narrator thinks of Brissenden as resembling "some fine old Velasquez or other portrait" (James 1953, 158).

The novel's thematics of portraiture is explored most fully in chapter four, in which the narrator, Server, Long, and the painter Ford Obert contemplate a portrait in the gallery at Newmarch. Server and the narrator come upon Long holding forth to Obert about the painting; Long's speech, which, ironically, the narrator cannot hear, leads the narrator to suspect that Server has sacrificed more intelligence than she had originally to give; her reaction to Long's displays appears uncharacteristically reserved. His suspicion about May's depleted resources undermines the narrator's anxious resolve to verify the completeness of exchange among his principals:

> "It's the picture, of all pictures, that most needs an interpreter. Don't we want," I asked of Mrs. Server, "to know what it means?" The figure represented is a young man in black, a quaint, tight black dress, fashioned in years long past; with a pale, lean, livid face and a stare, from eyes without eyebrows, like that of some whitened old-world clown. In his hand he holds an object that strikes the spectator at first simply as some obscure, ambiguous work of art, but that on a second view becomes a representation of a human face, modelled and coloured, in wax, in enamelled metal, in some substance not human. The object thus appears a complete mask, such as might have been fantastically fitted and worn.
>
> "Yes, what in the world does it mean?" Mrs. Server replied. "One could call it, though that doesn't get one much further, the Mask of Death."
>
> "Why so?" I demanded while we all again looked at the picture. "Isn't it much rather The Mask of Life? It's the man's own face that's Death. The other one, blooming and beautiful."
>
> "Ah, but with an awful grimace!" Mrs. Server broke in.
>
> "The other one, blooming and beautiful," I repeated, "is Life, and he's going to put it on; unless indeed he has just taken it off."
>
> "He's dreadful, he's awful that's what I mean," said Mrs. Server. But what does Mr. Long think?"
>
> "The artificial face, on the other hand," I went on, as Long now said nothing, "is extremely studied and, when you carefully look at it, charmingly pretty. I don't see the grimace" [James 1953, 55–56].

This episode is both an unmistakable allegory of reading and a *mise en abyme* of *The Sacred Fount*; for precisely this reason, "what it means" is anything but obvious. It is introduced by the narrator's comment that he did not wish to see Server studied by anyone other than himself "in the light of my theory"; knowing of "some pictures in one of the rooms that had not been lighted the previous evening," he seizes on this opportunity as a pretext to observe her (James 1953, 48–49). What light does this odd interlude shed on the aestheticist (sub)text of *The Sacred Fount?*

The passage "literalizes" the narrator's earlier metaphors of his gallery or museum of those who exemplify the law of the sacred fount, and gives concrete form to his recurring trope of the "picture," as in his reflection on what he takes to be May's distressed state: "Once my imagination had seen her in this light the touches it could add to the picture might be trusted to be telling"; and in the first chapter he "turn[s] ... around" the "picture" of Lady John's possible role in Long's transformation (James 1953, 96, 10; see also 13, 37, 39, 91, 96, 181, 204). Like the larger picture of the narrator's hermeneutic adventure, this one needs an interpreter; but its ambiguity stems in large part from its "already read" quality, which is underlined by the shift in tense with the description of the "decadent icon" (Freedman, 204) of the Pierrot, associated with a "perverse poetics" of artifice, disease, and death (William Stein, 168). The present tense ekphrasis of the generic and belated ("fashioned in years long past") harlequin underscores the received quality of the set piece describing this recognizable "figure," and the pointed absence of attribution to an artist in contrast to *The Outcry*'s detailed enumeration of historical painters counterintuitively underscores the highly mediated status of this moment: even though it has no accessible origin, the image is so familiar that no one in particular can be shown to have authored it. If anything, the passage gives the impression of being a transposition of recycled elements recalled from earlier in the text: the simile of the "clown bounding into the ring" (the narrator's remark that "I cast about for some light in which I could show that I—*à plus forte raison*—was a pantaloon" also aligns him with the Pierrot figure), his impression that Long and Brissenden respectively resemble "pliant wax" and "plastic wax in my hand," and his image of May as "an old dead pastel under glass" (James 1953, 18, 111, 17, 126, 51). James pushes the already-read status of the scene so far as to preempt its reading by means of the characters' own unverifiable critical commentary on it. Server, Obert, and the narrator bandy about the painting's more patent undecidabilities: does the mask represent life or death? Server and the narrator anticipate both positions. Has the man just removed the mask, or is he poised to put it on? Since the painting represents the mask as frozen in mid-air, this question is unanswerable. Does either the man or the mask resemble anyone at Newmarch? Obert asserts that the image recalls "some face among us here, on this occasion I mean some face in our party that I can't think of"

(James 1953, 57), identifying the image as a repetition whose original is occluded or nonexistent. In a manner reminiscent of *The Turn of the Screw*, virtually any critical response to the painting has been ironically preempted. And lest we are tempted to impute to this passage any metacritical authority beyond its articulation of these questions, the narrator's trope of painting as a figure for narrative itself (when he subsequently refers to himself as a "painter of my state" (James 1953, 94) reveals that painting and narrative stand in for each other in a way that privileges neither one nor the other: the idea that the painting accounts for the larger narrative carries no more explanatory power than the idea that the novel as a whole accounts for this passage describing the painting.

The relation between the human and the objective in the passage is vexed and undecidable. The narrator characterizes the object held by the "man with the mask in his hand" (James 1953, 54) as, ironically, "simply … some obscure, some ambiguous work of art," and this initial perception is displaced when the object then comes into focus as "a representation of a human face." The mask, then, is a doubling representation of a face that reverses the accepted valences of the human and the natural, displacing an oxymoronic "simply" obscure and ambiguous aesthetic object with an equally oxymoronic "artificial face." Or rather, the face may itself be artificial by its "nature," as suggested by the portraitist Oliver Lyon's reflection in "The Liar" that the face is a "human mask."

The narrator's reading of the painting of the man with the mask itself doubles his vampiristic theory of the sacred fount: he aligns the man's face with death, and life with the "blooming" (an adjective consistently associated with the recipients of the sacrificial resources of the fount) mask. The chiastic crossing suggested here of the categories of life and death, face and mask, is exemplary of a larger problematic of figurative language. The mask is a marker for prosopopoeia, the projection of a face or mask onto an inanimate other. Prosopopoeia, the technical term for personification, is the etymological positing of a face or mask (prosopon). The face of the man in the portrait, the representation of an icon rather than the portrait of an individual, is doubled by the mask he holds, which according to the narrator is "blooming and beautiful," as if it is feeding vampiristically off the face in a doubling representation of the narrator's theory of the sacred fount. As Paul de Man has taught us, defacement goes with the territory of prosopopoeia. The projection of a face onto the personified object potentially redounds with a violent reciprocity on the viewing subject, who is literally or figuratively defaced, struck dumb or dead.

If the man in the portrait is rendered a mere death mask by the prosopon that doubles and defaces him (Brissenden's "face and figure" are similarly "compromised" by the process of his sacrificial depletion by his wife [James 1953, 96–97]), this defacement is part of a larger pattern in which characters in *The Sacred Fount* are repeatedly seen from the back, "the less scrutable side of the human figure," in a playful negation of the notion that the face is an expression of the essential self. Thus Long's back appears "somehow replete for us, at the moment, with a guilty significance" (James 1953, 197, 38).

If prosopopoeia entails the defacement of the speaking or viewing subject, the picture of the man with a mask might be called a spatialized narrativization of this defacement, as in those medieval paintings that represent Christ's crucifixion, deposition, and resurrection in a single frame. In an ironic blazon that captures this disfiguring fragmentation of the face and the self, Mrs. Brissenden describes the exchange of properties posited by the narrator's theory—"what goes on whenever two persons are so much mixed up" as a metaphoric exchange of body parts: "'One of them you know the saying—gives the lips, the other gives the cheek.... It takes and keeps and uses all the lips give. The cheek, accordingly,' she continued to point out, 'is Mr. Long's. The lips are what we began by looking for. We've found them. They're drained, they're dry, the lips" (James 1953, 80–81). Since, like apostrophe, prosopopoeia entails the attribution both of a face and of a speaking mouth, this passage signifies something like the disfiguration of prosopopoeia, an anatomizing of its power of defacement. In *The Sacred Fount*, the decadent trope of vampirism narrativizes the disfiguring power of figuration itself.

Works Cited

Armstrong, Paul B. *The Challenge of Bewilderment: Understanding and Representation in James, Conrad, and Ford.* Ithaca: Cornell University Press, 1987.

Bollinger, Laurel. "'Miracles are Expensive': The Complicated Metaphors of Subjectivity in *The Sacred Fount*." *The Henry James Review* 20 (1999): 51–68.

Coulson, Victoria. "Sticky Realism: Armchair Hermeneutics in Late James." *The Henry James Review* 25 (2004): 115–26.

Cowley, Julian. "*The Sacred Fount* and Modernist Baroque." *The Henry James Review* 18 (1997): 273–79.

de Man, Paul. *The Rhetoric of Romanticism.* New York: Columbia University Press, 1984.

Freedman, Jonathan. *Professions of Taste: Henry James, British Aestheticism, and Commodity Culture.* Stanford: Stanford University Press, 1990.

Freud, Sigmund. *Character and Culture.* New York: Collier Books, 1963.

Giles, Paul. "Deterritorialization in *The Sacred Fount*." *The Henry James Review* 24 (2003): 225–32.

Humphreys, Kathryn. "The Artistic Exchange: Dorian Gray at *The Sacred Fount*." *Texas Studies in Language and Literature* 32 (1900): 522–35.

James, Henry. *The American*. London: Penguin Books, 1981.

_____. The Complete Notebooks of Henry James. Ed. Leon Edel and Lyall H. Powers. New York: Oxford University Press, 1987.

_____. *Complete Stories*. 1884–1891. New York: Library of America, 1999.

_____. *The Golden Bowl*. London: Penguin Books, 1966.

_____. *The Sacred Fount*. New York: Grove Press, 1953.

Miller, J. Hillis. *Ariadne's Thread: Story Lines*. New Haven: Yale University Press, 1992.

Version of Pygmalion. Cambridge and London: Harvard University Press, 1990.

Norrman, Ralf. *The Insecure World of Henry James's Fiction: Intensity and Ambiguity*. London: Macmillan Press, 1982.

Pryzbylowicz, Donna. *Desire and Repression: The Dialectic of Self and Other in the Late Works Of Henry James*. University, Alabama: University of Alabama Press, 1986.

Rimmon, Shlomith. *The Concept of Ambiguity: The Example of Henry James*. Chicago: University of Chicago Press, 1977.

Riquelme, John Paul. "Oscar Wilde's Aesthetic Gothic: Walter Pater, Dark Enlightenment, and *The Picture of Dorian Gray*." *Modern Fiction Studies* 46 (2000): 609–31.

_____. "Toward a History of Gothic and Modernism: Dark Modernity from Bram Stoker to Samuel Beckett." *Modern Fiction Studies* 46 (2000): 585–605.

Rowe, John Carlos. *Through the Custom-House: Nineteenth-Century American Literature and Modern Theory*. Baltimore: Johns Hopkins University Press, 1982.

Stein, Richard. *The Ritual of Interpretation: The Fine Arts as Literature in Ruskin, Rossetti, and Pater*. Cambridge: Harvard University Press, 1975.

Stein, William Bysshe. "*The Sacred Fount* and British Aestheticism: The Artist as Clown and Pornographer." *Arizona Quarterly* 27 (1971): 161–73.

Teahan, Sheila. "(De)Facing Aestheticism in The Outcry." *Symbiosis: A Journal of Anglo-American Literary Relations* 5 (2001): 159–71.

Figuring the Princess:
The Princess Casamassima and Pater's Mona Lisa

ANDREA CABUS-COLDWELL

The issue of aesthetics, especially in its relationship to artistic creation, is constantly present in the works of Henry James. Critics of his
work, including Jonathan Freedman, are quick to point out James's struggles throughout his career with Paterian aesthetic philosophy (see appendix, *Marius the Epicurean*). The idea of the aesthetic life seems to have both
drawn and troubled James. He ultimately attempted to strike a compromise
between his approval of Pater's ideas as an artistic way of perceiving life
and reading people, and his dissatisfaction with their implications if used
as a guide to leading one's life in place of traditional morality. Regardless
of his final evaluation, however, James's attempt to come to terms with aestheticism is visible throughout his work, most clearly through the various
characters who profess aspects of aesthetic theory.

The Princess Casamassima presents a number of expressions of James's
debates through the careers of the novel's main characters, Hyacinth Robinson and the Princess herself. Collin Meissner, author of "*The Princess
Casamassima*: 'a dirty intellectual fog,'" claims that Hyacinth "doesn't just
approximate James's sensibilities; he also embodies everything James felt
he'd outgrown as an artist" (53). A young man who, in good Paterian fashion, is "all beset and all perceptive," Hyacinth exists in part as a study of
the possibilities for the would-be aesthete in whose life money is an issue
(James, 34). More importantly, however, Hyacinth's attempts to live an aesthetic lifestyle allow James to compare Hyacinth—the immature aesthete

and would-be author—with himself through their individual attempts to frame and describe the Princess Casamassima.

Hyacinth's desire for authorship—for the ability to organize and define his world—is revealed to the reader early, through a conversation with Millicent Hemming, one of the women he will later attempt to define. Originally offended by her remarks about his work as a bookbinder, he relaxes under the influence of her company, and "by the time he reached her door he had confided to her that, in secret, he wrote: he had a dream of literary distinction" (112). Hyacinth continues to dream later in the novel, considering bookbinding a "resource" that could be given up when his debt to the Princess was paid, at which point "he proposed to himself to write something" (403). Although Hyacinth frequently mentions that he reads in both English and French, James's reader is offered only one tangible example of Hyacinth's own literary efforts. The letter he writes to the Princess Casamassima from Venice is important to their relationship and to Hyacinth's role as a possible political assassin, but it serves only as limited proof of Hyacinth's dream of authorship. Hyacinth's larger attempts at writing are made, like those of Gabriel Nash of *The Tragic Muse*, "in life" (*TM*, 105). As Elizabeth Allen demonstrates in *A Woman's Place in the Novels of Henry James*, Hyacinth plays out his efforts at aestheticism by "trying to sort out, label and define his impressions ... the mixed nature of society and of the individuals who make up society finally defeat this attempt at total purism" (98). In attempting to "work in life," to attach definitions and meanings to the figures around him, Hyacinth models his observation on the work of Walter Pater in his best known text, *The Renaissance*.

Although he attempts to offer meaning to the "types" of various figures in the novel, Hyacinth's most obvious and personally meaningful reification endeavor is that involving the Princess Casamassima. Here, he struggles to create an image to rival that of the Mona Lisa described by Pater in his chapter on Leonardo. In these paragraphs, Pater invests the figure in da Vinci's painting with all the knowledge and history of Western civilization—simultaneously creating a vampiric figure who cannot be moved because she embodies ultimate knowledge.

In his attempts to frame the Princess as a version of this figure, Hyacinth ignores the dangers inherent both to the figure he seeks to duplicate and to the process of transforming a woman into a cultural sign. Although Hyacinth is not alone in this classification of the Princess, his tenaciousness in salvaging his original impression of the Princess and in assimilating all of her later actions to fit this static ideal sets Hyacinth apart from other characters who attempt to refigure this woman as "sign" rather than as "subject of her own experience" (Allen, 85). For Hyacinth, this "fatally repetitive series of linguistic errors" leads to his death, as he continually refuses to accept the possibility that the Princess's political opinions may in fact be more than a whim (Teahan, 20).

Dangerous or not, the creation of an icon is clearly one of Hyacinth's goals from early in his relationship with the Princess Casamassima. Compelled to meet her by the claim of another of her disciples that she is "the most charming woman in the world" and "perhaps the most remarkable woman in Europe," Hyacinth comes to this initial encounter already armed with the information that will form a basis for his work of transforming the Princess into an aesthetic emblem (James, 186). The setting for this meeting, a box at the theatre, adds to Hyacinth's sense of the Princess as someone from a work of art; he sees his situation as "a play within a play" (192). "Dazzled" by her presence, Hyacinth, when he finds himself able to observe anything, decides that "she might well be a princess—it was impossible to conform more to the finest evocations of that romantic word" (191). The trio seated in the box is located, to Hyacinth's perception, on one side of a frame. He imagines that it is the stage which is being framed, but readers could just as easily envision the box as a frame for the group within, in the manner of a painting. Despite Hyacinth's ignorance of this possibility, the Princess does remind him of some work of art, "Which he had admired of old ... in a statue, in a picture, in a museum" (191).

Having once equated the Princess with a tangible work of art, Hyacinth attempts, in the true Paterian manner, to frame his discovery in such a way as to echo the Mona Lisa figure of *The Renaissance*. Pater claims for his "Lady Lisa" that "hers is the head upon which all 'the ends of the world are come,' and the eyelids are a little weary" and that "she has been dead many times, and learned the secrets of the grave" (Pater, 66). Similarly, the Princess, as perceived by Hyacinth, "might be divine, but he could see that she understood human needs ... there was something familiar in her smile, as if she had seen him many times before" (James, 192). Hyacinth's language echoes both the style of *The Renaissance* and Pater's description of the Mona Lisa as a world weary goddess figure—"The symbol of the modern idea" (Pater, 66).

This categorization completed, Hyacinth spends the rest of the novel trying to keep the Princess within the bounds of the role he has created for her. Philip Sicker demonstrates that "just as the Princess herself seems a work of art, so too she represents for Hyacinth the class that has produced and exhibited most of the art of our civilization" (68). Like the Mona Lisa, Hyacinth's figuration of the Princess is as an embodiment of history—

in this case, not of Western civilization in its broad sense but simply of its art. She is to be both muse and protector—someone whom Hyacinth will worship in return for an advanced form of patronage. His desire for this sort of relationship is clear through his "offering" of a beautifully bound copy of Tennyson, his own handiwork, as well as other volumes throughout the novel. His attempts to interest the Princess in the artistry of his profession represent not only an offering to her as a "divine" figure but also an opening through which he hopes to display his aesthetic abilities and gain support for his own imagined literary creations.

That Hyacinth's dreams of a patron/muse are hopeless can be seen well before the Princess chooses to ignore his elaborate offerings. During their memorable first encounter, the Princess establishes her lack of interest in the literary when she pleads that she has "already forgotten what they have been doing in the play ... someone or other was hurled over a precipice" (James, 195). The reader, who remembers this statement later although Hyacinth does not, recognizes that the Princess's interests, in terms of James's explanations of her behavior, lie more in observing as someone is "hurled over a precipice" than in questioning who that person might be or why he has been abandoned. Indeed, although Hyacinth expects that she will "save him" by "[flinging] a cloud about him, as the goddess-mother of the Trojan hero" had done—an act she claims she has in mind—the Princess does not act to save Hyacinth and derides Mr. Vetch for assuming she has the power to enact such salvation (384).

Although Hyacinth is finally disillusioned by his relationship with the Princess, he never realizes the real cause of his disappointment—the disparity between his icon and the Princess. Elizabeth Allen demonstrates that Hyacinth "seeks to establish a new, less bleak relationship to the world, through fixing the Princess as a value" (97). By investing the figure of the Princess with meaning, Hyacinth makes the figurative leap to authorship, which represents for him the possibility of controlling rather than being controlled by his society. This attitude necessitates the static nature of his figuration of the Princess. If the icon is inconsistent, then the author's authority is questionable. To the end of the novel, then, Hyacinth continues to understand the Princess as a work of art endowed with a meaning which he has discovered and elaborated in her. At the end of their intercourse, the Princess asks him, "Why am I so sacrosanct and so precious?'— revealing the limitedness of Hyacinth's vision of her. His only answer, "Simply because there is no one in the world, and there has never been any one in the world, like you," echoes his earlier statements about the necessity of saving art from the socialist revolutionaries (James, 574). In both cases it is the unique and lovely objects, which Hyacinth has invested with meaning, that must be saved.

Hyacinth's naive attempt at iconography fails because he depends on his limited view of "art," as personified in the Princess, to save him. This faith dooms him because it blinds him to this disjuncture between his lived world and the momentary aesthetic pleasure offered by art, according to Pater's philosophy. In presenting Hyacinth as sensitive but not consistently logical, James asks his readers to critique Pater's aesthetic. In following aesthetic philosophy, Hyacinth fails as a creator both in his inability to model an image of the Princess, in the vein of Pater's Mona Lisa, and in neglecting to write anything despite his evident desire for authorship. James, on the other hand, has proved his aptitude by offering his readers embodiments of "type" in both Hyacinth as the would-be aesthete and the Princess Casamassima as a variation on the Paterian female icon.

But is James really any more able than Hyacinth Robinson to create a concrete, ideologically invested figuration of the Princess? Certainly the novel urges the reader to regard her as an emotionless figure, with vampiric qualities reminiscent of Pater's "reading" of the Mona Lisa. This is most evident in the fact that, almost without exception, she is referred to by her title (also the novel's title), which instantly begins a process of reifying her, rather than by her given name, which would allow the reader to consider her as a person in her own right, thus breaking down attempts at objectification by the text. Although a character, in this objectified sense, the Princess becomes the tangible center of the text—the central object that reveals specific qualities in all of the characters that relate to it and thus organizes the range of opinions in the text. Having, as Philip Sicker suggests, "no lasting identity," the Princess becomes what other characters imagine her to be and, in doing so, reveals to James's reader the true desires of the characters that choose to define her (71). One example of this is Hyacinth's idea that she is the representative of beauty and genteel life, the very identifiers which he most desires for himself. A character's opinion of "the Princess" as a representational figure is intimately related to all other actions carried out by that character in the text, thus Hyacinth has the ability to see her as a muse for revolution as well as for literary art, the two competing desires in his life. His final attempts to protect her from her own revolutionary participation, to preserve the "beautiful woman," thus foreshadow his ultimate denial of revolutionary action as a possibility in his own life.

In embodying this role in James's narrative, the character of the Princess can hardly avoid being one who "poses" in various parts and, in doing so, appears to digest the experiences and personalities of those around her (Sicker, 71). This possibility is demonstrated by the Princess's opening remarks to Hyacinth on the night of the play, which suggests that she collects "types" so that she can talk them over with one another and gain additional experience from their reactions to one another (195). In the course of *The Princess Casamassima*, the reader encounters four men, including Hyacinth, who are, or have been, "involved" with the Princess and represent some of the "types" whose experiences she has observed. In each case, she appears to gain what she can, wealth in one case but more often unique experiences, and then to drop them when they cease to amuse.

It is from her husband, Prince Casamassima, that the Princess gains both her title and her wealth. Throughout the novel, James offers glimpses of this man who, like Hyacinth, saw the Princess as a beautiful woman who would bring honor and fame to his family and inherited fortune. Instead, he finds himself in possible disgrace as she revenges herself upon him, first by spending his money profligately, and then by using it to aid revolutionary causes that are antithetical to his own interests and beliefs. The Princess's second male companion, Captain Sholto, who understands her desires more accurately than her husband had, spends the entire novel finding "types" in an attempt to feed the Princess's insatiable interest in "collecting." As he tells Hyacinth,

> There was a time when I went in immensely for illuminated missals, and another when I collected horrible ghost-stories (she wanted to cultivate a belief in ghosts), all for her. The day I saw she was turning her attention to the rising democrats I began collecting little democrats. That's how I collected you [346].

In collecting democrats, Sholto introduces the Princess to Lady Aurora and Paul Muniment, who offer her more authentic experiences in humanitarian work and revolutionary politics respectively; as a character, he enables James to show the reader that the Princess prefers "cultivating" sensations over forming relationships.

James also presents the Princess as a potentially dangerous figure through the reactions of various characters who relate to her. Madame Grandoni, who is credited with understanding of the Princess by virtue of age and lengthy friendship, is shown either worrying or warning the various men against the Princess's capriciousness and unthinking behavior. She warns Hyacinth from the first not to "give up [himself]," and grows continuously more depressed throughout the book because of how "bad" things have become (James, 243). She finally leaves the Princess because she cannot stand to be complicit in her friend's actions. Prior to her departure, however, she discusses the Princess with both Sholto and the Prince.

Madame Grandoni's conversations with these men are important in revealing how "the Princess" figure emerges through James's text. The dangerous aspects of her relationships, and the highest criticism of her actions, are articulated by the various male figures placed throughout the novel. Although Sholto gives Hyacinth the first praise of the Princess, he is also quick to present his rival with her flaws. Some things, Sholto claims to Medley, cannot be understood "unless you happen to have a little heart. The Princess hasn't" (344). A few pages later, he is just as blunt with Madame Grandoni, remarking that Hyacinth "will have to be sacrificed" to the Princess's appetite for sensation and that when the Princess gets what she "deserves" it will be "whatever, in the future, may make her suffer" (350). Her husband finds her, by the novel's end, to be corrupted and scandalous, primarily through her unwomanly participation in revolutionary activity—going out at night with all variety of men, to dark dirty buildings. "Dear friend, she is the devil," he tells Madame Grandoni (511). Although Madame Grandoni disputes this on the grounds that the Princess "wishes to do good," it is the Prince's estimation that remains with the reader. Even Paul Muniment plants the idea, early on, that "she's an idle, bedizened jade" and "a monster" who "swallows" the fishes caught for her by Sholto, her "cat's paw" (207, 226–27).

Through his male characters, then, James attempts to portray the Princess as a beautiful but corruptive force, as a woman who, lacking a character of her own, must devour the characters of others regardless of the effect of such actions on those she "befriends." In doing so, he reveals to a certain extent the frustration of these men at not being able, completely, to limit and categorize the sphere of influence inhabited by the figure of the Princess Casamassima. That James faced this problem along with his characters raises the prospect that it may actually be impossible, even for James the experienced author and mature non-aesthete, to create a static figuration of the woman behind the Princess Casamassima. Unlike Pater's Mona Lisa, this dark beauty continually reveals the disparity between attempted aestheticizing descriptions of her and her own actions in the world of James's novel.

James claims to have brought the Princess, Christina Light, into the novel because he felt she had more of a role to play than that offered her in her first appearance in James's earlier novel, *Roderick Hudson*. James claims that "she had for so long ... been looking for a situation, awaiting a niche and a function" and that, "[revived] for him by a force or a whim" of her own, Christina asserted her right to a place in his new novel (44, 45). James tells readers in his preface to *The Princess Casamassima* that she had "made her desire felt ... to testify that she had not been—for what she was—completely recorded" (45). Against James's authorial will, Christina Light seems to take on a will of her own "Christina had felt herself, known herself, striking, in the earlier connexion, and couldn't resign herself not to strike again. Her pressure then was not to be resisted" (45). Regarding her relationship to Hyacinth, James notes that the Princess "was to serve for *his* experience in quite another and a more 'leading' sense than any in which he was to serve for hers" (italics mine) (46). That James should, in hindsight, express to his readers how events *were intended* to play out rather than how they actually occurred in the novel might lead these very readers to question his level of control over the character of the Princess.

James's own reading of the character of the Princess in his preface has been the major starting point for other critics of *The Princess Casamassima* and of the title character. It is in the preface that James solidifies the connection between the Princess and the Mona Lisa by concentrating on Christina's hatred of the "banal" and her "world weary" character which must be continually fed by experience, but never satiated (45). Philip Sicker follows suit when he tells his reader that "the sad irony of Hyacinth's adoring love is that ... it alienates the Princess" who is "incapable of genuine affection" (Sicker 68–9). Striking a similar note, Sheila Teahan presents the Princess primarily as an irritant to Hyacinth's already dangerous confusion regarding his class identity, which leads to his death (Teahan 26–7). For Collin Meissner, the Princess, like Lady Aurora, represents one of Hyacinth's escapist impulses, which prevent him from distinguishing between truth and reality.

A few readings of the novel do attempt to break free of James's prescriptions for reading this central character. Edward Wagenknecht, while dubbing Christina Light "James's *femme fatale*," also tries to retain a sense of balance when examining her character. Having just examined her relationship with her husband, he points out that "It is to her credit, though I have nowhere seen her receive credit for it, that she does not seem to hate anybody else" (60). This may, however, be merely damning her with faint praise, as he follows this observation by commenting on her complete lack of remorse over the case of Roderick Hudson. Wagenknecht's final conclusion is "that at heart she is not a cynical adventuress but a romantic idealist and for this very reason she is far more dangerous" (71). His last sentences show the continual confusion between Christina's figure and her personality:

> If she had been able to junk her ideals and accept herself for what she was (as her mother did), she would have been a much worse woman than she was, and there must have been much less hope for her as a spiritual being. But she would probably also have put much less pain into the world [72].

If nothing else, then, Wagenknecht's reading offers a possibility for a *character* of the Princess beyond the *characterizations* created by James and by his characters.

Of these critics, Elizabeth Allen goes the furthest in challenging James's limitations on the Princess. Her chapter on *The Princess Casamassima* focuses on "the dislocation between the woman as sign and the woman as subject of her own experience [that] is implied by making one character perform both functions" (85). The Princess is defined and "limited" by both James, in his attempt to make her character function, and Hyacinth, who refuses to look beyond his own impressions to discover hers. Allen goes on to explore the possibility that the Princess's consciousness could be examined, despite the distortions offered by Hyacinth's observation and interpretation of her throughout the novel.

What is revealed by the practice of considering the Princess outside of James's injunctions is the possibility of a humanity far greater than that shown by the Mona Lisa. Here, the reader recognizes not only the Princess's often hurtful ignorance of class issues but also her attempts to be personal and personable. She does remind Hyacinth that he "[ceases] to be insignificant from the moment [she] has anything to do with [him]," and frequently falls into the habit of treating him like "a curious animal" (James, 321, 247). Still, with her expression she also shows an ability to understand and "enter into" the challenges of Hyacinth's association with her and continually tries to make those around her comfortable or at ease (192). The same is true of her philanthropic attempts. Certainly she is driven by her (often rude) curiosity about the lower orders. She is able, however, to do a great deal of good once she gains the assistance and knowledge of Lady Aurora.

While Hyacinth may find her direct questioning rude, the Princess's straightforward manner means that those around her are seldom in doubt of her reactions to them—"she [is] not a person who [takes] the trouble to tell fibs" (470). Her anger, as well as her enchantment or boredom, are clearly communicated throughout the novel. Interestingly, her anger and her sarcastic vein are most evident in situations where she feels her personal mobility to be threatened by someone's idealization of her and not as a result of boredom. Thus she resents visits from the Prince, who would like to confine her to a traditional aristocratic lifestyle. The tension of her relationship with Hyacinth is also clearest at the moment when he attempts to save her from her revolutionary involvement because of her beauty (574). Even Paul Muniment faces her anger, although he does not believe it important, when he characterizes her as a woman dedicated more to money and comfort than to the cause she has taken up, coolly remarking "I don't want to aggravate you, but you *will* go back" (581).

In a similar manner, although the Princess is contemptuous of Hyacinth's adoration, she does not set out to destroy him. As early as their conversations at Medley, shortly after he pledges to commit murder if necessary to the cause, she begins to suspect that he has begun to lose interest in socialism. It is in response to this growing sense that she cries at his announcement and, he suspects, harbors plans to save him from his own promises. Though other friends begin to suspect this change, in his view "it was only with the Princess that he had permitted himself really to rail at the democracy and given the full measure of his skepticism" (553). Although the Princess tells Mr. Vetch that it is beyond her power to save Hyacinth from his choice, when she learns that Hyacinth has received his orders she turns pale and then attempts to claim the job herself rather than see Hyacinth sacrificed for a cause he does not support. She arrives at Hyacinth's lodgings in an evident attempt to dissuade him, "anxious" and "in a fever," and falls to her knees, apparently in despair, when she and Mr. Schinkel find Hyacinth dead (586).

In these few events, James's reader glimpses the Princess in situations that do not fit either Hyacinth's or James's definition of her character. Although James's attempt at framing her character is the more accurate, especially if the final scene is read as another triumph of her bloody and vampiric thirst for experience and sensation rather than as a moment of true feeling, neither description seems truly able to account entirely for the Princess. It is interesting that Christina, the title character, is positioned by James in such as way that both her spoken words and her observing consciousness are limited to a few short moments in this text. By burying Christina's consciousness beneath the layers of Hyacinth's flawed perceptions and his imaginative readings and rewritings of his interactions with the Princess, James makes it easier to categorize and limit her within his own authorial view.

When *The Princess Casamassima* is read in relation to James's preface, it is clear that, unless limited in the ways described above, the Christina Light outlined by James in the preface could easily have taken over the book. As a conscious character, the Princess would be unable to play the objective role that reveals other characters in relation to her fixed one. Her few moments of speech already have the power to reawaken "the vision of a great heroism" in Hyacinth "in all the splendour it had lost" (574). This influence, extended to the reader, as well as to Hyacinth, would unbalance James's text. The alternative to the Princess as a character with a voice and human possibilities is the Princess who *is* pictured in James's text—one who is most identifiable in all of her monstrous rebellion against the qualities of beauty and femininity that most of the characters attempt to make her represent. That she slips out of these constraints occasionally is a credit to James's understanding of the characters he creates, although it sometimes limits his revision of the Paterian icon.

By experimenting with the possibilities and risks of Pater's figure, James considers a number of issues in his own writing. He replays his debate with aestheticism through the limitations it places on Hyacinth Robinson and his desire for authorship. He also shows the limitations such categorization of aesthetic experience places on the author through the constrained characterization of the Princess Casamassima. Perhaps most importantly, for his own sense of himself as author, James realizes his ability to control his created characters despite their attempts to push beyond the limits of the story in which he has cast them. In being less completely static than the description of the Mona Lisa, the figure of the Princess allows for much more diverse and complex readings of the novel for which she forms the center.

Works Cited

Allen, Elizabeth. *A Woman's Place in the Novels of Henry James*. London: MacMillan Press, 1984.

Freedman, Jonathan. *Professions of Taste: Henry James, British Aestheticism, and Commodity Culture*. Stanford, CA: Stanford University Press, 1990.

James, Henry. *The Princess Casamassima*. London: Penguin Books, 1987.

Meissner, Collin. "*The Princess Casamassima*: 'a dirty intellectual fog.'" *The Henry James Review* 19 (1998): 53–71.

Pater, Walter. *The Renaissance. The English Literary Decadence: An Anthology*. Edited by Christopher Nassar. New York: University Press of America, 1999.

Sicker, Philip. *Love and The Quest for Identity in the Fiction of Henry James*. Princeton, NJ: Princeton University Press, 1980.

Teahan, Sheila. *The Rhetorical Logic of Henry James*. Baton Rouge: Louisiana State University Press, 1995.

Wagenknecht, Edward. *Eve and Henry James: Portraits of Women and Girls in His Fiction*. Norman: University of Oklahoma Press, 1978.

On Not Representing Milly Theale: Sacrificing for Art in *The Wings of the Dove*

Mark Conroy

Venice is the setting in which the dynamics of Henry James's late novel *The Wings of the Dove* come to a head. In part, this is just another instance of the way James's fictions migrate to strange locations to work themselves out. But the specific resonances of Venice are particularly rich for a novel whose preoccupation is the relationship of the aesthetic, the artistic mode, to the larger tendencies in life from which it would prefer to hold itself aloof. For how can the aesthetic moment, however evanescent, be detached from the practicalities of everyday striving on the one hand, or spiritual aspiration and devotion on the other? Sacrifice often enables art, whether it be the fleeting economizing recuperated by profit or absolute loss and death without recompense. Inevitably the issue of what is sacrificed to make something of beauty will concern the novelist as well as the novel. But our focus must be the fiction, the climax of which is aptly staged in Venice, that meeting place of love and death, of commerce and the sacred.

It is generally understood that art requires sacrifice. But whose sacrifice? Is just that of the artist required, or does it embrace his friends and lovers? Janet Malcolm says that journalists are always selling someone out, and this is equally true of artists. Leon Edel argues that in writing *The Wings of the Dove* James touched the mystery of Constance Fenimore Woolson, who had lived and died in Venice, and about whom more is said below.[1] But equally, by transforming a once living woman into a fictional portrait, James deepens the mystery, even though the subject of the book itself is, indeed, a living woman who is transformed into an exalted image. Milly Theale must be sacrificed for her image to be erected in Merton Densher's memory. And it is, in part, Merton Densher himself who must sacrifice her. It is neither in Milly Theale's character itself nor in Densher's that the mystery of inspiration for this novel can be glimpsed. Rather, it is, above all, in the duet between them.

In some ways James's novel is merely a very extensive novella, an elaboration on a series of characters who embody, as in a shorter tale, allegorical abstractions. This is heresy if we see James only as psychological realist, but the delicate touches are complemented by a sense of the larger architecture, here as elsewhere in the corpus. All three central figures, Kate Croy, Merton Densher and Milly Theale, can be said to embody different aspects of the aesthetic imagination, and, in particular, different conceptions of what must be sacrificed to it. Each employs a different sacrificial economy in thinking of the imagination and its products, and specifically they each have a different way of adjudicating the three grand registers of discourse in this novel—economics, art, and religion.[2] The varied approaches arise naturally from the divergent life situations of the characters themselves. But in addition, James does employ the worldviews that result from these situations in a kind of metanarrative. This metanarrative floats above the story of the characters' lives and interactions, but it depends upon that story all the same, for the fate of each is bound up with the others.

Milly Theale's conception of art and what is sacrificed for it is depicted in her famous confrontation with the Bronzino portrait in Matcham. Lord Mark himself has set the stage for this encounter by remarking on the likeness between Milly and the painting. What Milly gleans from this moment, which Jonathan Freedman accurately suggests is reminiscent of Lacan's mirror stage, is that her fulfillment as an image—as someone existing in the minds and, if possible, hearts of one's dear ones—will be predicated upon her own death. There is an obvious existential horror in this realization, limned in James's rare stylistic flourish of repeating the word "dead" three times. However, Milly leaves Matcham strangely reconciled to this idea, and even pleased by it.[3] She has the money and the aesthetic ability to be her own portrait painter, so that the temporal brevity with which she is confronted can become the stuff of her legend. She becomes a dove by flying away: other people's image of her will be bought by her physical sacrifice.

One of the reasons so many readers of this novel do not perceive Milly Theale as inhabiting the same story as Kate and Merton, or perhaps as inhabiting a recognizably novelistic world at all, is the starkness and simplicity of the economy above outlined, and the sacrifice. She is no mere victim or Joan of Arc heroine, the way some of her partisans, and some of James's critics, have contended. She is actively engaged in producing just the effect that she has on Densher, for instance, both in this world and conceivably from beyond the grave.[4] But her immense financial wealth and her severe existential poverty, though poignant in being yoked together, connive also in removing her from the scheming and machinations that people who must get on in the world, and who generally populate novels, must enter into.

This leads with a certain inevitability to Kate Croy. On the surface, and perhaps beneath it, Croy would seem a much better subject for a novelistic reality. Her version of the aesthetic is, in its way, almost as stark as Milly's, just in a rather different direction.[5] She views it as a necessary artifice, even a kind of lie, which will enable her to gain the sort of financial advantage that the Milly Theales of the world claim by natural right. She views herself, and is viewed by Aunt Maud, as an actress, perhaps in the tradition of her *boulevardier* father, of whom Kate reflects "there was no truth in him.... The inconvenience was not that you minded what was false, but that you missed what was true" (*19*, 7). When she proposes to Merton that he make love to Milly so that upon her death they can get her money, her worldview sees nothing so outrageous in the suggestion: playacting is exactly what she has been encouraged to do by her aunt anyway, and this just carries it into another realm. She separates the wheat of art from the chaff of commerce, rigorously preferring the chaff and assuming, at first correctly, that her view is shared by Merton Densher. She believes that this artifice will allow her to have both love and money, Merton's qualms to one side; the sacrifice of truth is well worth it. The artifice, she is careful to argue, costs nobody in material terms: Milly gets an affair of the heart to send her to the next world, Merton and Kate get her money when she leaves, and nobody is hurt unless the cover is blown. (Merton goes along with this notion, which is why at first he is able to transfer all of his own guilt onto Lord Mark for exposing the two of them.) For Kate Croy, the artifice of the aesthetic is a noble lie, or at least a harmless one: only truth is sacrificed by this art, and money is gained. By the novel's conclusion, her love for Merton Densher, which seems real enough at the outset and whose needs originally motivate her otherwise tawdry-sounding scheme, must also be sacrificed. Her version of the aesthetic is completely pragmatic, what one could call acting in order to accomplish an action. Her preference for the theatrical metaphor over the pictorial is apt in this respect. The play is the thing; however, the purpose behind it is not to catch anyone's conscience but to acquire the means for the real life one wishes to lead once offstage.

In this version of the aesthetic, the fictional, she is first tutored by Lionel Croy, and then by her Aunt Maud, whose hopes for her niece are likened to those of a stage mother for her daughter's aborning career:

> That was the story [for Densher]—that [Kate] was always, for her beneficent dragon, under arms; living up, every hour, but especially at festal hours, to the "value" Mrs. Lowder had attached to her.... he now recognised in it something like the artistic idea ... imposed ... in respect to a given character, on a distinguished actress. As such a person was to dress the part, to walk, to look, to speak, in every way to express the part, so all this was what Kate was to do.... Aunt Maud's appreciation of that tonight was indeed managerial, and the performer's own contribution fairly that of the faultless soldier on parade. Densher saw himself for the moment as in his purchased stall at the play; the watchful manager was in the depths of a box and the poor actress in the glare of the footlights. But she *passed....* It was as if the drama ... was between [aunt and niece] them quite preponderantly; with Merton Densher relegated to mere spectatorship, a paying place in front, and one of the most expensive [20, 34–35].

This passage is so lingered on that the narrator takes the rare expedient of justifying its length, in view of the fact that impressions such as this "come and go ... in very much less time than notation demands." It commingles the theatrical imagery with that of the arts of war, thus echoing Densher's first impressions of Aunt Maud and her home in Book Two; but it also underlines the way this passage has passed from aunt to niece, or perhaps back and forth between them. The imagery seems at first confused—Aunt Maud starts as the manager and ends up as a fellow performer of Kate's—even if that very double duty is appropriate to one who is a shill for her own creation. But the overwhelming point of this passage is Kate's deference to the requirements of simulation in some greater cause, to being a good actress the better to be a good soldier. By her own understanding, Kate's theatrical role is linked to her value as a commodity for Aunt Maud. As she puts it, "I *am* ... on the counter, when I'm not in the shop-window; in and out of which I'm thus conveniently, commercially whisked: the essence, all of it, of my position, and the price ... of my aunt's protection" (19, 279). This image of commodification, almost of prostitution, Kate offers up frankly, a token of her awareness of her own compromising role.

When she suggests to Merton that he make love to the dying Milly in the hope of securing her fortune (he eventually, and sadistically, forces her to enunciate this unworthy end explicitly) all she is doing is replicating through her lover her own aunt's pandering of her. Critics who stress the escape Kate hopes to make from the exigencies of her aunt are less inclined to observe that her means of doing so entail extending the logic of the world of Aunt Maud to a larger domain. The "admirable lucidity" for which Merton at first admires her does not admit of sentiment or even human emotion, at least not when it gets in the way of the goal.[6]

One nice way of balancing Kate Croy's aesthetic project with Milly Theale's is by pointing out the moment in her story that most recalls Milly's mirroring epiphany in Matcham. This moment occurs at the very outset of the novel, and here the mirror is not metaphorical but literal. Kate is, of course, prettier than Milly, which is one of the reasons why le tout London's worshipful response to Milly's coming out is assumed to be more about her fortune than about her face. But a mirror records not a dead person but a living one: her desideratum is not to be a memory for survivors but to enact a successful (i.e., profitable) performance for a living audience. While the Freudians among us could have some fun with the fact that the first performance for which we see this actor prepare is with her own father, the more sensible reading is that, for Kate Croy, life is a theatre piece, all the world a stage. The "waiting" with which she is tasked, and which is in a way her lot throughout the book, should not be seen as a detriment to her playacting self any more than Achilles sulking in his tent is anything but a gathering of mettle for the great battle. It is an inherent part of the dynamic, and one of the signs that Merton's relationship with her is deteriorating is the sense we have in Volume Two that when she talks with him she is no longer in any way backstage, as before, but now very much onstage.

To each of the women's aesthetic projects there corresponds a specific relation to place, as is so often the way with James. It is not only to Kate Croy that rooms seem to speak in this text, although they speak to her first, and most dramatically. The difference is that for Milly Theale the moment of apotheosis, which is also the revelation of that with which any conceivable living apotheosis will have to compete, has a local habitation and a name, Matcham; by contrast, for Kate the revelation she has is really about the world, the houses and rooms, that she will try to escape. The opening staging of her mirroring moment, where the surroundings seem to mock the loveliness of her figure and face, underscores her unsuitability to this background. Tellingly, it is the lack of fit with surroundings that makes for Kate's determination to find a place more worthy of her looks and intelligence, that in sum sets her course even before she meets up with her man or hatches her scheme.

It turns out that insofar as Kate can claim a specific place that figures her aesthetic project it would no doubt be her Aunt Maud's "tall rich heavy house at Lancaster Gate" (*19, 26*). This looming presence, which also impresses itself forcefully on Merton Densher, is formative for Kate Croy, both positively (she learns early on the importance of having the security that her very middle-class aunt has indicated is truly crucial) and negatively (she would like, if possible, to get this security in ways unrelated to her aunt's intentions, and particularly her intention that Kate marry the egregious Lord Mark). The issue of whether or how fully Kate ever really escapes the fate represented by Lancaster Gate is a fascinating one: the fact that she ends up apparently preferring Milly's inheritance to Densher's love may indicate that she was as helpless in her own way as Milly was in trying to make a countermove to fate. Still, the acutely felt disjunction between Kate's admirable qualities and the constricted world in which they were likely to manifest themselves provides the incitement to her to commence her theatrical, to become her own manager, in effect—and Merton's.

If Kate Croy is searching above all for a way to replicate the best aspects of Lancaster Gate without the less attractive ones, such as Aunt Maud herself and her Philistinism, then similarly Milly's project in Venice is to reproduce the apotheosis moment she briefly experiences in Matcham, only without the painful implications of her sense that her painted counterpart is "unaccompanied by a joy." Her ideal is to present herself in an improved setting, as hostess rather than guest, in a palazzo that will indicate her advantages of wealth and also of grace.[7] Her essence, as she hopes, can then radiate by means of a fair image, conveyed to others, and to one person above all others. Because she has had the advantage of both a moment of revelation and a great deal of money, Milly Theale is in the position to realize a certain kind of *nunc stans* image for herself and to construe it along specific lines. Palazzo Leporelli, in a vital sense, becomes a restaging of the Matcham apotheosis, proving that revelation to have been both soon and preparatory.[8]

Kate Croy, with neither a concrete revelation, aside from her love for Densher, nor independent means, has no perfect image to drive toward. All she is able to do is to mount a theatre piece whose end result will be wealth comparable to Milly's, in part because the money itself will be Milly's. What aesthetic project she then undertakes with Merton Densher, her vision of the good life, is left out of the story. In a way, this omission is the paradox toward which the novel's plot has driven, because it is at first the love between her and Merton, which James is at pains to present as quite real, that gives rise to the machinations that ultimately do them in as a couple.

There are intimations in Book Two that she delights in Merton's mind, in his otherness from the Philistine world of Aunt Maud: "He represented what her life had never given her and certainly, without some such aid as his, never would give her; all the high dim things she lumped together as of the mind" (19, 50). Likewise, Merton's interest in her intelligence also pleases her, perhaps lulling her into seeing their union as somehow spiritual, not just physical.[9] (This sense is one reason Merton's insistence that she sleep with him to "seal the deal" is already a potential sign that they are fraying at the edges.) One of the reasons so many readers root for Kate, and some are seemingly unable even to stop, is that at first she and Merton are in league against conventional society's requirements: Merton notes how "nothing could have served more to launch them, at special hours, on their small floating island than such an assumption that they were only making believe everywhere else" (19, 66). Kate has allowed Merton to furnish her offstage life with its implied purpose, that which is the reason for first her and then his playacting onstage. Milly seems the answer to Kate and Merton's dilemma: how to achieve worldly and personal happiness at once. But the longer Merton pursues his playacting with Milly the more vague his role in Kate's happiness becomes, as the money's role waxes.[10]

Thus, we can make a rough distinction between Milly and Kate on the basis of the way they position the aesthetic vis-à-vis the economic. Both encounter it as a kind of destiny, to be sure. But the essential distinction concerns their own relation to means, to money and the freedom it affords. In this respect, it is noteworthy that the only thing Kate adds to Merton's famous question (whether she is telling him that, if he acts the part of suitor to Milly, "when her death has taken place I shall in the natural course have money") is to say, "We shall in the natural course be free" (20, 225). Aside from assuming that Densher's regard will pay proper tribute to her beauty and brains, Kate Croy gives little sense of what concretely they wish to be free to do. Milly, of course, has all the money she can stand, arguably too much. One wonders if her affliction may recall that of Isabel Archer in *The Portrait of a Lady*, who seems also burdened by what her would-be benefactor, Ralph Touchett, thought would give her wings. In any event, she finds her fortune equal to the task of giving a sufficiently compelling gilt frame for her portrait as perfect hostess.[11] What is for one woman the path to acquiring means, via her admirer, is for the other woman the perfect excuse to sacrifice her means. This is the logical extension of what each has and lacks in life and in money: Kate has the former and lacks the latter, while Milly is short on the former and well endowed with the latter.

That Milly Theale seems at best indirectly marked as active is one of those paradoxes that confronts a novel whose heroine figure is marked as static, and who has taken stasis for a kind of project to boot.[12] Her lack of direct activity is part of what causes some readers to infer conspiratorial depths and sinister designs. This indirection is at least as much the author's puzzlement at exactly how to present novelistically this very un-novelistic character, who has all the money in the world, yet is in existential terms but a "poor girl ... with her rent to pay," in the famous formula (19, 253).[13] Insofar as she has a goal of the sort thought traditionally to impel the heroine of a novel, then it is that of becoming a timeless image, an eternal portrait, first in the eyes of a living admirer, then in his presumptive memory.

The aesthetic projects of both Kate Croy and Mildred Theale do not emerge fully formed, as if from their respective foreheads. They are made to germinate, to take shape gradually and with the aid of ever-greater clarity in the minds of the women about their situations in the world. In fact, this very gradualness worries the author a bit when he tells his correspondent, Ford Madox Hueffer (later Ford), that in taking pains to build up his edifice bit by bit, he "let my system betray me, and at any rate I feel I have welded my structure of rather too large and too heavy historic bricks" (Qtd. in Leon Edel, 119).[14] Kate Croy's vexed desire, which is to be both truly loved as well as rich, gradually presents itself as resolved via Milly; and only by the last book, arguably, are she and the reader quite clear that, true to her background, she prefers the reliability of material means to the more ethereal charms of people. (The suggestion that her background helps explain such a preference is furthered by the fact that she burns Milly's letter in the Condrips' fireplace. The baleful effects of the Condrip surroundings upon Kate Croy serve for one of Merton Densher's reveries, which begins Book Ten, Chapter IV.) But the logic of the last chapter is prepared for from the moment Kate and Merton encounter Milly: Kate herself warns Milly that Milly may rue the day she met them. Similarly, once Milly realizes she may be dying, and that, in her doctor's words, she could live "if she would," her own aesthetic project is all but engaged. It also follows its internal logic, as in a novella.[15]

It is, in truth, the aesthetic of Merton Densher that most smacks of the enigmatic in this text. For one thing, it changes, the clue to that being his shift of loyalties from Kate to Milly, with all that this shift implies in the foregoing aesthetic projects of the two women. Leo Bersani likens the three central consciousnesses to "three images of the self confronted with the alternatives of the world of the lioness and the world of the dove. And when Kate has chosen the former and Milly the latter, they allegorically become their choice for the final and most crucial spiritual performance, which is Densher's" (142).[16] The strange thing is that the basis for Densher's change of heart lies essentially hidden from view, suggesting "an awkward transition from a novel of social relationships to an allegory of spiritual appreciations," which allows Densher's narrator to "underplay the murderous implications of his hero's treatment of her as a distinct human being" (143).[17] Whether one accepts that James "lets off" his hero as Bersani charges—and it is doubtful since, among other things, being "let off" is exactly how Densher frames the matter to himself—there is no doubt that the turning of Densher, a *reversio* that gives him the aesthetic project with which he leaves us at the novel's end, is decidedly underspecified. This is particularly odd in a novel so replete with detail and characterization, built of so many solid blocks, as James would say.

The inevitable resort to Milly and Merton's final interview as the pivot for Merton's shift in loyalties gets us little further. That incident's gnomic dwelling place in James's novel, between Books Nine and Ten, has provoked far more discussion than the two principals could ever plausibly have generated by themselves. In some way, this resonating gap has become an emblem for the larger blank space where what motivates Merton Densher's transformation ought to be.

Into this space have rushed many Jamesians, each with partial explanations of varying probability. David McWhirter points to the sheer danger in the prolonged exposure of Densher to Milly Theale that Kate's slow-acting scheme ironically requires to take effect: "the intimacy which she [Milly] and Densher are engaged in creating, through their words, their awkward silences, the myriad choices involved in their simply being there together, is already on the way to becoming a reality in which Kate Croy has no place" (124).[18] If possession is not nine-tenths of the law—and the upshot of Kate and Densher's "bargain" implies it isn't—then proximity often is.

Holland by contrast makes much of the Venice dinner party, where hostess Milly's "sheer presence makes Densher aware of Kate's limitations; judgment is passed against Kate through Densher's consciousness.... he feels that Kate, when looking at Milly's pearls, is thinking not of their purity and genuineness, and what they reflect in Milly, but of the cash value which they represent while lending something of Milly's 'style'" (310).[19] For Holland, this moment of contrast is Densher's tipping point into the arms of Milly.

An even more unexpected source of conversion is sought by Michael Moon, who argues that it is the penetrating gaze of Theale's manservant, Eugenio, that emasculates Densher, sending him reeling into a "cult of phallic passivity" (436).[20] While admitting that "Eugenio's 'long looks' are at least on the surface signs of his disapproval of Densher's behavior," still this "does not explain why Densher repeatedly engages him in gazing matches" (437).[21] If this analysis not only plunges deep but also fetches far, the crepuscular outlines of the shift in Merton Densher's worldview give it leave to do so.

There are even genetic precursors to be sought for Densher's latter-day conversion to keeper of Milly's flame. The novel mentions early on that his mother's "distinguished industry" was that "she copied ... famous pictures in great museums" so faithfully that she "even deceived." To the mother's sensitivity to the image and fidelity in retaining it must be added the son's own capacity for retaining hers: "Her son, who had lost her, held her image sacred" (*19*, 93). This at least supplies a kind of precedent for Densher's will-ingness to make himself the repository for a beloved woman's memory, though apparently with none of his mother's painterly inclinations.

Such is the vagueness of motivation for this all-important change of heart that all of the above possibilities supply part of the answer. To these I would add my own speculations, taking as a point of departure Bersani's insight that with Densher's shift in loyalties the trajectory of the novel itself changes, moving with its hero from social relationships to spiritual appreciations. And appreciation is the term, because, unlike Milly Theale or Kate Croy, Densher does not honor his aesthetic project by what he does, but in the way of Jamesian renunciation by what he refrains from doing.

If Kate's guiding metaphorics are of the theatre and Milly's are of por-traiture, then the guiding forms for Merton's aesthetic at first are those of writing, specifically, the forms of journalism. When we are first introduced to Densher, he is plying that trade; his work is words, but his words are not art but craft. His profession has more in common with Kate's tasks at the hands of Aunt Maud, her manager, than he would care to admit, but what he prizes about it is his distance, his independence from bourgeois society and its proprieties.[22]

Densher's transcendent value is at first not aesthetic so much as intel-lectual. His writing is not necessarily deathless prose, just straight and hon-est. Even as he is wooing Milly Theale, he prides himself on not directly lying to her. He reflects, "Strange enough therefore it was that he could go too far—if it *was* too far—without being false," at least in his utterance (*20*, 86).[23] It is not surprising that he is attracted to the lucid Kate, who partly shares his bemusement at the rituals and hypocrisies of late Victorian society. The game they are working on Milly begins to seem not unlike the sorts of sham courtship an Aunt Maud would encourage; indeed, it appears she may be encouraging their designs on Milly, which would only confirm Merton's feelings of prostitution.[24] Along with the mysterious ways in which something fictional can assume the status of something actual, as Densher's courtship ritual proceeds, the growing sense of guilt is hard to ignore in determining just how his new aesthetic project—the perpetuation of the cult of Milly—finally emerges.

The myriad motives attributed to Densher by Jamesians through the years can almost all find some basis in the text, which is multilayered and, in the fashion of the master, subject to interpretation. No doubt there is somewhere, buried deep in the *écriture* perhaps, a scrap of a line to justify almost any motive. My suspicion that it is chiefly revulsion from the crass exploitation on which he and Kate are embarked comes in part from James's notebooks.[25]

But we all know how intentions, high and otherwise, get turned aside in the course of the creative process: for instance, the same notational entry, written in the months before James's infamous disaster with his play *Guy Domville* in January of 1895, seems to envision his eventual two-volume novel as a three-act play![26] The set piece from the novel itself that may best dramatize the essential role of Densher's own guilt in forming the basis for his aesthetic project has to be his lurching journey through Venice after being debarred from the Palazzo Leporelli. In one of James's Hawthorne-like modes, the very weather ministers to his distraught mood as Densher sees "a Venice all of evil" with its "cold lashing rain from a low black sky" and its "wicked wind" (20, 259). As he takes himself home in his banishment, Densher encounters St. Mark's Square, its "squares of red marble, greasy now with the salt spray," and in his foul mood sees the whole place as "more than ever like a great drawing-room, the drawing-room of Europe, profaned and bewildered by some reverse of fortune" (20, 261). This evocation of what Densher thinks of as his loss of margin is for James quite strong—has he before or since used the word "greasy?"—and it is the more powerful for echoing Densher's earlier propositioning of Kate, which happens also to occur in just this profaned square.

Some readers recall this scene as the one where Densher spies the sinister Lord Mark in Florian's, and attribute Merton's sensation of evil and contamination to the other man's presence. But, strictly speaking, Densher's nightmare vision of Europe's drawing room precedes his glimpse of Lord Mark. In fact, it has been suggested that in addition to solving the mystery of why Milly is so suddenly not "receiving" Merton, Lord Mark does Densher further service by supplying him with a convenient scapegoat. For one thing, he can tell himself that Milly's subsequent turn for the worse is not really caused by the original conspiracy so much as by Lord Mark's blowing of the conspiracy's cover.[27]

There is a further reason to suspect guilt as a motive, and that comes from the ways Densher's character rhymes eerily with that of the author.[28] The fact that the idea for the story comes to James so soon after the probable suicide of Constance Fenimore Woolson indicates that her life, her death and his conflicted relationship with both could well have provided as much inspiration for the Milly Theale figure as Minny Temple does.[29] James himself has done all he could to focus critics on the more distant figure of the long-ago cousin whose life was tragically cut short, from likening the dying heroine's name to hers, to opening his preface by claiming his novel "represents to my memory a very old—if I shouldn't perhaps rather say a very young—motive; I can scarce remember the time when the situation on which this long-drawn fiction mainly rests was not vividly present to me" (*19*, v). This is as clear an invitation to consider the heroine a replay of Minny Temple as could be extended. And many of the best Jamesians have accepted that invitation.[30]

It is not here suggested that Minny Temple must be removed from this inner pantheon and Constance Fenimore Woolson put in her place. Nor has James's history with her been entirely overlooked as forming a background to this novel. But the richness of implication in this association has not been pursued, partly because Milly's mode of death (natural causes) seems more apt for a consumptive than for a suicide, partly no doubt because James's own complicity in the life leading up to this death is somehow less savory to contemplate.[31] The fact that the author himself finds it hard to decide whether or not the Theale story is at the center of the novel or merely an excuse for Kate Croy and Merton Densher's relationship may suggest ambivalence toward a creative inspiration hard to distinguish from guilt.[32] Indeed, this pattern accords especially well with a tendency in James to encode a personal meaning within his fictional products.[33] It could be that Milly Theale and her forerunners are here twice encrypted: literally of course by novel's end, but symbolically throughout.

Even if, as seems unlikely, Densher's remorse over the death of a woman he has led on does not echo a comparable feeling on the part of his creator, there is still one crucial respect in which the two certainly do differ. Densher, who has lived by the pen, turns his heel not only on Kate and the money but also, it seems, on his previous occupation. At the very least, there is no indication—and it is very hard to imagine—that Densher would be mining his recent friendship with Milly Theale for its journalistic interest. In a way, that is, if one thinks about it, a bit strange for a writer; the shift in Merton's allegiances from Kate to Milly entails also a shift from writing to silence. One register of this shift from critique and interpretation to worshipful contemplation is in Merton's decision to assist at Christmas services at the Brompton Oratory. Indeed, if Milly's destiny is revealed to her at Matcham, then Densher's self-chosen role as assisting at the commemoration of a beautiful sacrifice has its great good place in Brompton Oratory.[34] As James puts it, Merton's "idea was really—as it struck him— consecrated" (20, 361).

Densher's aesthetic project, once it is finally "consecrated," is indeed far closer on the scale to the religious than to the economic and, indeed, requires the renunciation of the economic (and the erotic as well) as its precondition. In this, Densher only participates in the familiar Jamesian ritual of renunciation with which so many of his narratives seem to conclude. But this is a curious sort of project since, unlike both Kate and Milly, Densher's project does not entail doing anything apart from contemplation and what Bersani has called appreciation.[35] He will not profit in any way from Milly Theale's gift or her image, but will instead cherish it loyally, in reparation for his own betrayal of her.

If Milly Theale herself has a spectral and ambivalent relation to her real-life predecessors, then Densher has an equally vexed connection to his author. The journalist who makes use of his friendship with a dead woman would surely be the "publishing scoundrel" denounced by Julianna Bordereau (on behalf of the author, one assumes) in "The Aspern Papers" (1888). But is the same really true of a novelist who makes a fictional rendering based upon acquaintance with a dead woman, spurred as he would be by a guilt arising from her death? The sacrificial dynamic in the aesthetic projects of all three of this novel's major characters has eddied around how economic reality inflects and infects, indeed, gives rise to aesthetic ideals. That very ideal, as well, has been shown to be compounded of elements of commerce as well as quasi-religious admiration. Fitting then that Venice, famous for old cathedrals, art and commerce all at once, should be the setting for those scenes that bring the novel to a head; just as France, redolent of illicit love, is the appropriate place to resolve the tangle of pathology that is *What Maisie Knew* (1897).

Still, it must be noted that if Milly in any way recalls Fenimore, or Densher James, the author nonetheless does not mime the example of passive contemplation and refusal to profit set by the character. Insofar as any conceivable remorse over his relationship with Fenimore provides the author with his inspiration, the aesthetic project that results is active, not passive. The word is decidedly not renounced, and the resultant work is sent not to Brompton Oratory for contemplation but to the marketplace for sale. Unlike a memoir or piece of journalism, the novel does not, as such, betray (in either sense) its possible real-life model. Again, in James's late fiction, publishing in this form does not "out" the secret, but at most points to the existence of a secret that is being kept.[36] For all that, the trajectory commonly ascribed to Densher's aesthetic within the novel—from romantic love entangled with the economic to a retrospective contemplation divorced from the things of this world—is in the end not the one followed by the novel's author, for whatever reason.[37] This ambivalence toward that renunciation, which, we have noted, is indissociable from accepting one's own measure of guilt, may be what results in the encryption of Milly: a preservation that negates and occludes what it purports to honor.

When the aesthetic exaltation of a woman is founded upon the sublimation of a sexual desire the process is a familiar one: a living woman who is unattainable gets represented by a painting, a play, a poem. The sacrificial scene typically entails the foreclosure of direct erotic possibilities as the price for gaining purer aesthetic inspiration. Our post–Freudian age is rightly skeptical of this easy an economy, no doubt. But what about an aesthetic project that may be based on the guilt incurred by not having loved a (once) living woman enough, one who may be unattainable because one chose not to attain her? The strange double position that Milly occupies— central to the spiritual and practical drama of the novel, but offstage and almost willfully put to one side—would accord with this less traditional, less noble form of inspiration. For instance, the great impetus for Densher's subsequent fidelity to Milly, her great-hearted forgiveness of him, cannot be directly represented, not only because James probably had no real-life model for this interview, at least that we know of, but because the need for it is almost too shameful to acknowledge. Even Kate's overt act of betrayal in burning Milly's letter to accompany her bequest to the surviving couple has the convenient side effect of suppressing even a posthumous rendering up of her account in the matter.[38] Indeed, in this regard it could well be Kate Croy whose aesthetic project most traces that of the novel, at least concerning Milly, since she gleans the financial profit from the figure she had some role in betraying.

But this is to go too far, of course. There is no distinct and straightforward path from this novel, or any novel, to its antecedents. Like

Flaubert's human heart, the novel is a cemetery in which the names have been erased from all the tombstones. It is as futile to determine who is encrypted in Milly Theale as it is senseless to ask who is buried in Grant's tomb. All the same, the tendency in critical opinion to assume that Minny Temple is the primary or exclusive inspiration for this text has had the effect of muting a very important aspect of how Merton Densher's aesthetic project is actually formed, where self-disgust partakes of the admiring contemplation of someone else. Equally serious is the deflection of a more adult type of complicity in Jamesian creativity than that implied by the death of his cousin, in a motive both more recent and older than hers. After all, if part of the inspiration for this story was guilt about one's possible role in a suicide, then to turn the artistic product of that guilt into a marketable commodity is somehow more disturbing than merely exhuming once again the long distant story of Minny Temple. To avoid representing Milly Theale is then not so much to avoid representing Fenimore or Mary Temple; it is above all to avoid representing oneself, subjected to the very economic impulsions that one's textual *semblable* has transcended, and that the scapegoat Kate Croy has chosen over the love of others.[39]

James wants us to know only that there is a secret, not what it is. It may be a secret that has less to do with any woman than it does with the artist, and with the fate of any artist who must get on in the world, and use that world for his material.[40] So it is that I remind Jamesians of that other name effaced from its tombstone, for it tells a less heroic but equally necessary aesthetic tale. That tale might remind us of what Nietzsche has in mind when he wonders at "how much blood and cruelty lie at the bottom of all 'good things'" (62).[41] If the Minny Temple story, for all its dark aspects, is finally one of resurrection, of an old motive perpetually young, then Constance Fenimore Woolson's story is one of "the sacrifice of something sentient and throbbing, something that, for the spiritual ear, might have been audible as a faint far wail" (20, 396). We do well to recall that faint far wail, then, not because Fenimore is represented in Milly Theale but because she sums up so much of what is *not* represented in Milly Theale, and probably never could be.

Notes

1. Leon Edel, in his *Henry James: The Master, 1901–1916* (New York: Avon Books, 1972), says James "touched the whole mystery of Fenimore and the painful weeks of questioning and mourning when he had lived in Fenimore's Venetian apart-

ment—above all the great riddle of death" (122). He suggests that this realization "may explain" James's bouts of ill health while writing the book.

2. Laurence Holland's *Expense of Vision: Essays on the Craft of Henry James* (Princeton: Princeton University Press, 1964) notes that in The *Wings of the Dove*, the "language is shaped by three principal vocabularies—one commercial, one religious, and one aesthetic—which are defined by characteristic metaphors or phrases," and which partake of traditional institutions such as capitalism, the fine arts and "Judaeo-Christian tradition" (287). I take this register as my own, adding to it an interest in how each character weighs and puts into relation these three vocabularies, and the considerations they inscribe.

3. *The Novels and Tales of Henry James*, Vols. 19–20 (New York: Charles Scribner's Sons, 1909), Vol. 19: 220. Milly's exposure to the Bronzino painting is accompanied by her awareness of "the pink dawn of an apotheosis coming so curiously soon" (220). Of course, apotheosis for Roman emperors had to be preceded by death, hence the curious soonness. All further references given in the body of the text.

4. Holland refers to Milly's growing sense of style and self-possession as her "*acting as if*" (297, 302). Recent analyses of this novel have tended even further to emphasize Milly Theale's agency, the way she consciously adds pigment to the portrait others have of her. Some have even gone so far as to attribute to Milly almost *all* of the functional agency in her own victimization. Cf. Michael R. Martin's "Branding Milly Theale: The Capital Case of *The Wings of the Dove*" in *The Henry James Review* 24 (2003): 103–32. This highly imaginative reading suggests that Milly "elects to die in the Palazzo Leporelli because Venice's easily purchased cultural legacy ... magnifies her social power, and ... grants that power a permanence independent of her bodily existence... . She, in effect, uses the social power of art to coerce others, particularly Merton" (118). This prosecutorial language pervades the piece, which compares Milly's sinister project to the branding done by Nike, for contemporary liberals the sternest possible comparison to make. He does admit, in a rare concession to the skeptics, "James is not thinking of a new pair of Nike Air Zoom Ultralights" (124). After reading this thunderous indictment, one begins to wonder whether it is finally Martin who is branding James's heroine. But the "capital case" is made with such brio that one—almost—consigns Milly Theale to her capital punishment.

5. So different are their directions, indeed, that Millicent Bell's *Meaning in Henry James* (Cambridge, MA: Harvard University Press, 1991) finds in Milly and Kate the perfect counterpart to Bell's paradigmatic dyad of Isabel Archer versus Madame Merle in *The Portrait of a Lady* (1881): the pragmatist for whom the personality is determined by necessities, getting and spending, and the transcendentalist for whom character is in essence free and self-determined. "Kate is the heroine of the practical... . She is the ultimate expression of a society in which 'value' means the purchasing power of anything as determined by the market. To these attitudes and this world Milly opposes an older transcendental tradition of intrinsic personal being and a principle of moral behavior which stresses sacrifice rather than gain" (291).

6. There are some who have been about the business of rehabilitating Kate Croy in recent years. Some of the renovations are more lifelike than others, but one of the most imaginative comes from Doran Larson's article "Milly's Bargain: The Homosocial Economy in *The Wings of the Dove*," *Arizona Quarterly* 51 (1995): 81–110.

There she argues that, albeit with great indirection, Kate and Milly work out together a kind of positive economy where both in effect "win," and that reversing the traditional anthropology whereby men mediate their economic position through women, *they* in effect use *him* as a medium: "the struggle throughout the novel is not between Kate and Densher on one side, and Milly on the other. It is rather between Milly and Kate on one side, and Densher's conscience on the other: *Kate and Densher use Milly* becomes *Kate and Milly do things with Densher*" (101). As with most arguments that try to boost Kate Croy's moral stock, this one does so by attributing an inordinate amount of agency, to say nothing of intuition, to Milly Theale. In its use of Eve Sedgwick's theories to assert that Milly all but consents to Kate's scheme as a sisterly way of helping out a woman in trouble, Larson's argument acquires a novelty that cannot be equaled by plausibility.

7. Marcia Ian, in her "Elaboration of Privacy in *The Wings of the Dove*," *ELH* 51, no.1 (1984): 107–36, touches on the way Milly aspires to absorb her being into her reflection on others when she describes her "apotheosis" as entailing the process of becoming what "others see" (119).

8. John Goode's "Pervasive Mystery of Style: *The Wings of the Dove*, *The Air of Reality: New Essays on Henry James*," ed. John Goode (London: Methuen, 1972), 244–300, points to this fact among other things in saying that "Venice ... offers an ideal, lighted version of the London scene." But the need for Milly's money in order to realize this "ideal" also informs Goode's reading: "I don't think James is ironizing Milly, but I don't think either that he ever forgets that the ultimate symbol is money" (281). Milly's use of lavish means to try to transcend the mutable, fallen world is just the sort of paradox he has in mind when he notes "James's realization [in this text] of the interpenetration of economic and metaphysical values" (266).

9. Adding to this sense of romantic love is the idea that Merton not only has an unsuitable profession, that of journalist, but also an "aspect ... which made it almost impossible to name his profession" (19, 47). Kate is well aware that her choice of Merton could mean sacrificing social standing, and contrasts her knowledge in this regard to Milly's ignorance:

> "Milly ... has no natural sense of social values, doesn't in the least understand our differences or know who's who or what's what."
> "I see. That," Densher laughed, "is her reason for liking *me*."
> "Precisely. She doesn't resemble me," said Kate, "who at least know what I lose" (20, 60).

In this regard, we draw further fortification from *The Complete Notebooks of Henry James*, edited by Leon Edel and Lyall H. Powers (New York: Oxford University Press, 1987), where in writing up the first known sketch of the plot of *Wings*, James describes how Kate's refusal to make a "snobbish alliance" with Lord Mark is the "sacrifice [by which] she holds her lover." He qualifies this, though: "The girl's sacrifice is a sacrifice of that—but of nothing else" (106).

10. The tension between Milly's static moment of aesthetic revelation as opposed to Kate's fluidity and incompleteness is reminiscent of a long-standing concern on the part of James, especially in the latter years, with the gap between the two major figurations of art: as painting and as drama. The critic who has discussed this most thoroughly, at least in respect of *The Ambassadors*, is Nicola Bradbury. Cf. her "'The Still Point': Perspective in *The Ambassadors*," S. P. Rosenbaum, ed., *The Ambassadors*, 2nd ed. (New York: Norton, 1994), 473–501.

11. Holland remarks on Theale's spectacular Venice dinner party that it is "the dramatic scene for which the entire novel has been preparing" (305). Insofar as the novel coincides with Milly's aesthetic project, anyway, this is true, even though, as Holland notes, the woman herself is "scarcely even seen" (309). Yet another frame is invoked as setting off Milly Theale in this chapter as well: "The chapter's central action is enclosed in a frame outside (by the proposition which precedes [on St. Mark's Square where Merton demands that Kate sleep with him] and the assignation which follows [in his rooms where she obliges him])" (308). Their bargaining is juxtaposed with her gracious sacrificial largesse, the better to set it off.

12. Ian's article takes this tendency to its logical conclusion, arguing that Theale "is a romantic fantasy of self-annihilation [for the author], of escape from [James's] rigidly formalized consciousness, and an emblem for James's discomfort at being in the world" (127). Though Ian clearly means the author's discomfort at *his* [James] being in the world, it is possible that his *heroine's* being in the world troubles James almost as much. How to write a novel around this profoundly antinovelistic character was something that perturbed James a great deal throughout the writing.

13. Tessa Hadley's *Henry James and the Imagination of Pleasure* (Cambridge: Cambridge University Press, 2002) has discussed fruitfully the way James tried to square the circle of Milly Theale's sexuality, noting that as early as the nineties notebooks, he "deliberates at some length on the problems for decorum in representing this sexuality of a sick girl," her inference being that in "displacing" the consummation of sexual desire onto Kate, James obeys the dictates of the melodramatic good girl-bad girl convention with which the novel is still burdened: "What has prevented Milly [from getting sexual satisfaction] is that she has to be a 'dove,' she is the fair girl and not the dark one, she cannot be allowed to be sexual" (138–39). Within Hadley's reading of the two women as scapegoat figures out of René Girard (cf. 128–29), this makes a certain sense. In addition, though, sexual hunger places Milly right within the purview of prose narrative's standard urgencies; and James desires to place the aesthetic frame around her image, to freeze it. This ambivalence, along with the obvious quandary for the character as to whether any affair with Merton would get off the ground during her lifetime, only heightens the sense that Milly would, in the end, rather be an image for Merton than a lover, worshipped for eternity rather than taken in real time.

14. Cited in Leon Edel (119). The construction metaphor is also used in James's preface to the New York edition of the novel itself, where he speaks of the characters' various points of view as the "solid *blocks* of wrought material" he uses to build his effects (xii).

15. Goode says, "if the moral fable [undergirding the novel] is simple, it is also vague... . with this novel more than most.... accounts of its structure do not coincide with our experience of the book, because the book is so much an expansion from a simple plan" (245).

16. Leo Bersani, *A Future for Astyanax: Character and Desire in Literature* (Boston: Little, Brown, 1969), p.142.

17. Ibid., p. 143.

18. David McWhirter, *Desire and Love in Henry James: A Study of the Late Novels* (Cambridge: Cambridge University Press, 1989), p. 124.

19. *Expense of Vision*, p. 310.

20. Michael Moon, "Sexuality and Visual Terrorism in *The Wings of the Dove*," *Criticism* 28, no. 4 (Fall 1986): 427–43. Moon attempts to make this gaze "consti-

tutive of the same kind of relationship between them as has been said to exist between Densher and Kate Croy at the inception their intimacy" (436). Thus is a Sartrean standoff traded for a Freudian moment where Densher all but becomes Eugenio's "bitch!"

21. Ibid., p. 437. As with so much "queering" of James, this does not engage with whether what is under this surface is inaccessible to Densher's consciousness or to his author's. But so cursory is the essay's obligatory nod to the idea of Merton's guilt that it seems, well, almost guilty itself. Moon ultimately admits that the role of "the intense 'eye-games' he [Eugenio] plays with Densher in the broader scheme of the novel must remain speculative" (441). Even Moon's critique, it seems, is finally unmanned, a clean sweep for Eugenio.

22. Jonathan Freedman in his *Professions of Taste: Henry James, British Aestheticism, and Commodity Culture* (Stanford: Stanford University Press, 1990) has been especially useful in describing all the ways in which Densher, who "frequently muses ... on the question of cultural decline," loses his "essentially specious 'sense of independence'" by both his journalism, which "promotes the 'boom' he despises," and by his "passive participation in Kate's unfolding schemes." Significantly, Freedman notes Densher's "recourse to silence" as indicating his inability to take responsibility for his own complicity. But he also acknowledges "the impossibility of adopting any other attitude. For when civilization is defined as a perfected ... language and 'barbarism' as ... degraded or fallen speech, then the would-be cultural critic faces a situation where the only morally worthy speech is silence itself" (225). Whether this extreme a view is warranted or not, it does suggest a certain logic to Densher's gradual move from one defined by his words to one devoted to his silence.

23. McWhirter remarks, though, how "in an atmosphere where doing nothing is itself a determinant act, even the most casual words become deeds, replete with consequences for which the speaker is wholly accountable," and further, that "what is enacted, what is spoken, even when it is a pretense, takes on the full power of a reality" (122–23).

24. Julie Olin-Ammentorp in "'A Circle of Petticoats': The Feminization of Merton Densher," in *The Henry James Review* 15 (1994): 38–54, has pointed out that even Merton's gesture of taking charge, where he demands that Kate come to his rooms, can be seen to underscore the similarity between Kate's actions and his: "He is treating Kate as a prostitute—she must sleep with him in order to get the money—even while he is prostituting himself—agreeing to continue to 'please' Milly in exchange for Kate's sexual acquiescence" (45).

25. They are quite explicit about the connection between Densher's growing disgust at the plan they are working on Milly: "the young man learns from her that she *knows*—knows of his existing tie [to Kate]. This enables him to measure her devotion, her beauty of soul—and it produces a tremendous effect upon him. He becomes ashamed of his tacit assent to his fiancé's idea—conceives a horror of it. In that horror he draws close to the dying girl" (106). While it is worth admitting that even in this preliminary note James does disentangle Milly's beauty of soul from Densher's revulsion at the plan, and instead uses her forgiving response to it to throw the pettiness and cruelty of the plan into relief; nevertheless, the author clearly conceives of Densher's guilt as inextricable from the narrative of his falling in love with Milly, and then with what Kate calls "her memory" (20, 404).

26. Edel and Powers, ibid.

27. Olin-Ammentorp puts it this way: "Rather than accept the responsibility for his own actions, Densher uses Lord Mark as a scapegoat; when he hears that Milly is ill in the wake of Lord Mark's visit, he blames Lord Mark" (47).

28. Edel, for one, allows that the "personality of Morton Fullerton [the journalist who had been Edith Wharton's lover at one point] and the use of the name Merton permit us to speculate" that he is part of Densher's inspirational origin, but states nevertheless that "there is much of James's own moral feeling in Densher, his own reticence, his problems relating to women" (122). Freedman's reading of *Wings* relies upon a virtual identity between Densher and his author: for Freedman, even when James seems to be attacking some aspect of Densher's character, "the result of that attack is only to reinforce the homology between the positions of the author and character" (226).

29. Lyndall Gordon's *A Private Life of Henry James: Two Women and His Art* (New York: W. W. Norton, 1998) makes mention of a number of eerie resemblances between aspects of Fenimore's tragedy and James's *Wings* story. Among them, she underscores the original notebook entry of 1894: "James first imagined a death [for Milly] in Nice, Mentone, Cairo, or Corfu—the last two being the main scenes of Fenimore's Eastern journey in 1890, places James had not seen.... Her travel book, *Mentone, Cairo, Corfu*, was published posthumously in 1896" (315). Another, remoter but intriguing hint in this direction comes from R. W. B. Lewis's *The Jameses: A Family Narrative* (New York: Farrar, Straus, 1991), which notes that the Palazzo Barbaro, whose "staircase ... Gothic windows, [and] echoing voice" would all make its way into the rendering of Milly Theale's Venetian house, was the place James had moved to in summer of 1887, immediately after having resided for a lengthy stay at Fenimore's house in Florence (400–01).

30. McWhirter, for example, who is indeed among our best Jamesians, follows the master's lead by arguing that "in his final veneration for the memory of the woman he failed to love in life, Densher clearly echoes James's own strange satisfaction, so many years before, at seeing Minny Temple 'translated from the changing realm of fact to the steady realm of thought'" (140).

31. As Gordon points out, with perhaps undue melodrama, the letters James wrote in the aftermath of her death were to keep the recipients from implicating him in any way with the dead woman's state of mind: "The purpose is the same in all the letters: to fix on Fenimore the slur of uncontrollable *dementia*.... The James story [in these letters] is all about latent and emergent mania" (280–81).

32. It is striking how central Milly's psychology is to the notebooks, for instance (cf. the November 3, 1895, entry, which begins with her plight and her response to it [102–04]); whereas by contrast James tells Ford Madox Hueffer, by the time he has finished the novel, that the essential "subject was Densher's history with Kate Croy ... and Milly's history was but a thing involved and embroiled with that" (quoted in Edel, p. 119). Is James trying somehow to dissemble the centrality of Theale to the novel? Probably not, but this "now you see it, now you don't" dynamic is symptomatic of the way her story is both idealized and heightened, and also obscured and secreted, in the course of Volume Two.

33. One of the most cogent statements of this tendency comes from Donatella Izzo's *Portraying the Lady: Technologies of Gender in the Short Stories of Henry James* (Lincoln: University of Nebraska Press, 2001), which cites D. A. Miller's formula of a double bind, "a secrecy that must always be rigorously maintained in the face of a secret that everybody already knows, since this is the very condition that entitles

me to my subjectivity in the first place" (quoted in p. 241). Izzo uses this insight to suggest that, especially in late James, the desire both to keep a secret, about one-self presumably, and to let "everybody" know that one is keeping something secret, accounts for some of "the famously intransitive and abstract writing of the later style" (242). As significant as Izzo's formula itself may be the fact that it results from a reading of his late tale, "The Beast in the Jungle" (1903), another story thought by some to be "about" Fenimore.

34. Edwin Sill Fussell's book, *The Catholic Side of Henry James* (Cambridge: Cambridge Univ. Press, 1993), contends that Densher's decision to attend services at Brompton Oratory arises because Milly was Roman Catholic (153–54). His case for this intrigues, but I suspect the Oratory gesture has more to do with the sacrificial (and forgiving) nature of Milly's final bequest, and Densher's new role of quasi-religious dedication to her memory, than some denominational affiliation on her part. Admittedly, though, if she *were* Roman Catholic, that would make the *reversio* central to James's pairing of her and Kate—that the New World figure is the aristocrat and the Old World figure the middle class *arriviste*—more pointed.

35. Ian makes the case that "Densher's active, defensive, and retaliatory seeing ... makes him the novel's 'survivor'; it also makes him, decidedly, not the 'passive male' James's readers often find him" (125). True, perhaps, but this is only the effect of a decision to make passivity, in effect, into a lifelong discipline.

36. James does just this, I submit, when he says in his preface that "the false and deformed" second volume of *Wings* "bristles with 'dodges,'" though attributing all of the makeshift gimmickry to having to reduce the "scale of the exhibition" toward the end. He does add, however, "what a tangled web we weave when—well, when, through our mislaying or otherwise trifling with our blest pair of compasses, we have to produce the illusion of mass without the illusion of extent" (*19*, xviii-xix). James presents this deception as a mere matter of formal proportions getting out of hand, and that may be. But the moralizing tone suggests other sorts of deception as well.

37. It may seem a bit unfair to make too much of James's mercenary goals in publishing a novel such as *The Wings of the Dove*, given his notorious inability to turn a proper profit from his latter-day fiction, whose exiguous yield is given humorous illustration in a late letter of his to Edith Wharton, cited in Fred Kaplan's *Henry James: The Imagination of Genius* (New York: William Morrow, 1992): "Whereas she had purchased automobiles with royalties from her best-sellers, he had, he remarked ... been able to buy from royalties only the wheelbarrow used to bring visitors' luggage from the railroad station to Lamb House [where he lived in his last years]" (547). If hiding in plain sight was the secret to Jamesian secrecy at this point, then no doubt the best way to keep a secret was to publish it in a novel by James!

38. Bersani makes much of "Densher alone in his rooms with his conjectures of the 'turn' Milly might have given to the letter which he has given to Kate (without reading it himself) [as] perhaps the most powerful image of consciousness, once again, triumphantly and eerily self-sufficient" (144). It is also one of the few instances where Densher is prompted to even mental forms of verbal activity and his author is not. Under Merton's "consecration" to his new aesthetic project it is more the other way around.

39. The person who has most vividly put forth the idea that women, especially in James's late novels, were used essentially as scapegoats is Alfred Habegger in *Henry James and the 'Woman Business'* (Cambridge: Cambridge University Press, 1989).

40. In fairness one could further crowd this nameless cemetery by mentioning the death of Katherine Bronson, a Venetian hostess and old friend of James, in the year before he began *Wings*. He wrote a memorial tribute to her (Edel, 90), and the central place of the Bronzino could suggest a play on her family name. But this figure is less known to us, James's relation to her apparently more casual, than in the case of the other two.

41. *On the Genealogy of Morals*, ed. and trans. by Walter Kaufmann (New York: Vintage, 1969), p. 62.

Works Cited

Bell, Millicent. *Meaning in Henry James*. Cambridge, Mass.: Harvard University Press, 1991.

Bersani, Leo. *A Future for Astyanax: Character and Desire in Literature*. Boston: Little, Brown, 1969.

Bradbury, Nicola. "'The Still Point': Perspective in *The Ambassadors*." In *The Ambassadors*. 2nd ed. Edited by S. P. Rosenbaum. New York: Norton, 1994, 473–501.

Edel, Leon. *Henry James. The Master: 1901–1916*. New York: Avon Books, 1972.

Freedman, Jonathan. *Professions of Taste: Henry James, British Aestheticism, and Commodity Culture*. Stanford: Stanford University Press, 1990.

Goode, John. "Pervasive Mystery of Style: *The Wings of the Dove*." In *The Air of Reality: New Essays on Henry Jame*. Edited by John Goode. London: Methuen, 1972, 244–300.

Gordon, Lyndall. *A Private Life of Henry James: Two Women and His Art*. New York: W. W. Norton, 1998.

Habegger, Alfred. *Henry James and the 'Woman Business.'* Cambridge: Cambridge University Press, 1989.

Hadley, Tessa. *Henry James and the Imagination of Pleasure*. Cambridge: Cambridge University Press, 2002.

Holland, Laurence. *Expense of Vision: Essays on the Craft of Henry James*. Princeton: Princeton University Press, 1964.

Ian, Marcia. "Elaboration of Privacy in *The Wings of the Dove*." *ELH* 51, no.1 (1984): 107–36.

Izzo, Donatella. *Portraying the Lady: Technologies of Gender in the Short Stories of Henry James*. Lincoln: University of Nebraska Press, 2001.

James, Henry. *The Complete Notebooks of Henry James*. Edited by Leon Edel and Lyall H. Powers. New York: Oxford University Press, 1987.

_____. *The Novels and Tales of Henry James*. Vols. 19–20. New York: Charles Scribner's Sons, 1909.

Larson, Doran. "Milly's Bargain: The Homosocial Economy in *The Wings of the Dove*." *Arizona Quarterly* 51 (1995): 81–110.

Martin, Michael R. "Branding Milly Theale: The Capital Case of *The Wings of the Dove*." In *The Henry James Review* 24 (2003): 103–32.

McWhirter, David. *Desire and Love in Henry James: A Study of the Late Novels*. Cambridge: Cambridge University Press, 1989.

Moon, Michael. "Sexuality and Visual Terrorism in *The Wings of the Dove*." *Criticism* 28, no. 4 (Fall 1986): 427–43.

Olin-Ammentorp, Julie. "'A Circle of Petticoats': The Feminization of Merton Densher." *The Henry James Review* 15 (1994): 38–54,
Sill Fussell, Edwin. *The Catholic Side of Henry James.* Cambridge: Cambridge University Press, 1993.

"The Figure in the Carpet" as an Allegory of Reading

Vittoria Intonti

"The Figure in the Carpet" (1896) is one of a substantial and "homogeneous group" (James 1907–09, 1232) of tales all dealing with "the literary life" (1228), most of which were written during the last decade of the nineteenth century.[1] They were dramatic years for Henry James because of the failure of his theatrical experience, which exposed him to public derision.

As James himself wrote in his preface to a number of these tales included in the New York edition, what they have in common is "their reference to the troubled artistic consciousness" (228). Most of them were born of generalizations and are, as Edel puts it, "fables for critics" (Edel 1964, 15)—parables allegorizing the predicament of the fin de siècle artist and his increasing aloofness from the reality around him and from what, in "The Figure in the Carpet," James calls the bottomless vulgarity of the age" (James 1896, 300). The protagonists of these *Kunstler Novellen* are all writers and artists, with their anxieties, their search for form, their yearning for perfection, their delusions, and their problems living in a changing world that cannot appreciate their toil and their creative torment. The tales record the "romantic" disproportion between the artist's subjectivity and the world, the impossibility of reconciling art and life; what seems more significant is that the subject is often dealt with in the tones of comedy rather than in the tragic mood, which prevails in a tale like "The Middle Years" (1893).

The easiest approach to these tales is by way of the autobiographical impulse that underlies them. As a matter of fact, they are often read as

This essay originally appeared in RSA Journal 7 (1996): 27–37.

"mere fictional footnotes" (Vaid, 62) to James's life, and critical discussion is generally concerned with thematic aspects relating to the artistic convictions and traits of James himself. This is a legitimate concern, as the author declares in his preface that the tales were drawn "from the depths of the designer's own mind" (James 1907–09, 1228), from "his own intimate experience" (1229), even though he is unable to connect them with any specific "germ" or anecdote of his life. However, what is more interesting for the critic is to investigate how the writer was able to manipulate, objectify, and re-present the material drawn from his own experience; how he managed to overcome the autobiographical implications of his fables.

James abhorred what he calls in the prefaces the "terrible fluidity of self-revelation" (1316), and he succeeded in bypassing both the autobiographical problem and the intrinsic difficulty of making fictional characters out of artists through "an orchestration of the ironic note" (Vaid, 61). In the preface, he clearly states that "the studies here collected have their justification in the ironic spirit" (1229), and illustrates what he means by "applied irony" or "operative irony" (1229). "It implies and projects," he says, "the possible other case, the case rich and edifying where the actuality is pretentious and vain" (1229), which means that the irony in the "tales of the artist" derives from the discrepancy between the aspirations of the artist and the vulgar reality surrounding him. James's interest lies in the "ironic consciousness" (1235) of the artist "left wholly alone amid a chattering unperceiving world" (1235).

In some stories, irony works on more than one level. In a first-person narrative like "The Figure in the Carpet," but also in earlier tales such as "The Author of 'Beltraffio'" (1884) and "The Aspern Papers" (1888), which can be included in this group, the narrator himself appears as an ironic center of revelation, belonging to "the great race of critics" (James 1987, 137), the band of reviewers and readers James is exposing in the tale. He is "a newspaper man" (137) who writes in "cheap journalese" (James 1896, 366), a young reviewer with limited experience and a doubtful competence as a critic. The author's irony seems to be directed to that kind of criticism—the same that he censures in his essay "The Science of Criticism"[2] (1891)—"which is incapable of close and analytic appreciation" (James 1907–09, 1234) and "is apt to stand off from the intended sense of things" (1235). The reader—himself an object of irony—at the end of the tale has, as the critic Vaid puts it, to "adjust himself to the ambiguous position of the narrator so as not to accept him as an ideal critic" (Vaid 80–81) and impelled to reread the tale.

From the outset of the tale the reader finds himself in the world of literature. There is a novelist of great renown, Hugh Vereker; a young and hopeful critic who is also the unnamed narrator of the story; a second young and brilliant critic, George Corvick, and his intended, Gwendolen Erme, herself the author of a novel; a third less young and less brilliant critic, Drayton Deane; and a work to be reviewed.

Corvick has just asked the young critic-narrator to do a review of Vereker's latest novel, which Corvick himself would have done had he not been summoned to Paris by Gwendolen. The famous novelist dismisses the young reviewer's article as "the usual twaddle" (James 1896, 278) and in a crucial conversation with him explains that everybody misses what he calls "my little point" (280), by which he means "the particular thing I've written my book most for" (281). There is an idea in all of them which 'stretches ... from book to book," involves "the order, the form and the texture" and adds up to "an exquisite scheme" (282). He never dreamt of making a secret or a mystery of it, and he can't help the critic to detect it because "every page and line and letter gives him the clue; the thing's as concrete there as a bird in a cage, a bait on a hook, a piece of cheese in a mousetrap. It's stuck into every volume.... It governs every line, it chooses every word, it dots every *i*, it places every comma" (283–84). This sort of "buried treasure" (285), "something like a complex figure in a Persian carpet" (289), is the very thing for the critic, for the initiated, to find.

The narrator starts his *quest*—feverishly scrutinizes Vereker's novels in search of their "essence"—but can make nothing of all this and after "a maddening month" follows the writer's own advice and gives up his "ridiculous attempt" (286), even suspecting that Vereker had made a fool of him. He passes over the content of his conversation with Vereker to his friend Corvick, who communicates it to Gwendolen, and the pair devote themselves to discovering the secret, continuing the "chase" for which the narrator "had sounded the horn" (291). The advantage Corvick seems to have over the narrator is that he is in love with Gwendolen, so that "poor Vereker's inner meaning gave them endless occasion to put their young heads together" (291). The narrator imagines them as absorbed in a game of chess with the author who meanwhile has left England "for an indefinite absence" (293). Corvick, too, is sent abroad and cables Gwendolen from India saying that he has discovered the mystery, and again from Italy that he presented his solution to Vereker, who gave his assent. In an enigmatic letter to his beloved he declares, however, he will reveal the secret to her only, after their marriage, not before.

Corvick and Gwendolen get married after the death of the girl's mother, but Corvick himself dies on their honeymoon. Vereker and his wife have also died in the meantime. The narrator turns to Gwendolen for enlightenment, believing that Corvick passed the secret on to her after their marriage, and even wonders whether he should have to marry Mrs. Corvick to get what he wants. But Gwendolen decides to keep the secret for herself and never to "break the silence" (307).

Later, Gwendolen marries Drayton Deane, a minor scribbler, and dies with her second child. As his last hope, the narrator turns to Drayton, thinking that Gwendolen may have passed the secret on to her second husband. But Drayton's answer is a confession of ignorance; he has heard nothing about any figure in Vereker's work and has no reason even to suppose that there was one.

The tale comes to an abrupt end; it opens like an *enigma-story*, immediately activating what Barthes calls the *hermeneutic code*, but the gap opened up at the beginning is not filled at the end. The secret, the treasure. The figure woven into the warp and woof of the carpet/textus is not found and the reader's expectations are disappointed. In a well-known study on James's tales, Todorov argues that the secret of his stories is the very existence of an essential secret (Todorov 1978, 83) and that the story ends if the mystery is unveiled. Whether all of James's tales follow this pattern or not, in "The Figure in the Carpet" the quest does not come to an end because the secret is not disclosed and the quest goes on in the reader's mind and in the subsequent critical debate.

Throughout the story the reader is carried along by the prospective centrifugal movement of reception and identifies himself with the first-person narrator asking: *what is the figure in the carpet?* At the end, no secret having been discovered, he is forced to change this question into another: *is there a figure in the carpet?* A straightforward "pragmatic"[3] reception does not seem to be enough and the story requires a second reflexive reading, which, overcoming the linear structure, discloses other perspectives and other meanings.

Questioned again in a retrospective view and against the horizon of a second reading, the text discloses other meanings, meanings of unstable significance. The reader realizes that the answer to the implied question—is there really a figure in the carpet—is not unambiguous. The problem is amply debated in the text itself by the narrator, whose attitude is subject to continual oscillation. More than once he expresses the suspicion that there may be no mystery in Vereker's work and that the writer is lying. Soon after giving up his quest the narrator takes the view that "the buried treasure was a bad joke, the general intention a monstrous *pose"* (286), and when Gwendolen refuses to make him privy to the secret discovered by her husband, his immediate reaction is "1 know what to think then; it's nothing!" (307). Vereker himself employs two ambiguous images when he says that the figure in his work is like "a bait on a hook" or "a piece of cheese in a mouse-trap," suggesting that it may he interpreted as a trick to lure the critic and the reader.

The other characters seem to believe in the existence of the secret. Corvick thinks that "there was evidently in the writer's inmost art something to be understood" (287). What is more, he informs Gwendolen that he has found it while in India, from where he writes triumphantly, "Eureka. Immense" (296), adding that Vereker approved of it. The work, however, does not dramatize the meeting between Corvick and Vereker, and the reader does not hear the writer's approval of Corvick's theory, authorizing the suspicion that the latter has found no secret and that his only aim is to force Gwendolen into marriage since he says that only after marriage will he disclose the mystery to her.

Other unanswered or unanswerable questions are posed by the tale, in which frequent omissions of information, incomplete or doubly directed statements, enigmatic letters, elliptic cables, and a series of strange occurrences—like sudden departures and deaths which are never accompanied by any emotion—appear like mere rhetorical and delaying devices aimed at endlessly deferring the solution of the mystery. In this way, the text continually undermines the "dominant reading" ('there *is* a figure in Vereker's work') it constructs through the voice of the first-person narrator, but once the reader has become aware that the narrator's mind is unperceptive and that he can no longer align himself with the narrator, the reticence of the text, its blanks and ellipses, do not enable him to formulate an oppositional reading like *there is no figure in the carpet.* The gap opened at the beginning of the tale is permanent; it involves not only the superficial level of the *sjuzet* but also the deep level of the *fabula* and continues to exist after the end of the story. The issue is left open and the reader finds himself with two conflicting hypotheses in his mind between which he is unable to choose because they are both equally tenable but mutually exclusive and disjunctive. The second reflexive reading not having enabled the reader to reverse the perspective offered by the text through the dominant reading but only to question it, the reader finds himself in a very uncomfortable situation, in a sort of double bind, as the story on the one hand encourages the search for the secret and on the other frustrates it. James himself seems to entrust the reader with the final responsibility for the meaning of the tale when he states in the preface that "the question that ... comes up, the issue of the affair, can be but whether the very secret of perception hasn't been lost" (James 1907–09, 1235–36). The interrogation of the text has to go on and the reader asks now why the narrator fails in his quest. A simple answer is that there is something wrong in the narrator's method and he lacks "close and analytic appreciation" (1234). According to Iser,[4] through the first-person critic-narrator James is denouncing the traditional critical approach to literature, that sort of archeological method that considers meaning as something hidden in the text which has to be unearthed like "a sort of buried treasure" (James 1896, 285), a method Vereker seems to encourage. But the critic who adopts this method, who believes that literature is like "a game of skill" (296), is destined to get nowhere and find nothing but a blank space. Iser's opinion, on the contrary, is that meaning is something to be experienced and that this experience cannot be communicated, like "the new and intense experience" (297) Corvick undergoes in India, where "the figure in the carpet came out like a tigress out of the jungle" (297).

This, too, is a legitimate interpretation, which is functional to Iser's reader-oriented criticism but assumes that Corvick has really found the secret which, however, is never brought to the reader's knowledge and leaves out other questions the story poses, like the subsidiary theme of marriage and its relation to the secret, and the connection of the mystery with death.

What interests James here is not just the problem of criticism and interpretation, but the "psychology of obsession," an issue which is central to his fiction in general and especially to his ghostly tales. The critic's mistake, or his critical impotence, seems to be due not merely to his lack of critical insight, but also to other causes, such as his own self-deception and the confusion he makes between the love of literature and the love for human beings; it may be the result of his nourishing hidden, repressed or inexpressible feelings and desires in his unconscious. The narrator's obsession with the secret of Vereker's work, which James himself defines as "undiscovered, not to say undiscoverable" (James 1907–09, 1234), seems to cover other obsessions and his inability to feel sensations that are different from those deriving from the sense of sight. "All my life had taken refuge in my eyes" (James 1896, 303), he admits, and, on the other hand, what else is a critic to be, Vereker asks him, a "coerced spectator" (303), one who searches "in his neighbour's garden?" (282–283). James ambiguously suggests in the tale, as well as in the preface to it, that "what we call criticism" is nothing but a subsidiary and substitutive activity, an "exercise of penetration" which is apt to stand off from the intended sense of things (James

1907–09, 1235) and is destined to failure. As Kermode puts it, "the test undergone by the questors of his story is a test of critical potency" (Kermode, 26). The celibate narrator asks himself whether the figure in the carpet was traceable or describable only for husbands and wives, for lovers "supremely united" (James 1896, 306), and whether he "should have to marry Mrs. Corvick" (306) to manage to penetrate the text and see "the idol unveiled" (305).

Thus, "The Figure in the Carpet" appears to he like a *Vexierbild*—a picture with a secret such as those painted by Erhard Schon—combining two different pictures in one picture, or like a sort of *anamorphosis* such as in *The Ambassadors*, the famous painting by Hans Holbein, in which an optical subterfuge allows appearance to hide reality from the observer; however, the point of observation, the strange and obscure object which is at the feet of the two imposing characters represented in the picture, is disclosed and another figure emerges from the canvas. It is a skull—the sign of nothingness.[5]

In James's work, too, the figure changes, as in an anamorphosis, according to the point of view from which the reader looks at the story. If he detaches himself from the narrator's central perspective offered by the text and takes a "lateral" position, he perceives another figure and another possible meaning; he discovers sex and death. Now the narrator's viewpoint appears to he nothing but *le regard qui se voit*, as Lacan would put it, and the secret he is looking for is his own secret. Like an enigma-story, James's tale is based on *Line dualité*, as Todorov says of the detective story, and it "ne contient pas Line mais deux histoires: l'histoire du crime et l'histoire de l'enquéte" (Todorov 1978, 11), the crime here being the narrator's unpardonable sin—his emotional sterility, his refusal or inability to fully live his life.

The obscure link uniting the artwork, the truth, and death may even suggest that it is not advisable and wise for the puritanical narrator to go beyond the boundary and inquire into the mystery. As a matter of fact, the work will live only if it keeps its secret and the *recit* can go on. "Le récit egale la vie; l'absence de récit, la mort" (41), writes Todorov. Knowledge is the privilege of the dead and of the author, who chooses to die in his writing.

A competent reading of this kind of work "can only he reached," as Karlheinz Stierle states, "if the act of reading is accompanied by theoretical reflection" (Stierle, 87). The tale has a definite metaliterary dimension demanding a metareading, which finally discloses the story as a special case of *mise en abyme*. What the tale represents is not so much, or not only, an objective reality outside the text, but the communicative situation of literary discourse itself with its three main actants: the author-Vereker, the reader-critic and the message to he interpreted in Vereker's work. This triangle mirrors the triangle of real communication formed by the author—James, the real reader and "The Figure in the Carpet" as the work to be interpreted. The two parallel communicative situations mirror each other, forming a double bind, which closes the tale in a self-referential and self-sufficient metadiscourse. The story duplicates itself in the inevitable interplay with the reader, and just as the critic-narrator in the story searches for the figure in Vereker's carpet, so the real reader looks for the parallel figure in James's work. The role the reader has to perform is pre-structured in the text by the self-interpretative dimension of the story, which supplies the receiver with a mode of reading and an attitude to adopt in order not to fall into the mistake of the narrator, who in the end finds nothing but a blank space. This attitude entails the acceptance of the radical ambiguity of the tale whose composition finally turns into its very theme.

In this elliptical and multidimensional tale, the creative act is not merely a form of thematic representation as the tale allegorizes its own functioning and has itself *en abyme*. It is about itself and about us who read and interpret it. Anticipating the anti-symbolism and the skeptical epistemology of contemporary literature, it states the uselessness of looking for the "'essence," for a single unambiguous and reassuring meaning. As Butor puts it, the *repli interrogatif sur soi* of the *récit* marks *une response a un changement de l'image du monde* (Butor 18) and, in this Jamesian tale, the beginning of a tradition that considers auto-referentiality as an essential feature of fiction which "cannot be transformed any more into mere illusion" (Stierle, 104).

Notes

1. Several "literary tales" are included in the fifteenth and sixteenth volumes of the New York edition of James's works. Well-known among them are: "The Author of 'Beltraffio'" (1884), "The Lesson of the Master" (1888), 'The Private Life' (1892), "Graville Fane" (1892), "The Middle Years" (1893), "The Death of the Lion" (1894), "The Coxon Fund" (1894), "The Next Time" (1895),"The Figure in the Carpet" (1896). "John Delavoy" (1898), "The Great Good Place" (1900).

2. The possibly ironical title of James's essay "The Science of Criticism" (1891) was changed to "Criticism" when it was reprinted in *Essays in London and Elsewhere* in 1893. The subject of this short piece of writing is the condition of contemporary journalism and, in particular, "the great business of reviewing," a practice that, in James's opinion, "has nothing in common with criticism" (James, 95).

3. In his essay on "The Reading of Fictional Texts," Stierle analyzes the activity

of reading fictional texts, comparing it with pragmatic reception—that is, the reception of nonfictional texts. He writes: "Although fictional and pragmatic speech differ in status, the difference does not influence the actual reception of fictional texts. There is a form or reception with regard to fictional texts that one could call quasi-pragmatic. In the quasi-pragmatic reception the boundaries of the fictional text are transcended through an illusion created by the reader himself. This illusion may be compared to pragmatic reception in an attempt to fill the gap between word and world" (Stierle, 84).

4. Iser opens his essay on the act of reading with an analysis of James's "The Figure in the Carpet" by way of introduction.

5. James probably knew Holbein's painting, which was taken to the National Gallery in 1890. When he gave the title *The Ambassadors* to his great novel of 1901, he was perhaps influenced by Mary F. S. Hervey's book, *Holbein's Ambassadors and the Men*, published in 1900, in which the identity of the two characters represented in the picture was established in James's novel, which, as Jean Perrot argues, is itself anamorphosis, the story of "unchangement de perspective d'une lente anamorphose étalée sur plus de quatre cents pages que fait passer un individue du point de vue puritain utilitariste de la Nouvelle Angleterre à la vision estétique, cosmopolite de la bohème dore des ojsifs Parisiens" (Perrot, 206). The anamorphic vision is typical of James's fiction, in particular of a novel like *The Sacred Fount* and of such tales as "The Lesson of the Master," "The Figure in the Carpet," and "The Turn of the Screw," where the technical problem of narrative perspective or point of view becomes an epistemological issue.

Works Cited

Baltrusaitis, Jurgis. *Anamofosi o Taumaturgus Opticus*. Milano: Adelphi, 1990.

Barthes, Roland. *S/Z*. Torino: Einaudi, 1973.

Butor, Michel. *Repertoire III*. Paris: Les Editions de Minuit, 1968.

Edel, Leon, ed. "Introduction." In *The Complete Tales of Henry James*. London: Rupert Hart-Davis, 1964.

Iser, Wolfgang. *L'atto della lettura*. Bologna: il Molino, 1987.

James, Henry. "The Figure in the Carpet." 1896. In *The Complete Tales of Henry James*. Edited by Leon Edel. London: Rupert Han-Davis, 1964.

_____. "The Science of Criticism." 1891. *Literary Criticism*. 2 vols. New York: The Library of America, 1984.

_____. "The Prefaces to the New York Edition." 1907–09. *Ibid.*

_____. *The Complete Notebooks*. Edited by Leon Edel and Lyall H. Powers. New York: Oxford University Press, 1987.

Kermode, Frank, ed. "Introduction." In *The Figure in the Carpet and Other Stories*, by Henry James. Harmondsworth: Penguin, 1986.

Perrot, Jean. *Henry James: Une Ecriture Enigmatique*. Paris: Aubier Montaigne, 1982.

Stierle, Karlheinz. "The Reading of Fictional Texts." In *The Reader in the Text: Essays on Audience and Interpretation*. Princeton: Princeton University Press, 1980.

Todorov, Tzvetan. *Poetique de la prose*. Paris: Editions du Seuil, 1987.

Vaid, Krishna Baldev. *Technique in the Tales of Henry James*. Boston: Harvard University Press, 1964.

On the Ladder of
Social Observation: Images of
Decadence and Morality in
James's *Washington Square* and
Wilde's *An Ideal Husband*

JAMES FISHER

*In America in the nineteenth century, Henry James was alone in know-
ing that to scale the moral and aesthetic heights in the novel one had
to use the ladder of social observation.*

—Lionel Trilling (206)

Ascending the "ladder of social observation," as Lionel Trilling describes the Jamesian pursuit of the "moral and aesthetic" aspects of character, is, to an extent, similarly evident in the peerless comedies Oscar Wilde, the icon of literary and artistic decadence, crafted in the 1890s. The characters of James's novels and Wilde's plays might not at first seem comparable or compatible; certainly the tone of their works is markedly dissimilar, even if the whiff of social satire, the central paradigm of Wilde's comedy, is also present in James's writing. Moral decay—and perhaps its inevitability—is a conception that connects them.

James and Wilde display aspects of Victorian literary decadence in their individual representations of opportunistic, privileged young men of means (or in search of means) maintaining a façade of social propriety masking casual or calculated amorality. Two charmers, Lord Goring, of

Wilde's 1895 comedy *An Ideal Husband*, and Morris Townsend, of James's 1881 novel *Washington Square*, are, in many respects, kindred spirits, wearing masks of social propriety. In depicting these individual lives and the societies in which they find themselves, James and Wilde are able to explore the decadence in their characters and in the social contracts of the late Victorian period. Although James's examination of the decadence of his time is considerably subtler than Wilde's virtual celebration of it, both writers find ample evidence that decadence is more a matter of moral decay in the personas of individual characters than in the trappings of society, however corrupt those trappings may be.

James and Wilde often explored similar terrains of society, emotion, and character, contributing to an era of writers documenting the gilded decadence of the late Victorian era. Wilde's homosexuality and the resultant exposure of the brutality and hypocrisy of British society in responding to it, leading to his tragic imprisonment and subsequent death, in itself embodied this decadent age, masked by a rigid social order and clearly defined social roles. James was interested in Wilde's personal tragedy, if not his literary output. Of Wilde's scandalous trials, he wrote to Edmund Gosse:

> But the *fall*—from nearly twenty years of a really unique kind of "brilliant" conspicuity (wit, "art," conversation—"one of our two or three dramatists, etc.") to that sordid prison-cell and this gulf of obscenity over which the ghoulish public hangs and gloats—it is beyond any utterance of irony or any pang of compassion! He was never in the smallest degree interesting to me—but this hideous human history has made him so—in a manner [Quoted in Beckson, 220].

James sniffed at the openly decadent aspects of Wilde's work, as when he attended the opening performance of Wilde's play, *Lady Windermere's Fan*, and, in a letter to a friend, wrote

> ... there was so much drollery—that is, "cheeky" paradoxical wit of dialogue, and the pit and gallery are so pleased at finding themselves clever enough to "catch on" to four or five of the ingenious—too ingenious—mots in the dozen, that it makes them feel quite "decadent" ... [Quoted in Beckson, 14].

James's play *Guy Domville* opened in London the same week as Wilde's *An Ideal Husband*. A. B. Walkley, reviewing the plays jointly in *The Speaker* on January 12, 1895, noted that Wilde's play "received every token of success," while the James was "laboriously wrought" and "so despitefully used by many of the audience that the manager virtually went down on his marrowbones and sued for pardon." However, Walkley asserted that "the brilliant success is infinitely outweighed by the ostensible failure, not merely in actual achievement, but in significance, in promise for the future" (Walkley 43–44). *Guy Domville*'s failure at St. James's Theatre ended after a mere thirty-one performances and was taken off the stage to be replaced by a new Oscar Wilde comedy, *The Importance of Being Earnest*. Of *An Ideal Husband*, James minced no words in a letter to his brother, William James:

> I sat through it and saw it played with every appearance (so far as the crowded house was an appearance) of complete success, and that gave me the most fearful apprehension. The thing seemed to me so helpless, so crude, so bad, so clumsy, feeble and vulgar... [cited in Beckson, 183].

James's low opinion of Wilde's talents is amply documented; Wilde was similarly dismissive, believing that James "wrote fiction as if it were a painful duty" (Mikhail, 178). Despite their mutual distaste, there are distinct similarities in their decidedly different styles; both impose a strict order on their compositional style, reflecting the rigid social order they examine in their works, and both scale the ladder of social observation to probe the moral shadings of their time.

Images of fatigued sophistication, rejections of unshakable social conventions, ambiguous or illicit sexuality, and calculated manipulation are found in both James's and Wilde's male characters. The central women characters of *Washington Square* and *An Ideal Husband* are present, in part, to reveal the decadent natures of the men. Wilde's aging lothario, Lord Goring, luxuriating in the pleasures of London high society, inspires amusement as a stock figure burnished by a mildly pointed brand of social criticism typical of such Wilde plays as *Lady Windermere's Fan* (1892), *A Woman of No Importance* (1893), and *The Importance of Being Earnest* (1895). The last, Wilde's most enduring classic, lightly mocks social conventions. Its perversely ironic title insists that to survive contemporary society, "earnestness" is, in fact, the least desirable trait. However, in the end, surface morality prevails. *An Ideal Husband* reflects some similarities, but it is closer in spirit to *Lady Winderemere's Fan*, a moral comedy balanced on a simple social *faux pax*—a misplaced fan discovered at a compromising location shatters the illusion of a perfect marriage between two morally unassailable persons. Contrived plot twists allow Wilde to restore the Windermere marriage through their reluctant acceptance of a mutual imperfection. For Wilde, the ending must always be at least superficially reassuring. *An Ideal Husband* also employs contrived plot devices to expose the fact that moral (or immoral) behavior may not be enough—the *appearance* of morality is *essential*. The notoriously decadent Mrs. Cheveley, having lost her social standing, takes pleasure in manipulating the lives of a well-established group of friends, among whom is Lord Goring, a middle-aged bachelor targeted by several young women of means who can cleanse his growing notoriety through marriage. Taking the scandal associated with Mrs. Cheveley on himself to spare his respectable married friends, Goring is redeemed. In Wilde, a decadent man can reform—or at least conceal moral lapses— through a good deed wrapped in the cloak of propriety.

An *Ideal Husband*, like *The Importance of Being Earnest*, satirizes both marriage and courtship, but in An *Ideal Husband* the focus is on the reluctant husband, the eternal suitor or bachelor (hetero- or homosexual) who may live *in* society but is not truly *of* it. In this sense, An *Ideal Husband*'s Lord Goring is akin to the comic servants of ancient and Renaissance stage comedy; he is both *in* the play and *outside* it, observed and observer, commented on and commenting. The dispassionate, unnamed narrator of *Washington Square* is only in the story insofar as he seems part of the world in which Morris Townsend hopes to find a place through a profitable marriage.

Writing of depictions of marriage in the works of English and American writers, Carolyn G. Heilbrun contrasts James with George Meredith, unintentionally making a persuasive argument about the difference between Wilde's bachelor, who is drawn into society with some reluctance, and James's Townsend, who uses society only as a means to an end. When he fails, the novel's claustrophobic tragedy is set in motion. As Heilbrun writes, "Meredith was essentially a comic, James a tragic writer: the end of comedy is integration into society, the end of tragedy is isolation" (Heilbrun, 174). In An *Ideal Husband*, Lord Goring surrenders to the values of his society, however hypocritical they may seem to him, and, as such, the play falls completely into the realm of comedy. In *Washington Square*, the tragedy belongs to both Catherine Sloper and Morris Townsend, her lover. Ultimately convinced that Townsend is drawn to her mostly, if not exclusively, for her fortune, Catherine dismisses him with a finality that makes clear that she is forever terminating her search for love. To Charles Thomas Samuels, Catherine's tragedy also represents the "power of integrity" (Samuels, 146); in firmly locking herself away from integration into society she scores a moral triumph. Townsend's tragedy is that, in failing to marry Catherine, he can never succeed at belonging to a society otherwise closed to him and he certainly can never demonstrate an integrity he lacks.

There is no such draconian solution to Wilde's comedy. In the 1999 film version of An *Ideal Husband*, directed by Oliver Parker, Goring's image of decadence is underscored by the sumptuous visual environment of the movie, but also by some directorial amendments. Without any additional text, Goring's amoral existence is instantly established within the film's opening minutes. Goring is shown awakening in his lavish bedroom and a nude woman slips out of his bed as Goring's butler keeps his back discreetly turned away. This deft touch exposes this society's (or at least this character's) moral hypocrisy—in and of itself, it is a demonstration that within the Victorian era only the *appearance* of morality matters. If the butler does not "see" the nude woman, she is not there. This is a profound image of decadence; immorality does not matter unless it becomes a public scandal. The film's Lord Goring is not a closeted homosexual, but in Wilde's play this character is significantly more ambiguous. He exhibits, like James's Morris Townsend, the "self-complacency of the rosy-grilled bachelor," as Eve Kosofsky Sedgwick describes it, a "bachelor hero" who, "through his celibacy and selfishness, can seem the only human particle atomized enough to plump through unscathed" (192). Lord Goring does indeed plump through, but matters are more complex for Morris Townsend because his attributes do not help him succeed in attaining his goal.

The cinematic *An Ideal Husband* emphasizes the humor Wilde finds in this decadent middle-aged bachelor being brought (albeit reluctantly) into social acceptability through a marriage he resists until he can resist no longer. The inherent decadence of Goring's persona and behavior are comically exploited by the character's father, Lord Caversham, who can see only his (otherwise good-hearted) son's failures to conform to social expectations. Caversham's first line, "Has my good-for-nothing young son been here?" (223), certainly establishes his attitude. Goring has not embraced the social contract and, as such, can only be a disappointing, exasperating son. Unfettered by social expectations, Goring falls subject to his father's blustering recriminations and both the play itself and the film emphasize the decadent hypocrisy of this situation. The following exchange from the play is typical of their relationship—and the air of studied decadence with which Wilde imbues the character of Goring:

> LORD CAVERSHAM: Well, sir! what are you doing here? Wasting your life as usual! You should be in bed, sir. You keep too late hours! I heard of you the other night at Lady Rufford's dancing till four o'clock in the morning!
>
> LORD GORING: Only a quarter to four, father.
>
> LORD CAVERSHAM: Can't make out how you stand London society. The thing has gone to the dogs, a lot of damned nobodies talking about nothing.

LORD GORING: I love talking about nothing, father. It is the only
thing I know anything about.
LORD CAVERSHAM: You seem to me to be living entirely for pleasure.
LORD GORING: What else is there to live for, father? Nothing ages
like happiness.
LORD CAVERSHAM: You are heartless, sir, very heartless! [Wilde,
234–235].

Once it is revealed that Goring will marry Mabel Chiltern, Caversham's
censure is instantaneously transformed into unquestioning (if slightly confused) approval.

Mabel, who will eventually win Goring's heart (and confesses that she
delights in his "bad qualities" [233]), shares something of his bemused attitude toward a society that, according to Mabel, "is entirely composed now
of beautiful idiots and brilliant lunatics. Just what society should be" (224).
Mabel's brother, Robert Chiltern, and his wife Gertrude are bastions of
London society and do not conform to Mabel's description. They are attractive, serious, and well-intentioned, but have allowed the expectations of
their society—and their usually unerring ability to perfectly meet those
expectations—to block out their ability to accept imperfection in anyone,
including each other. In describing Chiltern, Wilde notes that he displays
a manner "of perfect distinction, with a slight touch of pride" (226) and
it becomes clear that the "touch of pride" is what Chiltern would have to
face. He discovers not only his wife's lack of perfection but also his own.
Neither Chiltern can see Goring's fundamental goodness, even though he
is prepared to sacrifice himself for them. Wilde retains them as his leading characters, but his interest is clearly focused on Goring, his relationship with Mabel, and, more importantly, his relationship with society's
values. As the play's central "decadent," Goring's reformation, however
implausible, is where the play's heart rests.

If Wilde's Lord Goring is, in fact, a deeply moral man masquerading
as a wastrel, James's Morris Townsend is the reverse. Avoiding the melodramatic triumph of goodness over evil, James prefers to envision Townsend
as something of a moral question mark. The well-heeled Dr. Austin Sloper
may be certain of Townsend's avaricious intentions, but the reader, like
Catherine, Sloper's socially awkward daughter, may not be as certain.
Townsend becomes the conduit for James's imagery of a decadent society;
if Sloper's belief that Townsend is drawn only to his daughter's wealth is
accurate, then James's portrait of Townsend is an exquisitely malign image
of amorality and decadence.

William Veeder describes the inauthentic Townsend as a "Dandy-

Rake" (188), a label that certainly ties him to Wilde's Lord Goring, described at his first entrance as a "flawless dandy" who "would be annoyed if he were considered romantic" (231). As Veeder also points out, Townsend also strongly resembles his great adversary, Sloper, who similarly dominates most situations with an air of studied superiority and surface charm. Townsend combines aspects of the social insider, although he has not managed to fully enter society, and the lifelong outsider. Does Townsend's decadence result, in part, from his exclusion from the rarified social world of *Washington Square?* The novel's small and claustrophobic world suggests, despite the Sloper's trip to Europe, that, "there is nothing beyond the Square" (Tanner, 120). If Townsend does not find his place there, James seems to suggest, then there is no place for him. Veeder sees Washington Square as a realm of "social determinism" in which Townsend is the resulting product of such a society: "the name towns=end, plus Morris' Byronic wanderings, suggest that he is indeed an outsider" (201). Veeder stresses, however, that Sloper does not reject Townsend simply because he is an outsider, but because he is, in Sloper's estimation, "finally worthless" (202). Additionally, Townsend's decadent dream of becoming an insider through a profitable marriage to Catherine is unveiled by James in the symbol of Townsend's lush hair, noticed immediately by Catherine during their first encounter, and the receding hairline he has when he comes to Catherine years later. This, according to Veeder, represents "the unmasking of a specious dream" (126).

Such symbolism suggests a theatricalism in the novel. The plot of *Washington Square* unfolds more like a stage drama than a novel, and its characters, particularly the novel's heroine, Catherine Sloper, are provided with interior monologues allowing the reader access to their complex, often contradictory, desires and values. Catherine is a profoundly moral woman, a genuinely dutiful daughter whose search for approval from a distant, mildly disapproving father leads directly to a relationship with Townsend, which culminates in her conclusion that love has eluded her. James effectively makes Catherine's unspoken suffering the equivalent of a tragic fall; she has held it all in her hands—wealth, a handsome lover, and a dutiful father—but all of these prizes is ultimately meaningless. Her wealth poisons everything: the handsome lover may or may not be merely a fortune hunter and the dutiful father is revealed as a cold martinet who prizes his public dignity more than his daughter's happiness.

Sloper's underestimation of Catherine is his most significant error; she is not the dull girl he believes her to be, in fact, she is far from it. The inherent decadence in this male-dominated society is that Sloper can be wrong, domineering, and inflexible without ever being challenged for his errors of judgment and his weaknesses, while Catherine, because she is uncomfortable in social circumstances, is generally condemned, or at least marginalized, in her world. Although Charles Thomas Samuels believes that Catherine is "precisely the dullard her father thinks" (145), it seems more the case that she is merely socially uncomfortable. James skillfully accentuates this by making her aware of her social failings so that, as Walter F. Wright suggests, "the pathos is emphasized to a point of painfulness" (138). James amply demonstrates that the adept social chatter, at which Catherine is so inept, is, as Carren O. Kaston writes, "disconnected from felt emotion" (267). As a woman capable of deep feeling, Catherine's social failure becomes empowering; it is a badge of honor in her moral triumph over the decadence of her father, aunt, and Townsend. By the novel's end, Catherine proves to be spirited and intelligent (or at least perceptive), and it is clear that her yearning for an emotional connection sets her apart from the others in the novel. Muriel G. Shine declares that Catherine's "capacity to love and be loved has been destroyed" (46), but it is more the case, as Veeder explains, that Catherine finally triumphs because her fundamentally moral personality has changed so little. Veeder writes that she "gains in awareness and courage, but basic integrity and worthiness were hers from the beginning. She, finally, develops less than we because she has less need to. And in her triumph, Catherine carries us ahead with her—probably not, however, for life as it will be" (205).

The theatricalism of *Washington Square* extends to Catherine's character; she emerges as something like a character from a late nineteenth century drama by Henrik Ibsen or George Bernard Shaw. Her dilemma is an intensely theatrical one, not one that would interest Wilde as much as it might Ibsen, for her options are impossible and the constraints of her era dictate much of her tragedy. The question arises as to why James did not make a stage work of *Washington Square*. When Ruth and Augustus Goetz dramatized the play as *The Heiress* in 1947, it became an enduring stage classic, and two years later a screen success.

James's predominance as a novelist obscured his failures as a dramatist, despite considerable experience writing dramatic criticism and theoretical essays (notably collected and edited by Alan Wade as *The Scenic Art* [1948]). James attempted drama first in the late 1860s with a few minor short plays (*Pyramus and Thisbe, Still Waters,* and *A Change of Heart*) and went on to adapt several of his novels and short stories, including *Daisy Miller* in 1882 and *The American* in 1891, and to write original plays, including *Tenants* (1890). Critics note that some of James's later plays, including *The*

Other House, which he first wrote as a play then revised as a novel before finally adapting it back into a play in 1908, were influenced by the innovations of Ibsen and Shaw. He had no interest in the melodramatic works that crowded mid to late nineteenth-century stages.

Catherine, Sloper, and Townsend are American characters Ibsen or Shaw might have admired for the conflicting images of the struggles between society's demands and the desires inherent in each character. The dramatists of the emerging realist/naturalist stage, as well as the symbolist theater in this period, were logical inspirations for James, but he regarded the American theater of the late nineteenth century with disdain. He resisted its simplistic melodramatic trappings and broadly drawn stock characters, which proved a significant reason that his dramas failed to find favor. In search of a more refined, subtle approach to character and plot, James did not succeed in reforming the American stage of his time, although his theatrical inclination clearly informs his novels and short stories. It is perhaps not surprising that, despite his own missteps in the dramatic realm, James's novels found a place on stages in effective adaptations by others, including John Balderston's and J. C. Squire's 1928 adaptation of *The Sense of the Past* as *Berkeley Square* and William Archibald's 1950 adaptation of *The Turn of the Screw* as *The Innocents*. (Others include *The Spoils*, adapted from *The Spoils of Poynton*, and *Watch and Ward*, adapted from *A Boston Story*, both in 1968.)

Washington Square, and its subsequent stage and screen adaptations, exudes James's fascination with, and cynicism about, "the uniqueness of the American scene" (Pippin, 53). James sees America as a place where romance and reason, morality and liberation, trust and opportunism are not easily distinguishable. Such a contradictory, ambiguous environment provides a logical setting for subtly decadent characters through whom he can expose the hypocrisies and treacheries of the established social order.

Robert B. Pippin finds in *Washington Square* a stock plot, the "familiar triangle of the heiress, fortune hunter, and the duplicitous accomplice, all often complicated by the despotic father" (81), but the plot's stock elements are elevated by James's perceptive treatment of "self-exposure, the risks of love or even moral acknowledgment" which are all made "difficult, potentially painful, even frightening" (81). On first glance, this is all exposed through Catherine's persona, but on closer examination these issues can be found in all of the novel's central figures, including Townsend, Sloper, and Sloper's ever-present sister, Mrs. Penniman. Sloper's late wife, who is deceased before the novel begins, also contributes to Catherine's dilemma; her presence hangs heavily over the novel, and particularly over Catherine.

As James describes her, Catherine's mother was "amiable, accomplished, elegant" (James, 2), everything Catherine is not. James immediately and poignantly establishes that, to her family and social circle, Catherine is "a disappointment" (3).

Catherine's seemingly (and sternly) caring father, Dr. Sloper, allows James to explore "intelligence and its insufficiency" (Pippin, 49) through Sloper's rational but unfeeling response to Catherine's relationship with Townsend. Sloper believes that "only human will and reason can fashion an acceptable life" (Pippin, 53); the possibilities of human emotion and compassion are subverted to cold reason. Sloper eventually loses the affection of his only child through his inability to demonstrate a genuine love for her; to him, Catherine's "bland and dangerous innocence" (Pippin, 53) is only a potential embarrassment. If the members of *Washington Square*'s insulated society should become aware that Catherine has been deceived by Townsend, Sloper fears he will be seen as a fool. His daughter's potential happiness is not his central concern, or even a significant one, despite his comments to the contrary; to Sloper, a woman is merely an enhancement to a man's attributes. In his eyes, Catherine offers no enhancements, so she can only be viewed as a liability. Her social ineptitude is embarrassing enough, but her romance with Townsend promises to be an unparalleled social humiliation. This Sloper cannot abide.

Sallie Sears calls Sloper's behavior nothing less than "parental abuse" (87), in his creation of a "tyrannical environment" (Tanner, 120) and his domineering imperviousness to Catherine's needs and desires. As Veeder points out, Sloper is "repeatedly wrong" (191), and it is a wrongness that is cruel and destructive. Sloper imagines himself an elegantly subtle man, but his decadence is all too obvious to the reader. A product of a hypocritical, amoral society, Sloper cloaks himself in an air of male superiority punctured only when his daughter defies his wishes regarding Townsend. The novel's subtle depiction of moral decadence extends even to Sloper's widowed sister, Mrs. Penniman, who exudes a particularly American "susceptibility to romance" (Pippin, 53), a trait with which James does not sympathize. Variant qualities are apparent in Mrs. Penniman, and some of her impulses, particularly regarding her niece's happiness, may be genuine. The reader's ultimate impression, however, is that Mrs. Penniman is merely a meddling fool created by a society unable to find other uses for a mature widow of limited means. Townsend's physical attractiveness, calculated social skills, and seemingly romantic attitudes take her in completely. Mrs. Penniman cannot possibly imagine that the bland, socially graceless Catherine could attract a better match, and, in fact, she seems to be suffering from shock at the mere fact that Townsend would be at all interested in her niece. If Townsend is mostly interested in Catherine's fortune, Mrs. Penniman finds it acceptable—even appropriate; Catherine's fortune is an asset to be exploited, like wit, social grace, or physical beauty, and, as such, Mrs. Penniman is satisfied that what she (and Sloper) regard as Catherine's sole attribute should be used to purchase a suitor, even if what those riches buy is superficial.

Sloper does not view Catherine's asset in the same light; in fact, he does not agree with his sister about much in regard to Catherine. Mrs. Penniman has resided in Sloper's home to raise the girl after her mother's death, but, as James pointedly indicates, Sloper "had never been dazzled by his sister's intellectual luster" (5). In fact, he had "never been dazzled, indeed, by any feminine characteristics whatever; and though he was to a certain extent what is called a ladies' doctor, his private opinion of the more complicated sex was not exalted" (James, 5), despite the fact that he has idealized the memory of his late wife. James does not expend much attention on Catherine's mother except to note that she was a beautiful and charming woman. What her relationship with Sloper was like—and what Sloper himself was like in that relationship—is not examined. It is possible that James is simply not interested in this character other than as an ideal Catherine can never attain. Martha and Charles Masinton stress that American novelists have "always emphasized the masculine and neglected the feminine" (298), citing Nathaniel Hawthorne and James as notable exceptions, but it is possible to argue that James is at least as interested in exploring the psyches of his male characters as he is in those of his women.

Graham Greene regarded *Washington Square* as James's assault on the "feminine" field of novels dominated by Jane Austen, but this view too narrowly categorizes this work. Although its events are seen mostly from the perspective of Catherine, this is not exclusively a "feminine" novel; the characters of Sloper and Townsend are both explored with similar depth and dimension, each, in turn, dominating a portion of the novel. More importantly, the male characters are essential in establishing the decadent imagery James has subtly woven into *Washington Square*. Sloper's smug superiority and inherent unfeelingness, displayed on several occasions in the novel, underscore the decaying stagnancy of the novel's society. Even if Catherine were a dazzling charmer, the thorough male dominance of the novel's world suggests that Sloper would be incapable of respecting Catherine or his sister, Mrs. Penniman, or, in fact, any of the other women he encounters, including his other sister, Mrs. Almond, and Morris Townsend's long-suffering sister, Mrs. Montgomery. Sloper's barely hidden resentment of Catherine's birth, which brought on her mother's death, is certainly at the root of the disappointment in her that he clings to regardless of the occasionally surprising bursts of spirit she exhibits. James stresses that Sloper determined that "though she was not what he had desired, he proposed to himself to make the best of her" (4). Only periodically does he manage to do this.

Sloper's self-satisfaction—a decadent absolutism in all matters, regardless of contradicting evidence—certainly influences his dominating grasp on his daughter, whom he cares for but with a thinly veiled contempt. On several occasions he acknowledges to himself that he sees her as a fool, in part resenting that he had produced such "a commonplace child" (8). Despite this, Sloper continues to hope Catherine may bloom into the sort of woman her mother had been. When Catherine reaches the age of twelve, Sloper implores Mrs. Penniman to "make a clever woman of her" (6), but he fears that no young man "will ever be in love with Catherine" (7), and in spite of this overture to Mrs. Penniman, Sloper convinces himself that his daughter cannot become what he wishes her to be. James pointedly establishes Catherine's dilemma: her father's lack of confidence in her, the memory of her mother's charms within her world, and her aunt's at once dispassionate and meddling care produce a strange mixture of qualities.

James stresses that Catherine was deeply attached to her father, but also terrified of him, and that in every respect, she was the definitive wallflower who had "no desire to shine" (7). Her father's total dominance sets in motion an erosion in their relationship. While on the European trip designed to make her forget Townsend, Catherine resolves to obey her father, but she no longer fears him and, in fact, no longer loves him. His profoundly decadent incapacity to love, forgive human frailty, or feel compassion for his daughter's dilemma costs him her loyalty and love.

In this stagnant, corrupted world, change is nearly impossible; Catherine is a preordained failure whose less obvious virtues have little or no currency in such an environment. The reader's awareness of Catherine stems almost entirely from her involvement in a decadent society in which her purity of spirit is ill-suited. This may explain her wish to be forever in the background, and why she is perceived by those around her as possessing a personality that is "shy, uncomfortably, painfully shy" (James, 9). However, a different Catherine emerges when she ultimately finds herself drawn to and courted by the handsome and socially skilled Townsend. To some extent, he tames this decadent society; he moves easily through its social rituals seeking ways to better his position through the social alliances he makes. Perhaps this renders him the most efficiently decadent creature in the novel. On stage or screen, and most certainly in the novel itself, Catherine is, as Robert B. Pippin describes her, one of the "deceived heiresses" (4), a type familiar from other James works such as *The Portrait of a Lady* and *The Golden Bowl*. This "paradigmatic" (Pippin, 4) figure draws the reader's focus, but in exposing complex images of Victorian decadence, James's paradigmatic characters are more likely those social climbers and opportunists of which Townsend is perhaps his subtlest example.

Once past the "difficult moment" (James, 14) of their first meeting, Catherine finds it surprisingly comfortable to listen silently while Townsend talks to her with "an easy smile, as if he had known her for a year" (14). Townsend effortlessly disarms her and she finds his familiarity "natural," in part because "he was so handsome, or, rather, as she phrased it to herself, so beautiful" (14). Her cheeks redden when they dance together, leading Townsend, in full command of his decadent slickness, to ask her, "in a tone of great kindness" (15), if the dancing had made her dizzy. Dancing had never made her dizzy before, she realizes, and as they move off the dance floor Catherine can hardly realize that Townsend's conquest of her—carefully calculated (although James may permit the more romantic among his readership to see this as an unconscious conquest)—is virtually complete. Within the confines of this first encounter, James efficiently establishes Townsend as a superficially perfect being within the demands and confines of this society and, as well, he implants Townsend's seemingly total victory over Catherine. James's depiction of Townsend is otherwise consistently ambiguous. From the start, Sloper disdainfully views Morris as nothing more than a social adventurer trolling for his dull daughter's fortune. How much this has to do with any action of Townsend's is somewhat questionable. Sloper's unshakable mistrust of Townsend arises directly from his lack of faith in his daughter's charms as well as his decadent notion that he is always right in all things.

The 1949 film version of *Washington Square*, retitled *The Heiress* and based on a 1947 stage play version by Ruth and Augustus Goetz, was directed by William Wyler and is, in many respects, faithful to *Washington Square*. Telescoping some of the plot, this handsomely mounted film features an original score by Aaron Copland. Any ambiguity that James has woven into Townsend's persona is enhanced in the casting of Townsend in Wyler's film. Montgomery Clift's interpretation of Townsend embodies an ambiguousness that encourages the viewer to decide whether or not Morris is indeed a wastrel and opportunist or is, in fact, truly drawn to Catherine, who is played with a touching earnestness by Olivia de Havilland in an Academy Award-winning performance.

Of the 1949 film, Julie H. Rivkin writes that "If in James's novel ultimately no one knows what Catherine knows, in Wyler's film Catherine makes it perfectly clear in the extravagant lessons of melodrama exactly what she knows and what impact her knowledge has upon those who have attempted to keep her in the dark" (148). However, whereas Catherine's thoughts and emotions are vividly expressed, Wyler makes Townsend a significantly more ambiguous figure. The viewer is never quite certain what Townsend thinks about anything, including the things he actually says and does. What he means and does not mean is never made explicit so that when, in the film's final moments, he is seen pounding desperately on the front door of the Sloper home, the viewer feels that the desperate frustration that surfaces may be the first genuine emotion the character has shown. How the filmmaker recodes the significant internal or the visually uncommunicated elements of the novel is, in itself, a revealing exercise, but in the case of this study, the recoding of the images of decadence requires examination.

The ambiguity with which James often imbues Townsend is underscored in Wyler's film, as Clift is often a beautiful blank. When he kisses the confused Catherine's hand in the shadows as she departs the party where they first meet, his face is a frozen mask betraying neither passion for Catherine nor the manipulative nature that may or may not be lurking beneath his façade. The subsequent two scenes, in which Townsend calls on Catherine for the third time in a single week and when he comes to dine with the Slopers, betray a more consciously ingratiating persona, leading Sloper to begin to catalogue his doubts about this young suitor. At the end of dinner, as in the novel, Townsend acknowledges to Catherine—correctly—that Sloper does not like him. The film telescopes Sloper's descent into a full mistrust of Townsend; a scene with Mrs. Montgomery, Townsend's sister, confirms his suspicions, leading to a confrontation when Townsend comes to ask for Catherine's hand in marriage. The scene includes much of the dialogue from James's novel, but plays somewhat more confrontationally on the screen than on the page. Again, Clift's performance betrays no definitive hint of the character's ulterior motives. Even in anger at Sloper's condescension he maintains an impassive mask, betraying no feelings except those carefully crafted replies to Sloper's accusations. Despite his romantic maneuvers directed at Catherine, Townsend also exudes a sexual ambiguity, and de Havilland's Catherine seems similarly sexless (unlike the nearly panting sexuality of Jennifer Jason Leigh's interpretation of Catherine in the 1997 film version of *Washington Square*).

Townsend's visits to Sloper's home continue during the time the doctor takes Catherine to Europe. Their six months on the continent are telescoped into two very brief scenes, establishing only that Catherine retains her feelings for Townsend, while his mask slips slightly, revealing only his frustration and impatience during her absence (as well as his enjoyment of the comforts of the Sloper home) and at the meddling of Mrs. Penniman, who has encouraged Townsend's visits while Catherine is away. The critical moment comes when, in a rain-soaked encounter outside the Sloper home, Townsend realizes that Catherine will never receive her father's estate, nor would Catherine accept it should it come her way. His mask slips, momentarily revealing a hardness as he goes off ostensibly to prepare for an immediate elopement with Catherine. Catherine's tragedy is enhanced in the film as she realizes that both her father and her aunt feel the same way about her, that in their eyes, she lacks beauty, charm, cleverness, so it could only be her money that Townsend seeks. She waits in vain for him to arrive to elope with her. He never comes and she later learns that he has departed for California. The film expands the novel's account of the end of Catherine's relationship with her father. She confronts him angrily as he sinks into his final illness, and, in a significant departure from James, refuses to go to her father's bedside as he dies.

An even more significant departure occurs in the film's final scenes. A few years have elapsed since Sloper's death and Catherine learns from Mrs. Penniman that Townsend is back in New York. Mrs. Penniman has, in fact, brought Townsend with her, but Catherine is immovable. She turns him away initially, but when she hears his voice she cannot resist inviting him in. Much of the dialogue of their final encounter is taken directly from the novel, but the melancholy tone of this final meeting is transformed into Catherine's ultimate revenge. Seemingly unmoved by Townsend's entreaties, Catherine finally agrees to marry him and sends him off to pack. While she is out of the room, Clift's portrayal of Townsend's subtle decadence is complete as he is shown walking through the splendid rooms of the Sloper home, rooms that he believes will soon be his own. When Townsend returns, Wyler creates another memorable moment that strips off Townsend's mask, so that we watch the character collapse from within. Townsend enthusiastically arrives at the Sloper front door, but hears the bolt lock barring his entrance. He repeatedly knocks. Catherine picks up a lamp and climbs the stairs to her bedroom as his knocking and entreaties become louder and more desperate. The novel's final moment is Catherine's, as she closes the door to Morris forever; the film, however, places the emphasis on the desperate Morris pounding on the door, leaving either an image of the heartbroken rejected suitor or of the opportunist who sees an extraordinary investment of time and energy failing to pay off.

The 1997 film version of *Washington Square*—directed by Agnieszka Holland and featuring Ben Chaplin as Townsend and Jennifer Jason Leigh as Catherine, with Albert Finney as Sloper, and Maggie Smith as Mrs. Penniman—returns to the novel's original name. It is not based on the Goetz play, but is instead adapted by Carol Doyle directly from the novel. It, too, has its wholly original moments, beginning with a somewhat graphic depiction of Catherine's birth and the death of her otherwise charmed mother, followed by scenes of Catherine as a chubby, awkward child failing to fulfill her father's wishes, including an embarrassing scene in which she panics when called upon to sing at a surprise birthday party for Sloper. In the 1949 film, Sloper's disapproval of his daughter does not become evident until well into the plot, but the 1997 movie emphasizes it from the beginning. In many respects, this version applies a too heavy hand to the relationship of Catherine and her father, who seems to literally terrorize her. He considers her "too simple," as he confides to Mrs. Montgomery, and "weak-willed," as he pointedly tells Townsend. Emphasis is placed on Catherine's awkwardness, initially for comic purposes. Olivia de Havilland toned down her own soft beauty and subtly indicated Catherine's shyness in Wyler's somber, brooding film, but Leigh carries both the physical and emotional awkwardness of Catherine to nearly farcical proportions. This seemingly odd choice is off-putting at first, but it pays off handsomely as Catherine learns that her father has refused to consent to her marriage with Townsend. Catherine, although remaining susceptible to Townsend, grows in self-possession, and the character's emotional progression is enhanced. This image of *Washington Square's* decadent world has no place for a young woman whose weaknesses and emotions are so open. Olivia de Havilland's restraint moves the viewer, but Leigh's plaintive neediness and urge to please are painful to watch. As mentioned earlier, this film also places a strong emphasis on the sexual attraction that draws Catherine to Townsend; she literally drops to the floor the first time he kisses her in the Sloper parlor, and their subsequent encounters similarly demonstrate the sexual power Townsend holds over her. His awareness of it is also evident, as their scenes alone are treated with an intimacy he fully exploits, especially on Catherine's return from a year in Europe.

Chaplin's Townsend is more obviously an opportunist than Clift's ambiguous interpretation of the character. More overtly ingratiating, his performance profits, to some extent, from the fact that the dialogue in most of his scenes is taken nearly verbatim from the novel. Secondary characters notice his physical appeal and his manipulative nature is more obvious. Townsend's avariciousness is more overtly underscored as well. In one brief moment, as Townsend awaits Catherine in the Sloper parlor, he looks admiringly at an elegant silver box. This Townsend is obviously aware of Catherine's lack of beauty and grace, as in a scene where his sister, Mrs. Montgomery, mistakes Catherine's attractive cousin for the girl that Townsend has presumably told her about. Townsend's dark, desperate reaction to his sister's apology indicates his fear that her understandable gaff will have an impact on his carefully laid plans. Townsend's petulant impatience in his clandestine meeting with Mrs. Penniman adds to a mounting sense of his manipulative nature. He is similarly petulant when Catherine tells him that she will journey to Europe with her father. Holland's film version lacks the ambiguities of both the novel and the Wyler version, but its more overt depiction of its decadent characters and their society is similarly potent.

That image of decadence is set against one element common to the novel and both film versions—the strength of Catherine's character in this decadent environment. Her character is consistent in her honesty and her courage in telling the truth even when it is painful for her. This is evidenced consistently throughout the novel in her scenes with Townsend, Sloper, and even in her frank assessment of Mrs. Penniman's interference in her relationship with Townsend.

Samuels believes that the ambiguity in Townsend's character, evidenced in the novel and the two screen adaptations, is settled in the scene in which he meets Mrs. Penniman to discuss ways to win Catherine and her father's estate. He is annoyed by Mrs. Penniman's request for some sort of message to Catherine, who is waiting in distress to hear from him; instead of joining Mrs. Penniman in planning a strategy to meet Catherine, "he gorges himself on a bowl of oysters" and Mrs. Penniman is "shocked to see a love-sick swain gormandizing" (Samuels, 142). Townsend's arrogance also asserts itself. When it becomes clear that he could wed Catherine anytime were he willing to accept her with just her mother's legacy, he is unwilling to give up hope that Catherine can manipulate Sloper out of disinheriting her. At his most decadent, Townsend has "a perfectly definite appreciation of his value, which seemed to him inadequately represented by the sum...." (lines from the novel) of Catherine's mother's legacy. He wants it all and, gets none.

The simple yet powerful ending of the novel may offer several possible interpretations, but Robert B. Pippin astutely notes that Catherine's display of a "kind of integrity and self-possession is also a moral necessity in this moral universe, even in acknowledgment of one's dependence" (80). James is asking his reader to turn away from the decadent world of Washington Square and toward Catherine, who represents a fundamentally principled ethic. To choose to sympathize with her is, as Veeder suggests, to choose "morally" (196).

Veeder writes of the novel's conflict between "the moral and the moralistic" (196). In fact, many of the literary and artistic achievements of the late nineteenth century may, in essence, explore this very conflict. Wilde's *An Ideal Husband*, as well as his other stage comedies, celebrate the triumph of a true morality over the moralizing tendencies of a rigidly constructed social order, but *Washington Square* presents a more complex journey in its depiction of a young woman's moral triumph—a triumph that is also her tragedy—over a master manipulator of a profoundly decadent social order. When Catherine Sloper closes the door to shut out Morris Townsend, the only lover she has ever possessed, or ever will possess, a hard-won moral standard is set by James. That her true morality wins her nothing but a cold and lonely life suggests a depth to the decadence of the world in which James has placed her.

Works Cited

Beckson, Karl. *London in the 1890s: A Cultural History.* New York: W. W. Norton, 1992.

_____. *Oscar Wilde. The Critical Heritage.* New York: Barnes and Noble, 1970.

Bloom, Harold, ed. *Henry James. Modern Critical Views.* New York: Chelsea House, 1987.

Heilbrun, Carolyn G. "Marriage Perceived: English Literature 1873–1941." In *What Manner of Woman: Essays on English and American Life and Literature.* Edited by Marlene Springer. New York: New York University Press, 1977.

James, Henry. *Washington Square.* New York: Barnes & Noble Classics, 2000.

Kaston, Carren O. *Imagination and Desire in the Novels of Henry James.* New Brunswick, NJ: Rutgers University Press, 1984.

Masinton, Martha, and Charles G. Masinton. "Second-class Citizenship: The Status of Women in Contemporary American Fiction." In *What Manner of Woman.*

Mikhail, E. H., ed. *Oscar Wilde: Interviews and Recollections.* Vol. 1. New York: Barnes & Noble, 1979.

Pippin, Robert B. *Henry James & Modern Moral Life.* New York: Cambridge University Press, 2000.

Rivkin, Julie H. "Prospects of Entertainment." In *Henry James Goes to the Movies.* Edited by Susan M. Griffin. Lexington: University Press of Kentucky, 2002.

Samuels, Charles Thomas. *The Ambiguity of Henry James.* Urbana: University of Illinois Press, 1971.

Sears, Sallie. *The Negative Imagination: Form and Perspective in the Novels of Henry James.* Ithaca, NY: Cornell University Press, 1968.

Sedgwick, Eve Kosofsky. *Epistemology of the Closet.* Berkeley: University of California Press, 1990.

Shine, Muriel G. *The Fictional Children of Henry James.* Chapel Hill: University of North Carolina Press, 1968.

Tanner, Tony. *Henry James.* Nashville, TN: Aurora Publishers, 1969.

Trilling, Lionel. *The Liberal Imagination.* Garden City, NY: Anchor Books, 1957.

Veeder, William. *Henry James—The Lessons of the Master: Popular Fiction and Personal Style in the Nineteenth Century.* Chicago: University of Chicago Press, 1975.

Wakeley, A. B. "Review." *The Speaker* 4 (January 12, 1895).

Wilde, Oscar. *The Plays of Oscar Wilde.* With a new introduction by John Lahr. New York: Vintage Books, 1988.

Wright, Walter F. *The Madness of Art: A Study of Henry James.* Lincoln: University of Nebraska Press, 1962.

The Importance of
Being Henry James:
What the Master Learned
from Oscar Wilde

ROBERT COMBS

It seems part of Henry James's fate to be haunted by Oscar Wilde. From the time of their first meeting in Washington, D. C., in 1882, when Wilde piqued James by responding to his solicitous sincerity ("I am very homesick for London") with an aphorism ("Realism? You care for places? The World is my home"), James repeatedly experienced Wilde's flamboyance, his notoriety, his success in the theater—perhaps even his very existence—as potentially overwhelming. It is shocking for admirers of Jamesian reticence to hear James referring to Wilde in a letter to Mrs. Henry Adams as "a fatuous fool, tenth-rate cad, an unclean beast" (Ellmann, 218). But James's irritation would increase. In 1895, at the opening night of his own play, Guy Domville, James decided to attend a performance of Wilde's An Ideal Husband at the Haymarket; he returned to his own theater in time to take a curtain call, at which moment he was greeted with jeers from the audience. Closing after thirty-one performances, Guy Domville was replaced with Wilde's The Importance of Being Earnest. Again, James was dismayed. He had found An Ideal Husband "so helpless, so crude, so bad, so clumsy, feeble and vulgar" (qtd. in Ellmann, 224), yet audiences loved it. And now he was being replaced by Oscar Wilde, so to speak, on stage. Perhaps most disturbing was James's response to Wilde's trial, in which he saw only "squalid gratuitousness ... beyond any utterance of irony or any pang of compassion" (Ellman, 226). James's cruelty has been seen by some critics as generated by his extreme anxiety over being associated with Wilde as a homosexual (Matheson). Surely a deeply personal—though perhaps we could add a deeply philosophical—anxiety underlay James's overreaction to the triumphs and tragedies of Oscar Wilde.

The concern here is with the conflicts within the mind and art of James. There were no personal or literary feuds between James and Wilde, no mutual enmity between them. Wilde could be harsh about James, of course, as he could be about many others. In "The Decay of Lying," Wilde quips, "Mr. Henry James writes fiction as if it were a painful duty, and wastes upon mean motives and imperceptible 'points of view' his neat literary style, his felicitous phrases, his swift and caustic satire" (973). But such comments do not sink to name-calling, nor does Wilde attempt to distance himself from James out of any fear of association. Wilde continued to read James with serious interest his whole life (Ellman, 222). Wilde's remarks constitute witty, pertinent criticisms that allow James to remain who he is. James's remarks about Wilde are psychological, like ugly arguments people sometimes have in public that may correctly be interpreted as arguments each of the parties ought to be having in private within themselves. James's animosity toward Wilde represents a projected psychological issue that could be called "theatricality," in the sense of histrionics, or in a broader sense the requirement that people feel to play roles, with all the attendant hazards, in order to belong to society. Roles can be traps, as Oscar Wilde discovered quite tragically.

Surely theatricality is one of the great themes of James's writing. Sometimes his characters, like Daisy Miller, lose themselves in unfamiliar social settings, like actors without the proper scripts. And the revelations of consciousness in James's fiction tend to be intensely dramatic. Also, we must not forget that James was himself enamored of the career of playwright, for mercenary as well as egotistical reasons. Symbolically, the stage was for James a psychological location of great power, where Oscar Wilde seemed to exercise almost magical verbal powers (Salamensky, 276), created wealth and fame for himself, and suffered his greatest humiliation and defeat when, at his trial, his audience became the "ghoulish public [that] hangs and gloats...." (Ellmann, 226). Henry James's art was an interior one where intense dramas of intrigue, concealment, exposure, and deceit were played out. Oscar Wilde must have appeared to James as an attractive anti-type, a Mephistopheles, a force he would have to come to terms with (in himself).

In considering psychological struggles caused by projected insecurities, it is important to remember how pervasive pronouncements of ultimate moral justification were on artistic and literary subjects when James and Wilde wrote, and in the next century when critics wrote about them. In reviewing a Pre-Raphaelite painting by Burne-Jones, James felt the need to qualify his praise by pointing out a want of "manliness" in the painter's work (Ellmann, 216). In the 1920s, Van Wyck Brooks, finding a depth of moral failure in James's late style, described James's writing as "Magnificent pretentiousness, petty performances!—the fruits of an irresponsible imagination, of a deranged sense of values, of a mind working in the void, uncorrected by any clear consciousness of human cause and effect" (134). Striving to protect the world from the adulation of late James by T. S. Eliot and the New Critics, Maxwell Geisman in *Henry James and the Jacobites* pronounces, "No character in the later James fiction, the so-called 'later phase,' can lead either a normal or a full life because James was in absolute control of their behavior, their thought, their being; and James had no other life except this fabricated and manipulated world of his fiction" (7). Such a judgment, as vitriolic in its own way as James's assessments of Wilde, shows the limitations of experiencing or representing literary efforts in terms of their ultimate ethical soundness. Even a reader of James as sympathetic as Leo B. Levy sees James's achievement qualified by his inveterate allegiance to a morally simplistic view of life: "[James's] moral partisanship exists wholly within the imagined worlds of his novels and tales, where refinement of intention exists with an involuntary commitment to melodrama, the prevailing form of the bias and the limitation of James's vision" (11). It does not seem enough for such critics to interrogate a work of fiction; they must offer an absolute moral evaluation as well.

Nowhere do we see more pointedly the "bias and limitations" of criticism than in attempts to respond moralistically to works by the Aesthetes and Decadents of the late nineteenth century like Pater's *The Renaissance* (1873) and Wilde's *The Picture of Dorian Gray* (1890). And, to be fair, the authors of these works could outdo their critics in being moralistic. Pater withdrew the conclusion of *The Renaissance* for a time because "it might possibly mislead some of those young men into whose hands it might fall" (194). And Wilde, in spite of his statement in the preface to *The Picture of Dorian Gray* that "There is no such thing as a moral or an immoral book" (17), insisted after being attacked by the *St. James Gazette* that his novel did indeed contain a moral: "And the moral is this: All excess, as well as all renunciation, brings its own punishment" (Qtd. in Ericksen, 99). Perhaps because of Puritanical assumptions in the culture at large or for whatever reasons, art has not often been given a free hand to explore the human condition unsupervised. Or it might do so, but only at the risk of bringing ruin down upon its creator.

But there is more to aestheticism than the breaching of cultural or moral taboos. To appreciate the philosophical refinements possible within an aesthetic approach to life, we need only invoke Walter Pater, whose ideas form a bridge between James and Wilde, revealing their affinities and clarifying their differences.

James's famous essay "The Art of Fiction" (1884), in which he defines his own style of psychological realism, is rich in Paterian echoes:

> The power to guess the unseen from the seen, to trace the implications of things, to judge the whole piece by the pattern, the condition of feeling life so completely that you are well on your way to knowing any particular corner of it—this cluster of gifts may almost be said to constitute experience, and they occur in country and in town, and in the most differing stages of education. If experience consists of impressions, it be said that impressions are experience, just as (have we not seen it?) they are the very air we breathe [489].

In *The Renaissance*, Pater makes the same intriguing equation of experience with impressions:

> ... those impressions of the individual mind to which, for each one of us, experience dwindles down, are in perpetual flight; that each of them is limited by time, and that as time is infinitely divisible, each of them is infinitely divisible also; all that is actual in it being a single moment, gone while we try to apprehend it.... The service of philosophy, of speculative culture, towards the human spirit, is to rouse, to startle it to a life of constant and eager observation [196].

An impression is a momentary coherence of thought and sensation utterly private and free since it does not depend upon confirmation by another. It does not display itself. It is the opposite of what is implied by "making an impression." Therefore, it is anti-theatrical. An artist basing his work on a cultivated experience of impressions is trying, as James says, to be "one of the people on whom nothing is lost" ("The Art of Fiction," 489) or striving, as Pater says, to "burn with a hard gem-like flame" (*The Renaissance*, 197) for the sake of the moment, and the moment only could be said to be absolutely moral. For the artist withholds personal judgment and represents complex human lives only through indirect, character-oriented points of view.

The work of Pater that reads most like a primer of Jamesian narrative is *Plato and Platonism: A Series of Lectures*. For Pater, Plato's *Republic*, in delineating the ideal state, "does but elevate what Athens in particular, a ship so early going to pieces might well be forced to become for her salvation, were it still possible, into the eternal type of veritable statecraft, a city as such, 'a city at unity in itself,' defiant of time" (237–238). The evils that threaten Athens come from "an exaggerated assertion of the fluxional, flamboyant, centrifugal Ionian element in the Hellenic character. They could be cured only by a counter-assertion of the centripetal Dorian ideal..." (238). Pater sounds very much like James in his description of Plato's dialectical search for truth: "precisely because [truth] resembles some high kind of relationship of persons to persons, depends a good deal on the receiver; and must be, in that degree, elusive, provisional, contingent ... that it's partly a subjective attitude of mind" (187). Each of the dialogues resembles a portrait, Pater says, inasmuch as "all knowledge [is] like knowing a person" (129). Pater even asserts that Plato "would have been an excellent writer of fiction" comparable to Thackeray (132). An even stronger case could be made for comparing Socratic dialectic with the art of Henry James. James stills the "centrifugal" theatrics of modern life by focusing on those impressions that reveal characters to each other and to themselves. The paradox of James's genius is the same as Plato's: each is a seer with a "sensuous love of the unseen" (143).

James explores art-and-the-artist in numerous works, but *The Tragic Muse* deserves special attention for three reasons. First, James examines the ideals of art and the sacrifices necessary for them specifically in relation to the theater. Second, the novel's spokesperson for aestheticism, Gabriel Nash, is and is not Oscar Wilde; he is Henry James's Oscar Wilde, if you will. And third, Wilde's novel *The Picture of Dorian Gray*, published one month after the last installment of *The Tragic Muse*, though a very different story, contains fascinating parallels with *The Tragic Muse* that invite analysis. Taken together these works shed light on what Oscar Wilde—or many of his and Pater's shared ideas—meant to James, how he assimilated them into his own style of "Platonic" realism, and why ultimately Wilde was no threat to James on any level. Wilde's art was very different from that of James. Wilde was a brilliant ironist and social critic, a poseur with a point; James was the "aesthete," if one means by that term someone who experiences what is most valuable and most real about life through works of art. In other words, Wilde helped James, *The Tragic Muse* suggests, to appreciate the value and the necessity of being true to himself as his own kind of artist.

The Tragic Muse tells two stories. Nick Dormer, though pursuing a political career in the House of Commons and intending to marry a wealthy, influential widow and receive a large bequest from an old family friend for doing so, experiences his true calling as a portrait painter. In the course of the novel he follows his muse, renounces his political ambitions, breaks off his engagement, sacrifices his inheritance, and sets to work in earnest as a painter. The second story concerns Miriam Rooth, whose great passion is to become an actress. But she is not an introverted renunciant like Nick Dormer. She is a magpie, a chameleon who ruthlessly learns her trade from a Parisian acting coach and pulls herself and her comical stage mother out of poverty into a prosperous career. One senses that she is always acting, whether onstage or off, and that in theatricality she enjoys her own kind of personal integrity as well as her professional success. Julia Dallow, Nick's fiancée, and her brother, Peter Sherringham, are the "worldly" characters in the novel, who try to appropriate the artists to their worlds. Even at the end of the novel we are not certain Julia will succeed in acquiring Nick and turning him into a weekend painter. Meanwhile, Peter, a diplomat as well as a fan of the theater, has fallen in love with Miriam Rooth and begs her to marry him so that she can decorate his political life with her histrionic intensities. Practical to the end, Miriam marries her stage manager instead. And Peter marries Nick Dormer's sister Biddy. Together they depart for Peter's new diplomatic post in Central America.

Gabriel Nash, Nick Dormer's old Oxford friend, is the heart and soul of the novel; his occasional angelic appearances out of and back into the world at large are the occasions when the central question of the novel comes into focus—not what is the value of art, but what is the value of everything else? Gabriel articulates a quasi–Buddhist philosophy of "being" over "doing." His Paterian aestheticism—"We must feel everything we can" (722)—though, does not extend to the ugly or the personally compromising. Technically he is an "aesthete," though he rejects such a formula as merely "walking in one's hat," but he is not a "decadent," as Dorian Gray becomes in Wilde's novel. Everything one experiences has consequences in one's spirit, Gabriel insists. The goal, therefore, is to become a "fine consequence" (724). Gabriel's philosophy is a contemplative aestheticism whose goal is to free the self from illusions that are taken very seriously by political types like Julia Dallow and Peter Sherringham. Gabriel is a regenerate rather than a degenerate because he believes in the possibility of absolute independence, avoiding, at all costs, participating in the categorical "we" of political parties or schools of thought. What others perceive as Gabriel's "impertinence" is simply his refusal to yield to intellectual coercion or forces inherent in others' personalities (819).

Gabriel is particularly hard on the theater. Asked if he thinks it "important," he replies:

> Important, certainly, to managers and stage-carpenters who want
> to make money, to ladies and gentlemen who want to produce
> themselves in public by lime-light, and to other ladies and gentle-
> men who are bored and stupid and don't know what to do with
> their evening. It's a commercial and social convenience which may
> be infinitely worked. But important artistically, intellectually? How
> can it be—so poor, so limited a form? [746]

Gabriel is describing the social dimensions of theater, of course, but one could say equally well that he is describing the theatrical dimensions of society. Although he admires the dramatic genius of Madame Carre, Miriam Rooth's acting teacher, for the triumph of consciousness each of her performances represents, he regards the claptrap context in which she must perform as no better than Plato's cave, where shadows pass for realities in the minds of spectators who are basically asleep. And the theatrical dimensions of life for Gabriel are simply *maya*. They are much better resisted in the more private aesthetic experience of the novel, as practiced by Balzac, for example, who creates portraits in thought of individual forms of consciousness.

Miriam Rooth, master of the theatrical, never its slave, is the "tragic muse" of the novel. She is simultaneously the most and the least human of all the characters, as she illustrates, in a way, the tragedy (and the comedy) of the human condition that the novel envisions. To be a success on the stage of life one must take up various roles, which require suspending one's naïve experience of self. To the extent one succeeds at playing one's roles with "the insolence of conscious power" (813), to that extent one forfeits what most people more or less unconsciously experience as their true selves. It is Peter Sherringham who first sees the tragic muse in Miriam as she auditions for Madame Carre, though he does not grasp any implications of such an impression. He is merely impressed.

> She wore a black dress, which fell in straight folds; her face, under
> her mobile brows, was pale and regular, with a strange, strong, tragic
> beauty. "I don't know what's in her," he said to himself; "nothing,
> it would seem, from her persistent vacancy. But such a face as that,
> such a head, is a fortune! [787]

At first Miriam is awkward, amateurish, and embarrassingly eager to please. But as she matures in her art, Peter is brought to the brink of fear when he sees her refined powers of artistic transformation in action.

> It struck him abruptly that a woman whose only being was to "make
> believe," to make believe that she had any and every being that you
> liked, that would serve a purpose, produce a certain effect, and

> whose identity resided in the continuity of her personations, so that
> she had no moral privacy, as he phrased it to himself, but lived in
> a high wind of exhibition, of figuration—such a woman was a kind
> of monster, in whom of necessity there would be nothing to like,
> because there would be nothing to take hold of [832].

At the height of her success Gabriel Nash refers to Miriam, the "tragic muse" in the novel, as "the great modern personage" (981), a phrase which invites comparison with another of James's representative types of modern life, John Marcher in "The Beast in the Jungle," who, because he is so afraid of being devoured by life, never really lives it and so becomes "the man of his time, the man to whom nothing on earth was to have happened" (446).

Miriam Rooth is the opposite of John Marcher. He is alienated from himself in unconsciousness; she has consciously discovered how to control her personas in order to achieve her ends. Gabriel Nash represents an equally extreme form of consciousness that is determined to stay within its own experience of self even if it means that he must vanish from the stage of life. After serving his purpose as an inspiration for Nick Dormer and a catalyst for putting Nick on the path that is the right one for him, the path of art, Gabriel vanishes from the action of the novel, and his uncompleted image actually fades away, as if by magic, from the portrait of him Nick had begun. (See "Afterwords.") Julia Dallow and Peter Sherringham return to their mundane worlds. Nick Dormer occupies a middle distance at the end of the novel, having found what gives him joy in portrait painting, in a style that sounds remarkably like the realistic narrative style of Henry James:

> There it is, said Nick at last—"there's the naked, preposterous truth:
> that if I were to do exactly as I liked I should spend my years copy-
> ing the more or less vacuous countenances of my fellow-mortals. I
> should find peace and pleasure and wisdom and worth, I should
> find fascination and a measure of success in it: out of the din and
> the dust and the scramble, the world of party labels, party cries,
> party bargains and party treacheries—of humbuggery, hypocrisy and
> cant. The cleanness and quietness of it, the independent effort to
> do something, to leave something which shall give joy to man long
> after the howling has died away to the last ghost of an echo—such
> a vision solicits me at certain hours with an almost irresistible force
> [478].

Critics have attempted to find a source for Gabriel Nash in James's life and thus to clarify the importance of this character for the novel and its author. Leon Edel identifies Gabriel as the "character in the novel who speaks for—and even resembles physically—the novelist himself," especially as he criticizes English theater as "puerile and barbarous." Edel believes that James is attempting to "purge himself in [The Tragic Muse] of all his conflicts over the dramatic arts" (40). The case for Oscar Wilde as James's source is made by R. P. Blackmur, who believes James—although he began with Wilde—ended by creating simply a type of aesthetic personality that interested him (xx).

In the 1950s a debate was carried on in Nineteenth-Century Fiction over the question of Gabriel's "identity." Oscar Cargill amasses a good deal of evidence, both textual and biographical, for Wilde as James's source, even going so far as to conjecture that The Tragic Muse (serialized in the Atlantic from January 1889 until May 1890), was influenced by The Picture of Dorian Gray (published in Lippincott's Magazine in June 1890), not the other way around. He speculates on various channels of gossip through which news of Wilde's plans for his novel might have reached James before the novel appeared. For Cargill, Gabriel is a satirical portrait of Wilde, albeit an unaccountably "generous" one, considering James's reference to Wilde in a letter as a "tenth-rate cad." Aside from purposes of satire, Cargill finds Gabriel's presence in the novel puzzlingly "nonfunctional" (177). Lyall Powers argues against Cargill's evidence and reasoning, preferring Edel's view of Gabriel as a mouthpiece for James's ideas that could rationalize his decision to give up novel writing to become a playwright (345).

Quentin Anderson makes the fascinating argument—which Cargill pooh-poohs and Powers ignores—that Gabriel Nash is based on Henry James, Sr. The James children certainly breathed their father's Mystical-Swedenborgian-Emersonian inspirations from their earliest days. Undeniably, Gabriel sounds like the elder James, who believed the Artist to be "the only regenerate image of God in nature, the only living revelation of the Lord on earth" (98). In a deep sense, Anderson sees the elder James as the continuing inspiration of the novelist throughout his life. But Anderson also sees a criticism of the elder James in the representation of Gabriel Nash in The Tragic Muse. Both Gabriel and the elder James were caught in a "contradiction between dedication to life and the lack of any medium in which to express one's allegiance save that of behavior toward others" (119). Anderson believes that James, Jr., experienced his father as a talker and probably never read any of his works except the "Autobiographical Fragment" included in his brother William's introduction to Literary Remains (121). As a result, the elder James's ideas were only problematically incarnated. Nevertheless, Anderson argues that a full understanding of the novels of Henry James is possible only against a background of his father's philosophical ideas.

Most recent critics accept Oscar Wilde as James's model for Gabriel Nash, though some see the character as an amalgam of Wilde and James. Poststructuralist critics tend to focus on psychosocial dynamics that transcend or threaten personal identification, placing the politics of identity center stage. For Niell Matheson, Wilde haunts *The Turn of the Screw*. The ghosts in that story are "signifiers of shameful (and shameless) public exposure; their appearance invokes scandal as well as horror, suggesting both James's sense of the 'fearful exposure' associated with the Wilde trials and his derision of Wilde's flamboyance, associated strongly for James with Wilde's success in the theater" (732). Jonathan Freedman places the artistic struggles of Miriam Rooth and Nick Dormer in the context of an ascendant commodity culture. Gabriel's role in *The Tragic Muse* is to acknowledge the paradox that in such a world "aesthetic success and aesthetic failure are finally one and the same thing" (188). Joseph Litvak, following Michel Foucault, sees the society of the nineteenth and twentieth centuries as moving from "spectacle" to "surveillance" (1), so that each theatrical moment of representation, of looking and being looked at, can become an occasion of entrapment.

It seems a shame to think of Henry James trapped in an Oscar Wilde world as if he were Alice in Wonderland. But that fate was his briefly during his adventure in the theater. The plot of *Guy Domville* suggests as much. The eponymous hero is about to enter the Roman Catholic priesthood but he is tempted, when he hears of the death of a kinsman, to marry and take up his worldly responsibilities. In the second act he enters that world, apparently trying to sound like a character out of Oscar Wilde: "There's scarcely a rule I haven't utterly abjured—there's scarcely a trust I haven't rigidly betrayed—there's scarcely a vow I haven't scrupulously broken! What *more* can a man do for conscience?" (499). But soon he discovers he was only being duped, so he returns to his vocation. The play lacks the dramatic interest so richly present in virtually all of James's stories and novels. And it contains several sore-thumb theatrical moments that the audience on opening night found absurd. One was a large black velvet hat worn by Mrs. Domville in the second act. Someone in the audience sang out a line from a popular song: "Where did you get that hat." A drinking contest between Guy and his romantic rival had to be cut it was so incredible. And the last line of the play, "I'm the last, my lord, of the Domvilles," was greeted by another audience participant who answered back, "It's a bloody good thing y'are" (Edel 474–475). These painful memories from James's opening night have been repeated and commented upon by critics and historians of theater so often that they have all but eclipsed *Guy Domville* itself.

And the two Wilde plays that enveloped James's play, *An Ideal Husband*, which James attended on his own opening night, and *The Importance of Being Earnest*, which replaced *Guy Domville* at George Alexander's theater, seem to comment intertextually on the moral earnestness of James's play in an embarrassing way. The "ideal husband" of Wilde's play, Sir Robert Chiltern, has made his fortune by selling a government secret. When he is caught up in a blackmail plot, his wife, a puritanical type who feels compelled to see herself and her husband as beyond reproach, can no longer accept him as her husband. But when Lord Goring, the play's dandy, convinces Sir Robert to fight Mrs. Cheverly, the blackmailer, a series of revelations unfold that force Lady Chiltern to admit, "There is the same world for all of us, and good and evil, sin and innocence, go through it hand in hand." The anti-puritanical dandy has carved out a social space in the play where these two naifs can live, "where the roses are white and red" (429), that is, where moral ambiguities do not have to be faced. James's play looks rather thin, and terribly melodramatic, compared to Wilde's. When Guy Domville retreats from the corrupt world of his family and reenters the priesthood, it is as though he simply preferred not to think about the complexities explored in this play by Wilde.

The Importance of Being Earnest parodies not only all forms of ceremony and respectability, it even parodies Wilde's own high nonsense (Nassaar, 130). This "Trivial Play for Serious People" implies that a truly serious person will enjoy seeing through the pomposities and sentimentalities that abound in nineteenth-century life and in all the stock dramatic devices that the play parodies. "In a play as artificial and delightful as this one, the work's lack of seriousness or content is its point" (130). Without meaning or needing to, Wilde's play pulls the metaphysical rug out from under *Guy Domville*, whose escape into seriousness, a Jamesian renunciation, is rendered meaningless. Wilde's play is a critique of society and of art in the sense that he defines the role of criticism in "The Critic as Artist": "It is Criticism that, recognizing no position as final, and refusing to bind itself by the shallow shibboleths of any sect or school, creates that serene philosophic temper which loves truth for its own sake, and loves it not the less because it knows it to be unattainable" (1057).

What *Guy Domville* misses James routinely achieves in his prose narratives, the sense of deeply lived inner lives, and more than that, inner lives that complete themselves, emptying themselves of further possibilities through decision, action, conflict, and denouement, in other words, drama. James came to believe (Edel, 63), and Levy agrees with him (89), that his foray into dramatic writing strengthened his fiction, making it more scenic. But countless scenes throughout James's career attest to his dramatic grasp of the terrible freedom of single moments in his characters' lives. James's fiction is packed with such moments. But they do not sound like the brilliant talk of Oscar Wilde. They are dramatic but not theatrical; they would not necessarily make good theater.

The *Picture of Dorian Gray*, especially since it contains such striking parallels to *The Tragic Muse*, clearly highlights James's dramatic fiction against Wilde's theatricality. In Wilde's novel, the artist Basil Hallward has found in his model Dorian Gray the perfect expression of his own soul. He paints Dorian's portrait almost fearfully, lest anyone guess his secret, and he does not want the portrait exhibited publicly. His Mephistophelean friend, Lord Henry Wotton, is the novel's spokesperson for Paterian aestheticism, but, unlike Gabriel Nash, Lord Henry gives a very dark coloration to Pater's philosophy. He teaches Dorian that his beauty is already fading and that with the passage of time it will be totally lost. And he also teaches Dorian how to use his beauty to explore an infinite range of sensations uninhibited by moral scruples and how to use his beauty to gain power over others in order to satisfy his desires. Dorian makes a sort of Faustian pact with this Mephisto when he exclaims, "If it were I who was to be always young and the picture that was to grow old! I would give my soul for that!" (34)

Dorian-Faust's Marguerite is an actress named Sibyl Vane whom he falls in love with and ruins. She is happy as a second-class actress until Dorian becomes her Prince Charming. Then she longs so much for a "real" life with him that she loses her ability to enjoy her acting and to infuse her roles with make-believe. "I might mimic a passion I do not feel, but I cannot mimic one that burns like fire" (75), she says. Ironically, she kills Dorian's love for her when she gives up make-believe passion for the real thing. After her suicide, Dorian spirals downward, murdering Basil Hallward, the artist who began Dorian's alienation from self by painting him. Dorian tries to destroy his own conscience by destroying the painting that has magically taken on all the ugliness of his life and deeds. But in this final act he kills himself.

The *Tragic Muse* and *The Picture of Dorian Gray* have a painter, an aesthete and an actress as their three main characters. And there is a painting in each novel that has the power to transform itself in sympathy with a human being. Richard Ellman points out that one of Miriam Rooth's stage names is Gladys Vane and that even Miriam Rooth's Jewish heritage finds an echo in Sibyl Vane's Jewish theater manager (222). Joseph Litvak finds a further parallel between Peter Sherringham and Dorian Gray, who both love and try to possess tragic actresses (272). The possibilities for inter-textual reading are complex, as Litvak points out.

There is one contrast between the two authors' approaches to charac-ter and incident that illustrates the difference between their dramatic and theatrical styles. James's style has been called "melodramatic" because of the palpable sense of evil threatening characters that appear to be inno-cent (Levy, 2). Yet James's characters, upon close inspection, turn out to be quite complex and their circumstances highly ambiguous. James creates a suspenseful tone for his tales in order to draw his readers in, but ulti-mately the conditions that prevail in James's characters and incidents must be thought very hard about; they are not merely sensational, as melodrama is. But Wilde's novel is truly driven by melodrama because an evil pervades the story on every level—alienation from self. Basil Hallward does not expe-rience his own soul except through its image in Dorian Gray. Lord Henry Wotton does not live out the implications of his own decadent philoso-phies. He uses Dorian to achieve his results, which are matters chiefly of intellectual curiosity to him. Sibyl Vane is not a conscious artist like Miriam Rooth. She loses herself in her roles and enjoys a richly vicarious, alien-ated existence until Dorian discovers her. All characters in Wilde's novel, even the portrait perhaps, live only for or through others. For Wilde this melodramatic evil of alienation is inherent and inescapable in society itself. His characters are simply various sensational, thought-provoking examples of this evil. In "The Soul of Man under Socialism," Wilde advocates the need for every person to escape "the sordid necessity of living for others" (1079). But this kind of freedom is far in the future; therefore, the age of alienation and enslavement—the nineteenth century—needs a brilliant the-atrical ironist like Oscar Wilde to impress upon the world the seriousness of its soulless condition.

James, on the other hand, has incorporated what Pater refers to as aesthetic patience in his constantly reconsidering the style of narration. Speaking of Plato's prose, Pater says,

> His prose is a practical illustration of the value of that capacity
> for correction, of the effort, the intellectual astringency, which
> he demands of the poet also, the musician, of all true citizens
> of the ideal Republic, enhancing the sense of power in one's self,
> and its effect upon others, by a certain crafty reserve in its exercise,
> after the manner of a true expert.... Patience, "infinite patience,"
> may or may not be, as was said, of the very essence of genius; but
> is certainly, quite as much as fire, of the mood of all true lovers
> [283].

James's fiction also strives to wait for the true nature of his characters to reveal themselves, not in melodramatic self-exposures, but in carefully thought-out conclusions that must occur ultimately in the mind of the reader. Miriam Rooth is like Lord Henry's description of a great poet: "the most unpoetical of all creatures" (55), while Sibyl Vane is like his description of inferior poets: "absolutely fascinating. The worse their rhymes are, the more picturesque they look" (55). Miriam achieves her full human potential in her everyday labors to master her craft. Nick Dormer, having had a more privileged upbringing than Miriam, needs the gospel of freedom to be preached to him by Gabriel Nash so he can cease living for Julia Dallow, Mr. Carteret, his mother and all the others, and eventually find himself in the labors of a portrait painter. He does not lose himself in painting his soul as Basil Hallward does. And Gabriel Nash does not experiment with Nick Dormer for the fulfillment of his own will to power, as Lord Henry does with Dorian. Very like Wilde, Gabriel Nash understands and uses the instrument he has been given: "To speak to people just as I am speaking to you. To prevent for instance a great wrong being done ... to the human race. I talk—I talk; I say things that other people don't, that they can't, that they won't.... " to which Nick can only reply, "If it's a question of mastery and perfection, you certainly have them... " (975). This could be read as a fine tribute to Oscar Wilde.

James's instrument was his own thought—dramatic prose. Perhaps his debacle in the theater was lucky for him. It sent him back to his true genius and to his true self.

As he says in his notebook, January 23, 1895:

> I take up my *own* old pen again—the pen of all my old unforgettable efforts and sacred struggles. To myself—today—I need say no more. Large and full and high the future still opens. It is now indeed that I may do the work of my life. And I will [Edel, 60].

Works Cited

Anderson, Quentin. *The American Henry James*. New Brunswick: Rutgers University Press, 1957.

Blackmur, Richard P. "Introduction." In *The Art of the Novel: Critical Prefaces*, by Henry James, vii-xxxix. New York: Charles Scribner's Sons, 1935.

Brooks, Van Wyck. *The Pilgrimage of Henry James*. New York: E. P. Dutton, 1925.

Cargill, Oscar. "Mr. James's Aesthetic Mr. Nash." *Nineteenth-Century Fiction* 12, no. 3 (December 1957): 177–187.

Edel, Leon. "Henry James: The Dramatic Years." In *The Complete Plays of Henry James*. Edited by Leon Edel. London: Rupert Hart-Davis, 1949.

Ellmann, Richard. "Henry James Among the Aesthetes." In *Proceedings of the British Academy*. Vol. 64 (1983): 209–228. London: Oxford University Press, 1984.

Ericksen, Donald H. *Oscar Wilde*. Boston: Twayne, 1977.

Freedman, Jonathan. *Professions of Taste: Henry James, British Aestheticism, and Commodity Culture*. Stanford: Stanford University Press, 1990.

Geismar, Maxwell. *Henry James and the Jacobites*. Boston: Houghton Mifflin, 1963.

James, Henry. "The Art of Fiction." In *The Norton Anthology of American Literature*, Vol. 2. Edited by Ronald Gottesman. New York: W. W. Norton, 1979.

_____. "The Beast in the Jungle." *The Norton Anthology of Literature*.

_____. *Guy Domville. The Complete Plays of Henry James*. Edited by Leon Edel. London: Rupert Hart-David, 1949.

_____. *The Tragic Muse, Novels 1886–1890*. New York: Library of America, 1989.

Levy, Leo B. *Versions of Melodrama: A Study of the Fiction and Drama of Henry James, 1865–1897*. Berkeley: University of California Press, 1957.

Litvak, Joseph. *Caught in the Act: Theatricality in the Nineteenth-Century English Novel*. Berkeley: University of California Press, 1992.

Matheson, Neill. "Talking Horrors: James, Euphemism, and the Specter of Wilde." *American Literature* 71, no. 4 (December 1999): 709–750.

Nassaar, Christopher S. *Into the Demon Universe: A Literary Exploration of Oscar Wilde*. New Haven CT: Yale University Press, 1974.

Pater, Walter. *Plato and Platonism: A Series of Lectures*. New York: Greenwood Press, 1969.

_____. *The Renaissance*. New York: Modern Library, 1919.

Powers, Lyall. "Mr. James's Aesthetic Mr. Nash—Again." *Nineteenth-Century Fiction* 13, no. 4 (March 1959): 341–349.

Salamensky, Shelly. ""Henry James, Oscar Wilde, and 'Fin-de-Siecle Talk': A Brief Reading." *The Henry James Review* 20 (1999): 275–281.

Wilde, Oscar. "The Critic as Artist." In *Complete Works of Oscar Wilde*. London: Collins, 1973.

_____. "The Decay of Lying." In *Complete Works*.

_____. *An Ideal Husband*. In *Complete Works*.

_____. *The Importance of Being Earnest*. In *Complete Works*.

_____. *The Picture of Dorian Gray*. In *Complete Works*.

_____. "The Soul of Man under Socialism." In *Complete Works*.

Papa, Postcards, Perfume, Phallic Keys: James, Symonds, and Late-Victorian Fictions of Homosexuality

Stephen da Silva

In Henry James's "The Figure in the Carpet," the narrator, deluded by the transferential desire that Hugh Vereker knows the mystificatory principle that supposedly unifies his work, ludicrously attempts to explicate that "figure": "'Perhaps it's a preference for the letter 'P!' I ventured ... 'Papa, potato, prunes, that sort of thing'" (368).[1] As my title indicates, I am appropriating and revising the narrator's absurd catalog in order to read an earlier Jamesian tale, "The Author of 'Beltraffio'" (1884), and beyond that tale itself to read the limited but complex and ambivalent relationship between James and the late–Victorian homosexual apologist John Addington Symonds, who is represented as the writer Mark Ambient in the tale.

When discussing the relationship between younger male writers and their literary papas or precursors, one almost inevitably turns to Harold Bloom's celebrated model of authorial influence.[2] Bloom theorizes that a younger male writer affects an Oedipal distance from his precursor by carrying out one of a series of complex revisionary literary swerves. My reading will show that James does indeed attempt to distance himself from Symonds by feminizing and pathologizing the older writer. However, while Bloom's model tends to visualize two agonistic figures, literary son struggling against literary father,[3] James tends to frame that drama in triangular configurations involving the splitting of the paternal function. Or, to put it put more directly, James tends to distance himself from Symonds, the weak feminized father, by dismissing the older writer to some other idealized or feared father figure, the good or strong father, if you will.

However, one of the distinct limitations of Bloom's model, as Thomas Yingling, among others, has pointed out, is its narrowly familial focus, its resolute insulation from the realm of public discourse (21). That limitation becomes particularly evident when one discusses two writers whose masculinity bears a vexed relationship to the cultural norm. As mentioned above, Symonds was a discreetly closeted, married, male homosexual and an apologist for a virile strain of homosexuality affiliated with a Hellenic tradition. James, whose own passionate, though probably sublimated, affective investment in young men was simultaneously concealed and artfully articulated in many of his works,[4] in representing his relationship with the older writer partially revises and partially reiterates some of the contradictions of male homosexuality and the closet within which both he and Symonds were inscribed. Specifically, I will focus on James's ambivalent relationship to what Eve Kosofsky Sedgwick has called gender integrative and gender separatist paradigms of male homosexuality (Epistemology, 1–2). To put it slightly reductively: Is the male homosexual in flight from constraining feminine domesticity, or is he an invert, an effeminized man? James draws on both models in representing Symonds and his relationship with Symonds. James's anxious contradictions about the relationship of gender to homosexuality replicate some of the contradictions in Symonds's own writing, and they mirror the larger contradictions of late–Victorian discourses regarding male same-sex desire. Unlike the narrator in "The Figure in the Carpet," I am not seeking to uncover a unifying figure that will unlock the mysteries of the Jamesian oeuvre. On the contrary, I am interested precisely in the contradictions and ambivalences that simultaneously constrained and enabled James to articulate his relationship with Symonds, and more broadly to represent affectively charged male same-sex bonds.

The Immediate Crudity of What Happened

To begin, I will chronologically retrace James and Symonds's brief and mediated relationship; then I will linger (to use a favorite Jamesian term, particularly in relation to his discussion of Venice in Italian Hours) over that relationship and read its significance, for as James points out in The

American Scene, "history is never, in any rich sense, the immediate crudity of what 'happens' but the much finer complexity of what we read into it and think of in connection with it" (453). In 1877, Andrew Lang took James to lunch at his club to meet Symonds.[5] In a letter to William James, Henry James described Symonds as "a mild, cultured man with an Oxford perfume, who invited me to visit him at Clifton" (*Letters II,* 101). By all indications, James did not take up Symonds' invitation.

The two writers' literary connections seemed closer than their personal bond. Fred Kaplan points out that "James read with great admiration [Symonds's] *The Renaissance in Italy*" (302), and Robert Gale points out that "James's library contained twenty books by Symonds, as well as Brown's biography of Symonds" (642). Impressed by Symonds's passion for Italy and for Venice in particular, James sent his own essay on Venice to Symonds as soon as it appeared in *The Century* late in 1882 (Kaplan, 302). Symonds replied to praise James, "and according to a letter from James to Gosse later (16 September 1901), Symonds called it 'the best image of V. he had ever seen made'" (Gale, 642). James replied to Symonds's letter on 22 February 1884, thanking the older man and affirming the love of Italy they shared in revealing terms that I will discuss at greater length later in the essay. The differences between Symonds and his wife over his art also inspired a tale by James as we learn from a *Notebook* entry of 26 March 1884. Learning from Gosse that Symonds' deeply religious wife disliked his writings, which she perceived as pagan and immoral, James derived the germ for "The Author of 'Beltraffio.'"[6]

James also got to read Symonds's unpublished apologetics for male homosexuality. Gosse gave him Symonds's *A Problem in Modern Ethics,* and in a January 7, 1893, letter, James called it "infinitely remarkable" but declared that "he wished [Symonds] more humour; it really is the saving salt" (*Letters III,* 398). When Symonds died that same year, James wrote to Gosse again on 21 April 1893 and was curious to learn "any circumstances about Symonds—or about his death that may be interesting" (410). In 1894, James also told Gosse that he read Horatio Brown's 1894 biography of Symonds with "the liveliest—and almost painful—interest" (502). Presumably, it was James's "painful" relationship to Symonds's private life that caused him resolutely to decline the opportunity to write about Symonds later that year. Symonds would be resurrected by James like a paternal specter in the aftermath of the Wilde trials. Writing to Gosse in 1895 about Wilde's sentence, James would scribble a postscript in French about Symonds on the envelope.

The critical and biographical assessments of James and Symonds's relationship are surprisingly divergent. To cite two examples from opposite ends of the interpretive spectrum: With a confidence and tone verging on the homophobic, Leon Edel declares that James showed nothing but "amused irony ... for the ardent invert John Addington Symonds" (233). By contrast, Wendy Graham has a far more upbeat assessment of the two writers' relationship. She tells us that "James clearly regarded [A Problem in Modern Ethics] as a work of importance, interest, and daring" (30) and maintains that in his 1893 letter to Gosse, "James was declaring his fealty to Symonds and men like him" (31). Clearly, "amused irony" has no place in Graham's narrative; her James seems a loyal recruit in the army of homosexual identity politics, ready to follow Symonds and men like him to the anti-homophobic ramparts.

Neither critic is persuasive because neither registers ambivalence. In that regard, their language is symptomatically revealing: Edel uses the adverb "simply": "For the young Oscar Wilde [James] would show contempt; for the ardent invert John Addington Symonds *simply* amused irony" (233, emphasis added). I would contend that there is nothing simple about James's feelings toward Symonds. Graham's complacent "clearly" is equally revealing. James's view of A Problem in Modern Ethics is far from clear; it is as clouded and murky as the canal water in parts of his beloved Venice.

Undoubtedly, there is some truth to both critics' positions: James does try to persuade surrogate father figures that he despises Symonds, and although James does not use Edel's term "invert," he does amusedly mock Symonds's effeminacy. However, as we shall see, there are various contradictions and incoherences in his position that undermine his desired stance of amused irony. Graham is correct that James reveals a great deal of fascination with A Problem in Modern Ethics and a strong degree of identification with Symonds. Simultaneously, however, he tries to distance himself from those feelings and undercut Symonds' authority. As we will see, Symonds and James associate masculinity with clarity and clear-cut boundaries; by contrast they associate femininity with a seductive, deadly liquidity. In ignoring Jamesian ambivalence, critics like Edel and Graham might be described as being complicit with a masculinist, phallocentric logic, a particularly ironic complicity in Graham's case, considering her explicitly feminist, anti-homophobic critical orientation.[7]

Triangular Variations on a Bloomian Theme

James's father, Henry James, plays a rather indirect role in the writer's Oedipal distancing from Symonds. Symonds was associated with an Oxonian strain of aestheticism, and James makes it a point to dismiss the effeminacy and intellectual nullity of that strain of aestheticism in writing to his father. Describing the Oxonian aesthete Lecky to his father, James writes, "The drooping, lackadaisical Lecky stands before me at this instant, and if I had only the pen of a Du Maurier, I would make you die with laughing at his languid eyes and his willowy limbs" (James qtd. in Novick, 370). The verbal caricature of Lecky is, in part, an opportunity for James to affirm his own masculinity to his father. The more he mocks the drooping, willowy nature of Oxonian aestheticism, the more he implicitly attempts to assert his own proper phallic rigidity. Such a strategy is dangerous, however. As Jacques Lacan has pointed out, phallic authority is unstated, assumed, "veiled." Paradoxically, striking a hypermasculine attitude can feminize a man (692).

The triangular configuration among Oxford aestheticism, James's father, and James works in the opposite direction as well. That is, James bonds with his pederastic papa, Symonds, by distancing himself from his own father and his powerful literary precursor, John Ruskin, whom he associated with patriarchal authority. We have seen that, although James met Symonds in 1877, it was James's essay on Venice published in 1882 that provided the real conduit between the two writers. But this was not James's first essay on Venice. His first essay on Venice was published in 1872. As Adam Parkes points out, " [Ruskin] praised the essay to his friend and former teacher at Harvard, Charles Eliot Norton, who in turn informed James." Significantly, "the young American ... sent Norton's note to his father, asking him to guard it 'privately and jealously'" (Parkes, 160). Ruskin's praise, mediated through a former teacher and a contemporary of his father, becomes a textual token of intimacy between father and son.

Parkes astutely connects James's moralistic reading of Tintoretto in the 1872 essay to Ruskin's mode of reading (160),[8] but he does not comment on James's idealization of Tintoretto's virile intensity and clarity of vision: "Tintoretto's great merit ... was his unequalled distinctness of vision. When once he had conceived the germ of a scene it defined itself to his imagination with an intensity, an amplitude, an individuality of expression, which make one's observation of his pictures seem less an operation of the mind than a kind of supplementary experience of life" (*Italian Hours*, 342). Sheldon Novick suggestively figures Tintoretto's power, as read by Ruskin and James, in explicitly phallic, penetrative terms—"At this time [James] sought principally to understand Tintoretto, whose work Ruskin had praised above all the others. Little was known of the painter himself, but as Henry studied the dozens of works Tintoretto had executed, the man himself began to appear to him, a great shadowed figure of genius and bottomless energy whose bleak vision seemed ... to penetrate every recess" (199). So James in this first essay on Venice affirms the masculinity of Tintoretto, an artist he synecdochically links to the city, and the effort gains the praise of his daunting literary precursor Ruskin, praise that the younger writer uses to gain his father's approval.

However, in the 1882 essay, as Parkes points out, James aggressively "quarrel[s]" with Ruskin (161). Specifically, James figures Ruskin as a contagion—"Fortunately, one reacts against the Ruskinian contagion, and one hour of the lagoon is worth a hundred pages of demoralized prose" (*Italian Hours*, 8)—and associates his insistent moralizing with the narrow provincialism of a governess—"much of [Ruskin's prose] appears to be addressed to children of tender age. It is pitched in the nursery-key, and might be supposed to emanate from an angry governess" (8). While Venice's association with the East, including its supposed dangerous malarial contagions, add to its seductively dangerous, Oriental strain of femininity for both Symonds and James, here Ruskin is linked to a contagion of narrowly patriarchal moralizing. Similarly, while Venice will provide the feminized, liquid landscape in which Symonds and James can surrender their phallic integrity, here Ruskin is figured as a grotesquely inverted but angrily judgmental governess. In part, through humiliating Ruskin and, by implication, his father, James bonds with Symonds over the 1883 essay. It is also worth pointing out that in 1882 Henry James, Senior, died, and as Kelley Cannon points out, James for the first time dropped the term "Junior" (128). Partially shaking off the name of the father, James reaches out to a homosexual predecessor through the mediation of an essay on Venice.

Parkes also points out that when James reprinted his Venetian essays in *Italian Hours*, published in 1909, he muddled the chronology. The collection begins with the 1882 essay; the 1873 essay will appear third in the travel anthology. For Parkes, the primacy given the 1882 essay in the book's arrangement indicates the importance that James gave to distancing himself from Ruskin (149). This is a convincing reading as far as an Oedipal account goes, but one could also plausibly read the temporal reversal as a sodomitic gesture. Lee Edelman has argued that sodomy has long been culturally linked to a preposterous temporal confusion—just as a sodomite supposedly confuses what lies in front with what lies behind, so, too, he is culturally perceived as one who conflates what should come before with what comes after (183). James repeatedly shows an endearingly perverse skepticism about the relationship between what supposedly lies before and what comes after. In fact, in "The Author of 'Beltraffio,'" the narrator seems proleptically to stumble upon what Freud will theorize as deferred action, or *Nachtraglichkeit*, in the Wolf Man case history, written a good twenty-six years after "The Author of 'Beltraffio.'" In the tale, the narrator perceptively recognizes how difficult it is to insulate past and present, how difficult it is to avoid projecting onto the past things subsequently discovered: "In looking back upon these first moments of my visit, I find it important to avoid the error of appearing to have fully measured the situation from the first or made out the signs of things mastered only afterwards. This later knowledge throws a backward light " (71). James, as Sedgwick has pointed out, deeply imaginatively invested in anal pleasure ("Inside Henry Ja: 131–132), in arranging his Italian essays, temporally reversed them in order to give priority to a later essay on Venice, a city he associated with passive anality, one, moreover, which he used to bond with his pederastic precursor Symonds.

Thus far we have opposed Symonds to James's father. However, Henry's brother William James was in many ways a more daunting representative of paternal authority than Henry James's literal father. Cannon points out that James "perceived his father as someone amputated both physically and emotionally" (127). By contrast, "Henry James saw his elder brother as forever outdoing him. He wrote that his brother 'had gained such an advantage of me, in his sixteen months' experience of the world before mine began that I never for all the ties of childhood and youth in the least caught up with him or overtook him'" (Cannon, 129; James quotation from *Letters* 4, 59). Further, the age difference between Henry James and Symonds was much closer to that between Henry and William James, than that between Henry and his father—Symonds was born in 1840, so he was about three years older than Henry James; William was about one and half years older than his brother. It is not surprising that Henry should use William as a foil in denigrating Symonds.

One way in which William James made Henry feel inadequate was by commenting on his effeminacy. For instance, Novick points out that "in William's last letters to Henry, after remarking on how Henry James seemed to be settled on the 'gilded and snobbish heights of Paris, he admired the manly English and deprecated the effeminate French influence on Henry's letters" (505). William's critique must have resonated with Henry James, who clearly had internalized his own version of this gendered nationalist myth, associating England with virility and the continent, and Italy, in particular, with passive pleasure. In a letter to his sister Alice, Henry writes, "To live in England ... you have somehow to draw more heavily on your manhood ... than in other countries—how much more, alas, than in sweet relaxing Italy. But I wish my pen had the power to make you feel the land as I felt it this evening" (Henry James in an unpublished letter, February 27, 1870, qtd. in Novick, 220). Henry's letter reveals his complex resistance to, and investment in, William's suspicion of continental effeminacy and passivity. On the one hand, writing to his sister, Henry undercuts the values of his brother and father by affirming "sweet relaxing Italy," as opposed to England where one has to draw more heavily on one's manhood. On the other hand, when James declares in the next sentence that his "pen" does not have "the power" to represent Italy's ineffable charms, at an unconscious level he seems to be confirming William's judgment. "Sweet relaxing Italy" has sapped the power from his artistic "pen."

Even when William is affectionately joking about his relationship with Henry, the accusation of effeminacy, and an effeminacy associated with the Continent and Italy in particular, often hovers in the air. For instance, writing from Rome to their brother Wilkie, William jokes, "At present Henry is my spouse ... " (286). Such a statement is undoubtedly flirtatious, and Sedgwick, among others, has rightly pointed out that there was a strong homoerotic bond between William and Henry, as evidenced in part by their obsessive and fascinated correspondence on supposed shared anal maladies ("Inside Henry James," 131–132). But the flirting precariously coexists with the threat of emasculation—to put it simplistically, Italy has emasculated Henry; hence, in Rome, he can be described as William's "spouse," the third feminized term in an epistolary homosocial triangle among brothers.

Henry's decision to live in Europe, some biographers suggest, "represented his attempt to combat all patriarchal influences, particularly that of his brother" (Cannon, 130). According to Novick, Henry found William's rare visits to Europe traumatic. When William visited Henry in Rome in 1873, he left Henry ostensibly for health reasons and moved to Florence. Henry joined his brother in Florence but resented leaving Rome and disclosed that resentment in a letter to Alice, "I wish I could portray for your sisterly soul the emotions of one who is called upon suddenly in midwinter to substitute Florence the meager for Rome the magnificent. [To] wake up and see the dirty ice floating down the prosy Arno ... this is a trial to test the most angelic philosophy" (Henry James qtd. in Novick, 288). Note the role that water plays in this half-joking complaint. If Henry associates the feminizing, seductive charms of Italy with water, paradigmatically the canals of Venice, it is the visit of his patriarchal brother that forces him to move by a "prosy river" which has "dirty ice" floating down it.

Novick describes how William left with enormous haste "without any further explanation and went north to Germany. He visited Dresden briefly and then returned to the United States ... He appeared to believe that Henry would be following him shortly" (Novick, 288). According to Novick, Henry used William's disapproving visit to Italy in a transmuted form in various works, including *The American*. Indeed, several of the brothers' mutual friends recognized aspects of William in Mr. Babcock (Novick, 289). In the novel, Mr. Babcock leaves Italy abruptly and writes a letter to Christopher Newman explaining his abrupt departure: "I am afraid my conduct at Venice a week ago seemed strange and ungrateful ... I have a high sense of responsibility. You seem to call only for the pleasure of the hour and you give yourself up to it with a violence which I confess I am not able to emulate" (581). Note how Henry transfers the city of fraternal contention from Rome to Venice, which becomes associated with a Pateresque (see appendix on *Marius the Epicurean*) reveling in the pleasures of the hour and a certain violent passivity ("you give yourself up to [pleasure]"). That this passivity is feminizing is further suggested in the novel in the discussion between Christopher Newman and Mr. Tristram. The moment Newman evinces interest in Venice, the commonsensical American businessman suggests that the young man needs to meet Mrs. Tristram, as though Venice properly belongs in the feminine realm:

> "Oh I want to see ... a lot of places. Venice in particular. I have great ideas ... about Venice."
> "Ah," said Mr. Tristram rising, "I see I shall have to introduce you to my wife" [537–538].

Mr. Tristram's curt response abruptly cuts off his long dialogue with Newman and ends chapter II, almost as though Newman's symbolic feminization is being mirrored in a literary, formal castration. Newman does indeed identify with women, and again that identification is figured in aquatic terms, terms that resonate with Venice: "Newman was fond under all circumstances of the society of women ... He was simply swimming in a sea of rapture" (541). In fictionally reworking William's visit to Italy, Henry represents him as a force that obstructs the liquid, feminizing pleasures that he associates with Venice.[9]

It makes a certain perverse sense, then, that in dismissing Symonds, Henry should turn to William. Thus, in his letter to William he describes Symonds rather condescendingly as "a mild cultured man with the Oxford perfume."[10] "Perfume" has feminine connotations, and later in the same letter, James half-jokingly and half-flirtatiously will evoke his intimacy with a patriarchal Victorian sage in order to make William envious and implicitly to distance himself from feminized Symonds: "I often take an afternoon nap beside Herbert Spencer at the Athaneum, and I feel as if I am robbing *you* of the privilege" (*Letters II*, 102). Henry tells us in his autobiography that as a boy, William would reject his younger brother's company, declaring, "I play with boys who curse and swear" (*Autobiography*, 147, Henry James's emphasis). It's highly unlikely that the Victorian sage Spencer ever cursed or swore, but he is being used by Henry as a signifier for an idealized virility, as opposed to the ineffectual femininity represented by Symonds.

Ironically, years later, in 1907, responding to *The American Scene* and criticizing what he saw as Henry's affected style, William appropriates his brother's metaphor of perfume: "For gleams and innuendos and felicitous verbal insinuations you are unapproachable, but the *core* of literature is solid ... The bare perfume of things will not support existence, and the effect of solidity you reach is but perfume and simulacrum" (William James qtd. in Edel, 616; emphasis William's). William insinuates that, unable to reach the phallic solidity of reality, Henry relies on the feminizing artifice of a perfumed style. Clearly, the charge of male effeminacy is a highly mobile and dangerous one. The strategy of labeling another man as effeminate in an attempt to prove one's masculine credentials does not insulate one from having that charge leveled at oneself in turn.

While "perfume" has feminine connotations, the qualifying adjective "Oxford" also obliquely evokes the odor of sodomy. Linda Dowling has explored the passionate, if most often sublimated, male homoerotic bonds between mentors and pupils that prevailed at Oxford in the nineteenth century, bonds that were sustained by a passionate commitment to classical Greek culture, and the work of Plato in particular. Symonds, Dowling explains, was a key figure in that tradition; a passionate student of Benjamin Jowett, the works of Plato epitomized for him the refining spiritual qualities of Hellenic pederasty (67). However, the role that Hellenism occupied in British male homosocial culture was an unstable one; one was expected to affirm the spiritual qualities of male bonds but repudiate the carnal vices of the Greeks, and as Dowling points out, by the end of his life Symonds would reproach Jowett for the cruelly repressive double bind in which the culture of Oxford placed male homosexuals who wanted physically to realize their desires (89). The vicious, if witty, association of Oxonian Hellenism with "the higher sodomy" would come long after Symonds and James's meeting, after the scandal of the Wilde trials. However, even in the 1870s, there was a muted connection between reprobated sodomy and the refining "Oxford perfume."

Symonds miscalculated how far one could go in affirming the Platonic tradition. His 1873 scholarly work *The Study of Greek Poets* scandalously desublimated the Hellenic tradition, incarnating it in the figure of a beautiful young Greek wrestler untouched by the pain of guilt of a Judaeo-Christian tradition, "Like a young man newly come from the wrestling ground, anointed, chapleted and very calm the Genius of the Greeks appears before us. Upon his soul there is no burden of the world's pain; the whole creation that groaneth and travaileth together, has touched him with no sense of anguish; nor he yet felt sin" (399). In that same text, Symonds celebrates Walt Whitman as being "more truly Greek than any man of modern times" (422). Dowling and Richard Dellamora have explored how Symonds's miscalculation cost him the Oxford professorship of poetry. In 1877, the year of James and Symonds's meeting, Richard St. John Tyrwhitt attacked "The Greek Spirit in Modern Literature." As Dowling points out, Tyrwhitt elaborately assured his audience that "Mr. Symonds is probably the most innocent of men," being fully aware that Symonds had been "falsely accused ... of having corrupted Magdalen College choirboys" and probably recognizing that his readers would make the connection between that scandal and the coy adverb "probably." Tyrwhitt then goes on bluntly to link sodomy and Platonic Hellenism, the "emotions of Socrates at the sight of the beauty of young Charmides are not natural: and it is well known that the Greek love of nature and beauty went frequently against nature" (St. John Tyrwhitt qtd. in Dowling, 91). Whether James literally read the review or not, the association of sodomy and Oxonian Hellenism was in the cultural air in 1877, so when James dismisses Symonds as having an "Oxford perfume" he is by implication condemning his sodomitic practices and distancing himself from those practices to gain the approval of patriarchal William.

In working out his ideas for "The Author of 'Beltraffio'" James also undercuts the Hellenic tradition that Symonds affirms. Based on their reading of Plato's *Symposium*, Oxonian Platonists like Symonds valorized the spiritual procreancy of ideas generated between men over the mere physical reproduction characterizing relations between men and women. James, in sketching out the plan for his tale, characterizes the relationship between Symonds and his wife as follows: "the opposition between the narrow, cold Calvinistic wife, a rigid moralist; and the husband impregnated—even to morbidness with the spirit of Italy, the love of beauty" (*Notebooks*, 25). We have moved from the language of Plato to the pathologizing language of sexology: Symonds is not impregnated with Greek ideals; he is impregnated with a morbid aesthetic passion for Italy.

Of Postcards—Venetian and Otherwise

James, in his letter to William, tries to make Symonds completely other; he is an emasculated man ("mild") redolent of Oxford's sodomitic perfume. And yet the sodomitic perfume of Venice fascinates James, and it is precisely the shared passion for Venice that binds James and Symonds. James repeatedly associates Venice both with sublime beauty and with "queer smells," sliminess, dirt, and a miasmic atmospheric denseness. He tells us in the essay he shared with Symonds that rather than associating the name of Venice with "the Great Square" or "St. Mark's,"

> I simply see a narrow canal in the heart of the city—a patch of green water and a surface of pink wall.... The pink of the old wall seems to fill the whole place; it sinks even into the opaque water. Behind the wall is garden out of which the long arm of a white June rose ... has flung itself by way of spontaneous ornament. On the other side of this small water-way is a great shabby façade of Gothic windows and balconies—balconies on which dirty clothes are hung and under which a cavernous looking doorway opens from a low flight of slimy water-steps.... the canal has a queer smell, and the whole place is enchanting [*Italian Hours*, 297].

While one might imagine that the "white June rose" would stand in opposition to the dirt, slime, and queer smell, it is clear that the two are, in fact, associated. Venice's enchantment lies precisely in its combination of the June rose's vitality and an alluringly anal landscape. Note the spatial insistence on that which lies behind and below; note, too, the insistence on dirt and queer smells; the scene is redolent of the disavowed Oxford perfume. To reach the seductive "narrow canal" and the "heart of the city," James's "gondola" "gives a great smooth swerve." Perversely swerving from the norm, traversing through the narrow canal, evocative of a tight rectal passage, one finds one's way to the "enchanting" "dirt," "slime," and "queer smell" of Venice.[11]

In James's earliest essay on Venice, dirt and slime also make an appearance, and here also are linked to a seductive passivity:

> The mere use of one's eyes in Venice is happiness enough, and generous observers find it hard to keep an account of their profits in this line. Everything the attention touches holds it, keeps playing with it.... Your brown skinned, white shirted gondolier, twisting himself in the light, seems to you, as you lie in contemplation beneath your awning, a perpetual symbol of Venetian "effect." ... You should see in places the material with which [Venetian light] deals—slimy brick, marble battered and befouled, rags, dirt, decay [*Italian Hours*, 237].

The image of the "brown skinned, white-shirted gondolier" might seem to belong to a familiar imperialistic tourist gaze. However, James's passive voice prose refuses to allow us to imagine a masterful male subject gazing at an objectified Venetian. The appropriative "your" is undercut by the fact that the owner of the gondola is the object of the sentence, "Your gondolier ... seems to you," and he lies passively, contemplatively below the figure of the upright gondolier. Truly enjoying the dangerously dirty pleasures of Venice seems to involve phallic dispossession, a surrender to an abjected anality.

Even Tintoretto, whose virile clarity James celebrates elsewhere in *Italian Hours* cannot escape the seductive anality of Venice. At the Scuola di San Rocco, the Tintoretto pictures are in disrepair; they have "turned to blackness and are positively rotting in their frames.... Solemn indeed is the place ... for the simple reason that we shall scarcely find four walls elsewhere that enclose within a like area an *equal* quantity of genius. The air is thick with it and dense and difficult to breathe" (306). While James is ostensibly bemoaning the deterioration of Tintoretto's pictures, there is an erotic energy to his description of that thick, enveloping, deadly atmosphere of genius. Here Tintoretto is associated not with clarity and light but with a seductive deathly anality. Elsewhere in the Venetian essays James will suffer Oedipal anxieties about the impossibility of saying anything original about Venice. But here he does not want to escape Tintoretto; he wants to sink into that enveloping, miasmic atmosphere of genius, allow himself to be taken over, dispossessed by his great artistic precursor.

While Symonds and James bond over Venice, the imagery that James uses to describe that shared intimacy is evocative of homosexual cruising rather than the male homosocial exchange of a mediating woman. Thanking Symonds for his praise of the 1882 Venetian essay, James wrote,

> I sent [my 1882 essay on Venice] to you because it was a constructive way of expressing the good will I felt for you in consequence of what you have written about the land of Italy—and of intimating to you, somewhat dumbly, that I ... nourish for the said Italy an unspeakably tender passion.... it seemed to me that the victims of a common passion should sometimes exchange a look [*Letters III*, 29–30].

The "unspeakably tender passion" that Symonds and James share for Italy, and Venice in particular, evokes the idiom of sodomy, traditionally described by the periphrasis that love which might not be spoken among Christians. This description would be invoked and partially transvalued by Symonds in *A Problem in Modern Ethics*: "There is a passion, or perversion of appetite, which like all human passions, has played a considerable part in the world's history.... Yet no one dares to speak of it.... surely it deserves a name" (79–80)—and would be further majestically transformed by Wilde at his second trial in which he eloquently defended the love that dare not speak its name. The intimately shared look also suggestively draws on the Platonic homoerotic tradition, which is so salient to Symonds's theorizing of male same-sex love. Italy allows the two men to gaze through the optical windows into each other's souls. Note, though, that, while the two men actively exchange a look, they are "victims of a common passion." Venice's "unspeakably tender passion" seems to deprive them of control.

Fittingly, when James wants to distance himself from Symonds, he will return to a visual metaphor. Responding to Edmund Gosse's news about Symonds's death, James writes in April 1893, "poor forevermore silent J. A. S. I had never even (clearly) seen him—but somehow I, too, can't help feeling the news with a pang—and with a personal emotion. It almost seemed as if I *might* know him" (*Letters III*, 409; James's emphasis). On the one hand, James acknowledges the "pang" he feels at the loss of Symonds; on the other, the look they shared over Venice is disavowed. Not only does James deny visual intimacy, he also turns Symonds into the object of his gaze. Symonds becomes an object that James was unable to see; or, perhaps, the cagey parenthesis concedes, was unable to see "clearly." In characteristically ambivalent fashion, James simultaneously wants to disavow his bond with Symonds and gesture toward an imaginary homoerotic intimacy (note the biblical sexual overtones to the verb "know"), hedged in by qualifiers and the subjunctive, "It *almost seemed* as if I *might* know him" (409).

There is a distinct tension between James's desire to portray Symonds as a mere object for epistemological investigation, the cool tonal irony that Edel notes, and an unseemly betrayal of how his own desire is implicated with that investigation. When James learned that Arthur Benson was writing on Symonds, leaving "the disagreeable side out," he responded with a joking fictional mini-dialogue, "Symonds Without the Key" (Kaplan, 539). The title suggests that James has the "key" to Symonds if he chose to disclose it, and his metaphor resonates with the discourse of scientistic mastery in the late nineteenth and early twentieth centuries. Wayne Koestenbaum has explored how important the key metaphor was for Symonds's collaborator on *Sexual Inversion*, Havelock Ellis. Ellis saw himself as a disinterested scientist unlocking the mystery of sexual inversion through examining and objectifying Symonds (48), and in a similar vein, Jane Gallop has shown how important the metaphor was for Freud in disavowing his counter transference onto Dora. In possession of the phallic key to Symonds, James would seem to be masterfully in control.[12] That sense of mastery also comes across in James's discussion of "The Author of 'Beltraffio'" in his *Notebooks*. Symonds is portrayed there purely as a literary problem, a representational challenge for a great artist: "I think I shall try it [representing Symonds's aesthetic differences with his wife]; for the general idea is full of interest and very typical of certain modern situations" (25). The artist will take the challenge of moving beyond the particularity of Symonds's situation to capture an idea typical of certain modern situations. Symonds is merely data, raw material for the artist.

Note, however, how much more unstable and ambivalent the tone of James's 1884 letter to Gosse is. Gosse had written to congratulate James on his tale, and James responds genially and expansively, "I am delighted you see some life in it and have an appetite for the rest." As a disinterested artist, he draws back and objectively evaluates his work, "the 2d part is better written than the 1st, and I agree with you in thinking the thing is more solid than many of my things.... But I shall do better yet" (Horne, 157). The tale is solidly written (no vaporous perfumes or Venetian wateriness here), and the master is confident that he can do better yet. The tone shifts in the postscript, though, and this is particularly significant because poststructuralist readers recognize the importance of that which is supposedly an afterthought, a mere supplement, for as Jacques Derrida has pointed out in *Of Grammatology*, the supplement has the power to call into question and displace the structure to which it is supposedly ancillary. In the postscript James writes, "Perhaps I have divined the innermost cause of J. A. S.'s discomfort—but I don't think I seize, on page 571, exactly the allusion you refer to. I am devoured with curiosity as to this further revelation. Even a post-card (in covert words) would relieve the suspense of the perhaps-already-too-indiscreet—HJ" (Horne, 157). If in the body of the letter it is Gosse and we readers who have an appetite for the artist's transmutation of Symonds's particular situation, here we have James "devoured with curiosity" regarding further revelations about "JAS." With Sedgwick, we should recall the importance of alimentary/excremental metaphors for James's figuring of homoeroticism ("Inside Henry James," 131–132). James's curiosity here is involved in a dispossessing, emasculating homoerotic desire. Note, too, that in the postscript the identification between Henry James and Symonds is underlined by the two sets of initials, "JAS" and "HJ." The masterful observing artist "Henry James," the signature at the end of the letter, becomes "HJ," a figure whose desires are complicit with the object of his investigation, "JAS."

James tells Gosse that "*even* a post-card" would help assuage his curiosity, but I would go further and suggest that a postcard is a particularly apt genre for discussing male same-sex desire. As Derrida points out in *The Postcard*, postcards are "half-private, half-public, neither the one, nor the other" (62), a monstrously hybrid construction similar to homosexuality. At times, James tries desperately to keep some writing on homosexuality private and secret to protect himself. Deciding to return Gosse's copy of Symonds's *A Problem of Modern Ethics* at the height of the Wilde trial, James writes to Gosse, "these are days in which one's modesty is in every direction much exposed, and one should be thankful for every veil that one can hastily snatch up.... It is strictly congruous with these remarks that I should mention that there go to you tomorrow a. m. in two registered envelopes, at 1 Whitehall the fond outpourings of poor J. A. S." (Bradley, 89). However, as though impelled to raise the veil slightly, James then scribbles a message in French regarding Wilde on the back of the envelope. Like a postcard, the writing on the back of the envelope straddles the borders of public and private. Just as the supposed private secret of homosexuality is in fact a cultural construction predicated upon the public/private division, so too James's writing about homosexuality constitutes a kind of postcard straddling the boundaries between the private enclosed space within the envelope and public discourse. Just as the meanings attached to the forbidden, supposedly deeply private pleasures associated with the backside are cultural constructions, so too James's French postscript on the back of the envelope is intricately connected with the discourse surrounding male homosexuality that can be written in public.[13]

The postscript at the back of the envelope reads "Quel Dommage, mais quell Bonheur—que J. A. S. ne soit plus de ce monde?" which Horne translates as "What a shame—but what a relief—that J. A. S. should no longer be in the world" (Horne, 280). French, it turns out, allows one tentatively to broach issues relating to the love that supposedly dare not speak its name. Critics like Richard Ellman and Jonathan Freedman have pointed to James's intense disidentification from Wilde. James notoriously described Wilde as "an unclean beast." And even though that description resonates at an unconscious level with his fascination with the filthy delights of Venice, at a conscious level it is an energetic distancing from Wilde. At the back of the envelope, though, James uses the figure of dead Symonds to insinuate a connection to Wilde.[14] Symonds, whom James has sometimes used as a foil to patriarchal precursors, now becomes a mediating figure who allows James to make the most tentative of gestures of connection to other homosexual men. James, his correspondent Gosse, and Wilde, the object of their correspondence, all occupy the vexed space of the closet, and it is through the figure of the dead Symonds that James is able to hint that there is any connection among them. This is a far cry from Graham's view of James embracing the logic of identity politics and affiliating himself with the views of Symonds and men like him, but it is a limited gesture of connection, the kind of limited gesture allowed by the cramped space of a postcard or the back of an envelope.

Gosse was probably far too discreet to send James a postcard regarding Symonds, and yet in a way, "The Author of 'Beltraffio'" itself might be regarded as a Jamesian postcard, approaching the question of Symonds's heterodox desires through an idiom that is both complicit with and slightly different from the norm. Specifically, this Jamesian postcard shares the broader culture's ambivalence about male homosexuality's relation to gender difference. Gender separatist paradigms of male homosexuality see the homosexual as a quintessential man in flight from the constraints of feminizing domesticity. Clearly, this mythology has great power for James. One repeated fantasy in his works is the idea of an all male family that can provide an alternative to the Oedipal nuclear family. In this configuration, the constraining power of the law gets aligned with a phallic woman, and the liberating possibilities of beauty and intimacy are shared among men. In "The Author of 'Beltraffio,'" the narrator, Mark Ambient, and Ambient's beautiful son Dolcino, form an erotic triangle that is repeatedly figured in terms of shared visual intimacy: at one point in the tale, Ambient and his wife approach the narrator. Ambient is carrying his son Dolcino, and the boy is gazing at his mother. As they approach the narrator, "Dolcino twisted himself about. His enchanting eyes showed me a smile of recognition" (96). The language of turning—"twisted about"—evokes the idioms of perversion and inversion, and yet the tale idealizes the bond among Ambient, Dolcino, and the narrator. The truly perverse tie is that between the phallic mother Beatrice and her son. Another idealized glance is shared among men a few pages later: after Ambient describes Dolcino as "agreeable," the boy's "exaggerated eyes" ("exaggerated" has the overtone of flirtation) "caught [the narrator's] own as I watched him. 'Do you think me agreeable?' he enquired with the candour of his age and with a look that made his father turn around to me laughing and ask, without saying it, 'Isn't he adorable?'" (99). Just as James and Symonds share an intimate look over mediating Venice, here Dolcino and the narrator's shared look affectively bind the narrator, Ambient, and Dolcino.

At one point in the tale, the narrator offers to rescue Dolcino from the murderous tug of war between husband and wife, and Mark Ambient responds positively to the offer, "'You had better give him to me to keep for you,' I said. 'Let me remove the apple of discord!'.... he had the air of being perfectly serious. 'It would be quite the best thing we could do'" (73). While they are discussing, setting up this alternative male family, Ambient's "expressive eyes" were "looking straight into mine" (73).[15] This fantasy of a male rescuer will reappear in a later James tale, "The Pupil." In this tale, as Cannon points out, the father is a deeply inadequate, almost absent figure, quite unlike the seductive Mark Ambient. But here also, young tutor Pemberton offers the young boy Morgan an escape from the murderously limiting constraints of his vulgar mother: "'We ought to go off and live somewhere together,' the young man said. 'I'll go like a shot if you take me'" (545).[16]

Even the intertextual allusions in the tale evoke an idealized male community. For instance, the narrator compares Mark Ambient to Quentin Durward (61). The protagonist of Sir Walter Scott's novel is deeply committed to a patriarchal code of chivalry that is dying out, and his disillusionment with the calculating Louis XI is figured as a form of filial disappointment. Quentin is equally horrified by the Duke of Gueldres, "who keeps his own father imprisoned, and ... he has even struck him" (70). Significantly, Scott opens the novel with an epigraph from *Hamlet*: "Look here upon the picture, and on this / The counterfeit presentment of two brothers" (39). Just as Hamlet mourns an idealized dead father, so Quentin Durward, confronted by Claudius-like Louis XI and the impious parricidal standards of contemporary France, mourns the debased standards of patriarchal chivalry, and so also Ambient, the narrator, and Dolcino long to flee to an idealized all male realm of pederasty, where fathers and sons, *erastes* and *eromenoi*, can escape the debased, feminized world represented by Beatrice Ambient or Gertrude, even though the forms of debasement that the two women represent are clearly very different. (Beatrice is linked to a deadly asceticism and Gertrude to an excessive female carnality.)

In this idealized male community, aesthetic value is associated with traditionally phallic qualities. The narrator represents his beloved Ambient's artistry in terms that evoke penetration and a certain autoerotic self-sufficiency: "To sink your shaft deep and polish the plate through which people look into it—that's what your work consists of" (88). Ambient responds by extolling the qualities of hardness and firmness in great art: "Life's really too short for art. One hasn't time to make one's shell ideally hard. Firm and bright, firm and bright" (88). The murky, liquid pleasures of Venice have no place in this male homosexual aesthetic community.

James's male separatist family myth resonates with Symonds's own apologies for male homosexuality. In *A Problem in Greek Ethics*, Symonds affirms the "masculine passion" of Hellenic pederasty (51). He strives sharply to distinguish it from the "effeminacies, brutalities, and gross sensualities which can be noticed alike in imperfectly civilized and in luxuriously corrupt communities" (19). Symonds uses the term "sexual inversion" in his subtitle, "An Inquiry into the Phenomenon of Sexual Inversion," but he uses it to describe object choice, not to describe the nature of the homosexual subject. In other words, he is not interested in the third sex paradigm promoted by figures like Ulrichs. He does not conceptualize same-sex desire in terms of gender inversion; he is primarily interested in the mutually virile bonds between men, whether they are coevals or share an age difference, and strives to insulate that desire from any form of effeminacy. In a rather moving passage in *Studies of Greek Poets*, Symonds refers to Greece as a "lost fatherland" (144). Like Symonds, in the tale James seems to hold out the offer of an all male community, a fatherland, but Greece does not have the same salience for him as it does for Symonds. It is true that Mrs. Ambient perceives Mark Ambient as "no better than an ancient Greek" (90). But neither Ambient nor the narrator appeals specifically to a Hellenic pederastic tradition. A significant moment in the short story "The Pupil" suggests why James is more reluctant to turn to Greece than Symonds. In the tale, Morgan looks up "the Greek for awful whopper" in a "Greek lexicon. He used Greek-German—to look for a word instead of asking it of Pemberton" (536). This passage indicates James's self-consciousness about the complicated mediation by which one inevitably encounters Greece. There is no shared lost fatherland which Pemberton and Morgan can turn to; multiple layers of cultural and linguistic mediation lie between them and that mythic fatherland. In a complex Jamesian universe, there is no truth to be recovered in a lost Hellenic fatherland, only multiple "whoppers," culturally mediated imaginative reconstructions of the past, whether it be the classical Hellenic past, which is so important to Symonds, or the mythologized version of Italy which is so important to both Symonds and himself.

In the Jamesian inversion of the Oedipal myth, it is the mother, Mrs. Ambient, who blocks the formation of a forbidden male separatist erotic community. Mrs. Ambient's phallic consistency is emphasized. Mark Ambient's sister gives the narrator the following tautology, "Beatrice is always ... Beatrice" (108). Another indication of her phallic integrity is her insistence on maintaining rigid, distinct boundaries even between the words she speaks, "These declarations fell successively and very distinctly from Mrs. Ambient's lips" (66). Beatrice's rigid consistency ends up petrifying her lively, vital little son. It is particularly ironic, of course, that she be named Beatrice. In texts like In a Key of Blue, Symonds developed an extended analogy between Dante's idealized Platonic love of Beatrice and Hellenic pederasty, but this Beatrice is anything but a representative of an idealized Platonic spirit. The irony works both ways: its misogynistic ally phallicizes Mrs. Ambient, but it also undercuts the Platonism that informs Symonds's male separatist mythology.

Mrs. Ambient is represented as blocking her son's intimacy with other men. For instance, when Mark calls his son, using language that has erotic overtones, "Dolcino, come and see your daddy" (62, my emphasis), Mrs. Ambient responds by clinging to Dolcino. Similarly, when the narrator offers "to carry [Dolcino] and opened my arms for the purpose" "she turned away with the child in her embrace ... so I never laid a longing hand on Dolcino" (101–102). As Mark Ambient points out, Mrs. Ambient "won't let [Dolcino] come to other men" (63), but James shrewdly recognizes that prohibition can be a form of eroticism also: "Dolcino struggled in the maternal embrace; but too tightly held, he after two or three fruitless efforts jerked about and buried his head deep in his mother's lap" (63). One might read this description as indicating that Mrs. Ambient derives a certain erotic pleasure from her maternal protectiveness, but one could also read this image as indicating that structurally this Jamesian inverted Oedipal myth needs the figure of the phallic mother prohibiting homoerotic desire to generate an erotic frisson. Mrs. Ambient, who is represented as blocking male homoerotic desire, may be structurally needed to facilitate a Jamesian myth of homoerotic desire.

Like James and Symonds, Ambient and the narrator share a passion for Italy. It is the narrator's "visit to Italy" that "opened my eyes to ... the beauty of certain pages in the works of Mark Ambient" (58). The phrase "opened my eyes" might remind us of the shared glance of textual intimacy between James and Symonds mediated by Italian Hours. And indeed, the tale relies on terms and figures that tantalizingly hint at Venice, James and Symonds's shared passion. For instance, Mark Ambient is described as being "saturated with what painters call the feeling of [Italy]" (58). "Saturated" irresistibly evokes the liquid element of Venice. Again, Ambient is repeatedly associated with knowledge of the East (58), and in characteristically Orientalist fashion, James associates Venice with the mysteriously decadent, feminizing qualities of the East. Even some of the dangerous qualities that Mrs. Ambient associates with her husband's perverse decadence have resonances with the terms that James usually uses to figure Venice. Miss Ambient tells the narrator that Beatrice sees her husband as emanating "a subtle poison or contagion" (84) that will morally corrupt Dolcino, and we have seen how in *Italian Hours*, James associates Venice with a miasmic, poisonous but seductively contagious surrender to passive anality. Despite all these hints of Venice, the city that actually formed the conduit of intimacy between James and Symonds never specifically appears in the tale. Instead, the Italian cities that are explicitly evoked are Rome and Florence (59). The text represses Venice because its liquid feminizing element and its seductive poisonous perfumes threaten to erode the myth of gender separatism that is central to the tale.

James replicates cultural contradictions regarding representations of homosexuality, but he also partially undoes them. In that sense, he is far more self-conscious and distanced from ideology than Symonds is. Mark Ambient's sister, for instance, forms an uncomfortable supplementary term in his tale that throws the gender separatist and integrative division into confusion. She is allied with aestheticism, and yet she cannot be fit into the myth of an all male community fleeing feminizing domesticity. She is a woman, and yet she cannot be pegged as a phallic woman like Beatrice. Aesthetically or formally, she is not effectively integrated into the tale precisely because she troubles, in the productive Butlerian sense of the word, the gender separatist mythology on which the tale relies.

If the character Miss Ambient fails aesthetically, the tale "The Author of 'Beltraffio'" has been condemned by some anti-homophobic critics as failing politically. Colm Toibin disapprovingly comments, "It is astonishing how James managed to withhold his homosexuality from his work.... James could have altered the entire meaning of these two stories ["The Author of 'Beltraffio'" and "The Pupil"] by adding a few sentences, or even a few words" (32). In Toibin's account, James's omission of those "few sentences" or "few words," which would unequivocally signify homosexuality, would politically castrate him. Toibin is reacting to Kaplan, who evaluates the tale very differently as one "of his most powerful short stories." For Kaplan, the tale has more to do with James's psychosexual needs than with his political concerns; the tale "express [es] his homoerotic sensuality that had no other outlet" (301). Kaplan's hydraulic account has uncanny resonances with James's treatment of Symonds; James often figures Symonds's writings, particularly his defense of homosexuality in *A Problem of Modern Ethics* as "outpourings," as though they are expressive emanations, seminal emissions over which he has no control. Unlike Kaplan, Cameron sees a relationship between larger cultural concerns and James's tales, maintaining that "James's marginal males' ... private fantasies are not really private at all, but mirror the wishes of a society too long repressed" (160). None of these critics get it quite right, I would argue, and in order to situate my reading in relation to theirs, I will make a small detour through a reading of a passage in "The Author of 'Beltraffio.'"

When Ambient meets the narrator, "He took me by the hand and said, 'You must be—a—you'" (60). Critics like Toibin want to erase those hyphens and fill in a positive identity. Symonds and James in their accounts ought to identify seamlessly. In their story, the line should unambiguously read "You must be a fellow homosexual," let's say. That identitarian logic resembles the phallic standards of Beatrice Ambient—"Beatrice is always Beatrice."

A humanist reading this passage might gloss it as referring to the irreducible singularity of the narrator. The narrator in such an account would transcend categories, would be irreducibly himself. And yet the tale repeatedly calls into question such humanist pieties. Like Wilde, James suggests that art does not simply mimetically copy experience; rather reality and the categories on which we depend are inescapably culturally mediated, secondary constructions, "It was not the picture, the poem, the fictive page that seemed to me [the narrator] a copy; these things were the originals, and the life of happy and distinguished people was fashioned in their image" (61). I would suggest that we read the blanks or hyphens as indicating the contradictions and tensions that inform the category homosexuality. Unlike Kaplan and Cameron, I neither see the hyphens as a private, compensatory psychosexual outlet for James nor as a liberatory alternative offered to a repressed culture. Looking for a reassuring figure, "Papa, potato, prunes," to cover over those hyphens would be a mistake; it would be equally deluded to try and flee to some space that supposedly dissolves contradictions, a space called Venice, say. Like the aesthetes, that Freedman claims shared "the desire to embrace contradictions, indeed the desire to seek them out the better to play with the possibilities they afforded" (6), we need to read both the constraints and possibilities offered by those hyphens.

Here, I am reminded of James's letter to Gosse, which I quoted earlier, describing his response to Horatio Brown's biography of Symonds: James says he read the biography with "the liveliest—and almost painful—interest." The contradictory myths regarding homosexuality that I am associating with those hyphens both generate pleasure ("liveliest interest") and pain ("almost painful"). They both constrained and enabled bonds between Symonds and James, as, indeed, they continue to constrain and enable the anti-homophobic pleasure and politics of those other late–Victorians, ourselves.[17]

Notes

1. For a fine reading of "The Figure in the Carpet" framed in terms of Lacanian theories of transference see Foster. I am tempted half-jokingly to suggest that "papa, potatoes, and prunes" might not be entirely irrelevant to the Jamesian figure in the carpet. My reading will suggest that James's strain of homoeroticism is informed by complex negative Oedipal currents ("papa"); further, there is the Jamesian Irish connection ("potatoes"?); and there is a growing body of scholarship on the connection between James's life-long problems with constipation and his homoeroticism and theories of artistic production (we are all aware of the deserved reputation of "prunes").

2. Bloom most cogently theorizes his Oedipal theory of literary influence in *The Anxiety of Influence* and *A Map of Misreading*.

3. In *The Anxiety of Influence* Bloom frames the drama in triangular terms, but the triangle is one among two men—"the Poetic Father" and the poet—and a mediating "Muse," the poet's "mother" (37), fitting the Oedipal familial paradigm or perhaps more aptly the male homosocial paradigm theorized by Eve Kosofsky Sedgwick in *Between Men: English Literature and Male Homosocial Desire*.

4. John Bradley rehearses the debate within Jamesian scholarship regarding precisely how physically realized James's homosexuality was (1–30). The general critical consensus is that James probably did not genitally realize his desires. One notable exception is the biographer Sheldon Novick, who argues rather unpersuasively that James had sex with Oliver Wendell Holmes. Undoubtedly, Novick's argument is reductive, but the panic and offense his book provoked in Jamesian scholarly circles is revealing both of the transferential investment critics still have in the master and the degree of homophobia that still energizes traditional scholarship.

5. Curiously, while James in a letter to his brother describes meeting John Addington Symonds at lunch, Fred Kaplan has them meeting for breakfast (178). The error is probably trivial, but given James's love of intricate realist social detail in his fiction, I felt compelled to note it. A historic breakfast meeting in a James novel would probably have a subtly different resonance from a historic lunch.

6. Wendy Graham persuasively suggests that the figure of Mark Ambient in "The Author of 'Beltraffio'" is a composite of John Addington Symonds and Robert Louis Stevenson (32 passim). My focus in this essay is the vexed relationship between James and Symonds, so I do not consider Stevenson's role in the tale's genesis or the admittedly interesting question of why James should not recognize or choose to acknowledge that role. In the essay, I do consider why James chooses to acknowledge Symonds's role in the tale's genesis in his *Notebooks* but implicitly denies the connection in a letter to his brother William.

7. Reading my draft, I was struck with the tonal force with which I criticize Wendy Graham's account of James and Symonds's relationship. While I stand by my critique, perhaps there is some unconscious anxiety of influence tonally energizing that critique; after all, Graham's book has been an influential antihomophobic reconsideration of James. I would prefer not to censor this unseemly trace of anxiety, for it reveals my complicity with James's anxieties.

8. While I am greatly indebted to Parkes's fine account of James's revisionary treatment of Ruskin, Parkes sometimes does not read sufficiently closely. For instance, commenting on James's account of Tintoretto "whose indefatigable hand

never drew a line that was not, as one may say, a moral line," Parkes declares that James's line sounds "thoroughly Ruskinian" (160). However, he does not pick up on the equivocation ("as one may say" coyly refuses directly to affirm—and negation—"never drew a line that was not moral" might logically translate into the formulation "always drew moral lines," but with its insistent foregrounding of the negative hardly has the same rhetorical effect as the affirmative translation) of James's characteristically cagey syntax. To me, James's syntax suggests that he has a more ambivalent distance from Ruskin even in the first Venetian essay than Parkes's account allows.

9. While James usually tends to associate fluidity with femininity and hence associates Venice with a feminizing strain of homosexuality, water plays a somewhat different role in his essay on Shakespeare's *The Tempest*. In that exercise in transferential Bardolatry, James, drawing on and transforming the speech "full fathom five thy father lies," figures Shakespeare as a submerged father, an artist who takes the risk of submerging his personality in his characters. However, the liquid element that entombs Shakespeare is his perfect style, so rather than dispossessing him, his oceanic grave confirms his transcendent mastery: "In *The Tempest* ... there is no violence; [Shakespeare] sinks as deep as we like, but what he sinks into, beyond all else, is the lucid stillness of his style" (301). On the one hand, Shakespeare has absolute mastery submerged in the lucid stillness of his style; on the other, his mastery depends on his being entombed, serenely masterfully entombed, no doubt, but still entombed. Thus, James in the act of celebrating the Bard's mastery also wreaks Oedipal violence on him.

10. Ironically, while Henry uses the adjective "mild" to insinuate to William that Symonds lacks nerve, we know from Symonds's *Memoirs* that in the same year he met James he had sex with a man for the first time, at considerable legal and emotional risk to himself: in February 1877 after, significantly, giving a lecture on Italy, Symonds went "to a male brothel near the Regent's Park Barracks" and later that afternoon had sex "with a brawny young soldier" (*Memoirs*, 253). Like Symonds, the young James was drawn to soldiers, and "one afternoon [in 1864, Henry James and Sargent Perry] went 'to a vast gathering of invalid and convalescent troops under canvas and in roughly improvised shanties' on the Rhode Island shore, at Portsmouth Grove. There, Henry talked with the men, strolled with them, sat by the improvised couches 'of their languid rest.' He drew from 'each his troubled tale,' and emptied his pockets for them of whatever cash he had" (Edel, 57). James connected the incident with Whitman's nurturing visits to the troops; however, I think there are also affinities between Symonds's visit to the male brothel and James's visit to the hospital. Both Symonds and James seem to derive an erotic frisson from giving soldiers money, but while Symonds goes on to enjoy a physical encounter with a soldier, James is too mild, perhaps, to risk the entanglement of physical intimacy.

11. My account of James's association of Venice with the passive pleasures of sodomy is indebted to Colleen Lamos's fine account of Proust's similar erotic investments in Venice.

12. James uses the metaphor of the phallic key more complexly elsewhere. In *Hawthorne*, for instance, he implies that Hawthorne's discretion in displaying his authorial key adds to his stature as an artist: "[Hawthorne] has all the ease ... of a regular dweller in the moral psychological realm, he goes to and fro in it, as a man who knows his way. His tread is a light and modest one, but he keeps the key in

his pocket" (51). In his introduction to the New York Edition of *The Wings of the Dove*, James complicatedly dephallicizes the metaphor of the key: "it was ... my 'key' ... that though my regenerate New Yorker [Milly] and what might depend on her should form my center, my circumference was every whit as treatable ... one began, in the event with the outer ring, approaching the center thus by narrowing circumvallations" (qtd. in Sedgwick, "Inside Henry James," 135). Here James both denaturalizes the metaphor of the key, enclosing it in scare quotation marks and then goes on to transform the key into an image of multiplicity that somehow embraces center and circumference.

13. The metaphorics of letters and letter writing also play an intricate role in James's complex relationship with his precursor Hawthorne. Criticizing Hawthorne's notebooks, James snidely writes, "the simplest way to describe the tone of these extremely objective journals is to say that they read like a series of very pleasant, though rather dullish and decidedly formal letters addressed to himself by a man who, having suspicions that they might be opened in the post, should have determined to insert nothing compromising" (33). James might dangerously negotiate the space between public and private in the space of a postcard, but Hawthorne in this reading refuses to compromise himself. And yet, James figures *The Scarlet Letter* as a missive that he receives in the mail from his precursor: "He [the young James] was too young to read it himself, but the title upon which he fixed his eyes as it lay upon the table had a mysterious charm. He had a vague belief indeed that the 'letter' in question was one of the documents that had come by the post" (87). If James as a child imagined that the scarlet A had been sent to him in the mail by Hawthorne, we might think of *Hawthorne* as a reply of his precursor, a letter that is simultaneously affectionate and Oedipally energized by the need to displace his precursor and leave America behind (to move beyond A, as it were) as he embarks on a cosmopolitan authorial career.

14. In "The Author of 'Beltraffio,'" Wilde makes an indirect appearance through the figure of paradox. Ambient and the narrator "sat and smoked on stiles broaching paradoxes" (86). In *De Profundis*, Wilde notoriously linked his sexual transgressions to his taste for paradox: "What paradox was to me in the sphere of thought, perversity became to me in the sphere of passion" (466). Walter Pater makes an equally indirect appearance through the association of Ambient's art with literary impressionism (39), a school of reading and artistic production arguably founded by Pater. However, these perverse precursors are domesticated. Ambient and the narrator may broach Wildean paradoxes, but they do so "in the decent English air" (86). Decent English pastoralism defangs the subversive formal strategies of that ethnically hybrid pervert Wilde.

15. Bradley finds "The Author of 'Beltraffio'" ethically disturbing because it insinuates, however indirectly, an erotic bond between adult men and a seven-year-old boy. Further, the death of Dolcino seems predatory and exploitative, a child being sacrificed to gratify the diverging agenda of two adults (87–88). While not dismissing these concerns, I would suggest that it is a mistake to read Dolcino characterologically, as a "real" child. He functions more like an allegorical figure, possessing no psychological interiority (unlike complex Jamesian children such as Masie). Bradley's ethical qualms are properly laid at the feet of post-Victorian culture than at the feet of James, for the figure of the beautiful, supposedly innocent and hence inevitably violated child is a post-Victorian cultural construction that allows us both to eroticize the child and demonize the figure of the monstrous

pederast (see Kincaid). David Lee Miller has also explored the enduring topos in Western literature of the father witnessing the sacrificial death of his son. Miller argues that the death of a son structurally allows the culture to embody paternity, which is otherwise a purely symbolic fiction (2). I would contend that the death of young boys, which is such a staple topos of Uranian literature, plays a related role: male homosexuality is deemed unspeakable and is associated with a passing adolescent phase. There is a certain cultural (il-) logic, then, that the death of a young boy becomes a representational structure that both allows a writer to embody homosexual desire and to legitimate that representation by simultaneously erasing that desire. Unlike sensational Uranian tales like "The Acolyte," "The Author of 'Beltraffio'" does not allow the reader to witness Dolcino's death. I am tempted to read this omission as indicating James's half-hearted adherence to this homophobic and sensationally homoerotic convention. He will sacrifice Dolcino but the sacrifice will be offstage.

16. The rescue and formation of an all-male community does not work out, and like Dolcino, Morgan dies at the end of the tale. Tony Tanner points out that "James situates the final degrading scene or scene of degradation in Venice, but a Venice turned ugly and desolate" (193). The fantasy of the separatist male homosexuality having collapsed, the idealized gender transitive view of homosexuality represented by Venice also gets undermined.

17. I am indebted to Michel Foucault's History of Sexuality for seeing the kinship between us and the Victorians. Using the phrase "we other Victorians," Foucault wittily critiques Steven Marcus's description of a repressed Victorian culture, supposedly completely other to contemporary, sexually enlightened Anglo-American society.

Works Cited

Bloom, Harold. The Anxiety of Influence. New York: Oxford University Press, 1973.
_____. A Map of Misreading. New York: Oxford University Press, 1975.
Bradley, John R. Henry James's Permanent Adolescence. N.p. Palgrave, 2000.
Cannon, Kelley. Henry James and Masculinity at the Margins. New York: St. Martin's Press, 1994.
Dellamora, Richard. Masculine Desire: Sexual Politics of Victorian Aestheticism. Chapel Hill: University of North Carolina Press, 1990.
Dowling, Linda. Hellenism and Homosexuality in Victorian Oxford. Ithaca, NY: Cornell University Press, 1994.
Edelman, Lee. Homographesis. New York: Routledge, 1994.
Ellman, Richard. "Henry James among the Aesthetes." In Proceedings of the British Academy. Vol. 69 (1983): 209–228.
Foster, Dennis A. "Confession and Revenge: James's 'Figure in the Carpet.'" In Confession and Complicity in Narrative. Cambridge: Cambridge University Press, 1987.
Freedman, Jonathan. Professions of Taste: Henry James, British Aestheticism, and Commodity Culture. Stanford: Stanford University Press, 1990.
Gale, Robert L. A Henry James Encyclopedia. New York: Greenwood Press, 1989.
Gallop, Jane. "Keys to Dora." In The Daughter's Seduction. Ithaca, NY: Cornell University Press, 1982.

Graham, Wendy. *Henry James's Thwarted Love.* Stanford: Stanford University Press, 1999.

Horne, Philip. Henry James: A Life in Letters. N.p. Viking, 1999.

James, Henry. *The American: Henry James Novels, 1871–1880.* New York: The Library of America, 1983.

_____. *Autobiography: A Small Boy and Others, Notes of a Son and Brother, The Middle Years.* Princeton: Princeton University Press, 1983.

_____. *The American Scene.* Edited by John F. Sears. Harmondsworth: Penguin, 1994.

_____. *The Complete Notebooks.* Edited by Leon Edel and Lyall H. Powers. New York: Oxford University Press, 1987.

_____. "The Author of 'Beltraffio.'" In *The Figure in the Carpet and Other Stories.* Penguin Books, 1986.

_____. "The Figure in the Carpet." In *The Figure in the Carpet and Other Stories.* Penguin Books, 1986.

_____. *Hawthorne.* 1879. Ithaca, NY: Great Seal Books, 1963.

_____. *Italian Hours, Collected Travel Writings: The Continent.* N.p. The Library of America, 1993.

_____. *Letters: Volume II, 1875–1883.* Edited by Leon Edel. Cambridge, MA: Belknap Press of Harvard University Press, 1975.

_____. *Letters: Volume III, 1884–1895.*

_____. *Letters: Volume IV, 1895–1965.*

_____. "The Tempest." In *Selected Literary Criticism.* Edited by Morris Shapira. New York: Horizon Press, 1964.

Kaplan, Fred. *Henry James: The Imagination of Genius.* London: The Johns Hopkins University Press, 1992.

Kincaid, James. *Child-Loving: The Erotic Child and Victorian Culture.* New York: Routledge, 1992.

Koestenbaum, Wayne. "Unlocking Symonds: *Sexual Inversion.*" In *Double Talk: The Erotics of Male Literary Collaboration.* New York: Routledge, 1989.

Lacan, Jacques. *Ecrits: A Selection.* Translated by Alan Sheridan. London: Hogarth and Norton, 1976.

Lamos, Colleen. "Errors of Affection: Ruskin, Venice, and Reading." In *Remembrance of Things Past, Deviant Modernism: Sexual and Textual Errancy in T. S. Eliot, James Joyce, and Marcel Proust.* Cambridge: Cambridge University Press, 1998.

Miller, David Lee. *Dream of the Burning Child: Sacrificial Sons and the Father's Witness.* Ithaca: Cornell University Press, 2003

Novick, Sheldon M. *Henry James, The Young Master.* New York: Random House, 1996.

Parkes, Adam. "Henry James's *Italian Hours* and the 'Ruskinian Contagion.'" *Roman Holidays: American Writers and Artists in Nineteenth-Century Italy.* Edited by Robert K. Martin and Leland S. Person. Iowa City: University of Iowa Press, 2002.

Scott, Walter. *Quentin Durward.* 1823. Oxford: Oxford University Press, 1992.

Sedgwick, Eve Kosofsky. *Between Men: English Literature and Male Homosocial Desire.* New York: Columbia University Press, 1985.

_____. *Epistemology of the Closet.* Berkeley: University of California Press, 1990.

_____. "Inside Henry James: Towards a Lexicon for *The Art of the Novel.*" In *Negotiating Lesbian and Gay Subjects.* Edited by Monica Dorenkamp and Richard Henke. New York: Routledge, 1995.

Symonds, John Addington. *The Memoirs of John Addington Symonds: The Secret Homosexual Life of a Leading Nineteenth-Century Man of Letters.* Edited by Phyllis Grosskurth. Chicago: University of Chicago Press, 1986.

_____. *A Problem in Greek Ethics: Male Love.* Edited by John Lauritsen. New York: Pagan Press, 1983.

_____. *A Problem in Modern Ethics: Male Love.*

_____. *Studies of the Greek Poets.* London: Smith, 1873.

Tanner, Tony. *Venice Desired.* Oxford: Blackwell, 1992.

Toibin, Colm. *Love in a Dark Time and Other Explorations of Gay Lives and Literature.* New York: Scribner, 2002.

Wilde, Oscar. *De Profundis: The Letters of Oscar Wilde.* Edited by Rupert Hart Davis. New York: Harcourt Brace and World, 1962.

Yingling, Thomas. *Hart Crane and the Homosexual Text.* Chicago: University of Chicago Press, 1990.

A Pair of Afterwords

DAVID GARRETT IZZO

The Disappearing Act of Gabriel Nash, or How His "Wilde-ness" Got the Better of Him

Gabriel Nash of Henry James's *The Tragic Muse* is certainly a satire of *somebody!* James is too clever to have made Nash inadvertently funny. One will not wander far off to say he is Walter Pater as interpreted by Oscar Wilde, as pointed out by, among others, Maurizio Ascari in "Gabriel Nash the Itinerant Aesthete," and Fred Kaplan in his James biography in which he writes, "With touches of Oscar Wilde, who appears in different ways in some of the ideas of the novel and in some of the metaphors, Nash wants to make his life a work of art. He wants to live life at the highest level of pure flame, like a Paterean bright light that burns without being consumed or consuming, without a product, without a thing to be called a work of art other than the artist himself" (333). This sounds serious, but could James, as Ascari points out, have possibly written these lines for Nash with a straight face, such as when Nash is asked if he is an aesthete? "I've no profession, my dear young lady. I've no *état civil*.... Merely to be is such a *métier* to live such an art; to feel such a career!" (*Muse VII*, 33); or, "Being is doing, and if doing is duty being is duty" (*Muse VIII*, 26); or, "People's actions, I know, are for the most part the things they do—but mine are all the things *I don't* do.... All my behaviour consists of my feelings" (*Muse VII*, 31). The pastiche of Pater via Wilde is done with exceeding cleverness as James imitates what Harold Bloom called Wilde's vulgarization of Pater rather than Pater himself, who would have agreed with James about how Wilde had corrupted Pater's intentions; hence, Pater's correction in *Marius the Epicurean* (to follow). There is, in addition to James's darts at Pater/

Wilde, a subtle scalpel edge applied acutely to British bourgeois society. Indeed, Edel notes that it was James's role as a visitor looking in at English society that gives *The Tragic Muse* its sharpness. "London critics observed that no English writer would look as closely at manners as James had done. It took an outsider to do that.... He has nowhere evoked better the scene of London streets or Parisian boulevards.... *The Tragic Muse* is as much a series of rich prose pictures of scenes and of people as an easy-going drama of art and the world" (viii–ix).

James's observations of his adopted society are astute enough that he knew that Nash is *not* Pater but rather the injustice done to Pater by Wilde— and the injustice Wilde did to James's artistic sensibility by Wilde's "vulgar" success that James abhorred. What Nick's sister Biddy says of Nash really has Wilde in view. To Biddy, he is "a gentleman unlike any other gentleman she had ever seen" (*Muse VII*, 22); moreover, his manner of speaking English is so affected that he might be mistaken for a foreigner. Many also thought Wilde was from another planet.

Nash's presence/absence divides *The Tragic Muse* into James's vision of (1) a Wildean superfluity of an overweening solipsistic romanticism, and (2) an anti–Wildean vision of what happens when the Wildean vision of superfluity spills over and leaves a mess that needs cleaning up. One cannot get one's hands dirty and this is one of the things Nash doesn't do— get dirty; so he exits, although he may be the one who kicked over Nick Dormer's paint can in the first place.

Speaking of Dormer, is it not Nash who, by his purple effusiveness, wrings the necessary guilt from Dormer that convinces Nick to give up Parliament for painting? (As if one could not be in Parliament—certainly not a nine-to-five job—and paint as well. Ah, but that would not be "pure" and that sort of worldliness could not possibly produce good art. What would Nash have thought of the insurance executive Wallace Stevens?) Art is certainly a major theme in *The Tragic Muse*, and even though James's pastiche of Nash/Wilde may be humorous, the impetus that Nash provides topples dominos that land on Nick, Miriam Rooth, Peter Sherringham, Julia Dallow, et al., with much greater seriousness. James said the main subjects of his *Muse* were "my theatrical case" and "my political case" (qtd. in Edel, ix); yet, Edel believes that in *Muse*, as well as *The Bostonians* and *The Princess Casamassima*,

> the underlying subject of the three novels is in reality that of the coercion of the artist-individual into forms of action alien to himself. What James is saying then, is that if society were to have its way it would destroy the artist rather than allow him self-fulfillment;

and that the artist must rebel in self-defense even at the risk of being destroyed by his own rebellion. An artist such as James, however, also is devoted to a society which nourishes him. The last thing he wants to do is to change it. He likes nothing better than the *status quo*—'the spectacle of life'—upon which he looks with never-ending satisfaction. His conflict, therefore, is that he must defy the very things to which he is attached: family, convention, tradition, the social institutions, even the men and women who, if they are his friends and relations, can also be his enemies [xi–xii].

James's conflict, as defined by Edel, can also define the conflict in *The Tragic Muse* that explains why Nash exerts so much influence in the first half but then slides sideways off the page in the second half; that is, his "purple effusiveness," like a naughty child, has been sent to its room. But we nonetheless know that, even if neither seen nor heard, it is lurking about out of sight but not out of consciousness, rubbing its hands over "the spectacle of life" it helped to put into motion.

Gabriel Nash is the character in the novel who expresses most memorably and insistently the aesthetic point of view of the decadent imagination. James here is making fun of the "decadent imagination" but not of the artistic imagination, which he believes in to the marrow of his existence as defined most notably in his prefaces. Moreover, he believes in the rebellion of the artist in society as Edel asserts. But unlike the decadents, who included society itself as a picture to be remade by their broad strokes of the overturned paint can, James would rather rebel *within* society through a mutual accommodation that, in his case, he achieved by attending endless parties and social events—so prominent and wonderfully depicted in *Muse*—and then, as he did in *Muse*, assert his rebellious artistic independence by recreating what he observed in his art, which would also display, through parable, the society's faults and contradictions.

James is the subversive rebel who uses Nash as his vehicle to set up contradictory predicaments in the first half that need a good deal of sorting out in the second half when Nash is offstage, perhaps also in "complete solitude" subversively observing what he has wrought. In fact, James's cleverly subversive subterfuge may have been, according to Edel, a double pastiche:

> The Tragic Muse ... is outwardly a story of politics and painting and the stage; it is in effect James's continuing story of the artist-dilemma in his society. The spokesman for James's views ... is the intrusive Gabriel Nash, one of James's most charming and at the same time exasperating characters. Various critics have seen Nash as possessing some of the qualities of Henry James's vision-haunted

and talkative father, or the aestheticism of Oscar Wilde. I dare say that one can find ingredients of both: but behind his suavity and his epigrams, his Walter Paterism and his *dolce far niente*, Gabriel Nash talks undiluted Henry James. His very appearance has something in it of his progenitor: his middle stature, his plumpness, his short beard and the 'mere reminiscence of hair' on his crown. This is the Henry James of the middle phase; moreover the conspicuous and aggressive perfection of Gabriel's speech corresponds to what we know of the speech of the novelist during the 1880s [xiv–xv].

Edel goes on to note that Nash is also based on James's brother William's friend, Herbert Pratt, and quotes James writing that "A good deal might be done with Herbert Pratt," of which Edel writes, "Nash is an unusually fine example of how a novelist, seizing upon a sympathetic personality, makes him an extension of himself.... James would have liked to be able to take life as easily as Pratt did.... he could make Gabriel Nash plead for many things dear to his own heart. Perhaps the most significant example of this is Gabriel's great defense of style—of Henry James's own way of seeing and writing" (xvi).

James was not only satirizing Pater and Wilde (and maybe his father and Pratt), he was also satirizing Henry James by putting his own tongue in Nash's cheek. Conversely, James never wanted to draw attention to his persona in lieu of his art, but only in conjunction with his art on its merit, which is why Nash must leave the scene in the second half, for he has produced nothing, except trouble for those who listened to him in the first half. This is not to say that what Nash says has no value—it does—but its value must be in an application (art, criticism) derived from a common sense that, instead of promoting both a self-destructive and outwardly destructive egoism, promotes a common sense that says: look at the product (art and criticism) and learn from it, *not* look at *me*.

Walter Pater: From Renaissance *to* Mysticism *in* Marius the Epicurean

This volume of essays centers on James's reaction to Victorian aestheticism. Victorian aestheticism begins with Walter Pater, to whom all the subsequent aestheticists reacted—but not necessarily in the way he might have wanted them to. Harold Bloom, in his introduction to the *Selected Writings of Walter Pater*, states that Oscar Wilde "brilliantly vulgarized" (iii) Pater, much to Pater's enduring regret. Bloom chooses from Pater's preface to *The Renaissance* (1873) the following epigram to precede his introduction:

> ... what is this song or picture, this engaging personality presented in life or in a book, to *me*? What effect does it really produce on me? Does it give me pleasure? And if so, what sort or degree of pleasure? [3]

Bloom does not stop here, but one can see that Wilde, in a sense, *did* stop here, and derived that Pater saw art as an end in itself. Bloom also adds this next sentence of Pater's that immediately follows Pater's last sentence above: "How is my nature modified by its [art's] presence, and under its influence?" (3). Wilde seemed to skip this sentence or certainly skipped the inference of the sentence. For Pater to ask "How is my nature modified" signifies that one's nature, and the improvement of one's nature through art, is the desired end, while art is a means to this end. Pater extols the artist for his heroic ability to be the medium that allows art to cause improvements in human consciousness. Wilde was more concerned with *appearing* heroic, with all of the narcissistic, vainglorious, ego-filled aspects of what Isherwood and Auden called *The Truly Weak Man* instead of *being* heroic in the self-effacing, egoless manner of *The Truly Strong Man*. (Wilde may have believed his trial was heroic despite the result.)

Pater believed art creates pleasure via sensation and stimulates ideas. He asserts in his essay on da Vinci that "The fancy of a perpetual life, sweeping together ten thousand experiences, is an old one; and modern philosophy has conceived the idea of humanity as wrought upon by, and summing up in itself, all modes of thought and life. Certainly Lady Lisa might stand as the embodiment of the old fancy, the symbol of the modern idea" (80).

For Pater, the "Lady Lisa" is an iconic symbol that evokes through its beauty a sense of "otherness" in the admirer that allows one to empty out his limited, self-identified mind so that it can become a conduit to receive— as the mystic views it—"a summing up in itself, all modes of thought and life." And in Pater's *Marius the Epicurean* (1885), it is no less than the universe that Marius wishes to investigate. This novel has the additional subtitle, *His Sensations and Ideas*. The "and ideas" is Pater's important distinction that he had not meant for readers (Wilde) to leave out of their interpretations of *The Renaissance*, in which the role of sensations is to inspire changes in one's nature by arousing the aesthetic imagination to think, and by thinking, to derive from symbolic ideals like the *Mona Lisa* new ideas as prelude to an advance in the evolution of personal and collective consciousness.

In his chapter "Marius and the Necessity of Religion," David DeLaura writes:

> *Marius the Epicurean* is not only the supreme intellectual and artis-
> tic effort of Pater's career, but it represents the ultimate reach of
> the dialectical impulse that had governed so much of his earlier
> career.... Marius becomes a thoroughgoing revision or at least
> reshaping of Pater's characteristic positions in the *Renaissance* and
> elsewhere; and his basic dichotomy between culture and religion is
> worked out ... each alternative view of life is tested ... and each,
> found wanting. Marius moves from the traditional religion and
> ethic, through a pleasurable paganism, to the apparent stability of
> Pater's partially hedonistic New Cyrenaicism; Stoicism then attracts
> him by its claim of a more complete life of "active serenity," and ...
> the possibility of union with a transcendent power [90].

Marius is a restless young man with a desire for ideas who goes on a
quest for more and more knowledge and more and more experiences to
fill his mind with both sensations and philosophy.[1] Pater's chapter titles
say much in themselves about Marius's pilgrimage: The Religion of Numa,
White Nights, Change of Air, The Tree of Knowledge, The Golden Book,
Euphuism, A Pagan End, Animula Vagula, New Cyrenaicism, On the Way,
The Most Religious City in the World, The Divinity that Doth Hedge a
King, The Mistress and Mother of Palaces, Manly Amusement, Stoicism at
Court, Second Thoughts, Beata Urbs, The Ceremony of the Dart, The
Will as Vision, Two Curious Houses—i: Guests, Two Curious Houses—ii:
The Church in Cecilia's House, The Minor Peace of the House, Divine
Service, A Conversation Not Imaginary (reference to Pater's *Imaginary Por-
traits*), Sunt Lacrimae Rerum, The Martyrs, The Triumph of Marcus Aure-
lius, and the last chapter, Anima Naturaliter Christiana.

Billie Inman considers the oppositions that evolve in Marius's progress
from Paganism to Christiana:

> Paganism, in his scheme, corresponds to the head and Christian-
> ity to the heart. Pater details three sides of this general conflict: (1)
> against the consuming concern of paganism for perfection in exter-
> nal display he places a Christian reverence for inner virtues; (2)
> against paganism's haunting sense of futility he places Christian
> hopefulness; (3) against paganism's philosophic indifference to pain
> and its vulgar delight in brutality to animals he places Christian
> sympathy for all creatures. Each of these conflicts has a correspon-
> dent in the mind of Marius: (1) pure aesthetic judgment vies with
> moral concern; (2) a skepticism which engenders despair vies with
> a mysticism which engenders hope; (3) a tendency to develop the
> mind in detachment vies with a sympathy for the suffering of all
> creatures [484].

Delaura notes that Inman "finds this continuing oscillation between the
aesthetic and skeptical view of life, and the moral and even mystical view,

persisting to the very end.... But she does concede that in one aspect of this conflict of heart and head—intellectual detachment versus sympathetic feeling—that the heart wins" (99).

One can see that "A Pagan End" (or end of paganism), which concludes, "Part the First," will evolve its way to the "Christiana" of "Part the Fourth." Indeed, in the very first chapter, "The Religion of Numa," Pater as narrator begins, "As, in the triumph of Christianity, the old religion lingered latest in the country, and died out at last as but paganism—the religion of the villagers, before the advance of the Christian Church" (1). Hence, Pater forecasts the direction toward which Pater, Marius, and the reader will be going. Pater says of Marius two pages later,

> A sense of conscious powers external to ourselves, pleased or displeased by the right or wrong conduct of every circumstance of daily life—that *conscience* [Pater's italics], of which the old Roman religion was a formal habitual recognition, was become in him a powerful current of feeling and observance. The old fashioned, partly puritanical awe, the power of which Wordsworth noted and valued so highly in a northern peasantry, had its counterpart in the feeling of the Roman lad, as he passed the spot "touched of Heaven," where the lightning had struck dead an aged laborer in the field: an upright stone, still with moldering garlands about it, marked the place. He brought to that system of symbolic usages, and they in turn developed in him further, a great seriousness—an impressibility to the sacredness of time, of life and its events, and the circumstances of family fellowship; of such gifts to men as fire, water, the earth, from labor on which they live, really understood by him as gifts—a sense of religious responsibility in the reception of them [3].

This early passage in the very first chapter is—much like the preface of *The Renaissance*—rich in declaring Pater's intentions. The last sentence above refutes Wilde directly, as Pater does not talk about the impressions of art only, but rather argues for the impressions received from nature and humanity that will lead to and then include art with art as a reaction to nature and humanity. And from these "gifts"—and from the aesthetic impressions derived from these gifts—one must have "a sense of responsibility in reception of them." So it is not "art for art's sake" as its own end but art for the sake of achieving a truer end, which is to inspire a sense of mystical consciousness.

When Pater praises Wordsworth and "puritanical awe" he is doing so in a book about a "Roman lad" to signify that the book is not really about Rome but applies metaphorically to Victorian England, as noted by R. V. Osbourn: "the historical setting is primarily of importance as a disguise for an autobiographical and philosophical progress in the nineteenth century.... " (392). Pater also infers an antielitism that might have been a counter to Wilde and his peers by invoking Wordsworth's "northern peasantry." Religion herein is not the religion of dogma and dogmatists but an individual's responsibility to seek the spirit within that unifies with mystical consciousness.

Marius, further motivated by the death of his mother, proceeds to seek spiritual truth in a variety of ideas and philosophies that Pater presents with great detail (and purple effusion), and which Marius will absorb one by one until the last chapter, "Anima Naturaliter Christiana," when he has an extended epiphany that precedes his slow death from illness:[2]

> [Pater's italics] Revelation, vision, the discovery of a vision, the *seeing* of a perfect humanity, in a perfect world—through all his alternations of mind, by some dominant instinct, determined by the original necessities of his own nature and character, he always set that above the *having*, or even the *doing*, of anything. For, such a vision, if received with due attitude on his part, was, in reality, the *being* something, and as such was surely a pleasant offering or sacrifice to whatever gods there might be, observant of him. And how goodly had the vision been!—one long unfolding of beauty and energy in things... [378].
>
> ... in the deep isolation of spirit which was now creeping upon Marius, the faces of these people, casually visible, took a strange hold on his affections; the link of general brotherhood, the feeling of human kinship. Asserting itself most strongly when it was about to be severed forever... [377].
>
> ... At this moment, his unclouded receptivity of soul, grown so steadily through all those years, from experience to experience, was at its height.... And was not this precisely the condition, the attitude of mind, to which something higher than he, yet akin to him, would be likely to reveal itself... [380].

For Pater and Marius, "unclouded receptivity of soul" signifies the tearing down and emptying out of adulterated influences to a state of an unadulterated Zen *no mind* that can now receive the mystical vision of the timeless undifferentiated unity. This revelation takes effect as a vision of *agape*—the love of all existence:

> ... to which that influence he had felt now and again like a friendly hand upon his shoulder, amid the actual obscurities of the world, would likely to make a further explanation. Surely, the aim of a true philosophy must lie, not in futile efforts towards the completer accommodation of man to the circumstances in which he chances to find himself, but in maintenance of a kind of candid discontent, in the face of the very highest achievement; the unclouded and

> receptive soul quitting the world with the same fresh wonder with
> which it had entered the world unimpaired, and going on its blind
> way at last with the consciousness of some profound enigma in
> things, as but a pledge of something further to come [380].

Marius also understands that this "something further" oversees human
nature and protects humanity's evolving consciousness from stagnancy by
giving man the power of a questing and questioning imagination. "There
had been a permanent protest established in the world, a plea, a perpetual
after-thought, which humanity would ever possess in reserve, against any
wholly mechanical and disheartening theory of itself and its conditions..."
(381).

The questors within the whole of humanity, despite the material evidence of a world that holds much pain and disappointment, continue, generation after generation, to persist in striving for a better world. This passage
would also seem to be a Paterian amendment to *Renaissance* in clarifying
Pater's intentions in that work; it is also anti–Wilde and a rebuttal of what
Wilde did to Pater's reputation, which Pater hopes will be corrected in the
course of humanity's "perpetual after-thought."

Marius here feels a great solace from his vision of agape and in contemplating how this vision will continue in those who follow him in his
quest: "That is nature's way of easing death to us. It was thus too, surprised, delighted, that Marius under the power of that new hope among
men, could think of the generations that would come after him. Without
it, dim in truth as it was, he could hardly have pondered the world which
limited all he really knew, as it would be when he should have departed
from it" (382).

> The people around his bed were praying fervently—*Abi! Abi! Anima
> Christiana!* In the moments of his extreme helplessness their mys-
> tic bread had been placed, had descended like a snow-flake from
> the sky, between his lips. Gentle fingers had applied to his hands
> and feet, to all those old passage ways of the senses, through which
> the world had come and gone from him, now so dim and ob-
> structed, medicinable oil. It was the same people who, in the grey,
> austere evening of that day, took up his remains, and buried them
> secretly, with their accustomed prayers; but with joy also, holding
> his death, according to their generous view in this matter, to have
> been of the nature of a martyrdom, as the church always said, a
> kind of sacrament of plenary grace [383].

For the Roman equivalent of Wordsworth's "northern peasantry,"
the death of the learned man who had given his life to a quest for knowledge was a martyr's death. Perhaps Pater, and the misinterpretation of

his intentions that Bloom says Wilde "brilliantly vulgarized," was also a martyr.

In *Marius the Epicurean*, Pater restates the intentions of *The Renaissance* but ultimately adds the more definitive vision of what he really meant to say, which, in fact, he had already said: "How is my nature modified by its [art's] presence, and under its influence." In *Marius*, art is just one influence among all of the influences described that together are the means to Pater's true end—mystical unity with all of existence.

James, in his fashion, wanted a mystical union with all of literature.

Notes

1. Huysmans's *A Rebours* seems a response to *Marius* as it is also about a pilgrimage, but one that is a perverse reversal of how Pater goes about his questing. Marius feels "awe" as he quests; conversely, Des Esseintes feels awful—disgusted and cynical. Nonetheless, both quests ultimately arrive at similar conclusions.

2. The passages of the thoughts of a person dying are emulated in Cather's *Death Comes for the Archbishop* (1928), Huxley's *Time Must Have a Stop* (1944), and Isherwood's *A Single Man* (1964).

Works Cited

Bloom, Harold. "Introduction." In *Selected Writings of Walter Pater*. New York: Columbia University Press, 1974.

DeLaura, David. *Hebrew and Hellene in Victorian England: Newman, Arnold, and Pater*. Austin: University of Texas Press, 1969.

Edel, Leon. "Introduction." In *The Tragic Muse*. New York: Harper Torchbooks, 1960.

Inman, Billie Andrew. "The Organic Structure of *Marius the Epicurean*." *Philological Quarterly* 41 (April 1962): 475–491.

Kaplan, Fred. *Henry James: The Imagination of Genius, A Biography*. New York: William Morrow and Company, 1992.

Pater, Walter. *Marius the Epicurean*. New York: Modern Library, 1920.

_____. *The Renaissance: Studies in Art and Poetry*. In *The English Literary Decadence*. Lanham, MD: University Press of America, 1999.

_____. *Selected Writings of Walter Pater*. Edited by Harold Bloom. New York: Columbia University Press, 1974.

About the Contributors

David Garrett Izzo has published nine books and more than forty articles concerning twentieth-century literature, including *The Writings of Richard Stern, W.H. Auden Encyclopedia, Christopher Isherwood Encyclopedia,* and *Stephen Vincent Benet: His Life and Work* (coeditor with Lincoln Konkle). He has also published two novels and two plays. He has a Ph.D. from Temple University and is a professor at Fayetteville State University in North Carolina. Learn more about David and his work at *www.davidgarrettizzo.com.*

Daniel T. O'Hara is the first Mellon Term Professor of Humanities in the College of Liberal Arts and professor of English at Temple University. He is the author of five books, the most recent being *Empire Burlesque: The Fate of Critical Culture in Global America* (Duke, 2003). He is also the editor or coeditor of five other volumes. In October 2005, Barnes and Noble Classics published a new edition of Freud's *The Interpretation of Dreams,* edited by O'Hara and Gina Masucci MacKenzie. The two are also coauthoring a book on the poetics of terror in modern culture.

Maurizio Ascari has lent his Italian point of view to a long record of publication in English and American literature, with previous articles on James, as well as W.H. Auden, Wilkie Collins, Katherine Mansfield, Walter Pater, William Faulkner, and many more. His most recent book was his collected essays on James, *In the Palatial Chamber of the Mind: Comparative Essays on Henry James.* He is a professor at the University of Bologna. Ascari is a member of AISNA, the Italian Association of North American Studies, as are Vittoria Intonti and Donatella Izzo to follow.

Andrea Cabus-Coldwell is a doctoral student in English literature and a teacher at Temple University.

Robert Combs is the author of *Vision and Voyage: Hart Crane and the Psychology of Romanticism* and articles on modern American dramatists, including Israel Horovitz, David Mamet, and Wallace Shawn. Combs contributed an essay to *Stephen Vincent Benét: His Life and Work*, edited by David Garrett Izzo and L. Konkle.

Mark Conroy teaches English at Ohio State University, specializing in the modern novel and critical theory. His books are *Modernism and Authority*, on Flaubert and Conrad, and the forthcoming *Muse in the Machine*, on American fiction and mass publicity from Henry James to Don DeLillo.

Stephen da Silva received his Ph.D. in English from Rice University. He has published essays on E. M. Forster and Christopher Isherwood and is working on a book titled *Boyish Affiliations*, which examines how late–Victorian and modernist writers challenged associating homosexuality with arrested development, drawing on the idioms of primitivism and Hellenism.

James Fisher, professor of theatre at Wabash College, has authored five books, including *The Theater of Tony Kushner: Living Past Hope* (New York: Routledge, 2001), and has published articles and reviews in numerous periodicals. He has published essays and reviews in a variety of publications, is a director and actor, has held several research fellowships, edits *The Puppetry Yearbook*, and is book review editor of the *Journal of Dramatic Theory & Criticism*. Fisher was 1999–2000 McLain-McTurnan-Arnold Research Scholar at Wabash College and was named "Indiana Theatre Person of the Year" by the Indiana Theatre Association in 1997.

Vittoria Intonti is a professor of American literature at the University of Bari. Intonti is the editor of *L'Arte della Short Story: Il Racconto AngloAmericano* and is a member of AISNA, the Italian Association of North American Studies.

Donatella Izzo is professor of comparative literature at Università degli Studi di Napoli l'Orientale, Italy. She has published books and essays on U.S. authors of the nineteenth and twentieth centuries and is the editor of several volumes of literary criticism and theory. Her latest books are *Portraying the Lady: Technologies of Gender in the Short Stories of Henry James* (Lincoln: University of Nebraska Press, 2001) and (edited with Elena Spandri)

Contact Zones: Rewriting Genre across the East-West Border (Naples: Liguori, 2003). Izzo is president of AISNA, the Italian Association of North American Studies. (Donatella Izzo is not known to be related to coeditor David Izzo.)

Solveig C. Robinson is assistant professor of English and director of the Publishing and Printing Arts (PPA) Program at Pacific Lutheran University in Tacoma, Washington. She is the editor of *A Serious Occupation: Literary Criticism by Victorian Women Writers* (Broadview, 2003) and has published articles on Victorian women editors and journalists in *Victorian Periodicals Review* and *Victorian Poetry*.

Sheila Teahan, associate professor of English at Michigan State University, is the author of *The Rhetorical Logic of Henry James* (1995) and of essays in the *Arizona Quarterly, The Henry James Review*, the Bedford/St. Martin's edition of *The Turn of the Screw*, and elsewhere. She was president of the Henry James Society in 2001.

Index

Chapter One

Ella

"How was the car?"

I smile. Trust my brother Drew to ask about my new car first, rather than me, or my job, or my new apartment.

"The car was fine."

"Remind me again... why did you choose bright red?"

"Because I liked it." I liked having the wind in my hair, too... not that it's long enough to notice.

"And how's the apartment?" Finally... something worth talking about.

"Empty. None of the furniture's getting here until later." I look around the vast space, my voice echoing off the blank walls. I kicked off my shoes almost as soon as I got here, hating the sound they made on the wooden floors.

"Are you okay?" he asks.

"I'm fine."

"You don't sound it."

How is it he can read me so well... even though he's in New York, and I'm in Boston? Whatever the reason, there's no point in trying to hide anything from him.

"I'm nervous."

"Why?"

"Because I'm due to start my new job on Monday, and I don't have a clue what I'm doing."

"Well… if you'd tell me what the job is, I might be able to help."

"I'd love to, but…"

"I know. You're not allowed." He chuckles. "It seems strange that a chef can't talk about their work."

"That's because I'm not just being employed as a chef."

"Ahh," he says, and I can almost see him nodding his head and grinning. "Does this mean you're gonna be working as a secret agent on the side?"

"Of course not, you idiot."

I'm fed up with hearing my own voice reverberate back at me, so I wander through to the kitchen, hoping it won't have as much of an echo. This room is the main reason I chose my new apartment, although I also like the view from the top floor. My life revolves around cooking, though; it has done ever since I first stood at Pat's side and watched her in the kitchen at home. Pat isn't my mother, but she's the closest thing to a mother I've ever known and it's thanks to her I have such a passion for food, and for cooking it.

I run my fingers along the granite countertop, admiring the shiny gray cabinets and wide six-burner hob. There's a space over by the floor-to-ceiling windows where my new table and chairs will fit, but I'm less interested in that than the cooking area. It's my domain.

It's where I belong.

"Did Hunter tell you about the engagement?" I ask, putting my phone onto speaker, and resting it on the countertop while I sit up next to it.

"Yeah. I saw him on Saturday morning, before I left Newport. He's so pleased with himself."

"I'm not surprised. Considering how close he came to losing Livia, he's a lucky man."

"I don't think he intends to forget it... or to make a mistake like that again."

"No..."

I know we're both remembering how broken our brother was when he and Livia split up a few weeks ago. I've never seen him like that before, and even if the situation was entirely of his own making, I felt sorry for him. Still, they're engaged now, and deliriously happy... thank God.

"Speaking of mistakes..." I say, waiting for Drew to take the bait.

"Yeah?" He doesn't, so I'll have to ask outright...

"How are things going with Lexi?"

"Don't." He sounds pained.

"Don't what?"

"Remind me of the errors of my ways."

"This isn't the error of your ways. Not entirely. It takes two to make a baby, Drew." He doesn't reply. "So? What's happening? I take it you've seen her?"

"Yeah. We met for lunch on Saturday, as planned. She was busy on Sunday, but we still had things to discuss, so I saw her again yesterday."

"And?" God... this is like getting blood from a stone.

"I've told her I'll support her."

"Financially?"

"In any way she wants," he says.

"You're not getting back together, are you?"

"No. Even if I wasn't in love with her sister, the fact that Lexi's having my baby isn't suddenly going to make our failed relationship a successful one... if what we had could even have been called a relationship."

"But you're gonna be there for her?"

"Of course. I'm not shirking my responsibilities."

I'd never say this to his face, but I'm a little surprised by that… and ashamed to admit it. Drew's my brother, and I love him, but his reputation with women is hardly something to be proud of.

Until now, it seems.

"It's not entirely your responsibility, Drew. Like I just said, it takes two…"

"I know. Lexi said the same thing. She told me she was really scared about calling me."

"Scared?"

"Yeah. She was worried I'd think she was trying to trap me, because of me being a multi-millionaire."

"Oh. I hadn't thought about that."

"Surely, when you've dated guys, it's crossed your mind that they might only be interested in your money?"

"Thanks for that. I prefer to think men might be more interested in me than my bank balance." I can't tell him I've never dated anyone. He'd never believe me. Taking offense seems like a far better route.

"Sorry. I didn't mean that to sound like an insult. But, to be honest, it's one of the reasons I've always kept women at arm's length."

"And Hunter? Did he feel the same… before he met Livia?"

"I don't know. You'd have to ask him."

"Is that why you both slept around?"

He falls silent for a moment, and I wonder if it's his turn to be insulted… not that I've said anything that isn't true.

"I can't speak for Hunter, but in my case it was simply that I like sex."

I can feel myself blush, and I'm grateful he can't see me. "Oh… I see." I need to change the subject, to cover my embarrassment. "Did you put Lexi's mind at rest?"

"About what?"

"About the fact that you didn't think she was trying to trap you."

"Yeah, I did. She said she still felt responsible, though... because she knew she'd been sick, and I didn't."

"Had she realized her birth control wouldn't work?"

"No."

"Then I don't see how she can feel responsible."

"That's what I said to her. This is on me, Ella."

"I don't think either of you should take the blame. It feels wrong when there's a new life involved."

"I know. But the circumstances are hardly ideal."

"Have you spoken to Lexi's sister?" I ask, guessing that's the 'circumstance' he's referring to. Falling for her certainly wasn't ideal, although we all know you can't help who you fall in love with... or when.

"Not since Lexi told me she's pregnant, no."

"So you don't know if she's aware of what's going on?"

"On the contrary. I know she is."

"How?"

"Because Lexi told me it was her sister who persuaded her to tell me. She convinced Lexi I had a right to know I'm gonna be a father... and I guess that tells me everything I need to know."

"In what way?"

"I suppose I'd kinda hoped it might not be too late for us. We were getting along really well. She even seemed a little disappointed that I was going away to Hawaii, and we couldn't make any definite plans to meet up again. I stupidly let myself believe that meant something."

"Maybe it did."

"How can it have done? How can she have wanted to be with me, and then have been so keen for Lexi to tell me about the

baby? She must have realized that Lexi's news was gonna mean the end for us."

"Maybe she decided to put Lexi's feelings first… and those of her unborn nephew or niece."

He sighs. "Nobody's that selfless, Ella."

I can hear the despondency in his voice.

"Are you okay, Drew?"

"No."

I have no experience of romance, so I can't imagine how he must be feeling. All I know is he felt guilty about wanting Lexi's sister so much. If he hadn't, he'd never have asked for advice. The thing is, he did, and Hunter and I told him, the only thing he could hope to do was to befriend Lexi's sister, and see where it took them.

It seems that's what he's been doing over the last few weeks, and it sounds as though it was going well, which makes it even more difficult to have it snatched away.

"How long are you staying in New York?" I ask, sensing a need to change the subject.

"Just a couple more days. I've got to be back in Boston before the weekend. I've got a new client, and they've lined up my first job for next week." He sounds a little more cheerful already, but talking about work does that for Drew. He loves being a photographer and always has.

"If you're not starting with them until next week, why don't you spend a few days in Newport first?"

"Because I've got some paperwork to do."

"So? You could work on your laptop, couldn't you?"

"I will. But if I take it down to Newport, I'll just end up sitting by the pool and thinking. Being in the city makes me more inclined to work."

I can understand that. Our house in Newport is the most relaxing place in the world. I always feel like I can breathe more

easily when I'm there. Hunter and Drew feel the same way, I think.

"I have to admit, I'm dreading living here," I say.

"Why?" he asks, sounding surprised. "You've lived in big cities before."

"You're talking about London, and Madrid, and Paris. They're different."

"They're still cities, and you went to each of them all by yourself. Why does being in Boston make you so nervous?"

"I don't know. Maybe it's not the city itself, but what I'm going to be doing here."

"The job, you mean?"

"Yeah."

"Then why did you take it? You didn't have to. Not having to work for a living is one of the advantages of being a multimillionaire, in case you haven't noticed. Just because Hunter and I work doesn't mean you have to. Not if it's making you this anxious."

"I suppose I feel like I have a point to prove."

"To whom? Not us, I hope."

"To myself." And to them, and everyone else, I guess, although I'm not about to say that. "I've always been a bit of a flake, Drew... drifting from one thing to another. But I can cook, and I guess I want to prove I can make something of that."

"You don't have to prove anything, Ella. Hunter and I will always love you, whatever you do."

Oh... I wish he hadn't said that. I'm not normally a tearful person, but my eyes are stinging, and I cough away the lump in my throat.

"I guess I can go back to Newport on the weekends, if I get time." I doubt I will, especially not at the start of my contract, while I'm getting used to my new role.

"I'm not sure I would, if I were you. Not if you're looking for peace and quiet, anyway."

"Why's that?" What's he saying?

"I was talking to Hunter the morning before I left…"

"Oh," I interrupt. "I suppose he and Livia want the place to themselves for a while, do they?"

"No. It's nothing to do with that. You've got your own apartment down there, and believe me, if Hunter wants privacy, he'll find it."

I'm sure that's true enough. "In that case, why should I avoid going home?"

"Because he's having some construction work done."

"He is?" He didn't mention anything to me before he left to come back to Boston on Sunday evening. "How many kids are he and Livia thinking of having? There are six guest bedrooms already, so…"

"It's got nothing to do with them having kids," he says, interrupting me this time. "It's about Livia's parents."

"Oh?"

"Yeah. Do you remember Hunter telling us about Livia's dad having a stroke?"

In reality, the man we're talking about is Livia's step-father, but to her he's 'dad', and always has been. Her natural father was a stranger to her until very recently. But the least said about him, the better…

"Yeah. What about it?"

"It's left him with mobility problems, and he can't work anymore. Hunter was explaining that Livia's mom's doing an amazing job, but that he wanted to help them out, and Livia wants to be able to see more of them. So, he's building them a house."

"At our place?"

"Yeah. I'm not sure exactly where in the grounds it's going to be. We didn't go into that much detail."

"I don't care where it is. I think it's a fabulous idea."

"I told him the same thing, but he said he'd talk it through with us… once Livia's parents have agreed."

"You mean, he hasn't discussed it with them yet?"

"No, he and Livia are going up to Maine next weekend to tell them about the engagement and see what they say about the house. To be honest, I think he's kinda nervous about it."

"Which part? The engagement, or the house?"

"Both. From what he was saying, Livia doesn't think her mom will be too happy about the house."

"Why not?"

"She thinks her mom will see it as charity."

"Hmm… I suppose that makes sense. And I guess he's worried about the engagement because it's all happened so quickly. Let's face it, they only got back together again a few weeks ago."

"I know, but they're so in love…" His voice fades again, and I know he's got to be thinking about his situation with Lexi's sister. Even if she wasn't in love with him, that doesn't change how he feels about her.

I wonder for a moment what it must be like to be in love. Based on my brothers' experiences, I'm not sure I want to be. I may have fantasized about it often enough, in the privacy of my own bedroom, but it sounds horrendous in reality. Okay, so Hunter's happy now, but he went through hell to get here, and although he might say it was worth it, I'm not so sure. I mean… how can that level of pain be worth anything?

Mac

We take our third bow, the applause ringing in our ears, and as the curtain falls, the leading man looks along at the rest of us and gives a nod of his head. We're done. The audience might still be clapping and cheering, but there is such a thing as milking it, and three curtain calls are more than enough. It's enough for me, anyway, and I feel my shoulders sag, the fake smile falling from my lips.

"Don't look so relieved," Calvin whispers in my ear.

"Why not? I am relieved."

He smiles. "I don't know why. It's straight into rehearsals again next week."

I pat him on the shoulder. "Not for me, my friend."

He rolls his eyes. "You don't have to remind me..."

We head off stage, a ripple of gentle applause still echoing through the corridors of the theatre as we make our way back to our shared dressing room. It's only a tiny theatre, but I like it here and I'm going to miss it. I love the atmosphere of the place, the smell of the greasepaint, the heat from the lights. Still... it's time to move on, and I open the door, letting Calvin pass through ahead of me.

"We'd better change quickly," he says, pulling off his jacket. "Everyone will be along soon."

"They will?"

"Of course. You didn't think you were going to get away without a party, did you?"

I'm not sure I'm in the mood for a party, but I smile anyway, and step out of my costume, throwing it into the wicker basket in the corner. When Calvin and I first met about eighteen months

ago, we were a little more shy and would take it in turns to change behind the screen in the corner. Now we just use it to hang things over, stripping down to our underwear without a care in the world. Having done that, I pull on my jeans and t-shirt before sitting down to remove my make-up. At least if someone comes in now, I'll be decent.

"You will stay in touch, won't you?" Calvin says, sitting beside me and rubbing a cleansing wipe over his face, although he's looking at my reflection, rather than his own.

"Of course."

"Even though you've made the big time?"

"You don't know what I've made. I haven't told you."

I haven't told anyone yet. I'm under strict, contractual instructions not to breathe a word about my new job to a living soul. It feels a little melodramatic to me, but I suppose if it's what they want, who am I to argue?

"No, you haven't. But it's gotta be something spectacular to take you away from all this." He waves his arm around the slightly shabby dressing room, a broad grin settling on his lips. He celebrated his thirtieth birthday a couple of months ago, which is how I know he's three years younger than me, and is continually complaining about the fact that his red hair limits the roles he gets offered. I always remind him that it never stood in the way of countless other red-headed actors, but he usually greets my reply with a scowl.

"It was a tough decision," I lie. It wasn't, although I still have to pinch myself every so often, just because it all seems so surreal.

The offer came out of the blue a couple of months ago, and although I asked my agent to repeat it several times over, to make sure I hadn't mis-heard, I still couldn't believe what she was saying. She's based in New York and is called Delilah Dunn. I've always imagined her name to be made-up, but I've never dared say so, or even ask about it. She's way too scary. She's in her mid-

forties, and – like Calvin – has bright red hair, although hers is artificial and matches her nails and lipstick. Delilah was adamant about the offer, though… the part she'd sent me to audition for was definitely mine.

"They know I'm British, right?" I asked once the news had sunk in.

"Of course they do. They're not deaf. They said they were impressed by your American accent." Her own was dripping into my ear. "I'll e-mail you the contract, but I've read it through and there's nothing to worry about."

"Okay. Before you go, have you had any luck with finding a publisher for my book yet?"

I ask her that question every time we speak, and her answer is always the same… just like it was that afternoon. A resounding, "No."

She's had my manuscript for over two years and sometimes I wonder if she's even trying to get it published. I know she makes more money out of my acting – as do I – but this isn't what I want to do, and she knows it.

The problem is, I didn't slave over my laptop for months on end to have my novel sitting on my agent's desk, gathering dust, while I tread the boards, keeping the wolf from the door.

"Shall I try another agent?" I said, knowing it would rile her.

"It won't get you anywhere." Her voice was harsher. I knew what was coming next and braced myself. "Your plot isn't original enough. I've told you over and over. You need to re-write it."

"But I like it." I like it exactly as it is. If I didn't, I wouldn't have written it that way.

"It's not about what you like… it's about what will sell, and country house murder mysteries have been done to death."

I refused to listen, just like I'd been refusing ever since she first raised the point, shortly after reading through my manuscript.

Regardless of everything she says, there's nothing wrong with my novel. I know I'm not exactly re-inventing the wheel, but my detective is at least a little different, no matter what Delilah says. He's a doctor, who enjoys reading mystery stories, and when a murder happens right under his nose, he sets about solving it. He has little choice, as there's a convenient snow-storm, stranding the inhabitants of the remote country house where the weekend party is being held, meaning the official police can't get to them. I've set the story in the mid-1920s, when house parties were all the rage, and created some interesting characters... at least, I think they're interesting, even if Delilah doesn't.

But that's because the woman clearly doesn't know what she's talking about.

I lean a little closer to the mirror to double-check I've removed all the make-up, then pick up the pile of cotton pads I've used for cleaning my face, and dump them into the bin. It's moisturiser next, and I apply it liberally, wondering whether I'll need to use so much make-up in my next job. I'm just replacing the lid on the pot when the door crashes open, at least half a dozen people vying to get through it at the same time.

"Knock, why don't you?" I mutter under my breath, although I paint a smile on my face. They mean well, even if they don't understand the word 'privacy'.

Ozzy leads the way, which isn't at all unusual for him. He's carrying a couple of bottles of champagne, swinging them wildly, which won't do the contents any good. Not that he seems to care. He's not the youngest member of the company; he just behaves like he is. Behind him is Anna, the leading lady. She's in her late forties, if I'm being kind... which I am, because I'm nearly always kind to ladies. It's not a trait shared by Ozzy, who's just crashed through the door ahead of her, while the rest of the company wait their turn, giving Anna due deference.

I stand, offering her my seat, and she smiles up at me.

"Why, thank you."

She has a slight southern drawl, and without the awful blonde wig and excessive make-up required for the role she's been playing on the stage, she's a very attractive woman.

The next person into the room is Desmond... our leading man. He's probably ten years older than Anna, although he doesn't look it when made-up, and while he doesn't run the company, he's very much in charge of the actors, and we all look up to him. He comes straight towards me, offering his hand, which I shake.

"It's been a pleasure working with you," he says with a smile.

"Likewise. I've learned a lot from you, Desmond."

"And I from you."

I doubt that, but I'm not surprised by him saying it. It's just the kind of thing he would say. He's forever encouraging younger actors to work harder... to be better.

A few more people pile into the room, but the next one to come over to me is the director. His name is Shawn. At twenty-seven, he's younger than I'd expect most directors to be, but he has a commanding presence, both on and off the stage.

"We're going to miss you," he says, patting me on the arm.

"I'm going to miss all of you, too." That's not a lie. I've made friends here, and although I know I'll stay in touch with Calvin, I doubt I'll be back. Like I said, this isn't what I want to do.

Calvin nudges me. "Uh-oh... here comes trouble."

I look up and see Maggie approaching, and wonder if I can hide somewhere. I glance around, except there's nowhere... other than behind the screen. That won't work, though, because I'm fairly sure she'd follow me, and God knows what she'd expect to happen then. She's been chasing after me since I got here, and if that sounds big-headed, it's not meant to. Maggie chases after everyone. She's about the same age as me and is

attractive enough, in a rather obvious way. To my knowledge, though, there's nothing wrong with her… other than the fact that she's slept with every other male actor in the company, including Calvin.

And Desmond, I believe.

"It won't be the same without you," she murmurs, coming right up to me and brushing her hand up my arm.

"Yeah, it will. You won't even notice I've gone."

"I will." She moves even closer, her body crushed against mine. Then she sighs, ensuring that her ample breasts press into me, and I take a step back, which seems to disappoint her. At that moment, Ozzy comes over, offering glasses of champagne to me and Calvin. "Where's mine?" Maggie asks, pouting at him.

"Over here." He nods towards the table on the far side of the room, and although she seems reluctant to go, she follows him, leaving me to sigh out my relief.

"There's an easy way to get rid of her," Calvin whispers, clinking his glass against mine.

"Oh?"

"Just fuck her. She'll leave you alone then. That's what happened with me."

"It's a nice idea… but I'm leaving, remember? She won't be a problem after tonight."

He chuckles and I take a sip of champagne. I've never 'just fucked' anyone in my life, but I'm not about to say that. I'm not about to admit I haven't had sex since moving here, either. Working in the theatre, learning lines, and keeping very anti-social hours have made it difficult to meet new people. Those all sound like pathetic excuses, I know, but they're genuine enough. And besides, I've always preferred to get to know the women I sleep with. That probably explains why the last woman to share my bed was Moira… the woman I left behind in London. I

wasn't in love with her, or anything like that, but she was my most serious girlfriend to date. We'd been together for nearly eighteen months when I was given the chance to come here. As far as I was concerned, even if acting wasn't my 'thing', it was an adventure, and one I wasn't about to turn down. Moira didn't see it that way. Unlike me, she had family ties, and asking her to leave them all behind was clearly too much.

I wasn't sorry, even if she made our parting more difficult than I felt it needed to be. It worked out for the best in the end. I'm rarely at home, so I'm not sure how much we'd have seen of each other… and if I'm being honest, I don't think we'd have lasted. We had fun together, but she was never 'it' for me.

"Do you think anyone would notice if I snuck out?" I whisper to Calvin, and he looks up at me, frowning slightly.

"Why?"

"I don't want to hang around for a fond farewell." I'm not sure there will be one, but Ozzy's just gone to find more alcohol, and the more drunk they all get, the more likely it is that this gathering will end in tears. They won't be mine, but I'd rather just sneak out, anyway. I'm done here now.

"It'll be fine," he says as he waves towards the door. "Just don't forget us when you're rich and famous."

"I'll never forget you, Calvin."

He chuckles and, keeping my head down to avoid making eye contact, I surreptitiously slip from the room, making it to the corridor with surprising ease.

The stage door is to my right, and I open it, sucking in a lungfull of fresh air, before pulling it closed behind me. I feel ludicrously light-headed, considering I've only had a small glass of champagne. It's not alcohol that's making me feel like that, though… it's a combination of nerves and excitement. I'm terrified about the new job I'm about to start, but to me, that just makes it even more of an adventure.

My apartment isn't far from the theatre, and I let myself in, standing on the threshold for a moment, absorbing the space.

I love it here, and I know how lucky I am to have found this place. When I first came to Boston, the production company I was working for financed my accommodation. The budget wasn't huge, but it ran to a one-bedroom apartment in a fairly nice part of town, not too far from the studios where I worked. That contract duly ended, and when it did, I knew I'd have to find somewhere else to live. I may have fallen in with the theatre company, but they couldn't afford to pay me very much, which meant I couldn't keep my apartment. Luckily, Anna said she knew someone, who knew someone, who might be able to help, and while I was grateful, I fully expected to find myself in a shoebox in a rundown area of Boston. I never anticipated a loft apartment that used to be a dance studio, just a ten minute walk from the theatre, where even at midnight, the light is incredible. The open plan layout helps with that, although I have the privacy of a mezzanine for my bedroom, with everything else, including the bathroom, on this lower level.

I close the door, the moonlight flooding in through the expansive windows, and make my way across to the kitchen, pouring myself a glass of wine. I don't care how late it is, I'm still too wired to go to bed, and I sit on the sofa, put my feet up, and lean back, staring at the high ceiling with a smile on my face.

Life's good. It's really good.

And I think it's about to get a lot better.

Chapter Two

Ella

I hold up my jeans, staring at them. Are they really appropriate for my first day at work? It's so hard to tell, and I sigh, sitting down on the couch in my dressing room. Why didn't I decide what to wear last night? It would have made this morning so much easier.

I know the answer to that, of course. It was because Hunter and Livia came over for dinner. It wasn't something we'd planned, but Hunter called in the afternoon, and I ended up inviting them… probably because I didn't want to spend another evening on my own, worrying about my new job, especially as starting it was so imminent.

They hadn't seen my apartment before, and both seemed impressed when I showed them in. I have to admit, now it's furnished and I've had a few days to get used to the place, I'm really quite pleased with it myself.

We ordered in, and while we were waiting for our food to arrive, and drinking wine in the living room, Hunter told me about their trip to Falmouth to see Livia's parents.

"I'm surprised you're not still there," I said, looking across at them. They were sitting together on one of the couches, while I was on another, opposite them.

He shook his head. "We came home early. I think between us telling them about our engagement and discussing the plans for the house, it was all a bit too much for Livia's dad. He was exhausted this morning, so we thought we'd leave them to it."

"It's sometimes better that way," Livia explained. "I hate feeling like I've abandoned them, but..."

"You won't have to feel like that for much longer." Hunter let go of her hand and put his arm around her instead. I had to smile to myself. It was lovely seeing my brother so happy.

"So they've agreed to the plans?"

He turned to look at me. "How did you know about it?"

"Aside from the fact you just mentioned it, Drew told me."

He nodded his head. "And you're okay with it?"

"Of course. I think it's a fabulous idea."

"I'm sorry I didn't get the chance to discuss it with you, but..."

"You've got nothing to apologize for. I honestly don't mind."

He smiled. "Well... Livia's mom took a little more persuading than you, but we got there in the end, didn't we?" He turned back to Livia again and she gazed up at him, nodding her head.

"When does the work start?" I asked.

"I don't know exactly. Hopefully sometime in the next couple of weeks."

"And how did they react to hearing about your engagement?"

"They seemed pleased."

Livia nudged into him. "They were thrilled. It was just that Dad was getting tired by then. We talked about the house first, which was probably a mistake."

"No, it wasn't. It was intentional. I know I said I wanted to put it to them as your fiancé, but I realized when we were driving up there that it would be better to talk it through while your dad was alert enough to understand. It seemed to me, if we'd broken the news of our engagement first, he'd have been too tired to think

about anything else, and that might have backfired if we'd needed him to help persuade your mom about the house."

"Which was exactly how it happened."

"So, have you set a date?" I asked.

"For the wedding?" I nodded. "Not an actual date, no," Hunter said, smiling down at Livia. "But the architect assures me the house will take around five months to build, so sometime in February, probably…once Livia's parents have moved in. We want them to be there without it tiring them out."

"You're having the wedding at home?"

"Of course."

I wasn't that surprised. We all look on the house in Newport as 'home' even though each of us has an apartment in Boston… including me now.

"Have you heard from Drew?" I asked. "I haven't spoken to him for a few days."

Hunter nodded his head. "We've been talking fairly regularly."

"How do you think he is?"

"In a bad place. He feels guilty for getting Lexi pregnant. He's hurting because he can't even be friends with her sister anymore, let alone have a relationship with her… and he's got no idea what the future holds."

"Is he back from New York?"

"Yeah. He came back on Thursday." He frowned at me, tilting his head. "Don't look so offended." I hadn't been aware that I was, but Hunter could always read me like a book.

"I'm just surprised I haven't seen him, that's all."

"He's not feeling very sociable."

"But he's talking to you on the phone?"

He sighed. "Yeah." He released Livia and leaned forward, his elbows on his knees, his eyes fixed on mine. "It's not personal, Ella. And by that I mean, you shouldn't take his silence

personally. This is all very personal to him, but I think he needs to talk things through with another man... with someone who knows what it feels like to lose the person they love most." He sat back again, taking Livia's hand in his.

"I think it's also not something you or I can understand," Livia said, and I looked over at her.

"Why not?"

"Because I think men have a difference perspective in this situation."

Hunter looked down at her. "Just so you know, I've never been in Drew's situation myself."

She smiled. "I know. I'm just saying I think it's probably easier for you to put yourself in his shoes than it is for Ella and me."

He nodded his head, and I did, too. I could see what she meant, and why my big brother loves her so much.

"Do you think he'll travel around as much as he did before?" I asked. Drew's job has always involved him traveling far and wide. It was one of the things that most appealed to him when he started out. Obviously, he can afford to go wherever he wants, but he once told me he liked the idea of traveling with a purpose, rather than aimlessly... and I guess that makes sense. At least, it does when you've got as much money as we have, and can do whatever you please.

"He said he'll be going to New York a lot more, but as for everything else, he hasn't decided yet. I imagine he'll carry on as before until the baby's born, but nothing's set in stone. He and Lexi haven't decided what they're going to do yet... how they're going to live."

"Not together, I'm guessing."

"No... not together. That much is for certain." He shook his head. "Drew's still getting his head around losing Lexi's sister, let alone the whole concept of becoming a father."

"It's such a mess, isn't it?"

It is a mess, but so am I, and I need to stop sitting here daydreaming about last night and get dressed.

I'm still not sure about jeans and I throw them down on the couch and go back to my closet, standing with my hands on my hips. I'm only wearing the towel I wrapped around myself when I came out of the shower, but I can't even choose my underwear until I've decided about the clothes. Practicality is essential, given what I think I'll be doing, but I also want to be smart… so maybe a dress?

I turn, opening the closet behind me. It's warm today, so a summer dress would do, and I pull out the yellow one with blue piping, holding it up. It's new, and French… like a lot of my clothes. I'd gained a few pounds while I was in Paris. It was one of the hazards of learning to cook, I guess. Before I came home, I wanted to get back in shape, and as well as watching what I ate, I joined a gym for the first time in my life. As a result, most of my old clothes didn't fit… and that gave me the perfect excuse to go out and buy some new ones.

This dress came from a lovely little boutique I discovered on the Boulevard St. Germain. It's quite fitted, but stretchy, so I can move around easily in it, and it's informal enough that it shouldn't look like I'm trying too hard.

"Perfect."

A white bra and panties will be fine, and I grab them, heading back to the bedroom, where I throw everything onto the bed and start styling my hair. I don't know who thought short hair was easier to maintain, but they were wrong. I keep mine this length because it saves me having to tie it up in the kitchen, but it still takes me a good twenty minutes to straighten it into the pixie style I like, and then work through the smoothing oil, to make it look messed up. If I'm not going anywhere, I can just let it dry naturally, and I often do, but I'm trying to create the right

impression today... even if I'm not entirely sure what that impression is.

One thing I do know as an absolute certainty is that I'm not wearing heels today. I fully expect I'll be on my feet until the time I get back here tonight, so I'm going for comfort, and once I'm dressed, I wander back into the dressing room to find my navy slingback ballerina flats. They have huge blue buckles on the front, and I love them.

Finally, I grab a cardigan. My dress is sleeveless and if I end up working late, I might get chilly...

My stomach is churning with nerves, so I skip breakfast, making myself a coffee and pouring it into a travel mug. I'm running a little later than I'd hoped, thanks to my indecision – and my daydreaming – and I grab my purse and knife case, and head out the door.

I've been sent a list of instructions, which include the code for the parking garage, and I input it into the device by the barrier, waiting until it rises, and I can drive through. None of the spaces seem to be numbered, or have anyone's name by them, and I park beside a Lexus, making for the elevators in the corner. The instructions say to go to the fourth floor, so I press the button numbered '4', and suck in a breath, trying to calm my nerves as the doors close.

Unfortunately, they open again within moments, before I've had time to release that breath, and I step out to face a long, light wood reception desk. Standing behind it is a pretty blonde, who turns to me with a smile.

"Can I help?"

"I'm Ella Bennett. Kennedy Black is expecting me."

Her smile widens. "Ahh, yes." She nods over my shoulder. "If you want to take a seat, I'll let Ms. Black know you're both here now."

Both? I turn as she picks up a telephone, to see a dark-haired man already sitting on one of two couches. He's casually dressed in jeans and a white button-down shirt, and I'm wondering if I should have gone with my first instinct, and worn jeans too.

He glances up as I approach, then stands in a most gentlemanly way, and I struggle not to gasp. He's heavenly… and he has the most perfect smile. It seems to match his deep blue eyes, which are currently roaming over me, in a heated gaze. I ought to be offended… I know that. I should probably tell him I'm not a piece of meat, or an object to be judged. But I can't, because my eyes are wandering, too, so to tell him off would be something of a double standard. He has to be at least six foot five, and while I've always thought of my brothers as muscular, this man takes it to a completely different level, his biceps positively bulging as he raises his right hand, pushing his fingers back through his thick, dark brown hair.

"Ms. Black will be along in a moment." The woman's voice startles me back to reality, and without a word, I take a seat at the opposite end of the couch, putting my knife case down by my feet. The man sits back down too, and I wonder if I should say something… maybe introduce myself, as it seems we're both here to see Kennedy Black. Except I'm not sure my voice will work properly. My nerves are still threatening to get the better of me… and he's not making any effort, so why should I?

The silence is just becoming awkward when I look up to see Kennedy Black walking toward us. In her precarious heels, she's around five foot nine – so about the same height as me, except I'm wearing flats – and she has unnaturally blonde hair, which she wears tied up in a neat but fairly stark bun behind her head. Her stick-thin body is encased in a tight black dress that's practically glued to her. She's wearing a lot of makeup, perfectly applied to flawless skin, and it's impossible to say how old she is.

If I had to guess, I'd say she's in her early forties, but luckily, I don't have to guess.

Before I can even flinch, the man beside me quickly leaps to his feet, and I copy him, both of us holding out our hands, although it's mine that Kennedy reaches for.

"Welcome, Ella."

"Thanks."

She turns to the man and although I know I'm being childish, I can't help feeling a stupid sense of triumph that Kennedy greeted me first.

"Have you two introduced yourselves?" she asks, letting go of his hand.

"No." He shakes his head, looking down at me. I half expect him to say I've only just arrived, but he doesn't.

"Well… let me do it for you." She tilts her head toward me. "Ella Bennett, meet Blake MacKenzie."

I turn, and he offers me his hand, which I accept. "My friends call me Mac," he says and I notice his British accent. It's unmistakable and very sexy. "What do your friends call you?"

"Ella."

"Okay." He frowns, turning back to Kennedy. What's his problem? I don't have a nickname. I never have had, so I'm not being standoffish… just honest. Don't tell me he's going to be super-sensitive to everything I say? That's the last thing I need. Not that I know who he is, or if we're even going to be working closely together. Kennedy hasn't been forthcoming with that piece of information yet.

She looks at the gold watch on her wrist and then back up at us again, her eyes settling on me. "We need to get on." I nod my head, because I feel it's expected, and she turns away. "I've set up a meeting," she says as she walks back down the hall. It seems we're supposed to follow, so I quickly grab my knife case, and

Blake and I catch up to her while she talks to us – or rather at us – over her shoulder. "I'll introduce you to the team, so you can find out who you'll be working with, but don't worry about remembering who they all are."

I wonder if the people who work for her mind being dismissed so readily, although I doubt they have a choice.

At the end of the hall, she opens the door on the left, going in first. Blake waits and I pass through ahead of him, although I wish I hadn't when I see how many people are in the room. There must be at least twenty of them, either seated at the enormous oval-shaped table, or in chairs around the edge of the room, and they all stand and look at us.

I can feel myself blushing as Kennedy walks over to the head of the table, taking a seat.

"Ella, sit here beside me," she says, and I do as I'm told, while she indicates that Blake should take the seat next to mine. Everyone else sits down, too, and although I feel like they're all staring at me, I know they're not. Blake is getting just as much attention. In fact, he's getting a lot more… especially from the women in the room.

Kennedy coughs, and all heads turn in her direction, which makes her smile.

"Good morning," she says, and I half expect the assembled group to reply, 'Good morning, Miss,' like they were still in school. They don't. They simply nod their heads, some of them smiling. "This is the Meal Master team." I'm not sure who Kennedy's talking to, but she holds out her arms in a collective acknowledgement, and I struggle not to laugh. 'Meal Master'? Is that the best name they could come up with? It's awful… "I think we'll start with introductions."

She turns to the lady on the other side of Blake, who leans forward and smiles in my direction. "I'm Ruby. I'm the floor manager."

She's probably in her mid-thirties, with dark blonde hair, and she gives me a sympathetic look, like she knows how nervous I am. I nod my head, trying to appear grateful and knowledgeable at the same time, when I realize the man beside her is talking.

"Vince... sound," he says, in a deep, monosyllabic voice, which matches his dour appearance. He's quite young to be wearing such a stern expression, and as he glances at his watch, I wonder if this meeting has interrupted something more important.

In studying him, I've missed the next two people, and I realize Kennedy was right; I'm never going to remember everyone, or their titles. Instead, I let their words drift over me, nodding my head and trying to look polite. I'll have to catch up with who they are later.

Eventually, we've made it around the room, and although my head is spinning, I focus on Kennedy for a moment or two before it becomes clear she's got no intention of introducing herself. I suppose she doesn't need to. Everyone knows who she is... and that she's the executive producer. In other words, she's in charge, and I get the impression no-one is allowed to forget it.

She looks at me. It's my turn to say something, and I lick my lips, my throat drying, although I croak out, "My name's Ella. I'm the culinary consultant." I feel a little pompous saying that, when I'm really a chef. But the title on my contract says 'culinary consultant', and I get the feeling that, if I called myself a 'chef', Kennedy would correct me. She seems like that kind of woman. And besides, the man beside me is the real chef...

I twist in my seat slightly, the spotlight now on him, and he stares at me for a moment before turning and facing the assembled group. "Hi. I'm Blake MacKenzie. I guess I'm the presenter."

Mac

I look around at the sea of faces, none of their names registering with me, nor their job titles, for that matter. I've never been a great one for titles… especially not 'Meal Master'. Who the hell thought of that monstrosity? Frankly, I'd like to wring their neck. As for names, I rarely use the one I was given at birth, preferring to stick with the nickname I was awarded at school… although Ella Bennett didn't seem to appreciate that when I told her. Instead, she just stared at me, like I'd grown a second head.

She may be aloof, but she's beautiful, there's no denying that. Her short dark hair fits neatly around her lovely face, and I know from years of experience that she will have spent ages perfecting that style. I've spent far too long waiting around for girlfriends to get ready, to underestimate the time these things take. In Ella's case, the effect she's achieved is like someone has been running their fingers through her hair… or she's just got out of bed, which makes me wonder what she looks like first thing in the morning. I know what she looks like right now, in that figure-hugging dress. She looks divine. When I first heard her speak, telling the receptionist she was here to see Kennedy Black, I looked up from my seat, simply because I was here to see Kennedy as well. I hadn't caught her name, even though I was fairly sure she'd said it. I couldn't be absolutely certain about that, though, because I was distracted at the time by the sight of her delectable backside. My cock twitched in acknowledgement of the vision before me. Although in my defence, she was leaning over slightly, and her dress was quite tight, so there wasn't really anywhere else to look. She turned around moments later, and I wasn't disappointed. As

I say… she's beautiful, and I couldn't help admiring her, or smiling to myself when I noticed her eyes taking a tour.

I wondered if we should shake hands then, but I couldn't decide what to say and ended up pushing my fingers back through my hair instead, in a very uncool move. Luckily, Kennedy arrived a few minutes later, so what was merely awkward avoided becoming embarrassing.

Now, Ella is sitting beside me in this brightly lit room, with her silver case on the floor between us. We're close enough that I can see her amber coloured eyes have flecks of green in them, and that although her skin is porcelain smooth, she's barely wearing any make-up at all.

The woman beside Kennedy sits forward slightly. She's probably in her late-twenties with long, straight brown hair, and much darker brown eyes. "I'm Diana… the make-up artist, so you'll be seeing quite a lot of me." She looks at me as she's speaking, which makes sense. We'll be the ones working together, after all.

The next in line would be Kennedy, but she doesn't introduce herself and simply turns to Ella, who pauses for a second or two, then licks her lips, taking her time. She seems even more nervous now than she was before.

"My name's Ella. I'm the culinary consultant." Her voice is a little hoarse, and she blushes as she speaks, although I don't know why. Without her, none of this is going to happen. Believe me.

She turns, facing me, and I stare at her glistening lips, mesmerised… perhaps even a little enchanted. Then I remember where I am and look back at everyone else.

"Hi… I'm Blake MacKenzie. I guess I'm the presenter."

I thought for a moment then about saying, 'I'm the actor', or even 'I'm the fraud'. I'm starting to feel like one in the present company. Everyone else in the room seems to know what they're doing, while I'm less and less sure why I'm even here.

Kennedy clears her throat, getting the attention back on her again, and she places her hands, palms down, flat on the table in front of her.

"This first season will be ten episodes long," she says, even though I'm pretty sure everyone here already knows that. I do. It was in the contract. "If we're gonna persuade the network to give us a shot at a second season, then trust me, we need to ensure this one is perfect."

Perfect? Could she set the bar a little higher? A few faces turn to me, and I feel the pressure mounting. We may be a team, but the weight of getting it 'perfect' is going to fall on me. We all know that. Even so, I try to stay focused, not wanting to miss anything important.

"As you all know," Kennedy continues, "the format is simple. Each week, a different guest will present us with their culinary problem, and Blake – or Blain as he's going to be known for our purposes – will solve it for them… on air."

I raise my hand, feeling a little childish, except that I need to stop her talking and this seems like the only way.

"Excuse me?"

She turns, her eyes narrowing. "Yes?"

"Did you just say 'Blain'?"

"Yes, I did. That's what we've decided to call you."

"Blain MacKenzie?"

"No. Just Blain. You won't have a last name. We think it'll make you sound more interesting."

"I didn't realise I was boring."

She smiles at me, in the same way you might smile at a small child who's failed to understand the simple concept of adding one plus one. "It'll be better for the show… trust me."

She looks down at the table, but I raise my hand again, and she sighs, tilting her head at me. "When you said I would solve each

guest's problem on air, you didn't mean it would be live, did you?"

There's a slight ripple of laughter around the table, and I feel stupid now for having asked the question.

"No," she says, and I can hear the impatience in her voice. "We'll record in advance, one episode per week."

The woman sitting beside me leans a little closer. "Recordings take place on a Thursday." I can't remember her name, but I know she said she was the floor manager, which even I realise means she's pretty much in charge of everything that happens in the studio.

"Thursday?"

She nods her head. "Most of the week will be taken up with preparations and rehearsals, we'll record on Thursdays and allow Fridays to pick up any continuity errors or other mistakes that need re-recording, and also for Ella to begin work on the following week's content."

I feel a hand on my arm and turn to see Kennedy leaning right over, across Ella, which strikes me as rude. Her eyes are fixed on mine, though, in a way that tells me I need to keep quiet.

"I know you're new to this, but trust me, it'll be fine."

I'm not entirely 'new' to this, but I refrain from telling her that and I smile and nod my head, wondering why she keeps saying 'trust me', like that. In my experience, when someone feels the need to repeat those two words, it usually means 'run... run as fast as you can, and don't look back', and while I'm tempted, I like to eat, so I'm staying put.

She sits back and opens her mouth to say something else, just as Ella raises her hand, copying my earlier action. Kennedy turns to her, her face like thunder at yet another interruption. Not that Ella seems to notice.

"Can I ask..." she says.

"Ask what?"

Kennedy's impatience is getting the better of her and I half expect Ella to blush and say it doesn't matter. She doesn't, though. She frowns and says, "About the guests and their questions. Will I have any input in choosing which ones are selected for each episode? And will I get to meet the people first?"

Kennedy rolls her eyes. "You don't need to worry about any of that. The selections have already been made…"

"By whom?" Ella interrupts her, and I bite my lip, trying not to smile. She might have been nervous before, but she's got the bit between her teeth now, and she's not letting go.

"By me."

"I see. Your knowledge and experience of cookery being…?" Ella leaves her question hanging and I – along with just about everyone else in the room – brace myself for Kennedy's response. It won't be good. That much is obvious from the dark expression on her face.

"Irrelevant," she snaps. "The questions have been chosen because they'll make good television."

"And the guests?" Ella persists. "The members of the public?"

"They're not members of the public. They're actors."

"Seriously?" The word leaves my lips and everyone turns to me. I knew the whole thing was a sham – I'm evidence of that – but they're not even going to use real guests?

"Yes, seriously." Kennedy huffs, shaking her head. I guess she's not used to justifying herself. "In a situation like ours, involving members of the public is fraught with all kinds of dangers. We're going to use genuine problems, sent in by viewers, but have actors play the parts of the people presenting them." She pushes a blue folder across the table in Ella's direction, as though the subject is now closed. "This is the list of questions you're going to be working on during this season."

Ella hesitates for a moment, like she's not sure whether she's supposed to open the file now, but Kennedy looks down at it rather pointedly, and Ella folds back the flap, pulling out the top sheet, and glancing down at it. The room falls to silence, all eyes fixed on her, which is unfortunate, because it means we all hear her snort of laughter.

"What's wrong?" Kennedy says, frowning and sitting forward in her seat.

Ella looks up. "This…" She taps the piece of paper. "It isn't a problem, and even if it were, the answer is common sense, and certainly doesn't need explaining on a television show."

Kennedy glances over, presumably to refresh her memory, as she's just told us she selected the 'problems' herself. "It might be common sense to you, dear, but it isn't to everyone. That's the whole point of the show. We're taking cookery back to basics."

She looks around the table for support and gets it in the form of nodding heads and sycophantic smiles. Ella blushes and I feel sorry for her, watching as she puts the piece of paper back into the folder again. I wonder about saying something, even if it's just to ask what the 'problem' is, but that would probably only make matters worse, and I think in her shoes, I'd rather forget the whole thing.

The woman sitting beside me leans forward. "Shall I show Ella and Blake around the studio?" She's looking at Kennedy, but I sense a solidarity with Ella and myself… or maybe that's just wishful thinking. I'm feeling very much on the outside here.

"I think that would be an excellent idea." Kennedy's reply makes me think she'll be glad to see the back of us, especially as she stands the moment she's finished speaking. The others follow suit, filing from the room, until we're left alone, just the three of us.

I get the feeling Ella's still smarting from Kennedy's remarks, and it wouldn't hurt to take some of the heat from her, so I turn

to the other woman. "Forgive me… I can't remember your name."

She smiles. "I'm Ruby."

"The floor manager, right?"

"That's it."

She gets to her feet, revealing that she's around five foot seven tall, and is wearing casual grey trousers and a white blouse. I stand up too, as does Ella, grabbing the folder at the same time, and holding it close to her chest.

"I'm sorry," she says, biting on her lip, which is only a little distracting, "but what exactly is a floor manager?"

Ruby chuckles. "That depends who you ask. The director would tell you I'm just here to fulfil his or her wishes. My assistant would say I'm here to boss them around. In reality, it's my job to make sure everything runs smoothly, so we stick to the schedule."

"And how do you do that?" Ella asks.

"By knowing what's happening at all times. No-one's even allowed into the studio without checking in with me first."

"So, you're in charge?"

Ruby laughs a little louder. "Hell, no. Kennedy's in charge. She's the executive producer, and the buck stops with her. In terms of creating the show, the director calls the shots… quite literally. But I'm the one who makes it all happen. Although it's probably best if you don't tell either of them I said that."

Ella nods her head, although she's frowning slightly. "What's wrong?" I ask her and she looks up at me.

"I don't remember anyone saying they were the director. Or did I miss that?"

I wrack my brain, trying to recall all the names and job titles, but I can't think who it was either, and we both turn to Ruby, who's smiling at us.

"That's because he's not here. Linus Hicks is our director." I'm not sure if we're supposed to recognise the name, but it's not

familiar to me, and judging by the blank expression on Ella's face, I'd say she's never heard of him either. "He's done a couple of cookery shows before, but he made his name in daytime quizzes."

"Is that significant?" It doesn't sound like a claim to fame to me, but what do I know?

"It means he's used to working quickly. The turnaround time on a daytime quiz is next to nothing."

"I see."

"When will we meet him?" Ella asks.

"Not until rehearsals start, and then obviously he'll be here for the recording sessions." She glances at Ella and then up at me. "Don't look so worried." She pats my arm and I try to change my expression, unaware that I'd given myself away so easily. "Linus is a pussycat, and in any case, he'll be up in the booth. I'll be the one pushing you around in the studio."

Ruby doesn't seem the type to push anyone around, although I'm still surprised that the director won't be putting in an appearance until so late in the schedule.

"Is it normal for the director not to take part in the planning?" I ask, unable to help myself.

She hesitates for a moment and sighs, shrugging her shoulders slightly. "I wouldn't say it's normal, no, but you need to remember, this is a new show. Budgets are tight, and Kennedy's argument is there's no point in paying a director's fee when we can manage perfectly well without him."

"So what does he do in the meantime? Sit around at home waiting for us to call and say we're ready for him?" I ask.

She smiles. "No. He's a freelance, like a lot of directors these days. He has other projects he's working on and he's fitting in around our schedule."

"I see." I nod my head. "What about scriptwriters?"

"You mean scriptwriter… singular. That would be Gavin. He was in the meeting, sitting next to Vivian."

"And who was Vivian?"

"My assistant."

I shake my head. "I don't remember her… sorry."

"Don't worry about it. It's a lot to take on board."

"Why is there only one scriptwriter?" Ella asks, as though she'd been expecting more. I had too… but I've got more experience of this than she has.

"Again, it's a budgeting necessity. And…" She pauses and we both look at her. She's focusing on Ella, though, and I wonder what's coming next. "And Kennedy thought you'd want to have some input into the scripts."

"Me? I know nothing about writing."

"You don't have to, really… not in this instance. Gavin's very good at what he does. But your culinary expertise will be invaluable."

Ella frowns, but I don't know why. I'd love the chance to get involved in the writing. I doubt I'll be given it, though. And in any case, I feel like I've already got my hands full.

Ruby starts for the door, perhaps hoping to halt our questions, and I take the chance to lean in to Ella. "Are you okay?"

She turns, her frown deepening as she looks up at me. "I'm fine."

That was a little dismissive. I was only being friendly… or trying to, and I watch her walk away, shrugging my shoulders. Beautiful or not, she can be really frosty.

I follow Ella to the door, which Ruby is holding open, making it there just in time to see Ruby smile at her and place a hand on her bare arm.

"Don't worry too much about Kennedy," she says, keeping her voice quiet. "She can be abrupt sometimes."

"I noticed."

"You have to bear in mind, she's got a lot riding on this show."

I'm not sure that's a good enough excuse for deliberately belittling someone, but I don't comment. It seems Ella can be quite abrupt too, when she wants to be.

As I step outside and we start along the corridor, she hangs back a little, and I hear a slight sniffle. When I turn, she's pulling a tissue from her handbag, and I'd swear there are tears in her eyes. I want to ask if she's okay again, but I doubt she'd thank me. She seems embarrassed about being upset... and having me draw attention to it won't help. I turn away to give her some privacy, but I'm wondering if I might have misjudged her. Perhaps she's not so frosty after all. Maybe it's Kennedy's attitude that's made her defensive...

"I'm just gonna focus on the areas you really need to know about." Ruby stops walking and turns around as she's speaking and I step just slightly to my right, to block her view of Ella, and hopefully give her the chance to compose herself before she catches up with us. It seems to work. Within seconds, she's by my side, and when I glance at her, she looks perfectly normal... and very beautiful.

We're standing by a door and Ruby opens it to reveal a make-up room.

"This obviously concerns Blake more than you," she says, turning to Ella with a smile before she looks at me. "I think you're familiar with what goes on in here?"

"I am."

I glance inside, noting the three make-up stations, their chairs tucked neatly beneath the black surfaces. The lights around the mirrors are switched off, making it feel dull and lifeless, and I'm about to step inside when I notice Ella, standing right beside me.

"I never realised they actually had lights around the mirrors like that," she says, sounding intrigued. "I thought that was just something they did in the movies."

"It's to replicate the lights in the studio." I look down at her, studying her enquiring face, her full, rose-pink lips and flawless skin.

"Oh… I see." She frowns, tilting her head slightly. "Will you need to wear make-up then?"

"Yes, he will."

We both spin around at the sound of a voice and see a woman coming towards us. I recognise her from this morning's meeting. She was the make-up artist, although I cannot, for the life of me, remember her name. Now she's standing up, though, I can see she's around five foot six tall, and like most people here, she's casually dressed in black jeans and a grey t-shirt.

"Ahh… Diana," Ruby says, saving me the trouble of asking. "I'm sorry we've intruded. I was just showing Blake and Ella where hair and make-up is."

"Well… Ella won't be needing my services," she says with a smile and then turns to me, narrowing her eyes as she assesses my face with a professional eye. "And I know I said you'd be seeing quite a lot of me, but on second thoughts, I don't think you will." She sighs. "Such beautiful eyes… and perfect skin…"

I'm not sure how to reply to that, but Ruby saves me the trouble. "We'd better be getting along."

Diana nods her head and we step out of her doorway, allowing her to move inside the room, as we pass on down the hallway, going through a set of double doors. Here, the corridor widens and although there are several doors on our right, there's only one on the left.

"The men's room is just here," Ruby says, nodding to the first door on the right. "And the ladies' room is at the other end." She stops by the solitary door on the left and opens it. "This is the rehearsal studio."

We all move inside, and she flicks on the lights to reveal a vast room. It has a high ceiling and is mostly empty, other than the

large kitchen area at the back, and the table right in front of us, which is surrounded by half a dozen chairs. Between the two is an empty space, which I know is where the cameras would be in a real studio.

Ella wanders over to the kitchen, putting her folder down on the work surface and turning around to face us. "I appreciate this is for rehearsing, but is everything real? I mean, the ovens are fully functioning, and there's running water, and a working refrigerator, isn't there?"

"It's an exact replica of how the kitchen will look in the main studio," Ruby says, going over to her. "Blake needs to get used to where all the equipment is, so every detail is identical."

Ella nods her head, and Ruby wanders to a door in the corner of the room, which I hadn't noticed until now. She opens it, revealing yet another kitchen.

"What's that for?" I ask.

"It's for your personal use," she says. "You'll be spending a lot of time in here, so if you want to make a coffee…"

"We can't just make it over there?" I nod towards the professional kitchen and she smiles, shaking her head.

"It's gonna be best if you keep that for rehearsing… for the show."

I'm not sure I understand why, but I go along with her. She seems to know what she's doing. There's not very much more to see in here, and although I can tell Ella is itching to spend more time in the kitchen, there seem to be other things that Ruby wants to show us, and she makes her way back to the door, clearly expecting us to follow.

Ella picks up her folder again, and I wait for her to pass through the door, closing it behind me.

Outside, Ruby takes us through yet another set of double doors into an equally wide corridor, with just two doors; one on either side.

"We'll be filming in here," she says, opening the door to our right, and letting us into what is essentially a large, very dark, very empty room.

"Where's the kitchen?" Ella asks, getting in the obvious question before I can.

"Unfortunately, the studios are used for filming other shows during the rest of the week, so we'll install it on Wednesday evenings, in time for filming to start on Thursdays... and then take it out again on Fridays as soon as everything's wrapped."

Ella frowns, but remains silent, and so do I, even though that sounds like an inordinate waste of time to me. Ruby reiterates how tight the schedules are, which I feel has been said a dozen times already, and I turn around and almost gasp out loud when I see the banked seating behind me.

"I—I know Kennedy said the shows weren't going out live, but we're not recording in front of an audience, are we?"

"No." Ruby shakes her head. "Each show will probably take the entire day to shoot, and they'll be full-on days. It's going to be stressful enough as it is, without throwing a live audience into the mix."

I've never felt so relieved in my life. Acting in front of an audience is one thing... and I'm quite used to it, after my experiences in the theatre. Playing the role of an alcoholic chef was challenging. I got by, though. It was how I landed this part. But cooking for real, with people actually watching me? I'd be terrified...

I'm all for adventures, but even I have my limits.

Chapter Three

‑⁓‑

Ella

Is it me, or does it seem really dumb that the person who has to create the content for theses cookery shows, and who bears the title 'culinary consultant', gets no say in what will actually be cooked?

I understand that Kennedy's choices might make 'good television', but based on the first one, they're going to be pretty damn hard to make interesting... or even watchable. And if they're all like that. The next ten weeks are going to be a lot more challenging than I'd expected.

Kennedy's responses seemed uncalled-for, and even if Ruby and Blake tried to be kind about it, I wasn't really in the mood for kindness, or for discussing it anymore. I hope neither of them thought I was being dismissive. Because I wasn't. I was just trying not to cry. It wouldn't have looked good on my first day, and although there were tears in my eyes, I kept them at bay, and with any luck, neither of them noticed.

One thing I couldn't fail to notice was how differently Kennedy behaved toward Blake. Sure, she was a little testy in her replies, but she was nowhere near as scathing to him as she was

to me. Was that because he's the 'talent'? He so clearly is, judging by the way everyone fawned over him in the meeting, and the makeup artist doted on his 'perfect' skin, and 'beautiful' eyes just now. And while I'm not saying he doesn't have perfect skin, or beautiful eyes, I'm feeling belittled and humiliated, when the reality of the situation is his skin and eyes won't count for anything, if I can't come up with exciting content for the shows.

As I look around the studio, I'm still struggling to understand why they'd bother to deconstruct and re-construct the kitchen so often… but I'm not about to query their decisions anymore. I've learned my lesson.

Blake is looking around too, while Ruby repeats the mantra she's spoken several times so far this morning, about the schedules being tight, and I wonder for a moment why he introduced himself as 'the presenter', rather than 'the chef'. It seems like an odd way for him to have described himself, but maybe he was concerned about there being two chefs on this project, and didn't want to appear to be stealing the limelight… not that it matters to me. I always knew I'd be working with someone else. It was my primary concern when I was interviewed. I had no desire to appear before the cameras, and I still don't. It's never appealed to me, and I told Kennedy that when she interviewed me. I was still in Paris at the time, and was reeling from the fact that one of my tutors had recommended me for this job. Pierre had never seemed that impressed with my abilities. In fact, he'd been quite dismissive, and I'd assumed he'd thought of me as a waste of space; someone who was only there because she couldn't think of anything else to do… a poor little rich kid, I guess. When he told me he'd been made aware of this opportunity and had put my name forward for it, I was speechless… grateful, but speechless. I was excited too. Despite my training, I had no interest in working in a hotel or restaurant.

The hours really didn't appeal, and neither did the atmosphere. It wasn't until I'd thanked Pierre that I started to worry... would they want me to be on camera? The thought was terrifying. It was the first question I asked Kennedy during my interview, and she was very reassuring. My role would be strictly 'behind the scenes'. It would be my responsibility to create the menus and recipes, cook the dishes that would be used on the shows, and assist the chef. She used the word 'chef', even though Blake didn't, and I suppose it was that, and her insistence on so much secrecy, that made me wonder if the 'chef' might be a celebrity.

Except it seems not, because I don't recognize Blake at all.

One thing Kennedy didn't mention at any point, was scriptwriting. I have no idea what that might entail, but I find it odd that I'm not allowed any input into deciding which questions will form the content of the shows, but my 'culinary knowledge' is evidently going to be 'invaluable' in writing the scripts.

Go figure...

"I—I know Kennedy said the shows weren't going out live, but we're not recording in front of an audience, are we?"

For the first time this morning, it's Blake's turn to sound nervous and I turn to look at him. He's frowning at Ruby, and I can see why now. Behind him, there are rows and rows of seats... probably enough for at least two hundred people.

Ruby shakes her head, seemingly as patient with him as she's been with me, even though I get the feeling he's much more experienced in the ways of a television studio than I am. "No. Each show will probably take the entire day to shoot, and they'll be full-on days. It's going to be stressful enough as it is, without throwing a live audience into the mix."

Blake seems relieved by her answer, nodding his head, and relaxing. For myself, I'm not sure I like the sound of what she's saying. It all sounds very pressured... and I'm feeling enough of

that on my own account. I suppose I should be grateful, though. At least there won't be an audience to witness my inevitable mistakes.

We head for the door again, and I wonder where we're going to be taken next. I'm getting sick of carrying my knife case around, I could murder a cup of coffee, my head is already spinning, and even though I've got something of a reputation for being outgoing, I've never felt more like running away and hiding. I feel so completely out of my depth.

Once we're out in the hall, we retrace our steps, going back through the double doors, and coming to a halt outside the rehearsal room.

"I'm gonna leave you to get on," Ruby says. "Unfortunately, even though schedules are normally tight, this week is gonna be even more crazy."

"It is?" Blake frowns down at her.

"Yeah. As I said in the meeting just now, the way we've organized this is that, in a normal schedule, Ella will have planned out the following week's content on the previous Friday."

"When the rest of us are re-recording any problems that might have arisen the previous day?" he says and Ruby nods her head.

"Won't I be needed in the studio?" I ask.

"You might," Ruby says. "But there should still be plenty of time for you to do your planning, so when you guys arrive on the Monday morning, your ingredients would be set up and everything would be ready for you to get straight down to work, practicing the dishes. Then, sometime on Monday afternoon, the rest of the team would join you and we'd start working on the script, so we could begin full rehearsals as soon as possible. Everything has to slot into place, you see…" She turns to face me. "As it is, we're running late."

The clock is ticking and I'm not allowed to forget it.

"Where do we work?" I ask, as it hits me that, not only are we going to be recording this week, which I hadn't expected, but I have less time than I usually would to do my job... a job I don't fully understand yet.

"In there," she says, nodding toward the rehearsal room, her eyes darting from me to Blake and back again. "Don't look so worried. My office is just across the hall... here." She turns, taking a step back, and opens the door behind her. "If you need anything, just ask."

There are so many questions... like why I thought I was good enough to do this job in the first place... who was the idiot who thought we'd be ready to record our first show just three days from now... and why I'm wasting time standing in the hall, when I should be working...

"Shall we?" Blake says, and I startle, realizing Ruby's office door is closed. She must have gone inside, and I didn't even notice. Blake is standing by the door to the rehearsal room, holding it open, and I pass through, taking a deep breath to calm myself.

I can do this.

I gaze at the table for a moment, but by-pass it and wander over to the kitchen area. It's my natural domain and I feel more at home here. Blake follows, standing on the opposite side of the island unit. Between us is a five-ring hob and plenty of preparation space, which I suppose makes sense. This is a replica of the kitchen that will be used in the show, which means I'm standing where he would be when he's presenting. Just thinking that makes me feel nervous again, and I put my knife case on the countertop, placing the file Kennedy gave me on top.

"Do you have your own set of knives?" I ask, looking up at Blake.

"No," he says, frowning and evidently surprised by my question. "Do you?"

"Of course." I may not have paid as much attention as I should during all of my classes, but one thing I can remember is that all self-respecting chefs own their own knives. I bought mine the day after I graduated, by way of celebration. To prove the point, I push the blue file to one side and open my silver knife case, revealing the blades inside. Blake leans over, getting a good look, and then stares down at me again.

"Impressive," he says, smiling.

I can't see why he'd be impressed by a set of knives, but that's the least of my problems, and I close the lid again, letting out a sigh. "Is it me, or does this all feel a bit rushed?"

"It feels very rushed. I hadn't realized we were going to be recording this week."

"No. Neither had I."

He shakes his head, his smile fading. "I'd assumed there would be a more gentle breaking-in for both of us … with a few production meetings first, before we got down to recording next week."

He seems to understand the process a lot better than I do, but I nod my head anyway. "I think they must have had the production meetings in our absence, don't you?"

"I'd like to think so. But if that were the case, they ought to be more prepared than this."

My stomach churns, my nerves returning, as I realize how much of this process depends on me. "I suppose we should get on, really …"

I open the file, pulling out the sheet of paper I glanced at earlier.

"How complicated is the first question?" he asks, before I even have time to look at it again, and for a second or two, I wonder

if he's being facetious, trying to remind me of Kennedy's reaction in the meeting. I don't comment, but hand the page over to him. He looks down, reading it to himself, and then looks up again. "You think the answer to this is common sense, do you?"

"Of course it is." I can't see why he wouldn't think so, too. "It's just logic."

"Not to me, it's not."

What's he talking about? Have I given him the wrong document? Is there something more complicated to come later in the season? I hope so…

I hold out my hand and he gives it back to me, waiting while I read it for myself…

'My boyfriend has invited his parents for dinner, and his dad's favorite dish is roast lamb. I've never cooked a roast dinner before, and I'm terrified I won't be able to get everything ready at the same time. I'm desperate to make a good impression… please help!'

I look up at him again, tilting my head to one side as I put down the piece of paper. "Are you seriously saying you couldn't prepare a roast dinner and get all the components ready at the same time?"

He chuckles, shaking his head. "No. I'm saying I couldn't get any kind of dinner ready."

"Why on earth not?"

"Probably because I can't cook," he says, still smiling.

I take a half step back, unable to help myself. "Y—You can't cook?"

"No."

"But you're a chef."

"No, I'm not. I'm an actor."

Mac

Her expression is priceless. It's a cross between blank bewilderment and building anger. She struggles, one emotion fighting it out with the other, until, in the end, anger wins.

"W—What do you mean, you're an actor?" She stammers over her words, pushing her fingers back through her hair, and while I try to focus on what she's saying, it just got seriously complicated. She looked amazing before, but now she's messed up her hair a little more, she looks insanely hot, and it's taking all my willpower not to walk around the island unit, grab hold of her, and kiss her. That's not something I'd normally do, but she's disturbing the hell out of me. "Well?" she says and I realise she's waiting for an answer, and being distracted isn't helping.

"I'm an actor," I say, trying to focus. "I don't know how else to phrase that."

"But what are you doing here?"

"Acting, I guess." She narrows her eyes at me, but before she can yell at me for being flippant, I hold up my hands. "I don't know any more than you do, Ella. I was hired to present a cookery show."

"Even though you can't cook?"

"Yes. I told Kennedy when she auditioned me. I made it very clear I wasn't kidding, or being modest. Boiling water is a struggle for me. She said it didn't matter, and that someone else would take care of the cooking. All I had to do was speak my lines and act out the cooking part." I smile at her, tilting my head slightly. "I guess you're the 'someone else'."

She rests her hands on the work surface, leaning over slightly and shaking her head. "I suppose I must be." She stares at me for

a moment and then looks down at the piece of paper in front of her. "Would you excuse me for a moment?" she says, although she doesn't look up as she speaks, but steps away toward the end of the island unit. I meet her there, grabbing her arm before she can make her escape. Her skin is feather-soft, and we both seem to gasp at the same time, although she looks down at my hand, and I quickly remove it, wondering if I've overstepped the mark.

"Sorry... but where are you going?"

"To find out what's going on here."

"In that case, I think I'll come with you. I'd quite like to know myself."

She pauses for a second or two and then nods her head and turns, walking away. I follow – not that I was asking her permission – and we head for the door. She almost yanks it off of its hinges, and steps out into the hallway, stopping abruptly.

"What's wrong?" I ask, and she glares up at me, although she doesn't say a word, and I decide to keep quiet. She's gone frosty on me again, and she glances up and down the corridor, looking left and right, before she seems to reach a decision, and marches across the hall, to Ruby's door. She offered to help earlier, when she pointed out her office to us, but I'm not sure she anticipated Ella would barge right in there just a few minutes later. That's exactly what she does, though, without knocking.

I'm right behind her, so I'm there to see Ruby look up from behind her desk, her eyebrows raised in surprise. The room itself is small and sterile, with just her desk, and a couple of chairs in front of it, a tall cupboard against the wall behind Ruby, and a view through the windows, across the city.

"Can I help?" she asks.

"I don't know." Ella stands in front of her and takes a breath, like she needs to compose herself.

"What's wrong?" Ruby asks, sitting forward slightly. "Has something happened?"

Ella shakes her head. "Not as such, but I'd like to know why I wasn't told that Blake can't cook... and why you hired an actor, rather than a chef. I hadn't realised that training him to cook would be part of my role, but I've only got three days until we start rec—"

"You don't have to train him." The voice in the doorway makes us all jump and Ruby looks up, while Ella and I turn around to see Kennedy standing there, her face like thunder. I wish I'd closed the door now, especially as she takes her time stepping across the threshold while glaring at Ella. It's a tight squeeze for all of us to fit in here, and I move over, so I'm behind Ella, giving Kennedy space. "Cooking is your responsibility," she says, "and no-one else's. We hired an actor because this show isn't just about the food; it's about interacting with the guest who's brought in their problem, and knowing how to connect with the audience, through the camera." She tilts her head, narrowing her eyes slightly. "In future, Miss Bennett, if you have any questions about the set-up, perhaps you'd be kind enough to bring them to me, rather than bothering Ruby with them?" She's positively dripping with sarcasm, the smirk on her lips finishing the picture to perfection.

Ella takes a half-step closer to Kennedy.

"I would have done, but I didn't know where your office was."

"Then you should have made it your business to find out."

"I don't have time," Ella snaps, giving as good as she gets, which makes me smile. "You've hired a puppet, it seems, and you're leaving me to work out how to pull his strings."

Ouch...

My smile fades. Okay, so she's only saying the same thing as I've been thinking myself, but hearing the words on someone else's lips – especially when that someone is a comparative stranger – is a sobering experience.

I clear my throat and everyone turns to look at me. Ella's eyes lock with mine for a second, and I'm almost certain I see sorrow behind them... although I can't be sure, and even if I could, there's no way of knowing what she's sorry about. It could be her insult towards me, or that she's regretting taking this job... or just Kennedy's attitude to her, which sucks.

"I seem to be the problem here," I say. "But I——"

"Don't you dare say you're gonna leave." Kennedy interrupts me, stepping closer, so she's right beside Ella. She looks up at me, a pleading expression on her face as she shakes her head, and for a split second, I almost feel valued. "There's no time to find a replacement," she says, crushing the last vestiges of my ego.

"I wasn't going to say I'd leave." Apart from anything else, I've left the theatre company behind, and I need this job just to keep a roof over my head. "What I was going to say was, I'm a quick learner. I might never have succeeded at cooking anything in my life, but I'm sure I'll cope." I'm about to add, 'It can't be that hard,' when I think better of it. Ella might have called me a puppet, but that's no reason for me to insult her... or her profession.

Ruby stands up. "This is my fault," she says and we all turn to look at her. She glances at me, then at Ella, smiling slightly, before she turns her gaze on Kennedy. "I forgot to show Ella and Blake where your office is, and I made a point of saying they could come to me if they had any problems, so Ella was just doing what I'd told her."

Kennedy sucks in a breath. "You're not responsible for personnel decisions, Ruby. You know that... and if Miss Bennett has an issue about her employment, or her contract, then she ought to have realised it should be brought to me, not you."

"How?" Ella says, raising her voice slightly. "How would I realise that?"

Kennedy turns to her, that smirk back on her lips again. "It's common sense."

"It might be common sense to you, Ms Black, but it isn't to everyone." That's almost exactly what Kennedy said to Ella earlier, in the meeting, and I can see the anger rising in Kennedy's face. Ella's taking tremendous risks here, unless she's trying to get herself fired.

"I think it's best if you leave me to handle this," Ruby says, trying to calm the situation. "It's not really a contractual issue. It's more of a… a time-management one." She struggles to find the right phrase to placate Kennedy, but gets there eventually.

"You're not wrong," Kennedy says, backing up towards the door. "Time is money. And so far, all you're doing is wasting it." Her eyes are fixed on Ella as she's talking. "I expect to see some results, young lady," she says, with a threatening tone to her voice, and then she turns and leaves the room.

"Well… that was only slightly patronising," I murmur, quietly enough that she won't have heard.

"Hmm… Kennedy's good at patronising." Ruby looks up at me, and then sits down again, sinking into her chair.

"I'm sorry." We both turn to Ella as she speaks. She's looking down at Ruby, biting her bottom lip. "I didn't mean to get you in trouble."

"Don't worry about it. Kennedy and I have these battles now and then, but she and I both know she can't afford to fire me."

"She can't?" I ask, feeling confused. "I wouldn't have thought Kennedy would let anyone have a hold over her."

"I don't have a hold over her, as such," Ruby says with a smile, and then leans forward, resting her elbows on her desk. "You've probably noticed that Kennedy doesn't pay very well."

"It hadn't escaped my attention," I say. "Although I'm getting more here than I was in my last job."

Ella looks up at me, a little confused, and then turns back to Ruby. "I can't say I'd noticed," she says with a shrug of her shoulders.

"Well, she doesn't... except in two departments."

"What are they?" I ask. "Certainly not acting."

"No. She thinks actors are two a penny."

"Thanks. I only came here to get insulted."

Ruby smiles. "Sorry. It's her opinion, not mine. The only people to whom she's prepared to pay the going rate, are directors and scriptwriters. She says they're the ones who can make or break a show. The rest of us are eminently replaceable."

"And you put up with that?" Ella's clearly shocked.

"Yes, but only because it suits me. I enjoy working here, because I actually get to see my husband." I don't think Ella or I do a very good job of hiding our surprise, judging by the smile on Ruby's face.

"Who's your husband?" I ask.

"Gavin."

"The scriptwriter?" Ella says.

"Yes. And that's why Kennedy can't afford to fire me. She knows if I go, Gavin will leave, too... and he's one of the best in the business."

"So, not eminently replaceable?"

"Anything but..."

"Did you meet here?" I ask, feeling intrigued, even though I know it's a personal question.

"Yes. Three years ago. That was when I started here. We've been married for eighteen months, but with the hours we have to keep, if we didn't work together, we'd never see each other."

"I don't think I've ever met a couple who worked together, as well as lived together... not successfully." I can't think of anyone, anyway, and I know I'd never have been able to do it with any of my exes.

"I have," Ella says, and I turn to look at her. "My brother's just got engaged to his PA."

"You see? It can be done," Ruby says, and we both look back at her to find she's smiling up at us. "Now… before Kennedy comes back and finds us all still talking, I think you two had better get back to work, don't you?"

Ella nods her head with a half-hearted smile and heads for the door. "I'll bring my ideas over as soon as they're ready," she says, although her lack of enthusiasm is hard to miss, and I follow her from the room, closing the door behind me.

Back in the rehearsal studio, Ella flops down into one of the chairs, puts her elbows on the table, and dips her head, resting it on her upturned hands. She's a picture of dejection and I wander over, standing beside her.

"I'm sorry," I say, resisting the urge to put a hand on her shoulder.

She looks up, frowning. "What are you sorry for? I'm the one who called you a puppet."

"I know, but it's not your fault."

"It's not yours either."

She's not wrong. I didn't ask to be here, or to be a puppet, but she's upset and I want to help.

She sighs, shaking her head. "I can't believe this…"

"Believe what?" I ask.

"This…" She waves her arm around the room, sitting back. "Doing this job was going to be complicated enough as it was, but I assumed I'd be working with a professional."

"Thanks…" I was trying to be nice, but I don't know why I bothered.

"What for?" She frowns up at me again.

"The half-arsed apology."

"Half-arsed?"

"Yes. You apologise for calling me a puppet, and then tell me I'm unprofessional."

She looks up. "Well, it's true. You're not a chef. You can't even cook."

I lean down slightly. "Maybe not, but from what I've seen, you know nothing about acting, or TV production, which I guess makes us even."

Things don't feel very 'even', despite my words, and rather than risk any further insults, I beat a hasty retreat to the side kitchen to make a pot of coffee.

As I pour the water into the machine, I do my best to calm down. Ella has a point, after all. She wasn't told that I can't cook, so she'd expected to be working alongside a chef, not an actor. That's the aspect of this job that's been worrying me the most, ever since I was told I'd landed the role. Even so, I don't see why she needs to be so rude. We could be working together... helping each other. Let's face it, I wasn't wrong. My knowledge of TV production may not be all-encompassing, but it's greater than hers.

I grab a cup from the cupboard and consider taking down a second one. Should I offer her a coffee? I hesitate and then close the cupboard door again. What's the point? She'd only tell me I'd made it wrong.

Chapter Four

Ella

I'd decided against querying any more decisions, so why couldn't I just stick to that? Why did I have to go in, guns blazing?

I'm angry about the way Kennedy's handled things, but I'm not sure my attitude helped the situation, and now, although I almost never cry, I'm getting really close again, for the second time in as many hours.

I'm not going to, though, if only because I refuse to let Blake – or anyone else – see how much Kennedy got to me back then.

I get up, wandering over to the kitchen area, and I bring back the folder and the sheet of paper I left on the countertop earlier... although I leave behind my knives. I won't be needing them for a while yet, and sitting back down at the table, I study the question, trying to concentrate on my job, and deal with the tasks at hand... ideally in order of importance. Solving this supposed 'problem' is the number one priority. I can worry about Blake and his inabilities later.

Although, thinking of Blake, I notice he hasn't returned from the side kitchen yet, and I bend forward slightly so I can see him. He's leaning against the countertop, a cup of coffee in one hand,

while the other is in his pocket. I can't see his face clearly from here, but his pose tells me he's thinking. There's even something pensive about the slow, deliberate way he lifts the cup to his lips.

He didn't offer to bring me a coffee, and a tiny part of me feels offended by that, especially as I'm gasping for one. My offense – and my thirst – are overshadowed by my guilt, though. I can't blame him for ignoring me, can I? I did just call him a puppet, after all. And he was right. My apology, such as it was, was laced with another insult. He may not be a chef, but that was no excuse for calling him unprofessional. It's just that our professions are different, and I wasn't expecting to tutor him in the rudiments of cooking, as well as everything else.

Still… that's not his fault.

It's Kennedy's.

I know I didn't handle that situation very well, but there's no getting away from it. I don't like her. It's pretty clear she doesn't like me very much either, but sitting here contemplating that, and my 'half-arsed' apology to Blake, won't get anything done.

I don't have any writing paper, or a pen, but I have my phone, and I pull it out, noting down the first idea that comes into my head in response to the question about preparing a roast dinner. It's the simplest thing I can think of, but I guess simple is going to be best. I need to keep it interesting, though, so although I don't make any more notes, I give some thought to how I can employ easy cooking methods, and tasty ingredients, to achieve what I'm looking for.

It isn't that difficult in the end, and after just a few minutes, I get up from the table, pocketing my phone and putting the piece of paper back into the folder. I won't need to take it with me… I know the question backwards now, but I guess I'd better see if Blake wants to come with me. He ought to, really, so he knows what he'll have to do.

He still hasn't surfaced, so I wander over to the side kitchen to find he's standing in exactly the same position, his head slightly bent. I cough to attract his attention and he turns, looking at me, although he doesn't smile.

"I'm just going to see Ruby."

"Again?" he says, frowning. "What's wrong now?"

I'm not sure that was entirely called for. "Nothing's wrong. I've just been doing my job." *Rather than standing around drinking coffee.* "I've got an idea for this supposedly problematic roast dinner, and I was told to present it to her."

"Okay."

"Don't you want to come with me?"

He shrugs his shoulders. "Why?"

Do I have to spell it out to him? For heaven's sake, if he's going to be this difficult, how am I going to teach him to cook? "Because this is supposed to be your show. I assumed you'd want to be involved."

"And I assumed you'd want to keep the conversation between the professionals."

I stare at him for a moment, and although part of me wants to tell him to grow up, I can't blame him for being bitter. My remarks were quite derogatory.

"I'm sorry if what I said offended you. It wasn't meant that way. But if you'd rather stay here and sulk, that's fine. I'm sure I'll manage by myself."

I turn away, aware that my apology didn't come out quite right – again – but before I've taken two steps, I feel his hand on my shoulder, spinning me around. I look up into his face, wondering how anyone can have eyes the color of sapphires, as he leans in close enough for me to feel his breath on my cheek.

"What is it with you? Can't you even say 'sorry' without being obnoxious?"

"Obnoxious?" *Seriously? God, he's sensitive.*

"Okay... maybe obnoxious is too strong a word, but you've apologized to me twice now, and both times you've seasoned your words with a further insult."

"That wasn't an insult."

"What was it then?" he says, shaking his head. "Unless I'm much mistaken, you just accused me of sulking."

"And? If you haven't been sulking, what have you been doing in there for the last twenty minutes?" I nod toward the kitchen behind him.

He pauses for a second. "Thinking."

"Okay... I'll rephrase my sentence then, shall I? If you'd rather stay here to think, that's fine by me. Happy now?"

"You forgot to reiterate that you can manage by yourself."

"It looks like I'm gonna have to," I mumble under my breath, pulling free of him and striding to the door.

I hadn't even realized until just then that he still had a hold of my shoulder, or how close we were standing... so close that I could feel the heat from his body leaching into mine. I hadn't realized his lips were only an inch or two from my own, but as I open the door and step outside into the hall, I take a deep breath, letting it out slowly. He might have been angry, and so might I, but there's no denying, he's the most beautiful man I've ever seen.

I shake my head. *Stop being so superficial, Ella, and get on with what you're supposed to be doing. It's not like you have all day.*

I step across the hall, just as the door behind me opens and I turn to see Blake coming out. Although I half expect him to ignore me and wander off down the hall, he doesn't. He steps up behind me, making it clear he intends coming with me to see Ruby.

"I thought you were staying behind to think." I can't help my sarcasm. It's brought on by nerves, I think... although I can't be entirely sure. I've never been in a situation like this before.

"I changed my mind."

"So you're interested now?"

He tilts his head and studies me for a moment before he says, "I think I've always been interested."

I decide against replying, in case I say the wrong thing… which seems quite likely at the moment, and turn around again, facing Ruby's door. I knock, and this time, I wait until I hear her call out, "Come in."

As I go to open the door, Blake surprises me, stepping up beside me and turning the handle. He gives the door a push, and I turn my head, looking up into his eyes again.

"After you," he says, nodding toward Ruby's office.

"Thank you." It's not the first time he's behaved like a gentleman, and I want to apologize again for my ungracious behavior. I don't, because I'm almost certain I'll get it wrong, but I resolve to try harder not to let my nerves get the better of me with him.

He follows me into the room, closing the door behind him, and we step up to Ruby's desk.

"Please… sit down," she says, as she looks up from her computer screen.

Blake waits for me to sit, then copies me and they both stare at me, waiting.

"I—I've come up with a couple of ideas… for the show." For heaven's sake. I need to stop stumbling over my words. I sit up a little straighter, hoping that giving the appearance of having a backbone will help.

"That's good." Ruby gives me an encouraging smile, but I know she's waiting for more.

"The problem is, how to cook a roast dinner and get all the components ready on time." She nods her head. "The easiest solution to that is to roast all the vegetables together, so you're only worrying about two dishes instead of several."

"Two dishes?" Blake sounds confused, and I turn to face him.

"Yes. The lamb and the vegetables."

"Oh... sorry. I forgot about the lamb."

I don't comment, just in case I say something mean to him again, and instead I turn back to Ruby, who's frowning at me. "Don't you like it?" I feel sick with doubt now.

"It's fine," she says. "But the show is an hour long. Is it really going to take an hour to demonstrate that?"

"No. That's why I said I had a couple of ideas. I thought we could offer two recipes, both of which answer the problem just as well. That way, the viewers who want to can go for the slightly more complicated solution."

"And what's the slightly more complicated solution?" she asks, tilting her head.

"There is only one. We can't reinvent the wheel in this instance. That's why I said it was common sense. A roast is a roast, so there's not much point in us preparing a lamb stew, just because it's easier."

Ruby smiles. "I take your point, but you still haven't explained what we're gonna be doing."

"Making roast lamb in the usual way." I'm amazed I needed to explain that, but judging by the expressions on hers and Blake's faces, it seems they're still looking for more. I sit forward and let out a sigh. "Blake would show how to time the meal, counting backwards from when it's due to be served, and demonstrating all the advanced preparations that can be done. Obviously, that takes a lot longer than an hour, but I guess you have ways of accommodating that, so it all fits into the running time for the show?" I raise my eyebrows, focusing on Ruby, and she nods.

"Yes, we do." She gets up, surprising me. "This should work well."

I feel myself sag with relief. "You're sure?"

"Positive," she says, nodding her head. "Ordinarily, you'd already be practicing the dishes for this week's show, and we'd work on the script this afternoon, but you don't have any ingredients to practice with, so I think it's gonna be best if we bring forward the production meeting, so at least we can make a start on something."

"Bring it forward to when?" I ask, getting to my feet.

"Now. I'll gather everyone together and we'll join you in the rehearsal studio." She stops talking and looks at Blake. "I almost forgot, Kennedy wants to see you."

"Me?" He sounds surprised. "What about?"

"I don't know. She sent me an email just before you came in here, asking if you'd go to her office. I was about to come and tell you when you knocked on my door."

Blake stands up too. "Where's her office?" he asks.

"Do you remember where the meeting room was?"

"Yes."

"Okay. Find your way back there, and Kennedy's office is opposite."

Blake nods his head, then without another word, he leaves the room. I feel like calling out 'good luck', but I'm sure he doesn't need it. Kennedy seems to like him. It's me she hates.

"If you want to go back to the rehearsal studio, I'll join you in a minute," Ruby says, and I turn back to her.

"Okay."

"In the meantime, can you write out a list of the ingredients you're going to need?"

"Of course, although I don't have anything to write on, or with, for that matter."

She smiles, turning around to open the cabinet behind her, then pulls out a notepad, handing it over to me, before grabbing a pen from her desk, which she offers. I take it, glancing at my watch, and I try not to register my surprise when I see that it's

only just gone eleven. How is that possible? I feel like so much has happened already, and it's not even lunchtime.

"If you head back, I'll round everyone up," Ruby says and I come to my senses. It might feel as though a lot has happened, but in reality, we've achieved almost nothing.

"See you in a minute."

I leave her office and cross the hall, going back into the rehearsal studio, and after dropping the notepad and pen on the table, I make my way into the kitchen and fix myself a coffee. I've barely sat down again when the door opens and Ruby comes in.

"They won't be long," she says, sitting opposite me, and I take the lid off the pen and start writing, just as a thought occurs.

"How many times are we going to need to practice this and rehearse it?" I ask. "Just so I know how much of everything to ask for."

"Just put down what you need to cook it all once, and we'll work it out."

I nod my head, although I wish she'd answered my question. It would have been interesting, and useful, to know how many times I'll be expected to cook these dishes in the next few days. Still, I expect I'll find out, eventually.

The door opens again within moments, and several people come in, talking among themselves. I recognize some of them from this morning's meetings, although I can't remember their names, or what they do. They all settle around the table, except one of the men, who goes straight back out again, returning a few moments later with a couple more chairs. One of the women goes into the side room, bringing back several cups of coffee, which she dumps in the middle of the table. A few people take one, and a silence descends.

"Thanks for coming, everyone," Ruby says. "Ella's got our menu ready, and as we're short of time, I thought we'd make a start."

"So, what's cooking?" One of the men says and Ruby smiles at him in such a way, I can't help wondering if he might be her husband, Gavin.

I go to open my mouth, but Ruby holds up her hand. "You carry on with what you're doing. I can explain." I nod my head and get back to writing my list, which is getting ever longer, while Ruby gives them a very brief outline of what I described earlier… not that it needs much explanation. It's very simple.

"Is that it?" A female voice speaks out, and I look up, unable to tell who spoke.

"I'm sorry?" I don't give Ruby time to respond, and a young woman who's sitting at the other end of the table leans forward.

"I said, is that it?"

"What were you expecting? Crepes Suzette? It's a roast dinner."

There's a ripple of laughter and two dots of red appear on the woman's cheeks as she narrows her eyes at me. "Is that a reason to make it boring? Surely you can teach people to cook roast lamb and still keep it interesting, can't you?"

Who does this woman think she is? "You've never tasted my food, but I guarantee it'll be interesting."

She shakes her head as Ruby leans forward. "I'm sure it'll be lovely, and in any case, we don't have time to argue about it."

The woman doesn't seem convinced, and as I look back down at my ingredients list, assessing the spices I was adding before I was interrupted, I can't help wondering if she's going to be trouble. She's very pretty, and not a lot older than me, I'd have said, with blonde hair and blue eyes. They're not a warm blue, like Blake's, though. Hers are a steely blue… as cold as ice.

"Are you ready yet, Ella?" Ruby's words interrupt my train of thought.

"Just about."

I check over the ingredients list one last time and tear off the sheet of paper, handing it across to her.

"Thanks." She doesn't even look down at it, but puts it on the table in front of her and glances around, before her eyes settle on the man who asked what was cooking, her lips twisting into a smile again. "I think it would make sense if you came and sat beside Ella, don't you, Gavin?"

He smiles back and stands, bringing his chair with him. The woman beside me gets up, shifting a little further away, and Gavin sits beside me, holding out his hand.

"We haven't been formally introduced, but I'm Gavin."

"Ella."

He nods his head and we shake hands, before we both look back at Ruby. "We're gonna take the premise of your plan and fire ideas around the table. Gavin will make notes that will eventually become the script. I want you to jump in whenever you feel like it, Ella… especially if we're getting something wrong."

"Okay."

That all sounds very chaotic to me, but I assume they know what they're doing, and I take a sip of cool coffee as they all pitch in.

"Obviously, there needs to be an introduction piece." A man further down the table leans forward, trying to get Gavin's attention.

"That goes without saying. I can write that later… maybe with Blake's input."

It strikes me as odd that Blake's taking so long with Kennedy, and that we're not waiting for him. This is supposed to be his show, after all…

Mac

I make my way along the corridor, wondering what Kennedy can want with me, while trying not to beat myself up too much over what just happened with Ella.

I wasn't very gentlemanly to her, but in all fairness, I hadn't been expecting her to appear at the kitchen door and invite me to come to Ruby's office with her. I'd been deep in thought at the time, and hearing her voice took me by surprise. Even so, my response wasn't what it should have been, and it set the tone for what followed… which was yet more acrimony.

Did Ella need to imply I hadn't been doing my job? Probably not. Was it true? Absolutely it was. I'd been drinking coffee and avoiding her. But I didn't need to make that sarcastic comment about her keeping the conversation between professionals. I don't even know why I said it… other than the confusion that was rolling over me at the time. She was mocking me – or that was how it felt – and that jarred with the thoughts that had been running through my head. I wasn't about to explain that to her, although I didn't need another half-hearted apology either… not when I'd barely recovered from the first one.

When she turned away, I had to go after her, and although I did little more than continue our argument, that was a cover. At least it was for me. I wasn't really offended, so much as I was completely bewildered. Her accusation of sulking might have been inaccurate, but what was I supposed to say? That sulking had been the last thing on my mind, because it was full of thoughts of her? That I'd spent the last twenty minutes wondering how she could wind me up, and turn me on at the

same time, and with so little effort? Or maybe that I wanted to close the narrow gap between us and kiss her? There was no way I was about to say any of that out loud, although what came out of my mouth instead was hardly helpful.

She pulled away from me then, and my initial reaction was to stay behind... not to lick my wounds, but to put some necessary space between us. Except that was when I realised she was right. She'd been doing her job, and I hadn't. Admittedly, that was mostly because I've got no idea what my job is supposed to be. But while I'd been in the kitchen, day-dreaming about her, she'd been getting the work done. While I'd been wondering what it might be like to kiss her – and whether we might stop fighting long enough for me to find out – she'd been more diligent.

It was time to pull my weight.

So, I followed her out into the corridor. And when she asked – with customary sarcasm – if I was interested in what was going on, I couldn't help myself. I had to tell her that I think I've always been interested. I don't think for one second she understood what I meant. She didn't get that the 'interest' I was talking about was in her. It hadn't really occurred to me before that moment, but I've been interested in her since the first time I saw her. Is that because of her delectable backside? Possibly. I don't claim to be any less superficial than the next man. But there's more to it than that. I know there is. We might have done little more than argue since we met, but there's something about her that I'm finding harder and harder to resist... and I wonder if it's worth trying.

I reach Kennedy's office, although now I'm here, I'm even less sure why I've been summoned. Is it because I've done something wrong? Or have they changed their minds and decided Ella's right, and that they need someone who at least knows what to do with the sharp end of a knife? It wouldn't surprise me. I might have boasted to Ella that I have a knowledge of TV production,

but in reality, it's very limited… and maybe they've worked that out.

I guess there's only one way to find out, and although the prospect of not working with Ella makes me unusually depressed, I knock on the door.

"Come in." Kennedy's strident tones echo straight back at me, and I enter her office. It contrasts harshly with Ruby's and I stand for a moment, taking in the size of it – which is enormous – as well as the slightly over-the-top furnishings. Her desk looks as though it would have been more at home in a 1960s spy thriller, with its modular design, and I have no doubt she – or someone, at least – paid a small fortune for it.

She doesn't stand, but holds out her hand, indicating the two seats in front of her, and I close the door, crossing the room to sit.

"How are you getting along?" She seems genuinely interested in hearing the answer to her question, and I realise I'm not about to be fired.

"Fine." I don't tell her I haven't done anything yet. I doubt that's what she wants to hear, and it won't do me any favours.

"I'm glad to hear it," she says. "We know we haven't given you much time to prepare, considering it's the first show, but it can't be helped, I'm afraid."

I nod my head, feeling fairly sure she's not expecting an answer, although I note she doesn't take personal responsibility for the lack of preparation time. It seems that must be born collectively.

She surprises me by getting to her feet and smiling down at me. "I need you to come with me."

I stand up too, unsure why she invited me to sit if she was only going to take me somewhere else almost immediately.

She doesn't say another word, but heads for the door, and I follow, noticing when I turn around that, across the other side of

the room, is an enormous white couch. It has the same retro feel to it as Kennedy's desk, and although she doesn't dress like someone out of *The Man From Uncle*, I can't help asking myself if this is her style. It's not mine... but each to their own, I suppose.

Out in the hallway, she turns to her right, walking away from the rehearsal studio and back toward the reception area, although before we get there, she stops at a door on the left, which she opens without knocking.

The room inside is quite large and, other than a couple of chairs over by the window, is devoid of furniture, although as I come further inside, I notice that, at the far end, there's a dark backdrop and some lights, all set up around a man, who I assume is a photographer. He's currently doing something with a tripod and has his back to me.

I look down at Kennedy, frowning.

"We need some publicity shots," she says, clearly noting my expression and explaining my presence.

"Oh... okay." I guess that makes sense.

She doesn't wait for me to say anything else, and wanders over to the photographer, who turns as she approaches. He's tall, although not as tall as me, with dark hair and a handsome face, and he smiles his greeting. She says something to him in a soft whisper, and he steps back, picking something up from a stool that's positioned in front of the backdrop. He hands it to her with a nod of his head before he returns to his tripod and she comes back to me.

"We need you to wear this," she says, holding out the 'something' in her hand. I take it from her, unfolding it to reveal a bright red apron with the words 'Meal Master' emblazoned on the front in bright white lettering. It's incredibly tacky, but I suppose needs must, and I turn it around to put it over my head, just as Kennedy reaches out and grabs my arm. I stop, looking

down at her, but she leaves her hand on my bicep, and I'm tempted to ask her to move it. She's got my attention, so why does she need to touch me?

"What's wrong?" I ask, and take the opportunity to step away from her, forcing her to release me in the process.

"You need to take your shirt off first."

"Um... excuse me?"

"We're going for a particular theme with this show, and we'd like you to take your shirt off."

"What's the theme? Cooking half naked?"

She laughs, although it's forced and completely unnatural. "Of course not." She steps closer again, and once more, she rests her hand on my arm, gazing up into my face. "But you're a very attractive man, Blain... and we might as well capitalise on that."

"My name is Blake, not Blain." Ordinarily, I'd say my name is 'Mac', but Kennedy doesn't strke me as someone I'd ever call a friend, so we'll stick with Blake.

"While you're working here, it's Blain." There's a harder edge to her voice, and I can hear the underlying implication that she holds all the cards.

I want to argue that it isn't, but decide it's best to pick my battles, and in this instance, the battle is about what I'm wearing, or not wearing, to present this show.

"Can I get one thing straight here, Kennedy... are you expecting me to present this show wearing nothing but an apron and a pair of jeans?" If they are, she won't need to fire me. I'll quit.

She smiles again, but if anything, I feel slightly less comfortable. The look in her eyes speaks of appetites that have nothing to do with the food I'll be pretending to cook.

"No, but the production team have decided a black t-shirt will look really good with the red apron, so we've ordered some in... and we'd like you to wear black pants, too."

"By 'pants', I assume you mean jeans or trousers?"

She laughs, with a little more authenticity, and caresses my arm while nodding her head. "I keep forgetting you're British." I can't see how. My accent is a huge giveaway, I would have thought. "Black jeans would be fine," she says. "They won't be seen very much, anyway."

"Why don't you leave us to it?" I turn as the photographer speaks, and see he's wandering over, his hands in his pockets. He's wearing stonewashed jeans, and a dark grey t-shirt, and although he's talking to Kennedy, he's looking at me with a friendly smile on his face. Now he's closer, I can see he's probably a few years younger than me, although he has an air of professionalism that makes him seem older.

"You don't need me to stay?" She releases my arm at last and turns towards him, the disappointment obvious in her voice and demeanour.

"No. We'll be fine. I know what you're looking for."

I think I do, too… but she's not getting it.

"I could stay, just in case you have any questions," she says, but he shakes his head.

"I work better alone." As he speaks, he folds his arms across his broad chest, his feet set firm on the floor. This is a battle of wills and although Kennedy isn't renowned for backing down, I get the feeling he won't budge, either. After just a few seconds, she steps away, relenting, and moves towards the door.

"I'll be in my office if you need me."

He nods his head. "I'll come find you when we're through."

She frowns, but doesn't say a word, and finally leaves the room.

I turn to the photographer, letting out a sigh of relief. "Thanks for that."

He smiles. "My pleasure. Believe me, I didn't want her hanging around here any more than you did."

"For different reasons, I imagine."

"Yeah," he says. "In my case, she'd have just gotten in the way. In your case…"

"She's only interested in the packaging… or so it seems." I hold up the apron. "Is this really necessary?"

"You mean, do you have to take your shirt off and put that damn silly apron on?"

"Yes."

"To get what they want? Yeah, you do. Didn't they tell you this was part of the deal?"

"No, they didn't. And, before you say anything, I know I won't be naked in the pictures. It's just that…"

"You didn't sign up for this?"

"Exactly. Don't get me wrong, I'm not worried about being topless in front of you, but…"

"It's the principle?" he says, tilting his head.

"Yeah. I don't like being kept in the dark, and I'm concerned about how bad the end result is gonna look."

He smiles. "I'll make it as tasteful as I can."

I shake my head. "Bearing in mind that the apron has 'Meal Master' written all over it, that's going to be a challenge."

He chuckles. "Do you have any alternatives?"

"Like what?"

"Like putting principles first and quitting?" he says, raising his eyebrows.

"That's not an option. I've grown accustomed to having at least two, and sometimes even three meals a day."

"In which case, shall we get on?"

"Sure."

I guess time is money for him, and I hand him the apron while I unbutton my shirt, shrugging it off, then look around for somewhere to put it in this virtually empty room. The chairs by

the window are my only option and I saunter over, laying it across the back of one of them, and then return, putting on the apron.

"Do you mind if I do it up?" The photographer steps forward and I frown at him. He smiles, holding up his hands. "I need to make absolutely sure the logo appears in the centre and isn't skewed by the way the apron is tied."

"Oh… I see."

I turn around and he takes his time, doing it up behind me, and then walks around in front, eyeing me closely, adjusting the strap around my neck by a fraction of an inch, and nodding his head.

"Okay. Let's get started."

"Where do you want me?"

He leads me over to the backdrop, setting the stool to one side. "We're not gonna need that, after all," he says, almost to himself, and I step to my left, keeping out of the way, while he adjusts the position of the lights by a few inches in each case. "Okay… come stand over here." He shifts to one side and I take his place, feeling self-conscious.

He moves behind the camera, looking through the viewfinder, and then steps out again, coming up to me.

"Do you mind?" he says.

"Mind what?"

"If I move you around a little?"

"Not at all. Go ahead."

He smiles and puts his hands on my shoulders, shifting me to my left and turning my body, so it's at an angle to the camera.

Once he's happy, he moves away again, returning to the other side of the tripod. "That's better," he murmurs and I hear the shutter click a few times. "Fold your arms across your chest," he says, and I do as he says while he takes another few photographs. "You'll like those. The logo is completely obscured."

"Yeah… but that means Kennedy won't use them."

"Probably not, but she's got the option. Okay… now… let's try this…"

He steps aside, crouching down to a small bag, and pulls out a rolling pin, coming over and handing it to me.

"Are you sure this shouldn't be a riding crop or a flogger?" I ask, and he laughs.

"We'll get around to that later." Once again, he manoeuvres me into position before getting back behind the camera. "Can you try looking masterful?"

"Masterful?"

"Yeah… like the name of the show."

"I'll try it."

It's at times like this I'm grateful for my acting experience, and I take a deep breath, trying not to shift my body at all, but puffing myself up and glaring down the camera lens.

"That's perfect." He snaps away. "How long have you lived over here?" he asks, making conversation, which I guess is to help me relax.

"A couple of years."

He nods his head, coming back to me and taking away the rolling pin, only to replace it with a large whisk. I glance at him and he shrugs his shoulders, smiling. "Just doing as I'm told."

"Fine…"

Once he's happy with the way I'm standing, he moves away again. "Can you just tilt your head slightly to your left?" I do as he says. "So, how did you end up working on the show?" he asks.

"I was with a theatre company, playing the part of an alcoholic chef, and unbeknownst to me, someone from the studio must have been in the audience. The next thing I knew, I got a call from my agent, telling me to come here for an audition… and the rest, as they say, is history."

He stands, looking over the top of his camera. "So, you're an actor?"

"Yes."

"You're not a chef?"

"You sound almost as surprised as the woman I've just started working with."

He smiles. "Didn't she know?"

"No. She was hired as the culinary consultant, and it seems no-one mentioned to her that she'd be working with a total amateur."

"How did she take it?"

"Not well. Although I can't blame her, really."

He looks back through the view-finder and then stands up straight again. "What happened to that masterful look?"

"Oh… sorry."

He shakes his head, smiling. "Can I guess that the dreamy expression on your face has something to do with the culinary consultant?"

"It might do."

"So, she doesn't blame you, either?"

"I don't know. I think she might. She seems to be pretty angry with me most of the time, and all we've done so far is argue. But that doesn't mean I'm not in danger of falling for her."

"It's incredible when it happens, isn't it?"

"I wouldn't know. I've never fallen for anyone before."

"Neither had I, but when I did…" He stops talking, his brow furrowing.

"Can I assume it didn't end well?"

"You can."

"I'm sorry."

He shrugs his shoulders. "I'll get over it," he says, although there's absolutely no conviction in his voice, and I wonder if he

believes a word of what he's saying. "We'd better get on with this."

I nod my head and do my best to put that 'masterful' expression back on my face, while he gets on with taking more photographs, changing the whisk for a long-handled ladle, which makes me smile. He does too, although he's shaking his head.

"Don't blame me for the props. Kennedy supplied them. I guess this is the image she's going for."

"Making me look like an idiot, you mean?"

"I think she's going more along the lines of sex symbol…" I nod my head, a thought taking shape in my mind. "You need to raise your head again," he says, and I realise I've let it drop. "And if you can look over my shoulder, rather than directly at the camera for this one?" I do as he says, although I'm not concentrating, and it obviously shows. "What's wrong?" He stands again, letting out a sigh.

"I'm sorry. I can't focus."

"Why not?"

"Because I've just had a thought." He tilts his head, like he's waiting for me to elaborate, and I realise it can't hurt to tell him… in fact, it might even help. "I was just wondering… am I so very different to Kennedy?"

He smiles, just slightly. "I can think of several ways in which you're vastly different."

I shake my head. "Obviously. But what I mean is, I've been admiring the show's culinary consultant ever since I met her. That's only a few hours ago, I'll admit, but even so, is that any different to the way Kennedy behaves around me?"

He thinks for a moment or two. "I guess that depends."

"On what?"

"On what you're doing about it?"

"Like I said, other than arguing with her, I'm not doing anything. I'm just admiring from afar at the moment."

"In which case, I don't see what your problem is."

"That I think I'd like to do a lot more than argue and admire?"

He smiles. "I get that," he says. "But the point is, how would you respond if you were to get the chance to do more, and she said she wasn't interested?"

"I'd apologise and back off, of course."

"Exactly. And that's the difference. I saw the way you reacted to Kennedy. You made it very clear you weren't happy with her touching you, and you had every right not to be. She didn't pay any attention, though, and came on to you again."

"Hmm… I noticed."

"The thing is, she's your boss, and she clearly thinks that gives her rights."

"It damn well doesn't."

"I know. And that's why the two situations are different. You're finding out about the woman you work with, getting to know her, and maybe at some stage, you'll take it further… with her consent. Kennedy is using her position as your boss to her advantage. If a man did that, it would be called sexual harassment, but in reality, there's no difference."

"Are you speaking from personal experience?"

"Kind of. It's never been done to me, but I work with models all the time. Exploitation is never far from my lens."

I nod my head, realising why he asked before he touched just now, and perhaps why he placed so much emphasis on Kennedy leaving us alone. I hadn't fully appreciated any of that before, but I do now, and I'm grateful for it.

"I guess we'd better take these photographs."

"Probably." He smiles. "Otherwise Kennedy might come find us, and if she sees you looking like that, I dread to think what she'd want to do with that ladle."

I have to chuckle, although the reality is, I'm not finding this very funny.

It's only when I'm walking back to the rehearsal studio, having thanked the photographer for making me feel at ease, that I realise I forgot to ask his name.

Still… I doubt I'll meet him again, and I check my buttons are all fastened before opening the door, to be greeted with a wall of noise. There are ten or twelve people sitting around the table, which I guess means someone must have found some more chairs and brought them in. They all seem to be talking at once, too, and I can't make out anything they're saying.

Ella looks up, just briefly, but doesn't acknowledge me. Instead, she turns towards a blonde woman at the other end of the table, who's berating her over something, although I'm not sure what. I vaguely remember her from this morning's meeting, but I can't recall her name or what she does. Either way, she's not shy in saying what she thinks, and although I can't hear very much above the din, I make out the words "undercooked," and "raw lamb."

"It won't be raw." Ella raises her voice, sufficient that everyone can hear, and they all stop talking. She blushes, evidently surprised to have become the centre of attention.

"What will it be, then?" The blonde narrows her eyes.

"It'll be pink, just as it should be. Blake can give instructions for those who want it well-done, but I'm not serving lamb like that… and if you don't agree, then someone a little further up the managerial ladder is welcome to fire me."

"Okay… okay." Ruby holds up her hands, like she's trying to get control of the situation, and then she turns to the blonde. "Ella's the expert, Vivian, so I think we'll let her decide how she wants to cook the lamb, don't you?"

Vivian…? I remember Ruby saying she was her assistant, but judging from her expression, I don't think she appreciated being told off in front of everyone. She sits back, clearly angry, but rather than gloating or enjoying her moment of glory, Ella just slumps into her seat like she's exhausted. I can't help feeling sorry for her – again – although there's no denying my attraction to her now. My cock won't let me. In my defence, Ella looked really sexy just now, with her eyes on fire. Between that, her tousled hair, and her incredible backside, I'm going to need to learn a little more self-control around her…

She looks up at me again, and all thoughts of self-control are immediately forgotten. How can I even consider such a thing when gazing into those perfect amber eyes? I smile, but rather than returning the gesture, she simply takes a breath, letting it out slowly. Then she sits forward again, looking at the notes in front of her, making it very clear she neither needs nor welcomes my sympathies.

Chapter Five

Ella

I've never felt so tired in my life.

Somehow I've made it home, and I kick off my shoes, my feet killing me. I drop my purse to the floor, rolling my shoulders to relieve the tension. As for my head… it feels like it's full of cotton candy, and although I'm tempted to open a bottle of wine, I don't think it'll help.

I pad through to the living room, falling onto the couch and while I'm very far from comfortable, I can't move a muscle. My limbs won't work.

Was that really only one day?

I know it was… just like I know tomorrow is going to be so much worse. How that's possible, I'm not sure, but before I left the studios, while Blake was talking to Gavin about the script, Ruby took me to one side and explained the schedule.

"I know you're doing your best, but we're behind where we need to be," she said, frowning at me, even though none of the hold-ups had been of my making. "You and Blake haven't been able to practice any of the dishes yet, and even though Gavin will work up the script as quickly as he can, I doubt you'll get it before

late tomorrow afternoon, so I need you to go through things with Blake as thoroughly as you can tomorrow morning, so we can catch up and get started with full rehearsals on Wednesday."

"Okay. But you need to remember, I'll be teaching him to cook, on top of everything else."

"He doesn't need to cook," she said. "He just needs to add the finishing touches."

"Plate-up, you mean?" I was too tired to make sense of what she was saying.

"No. But, for example, with the roasted vegetables, you can prepare nine tenths of them, and just have him add a few at the end, while he's talking to camera."

"I appreciate that, but if he doesn't know how to cut up a potato properly, I'll have to show him what to do, or he'll end up looking like an amateur."

"Hmm… I suppose, but you can't let the niceties of cooking impede the schedule."

"I'm not responsible for the schedule… or for the fact that it's running behind. I'm responsible for the food, and it'll be prepared properly, or not at all." To be honest, I'd had enough by then. Between Kennedy's attitude, and Vivian's criticisms, I didn't need anyone else blaming me for something I hadn't done.

"Fine. Just keep me informed about where you're at."

Personally, I thought it would have made more sense for me to get on with doing my job, rather than reporting to her all the time, but I nodded my head and gathered my things together, desperate to get out of there.

I'm relieved to be home, but lying here is getting seriously uncomfortable, and I need to shower and eat something before I fall asleep.

It's a struggle, but I get to my feet again, feeling a little light-headed, although that's not an enormous surprise. I haven't eaten all day.

"Note to self," I murmur as I head for my bedroom. "Eat breakfast."

I strip out of my dress and underwear, leaving them on the floor, and walk straight into the bathroom. The shower feels fantastic, but I don't take all day over it. Not only am I hungry and tired, but I'm thirsty, too. I barely drank anything today, either, and I make another mental note… to take a bottle of water with me tomorrow.

Once I've washed and shampooed my hair, I step out, wrapping myself in a fluffy bathrobe, and going back into my bedroom. Having such short hair has tremendous advantages at times like this, and I only pause to pick up my clothes and throw them into the laundry hamper before heading straight for the kitchen.

I could order in, and to be honest, I would… if it wasn't for the fact that cooking is the best therapy I know, and I need to let off steam.

I grab a few ingredients from the refrigerator, along with a chopping board and knife, and set about preparing a stir-fry while contemplating some of the more worrying aspects of my day. Looking back, I suppose Kennedy set the tone, and everything seemed to go steadily downhill from there. Still, she's the boss, and I guess if she wants to adopt that kind of attitude, she can. I never expected 'star' treatment… I'm not the 'star', after all. But the total disdain I received from Vivian was something else. What started as a criticism of my idea became a fault-finding exercise over everything I said and did. I swear, if I'd told her the sky was blue, she'd have argued with me that it was green. It took me a while to even find out who she was, but I eventually learned her name, along with the fact that she's Ruby's assistant. I don't know what that means, or what her job entails, but she seemed to think it entitled her to criticize me.

Personally, I just hope we won't be working together too closely, because I don't think I've ever met anyone so openly hostile... and I've got enough to cope with as it is.

The vegetables are all prepared now and I heat some oil in a wok, waiting until it's hot before adding them. I turn them over and over, until they're almost tender and then add some pre-cooked noodles and quickly whisk up some soy sauce, garlic, brown sugar, sesame oil, chicken broth and cornstarch in a small bowl, before adding that to the vegetables, too. It sizzles and I stir it again, giving it a few minutes to coat the veggies and thicken before turning it out into a bowl and garnishing it with some sesame seeds.

I could have a glass of wine, but I'm too tired to enjoy it, so I pour myself a glass of ice cold water and carry it through to the living room, settling onto the couch. I don't turn on the television, though. There's no way I can handle any more noise today, and instead, I sit back and eat while thinking about the other thing that's been bothering me...

Blake.

I feel a little guilty about the way I handled things with him. I wasn't as kind as I could have been, and I let my nerves and the situation get the better of me on more than one occasion. Let's face it, even when he smiled so supportively at me, after Vivian was being such a bitch over the lamb, I couldn't raise the enthusiasm to smile back. I just wanted to get finished and get out of there... but I'm fairly sure that came across as ignoring him.

The problem is, even if he is eminently adorable, I can't escape my worries... the foremost of which is that the man can't cook.

I still don't understand why nobody made me aware of that in advance. He said he'd told Kennedy, so it's not like they were oblivious, and there was nothing to be gained by them keeping

it a secret from me. The only reason I can think of is that they thought I might not take the job if I'd realized what was involved... and they'd have been right. Maybe they'd tried other chefs, told them the truth about Blake, and been turned down. Maybe that was why they kept quiet. Who knows?

Whatever the reason, it doesn't alter the fact that I could still walk away if I felt like it.

It's not as though I need the money.

Kennedy might not know that, but does she honestly think humiliating me in public is a good idea? Surely she has to realize that, if I walk out on her, she won't have a show, and while I may not be the 'star', replacing me won't be easy... especially at this stage of the production.

None of it makes much sense to me, but I suppose I need to allow for the fact that I'm tired, and that I don't really understand how the television industry works.

I finish my stir-fry, taking my bowl and glass out to the kitchen and putting them into the dishwasher. There's nothing much to stay up for, and although it's only eight-thirty, I check everything is switched off and make my way back through to the bedroom, pulling off my bathrobe and climbing into bed.

My head hits the pillow, tiredness overwhelming me, and just before I fall asleep, I think about the prospect of walking out of my job, after just one day...

I won't do it, simply because I think it's what Vivian would like most in the world, and I'm stubborn like that. But as my eyes flutter closed, I resolve not to take any more crap... from anyone. If I know I'm right about something, I'm going to stick to my guns from now on, just like I did over the lamb. I don't care whether I'm dealing with Vivian or Kennedy. I'm not going to let them talk down to me anymore, and if they don't like it, they can find another culinary consultant.

*

When I arrive at the rehearsal studio, Blake is already sitting at the table with an iPad in his hand and a cup of coffee in front of him.

"Good morning," I say, doing my best to sound cheerful, to make up for yesterday's unkindnesses, even though a good night's sleep has done very little to calm my nerves.

"Hi." He looks up, frowning, before returning his attention to the iPad.

That was abrupt. Surely he can't still be put out because I ignored him yesterday. If he is, he needs to grow up.

I put down my purse and the bottle of water I brought with me from home, and head into the side kitchen, pouring myself a cup of coffee. Once I return, I stare down at Blake for a moment, but he doesn't move and I realize I'm going to have to break the silence.

"How are you today?"

"Okay." He seems distant, and I wonder why I'm bothering to make the effort.

"Shall we get on?"

"Just give me one minute…" He frowns, then quickly taps something into the iPad, focusing hard on the screen before he nods his head and turns it off. Once he's put it down, he looks up at me, his face clearing. "Sorry about that. I just needed to finish something."

Oh… so he wasn't being rude. Just busy.

"I see." He's obviously not about to tell me what the 'something' is, and I guess that's none of my business, either. Instead, he takes a sip of coffee, and stands up, looking down at me. He's frowning again, and for the first time, I notice what he's wearing, which is black jeans and a pale gray t-shirt… and I have to say, he looks utterly divine.

"Are you as nervous about today as I am?" he says, and I wonder if anxiety is the answer to his strange mood.

"Yes."

He smiles. "In that case, let's see how much of this I can get wrong, shall we?"

That hardly fills me with confidence, but I nod my head, relieved he's no longer frowning at me, and turn around, making my way across to the kitchen. Blake follows, and we both put our cups on the countertop, where there's a box next to my knife case. I pull it closer and look inside. On top, there's a bag which says 'For Blain' on the outside, and I reach in, handing it over to him.

"This must be for you."

He takes it, rolling his eyes, and opens it up, glancing inside. "Oh, great." He pulls out a red apron, which he unfolds to reveal the name of the show in white lettering on the front. It looks absolutely awful, but I keep a straight face, for his sake. He's got to wear it, the poor man.

"Is there anything else?" I ask.

"Yeah… this." He puts down the apron and holds up a black t-shirt, which looks far too small for him.

"Are you supposed to wear that as well, do you think?"

"For the show, yes… but for what we're about to do, I can't see the point."

I have to agree with him, and watch while he puts both items back into the bag and sets it on the countertop.

"I guess we'd better get on with unpacking everything."

He nods his head. "Why don't I hand you things and you can decide where you want to put them?"

"Okay."

I'm perfectly capable of unpacking the box by myself, but at least he's being helpful… and willing. I step aside, and he delves

into the box, handing me a few jars of spices, which I put at the back of the countertop, followed by bell peppers, onions, eggplants, zucchini, green beans, tomatoes, olives, fresh herbs, and potatoes.

"Where do you want this?" he says, holding up a leg of lamb in a large plastic storage bag, with a slider seal at the top.

"What on earth is that doing in there?"

He frowns. "I don't know. It was just sitting here in the box. Why?"

"Because I'd assumed that whoever delivered the box would have had the intelligence to put the meat into the refrigerator, rather than leaving it out here to warm up."

His frown deepens. "Is it going to be okay?"

I reach over, rubbing my hand over its surface. "It seems fairly cold still. Can you put it away?"

"In the fridge?"

"Yes. We won't be needing it for a while."

He nods his head and carries the lamb over to the other side of the kitchen, to the tall refrigerator, with a deep-freeze beneath. As he opens the door, I turn back to the box, pulling out a bottle of olive oil, just as I hear him let out a slight chuckle.

"What's wrong?"

He puts the lamb inside, closing the door again. "Oh, nothing... it's just odd seeing a fridge that's even emptier than mine."

I stop, absolutely still, the oil still in my hand. "A—Are you telling me there's nothing in there?"

"Not anymore. It's got the lamb in it now."

I put down the olive oil and walk over, yanking the door open, to see he's not wrong. Other than the lamb which is resting on the middle shelf, the refrigerator is completely empty.

"I can't believe this."

He comes and stands behind me, and I close the door again and turn to be confronted by his broad, muscular chest. He's closer than I thought, and I take a moment to recover and look up into his bewildered eyes. "I'd expected them to supply us with a few basics. You know… milk, butter, eggs…"

"Is this going to be a problem?"

I think for a second or two, recalling what we're going to be cooking. "Not for this morning, no. But I'll have to speak to someone about it… and about them leaving out the meat as well."

He nods his head. "Yeah. Especially as the studio will be a lot hotter than it is in here."

"It will?"

"Hmm… because of the lights."

I feel silly for not knowing that. He explained about the lights in the makeup room yesterday, so I should have remembered. Still, we've got bigger things to think about now, and I wander back to the countertop. Blake follows, checking inside the box.

"Oh… look," he says, pulling out a brand new set of knives, still in their box. They're not the best brand in the world, but I guess it doesn't matter. It's only for show, after all.

"They'll be for you."

"Yes, because you've got your own."

I glance up at him, wondering if he's being sarcastic, but he's smiling, and I smile back.

"Hmm… but what they haven't provided you with is a spare apron."

"Will I need one?"

"Yes. Cooking can be a messy business."

"Well… if you think I'm wearing that awful red thing, you can think again."

"I wasn't thinking anything of the sort. I don't want to look at it any more than you want to wear it."

"In that case…" he says, his lips twitching upward.

"It's lucky for you I always carry a spare."

He looks me up and down, taking his time about it, and I let him, my body heating under his gaze. "Where?" he says, and I'd swear his voice is a little deeper than usual.

"Not literally about my person." I reach over, pulling my knife case forward. "It's in here."

I flip open the lid, and delve into the pouch inside, pulling out two navy blue fabric aprons, handing one to Blake.

He takes a little longer than me to put his on, but once we're both ready, I clear the countertop and get out a large chopping board, then unpack his new knives, laying them in front of him, while I grab a few knives from my case and put it away to give us more space.

"The first thing we're gonna do is prepare the vegetables."

He nods his head. "Okay. What do I need to do?"

"You're just gonna watch for the best part."

"Don't I need to know how to cut things up?"

"Yes, but in reality, when it comes to the recordings, I'll have done most of the work for you, and you'll just add a few vegetables at the end, before mixing in the spices. So, that's what I'm going to teach you."

"How do you know all this? About the show, I mean, not the cooking."

"Ruby explained it to me yesterday while you were talking to Gavin. I was also told I have to report to Ruby about how we're progressing, which seemed like an enormous waste of time to me."

"I agree. It feels like we've already got more than enough to do… or you have, really. I'm just observing."

It's good to know he agrees with me, but we need to get started, or all I'll be reporting to Ruby is that we've achieved little more than unpacking the food.

"First, we have to turn on the oven." I go over and switch it on, then turn back to him. "You won't need to worry about that. Gavin told me yesterday that, for the show, the ovens will be on permanently, and they'll be set to the correct temperatures, which will be in the script."

"Okay."

"And now, I just need to find a large roasting pan…"

"Where will it be?" he asks.

"God knows. Whoever organized this kitchen doesn't seem to have used very much logic so far…" I wander over to the oven, checking inside, but there's nothing there, so I check the drawer beneath and that's also empty. Helpful…

"What about this?" I turn to see Blake, standing by the refrigerator, holding up a very large roasting pan.

"It's perfect, but where did you find it?"

"In this cupboard." He peers inside the cabinet beside the refrigerator. "There's another one just like it, and two slightly smaller ones."

"And, of course, it makes perfect sense to put them all the way over there."

"Like you said, it's not logical."

He comes back, bringing the pan with him, and puts it down on the countertop. "Okay… I think we're ready." He stands right beside me and I pick up my chef's knife. "I'm not gonna bore you with the purposes and practicalities of every knife, but you need to understand the basics so you don't pick up the wrong one during the recordings. Believe me, someone out there will know if you make a mistake, and probably write in."

"They won't write in… they'll plaster it all over social media."

"Exactly. So we can't afford to slip up."

He nods his head. "Okay, so what's that knife?" he asks.

"It's called a chef's knife, and the clue is in the name. It's the knife most chefs use for just about everything. The blade is

slightly curved, so you can rock it while chopping, and because it's heavy and has a thick heel, you can use it for grinding or mincing, too."

"Heel?" He sounds confused already.

"Yes." I hold out the knife, showing him the part of the blade furthest away from the tip. "Here, close to the handle, where the blade is at its widest."

"Okay."

"I'll tell you about the other knives when we use them, but we'll begin with preparing the onions." I reach out for one, putting it onto the chopping board, root side up. "If you cut it in half," I say, putting actions to my words and slicing through the onion from root to tip, "you can lay it flat and make it easier to cut. The root will hold it together while you're working."

"I'd love to say I know what you're talking about, but okay."

I turn the onion, so it's flat-side down and cut off the top. "We're gonna take off the outer layers and then quarter it." He watches closely. "Then we can cut off the root."

"Because its done its job?" he says.

"Yes. We're leaving our vegetables chunky because it suits the timing of the recipe, but I'll explain that to you later. For now, we'll just focus on techniques. So, why don't you do the next onion?"

I step aside and he picks up the chef's knife from his own set. He's holding it far too tight, and I step forward again, stopping him.

"You need to relax."

"I'm holding a deadly weapon. I don't feel very relaxed."

"Then don't think of it as a weapon. Think of it as an extension of your hand."

He frowns at me and I pick up my own knife again, showing him how to hold it. He adjusts his grip, but still looks

uncomfortable. This isn't working, so I put down my knife and move closer to him, picking up his paring knife, which has a much smaller handle.

"Put that down for a second." I nod toward his knife and he does as I say. "Now, come stand behind me." He steps closer, and I feel the heat from his body. "P—Put your hand over mine." I don't know why I'm stuttering, but he leans in even closer still, his hand covering my own.

"Like that?" he says, his breath whispering against my cheek.

"Yes."

"What now?"

"Just think about how gently you're holding the handle of the knife."

"But I'm not. I'm holding your hand."

"Okay. Imagine my hand is the knife."

"I don't have that much imagination."

"Yes, you do. You're an actor."

"I'm not acting now, Ella."

I'm not sure this is helping, and I'm struggling to breathe for some reason. "I—I think you've probably got it now. Try again with the chef's knife."

He releases my hand and steps back, letting me move out of the way, and he picks up the chef's knife again.

"I take it I'm supposed to imagine I'm holding your hand?" He looks at me with a slight smile touching at his lips.

"If it helps."

He adjusts the handle and I have to smile, because he's holding the knife perfectly now.

"Who taught you that?" he asks.

"Nobody."

"So you didn't have to hold your tutor's hand to learn how to use a knife?"

I chuckle. "No. He wasn't the hand-holding type. He just shouted at us when we got things wrong."

"Hmm... I think I prefer your approach."

I give him a second onion and watch while he repeats my earlier actions to perfection, needing no additional instructions. His techniques might be lacking, but he's got a great memory... I'll give him that.

"What do we do with them now?" he asks, standing back.

"Put them into the roasting pan." He does as I've said and I grab a couple of potatoes. "These are big, so we'll cut them into wedges instead of chunks." I demonstrate how to do that, and he copies me yet again.

"So, when we're recording this, there'll be a tray of vegetables already prepared, and I'll just cut up a few more and add them, while talking to camera?" he says, scattering the potatoes on top of the onions.

"Exactly. Like I say, you'll have to add the oil and spices by yourself, but I'll show you how to do that in a minute."

"Okay. What's next?"

"The bell peppers, please." He hands over the two large red ones, and I put them on the chopping board. "There are few different ways of preparing these, and while a lot of professional chefs would pour scorn on me, I'm going to show you the simplest way... just because you're less likely to cut yourself."

"Sounds good to me." I look up and he smiles down at me, although he quickly averts his gaze to the pepper as I show him how to take off the top and de-seed it, cutting it in half before I slice it.

"We don't want it too thin, or it'll burn before the potatoes are cooked."

I hand him the second pepper, and although he wastes a little more than I did and struggles with the de-seeding, he does a reasonable job and adds the slices to the pan.

"We'll have the zucchini next."

He stares at me, then looks at the remaining vegetables lying on the countertop. "Zucchini?"

"Yes."

"Sorry. What on earth is a zucchini?"

"Oh… I forgot. Even though we speak the same language, we sometimes don't." I reach over, picking one up. "It's a courgette to you."

"I'm sure it would be, if I knew what to do with it. But I'll need to remember to call it a zucchini during the recording."

"It might be useful if you could, yeah."

I slice it at an angle. "Why are you cutting it like that?" he asks.

"Because it gives the oil and spices more of a surface area… and it looks more interesting."

He copies me with the second zucchini, and although his slices are by no means uniform, and he takes a lot longer to cut them up, he gets there with reasonable results. The pan is fairly full and I mix up the vegetables, burying most of the peppers and zucchini.

"Why are you doing that?"

"To protect them from burning."

"I see. And is that it for the vegetables?"

"We've got enough, if that's what you mean."

"You're not going to use this?" He holds up the eggplant.

"Not for now. It won't fit into the pan. The potatoes and zucchini were larger than I expected, but we'll use the eggplant next time."

"So, it's an eggplant?"

"Yes, although you'd know it as an aubergine."

He shakes his head. "You probably shouldn't have told me that."

"Why not?"

"Because I didn't know it as anything, and now I'm likely to get confused." He has a point and I wish now I'd kept my mouth shut. He puts the eggplant down again and then looks up at me. "What do we do next?"

"We need to add the oil and spices, and some garlic."

"Oh good. I love garlic."

"Hmm… me too, but we have to allow for the fact that not everyone does, so we'll just put in one fat clove, and I think Gavin's going to put a proviso into the script that you're supposed to say it can be left out altogether."

"Yeah… if you're insane."

"I don't think you're supposed to say that on camera, but if I was making this at home, I'd probably use three, or even four cloves."

I pick up the bulb in front of me and put it on the chopping board, leaning hard on it to break it apart.

"So, how many of those are we using?" he asks.

"Just one… like I said." He frowns, looking confused, and I pick up a clove, holding it up to him. "This is a clove of garlic. The whole thing together is a bulb. Don't confuse the two. Even the most addicted of garlic lovers won't thank you."

"I'll bear that in mind."

"There are lots of ways of preparing garlic and I'll show you some of the others later on, but for now, we're going to make a paste, so we can add it to the spice mix." He nods his head, stepping closer again, and I place the garlic clove on the chopping board, putting the flat edge of my knife over it and leaning down hard on the blade to crush it. "If you do it this way, the skin comes away easily," I say, demonstrating the fact by removing the skin from the clove. "And because we don't need the clove to be whole, it doesn't matter that I've crushed it."

"Okay."

I look around the countertop, then double check the box, which is empty. "I don't believe this."

"What's wrong?"

"There's no salt… or pepper, for that matter."

"Do we need it?"

I stare at him for a moment. "Yes." I shake my head. "As if it wasn't bad enough that they didn't give us a few basic ingredients, to leave out salt and pepper is…"

"Unforgivable?"

"Something like that."

"Can we manage without, just for today?" he says.

"I guess we're gonna have to. You'll have to pretend I've added some salt to this, and just so you know, you do that to help with mashing it." I chop the garlic roughly, then place the blade of my knife over it and flatten it against the chopping board, scraping it back and forth. "It would work better with the salt, but you get the concept?"

"Sure."

"Okay, once that's done, we can put it into a bowl."

"Shall I find one?"

"If you can."

"How big does it need to be?"

I hold out my hands, making a circle with my fingers to show him. "Just a small one."

He nods his head and starts opening the cabinets, coming back after the third attempt with a glass bowl that's just the right size.

"At least they've given us the right equipment, even if we're short of ingredients."

I'm not in the mood for giving credit at the moment, so I take the bowl and add the garlic to it. "We're going to make a spice mix," I explain, taking the jars from the back of the countertop

and setting them out in front of us. "This will make the dish more interesting… because, according to Vivian, my ideas were boring."

"Did she really say that?"

"Yeah. I don't know what I'd done to offend her, but she seemed to take an instant dislike to me, and my food, even though she's never tasted it."

"Well… I'm glad to know it wasn't just me who they thought of as dull. And look on the bright side, at least they didn't change your name."

"That isn't permanent, you know. It's just for the show."

"That's what you think. Kennedy told me yesterday that all the time I'm here I'm to be known as Blain." He says the name with such scorn, it's hard not to smile.

"All the time?"

"Yeah."

"But that's ridiculous." I can't understand why it's so important he should be called 'Blain', other than in recordings… especially as he seems to hate the name so much.

"I know that, and you know that…"

I shake my head. "I guess we'd better get on," I say, tapping the tops of the spice jars. "We've got coriander, cumin, and turmeric, and we'll put a teaspoon of each into the bowl." I open the drawer and find some measuring spoons, thank God, using them to measure out the spices. Then I open the olive oil. "We need to make this into a runny paste, so we can use it to coat the vegetables," I say, pouring some into the bowl.

"How do you know how much to use?" he asks.

"Experience. But you don't need to worry. This will all be pre-prepared and waiting in a bowl. You'll just recite the ingredients and give them a final mix."

I hand him the bowl and a spoon from the drawer and he stirs it around a few times.

"Is that enough?"

"It'll do." I push everything to one side and pull the roasting pan forward. "Pour it over the vegetables…" He does as I say, setting the bowl aside. "Okay… now we get our hands dirty."

I tuck mine under the vegetables, lifting them slightly and letting them fall again.

"We have to do this with our hands, do we?"

"Yep… nothing better for mixing."

He nods his head and joins me. "It's weirdly satisfying," he says, as he helps to toss the vegetables, our hands touching every so often.

"Nowhere near as satisfying as kneading bread."

"If you say so."

We keep going until the vegetables are thoroughly coated and then wash our hands.

"Okay. You can put the pan into the oven now."

"Me?"

"Yes. You'll have to get used to it. I can't do everything for you."

He stares at me for a moment, and I wonder if that came across as sarcastic. I didn't mean it to, but before I can say anything, he grabs the pan of vegetables and turns away, putting it into the oven.

Mac

This is so frustrating.

Just when I think I'm getting somewhere, and finally breaking through the permafrost that seems to surround Ella, she closes down on me again.

I honestly thought I had no chance at all with her after she refused to even return my smile yesterday afternoon. I went home last night feeling quite depressed about the whole thing, bearing in mind we've got to work so closely together, and she seemed to want nothing to do with me. My mood was so low, I even contemplated changing my novel, just for the sake of getting Delilah to take it seriously, but when I started re-reading it, I still liked it, and I'm just tweaking a few bits as I work my way through the manuscript to keep myself occupied... and to take my mind off of Ella.

Except this morning, when she arrived, she was a completely different person... all sweetness and light. I might have been right in the middle of trying to re-write a tricky paragraph in chapter three, but I couldn't help wondering if yesterday's reactions might have had more to do with first day nerves and tiredness than with me. It was a possibility, and once I'd worked out how to phrase the end of that paragraph, I gave Ella my undivided attention. It wasn't hard. She looked fabulous in her skintight jeans and a pretty white blouse with a floral embroidered panel at the front.

We've had fun working together so far this morning. I especially enjoyed the part where she showed me how to hold a knife. It meant I got to hold her hand for a brief moment, until she got embarrassed. I don't know why she did that. There was

nothing to be embarrassed about, and her method seemed to work. The knife felt a lot more comfortable in my hand after her demonstration. Although I'd rather have gone on holding her hand instead.

Mixing up the vegetables in the spices was good, too. We touched hands quite a few times. She didn't seem to be so self-conscious about that... or maybe it was just that she didn't notice. Perhaps that was because she'd just been explaining what Vivian had said about her food. She seemed really affected by that, and I can't say I blame her. I thought it might have been another reason she was so deflated yesterday, and I tried to make her feel better by telling her that Kennedy was insisting I should be called Blain all the time. Ella seemed to find the idea just as ludicrous as I do, but we didn't dwell on it... perhaps because she'd sensed how much it was bothering me.

I'd like to think so. It would be good to think she's that in tune with me.

Even if she isn't, we still had fun mixing up the vegetables.

At least, I did, until she made that sarcastic remark about not being able to do everything for me. I mean... who's asking her to?

I'll admit, that took the edge off of what had been a fun morning, and since then, we've been clearing up in silence.

"We need to prepare the lamb," Ella says, breaking into my thoughts.

"Okay."

"I should probably explain... in the recording, you'll demonstrate the lamb preparation first."

"In that case, why did we do the vegetables before the lamb?"

"Because they're harder to prepare, so I wanted to get them out of the way early on."

"I see. So we're not doing this in the right order?"

"No."

I nod my head, although I've got no idea how I'm going to remember all this. It's confusing enough as it is, without doing it all backwards.

"Shall I get the lamb?"

"Yes, please." I go over to the fridge, pulling out the leg of lamb. "Can you grab another roasting pan while you're there?" she asks.

"Sure." I do as she says, bringing them both back to the countertop.

She takes the lamb from me, and I watch as she removes the meat from its bag, putting it into the pan.

"We're going to use the same lamb for both dishes," she says. "So you'll only need to do this once."

"Okay." The atmosphere between us isn't as easy-going as it was first thing this morning, and while I want to feel more relaxed, it's impossible when I'm waiting for the next bolt of sarcasm to hit me.

She reaches out, picking up a small-bladed knife, which she holds out, showing it to me. "This is called a paring knife, and it's used for peeling and slicing smaller vegetables and fruits. In this case, though, because it has a really sharp point and blade, we're going to use it to make holes in the lamb."

"Holes?"

"Yes." She demonstrates, sticking the knife into the lamb's flesh, about an inch or so deep before she repeats the process several times and then turns to me. "You try it."

I pick up the same knife from my own set and copy her actions. "Is that okay?"

"Yes, just don't go too deep."

She's a little snappy, but I ignore her tone and focus on what I'm doing, and on keeping my incisions more shallow, until the lamb leg is pitted all the way across.

"Now we're going to prepare some garlic." She reaches over, taking a few more cloves from the bulb she broke up earlier, and this time she peels them, rather than crushing them. "You won't need to do any of this," she says, and rather than giving me a chance to try, she gets on with it, until she's done three large cloves. "This time we're going to slice them, but again, I'll do it for you because most of this will have been prepared in advance, so you'll just need to finish it."

"Okay."

I watch while she thinly slices the garlic, forming a neat pile of slithers, and then she picks one up and stuffs it into one of the holes in the leg of lamb. "You'll have a leg which has been almost completely studded with garlic," she says, as she continues her work. "All you'll have to do is put in the last one or two, while you do your piece to camera, explaining the process."

"That doesn't seem too difficult."

"It's not."

She hands me a slice of garlic and I stick it into the last hole. "Does it go into the oven now?"

"Not quite. We need to rub it with olive oil. Again, that's something you'll have to do, because it can't be done until all the garlic has been inserted... so..." She grabs the oil bottle and holds it up. "You'll need to drizzle the oil, like this." She places her thumb over the top of the bottle, letting just a small trickle out as she tips it, and then hands it to me. I copy her, and although a little more seeps through, I manage okay. Once she's happy with the amount of oil, she rubs it in with her hands. "Your turn," she says, stepping back slightly, and I finish the job.

"Now I'm guessing we wash our hands again?"

She nods her head and we go over to the sink. I let her wash up first, and then clean my hands, drying them off on a towel.

"Ordinarily, we'd season the lamb with salt and pepper, but we don't have any, so I'll have to show you that next time around."

"Okay."

"So, if you imagine we've done that, you can put the lamb into the oven as well."

I do as she says, opening the oven door, to the delicious aroma of roasting spiced vegetables. "That smells incredible," I say as I close the door again and turn to face her.

She looks up at me, like she's waiting for something. I raise my eyebrows, expecting her to tell me I've done something wrong, and she opens her mouth and whispers, "I'm sorry." I wasn't expecting that and I frown down at her. "Aren't you going to ask what for?" she says, after the silence has stretched for a little too long.

"I was waiting for the insult that usually follows your apologies."

She blushes. "There isn't one. Not this time."

"In that case, why are you apologising?"

"Because I think I might have sounded a little sarcastic earlier… and because I know I'm being tetchy."

"Is there a reason for that?" There's no point in telling her she isn't, when we both know she is.

"I think it's just the realisation of how little time we've got, how much there is to do, and that we're working without all the ingredients we need. The pressure is…"

"Getting to you?"

"Yes, it is. But it's not your fault, and I'm sorry if I keep snapping at you."

"It's okay. I'm sorry, too."

"What on earth for?"

"For making your life harder than it needs to be. If I knew how to cook…"

"That's not your fault either, though, is it? Kennedy hired you. She should have known it would…"

I reach out, placing my fingertips on her lips, the softness taking me by surprise, as does her sharp intake of breath.

"I'm gonna stop you there, Ella, before you find another way to insult me. Okay?"

She nods her head, and I pull my hand away. For a second or two, she just stares at me while I regret my actions. I'm not sorry I prevented her from insulting me again. I don't think it would have done either of us any good. But I regret the way I did it. I wish I'd kissed her into silence. Still, the moment's passed now. It's too late for regrets... and kisses.

She seems to startle back to life, a blush creeping up her cheeks, and she turns back to the countertop.

"W—We've probably got a little while yet until the vegetables are ready, so why don't we make a start on the alternate roast?"

"Okay. What are we making for that? And when I say 'we', I'm using the word in its loosest sense. You're the one doing all the work."

She smiles up at me, her eyes twinkling. "We're gonna make garlic roast potatoes to start off with."

"I'm sold."

She chuckles. "That's just because you like garlic."

"There's nothing wrong with that."

"Which is just as well because it's in the vegetable dish as well."

"What vegetable dish?"

"The Provençal green beans that will be served with the lamb and roast potatoes."

"What exactly would Provençal green beans be, when they're at home?"

"Anything that's called 'Provençal' comes with a tomato sauce. It originates in the south of France."

"Is a lot of your cooking influenced by the French?" I ask.

"Yes," she says, nodding her head.

"And apart from tomatoes and garlic, what else goes into this sauce?"

"It usually includes onions, olive oil, Herbes de Provence, maybe some capers and a little white wine."

"Stop it. You're making me hungry."

"In which case, you'll be pleased to hear that you're going to need to taste all of this, so you can describe the flavours with more accuracy."

"Great… when do I start?"

She giggles, and the sound pulsates through my body. "When it's all cooked."

"Does that mean I've gotta wait?"

"Yes. Now, pass me a pan for the potatoes."

"What kind of pan?"

"One I can put water in, so I can parboil them."

I'm still none the wiser, and she rolls her eyes at me, although she's smiling, so I know she's not angry, or even about to get so. Instead, she walks around me, heading for the cupboard where I found the roasting pans, and she returns within moments, carrying a large saucepan. She puts it down on the work surface and turns to face me.

"For the show, the potatoes will already be peeled, so you'll just have to explain what to do from there on."

"Okay." I nod my head and watch while she peels two large potatoes, cutting them into chunks and putting them into the pan.

"The water needs to almost cover them," she says, nodding to the pan and I lift it to the sink, turning on the cold tap, and watching while it slowly drowns the potatoes. I stop it just in time and take it back to her. "Perfect." She smiles up at me just as the door opens, and we both look up to see Kennedy come into the studio. She's followed by Ruby and Vivian.

"How are things going?" Kennedy asks.

"Fine," Ella says, glancing up at me just briefly, the look in her eyes telling me she doesn't welcome this interruption any more than I do.

"The smells are driving us all crazy." Ruby smiles as they come over and stand on the other side of the island unit.

"That'll be the roasted vegetables." I try to make it sound like I know what I'm talking about, and from the looks on their faces, I seem to have succeeded.

Vivian leans over slightly, picking up a bunch of something green and leafy. "You didn't put the cilantro in, then?" She turns to Ella with a sly smile on her face. "I don't know why you asked for it, if you weren't going to use it."

"How do you know it's not for a different dish?" I ask, desperate to protect Ella from any more of Vivian's ridicule.

"Because it was listed under the ingredients for the roasted vegetables, and it makes sense to put it in there."

I wish I'd kept quiet now. I don't care about making myself look stupid, but I've failed to defend Ella, and I could kick myself for that.

"The cilantro is for the garnish," Ella says, crossing her arms. "We'll only add it to the dish at the very end. No-one in their right mind would add it to the dish before roasting. It would burn to a crisp." She turns to Ruby. "While we're discussing ingredients, though, I'd expected there to be a set of basic supplies… you know, flour, milk, eggs, butter. And at the very minimum, I would have thought you'd have given me some salt and pepper. Or do I have to ask for absolutely everything?"

Wow… she's not taking any prisoners today, and although I half expect Kennedy to tell her off for her tone, she doesn't, and instead it's Ruby who nods her head, leaning over the work surface slightly.

"I'm sorry. We should have seen to that." She turns, scowling at Vivian, and I guess it was her job… and that she failed to get

it right. "We'll make sure the kitchen is properly equipped before the morning."

"Thank you," Ella says, although her tone is still steely.

Kennedy reaches over, putting her hand on my arm, which makes me jump. "Why aren't you wearing your t-shirt and apron?" Her voice is a soft, worrying purr, and I step away, raising my hand and pushing my fingers through my hair.

"I assumed they were for the show, not for rehearsals."

"I'd like you to get used to wearing them... to being in character. That's why I'm insisting everyone refers to you as Blain."

"Even if that's not who he is?" Ella says, tilting her head at Kennedy.

"Yes. It's for our benefit as much as anything. We can't afford for there to be any slip-ups, so it's best if we just get used to calling him Blain."

"Is that what you'd normally do with an actor?" Ella asks, refusing to give up. "If they were taking part in a soap or drama, I mean? You'd call them by their character's name, even if you were having a coffee with them, off set?"

Kennedy narrows her eyes. "It's not that simple, dear. It's..."

Ella holds up her hand and Kennedy surprises me by falling silent. "Please don't call me 'dear'. It's incredibly patronising."

Something's changed here. I don't know what it is, but the dynamic has altered from how it was yesterday. When Kennedy spoke to Ella in that tone of voice during yesterday's meeting, she didn't react at all. Today, she's like a different woman.

She's feisty, and I like that. It makes me smile.

At that moment, Ruby's phone rings, and she pulls it from her pocket.

"Vince?" She listens for a moment or two. "Do we need to look at this now, or can it wait until we start rehearsals? I'm sure

it won't be long now." She frowns, giving Ella a quick glance, while Vince says something else, and then she nods her head. "Okay, I'll come along now."

She ends the call, returning the phone to her pocket, and looks up at us, smiling. "I've gotta check something with Vince."

"Is there a problem?" The panic in Kennedy's voice is obvious for us all to hear.

Ruby shakes her head. "I think he's just getting anxious about the schedule. I'll placate him."

I can't remember what Vince does now, but he's not the only one who's getting anxious. Kennedy seems to be doing a fairly good job of that herself, and it's rubbing off on everyone else.

"Okay," she says. "Let me know if there are any issues we need to address."

I can think of several… the most important being that they haven't allowed enough time to prepare this first show. I'm not about to say that, though… and clearly Ruby doesn't want to stick her head above the parapet, either. She just nods and leaves the room.

After a moment's silence, Kennedy turns back, taking a deep breath, her eyes settling on me.

"Okay, so before the next disaster strikes, do you think you could change into the t-shirt and put the apron on?"

"Now?"

She nods her head, and although Ella might be able to answer back, I don't feel I can. I need this job too much, and I guess maybe she's decided she doesn't. At least not enough to tolerate Kennedy's attitude. Maybe the hassle of it all is too much for her.

"Fine."

I grab the bag containing the t-shirt and apron and head for the door, making my way down the hall and through the double doors, before entering the men's room.

Once inside, I undo the apron Ella lent me, lifting it over my head, and yank off my t-shirt, dumping them both onto the white countertop, before I delve into the bag for the black one Kennedy supplied. Unfolding it, I can't help frowning. It's tiny, and I struggle to pull it on. I get there eventually, after a little huffing and puffing, but when I look at myself in the mirror, it's all I can do not to laugh. Sure, it shows off my muscles, but I look like a modern-day version of Popeye, and even when I've got the apron on, I still feel foolish, mainly because the logo on the front is so prominent. I don't feel like I'm the 'master' of anything at the moment, but I know the implication they're going for, and it's just not who I am.

I don't know if I want to walk back to the studio dressed like this, but I guess I'll have to get used to it.

"It's a character," I tell myself quietly, relieved there's no-one else in here. Kennedy's decided this is my 'costume', for want of a better word, and I'll be wearing it on screen soon enough, so I may as well get used to it.

Grabbing my t-shirt and Ella's apron, I poke my head out through the door, thankful there's no-one in sight, and I practically run back to the rehearsal studio. As I open the door, though, everyone turns to look at me, and I can feel myself blush.

Ella stares at me, like she's not entirely sure what to make of the change in my appearance. I'm not sure what to make of her reaction, either. If we were alone, I might be brave enough to ask, but we're not, and I glance at Vivian, whose eyes widen as she licks her lips. She couldn't look any more hungry if she tried, her eyes literally feasting on me, but I can't raise any enthusiasm for her response. She's attractive enough, I guess, but I don't like the way she treats Ella. I turn away, just as Kennedy pushes herself off of the island unit, and walks over. There's something in the swing of her hips that makes me nervous, though, and I back up to the door a little.

"That's so much better," she says, smiling, as she reaches me. "I just need to..." She grabs my hand, pulling me further into the room, and then walks around behind me. I can feel her fiddling with the ties, her hands in the small of my back.

"What are you doing?" I try to pull away, but she's got hold of the apron strings and isn't letting go. Short of striding away and probably pulling my boss to the floor as she clings on to me, I've got no option other than to stay where I am.

"I'm just adjusting the ties."

"Is that really necessary? I'm not on camera now."

"Maybe not. But there's no harm in getting things right."

She finishes what she's doing, taking another moment to straighten the strap around my neck, which I'm sure is just as unnecessary as everything else she's doing, and then she comes around in front of me again.

"Happy now?" I say, surprised by the sarcastic tone in my voice. Ella's boldness must be rubbing off on me... thank God.

"Yes."

"Well, I'm not. This t-shirt is way too small."

She looks me up and down, taking her time over it. "But that's exactly the look I wanted."

"Are you serious?"

"Yes." She runs her hand up my arm, letting it rest on my bicep. "We want people to see you properly, don't we?"

"Not particularly, no." And certainly not looking like this.

"I'm sorry to interrupt..." Ella's voice rings out and I look up, Kennedy turning to face her at the same time.

"What is it?" Kennedy says, although Ella's looking at me, not her.

"Everyone keeps telling me that the schedules are tight and budgets are restricted, so do you think Blake and I could get on with what we're supposed to be doing?"

I don't wait for Kennedy's answer, but take my chance to escape, putting my t-shirt and the apron on the table before I quickly make my way back to the other side of the studio, taking refuge behind the island unit. I notice the tray of roasted vegetables on the work surface, and realise Ella must have removed them from the oven in my absence. They smell delicious, but I've got other things on my mind. Given Ella's comments, I would have expected Kennedy and Vivian to leave, but they don't. Instead, they stand, staring at us both… or at me, to be precise. It's an unnerving experience and one that's making me more than a little uncomfortable. I feel like a prize exhibit.

"Was there anything else?" Ella's voice is surprisingly harsh and as she speaks, she moves a little closer, like she wants to protect me. That thought almost makes me smile. Except I'm being careful not to show any emotions right now. It seems important to remain impassive… like I don't care. Not for Ella's benefit, but for the sake of the two predators in the room.

"We're just interested in how things are going." Kennedy glares at her.

"I've already said, everything is fine… but it won't be, if you don't let us get on." She's really gunning for Kennedy, and I wonder if she's actively trying to get fired. I hope not… and not because the show would suffer, but because I'd miss her. Now I come to think about it, I'd miss her more than I would have thought possible, considering I've only known her for a little over twenty-four hours.

Vivian looks almost as surprised by Ella's tone as I am, but doesn't comment. Instead, she looks at Kennedy with a smug expression on her face, probably expecting our mutual boss to come back with some kind of put-down.

After what seems like an eternity, Kennedy lets out a sigh and nods her head. "We'll leave you in peace, then."

Even Ella seems surprised by that, and frowns. That obviously wasn't the response she expected. Vivian didn't either, and her face gives away her shock, although she follows Kennedy from the room without a word.

I wait until the door has closed behind them and turn to Ella. "Do you hate this job so much you want to get fired?"

"Not especially. But I'm done with being spoken down to." She shrugs her shoulders and looks up at me. I can tell she's itching to ask why I let Kennedy walk all over me just now, but I'm not in the mood for talking about it, especially as she's just shown herself to be so much more daring than me.

Instead, I pick up the bunch of green leaves Vivian had hold of earlier. "Are these called something different in England? Because I've never heard of cilantro before."

She takes them from me, picking off a leaf and holding it out to me between her thumb and forefinger. Rather than taking it, I grab her hand, keeping it steady and then dip my head, nibbling at the leaf, my lips caressing her skin until she releases it. She gasps, holding her breath, her eyes wide and fiery, and fixed on mine as I chew, and suddenly recognise the flavour.

"Oh… it's what they put on curries."

"Yes." She blinks, letting out that breath. "It's called coriander."

"Didn't we put some of that into the roasted vegetables?"

"Yes, but that was the seeds, ground to a powder."

"I see, and you call the leaves cilantro?"

"We do."

"Is that just to be difficult?"

"Something like that." She puts the coriander leaves down again, and turns back to me. "Shall we get back to the potatoes?"

I pull my t-shirt back on, gazing down at the black one, which is lying on the countertop in the men's room, alongside the red

apron. I refuse to think too hard about having to wear them. Instead, I'm just going to accept it for what it is: a costume. After all, there are too many other things to think about, and having made it to the end of the day, I'm too tired to care about Kennedy's desire to dress me up like a clown.

Gavin didn't bring the script along until half an hour ago, so I've barely had a chance to even glance at it. He was very apologetic about running so late, and while that meant I couldn't make a start on learning my lines, Ella and I have used the afternoon wisely. I've gone over a few of the things she's taught me, making sure I've understood them properly, and we've practiced certain techniques, so I look more like a chef who knows his way around a kitchen, and less like an actor who's playing a part. She's also shown me how to plate up both of the meals, because – like putting things into the ovens – that's something I'm going to have to manage without her. I hadn't realised how much precision went into doing that, but Ella drew me diagrams, showing which parts of the meal went where, so I couldn't forget. I got to taste everything, too, and although I liked the lamb with the roasted vegetables, the French-inspired version, with crispy roast potatoes and Provençal green beans was out of this world. They contained more garlic than should be legal, but I loved them.

Ella and I left the studio together, but the last I saw of her, she was talking to Ruby and Vivian as she walked towards the lifts, while I had to come and change before leaving the building. There was no way I was going to ride on the bus in that ridiculous t-shirt. Now I feel more like myself, though, I head home, trying not to think about how much work we've still got to do… and how little time there is left.

Instead, I use the bus ride to go through the script, and then continue with it in earnest once I've ordered a pizza.

I can't be late to bed, though, so once I've eaten, I take a shower and go upstairs. Not surprisingly, I'm asleep within moments of my head hitting the pillow.

I'm in a TV studio, although it's not the one Ella and I have been working in for the last couple of days. This one is set up for a chat show, and I'm waiting, while Aria White, the darling of daytime television, introduces me.

"You all know him as the Meal Master, and I've gotta say I wouldn't mind him giving me a few instructions." The audience laughs, and she smiles to the camera. "But following the phenomenal success of his show, let's meet the man who knows all the answers… ladies and gentlemen… here's Blain."

Deafening applause rings out as floor manager gives me a firm shove and I step forward, offering my hand to Aria. I feel self-conscious still, wearing the black t-shirt and red apron, but I'm under strict instructions from Kennedy that it must be worn for all publicity appearances, and I'm not about to disobey her now… not when the show's taken off like it has.

Aria doesn't really shake my hand, but holds it in hers, guiding me to the couch, and sitting in her chair, right beside me. Her eyes are sparkling and she looks at me appreciatively.

"I thought you looked great on the screen, but the reality…" she says, fanning her face with her hand, which makes the audience laugh. I smile, unsure how to answer her, but she covers my shyness with consummate professionalism. "So, Blain… it's okay if I call you Blain, isn't it?"

"It's my name."

Her smile widens. "Great. Tell me, what's your favourite ingredient to cook with?"

My mind goes blank. We didn't rehearse that question, and I can't think what to say. She's waiting, though, and I have to say something…

"I think it would have to be… courgettes."

She stares at me blankly. "Courgettes?"

"Zucchini!" I wake up, shouting the word, sweat pouring off of me as I glance around my bedroom, realising I'm at home. It was a dream. Or to be more precise, it was a nightmare… one that stands every chance of coming true, if I'm not careful. Not

that I'm assuming the show will be a success, or that I'll be asked onto chat shows, but I think there's a very real chance I could mess this up, simply by saying the wrong thing at the wrong time.

I turn over and check the time on my phone. It's five-thirty, and not worth going back to sleep. In any case, I'm concerned I'll drift back into my nightmare again, so I get up and go downstairs to take a shower, trying to put all thoughts of courgettes – or zucchini – out of my mind.

When I arrive at the studio, desperate for coffee, I'm not at all surprised to find Ella isn't at work yet. It's only just gone seven in the morning. What does surprise me is the pile of black t-shirts and red aprons waiting for me on the table. I guess this is Kennedy's way of getting her point across, and although I don't want to wear them today any more than I did yesterday, I also don't want another repetition of that scene with her. Rather than running the gauntlet of the men's room again, I shrug off my jacket, quickly undo my shirt, and pull on a tight black t-shirt. I don't bother with the apron yet, but wander into the side kitchen and make a pot of coffee, pouring myself one before I return to the studio.

Instead of going straight back to the table, I walk across to the kitchen, noticing there's no box of supplies today. I wonder if this is Vivian's idea of a joke... whether she's exacting some kind of revenge over Ella for showing her up in front of her boss, and I open the fridge and let out a sigh of relief. Inside, there are two legs of lamb lying on the middle shelf, along with eggs, butter, cheese, cream, and heaven only knows what else. If anything, I'd say we're over-equipped now, but I'm not about to complain. When I turn back, I note the salt and pepper mills beside the hob, along with the olive oil, and a bottle of what appears to be balsamic vinegar. I smile, sauntering over to the cupboards, where I find several types of flour and sugar, and more herbs and

spices than I could even begin to name, and I chuckle. It seems Vivian's done her job a hell of a lot better today.

Still, this isn't getting my job done at all, and I go back to the table and sit down. My script is in my jacket pocket and I pull it out, sitting back and turning over the title page to focus on learning my lines. I've always been quite good at this, even if acting was never my first love. It's a career I fell into more by luck than judgement, but thinking about it now, I suppose most of my roles have been more about my physical appearance than anything else. Except that last one, of course. Playing the part of an alcoholic chef involved me looking dishevelled and moody for at least ninety per cent of the play. The rest of the time, I just had to pretend to be asleep. When I was awake, though, I acted my socks off, and look where it's landed me… in yet another role where the only thing that matters is what's on the outside.

Great.

"One of the major benefits of roasting vegetables in this way is that, once you've done the preparation, they will look after themselves, while you look after your guests." I mutter the words under my breath, scanning the line a few times, so I'll remember it, before moving on to the next one, just as the door opens and Ella walks in. My breath catches, my stomach flipping over… the two combining to almost make me choke. God, she looks good today. Not that she didn't look good yesterday, in that white blouse, with the pretty embroidery at the front. The one she's wearing today is just as lovely. It's in a floral material, with a v-neck, and I put down my script and let my eyes wander for a moment. Her blouse might be beautiful, but there's something about her jeans… I noticed it yesterday. They do something to her legs and her backside that makes it really hard to concentrate. I raise my eyes again to find she's staring at my chest, which makes me smile. It's good to know I'm not the only one whose eyes are drifting…

She looked at me like this on Monday morning, when we first met, and although we got off to a frosty start, I think there's been a slow but definite thaw.

It started with yesterday's apology, progressed when I placed my fingers over her lips to stop her from insulting me again, deepened when I came back in here after changing into my costume, and really fell into place when I nibbled that piece of coriander leaf out of her hand. I can still remember the intense fire in her eyes when I did that, and the way she held her breath. I liked that reaction... nearly as much as I like her. She might speak her mind, but I'm not complaining. I hate women who fawn, like Vivian, almost as much as I hate women like Kennedy, who use their position to get what they want. That photographer I met on Monday was right about that... just like he was right about my attitude to Ella. It's different. She's different.

"Good morning." She smiles and I smile back.

This is promising.

"Good morning."

She dumps her handbag on the table. "Can I get you another coffee?" She nods towards my cup and I realise it's gone cold without me having touched it.

"Yes, please. But can I ask you something first?"

"Sure." She nods her head, waiting.

"I... um..." I don't know how to say this, but I've started now, so I'll just have to own up. "I had a dream last night."

She frowns. "You did?"

"Yes. It wasn't a very nice dream, either."

"Oh." She sounds disappointed and I wonder what she'd been expecting me to say, and whether she'd assumed my dream might have featured her. *If only...* "What happened?" she asks.

"I was appearing on a chat show."

"Why?"

"Good question. In my dream, the Meal Master show had been an enormous success, and I was having to do the rounds of publicity appearances… dressed like Blain."

"I see."

"As if that wasn't bad enough, the host of the show went off-script and asked me about my favourite food to cook with, and I blurted out that it was courgettes."

"Right… and?"

"I didn't say 'zucchini'."

"Oh. I see." She smiles.

"It's not funny, Ella. I'm scared."

She pulls out the chair beside me, sitting down. I can smell her scent. It's floral, but not sweet, with a kind of woody overtone and I inhale gently as she draws the chair a little nearer.

"What are you scared of?"

She's being serious now… all thoughts of amusement forgotten.

"I'm scared I'll say the wrong thing… that I'll call a cookie a biscuit or something."

"So you know there's a difference, then?"

"Only because I go to the supermarket, just like anyone else."

"Hmm… except a lot of people over here call it a grocery store."

I sit forward, resting my elbows on the table. "You see? That's my point entirely. I'm going to make an arse of myself."

"You mean 'ass'."

"Stop it, will you?"

She reaches out, placing her hand beside my elbow, the tips of her fingers almost touching me, and I forget all my fears as I struggle not to react. I wish she'd take that last step and let her fingers wander a little closer… maybe walk them up my arm and give me an excuse to clasp her face between my hands and crush my lips to hers…

"I won't let you make an ass of yourself, okay? I'll make sure you know the names of everything you're gonna be using."

Her words bring me back to reality, and although the desire doesn't go away, I focus on what she's saying, and I smile at her. "Sorry to be so pathetic."

"You're not pathetic. Hell... I'm terrified, and I won't be doing any of this in front of the cameras."

She pulls her hand away as she's speaking. I want to grab it back, but I don't. Time is moving on, and we need to move on with it...

"What are we doing today?" I ask as she gets up again, pushing the chair back under the table.

"That depends..."

"On what?"

"On how close you are to knowing your lines."

I tilt my head. "I could do with a little longer, if that's okay."

"It's fine. In fact, it's perfect."

"It is?"

"Yes. I was thinking I might prepare everything we're going to need in advance today, so it's more like it will be when you're doing the show for real."

"Okay."

"So, I can do that while you finish going through the script."

"Sounds like a plan."

"It will be... once I've made us both a coffee."

She wanders off to the side kitchen, but has only just got there when the door to the studio opens and Kennedy comes in, followed by Ruby. Fortunately, Vivian isn't with them today, but Kennedy is eyeing me closely already, and I wonder if she's about to ask why I'm not wearing my apron. She doesn't. Instead, she comes over to the table, standing right beside me.

"These arrived just now, from the photographer."

She puts down a pile of photographs, fanning them out, and then spreads them a little further, so I can see them better.

"What are they?" Ella comes back, standing on the other side of me, gazing down at the images of me, wearing nothing other than the apron and my jeans, and I feel myself blush, not daring to look up at her.

"They're the publicity stills for the show," Ruby says. "We asked the photographer to print them out, as well as sending us the digital images, so we can show them around more easily."

"They're magnificent, aren't they?" Kennedy's positively gushing.

I can't deny the photographer has done a fantastic job, although I'm not sure I like the idea of them being 'shown around'. "They're certainly atmospheric," I say, unable to think of another way to describe them.

Kennedy smiles and then surprises me by looking straight at Ella. "Can we talk... privately?"

Ella frowns. "If you insist."

"Perhaps through there?" Kennedy nods towards the side kitchen and the two of them walk away, leaving me alone with Ruby.

"What do you really think?" she says, glancing down at the pictures and then at me.

"I don't feel entirely comfortable about them, if you want me to be honest."

"I didn't think you did."

"Why? Does it show?" I look down at the pictures again, trying to discern any trace of discomfort in my face or body language.

"Not in the photographs. But I think you've made it pretty clear you don't like the way you're being presented."

"That's because I don't."

She smiles. "Look on the bright side... at least they're tasteful."

Other than the apron and its gaudy logo, she's probably right. Things could have ended up far worse.

"What are they going to be used for? And don't just say publicity. I got that much already."

"All sorts of things. We're running a social media campaign, and these will give it a real shot in the arm."

"If you insist. Which ones are you going to use?"

"We're gonna start off with the one where you're holding the rolling pin."

I nod my head, rifling through the photographs until I find one. I wonder what Ella's going to make of this, and turn toward the side kitchen, to see she's standing with her back against the work surface, while Kennedy's talking. There's something about Kennedy's demeanour that draws my attention. She seems positively obsequious, and I frown, recalling her change of attitude to Ella yesterday, and how she didn't bite when Ella argued with her. *What's that all about?*

They come out a few minutes later, and Kennedy walks over, gathering up the photographs. "We'll leave you to get on," she says. "I'm sure you've got a lot to do."

We have, there's no denying that, and while I'd love to ask Ella what that conversation was about, I guess it's none of my business. It was probably just something to do with work, and speaking of work... my lines are beckoning...

Chapter Six

Ella

Today isn't going as well as I'd hoped.

It started off okay until Kennedy had to interrupt us, yet again.

She'd come by with Ruby, to show us Blake's publicity photographs. I hadn't even realized they'd taken any, but I guessed that was where he'd disappeared to on Monday, when Ruby sent him to see Kennedy. The pictures themselves were fantastic, and I'd be the first to admit, Blake looked very sexy in them... but it was obvious he was uncomfortable about them. I was wondering about that, and if there was anything I could do or say to help the situation, when Kennedy asked to see me privately. I assumed I must have done something wrong, but couldn't say 'no', and we went into the side kitchen.

The moment we were in there, she turned to face me.

"Are you related to Drew Bennett?" she said, surprising me.

"Yes. He's my brother."

She frowned. "Why didn't you tell me?"

"Because I didn't realize you knew him. I'm not in the habit of going around telling people who I'm related to, just in case they happen to have met."

"That's not the point." She seemed flustered, although I couldn't work out why.

"Then what is?"

"That I didn't realize who you are…"

I knew then that she wasn't talking about me just being Drew's sibling, but his multi-millionaire sibling. I saw that fact registering on her face, even as we were speaking.

Her reaction has been bothering me ever since, and I've struggled to concentrate on anything else. I don't know how long she's been aware of the connection between myself and Drew, but I can't help wondering if that's why she didn't argue back yesterday when I told her to stop calling me 'dear'. If she'd begun to suspect who I am, maybe she thought better of bickering with me… and if that's the case, does it mean things between us will get better, or worse? They surely can't get any worse, can they? I suppose they could, if it transpires the connection between her and Drew is that they slept together. She didn't say anything about how she knows him, but would she, if they'd been in a relationship? And would Drew have slept with her in the first place? God… could it be that he turned her down? She's a lot older than him, but I know almost nothing about his taste in women. I'm not about to call him and ask, either. I'm not sure I want to know. Besides, I've got far too much to do. Aside from all the food I need to prepare, I'm very distracted today.

It's Blake who's the cause of that. I know he keeps looking at me, even though every time I glance in his direction, he seems to be focused on his script. I can still feel his eyes on me every so often, though. It's like there's a switch inside me that seems to flick on every time he looks at me.

I raise my head again, only this time, instead of finding him staring at his script, he's looking straight at me, and I pause, about to slice into the zucchini, my knife poised. He puts down

his script, but doesn't move, and just continues to stare for ages, his lips twisting into a smile. I smile back, and after a few moments more, he gets up, leaving his script behind, and walks over. He's not wearing his apron yet, and I can't help noticing the way his tight t-shirt clings to every contour of every muscle. It makes me wonder if the point of this show isn't so much about the food as about Blake himself… or Blain, as we're supposed to call him. I'm not going to… not now I know how much he hates it, which is almost as much as he seems to hate his costume.

Kennedy and Vivian's response to him yesterday, when he came back from the men's room, was almost feral, and it would have been amusing, if it wasn't for the fact that it clearly made Blake so uneasy. What was interesting, though, was that as soon as he could escape Kennedy's clutches, he came and stood right beside me, like I made him feel safe. I think that was when I realized that, in his shoes, if someone had insisted I had to wear something so revealing, I'd have felt exactly the same… and would almost certainly have refused. I thought then – and have thought even harder since – about the way Kennedy had behaved toward him, and it made me angry. She was using her authority and her power over him, and expecting him to be flattered. As he stood beside me, I understood my privileged position better than ever. I can afford to lose this job, I can answer back and take the consequences, just because I'm rich. Hell… I could probably afford to buy the studio, if I felt like it. But Blake has to take whatever Kennedy throws at him… and that's not fair.

"I noticed the food was already unpacked today," he says, coming around the island unit and standing quite close… although it's not as close as I'd like him to be.

"Yeah. I spoke to Ruby before I went home yesterday, and told her that whoever delivered the food needed to unpack it, too.

It seems it was Vivian's job to organize that, so she was told to make sure it was done properly today."

He chuckles. "I bet she loved that. Especially as she'd already been told off once in front of you."

"She wasn't entirely thrilled about it."

"We seem to have extra supplies… and two legs of lamb."

"I guess they're expecting us to do more than one run-through today."

He continues to stare at me, and I can't bring myself to break the moment and look away. There's something in his eyes which is different from yesterday, but I'm not sure what it is.

"Where do you want to start?" he says, breaking the moment for me, and although I'm disappointed by that, there's no escaping the fact that we've got work to do.

"I was wondering if you wanted to go through your lines first, and just act out the preparation elements, rather than having to actually do them?" I look up at him and he frowns slightly, staring down at the countertop, which is littered with vegetables, garlic and herbs.

"But you've done all this work."

"I know… and it'll keep. I just think, with hindsight, it might be best if we focus on one thing at a time, don't you?"

"Yes… as long as that's okay with you. I'm a lot more nervous about this than I thought I would be, and I think it'll help if I can get the lines right before I have to worry about pretending to be a chef again."

I move a little closer, although I take care not to touch him. "You've got nothing to be nervous about." His eyes widen and I hope my words have helped, not hindered.

"Do you want to take the part of the guest?" he says, smiling slightly.

"Sure, although I don't know what I'm supposed to say."

"I'll fetch my script." He wanders away, going back to the table.

"Won't you need it?" I ask as he starts back, bringing a stool for me to sit on, which he sets down at the end of the island unit.

"No. I'm hoping I know my lines well enough by now. But if I slip up, let me know."

He hands me the script, and I take my seat, waiting while he gets into position. Then he looks up to where the camera will probably be, and takes a breath before he delivers a perfectly worded welcome speech, introducing 'this week's guest', who's called 'Lyla'.

I stare at him, my mouth slightly open, and he spins around, looking at me.

"It's your turn," he says. "You just need to say 'hello'."

I startle. "I—I know, but you're talking with an American accent."

"No, I'm not."

"Okay, you're not now, but you were just then... when you were being Blain."

"I know. Blain is American. Didn't you know?"

"No. I assumed they'd chosen you because you were English."

He nods his head. "Ahh... so you didn't think they'd picked me for my incomparable acting abilities, either?"

He can hear the disappointment in his voice, and I can't say I'm surprised by it. After all, I've done nothing but insult him since the moment we first met. "I'm sorry." He looks at me like he's waiting, but I'm careful to limit myself to an apology this time, and after a few seconds, he smiles.

"Don't be. I guess I'd better get used to humiliating myself. It's going to be my face appearing on a show called 'Meal Master', and all the publicity material that goes with it."

"Do you think that's as bad as I do?"

"The name?" I nod my head and his smile widens. "Of course. But what can I say? They've decided on it already, and they're not about to change it."

"I'm just grateful I'm going to be hidden behind the cameras."

"Not for today, you're not…" He stares at me for a moment or two. "Shall we try that again?"

"Okay."

He takes another breath, like he needs it to get back into character again, and delivers his opening lines, his American accent no longer taking me by surprise, although I'm impressed by it. If I didn't know he was English, I'd never have guessed…

We work our way through the script and, with just one exception, Blake gets it word perfect. Even that exception is only very slight, and I don't pick him up on it at the time.

"How was that?" he says, when we get to the end.

"It was amazing. You remembered everything I showed you yesterday, and you were almost word perfect."

"Almost?" He frowns slightly.

"You said 'pour', instead of 'drizzle', when you were pretending to put the oil onto the lamb, but that doesn't matter. They both mean the same thing."

"Except 'drizzle' is more accurate."

"Maybe, but don't beat yourself up over it. You got everything else right."

He nods his head, letting out a breath. "What's the time?" he asks.

I put down the script and check my watch. "Just before noon."

He raises his eyebrows. "Not bad."

Considering we didn't start until ten-thirty, I think it's nothing short of a miracle. "I know. We got through that a lot quicker than I thought we would. I'm wondering if we should break for lunch and then go through it all again afterwards, but with the food this time. What do you think?"

His brow furrows. "I'm not sure. Maybe we ought to check with Ruby first. She said they like to start full rehearsals as early as possible, didn't she?"

I can see his point, but I'm not convinced. "You don't think we should run through it all again ourselves, before we invite everyone else in?"

"I'd love to say 'yes' to that, but I'm not sure we've got the luxury of that much time."

"Shall I go ask her?"

"I think it might be wise… but I'll go, if you like?"

"No, it's fine." I get down from the stool, and he reaches for the script, flipping over a couple of pages. I know he's checking on the 'drizzle' speech, and while I want to reiterate that it really doesn't matter, it'll make him feel better if he gets it right, so I leave him to it and exit the rehearsal studio, crossing the hall and knocking on Ruby's door.

"Come in." I push the door open and enter. She's sitting behind her desk and looks up at me, smiling. "Ella… what can I do for you?"

"I just came to let you know we've done our first run-through, without the food, and we wanted to ask whether we should do it all again, by ourselves, or whether you want to get the rest of the team involved?"

"I think we need to get started on rehearsals," she says, nodding her head. "Time's moving on, I'm afraid." She gives me a sympathetic look, which says she's not blaming me, and I feel guilty for my outburst on Monday, right before I went home. She's no more to blame for this situation than I am, but she got the brunt of my tiredness and bad mood.

"What do you want to do, then? Get everyone to come in now?"

She glances at her computer screen. "I think we can allow some time for lunch and start at… one-fifteen?"

"Okay."

"I'll send a message to the team to let them know they're needed in the rehearsal studio. We'll do a couple of dry runs, without the food, so we can work around Blain, and the lighting and camera angles. Then we'll go again…"

"With the food?"

"Not necessarily. I mean, I'm hoping it'll work out that way, but we'll keep going until everyone's happy with the set-up, and only then will we add the food. So, if you can make sure it's all prepared, because you won't get much warning."

"I already have."

She nods her head. "It's going to be a late finish, I'm afraid."

"Okay. I'll let Blake know."

A smile touches her lips. "You're supposed to call him 'Blain', don't forget."

I don't reply, but leave her office and head straight back to the rehearsal studio. Inside, Blake is sitting on the stool I vacated a short while ago, still thumbing through the script, but he looks up as I come in.

"How did it go?"

I walk over, standing a little distance from him, leaning against the island unit. "We're starting full rehearsals after lunch… at one-fifteen. To start with, you'll do dry runs, like we've just done, and when everyone's set up correctly, they'll bring in the food."

He nods his head, glancing at everything I prepared earlier, most of which is still on the countertop – except the lamb, which I put back into the refrigerator once I'd studded both legs with garlic. "Okay… but is everything going to keep for that long?"

"Most of it'll be fine." I grab the trays of vegetables and put them in the refrigerator, above the lamb.

"What about the green beans?" he calls from behind me.

"They'll be okay, and so will the potatoes. They're in water." I go back over to him. "We'll just move everything out of the

way." He helps me put the pans onto the table, so the countertop is clear, other than the spices and oils, which we push to the back. "I hope you didn't have any plans for this evening," I say, turning back to face him.

"No. Did you?"

I shake my head, wondering how I can ask if that's a permanent state of affairs for him, or whether it's just tonight that he's available, and he's normally busy... with someone. How can I, though? I'd be too embarrassed, and I'm worried he might give me an answer I don't want to hear.

"I guess I'd better be prepared to make a fool of myself in front of other people," he says, scratching his head and messing up his hair.

"Are you still feeling nervous?" I ask. "Even though you did so well earlier?"

"A little."

"You've got no reason to."

"That's easy for you to say. You know what you're doing."

"No, I don't. This is all new to me. It's my first job."

He frowns. "In television?"

"Anywhere."

His face clears, and he smiles. "It doesn't show." He looks at his watch. "I guess we'd better get some lunch before we run out of time."

"I can make us something, if you like?"

His smile widens. "Do we have enough ingredients?"

"Sure we do. We've got eggs, so I can make us an omelet, if nothing else."

"Okay." He nods toward the side kitchen. "Shall we?"

"I'm not cooking in there. The only thing in that kitchen that's worth using is the coffee machine." He laughs. "Why don't you sit?" I glance over at the stool, where his script is still lying on the countertop.

"And watch you work? That doesn't seem very fair."

"I'm pretty sure I can make omelets all by myself. They were one of the first things I learned to cook when I got to France."

He doesn't argue anymore, and wanders over to the stool, sitting down, and pushing his script aside as he gazes across at me.

"So that's where you studied cookery, is it… in France?"

I nod my head, then walk over to the refrigerator, grabbing some eggs and an omelet pan from the cabinet before I return to him.

"It wasn't just in France. I spent about six months in London, and then just over a year in Madrid, before I moved on to Paris."

"And how long did you spend there?" He watches, while I quickly get out two plates, and then put the pan on the stove to heat. After that, I crack three eggs into a small bowl that I put out earlier but didn't end up using, and start beating them with a whisk.

"A little over two years."

"Was that because you liked Paris the most?" He's teasing. That much is obvious from his smile… and I like it.

"No. It was because the course there was the longest… although I will admit, I loved living in Paris."

"More than London?"

I smile at him. "Maybe. Sorry."

I lean over toward him, grabbing a handful of fresh herbs from the pot, and he watches my every move. I'm usually a lot more self-conscious than this, but I enjoy being scrutinized by him. There's something oddly comforting about it.

I take my chef's knife and chop the herbs, running it back and forth over them. "How do you do that?" he says, shaking his head.

"It's about rolling the knife." I make my moves more slowly, demonstrating.

"Can I try?"

"Of course."

He gets up, coming around the island unit, and I hand him my knife.

"You're willing to let me use yours?" he says, staring down at me, with that teasing smile on his lips.

"Just this once."

I step aside, giving him space, and he makes a reasonable job of chopping the herbs.

"How's that?" he says.

"Pretty good. We'll make a chef of you yet."

He chuckles, handing me back my knife, and I put it down again, adding some butter to the pan, and watching while it sizzles and bubbles. I add half the herbs to the beaten eggs, stirring them around, and once the butter has melted, I pour in the egg mixture.

"What do you do now?" Blake asks.

"Wait."

"You just wait?"

"Only for a few minutes…" He moves closer to get a better view of the pan and I struggle to breathe.

"What are you waiting for?"

"This…" I grab a fork, teasing the omelet from the edges of the pan. "See? The eggs have started to cook."

He leans in, watching, our heads really close together, while I continue to pull the egg mixture into the middle of the pan until the whole thing is cooked, the top still slightly runny.

Then I tip the pan, folding the omelet into a perfect roll, and slide it onto one of the waiting plates, topping it with a sprig of fresh parsley, before I hand it to him.

"Voilà, monsieur… une omelette aux fines herbes," I say in my best French accent.

"Merci, mademoiselle." He surprises me with his response… his accent at least as good as mine.

"Please don't wait for me. It'll get cold."

I hand him a fork, and he takes a bite, closing his eyes as he chews. "God… that's so good."

I feel myself blush and, to cover my embarrassment, I mix up some more eggs and herbs, adding them to the pan to make my own omelet. It takes but a few minutes to prepare, and Blake hasn't eaten more than a couple of mouthfuls of his by the time I'm serving mine.

"Shall we sit at the table?" I suggest and he nods his head, leading the way, but holding out a chair for me when we get there, and waiting until I've sat down before he sits beside me. We both eat, and I have to admit, the omelet is good, Blake making 'hmm' noises after every mouthful. "Where did you learn to act?" I ask, looking up at him.

"You're assuming I was taught to do this?"

"You mean, you weren't?"

"No. Doesn't it show?"

"No. You were word perfect earlier."

"Almost," he says, rolling his eyes. "And learning lines is just about having a good memory. It's got nothing to do with acting."

"So you've never had any formal training?"

"None whatsoever. I studied English at university and always wanted to be a writer."

"Really?" I'm intrigued by that. He seems like such a natural when he's acting.

"Yes. When my parents died, I sold their house. It needed a lot of work doing to it, and I didn't want to live there. But it was on an enormous plot of land, so I did quite well out of the sale and once I'd paid off their mortgage, I was left with enough to keep a roof over my head for a few years, while I earned absolutely nothing and slaved over writing my first novel."

"You've written a novel?"

"Written, yes. Published, no."

"Oh."

He smiles. "It's funny. That's how most people react when I say that… with enormous disappointment."

I feel guilty now. "I—I didn't mean…"

"It's okay. I'm disappointed too."

"Have you thought about trying to find an agent?" I ask, wondering if he's lacking in contacts, rather than talent.

"I've got an agent. A friend of mine recommended her, and I sent her my book. We had a video call, during which she told me she thought my story wasn't original enough… and then the next thing I knew, she sent me a message, asking if I'd be interested in coming over here to do some TV work, for a commercial."

"To write it, you mean?"

"No, to act in it."

"But why? You had no experience in acting."

"That's not strictly true. I'd done some stage work in the UK, just for fun, and it was on my CV, which I'd sent to the agent."

"Your resume, you mean?"

"Yeah… I guess. In any case, there wasn't a great deal of acting involved in the commercial."

"Why? What was it for?"

"Fitness equipment. They had a 'before' guy, and an 'after' guy."

I can't help smiling. "Which were you?"

He smiles back. "I was the 'after' guy."

"I'm not surprised. You've got the perfect physique." I feel myself blush… again, but I don't regret my words, or the smile that's formed on his lips.

"Thank you… I think. It was hardly Hamlet, but it paid well, while it lasted."

"How long did it last, then?"

"Initially, they just brought me over to do the one commercial, but it went so well, they gave me a six-month contract."

"And you didn't think about going home, rather than signing it?" I ask as he finishes his omelet, pushing his plate aside.

"No. I'd decided to make the move here when I got their first offer."

"Even though it was just for one commercial?"

"Yes. I wasn't sure how I was going to make it work, but I felt like trying something new, and I certainly got to do that. I'd been here for about four months when I met a couple of people who belonged to a theater company, and when my contract for the TV commercials ended, I went to work with them."

"Here in Boston?"

"Yes."

"But what about your family? Don't you miss them?"

"I don't have any family."

I remember he said his parents were dead but… "You mean you've got no brothers or sisters?"

"No. I'm an only child," he says. "As were my parents. So there aren't even any uncles or aunts, or cousins."

"You said they died?" I say, lowering my voice, because it feels like the right thing to do.

He nods his head. "In a car accident."

"That must have been awful."

"It was."

"When did it happen?"

"Just after I finished my degree. I'd gone traveling in Europe to let off steam after all that studying, and I got a call from the police to say they'd been killed. Obviously, I went straight home again and dealt with everything. I hadn't been away for very long. I think I'd been in Paris for about four days."

"I'm so sorry."

"Why? Paris isn't that bad."

I shake my head, finishing my lunch. "I meant about your parents."

"I know, but it was a long time ago."

"Was it?"

"Yes. I'm older than I look." He's got a mischievous glint in his eyes and I can't help smiling.

"You can't be much over thirty."

"Add three years to that nice round figure, and you'd be spot on," he says.

"You're thirty-three?"

He nods his head. "Yes." That means he's nine years older than me… not that it matters.

"So, you moved your whole life to America? Just like that?"

"I did. But don't sound so surprised. You know how that feels. You moved to Europe."

"I know, but I came home from time to time, like at Christmas and during the summer, and I knew I'd be coming back permanently at some point. It was never going to be forever."

"I guess I didn't know it would be forever when I first came over here. I just knew I wasn't going straight back again. Not that my girlfriend understood any of that."

"Your girlfriend?"

"Yeah."

"Ah… so there was someone you left behind?"

"I didn't say there wasn't. I just said I didn't have any family. If we're talking about everyone, rather than just relatives, then you'd have to include my friends, and my godfather as well."

"Did they understand your reasons for coming here better than your girlfriend?"

"Yes, I think so. Some of them thought I was mad, but most of them – Henry especially – thought it was a great opportunity… an adventure."

"And your girlfriend didn't?" I ask, feeling intrigued by his past.

"No. She wasn't happy about me taking the initial contract, let alone my decision to make something long-term of it. She made it clear she thought I was being selfish, as well as professionally short-sighted, and that she wasn't going to come with me."

"So, what did you do?"

"I came anyway."

"You broke up with her?"

"Yes." He doesn't seem very upset about that, but I guess if they weren't that close, he wouldn't be, would he? The thought that he might have been close to her – or anyone else for that matter – is surprisingly difficult to contemplate, so I don't, and instead I get up, reaching for his plate.

"We should probably clear away."

"Let me," he says, standing up too. "Clearing up is the one thing I do well in the kitchen."

I can't help chuckling and he smiles down at me, taking the plates and carrying them to the island unit.

It's been lovely getting to know him.

I just wish we didn't have to stop so soon.

Blake cleans the dishes, while I wipe down the countertops, and between us we get the kitchen back to normal in no time at all, which is just as well, because he's only just put everything away when Ruby comes in the door. She's followed by several other people, including Vivian, and although I hadn't been feeling that nervous before, I am now. There's something about Vivian's presence that just sets me on edge.

Ruby comes straight over to me, looking around. "Have you prepared everything Blain will need?"

I nod my head. "It's all in the refrigerator."

She frowns. "What about the cooked versions?"

"Cooked versions?"

"Yes. When we do the show for real, you'll have cooked a set of everything in advance so Blain can magically pull it from the oven." Her brow furrows. "Are you telling me all the food is still raw?"

I could kick myself. "Yes."

"You didn't wonder why we gave you two of everything?"

"I assumed that was so we could do more than one run-through."

She sighs. "Okay. It's not the end of the world. As I explained earlier, we're gonna need to read through the script at least a couple of times for the technical set-up. You can cook one complete set of each dish in the meantime, can't you?"

"Sure."

She nods her head and I realize she's waiting for me to get on with it. I can't bring myself to look at anyone, although I catch Vivian's eye as I'm heading for the refrigerator and notice the smug smile on her lips. It's well deserved, though. I should have thought of this myself. They gave me additional ingredients for a reason, and I completely ignored the fact that Blake would need to plate up the prepared food, as well as pretending to cook it… all within the space of an hour.

I get busy putting things into the oven, and when I turn around again, I'm surprised to see three cameras in the space between the island unit and the table, and several people I've never seen before, all milling around. They seem to know what they're doing, and are busy going about it, and I stand aside, watching for a moment.

"Are you okay?" Blake's voice is a whisper in my ear, his breath a dusting against my skin and I turn to find him standing right behind me.

"No. I feel such a fool for forgetting to cook the food."

"You weren't to know. And anyway, there's no harm done, is there?"

"I suppose not."

"In which case, to repeat your advice to me… don't beat yourself up over it." I smile up at him, and our eyes lock, just for a moment, before he looks down at the apron in his hands. "I'm supposed to put this on. Do you think you could help me with the ties at the back? They're meant to be 'just right' according to Kennedy, so the logo is in the middle."

"Sure."

He puts the apron over his head and turns around, while I grab the ties, binding them in a neat bow behind his back. He turns around again, and I straighten the apron, making sure the logo is centered, and nod my head. "Perfect."

He smiles, shaking his head and while I want to say something to put him at ease, I can't seem to think of anything, so we just stare at each other for another moment.

"Blain?"

We both startle as Ruby approaches.

"Yes?" Blake says, turning to her.

"I've been calling you." She smiles up at him.

"Have you? I didn't hear."

"Probably because 'Blain' isn't your name," I say, and he grins down at me.

"That might have something to do with it."

"Well… you'll need to get used to it," Ruby replies, and nods over her shoulder. "We're ready for you."

"Okay." I hear him suck in a breath, although he gives the impression of being perfectly calm. "Who's playing the part of the guest?" he asks as he follows her onto the kitchen set.

"Vivian."

He turns to me, pulling a face. "Can't Ella do it? I practiced with her this morning."

"Unfortunately, now Ella's got everything in the oven, we need her behind the cameras, so she can tell us if we're going wrong in terms of where the food will be."

"Oh… okay." I can sense his disappointment, but that's not difficult. It matches my own, and while I wander over to the camera area, he steps up behind the island unit, where Ruby says a few words to him. They're too quiet for me to hear, but he nods his head, looking like he understands. Vivian marches forward, a script in her hand, and Ruby steps back.

"Do you need your script, Blake?" she asks as she moves away from him.

"No. I should be fine."

She seems a little surprised by that, but comes and stands beside me, looking around to check if everyone is ready. At that moment, Vivian leans forward, showing off her cleavage, and the cameraman to my right swears under his breath.

"Sit back, will you? You're blocking the shot."

Vivian does as she's told, and everyone settles again. Ruby clears her throat and says, "Okay… cue Blain in three, two… one…"

Mac

I'm not sure how, but we've made it through the first five shows.

Wednesdays and Thursdays are definitely the hardest in terms of the hours we have to work. It's relentless and full-on.

Linus Hicks might be a 'pussycat' in Ruby's eyes, but I've yet to see any evidence of it. He's a perfectionist, and although we rarely see him, because he's up in the director's booth, he picks up on even the slightest issue, making us go again, and again, until he's happy with everything. I have to be at the top of my game for both days, which can sometimes be fourteen or fifteen hours long. That's fourteen or fifteen hours of physical and mental exhaustion.

That first week was definitely a baptism of fire, and because we've been better organised and a little more knowledgeable about Linus and his standards, and what's expected of us since then, it's been slightly easier. That said, we're still having to put up with Kennedy coming by the studio all the time. I've noticed she seems a lot more friendly with Ella than she was, and of course, she doesn't leave me alone. Her attentions are getting more and more annoying, and I'm finding it harder and harder not to snap at her. I have to keep reminding myself she's my boss, and that losing my temper with her is unlikely to end well, but when the woman is literally pawing me, it's tough.

Then, of course, there's Vivian.

During the first week, she'd been less of an issue than Kennedy… at least until we got into rehearsals, when she started playing the part of the guest. She's done so ever since, and to be honest, she's driving me insane. She's constantly in the way and has taken to wearing ludicrously low-cut tops on rehearsal days, so when she leans over, I barely know where to look. The camera operators keep losing it with her, because she's continually getting in their way, too. I overheard a couple of them talking the other day and I gathered they're as relieved as I am when we get around to recording for real. There may be occasional problems with the guests – or at least, with the actors playing them – but at least they all know their lines, and where to sit.

As for Ella… she's been miraculous. She's so professional, and although I know she felt bad about not having everything ready for the first run-through we did in week one, she hasn't put a foot wrong since. Not only that, but her cooking is sublime. I haven't tasted a single thing yet that hasn't been mouthwatering.

It's more than that, though. Over the last few weeks, we've become so much closer… and I don't think I'm the only one who believes that. There's something in her eyes and her demeanour that tells me she's thinking the same thing, too.

I guess that all started in our second week, when she was showing me how to make pastry. I was being far too heavy-handed – according to Ella, anyway – and she took my hands in hers to demonstrate the lightness of touch required. She was talking at the time and it took her a moment or two to realise we were holding hands, to the extent that our fingers had become entwined… at which point she snatched her hands away.

"I'm sorry." She looked up at me, blushing. "I shouldn't have touched you."

"Why not? We've touched before."

She shook her head. "You've touched me." She bit her lip then, and I wondered if she was remembering the way I'd used my fingers to silence her. I hoped so, but I didn't make a big deal out of it. She seemed embarrassed enough already.

"I know, but we've touched by accident as well… like when we've been preparing foods."

"Even so, I don't want to make you feel uncomfortable."

I smiled at her. "I don't think you could, Ella."

Her blush deepened. "Are you sure about that? Because I— I noticed your reactions when Kennedy and Vivian have been around, and…"

"And you thought I had a problem with being touched in general?"

"It seemed that way."

"Well, I don't. I just prefer to choose who's doing the touching."

She smiled at me then. "Don't we all?"

It seemed to me that moment meant something significant… a mutual understanding, maybe? Or possibly that she felt as comfortable around me as I felt around her? I couldn't be sure, but whatever it meant, I liked it.

As I say, since then we've become closer, and although there's nothing overtly intimate about it, I love being near to her. I love spending so much time with her, too… and even though the job is hard work, I wouldn't have it any other way. She's made us lunch a few times since that first week, although it's always been a bit more rushed, and occasionally, other members of the crew have joined us, too. It's impossible for me to object to their presence, but I prefer it when we can be alone. I think she does, too.

If there is a cloud on the horizon, I guess it would have to be that I don't know whether she's free. I keep thinking she must be… especially when she looks at me the way she does. But then I remind myself that I could be over-thinking… over-interpreting, because I want her to want me, like I want her.

I've tried fishing several times, to find out if she's seeing anyone, but short of asking outright, I've not been able to discover anything. I don't know whether that's good or bad. All I do know is that, when we have to work late, she never seems to worry about what time she'll be getting home.

And that's got to be good… right?

I'm so relieved it's Friday, and we've almost finished for the day. It's been a tough week – nearly as difficult as our first one – and Ella's apologised for that so many times I've lost count. It's not her fault, though. The 'problem' we were given was someone

who wanted to cook and eat healthier versions of takeout food that didn't take too long to make. Ella was a genius, as usual, and came up with three different ideas, and while they all look and taste incredible, I've struggled with learning and remembering all the processes involved.

The sticky rice which is going with the Thai green curry had me flummoxed, and as for making pizza…

Ella went into lengthy explanations on Monday morning about how the pizza base would normally contain yeast, and take a lot longer to prepare. I pretended to pay attention, and to understand what she was talking about, while thinking that I'd missed seeing her over the weekend. I wished there was something I could do about that, and by the time I realised she'd moved on to actually making the dough, I'd missed the order she'd put everything into the mixing bowl, and she had to go through it all again. She didn't seem to mind and repeated it all to me with a smile on her face, which made it even harder to concentrate.

I found rolling out the dough really difficult, but we both knew it was something I'd have to master and 'perform' on the show, so we took our time, and I got there… eventually.

"You see? You can do it." Ella did her best to sound encouraging, even though it had taken me four attempts to get a reasonably circular round of pizza dough, which looked nowhere near as good as hers.

"Thanks to you, yes."

She nudged into me. "Stop putting yourself down. I've had years of training, and you're doing all this in a fraction of the time."

I hadn't been putting myself down at all. Don't get me wrong, I wasn't under the illusion that I was a budding culinary genius, but the only one in the room who deserved any credit for what

I'd achieved was Ella. I opened my mouth to say so, just as Gavin barged in with a technical question for Ella, and the moment was lost.

Fortunately, when it came to the recording yesterday, I rolled out the dough quite well... well enough for the cameras, anyway. In fact, most of the cookery elements went okay, but they were especially difficult, and I was tired, so I messed up quite a lot of my lines... which is why today has been so busy. We've been re-recording several sections, mostly of me just talking to camera and filling in gaps. All I've got left to do now is the final element... adding the garnish to the curried chicken that forms the basis of the last dish, while rounding off the show... because I didn't get that quite right yesterday, either.

The bowl of chicken is sitting in front of me, and on the chopping board are some pre-chopped coriander leaves.

Cilantro, not coriander. Cilantro, not coriander... I mutter the words in my head as Ruby counts me in for my final speech and I look up at the camera and plant a smile on my face.

"Okay, so we just need to scatter some chopped cilantro over the top..." I put actions to my words, picking up a handful of the leaves and sprinkling them over the chicken. "And there we have it." I push the dish over towards the 'guest'; a young woman, whose name for the purposes of the show is Amanda. "Three of the best take-away dishes in town, all made in the comfort of your own..."

"Cut!"

"What?" I look up to see Ruby frowning at me, her finger to her ear. On recording days, she wears an ear-piece so she can communicate with Linus in the booth, and she's nodding her head.

"Linus says you just said 'take-away' instead of 'takeout'."

"Did I?"

"Yeah, you did." One of the camera operators peers out from behind his camera, rolling his eyes.

"Oh… sorry." I haven't said 'take-away', even in real life, since about six months after I moved here. What on earth possessed me to say it now?

Ruby turns to Ella, who's standing off to one side. "Do we have any more of the curried chicken?"

She nods her head, rushing forward. "I prepared extra, just in case."

She takes away the bowl I've just garnished and prepares another one, filling it with creamy curry, then grabs some more coriander leaves and I step aside while she quickly chops them for me, leaving them in a neat pile.

Once she's finished, she smiles up at me, giving me a quick wink. "Okay?"

"Yes, thanks."

I feel guilty for getting it wrong, when I know everyone is desperate to get finished, but the last thing they need is for me to waste more time dwelling on it, so as Ella and Ruby step back behind the cameras, I resume my position.

"Okay everyone?" Ruby raises her voice, and the studio falls into silence. She pauses and then counts me in again.

I take a breath, then look into the camera, smiling. "Okay, so we just need to scatter some chopped cilantro over the top…" I repeat my actions with the freshly chopped coriander leaves. "And there we have it." Once again, I nudge the dish towards 'Amanda'. "Three of the best takeout dishes in town, all made in the comfort of your own home."

'Amanda' picks up the fork beside her and starts eating, making all the right noises about how good the food is, even though a couple of the dishes are stone cold by now, and I look back at the camera.

"Thanks for watching, folks, and we'll see you again next week for more masterful meal ideas… with me, Blain… your very own Meal Master."

I hate that line and struggle not to cringe as I say it, but I keep smiling until Ruby calls out, "And… cut!" and we all heave a sigh of relief.

"Sorry about that, everyone." It seems only fair that I should apologise for having messed up, but they all smile at me, and 'Amanda', whose name is really Bonnie, leans over the island unit, placing her hand on my arm.

"Don't sweat it," she says, gazing up into my eyes. "We all make mistakes."

I know she means well, but she's not the first of our 'guests' to cause me a problem. Like I said, they at least know their lines and how to behave on camera, but that doesn't stop them from being too tactile, too flirty, or too talkative when it stops rolling.

To be honest, I'm wondering what it is with the women around here.

"Thanks." I acknowledge her kindness, even though I step away at the same time, so she's forced to release me.

"Are you doing anything tonight?" she asks, tilting her head and blinking a few times.

Okay. That's different. None of the others have been quite so obvious.

"Yes. Sorry… I'm afraid I'm busy."

"Oh, that's a shame." She looks genuinely disappointed, but then her face suddenly brightens. "Can I call you?"

She doesn't have my number, so she's going to struggle, but I guess that's what she's asking for, and I lean a little closer to her, lowering my voice slightly.

"When I say I'm busy, I mean I'm with someone," I say, the lies falling from my lips with the consummate ease of an actor.

"Oh… okay." Her shoulders drop, and she climbs down from the stool. "I've enjoyed working with you."

"Me too."

She looks up again, giving me a smile, and I smile back, just to be polite, waiting for her to walk away, before I turn and find Ella standing right behind me. She looks bewildered, maybe even a little sad, and I wonder how much of that conversation she heard.

I wish I could hold her and tell her it was all lies, but I'm aware of where we are, and that we're surrounded by far too many people. I don't want her to leave, though, so I step a little closer. "Were you able to get all your preparations done for next week?" I ask. God, that's lame.

"Y—Yes," she stutters. "In between everything else."

"I'm sorry about that. If I hadn't made so many mistakes yesterday…"

"It's not your fault. I gave you a lot to do." Her voice is devoid of emotion, and I wish we'd never started this conversation now.

"What are we doing next week?"

"Salads."

"That should be easier… no cooking." I smile down at her, but she doesn't smile back.

"I wouldn't go that far."

I'm not sure what she means by that, but I'm done talking about work. I'm done seeing the hurt in her eyes, too. It's making my chest ache.

"Are you okay?" I ask, stepping even closer to her.

"I'm fine." She clearly isn't. Her reply was way too quick… way too artificial.

I want to reach out to her, but I can't. Not here. Not now. I feel the need to give her some kind of reassurance, though, so I just say, "I hate lying, don't you?"

"Lying?"

I nod my head. "Yes."

She frowns. "What are you talking about?"

"Just now… I was lying to Bonnie. And don't pretend you didn't overhear, because we both know you did."

She blushes and looks down at my chest… at the show's logo emblazoned on my apron, before she raises her eyes to mine again. "Which part were you lying about?"

"Being busy tonight… being with someone."

"So you're not?"

"No. I'm very free and very single. I just didn't want to accept her generous invitation, and telling her I was already taken seemed like the best and kindest way of achieving that."

"I see."

"So… are you okay?" I ask again, and she smiles.

"I'm fine."

This time I believe her, and I have to smile too.

"Do you wanna get out of here?"

She nods and, while everyone mills around us, clearing up and dismantling the studio, I grab her hand and quickly lead her from the room.

Outside in the hall, I pull the apron off over my head.

"Are you going to change?" she asks.

"Not tonight." I don't feel like wasting any more time than is strictly necessary. "But we both need to get our jackets."

"Hmm… and my purse."

We left our things in the rehearsal studio, and make our way back there, where I help Ella with her jacket, shrugging on my own, and leaving the apron on the table, before I pick up my shirt and we head for the elevator.

As we're riding down, I do up my jacket, and when I look up, she's staring at me.

"What's wrong?"

"Nothing. It's just that you usually change before you go home, so…"

I smile at her. "That's why I'm doing up my jacket… so no-one on the bus will notice the unusually tight t-shirt."

"You take the bus?"

"Yes."

"I—I can give you a ride, if you like."

I'm not about to say 'no' to an offer like that, and I undo my jacket again as I smile at her. "That would be great."

The elevator doors open and we step out.

"What made you say 'take-away' tonight?" Ella looks up at me as we stroll between the rows of cars.

"I've got no idea."

"I was going to ask if they really needed to make such a big deal of it. The phrase 'take-away' isn't unheard of over here."

"Maybe not. But we'd used 'takeout' all the way through the recording."

"I know. That's what I figured, and it's why I kept my mouth shut," she says, shrugging her shoulders. "Sorry."

"Don't apologise. It was my fault, not yours. I was thinking after I did it, I've been used to saying 'takeout' for ages," I say, shaking my head.

"Maybe you're just tired."

"Let's hope so. I don't need to keep screwing up like that."

She stops right beside a red Mercedes. It's a convertible, with a black canvas roof, which is currently closed, and I stare at it for a second.

"Is this yours?" I ask.

She nods her head. "It certainly is."

I'm surprised, but do my best not to show it as she opens the car and lets us in. It has that new car smell, and while I dread to think what it cost, I guess that's none of my business.

She starts the engine and looks over at me. "Where are we going?" she says.

"I'll give you directions."

She nods, reversing out of the parking space, and driving slowly from the car park and up onto the street. It's late, and there's less traffic than usual, which means it won't take as long as I'd like to get back to my apartment. We're about half-way there when Ella sighs and I look over at her, to see she's smiling.

"I don't know about you," she says, "but I thought that was a hard week."

"Apart from our first one, and maybe the Thanksgiving dinner last week, I thought it was the hardest yet... but please don't apologise again. It wasn't your fault."

"If you insist. Although I'm done with cooking. I'm gonna order something in for tonight, I think."

"Hmm... me too. My excuse is exhaustion, though. I can hardly claim to be done with cooking when I'm faking it." She laughs, and the sound somehow gives me courage where it's been lacking before. "W—Would you like to join me? We could order in together, couldn't we? Unless you need to be somewhere else?"

"No, I don't..."

That's still not a definite answer, but coupled with her reaction to what I said to Bonnie, it feels vaguely promising. Not conclusive, but promising.

"So... would you like to have dinner with me?"

"I'd love to."

That feels more than promising, and I tell her to turn left before we drive past my street.

"You can park anywhere down here."

She pulls into a space, switching off the engine, and we both get out of the car. I step around to her side and although I don't take her hand, we walk together to my apartment building. I

open the door, holding it for her, and she passes through ahead of me, waiting until I guide her towards the elevator.

Once inside, I avoid looking at her, knowing if I do, I'll have to kiss her. She's getting harder and harder to resist, and my self-control is waning.

Fortunately, it doesn't take long to get to the top floor, and the doors open onto the narrow corridor that leads to my apartment. I let her step out before me.

"There's just me up here," I say, as we make our way to my front door.

"Hmm… it's the same at my place. I have the whole top floor, too."

I nod my head, putting the key in the lock.

She steps inside and I flick on the lights before following her, feeling grateful that I've hardly been here this week, and haven't had the chance to make a mess.

"This is amazing." She spins around in the enormous space that forms my living area. Her enthusiasm is adorable, and I can't help smiling.

"I know. It used to be a dance studio, but I got lucky. The block is owned by a collective that will only rent to people who work in the creative arts."

"And that includes you?"

"Evidently. Acting counts, and so does writing. They subsidise the rent as well, which is a godsend. I'd never be able to afford somewhere like this otherwise."

I shrug off my jacket, and offer to take hers. She turns around, and I remove it, being careful not to touch her any more than is strictly necessary… which is a challenge in itself, and then I take our coats back to the front door, hooking them up.

"What would you like to eat?" I ask, and she tilts her head at me.

"Anything, as long as it's not curry, Thai, or pizza."

"So… Chinese?"

"Sounds perfect."

I pull out my phone and find the website for my usual Chinese takeout before handing it to Ella. "Take your pick. I'm just gonna go change my top, before this t-shirt cuts off my circulation."

She chuckles, looking down at my phone and I run up the stairs, peeling off the t-shirt as I go, and throwing it into the laundry hamper before pulling out a white shirt, rolling up the sleeves and buttoning it up.

As I make my way back down the stairs again, I notice my phone on the arm of the sofa and Ella standing over by the bookcase.

"Did you choose?" I ask.

She turns, nodding her head, and I pick up the phone, making my own selection. "Let me pay," she says, and I look up, frowning at her.

"I wouldn't dream of it. I invited you."

She opens her mouth, but closes it again, and I pay for the takeout, throwing my phone down on the couch before I look up at her again.

"You read a lot of detective stories," she says. "Is that what your novel is?"

"Yes. It's a country house murder mystery."

"I'd love to read it one day."

"If it ever gets published, I'll let you."

"If it ever gets published, I'll buy a copy, and you won't be able to stop me."

She has a point, although the thought of Ella reading my novel fills me with fear. I've written it to be read… just not necessarily by her. I dread to think what she'd make of my storyline. Would she agree with Delilah that it's lacking in originality?

"Can I get you something to drink?" I feel the need to change the subject.

"I'm driving, so I'd better stick to soda."

"If by that you mean Coke, then would you prefer it with or without caffeine?"

"Without, thanks."

I head for the kitchen, pouring two glasses of Coke, and return to the living area, where we both sit on the couch. I hand her a glass and she takes a sip, while I watch her, unable to stop myself from thinking about how much I want to kiss her. It's a constant thought now, but the problem is, I don't know for sure whether she's available.

I put my glass on the table in front of us, wondering how to go about this, and coming up empty. We can't sit in silence, though. I need to say something…

"Tell me about Paris." It feels like a reasonable starting point.

She tips her head slightly. "You've been there yourself. What do you want to know?"

Okay… that went well. "I don't know. I'm just making conversation."

"Why?"

"Because we can't sit here and say nothing all evening."

She turns in her seat, so she's facing me. "I know that. What I mean is, why don't you say what you're really thinking… because I don't think it's got anything to do with Paris."

"No, it hasn't."

"Okay…" She stares at me, waiting, and I decide I might as well tell her the truth… and be damned.

"I was thinking how much I want to kiss you." Her eyes widen. "But I'm not sure how you feel about that."

"Why don't you try it and see?"

My heart stills and I move closer, taking her glass and putting it beside my own. Then I lean in until my lips are almost touching hers.

"I'm not treading on anyone's toes, am I?" I have to know…

"What do you mean?"

"Are you seeing anyone? Is there a secret husband or boyfriend I don't know about?"

She shakes her head. "Do you think I'd have said you could kiss me if there was?"

I smile and, without another word, I close the gap between us, covering her lips with mine.

Having essentially been invited, I'm not expecting her to slap me, but neither am I expecting what happens next. No sooner have my lips touched hers than she sparks to life, her arms coming up around my neck, her breasts crushed against my chest. Our tongues clash and she moans into my mouth. There's nothing tentative about this, and I like it. I reach over, grabbing a hold of her, and pull her up onto my lap. She straddles me and shimmies closer still, my cock pressing hard against her core. God… this is hot. I flex my hips, cradling her backside, and she sighs, rocking against me. I know I should probably stop before we both get carried away and take our first kiss into something so much more. Except I don't want to stop, and I put my hand up inside the back of her blouse, skin against skin. She gasps, breaking the kiss just long enough to whisper, "Blake," and I pull back, gazing into her fiery eyes, both of us breathing hard.

"Will you do something for me?" I ask.

She blinks a couple of times and nibbles on her bottom lip, which is slightly swollen from our kiss. "What?"

"Will you call me 'Mac'? You've avoided calling me 'Blain' over the last few weeks, and I'm grateful for that, but like I said to you when we first met, my friends all call me 'Mac'."

"Am I a friend?" she says, with a hint of a tease in her voice.

"After a kiss like that, I damn well hope you're not an enemy."

I place my hand behind her head as I'm speaking and pull her in, renewing our kiss. She responds just the same as she did the

first time, my touch igniting something inside her. She clasps my face, her fingers delving through my hair as she rolls her hips against mine. I've kissed a few women in my thirty-three years, but I've never kissed, or been kissed like this, and I'm just wondering how much more I can take without stripping us both out of our clothes, when the doorbell rings, and Ella jumps back, startled.

"Hey… it's okay. It's just our takeout."

She nods her head, catching her breath, and climbs off of me so I can get up to answer the door. I don't feel happy about the interruption, or about leaving her behind, but I'm only gone a few minutes. When I return, she's sitting back on the couch, a blush on her cheeks, and she doesn't look up at me.

What's wrong?

I put down the takeout bag next to our drinks and sit beside her.

"Ella? Are you okay?"

She nods her head, but still won't look up.

"Are you sure?"

She raises her head, her eyes connecting with mine at last, and sucks in a breath. "I—I'm just not very hungry."

I'm suddenly overwhelmed with fear that she wants to leave, that she's embarrassed about what we've been doing. "I—I'm sorry. Did I go too far?" If I did, I wouldn't have been alone, but maybe she's embarrassed by that, too.

"No." Her voice is soft, her eyes sparkling. She looks sexier than she ever has, and I wonder if maybe I didn't go far enough… yet.

I take her hand in mine, moving a little closer. "Would you prefer to eat later?"

"Y—Yes." I can't help smiling and I stand up, pulling her to her feet. I'm just about to start towards the stairs when she pulls me back. "What about the food?"

"What about it?"

"If we're going to eat it later, we need to keep it warm. I can't think of anything worse than cold Chinese food."

I'm not sure I care, but I shrug my shoulders, looking down at the bag. "What should we do with it?"

"We can put it into a low oven," she says, confusing me.

"A low oven? What does that mean? My oven is quite low down as it is."

She shakes her head, grinning. "You're an idiot sometimes, you know?"

"Why? What did I say?"

"The word 'low' refers to the temperature of the oven, not its height."

"Oh… I see."

I grab the bag and, keeping hold of Ella, we go through to the kitchen, putting the Chinese food into the oven. I wait while she sets the temperature, and then as she stands, I capture her face between my hands, bending my head and kissing her again.

Without warning, she jumps up into my arms, wrapping her legs around me, and I hold on to her, not breaking the kiss as I carry her back through my living area and up the stairs.

My bedroom is completely open, up on the mezzanine floor, and I'm relieved I thought to make the bed this morning, even though there's a pile of folded laundry on the chair in the corner that I haven't had time to put away. Not that Ella seems to notice. As I break the kiss and lower her down my body, she keeps her eyes fixed on mine.

I bring my hands up between us, unfastening her blouse, noticing as I do that she's shaking. I stop, putting my arms around her and hold her close.

"We don't have to do this if you're not ready. You're allowed to change your mind."

She shakes her head. "I don't want to change my mind."

"Are you sure?"

"Yes."

I brush my lips over hers, just briefly, and she sighs, then watches as I finish my task, pushing her blouse from her shoulders and leaning down to kiss her neck. She shudders, and I reach around behind her, undoing her white lacy bra, letting it follow her blouse to the floor before cupping her breasts in my hands. She gasps and then squeals as I pinch her nipples and as she stares into my eyes, I notice she's already breathing hard. I could spend a lifetime just gazing at her, but I want to see more, and I kneel, unfastening her jeans and pulling them down, together with the white lace knickers she's wearing. She kicks them off, along with her shoes, and I take a moment to admire her. She has beautifully rounded breasts, a narrow waist and slightly flared hips... long, sexy legs, and a heavenly, shaved pussy. I'm tempted to lean in and taste her, but I want a better view, so I stand, lifting her off of her feet and carrying her to the bed, where I lay her down, shaking my head as I gaze upon her.

"You're so beautiful."

She smiles and I bend over, grabbing her legs and pulling her back towards the edge of the bed. She yelps in surprise, her eyes widening as I place my hands on her knees, parting her legs, then brush my fingers lazily down her thighs. When I reach her swollen lips, I part them and kneel, dipping my head and running my tongue from her clit to her entrance and back.

"Oh... oh, yes. Do that again... please?"

I oblige, tasting her succulent sweetness, and she shudders, bringing her hand down on the back of my head. I part her lips wider and focus on her swollen clit. She bucks her hips up into me and I flick my tongue over her.

"Yes... yes... right there. That's so good."

I repeat my actions, sweeping my tongue across her, over and over, and moving my hands, so I'm parting her with the fingers

of my left, while I reach up with my right, and pinch her nipple. She cries out, spreading her legs, and pushing my head down, clearly wanting more, so I nip at her clit with my teeth, and that pushes her over the edge. Her cry becomes a scream as she writhes and thrashes through her orgasm. I don't relent, but keep up the pressure on her clit until she finally calms, and I release her, staring up into her glazed eyes.

"You taste incredible."

"Do I?" She's breathing hard and I stand, leaning over her, my hands resting on either side of her head, as I bend my own and kiss her. I half expect her to hold back, but she doesn't. If anything, she's even more wild than before, her tongue darting into my mouth, devouring me. I let her for a while, and then I pull back, straightening my arms.

"I'm sorry, but I need to be inside you."

She stutters out a sigh, nodding her head, and I stand upright, lifting her in my arms and turning her around, moving her up the bed, so her head's on the pillows. Then I yank my shirt off over my head and undo my jeans. She watches while I lower them, and my boxers, her eyes widening, although she doesn't say a word. Her eyes don't waver, either, when I grab a condom from my bedside table and roll it along my length before I crawl up over her body.

With one hand up by her head again, I palm my cock with the other. I don't think I've ever been this hard, but I'm desperate for her now, and I rub the tip of my dick along her swollen folds, finding her entrance and nudging inside.

She sucks in a sharp breath, closing her eyes, and I feel her tense beneath me as I push further inward, her muscles tightening around me, until...

I stop, unsure of myself. This can't be right, can it?

I lean back, staring down at her. She opens her eyes, her brow furrowed, and I tilt my head slightly.

"Is this your first time, Ella?"

She blushes and slowly nods her head. "Yes, it is."

I know what she's saying is true, but I still can't believe it. "How is that possible?" I ask.

She frowns. "It's quite easy, really. You just don't have sex."

"I—I know that. What I mean is, how does someone who looks like you end up still a virgin at... how old are you?" How can I not know her age, when I'm practically inside her?

"Twenty-four. And I'm still a virgin because of my brothers."

"Okay. That didn't sound at all weird."

She smiles. "It's not," she says. "Honestly. It's just that I've got two older brothers who spent their younger years sleeping around... and as much as I love them, I always knew I didn't want to end up with a guy like that. I thought it was worth waiting until the right man came along."

I lean a little closer to her, so our lips are almost touching. "And you think I'm that man? The right man, I mean?"

"I—I hope so." She looks a little doubtful now, and I close the gap, my lips brushing over hers.

"So do I." We stare at each other for a moment or two, and then I straighten my arms again. "Are you sure about this?"

"About you?"

"No. About this. I want to be the right man for you, but that doesn't mean we have to do this... not straight away. If you'd rather wait..."

"I don't want to wait, Mac."

I smile. It's the first time she's called me that and it sounds great. "Sure?"

"Positive. I feel like I've been waiting so long already."

"Hmm... me too." She takes a deep breath and I move my right hand, cupping her face as I stroke her cheek with my thumb, leaning in closer. "Relax, Ella." She nods her head, and I push inside her, swallowing her cry with a kiss.

I wait, buried as deep as I can go, my lips caressing hers, until she lets out a long sigh, raising her hips just slightly off of the bed. I guess that means she's okay now, and I lean back up, pulling almost all the way out of her, before I edge back in, taking my time, savouring every second. Within moments, she's matched my rhythm, our bodies writhing in perfect harmony.

There's something new about this. Just like her kisses, I'm aware that it's never felt like this before, and I know – deep down – it's not just because she's so tight, she's gripping my cock, pulling me into her. It's not just because she's gazing up at me, her lips slightly open. Nor is it because her body is divine, yielding beneath me, her soft moans driving me crazy.

It's because I'm in love with her.

Chapter Seven

Ella

Would it ruin everything if I told him I love him?

We've only known each other a few weeks, and he'd probably think I'm mad. Hell… sometimes even I think I'm mad. Let's face it, when we first met, we didn't exactly hit it off, did we? We bickered and fought and antagonized each other… endlessly.

But over the last few weeks, that's all changed. It's changed so much that when he said he wanted to kiss me, I had to offer as much encouragement as I could. The kiss itself was everything I could have hoped for. It was magical and intense, romantic and passionate. I was carried away on a sea of need, and I whispered his name, wanting more, I think. That was when he asked me to call him 'Mac'. I know he'd already told me that all his friends call him that, but there was something about the way he said it… like it mattered to him, and I decided there and then, there's no way I'm going to call him 'Blake' anymore. I didn't tell him that, of course, but when we started kissing again, I put my hands on his face, letting my fingers twist back into his hair… in the hope he'd realize how seriously I was taking this… and him.

Of course, the takeout had to arrive not long after that, interrupting us, but I needed to let him know I didn't welcome

the interruption… just in case he decided against picking things up again.

And it seems he got the message.

Had I expected all this, though?

Had I thought he'd look into my eyes and tell me I could change my mind? I had no intention of doing so, but he was so considerate… so caring, it took my breath away. That had to mean something, didn't it?

Had I thought my heart would become his… just like my body? I suppose I should have guessed. I was half-way to falling in love with him already. If I hadn't been, I'd never have let things go as far as they did. But that feeling… that wondrous, heavenly feeling of being his and his alone… that was beyond my wildest expectations. It made me realize he's not just the right man. He's the only man.

He's moving so gently inside me, and I'm grateful for that. I moan, raising my hips a little higher, wanting more of him. It may have hurt to start with, but now it feels sublime.

"You feel so good." His voice seems deeper than usual and I smile up at him, raising my hands and caressing his taut biceps, before moving them up and over his shoulders and then down his back, letting them come to rest on his perfect ass. His eyes widen as I pull him into me, enjoying the way he stretches me with every stroke, and he sucks in a breath. "Are you trying to make me come?"

"I don't know. Am I?"

I pull him in again… a little harder this time.

"I—It feels like it."

He closes his eyes, groaning a little louder. I'm not sure if that's a good thing, and because I don't want this to end yet, I let my hands drop to my sides.

His eyes pop open, and he smiles. "Wise move."

"Was it?"

He nods his head. "That felt amazing, but I was struggling to hold on."

He reaches down, taking my hands in his, one at a time, and brings them up beside my head, pinning them there. That feels good, and I can't help sighing and parting my legs a little wider.

He smiles. "My turn now."

"Your turn to what?"

He bends his head, his mouth right beside my ear. "To make you come." I shudder and, holding my hands in place, while keeping up a slightly faster pace, he traces a line of kisses from my ear, along my jaw and down my neck, across the top of my breasts and finally, to my right nipple, which he licks and then bites, oh so gently. That seems to be all it takes, and I feel that familiar quivering deep inside me, bucking against him as my orgasm takes hold and rocks through me. I keep my eyes open long enough to see his expression change, his eyes closing and a look of perfect ecstasy crossing his face as he swells inside me. His howls and my screams mingle, the noise filling the room. Just when I think it's all too much, my pleasure ratchets up another notch and I lose control. Nothing exists but what he's doing to me... how it makes me feel... and I let it take me, and consume me, until eventually, it fades and I realize my hands are no longer trapped, and Mac's arms are tight around me.

The words, 'I love you' are poised on my lips and, even though I'm breathless, I open my mouth to say them, just as he whispers, "Stay? Please?"

What does that mean? Is he talking about tonight, or forever? I might be in love with him, but that doesn't mean he feels the same way, and I don't want to read too much into a simple invitation. Even so, I need to know.

"The night?" I ask, not daring to raise my expectations too high.

"Yes." He smiles and I smile back. It may not be 'I love you'. It might not be 'forever', but the smile on his lips and the look in his eyes feel like the next best thing.

The Chinese food stood up remarkably well to being kept warm for just over an hour, and once we've eaten it – in bed – Mac clears away all the cartons, taking them downstairs, before he comes back up and climbs into bed beside me. He pulls me across, closer to him, and I lie in his arms, my head resting on his toned chest.

He feels so good, and although it's only been an hour since he made me lose my mind, my body is humming with need again. I want him, but I don't know how to ask, or what to say.

"Is everything okay?" He leans away from me just slightly, and I look up at his concerned face.

"Yes. I was just wondering…"

"Wondering what?" he asks.

I guess there's no point in prevaricating. "When we can do that again?"

His face clears, and he smiles. "Eat Chinese food in bed?"

I slap him, just gently on his chest. "No… silly."

"Ahh… you mean you want to know when we can make love again?"

I nod my head, smiling at the way he said that, and he throws back the covers, revealing his erection. I can't help gasping. It's even bigger than I'd thought, and I tear my eyes away from his masculine perfection and look up into his eyes.

"Did that really fit inside me?"

"It did." He leans down and kisses me, cupping my chin with his hand as he whispers, "Like it was meant to be."

Oh… God.

My lips tremble as he kisses me. Can it be that he feels the same way I do? Am I daring to hope too much?

He pulls back, gazing into my eyes. "I've got a question for you."

"Oh?"

He nods his head. "Are you sore?"

"I don't think so."

He doesn't say another word, but sits up slightly and turns away, reaching over to the nightstand. When he turns back, he's holding a condom, and I lean up and watch avidly while he tears into the wrapper and then rolls it over his erection. I'm mesmerized by the way he touches himself, studying his fingers as they stroke his length, from base to bulbous tip. I'm so entranced, I yelp in surprise when he leans over and grabs me, moving me on top of him, although I instinctively part my legs and straddle him as he sets me down.

"I liked the way you kissed me downstairs," he says, his eyes twinkling mischievously.

"*I* kissed *you*?"

"Okay… I started it, but I liked what you made of it."

I can't help smiling. "I liked it, too."

He nods his head. "Care to make something of this?" He tilts his head toward his erection and I gaze on it for a moment or two, spellbound, until he says, "Need some help?"

I smile at him, and he places his hands on my ass, raising me up, then reaches between us, positioning the head of his erection right at my entrance. I don't need to be told what to do next, and I lower myself down, sucking in a breath as he stretches me.

"Take it slowly," he says, letting out a slight groan.

"I need to. You're so big."

His smile widens. "Unless I'm much mistaken, you don't have anything to judge that by, do you?"

"No. But you seem big to me." I lower myself a little further onto him, proving the point.

"Has it occurred to you that maybe you're tight?"

"I don't know. Is being tight a good thing?"

"In this situation, it's a fabulous thing."

"And I'm gonna assume you've got something to judge that by?" I'm not sure I like that thought. In fact, I'm pretty sure I hate it, but I finally settle onto him, swiveling my hips to get comfortable.

"Yeah, I have." He rests his hands flat on my thighs, like he feels the need to hold me in place, and looks into my eyes. "Do you want to know about it?"

"Your past?" He nods his head and I shrug my shoulders, wondering if now is the best time to have this conversation, or if we should even have started it. "I don't know. Do I?"

"If not knowing is going to make you look as doubtful as you do now, and make you worry, and imagine all kinds of things that aren't there, then maybe you do."

"How did you know I'm worried?"

He sits up so his chest is crushed against my breasts, his arms coming around me as he dusts his lips over mine. "Because I can see it in your eyes."

"I'm not sure if that's good or bad."

"It's good…"

"That I'm so transparent?"

"You're not transparent. You're open, and that's how it should be. We're not supposed to have secrets."

He's right. I'm in love with him, and I'd like to think he feels something for me, even if it isn't love yet. And that means there shouldn't be any secrets between us. "Okay… tell me."

"Don't sound so scared. There's nothing much to tell." He rests his forehead against mine for a moment and then leans back, although he keeps a tight hold on me. "First, I have to say, I don't sleep around. I never have."

"I'm glad to hear it. So… how many women have you slept with, other than me?"

"Eight."

"Over how many years?"

"Fifteen."

I nod my head. That seems reasonable to me… a lot more reasonable than my brothers, who probably used to get through that many women in a month.

"Were any of them serious?" I ask.

"I suppose you could say three of them were, in that we dated for more than six months."

"And did you live with any of them?"

"Yes. One. Her name was Moira."

I pull back just slightly. "D—Did you love her?"

"No." He shakes his head, as though he wants to make the point doubly clear.

"You mentioned having a girlfriend before you left England… was that Moira?"

"Yes, it was."

"I remember you saying she didn't want to come to the States with you… which I'm guessing means you asked her?"

"I did."

"But you didn't love her?"

He sits up a little straighter, holding my body tight against his. "No… but she loved me. And before you accuse me of being big-headed, she told me that herself."

"All the time?" I haven't said the words myself yet, and I suddenly hate the thought of someone else dripping them into his ear.

"No. She only said it once, just before I left. She begged me to stay and told me she loved me."

"It didn't make you want to give up your plans?"

"Not at all. I'd accepted the job over here. I'd made up my mind and wasn't going to change it. Sorry if that sounds ruthless, but I felt like she was playing games. She'd never mentioned love before, and it all seemed a bit contrived. It certainly made my departure a lot messier than it needed to be."

"Why did you ask her to come with you if you didn't love her?"

"It felt like the right thing to do at the time. I may have made it sound like I just abandoned her at the end, but it wasn't like that. It wasn't that simple. We'd been together for quite a long time, and I guess I felt obliged to ask her, out of loyalty, if nothing else. The thing was, she had family... parents, sisters, uncles, aunts... there were dozens of them, and I think I knew, deep down, she'd never leave them."

"That was a risk, wasn't it? What if she'd said 'yes'?"

"Then I'd have brought her with me."

"And fallen in love with her, eventually?"

"No. I don't think love works that way. I think you either know, or you don't... which is why I didn't believe her when she blurted it out like she did."

He leans in and kisses me, his lips skimming over mine in the gentlest of caresses.

"Is that it?" I murmur. "There's nothing more to tell?"

"That's everything. You've got nothing to fear from my past... I promise." He gazes into my eyes and flexes his hips, making me gasp as I feel him deep inside me. I raise myself up, then sink down again, groaning as I cling to his shoulders and grind in to him.

"God... that's good."

I repeat my movements, over and over, harder and harder, while he holds on to me, supporting my every move. I want to see him better, though, and I want him to see me, too. So, without disconnecting us, I release his shoulders, and sensing that I'll

have more control if I'm crouching, rather than kneeling, I adjust my legs, bringing them up and placing my feet flat on the mattress, my knees bent. He watches, tilting his head, as I lean back, resting my hands behind me, on his legs.

He gazes down at the place where we're joined, shaking his head. "That looks incredible... you look incredible." I'm about to move, but he puts his hands on my thighs, stopping me. "I've got this." I hold still, and supporting himself on his arms, he raises his hips, impaling me.

It's glorious, and as he increases the pace, I realize I don't just want him to see me... I want him to see the real me. So, I balance on my left arm and bring the right one around in front, my fingers finding my swollen clitoris.

I'm a little nervous. What if he's shocked? What if he thinks badly of me? It's too late to go back, though, and I circle my middle finger over and around myself, my fears evidently unfounded as his eyes mist over slightly and he whispers, "Oh... fuck... yes..." under this breath.

He takes me deeper, slamming into me as I rub myself, abandoning my insecurities in favor of passion... of love.

It doesn't take long before I feel my orgasm build, and as though he can feel it too, he takes me even harder, pushing me over the edge.

"Oh... yes!" I throw back my head, screaming his name. He keeps moving, unrelenting, and I clamp my legs together, struggling for control.

"No... let me see you." He takes his weight on one arm, placing his other hand on my knee to part my legs, then holding them open as I ride out the waves of pleasure, breathing hard, until I'm spent, and I collapse onto my back, between his legs.

Without giving me a moment to recover, he slides out from under me and kneels up and over me, entering me afresh.

"Oh, Mac... please."

"Please what?"

"Take me?"

He smiles. "Gladly."

He kneels back, grabbing hold of my ankles, and holds them wide apart, lifting me off of the mattress slightly, as he slams into me. The muscles in his arms and shoulders flex as he takes my weight, but he doesn't show any signs of strain and just stares down into my eyes.

"Rub your clit again."

I lower my hand between my legs, finding my exposed nub, and brush my fingers over it. I moan softly and he smiles. "Do you like watching me?"

"I love watching you." He tips his head slightly, holding still inside me. "I take it this is something you've done before... by yourself?" he says and I nod my head, blushing, as he puts my legs up on his shoulders, leaning over so his lips are nearly touching mine. I might be almost bent in half, but I'm surprised that I'm a lot more comfortable than I would have thought. "Don't be embarrassed." He kisses me. "I love that you know your own body... and that no-one else does, except me."

"I love that too." He smiles and starts to move again, making me yelp and move my hand away, up to my mouth, in shock. "God... that's deep."

He pulls back slightly and stops. "Too deep? We can change position, if you want?"

"No... I like it down here."

He smiles, taking it more gently. "Is that better?" I nod my head and he builds a slow, steady rhythm, being careful not to go too deep... not to hurt me. "When was the last time you touched yourself?" he asks.

"About thirty seconds ago."

He chuckles. "No. I mean before that."

I move my hands up, caressing his biceps as they contract and relax in time with his movements. "To be honest, I can't remember. I've been too tired to think about anything but work for the last few weeks."

"Hmm… I know what you mean."

I'm not sure I do, and I clasp my hands around his arms, as far as my fingers will go. "Do you… um…?" I nod downwards, hoping he'll understand, and he smiles.

"Are you asking if I masturbate?"

"Yes."

"Why do you want to know?"

I stare up at him. "Because I want to watch you, too."

He grins. "In that case, you'll be pleased to hear that I do."

I can't help laughing. "And when was the last time for you?"

"Ages ago. I would have thought that was obvious."

"Why?"

"Because I didn't last as long as I would have liked earlier. It's been a while and my staying power wasn't what it could have been."

"Really? I can't say I noticed."

He leans over, kissing me again. "Then you'll have to take my word for it. I'll last a lot longer this time." I suck in a breath at the thought of this going on… and on… and he gasps.

"What's wrong?"

"Nothing. It's just all your muscles tightened then."

"And that's a good thing?"

"It's an excellent thing. It's like when you come, and you grip my cock, from base to tip."

"I do?"

"Yes. It's the best feeling in the world."

I'm not sure what he means by that. Is he saying it feels like that all the time… with everyone? Or does he mean it just feels like that with me? I don't know… and I can't think how to ask. He

stops moving, gazing down at me and frowning, and then he lowers my legs, dropping to his elbows.

"Why have you stopped?" I ask.

"Because you look confused."

"I do?"

"Yes. And before that confusion puts you off what we're doing, I'm just going to say... it's never felt like this, Ella. What I just said about the way you make me feel, and what you do to me... I wasn't speaking in general terms, but in very specific ones... about you. Does that help ease your confusion?"

I nod my head. "The best feeling in the world?" I whisper.

"The very best there is."

He puts his arms around me, one behind my back and the other beneath my ass, holding me close, our bodies entwined as he moves inside me again. I'm so tempted to tell him I love him, but somehow it doesn't feel so necessary anymore... or at least not so urgent. If he can see my confusion, surely he must be able to see my love... and to feel it, too. I'm not holding anything back, and I don't think he is, either.

He raises my ass up slightly and swivels his hips, and I stop thinking and just enjoy the sensations he's creating... the tingling and throbbing at my core as he tips me into yet another orgasm. I cling to him, riding it out, pleasure rocking through my body.

"More," I whimper. "Please, Mac... give me more."

"You want more?" He leans up, staring down at me.

I've barely come back down to earth, but I nod my head and he kneels up, pulling out of me, and giving me no time at all to recover before he flips me over onto my front. My hands are caught beneath me, but he doesn't give me time to free them. He grabs my hips, pulling me up onto my knees. My ass is in the air, my shoulders pressed into the mattress, and he leans over, his front to my back.

"Tell me if this hurts... okay?"

"Okay." I feel a quiver of anticipation run through my body as he straightens, moving closer, and pushes my legs apart with his own. I feel defenseless, but I like it, and I let out a low groan of satisfaction when I feel him push inside me... yet again. He goes really deep, making me feel fuller than ever, and when he's buried as far as he can go, he stops.

"How's that?"

"Perfect."

"Sure? It doesn't hurt?"

"No." I rock back against him, just to prove the point, and he grabs my hips again, holding me steady, and after just a second's pause, he pulls all the way out of me, and then slams back in. I cry out, but he must be able to tell it's a cry of pleasure, not of pain, because he repeats his action, harder, faster, deeper. Even though I can't see him, there's something about this... about the way he's controlling my body. I love it, and how it makes me feel... like I'm his, which I am, of course.

"Tell me you're close." It sounds like he's talking through gritted teeth.

"W—Why?"

"Because I need to come."

"Then come."

"No... not before you do."

He reaches around me, his fingers finding my clitoris, although I'm not sure I can do anything about it. I know I said I wanted more, but I'm so tired. "Sorry, Mac. I can't. I've already..."

He hammers into me, really hard, stealing my breath and my words, his fingers working over me. "I need to feel you come again. I need you to give yourself to me... all of you. Now."

There's something about his words that gets to me. It's like he knows how I feel, and I forget my exhaustion, and do as he says, giving myself to his magical touch... his urgent need.

"Yes… yes… yes…"

I can't manage anything more coherent as he drives me on, into ecstasy.

"Oh, fuck… yeah. I'm coming…" His voice is strangled, filled with emotion, and he stills, swelling inside me, and then lets out a loud roar, which surrounds and envelops us in what has to be love. It must be. Nothing else could feel like this.

Finally, he collapses on top of me, spent, and then pulls us over, so we're lying, my back to his front, still joined, both breathless.

"Sorry about that," he murmurs, his arms tight around me.

"Why? Why would you be sorry?"

"Because I went a bit caveman on you at the end."

I chuckle. "I'm not complaining."

"Good. I don't think there's much I could have done about it." He kisses my neck and shoulders, and I twist around slightly, looking up at him. He smiles, then kisses my lips, slowly pulling out of me. "I won't be a minute. I just need the bathroom."

I nod my head and watch him walk to the stairs, disappearing down them. My body aches, but I shift back up the bed a little, my head resting on the pillows, and I straighten the covers, pulling them up over me, just as Mac returns, the smile still etched on his lips.

"You look so good in my bed." He climbs in beside me and I snuggle down, my head on his chest as he wraps me in his arms.

"This feels nice."

"Hmm… it does."

He kisses the top of my head and I listen to his heartbeat as my eyes flutter closed.

It's the sunlight on my face that wakes me, and I blink a few times, remembering where I am.

I'm at Mac's place, in his bed, and I can't help smiling as I stare across the expanse of his apartment to the windows beyond. It's very open-plan here, so although we're upstairs in his bedroom, the main wall, which is made entirely of glass panels, lets the morning sunshine into the entire apartment. We're not overlooked, though, and I gaze at the clear blue sky for a moment or two, stretching my arms and legs, my muscles aching, and my smile widens, as I recall all the things we did together last night… all the things we said.

"Are you awake?" I turn to find Mac staring down at me, his deep blue eyes fixing mine, as he reaches out, cups my face and leans in to kiss me. "I'll take that as a 'yes', shall I?"

I chuckle and snuggle up closer to him. He puts his arms around me, kissing me again, only this time, he deepens it, his tongue finding mine, and despite the aches, my body's already humming with need for him.

"Shall I make us breakfast?" he asks, pulling back eventually. "Or are you not particularly hungry again?"

"Not especially."

He licks his lips. "I'm so glad to hear that."

He leaps out of bed, grabbing my hand and pulling me with him, and he drags me to the stairs, leading me down them and toward the front door, stopping short of it, and taking me into the bathroom, on the right.

Inside, he guides me straight to the shower, switching on the water, and turns to face me, bending his head and kissing me, yet again. I bring my arms around his neck, my body crushed against his, and he cups my ass in his hands, pulling me onto his erection. I sigh in to him, and he groans, swiveling his hips as the water cascades between us.

After a few minutes, he pulls back, tilting his head, and without a word, he reaches for the soap. I feel a little disappointed. I guess

I'd hoped for something more than a wash, but I watch as he lathers up his hands, and then, without taking his eyes from mine, puts the soap back, and lowers them.

"You wanted to watch me... remember?"

He places his hands around his arousal, soaping it up, and then moves his left one away and leans back against the wall, his right hand stroking along his length. I stand, mesmerized, noting that every time he reaches the tip, he gives himself a gentle squeeze, and that he sometimes twists his hand just slightly, too. I raise my eyes to find he's staring at me, breathing hard.

"Do you want to join in?"

"In what way?" I'm not sure if he wants me to touch myself, or him, but he answers the question by reaching out and taking my hand, placing it around his erection, and then putting his back on top. He starts to move again, groaning as he guides me, and then he removes his hand and leaves me to my own devices. I move closer, standing slightly to one side and lean up to kiss him while he puts his arm around me, my breasts pressed hard against his chest as I pump him, harder and harder.

"Oh... fuck... I'm gonna come." I increase the pace, squeezing a little more firmly, and he lowers his hand, grabbing my ass. "Please, Ella... Yes!" His body tenses, he throws back his head, his erection hardening and thickening in my hand and then it jerks, jets of fluid spurting up the opposite wall in long, thick streams.

His chest is heaving as he struggles to breathe, but he's barely finished, when he lowers his head, his eyes boring into mine. I'm about to ask if it was okay, when he picks me up and turns me, slamming me up against the wall. Then he grabs my hands and pulls them up above my head, holding them there with one of his, while the other moves straight down between my legs. I spread them, but he kicks them a little wider apart, inserting a finger inside me, which makes me gasp, as he leans in.

"You're so wet."

"I know. I want you."

"You can have me… later. But for now, I need to make you come."

He adds a second finger to the first and then uses his thumb against my clitoris, rubbing hard, then circling more gently, the contrast driving me wild. I arch my back and he leans down, capturing my nipple between his teeth. I feel like I'm being consumed by pleasure, as though it's all around me, in every breath I'm struggling to take.

"Please, Mac…" I'm so close already.

He applies just a little more pressure with his thumb and I fall headlong into a mind-blowing, breath-snatching orgasm, my body surrendering to him. Sensing my predicament, he releases my hands, putting his arm around my waist to hold me up, until I've calmed sufficiently to take my own weight, although even then he doesn't let me go. He just pulls his fingers from me and raises them to his lips, licking them while staring into my eyes.

"Stay?" he whispers.

"I already did."

"That was just one night. I mean… stay."

Is he asking what I think he's asking? I'm too scared to ask if he means forever, just in case he doesn't. The disappointment would be too much. "Do you mean for the weekend?"

He pauses for a second or two and then nods his head, and although I smile and nod my agreement, I can't help wishing he'd said 'forever', instead.

Mac

What a weekend…

When we got back to my place on Friday night, I don't know what I was hoping for… other than a kiss, perhaps. The last thing I expected was for Ella to respond in the way she did, for that to be her first time, for her to want to stay… and for that to be the best two days of my life.

But that's exactly how it's been.

Her responses have been incredible… not just to our first kiss, but to everything, and I've revelled in her enjoyment of every sexual encounter. There's no doubting her enthusiasm, which is adorable, and although she sometimes gives away her inexperience, I love the fact that she knows her own body. She knows what she likes and isn't afraid to ask for it… or simply take it.

Watching her bring herself off was incredible. It's something I've done with previous partners, but it's never felt like that before. Like everything else with Ella, it's special… and very different.

That's why I asked her to stay. Not just on Friday night, after our first time, but on Saturday morning, in the shower. She'd just made me come – spectacularly – and I'd brought her to orgasm, but I wasn't ready to let her leave. It wasn't just about the sex, either. I'd loved sleeping with her, holding her, kissing her… everything about her. When she asked if I meant for the weekend, I so very nearly said, 'No, forever.' I would have meant it, too… even though I know it wouldn't have been long enough.

I want more than that.

As it was, I just nodded my head, knowing it was too soon for 'forever', just like it's too soon for 'I love you', which is the other thing that's been on my lips almost all the time. I've dropped a few hints about how I feel, because I want her to know, although I've tried not to be too obvious about it, just in case she's not ready to hear something like that. The last thing I want is to scare her off... except sometimes I wonder if she's just as ready for love as I am.

Every so often I catch something in her eyes; a look, or a smile that makes me wonder...

What would she have done if I'd revealed my true feelings... if I'd asked her to move in with me? She'd probably have said I was mad. Just a couple of days ago, we were little more than work colleagues, and now we're... well, I'm not sure what we are. We haven't talked about it, although I know this isn't casual for either of us. Ella made a point of telling me she'd waited for the right man, and that she hoped I was him. Then, on Saturday morning, after we'd finished our shower, I made some breakfast, which we ate in bed. Full up on toast and coffee, she was lying naked in my arms, and she looked up at me and frowned slightly.

"How are we going to handle this at work?"

"Handle what?"

"Us."

That meant there was an 'us', and I couldn't help smiling. It was only a little over twelve hours since we'd first made love, less than an hour since I'd asked her to stay, and already she was thinking beyond the weekend. She was looking to a future... with me.

"That depends. Do you want everyone to know, or would you rather we kept it to ourselves?"

"Would you mind if we kept it to ourselves? We've only got another five weeks of recordings."

I came down from my high with a bump. "What are we going to do after those five weeks?"

Her frown deepened, and she tipped her head. "Do we have to 'do' anything? I mean, the studio has the option to renew our contracts for another season, but that doesn't affect us, does it?" She'd said it again. It was just two letters, but when put together as a word, they meant everything. "We can still keep seeing each other, and if there is a second season, we can decide if we want everyone to know about us then, can't we?"

I don't think I've ever felt as happy as I did at that moment. "Of course we can," I said, holding her tighter.

"So, can we keep things to ourselves… just for now?"

"If that's what you want. Although I'm not sure how easy it's going to be, hiding how I feel about you from everyone else." That was one of those not-so-subtle hints, which made her smile and lit up her eyes… making me wonder.

I rolled her onto her back, raising myself above her, and she gazed up at me. "It'll be much harder for me," she said.

"How do you work that out?"

"Because you're an actor. You can pretend."

I leant down, brushing my lips against hers. "I never pretend with you… and besides, I'm not that good an actor." She giggled, and I deepened the kiss, swallowing that perfect sound.

Since then, we haven't talked about 'us' at all. We've been too busy enjoying ourselves.

I ought to feel exhausted, but I don't. I've never felt so alive in my life.

That's not surprising, though, is it?

I'm in love.

Now we're back at work, doing our best to behave 'normally'.

That means Ella's in the kitchen, preparing whatever it is we're working on today, and I'm sitting at the table, editing my

novel. I don't have my lines yet, because we haven't had our production meeting, so Gavin hasn't written them. But I'm not making a great job of doing any editing, either. I'm too preoccupied with staring at Ella. She's chopping something, her head bent, focused on the job in hand, and I smile. Beneath her apron, she's wearing exactly the same clothes as she was on Friday, because she hasn't been home since then. My smile widens as I recall her panic yesterday morning, when she realised she had nothing to wear to work today.

"I'll have to go home."

We were still lying in bed, contemplating a shower, and there was no way I was letting her go anywhere.

"We can wash your clothes. Nobody's gonna notice if you're wearing the same thing as you wore on Friday."

She looked up, her brow furrowing, less than convinced.

I leant in to her, lingering over a gentle kiss.

"Don't go."

I knew perfectly well that she wasn't talking about leaving for good, or even necessarily for the rest of the day. She could have gone home, collected some clothes, and then come back again, and for a moment I wondered if she was going to suggest that. I could have suggested it myself, and said I'd go with her, but the thing was, I didn't want to.

"Please, Ella. Stay here… with me…" I was about to add 'forever', but she pulled back and looked up at me, the emotion in her eyes silencing me. The air around us stilled, and then she clasped my face in her hands and kissed me so damn hard it took my breath away.

I'd have loved to prolong that kiss, or turn it into something more, but I knew that, if we were going to get her clothes washed and dried, I needed to get them into the machine. So, I reluctantly broke the kiss, gazing down into her flushed face.

"I'd better put your clothes on to wash."

"Oh... okay."

"Don't go anywhere."

She smiled. "I won't."

I got up, grabbing her clothes, and took them downstairs, putting them into the washing machine. Then I made a pot of coffee, deciding that our shower could wait a while longer, and carried two cups back up the stairs. When I got there, Ella was lying on the edge of the bed, on her side, facing me, and I wandered over, noting the smile on her lips as she eyed my erection. I'd only just put the cups down when she reached up, wrapping her hand around my cock, and I stood still, letting her stroke me for a while, before she shifted down the bed a little and leant forward, taking me in her mouth. I hadn't been expecting that, and I gazed down at her, holding still, while she bobbed her head back and forth, her perfect lips wrapped around my cock

"Have you done that before?" I asked, surprised by the rasp in my voice.

She released me, looking up. "No. I've never done anything before. I told you, I was waiting for the right man."

I smiled. "Me, you mean?"

"Yes."

"In that case, it was worth the wait. You're very good at that."

"I assume you have something to base that judgement on?" I recalled our conversation on Friday night and crouched down beside her.

"Yes, but we're not going to talk about my past anymore. I told you, you've got nothing to fear from it, and none of it matters... not now."

She nodded her head, a smile touching her lips, and I stood up, turning to walk around to the other side of the bed, just as she grabbed my cock.

"Can I have some more?"

"Of course, if you want."

She didn't say a word, but took me in her mouth again, and without thinking, I flexed my hips. I was about to apologise when she groaned and took me a little deeper.

"Do you like that?" She nodded, and I placed my hand behind her head. "Do you want me to take your mouth?" Her eyes widened, sparkling, and she nodded again. I stepped a little closer, using both hands on her head to hold her steady as I started to move. I took care not to go too deep, but the sensations were incredible, made better by her keeping her eyes fixed on mine, as she moaned out her pleasure. "Touch yourself... make yourself come," I said, and she didn't hesitate, but parted her legs wide, exposing her pussy, as she moved her hand down, rubbing her clit. That sight was almost too much for me, and I slowed my pace, giving her time, until I knew she was close, her breathing erratic, her fingers moving more ferociously over her swollen nub. I sucked in a breath, holding back... holding back, until I knew I was almost there. "Ella... I have to stop. I'm gonna come." I released her head and went to pull out of her mouth, but she gazed up, shaking her head just slightly, and took me deeper, my cock hitting the back of her throat as I let go, the pleasure almost tipping into pain. Almost. She came at the same time, writhing on the bed, and squealing as she swallowed me down.

I was close to collapse, struggling to breathe, and grateful I could kneel up on the bed and push Ella back into the mattress as I leant over her.

"Just so you know, I've never done anything like that in my life."

"You haven't?"

"Not to the same extent, no."

"You mean you've never...?"

She stopped talking, and I smiled at her inability to say the words, although I nodded my head. "I mean, I've never come in anyone's mouth, Ella."

"Why not?"

"Because no-one's ever wanted me to... until now."

She frowned, like she didn't understand, and then tipped her head to one side. "Does it make a difference?" she asked.

"It makes all the difference in the world."

"In a good way?"

"In the best way. Thank you."

She seemed surprised. "Why are you thanking me?"

"Because you're you, and you're everything I've ever wanted, or ever will want." I kissed her then, swallowing her gasp, and the memory of the look on her face makes me smile, even now...

"Why are you smiling?" Ella's voice brings me back to reality. She's staring at me, a tomato in one hand, and a small knife in the other.

"I was just thinking about you."

"And what's so funny about me?"

I get up, put down my iPad, and wander over, taking the knife and tomato from her hands, as I put my arms around her. "I wasn't smiling because you're funny."

"You weren't?" she says, gazing up at me.

"No. I was smiling because you make me so damned happy, Ella."

I think she was expecting me to tease her, and she blinks a couple of times, then swallows. "You make me happy, too."

I close the gap between us, kissing her hard, and she responds in an instant, her hands wandering up my back, over the too-tight black t-shirt. I let mine roam south, to her backside, resting them there and pulling her onto my erection. She lets out a low, satisfied moan, grinding her hips in to mine, just as the door crashes open and we leap apart.

"We'll use the meeting room." Kennedy is the first to enter the room, but she's talking to Ruby, who's behind her, and doesn't seem to notice Ella and myself straightening our clothes, or that I move right up to the island unit, using it to hide my very obvious arousal.

"Good idea." Ruby nods her head, even though she's checking something on her phone.

They're both smiling and, for a moment, I feel a little nervous. Kennedy's smile is inclined to do that to me, and she doesn't take her eyes off of me as they walk over. Fortunately, she stays on the other side of the island unit, fluttering her eyelashes as she looks me up and down.

"Can we help?" Ella says, moving a little closer to me.

Kennedy gives her a slight glance before returning her gaze to me. "Not really. I just wanted to let you know we'll be getting together on Wednesday to celebrate the airing of the first show."

I couldn't be less interested. "Is that when it goes out?"

She frowns. "Yes. At five. The schedules were sent round a couple of weeks ago."

"I must have missed that," I say, putting a sufficient level of nonchalance in my voice. Kennedy's frown deepens, like she can't understand my attitude to such a momentous event in her calendar, but what she doesn't realise is, I've been busy falling in love.

"Hmm… me too." I look down at Ella as she speaks, and she smiles up at me. The glint in her eyes makes wonder if she's been busy falling in love, too.

I hope so.

Kennedy seems quite cross now, and huffs out an exasperated sigh. "You both have to be there." It's clearly not optional, and we nod our heads. "I want the entire team to watch it together."

"The entire team?" I hadn't understood that was what she'd meant, and my stomach lurches.

"Of course." She glares at me, her earlier fluttering eyelashes a thing of the past. My acceptance is presumably a foregone conclusion, and without another word, she turns and leaves. Ruby follows, although I'm not sure why she was here in the first place, and once they're gone, I let out a sigh of relief, although it's tinged with fear.

"Are you okay?" Ella places her hand on my arm and I turn to face her.

"Not really."

"What's wrong?" She looks concerned, and I move closer, pulling her into my arms.

"The one great advantage of working on the stage is that you never have to watch yourself perform."

"Is this the first time you'll have seen yourself acting, then?"

"Yes. Even when I was in the commercials, I avoided seeing them."

"I'm sure it'll be fine." She looks up, tilting her head. "You're really good, you know?"

"Thanks. I'd just rather not have to see myself on the screen."

"I'll be there. I'll hold your hand."

"How? We're not supposed to let anyone know we're together."

She chuckles and stands up on her tiptoes, planting a kiss on my lips. "Don't worry… I'll find a way."

"Does it seem like today's been a lot easier than usual?" I ask as we clear away. We certainly got a lot more done. The production meeting was done by early afternoon, and Ruby announced as everyone left that the crew will be joining us first thing tomorrow, rather than waiting until after lunch.

"Yes." Ella says. "But that's probably because we're working on salads. Making dressings is a breeze compared with just about everything else we've done so far."

"Hmm…" I wander up behind her and put my arms around her waist, leaning in and kissing her neck, smiling as she moans and rocks her head back. "You don't think it's because there's no tension between us anymore?"

"Tension?" She turns in my arms, looking up at me. "Are you talking about when we first met?"

"In a way, yes. You have to admit, it was difficult."

"But I apologised for that. I know I said some things that…"

I raise my hand, placing my fingers over her lips to silence her. I've done this before, and just like the first time, her eyes widen. This time, though, I move my hand again, cupping her face and stroking her lips with my thumb.

"I'm not talking about our misunderstandings, Ella. I'm talking about the sexual tension… the fact that I wanted to kiss you from the moment I first saw you, and that after we'd resolved our differences, I wanted so much more."

"You did?"

"Yes. Why wouldn't I? I thought you were the most beautiful woman I'd ever seen."

She chuckles. "That's funny."

"Why?"

"Because I thought the same thing."

"That I was the most beautiful woman you'd ever seen?"

"No, silly. That you were the most beautiful man I'd ever seen."

I move a little closer, so our bodies are touching. "Did you want to kiss me, too?"

"No." I lean back slightly, unable to hide my disappointment. "But I wondered what it would be like to be kissed by you."

I smile, pulling her close again. "I hope I haven't disappointed?"

"Not at all."

"And did you want more, too?"

"I don't know that I was experienced enough to understand what 'more' entailed. But I know I wanted to find out."

"With me?"

"Naturally."

I tip her head back, covering her lips with mine. I keep the kiss a lot more brief than I'd like, knowing someone could walk through the door at any moment, and I pull back again, looking down into her eyes.

"Would you like to come back to my place?"

She nods her head with irresistible enthusiasm, and it occurs to me that, if I keep asking, and she keeps saying 'yes', we can turn this into forever without even trying.

"I'll need to go home to get some clothes," she says, after just a second's pause. "I can't keep wearing the same outfit every day."

That sounds like she's thinking of forever, too, and I nod my head in agreement. "Okay. Why don't I take the bus back to my apartment and meet you there later on?"

"Perfect. I'll probably be about an hour behind you." She leans up, kissing me, and I take a chance, deepening the kiss for a moment or two before I release her and she smiles up at me, breathless and beguiling.

We finish clearing up and gather our things together.

"Shall I leave before you?" she says.

"No. It doesn't matter if we leave together. We've done it before."

She nods her head, and I open the door, letting her walk out ahead of me. There are a few people in the corridor and we take care not to walk too close to each other, until we get to the elevators, where we join two other people, who are also waiting, and I turn to Ella.

"I'm not in the mood for this. I'm gonna take the stairs. See you tomorrow."

She frowns slightly, like she doesn't understand, and I give her a surreptitious smile, before turning away and heading for the stairwell. I had a good reason for doing that, but I wish now that I could have explained it to her. She looked so confused, but I don't even have her number, so I can't call her to justify why I parted from her before absolutely necessary.

I make my way down, ignoring the sign above the door that says 'lobby', and continue on to the one that leads to the car park. I can't leave Ella in the dark, not knowing why I did that.

I yank open the door, heading out into the fume-filled space and curse under my breath when I see her car pulling out and heading for the exit.

Damn… I'm too late.

I just hope she still comes over later and doesn't think I meant it when I said I wasn't in the mood, and I'd see her tomorrow… because not only do I not have her number, but I've got no idea where she lives, either.

I get off the bus, feeling a little dejected and wishing I'd been stronger…

As I start the short walk back to my apartment, I wonder what I'll do if Ella doesn't come over. I can't contact her, so I guess I'll just sit at home by myself, worrying… until tomorrow. God, what an awful thought. It's not one worth contemplating, and as I turn into my street, I realise I could be over-reacting. She could be at home, packing a bag, still feeling a little confused, but willing to come over for an explanation, if nothing else.

I stop in my tracks.

If that's the case, I need to get us something to eat. We ordered in over the weekend, both of us too busy enjoying each other to

bother with cooking, but I'd like for us to cook together tonight. The problem is, other than bread, milk and a few other essentials, my fridge is almost bare, and my cupboards aren't a great deal better. There's certainly nothing at my place Ella would be willing to eat, let alone cook.

I turn around, going back onto the main road, and picking up my pace. I daren't risk getting home too late. After what's just happened, I can't think of anything worse than Ella arriving at my place to find I'm not there.

There's a small supermarket – or grocery store, as Ella would call it – down here on the left, and I quickly decide the easiest thing is going to be for me to buy the ingredients we were using today, so we can recreate one of the dishes she showed me earlier. It's not very original, but I don't have the time or the ability for anything radical.

I grab what I need, hoping I got it right, and rush through the check-out before dashing home. There's no sign of Ella, or her car, and I let myself in, hook up my jacket and unpack the groceries, before quickly running upstairs to change out of my overly tight t-shirt and into a white one of my own, just as the doorbell rings.

I hurry back down and open the door to find Ella standing there, a holdall in one hand and a bag of groceries in the other.

"Here... let me."

I take the groceries and then her hand, pulling her into my apartment, and kicking the door shut, before I grab her holdall and put it down on the floor, bending to place the groceries alongside it.

As I stand, she looks up at me, and I reach out. She backs away, though, looking up into my eyes.

"What did you mean when you said you weren't in the mood? And why didn't you want to ride down in the elevator with me?"

she says, sounding so hurt my chest contracts, my breath catching in my throat.

"I did. And I would have done… but I'm not strong enough."

She takes a half step back, frowning. "What are you talking about?"

"I'm talking about not being in the mood for standing next to you and not touching you… not claiming you. I'm talking about being in a confined space, like an elevator, and not taking you in my arms and kissing you, or in some way giving away the fact that you're the best thing that's ever happened to me. It's about knowing my limitations, Ella. I'm…"

"Stop talking." Her voice is little more than a whisper, but I do as I'm told, and she stutters out a breath. "Now, kiss me. Please, Mac… just ki—"

I grab her and pull her hard against me, capturing her lips with mine, cutting off her words as I devour her, turning us both and walking her backwards until she hits the wall. We break the kiss, only to pull off each other's tops, and I undo her bra, releasing her breasts into my waiting hands. She unfastens my jeans and I do the same with hers, both of us kicking them off, along with our shoes.

"Condom," she murmurs into my mouth.

"Wallet." I pull off my boxers, finding my wallet in my jeans pocket, and pulling out a condom, while Ella removes her knickers, throwing them to one side, her eyes on fire as I roll the condom over my cock. She looks up at me, unsure what to do next, so I lift her, hooking her legs over my bent arms, and lower her onto my erection.

"Oh… God." She grinds out the words, her eyes closing as she adjusts to the penetration, and she leans back against the wall. I hold on to her, and with my hands on her backside, I pull almost all the way out, and then ram home. She screams in delight,

opening her eyes again and letting them lock with mine as I take her, harder and harder. I feel her body shudder and convulse, and I know she's losing control, coming hard, her loud scream of, "Yes, Mac... Yes..." filling the apartment.

That was quicker than I'd expected, but I want more... much more, and as she falls on to me, struggling for breath, I take her weight, turning, and carrying her into the living area, where I lay her down along the couch, kneeling up and giving her just a moment before I take her ankles, parting her legs wide, and start to move again.

"Touch yourself."

"You think I can come again? After that?"

"I know you can... now, touch yourself."

She moves her hand down, letting her fingers play across her exposed clit, and I watch, bewitched. I part her legs a little wider and she gasps, her nipples hardening, her legs tensing. She's close again already, and I hammer into her.

"I'm coming, Ella..." I give her fair warning, but she doesn't need it, and as I let go deep inside her, she tips over into a wild orgasm.

As she calms, her body still twitching, I lean over, sucking air into my lungs, and kiss her.

"I'm sorry."

"What for?"

"For what happened earlier... by the elevator."

She reaches up, cupping my face with her hand. "You don't need to be sorry. I understand now."

"I know, but I won't let it happen again. No matter how tempting you are, I won't let my weakness around you get the better of me. I'll try to be stronger."

She lets her hand drop, her fingers dusting over my arm, resting on my bicep.

"I don't think that's possible, is it?"

I smile and kiss her again. "I don't know… but one thing's for sure…"

"What's that?"

"Before we leave here tomorrow morning, you're going to give me your mobile number. I was going to call you, or text you, to explain and to let you know I hadn't meant to abandon you. Only I couldn't, because I don't have your number."

"I don't have yours, either."

"We'll put that right before the morning, but for now, I need the bathroom…"

She nods and I slowly pull out of her, straightening up and gazing down on her perfect body for a moment or two before I help her to her feet, and take her in my arms, just briefly, giving her a kiss, and then make my way to the bathroom.

Once I'm finished, I come back out again and notice her bag and groceries, still lying on the floor. Her bag can wait for now, but I pick up the groceries, cradling them in one arm as I wander back to the couch. Ella's sitting now, and looks up at me as I approach.

"What did you buy?" I ask.

"Something for dinner."

She sits forward, and I chuckle, holding out my hand to her. She takes it and I pull her to her feet and lead her into the kitchen, dumping her bag on the work surface before I open the fridge door wide and let her look inside at the salad and chicken breasts I picked up at the supermarket.

"Great minds think alike," I say.

She looks up at me and laughs, throwing her arms around my neck as I close the fridge door again. "Were you thinking of cooking?"

"God, no. I was thinking I'd help you cook… or try to."

She brings her hands between us, resting them on my chest, and looks up at me. "That sounds more like it."

"I know my limitations." I kiss her forehead. "So, what were you planning on making for dinner?"

"I bought the ingredients to make spaghetti with asparagus, sun-dried tomatoes and chicken."

"Wow... that sounds amazing."

"I wanted something that tastes good but is quick to prepare."

"Oh? Is there a reason for that?"

"Yes. But we've kinda covered that already."

I grind my hips into her, letting her feel my arousal. "Given my weakness for you, do you honestly think once will be enough?"

She bites on her bottom lip, gazing up at me through her eyelashes. "I hope not."

I can't help smiling. "I guess we can have dinner, and then..."

"And then what?"

"Then I'll take you to bed."

"Yes, please." She leans up to kiss me and as I deepen the kiss, I wonder if she has any idea how much I love her.

"What are we going to cook?" I ask, breaking the kiss eventually. "The pasta, or the salad?"

"The salad. The pasta will keep until tomorrow."

I pull her closer, my hands on her backside, my cock pressing hard against her. "You're thinking of coming here again tomorrow, are you?"

A shadow of doubt crosses her eyes. "I—Is that a problem?"

"Of course not. I'm teasing, Ella. You're welcome to come here any time you like. In fact, you can come here all the time, as far as I'm concerned." Does that sound too much like 'forever'? I don't know, but her eyes widen, and her smile returns.

"I'd like that."

"Good."

I don't care what it sounds like anymore, and I touch my lips to hers. She pulls back after just a few seconds. "Shall we cook?"

"I think you're being a little optimistic with your pronouns, but I'm happy to help."

She nods her head and I open the fridge again, pulling out all the things I bought, while she puts her ingredients inside. Once we're done, she turns to me, tilting her head to one side.

"Do you have honey and wholegrain mustard?"

"Of course I don't... but I bought some." I open the cupboard beside us, and she smiles up at me.

"Well done," she says, going over to the oven to turn it on.

"Don't congratulate me. I just went with the recipe you were teaching me today. It wasn't rocket science."

"No. But at least you remembered it."

She comes back and reaches down the honey and mustard, along with the oil, white wine vinegar, salt and pepper, and while she sets about preparing the chicken, I open the bottle of wine I bought.

"I got some wine, too," she says, looking up as I pour two glasses.

"I noticed, but mine's chilled."

She smiles, taking the glass I offer her and we clink them together, both taking a sip before we put them down on the work surface.

"Do you want to make the dressing?" she asks.

"Sure."

I step up beside her.

"Can you remember how it's done?"

"I think so." I find a small glass bowl and then realise there's a problem. "Oh dear... I don't have any measuring spoons."

"You surprise me," she says with a smile. "As we're not making a tv show, we'll do it by eye."

"Really?"

"Yeah." She moves closer, taking the oil. "If you pour it in for a count of three," she says, doing exactly as she's said, "that's roughly equivalent to three tablespoons."

"Okay."

She looks up at me. "So... how much vinegar do we need?"

"One tablespoon."

"Wow... you really were paying attention."

"I always pay attention. I have to remember it all... and besides, I enjoy learning from you."

She smiles and repeats the process of measuring out the vinegar.

"Now, you can add a teaspoon of mustard and a twist of salt and pepper."

I do as she says, stirring it all together, while she mixes up honey and mustard, and coats the sliced chicken with it, before spreading it out on a baking sheet and putting it into the oven.

"For someone who doesn't cook, your kitchen isn't badly equipped, you know?"

I stop stirring and look over at her. "I can't claim any credit. A lot of these things were here when I moved in. The previous tenant was from Europe as well, and they couldn't take everything back with them, so they just left it here. The dishes are mine, and the glasses and cutlery, but all the cooking equipment is inherited."

She smiles, shaking her head. "Somehow I'm not surprised."

I give the dressing one last stir. "Do you want to taste this?"

"If you like." I fetch another teaspoon from the drawer, dipping it into the bowl and holding it out for her. She lowers her head, tasting the dressing, but I pull the spoon away a little too quickly and a little of it trickles onto her chin. She reaches up to wipe it away, but I drop the spoon onto the work surface and take her hands in mind, holding them behind her back, as I step up close, my body against hers and bend my head, licking the

dribble of dressing from her chin, with just the very tip of my tongue. I feel the shiver rush through her and flick my tongue against her lips, delving inside and kissing her. She arches her back, her breasts hard against my chest, and I take her hands in one of mine, bringing up the other to cradle the back of her head.

"I told you," I whisper into her mouth. "I can't be in confined spaces with you. Not without losing control."

She pulls back slightly, looking around my kitchen. "This isn't that confined."

"It's confined enough for me." She chuckles and I kiss her again.

"Shall I get on with the dinner?" she asks, breaking the kiss eventually, both of us a little breathless.

"I think you'd better."

It doesn't take long before everything is ready, and Ella plates up two chicken salads with the dressing I made, and we eat in the living room, staring at each other. The food tastes great, but I know we're both impatient to be elsewhere, and as soon as we've finished, I clear away, and come back to her, taking her hand in mine and pulling her to her feet.

I grab her bag as we pass, and then lead her up the stairs… straight to my bed…

"Do you think we'll always shower together?" Ella asks, looking up at me as I wrap her in a towel before taking one for myself.

"I hope so."

She smiles, her eyes sparkling and my cock twitches at the memory of her bending over, her hands resting on the tiled wall, while I hammered into her, the water cascading over us, as she gazed at me over her shoulder, crying out for more.

"Why does it do that?" she says, looking down at my hardened cock, her eyes wide.

"Do what?"

"Twitch."

"Because it's thinking."

She smiles. "You're assuming it has a mind of its own?"

"I know it has a mind of its own... at least sometimes. I can't seem to control it, anyway... not around you." She giggles and tips her head.

"What's it thinking about?"

"You, with my cock in your mouth."

She moans and leans up, kissing me briefly before she whispers, "W—We don't have time..." a stutter in her voice, and leaves the room. I wrap the towel around my hips and follow behind her, sensing her regret and matching it with my own, although I can't help admiring the sway of her body as she climbs the stairs ahead of me and then watching as she bends over her holdall, pulling out a couple of tops, before she stands up straight, holding them in front of her, like she's trying to decide which one to wear.

I smile, and she frowns at me. "What's wrong?"

"Nothing." I walk over to her. "I just like the fact that you brought more than one top."

"Why?" she asks, tipping her head to one side.

"Because it suggests you intend to stay for more than one night."

She looks at the tops, and a blush creeps up her cheeks. "I—It wasn't that. I just couldn't decide which one to bring."

I take the tops from her, throwing them onto the bed, and pull her into my arms. "Hey... I don't mind. Bring as many of your things as you like. I want you to feel at home here."

She relaxes and leans up, kissing me, her towel falling away. I let mine drop too, and for a moment, we hug and kiss, our hands roaming.

"W—We can't," she says, pulling back again, just as her fingers wrap around my cock. "We're already running late."

I know she's right, and I reluctantly step back. "We'd better put some clothes on, before this gets out of hand."

I walk over and pick up one of her tops from the bed, handing it to her.

"I'm wearing this one, am I?"

"I'm going to picture you naked whatever you wear, so…" She chuckles and takes the top, turning to bend over her holdall again, and I groan. "You can't tell me we don't have time and then tempt me like that." I run my hand over her backside.

"I need to get my underwear."

"I need to be inside you."

She stands, turning around again, and I notice the pale blue bra and matching knickers she's now holding, as well as the top. To my untrained eye, they look expensive, but I guess a lot of her clothes are quite refined and delicate… and her underwear is no different.

"Can we pick this up again later?" she says, tilting her head, with a teasing smile on her lips.

"I guess so, although I'll probably go insane."

"And you think I won't? I want you too."

I smile at her. "I know."

"How?"

"There are a few signs."

"Such as?"

"Well… your nipples are rock hard." I pinch them between my thumbs and forefingers and she squeals, throwing back her head. "And your pussy lips are swollen." I reach down, rubbing my fingers through her folds, and she sucks in a breath. "And you're wet… soaking wet." I insert a finger into her and she parts her legs, rocking her hips forward. Using my thumb, I rub her

clit, and she drops her clothes, putting her arms around my neck and holding on.

"Mac... please..."

I press a little harder, add a second finger to the first, and brush them against the front wall of her vagina. She bucks against me.

"Do that again, Mac... whatever it was... do it again."

Her muscles tighten around my fingers as I repeat the action, over and over, circling my thumb, and she shudders against me, her body surrendering to ecstasy. Her juices flow over my hand, dripping to the floor as she clings to me, trembling and whimpering.

"Are you okay?" I ask.

She nods her head and looks up at me. "That was... so good."

"I know. I felt it."

"What about you, though?" she says, biting on her bottom lip.

"We don't have time for me."

"Then we'll make time."

She drops to her knees, gazing up into my eyes as she takes me in her mouth, although she doesn't move, and I think I know what she's waiting for, flexing my hips to check I'm right. She moans, nodding her head, and I smile down at her.

"Do you have any idea how good you look?" I whisper, and she sighs, reaching up to cup my balls as I slide back and forth. I'm careful not to go too deep, but what she's doing is too much. There's a tingling at the base of my spine, which is enough of a warning, and I slow my movements. "I—I'm gonna come, Ella." She squeezes my balls, and it's more than I can take. With a low groan, I let go down her throat, my legs barely able to take my weight as she sucks me dry.

She pauses for a second, then leans back, releasing me, and I pull her to her feet.

"Was that okay?" she asks. "I wasn't sure if I should touch you."

"You can touch me any time you like. What you did was perfect. It was better than perfect. But I'd have been happy to wait. Just watching you come is all I need, Ella. It's…" I struggle to find the word, and she smiles up at me.

"It's magical," she says and I nod my head.

"Yes, it is."

"I know. I feel the same."

She smiles and I hold her for a moment longer, relishing the feeling of her body, soft and warm, against my own, before I let her go.

"We need to get dressed," I say, and she nods her head.

"Unfortunately, we do."

I might love watching her come, but I can't watch her dress. I wish I could, but regardless of everything we've just done, I know that just the sight of her will drive me crazy. There's no way I won't be able to stride over to her and take her clothes straight off again. So, for the sake of our sanity, I turn away. I can hear her, though, moving about the room, as I pull on my jeans and I have to smile.

I love having her here.

When we're both ready, we go downstairs, gathering our things together, and putting on our jackets, before I grab my keys and we head out the door. We're holding hands, and I lead her to the top of the stairs.

"Is there a reason we're not taking the elevator?" she says, frowning up at me.

"Yes. You're way too tempting."

We're halfway down before she stops, pulling me back, and she tilts her head. "Is that why we took the stairs yesterday morning?"

"Yes. And it's probably why we'll be taking the stairs every morning."

"What about the evenings? I mean... on Friday, we were still just friends when we came up here, and last night, we arrived separately... so what's going to happen tonight, and every other night, come to that?"

I smile, thinking about coming back here with her 'every other night', and I lean in closer, my mouth beside her ear. "Wait and see..."

Chapter Eight

Ella

I don't know what to do… how to behave… what to say.

My body's humming, like I'm on fire, and it's not just with a need for Mac which seems to be ever-present; it's a longing to hear his words.

He hasn't said he loves me, but it feels as though he's skirting around it… like he wants to say it, but is holding back. Maybe that's just wishful thinking on my part, because I'm desperate to say the words myself, and I know if he does, I'll repeat them straight back at him. I suppose I could say them first, but I'm constantly aware of my inexperience, and that I could be overreacting, or at the very least, mistaking lust for love.

I couldn't have mistaken the words he said to me this morning, though. 'I want you to feel at home here.' He definitely said that, and he meant it, too. Couple that with what he said last night, when he suggested I could go to his place 'all the time', as far as he was concerned, and I have to wonder if he was asking me to move in with him… and taking the long way about getting there. I wish he could have been more obvious, and just asked me outright. I'd have said 'yes', without even thinking about it,

although with hindsight, I suppose it might be a little impractical, considering I've only just bought and furnished my apartment. But who cares about practicalities? If living with Mac means we get to spend all our time together, and spend more of it doing what we did this morning, then I certainly don't.

The problem is, I can't even ask him what he meant… not because I'm not brave enough, or because I'm scared of his answer, but because we're not alone.

We got so much done yesterday, and the dishes we're demonstrating this week are so simple, that the crew have been able to come in and start work with us already. Mac ran through position checks for the lighting and camera guys this morning, while I prepared the ingredients he'll need later on.

As usual, the first run-throughs will be without food. It gives everyone a chance to check over where they're meant to be, and what they're supposed to be doing. That, of course, includes Vivian, who relishes her role as the 'guest'. Considering it's October, and that it was overcast, with a chilly breeze when we arrived at work, she's wearing a ludicrously flimsy top that's so low-cut, she's almost falling out of it.

Mac is standing behind the island unit, wearing another of those tight black t-shirts that he hates so much, and the red apron with the show's logo on the front, and he's studying the script, his focus unwavering, despite all the surrounding activity.

I can't stop thinking about how it felt to cling to that perfect body this morning, while he used his fingers and thumb to take me to heaven, or how it felt to take him in my mouth, and watch that look of ecstasy on his face, when his orgasm claimed him. My body shudders, and as though he can sense my silent reaction to the memory, he looks up, his eyes meeting mine, and a slow smile forms on his lips. How did he know? His smile widens and I feel myself being drawn to him, even though I'm rooted to the spot. It's like there's a link between us… one that can't be broken.

"Okay, everybody… places, please." Ruby's voice rings out, making me jump, and Mac chuckles to himself, shaking his head. I narrow my eyes at him, and he tips his head just slightly, both of us enjoying our silent conversation.

People move around, getting into position and I step back so I'm right beside the camera, where I usually stand. Vivian sits up on the stool, her script in her hand, and Mac puts his down on the countertop, rolling his shoulders and tilting his head one way and then the other, like he's preparing himself.

The camera operator beside me lets out a loud sigh and moves aside.

"Vivian… how many times? The opening of the show is meant to be just Blain, standing in the kitchen, so can you please get your tits out of the shot?"

A few people chuckle and Vivian sits back, although she doesn't seem even remotely embarrassed. Mac doesn't appear to notice the commotion and just glances down at his script again, his lips moving, like he's whispering something to himself – his lines, I presume – and then Ruby slaps her hand against the clipboard she's carrying.

"Right… if we're all ready. Cue Blain in… five, four, three, two, one…"

Mac turns to the camera, a smile lighting up his face, and in his immaculate American accent says, "Hi and welcome to this week's episode of Meal Master. I'd like to introduce our guest…" He turns, his smile directed at Vivian. "This is Abigail."

"Hi," she says, beaming at him.

"Where are you from, Abi?"

Vivian glances at her script. "I've just moved to Boston, but originally I'm from Miami."

Blake smiles. "How are you enjoying the weather up here?"

Vivian gazes at him, letting out a sigh… and says absolutely nothing.

"Vivian... keep up, will you?" Ruby snaps and Vivian jumps, looking down at her script for a moment before she raises her eyes to Mac again.

"I—It's a little cooler than I'm used to."

"I'm sure it is. So, what made you choose to come and live here in Boston?"

"I'm studying at Berklee College of Music, and my boyfriend lives here. He already works in the music industry, so..."

"It's a marriage made in heaven?"

"Something like that."

Mac nods his head and smiles. "Okay... so, I understand you've come to us today with a question about eating more healthy meals. Is that right?"

Vivian lowers her head, having to read from her script now, although it hasn't escaped my attention that Mac hasn't looked at his at all.

"Yeah. I've been following a weight-loss plan for a few months, and it's been going quite well, but now the weather is turning colder..."

I wonder about that phrase. I'm not sure when this show will be aired and if the weather will be 'turning colder' by then, or if it will already be 'cold', and I make a note to check it with Ruby and Gavin after the run-through.

When I look up again, Mac is speaking. "... and of course, there are plenty of alternatives to salad, although serving something warm with dressed salad leaves is a great option, especially if – like Abigail – you lead a busy life and don't have much time to devote to cooking."

He moves away slightly, and Vivian leans forward, although none of the camera operators seem worried, which I guess means the angle of the shot has changed and she's not in the way anymore. Mac, meanwhile, is describing the first dish he's going

to prepare – or at least pretend to – and he pulls a baking sheet closer to him, while looking at the camera and describing how it's best to line it with aluminum foil, because the honey that will be used to baste the chicken can caramelize and stick.

I'm relieved he used the word 'aluminum' and not 'tin', or 'aluminium'. It was something I discussed with Gavin this morning, and although we both worried he might slip up, we decided to take a chance and hope Mac got it right… and he did.

"So, what made you decide to lose weight?" Mac's saying, while he pretends to stir something in an empty bowl.

"I'd always been a little on the heavy side, and decided the time had come to do something about it… for me, not my boyfriend, or anyone else." Vivian's reading from her script again, and sounds as wooden as the chair she's perched on, but when she's finished, she looks up at Mac.

He stops what he's doing and leans a little closer to her. "Good for you. That's the best reason there is, you know?"

"I know. My boyfriend says he loves me whatever size I am…" She lets her voice fade deliberately and gazes up at Mac again, fluttering her eyelashes. "He's always telling me how beautiful I am."

"You shouldn't doubt him."

What on earth possessed Gavin to put that line in the script? It's so sycophantic… although judging from the sparkle in Mac's eyes, and the smile on his lips, I have to wonder… is he acting anymore? Or does he believe what he's saying? Vivian seems to. She can't take her eyes from his.

I've always hated the way she plays up to Mac… even when he was still 'Blake' to me, but now, it feels so much worse, because he means so much more.

I can't focus, and their words drift over me as I try to work it out. Is he really that good? And if he is, has he been playing a part with me, too?

I've lost count of the number of times I've heard him say that line today… the number of times I've seen him look into Vivian's eyes, his own twinkling with what appears to be admiration. I can't recall how many times I've wanted to run from the room, to be by myself, to work out what's real, and what isn't. My head is spinning and I can't decide what, or who to believe. Did I imagine the look in his eyes this morning, when he told me that what I did to him was perfect and that watching me come was magical? Did I read too much into him saying I was too tempting for him to risk riding down in the elevator with me? Or am I right…? Am I mistaking lust for love?

"Okay, everyone…" Ruby raises her voice and we all turn to face her. "That was almost there. We won't be able to work late tomorrow, because we're all watching the show at five, so I think we'll move into the studio first thing, and start rehearsals at ten. Have a good night, everyone." People start to move around, packing up their things, and Ruby turns to me. "Does that give you enough time to get everything prepared in the morning?"

"Yes. That'll be fine."

"Good. It went well today, don't you think?"

I nod my head, watching Mac out of the corner of my eye. He's studying his script, and Vivian gets up, walking around the island unit, going up to him and pointing to the page. She's standing a lot closer than I feel comfortable with, but he doesn't move away. Instead, he shakes his head, flipping back a couple of pages and saying something to her, although I can't hear what.

I can't bear to watch anymore. I excuse myself to Ruby, and put my notepad on the table, going out of the rehearsal room and along the hall to the ladies' room. Inside, I shut myself into a stall, clenching my fists, telling myself over and over that Mac has done nothing wrong… that this is me, not him.

I hear the outer door open.

"Jeez… who the hell left the window open in here? It's freezing."

I don't reply. I'm not sure a response is expected, but I hear whoever it is closing the window before they enter the stall next to mine.

Suddenly, I remember the note I made about the weather, and I flush the toilet, even though I haven't used it, and quickly wash my hands, for no apparent reason, before rushing back to the rehearsal studio. A few people have left, but I look around, noting that Ruby has joined Vivian and Mac, and that Gavin is still sitting at the table. I dash over to him.

"Can I talk to you about something?"

He looks up. "Sure."

Even though I don't think I'll need it, I grab my notepad from the other end of the table and sit beside him. "It's just that, at the beginning of the show, Abigail has to say a line about the weather turning colder."

"Yeah. What about it?"

"Well… if this show won't be airing for a few weeks, then the weather will already be quite cold by then, won't it?"

He frowns, tilts his head and then pulls his copy of the script a little closer, flipping back to the beginning, and then he turns to the second page before he nods. "Yeah… I see what you mean."

"If we take out the word 'turning', it'll work better, won't it?"

He grabs his pen, scratching out the word 'turning' and then picks up the script and reads the speech aloud. "How's that?" he says as he finishes, looking up at me.

"I think that works."

"Have I referred to the weather anywhere else?" he says.

"Only where Abigail remarks that it's cooler here than in Miami, but I don't think that matters, does it?"

"No, I don't think so." He stands, putting his pen in his shirt pocket. "We'd better just go tell Blain and Vivian… and adjust their scripts."

I get to my feet, looking over to the kitchen, where Mac is staring at me, looking confused. I follow Gavin, and as we approach, Mac steps away from Vivian, moving closer to me.

"Is something wrong?" he says.

"No," Gavin replies, not giving me a chance to speak. "But our genius culinary consultant here has just pointed out a mistake in the script."

"Oh?" Mac gazes down at me, raising his eyebrows.

"It was just that I noticed Vivian's character has a line about the weather turning colder, and I realized that by the time the show airs, it will be later in the year…"

"And will already be cold," Gavin says, completing my sentence. "We've amended the script, just removing the word 'turning'."

Mac reaches over, taking Gavin's pen from his pocket, and changes his script, while Vivian goes to get hers from the countertop, and brings it back. She hands it to Gavin, and he takes back his pen and crosses out the word, while Ruby looks down at her clipboard.

"The actress playing Abigail is called Maya Larson." She glances up at Gavin. "If you send me the revised script, I'll forward it to her."

"Thanks." He hands Vivian back her script, replacing his pen in his pocket, and then nudges in to me. "I don't know what I'd do without you."

"Neither do I." Mac's words take me by surprise and I spin around, gazing up at him. He's smiling down at me, but I can't smile back. I don't feel like I know where I stand with him anymore… not that I really understood it before, but now I feel

like I'm wading through quicksand, even though I'm not moving.

"If that's it, I guess we should all head home. We've got a busy day tomorrow." Ruby steps away from the group and Gavin follows. Vivian seems to want to hang around, but Ruby calls her and she reluctantly goes with them… and as everyone else has already left, Mac and I are alone.

I ought to feel relieved about that, but instead I just feel nervous.

"Are you okay?" He steps closer, reaching out to me, but I move away.

"I'm fine. We should probably head home."

I wonder about suggesting that I go back to my place… alone. I could do with some space to think; but we've already got dinner at his, and I don't want him to see through my insecurities again. That's all they are, and I'll get over this… I'm sure I will.

I head back to the table, gather my things and shrug on my jacket. Mac follows, pulling off his apron, which he drops over the back of a chair, and then he clutches up his script and his iPad, and puts on his coat before he follows me from the room in silence.

On the way down in the elevator, I can feel his eyes on me, but we're not alone, so we don't have to make conversation or worry about being in a confined space together.

When we get to the car, I open it, and as we both climb in, he turns to face me. "What's wrong, Ella?"

"Nothing's wrong."

He sighs and I sense he doesn't believe me, but he opens his script and buries his head in it while I drive us back to his place, wondering if I can use that as an excuse to go home after we've eaten. He's got lines to learn and having me under his feet won't help…

I park my car outside his apartment block and get out before he can say anything. He climbs out, too, looking at me over the top of the car, although he still doesn't comment and we enter the building together. He moves toward the elevators, while I go for the stairs, and he coughs, drawing my attention.

"Don't you want to take the elevator?"

"No, thanks."

I put my foot on the first step, and he joins me, still not saying a word as we climb up to the top floor. He spoke yesterday about there not being any tension between us anymore, but right now, you could cut it with a knife... and it's all of my own making.

He lets us in, waiting while I enter the apartment ahead of him, and then closes the door behind us. I feel the tension mounting, but I don't know how to start a conversation with him. I can't think of what to say. Instead, I head for my refuge... the kitchen.

Maybe cooking will help me relax, and I find a large pan in the cabinet and put it on the stove, just as Mac grabs my shoulders, spinning me around.

"We need to talk." His voice is deep, his eyes concerned, and my stomach lurches. He doesn't wait for me to reply, but takes my hand and pulls me over to the couch, sitting me in the corner and flopping down alongside me. Then he turns, facing me, still holding my hand in his. "Tell me what's wrong, Ella. Is it something I've done?"

"Kind of."

He nods his head. "Was it because I agreed with Gavin when he said he didn't know what he'd do without you? Was that going too far in front of everyone?"

"No. It's nothing to do with that."

"Okay. Did I get something wrong in the rehearsals?"

I stare at him for a moment. "Not exactly. Not in the way you mean."

"Ella… I can sit here all day and all night trying to second guess when and how I've screwed up, but it'd be so much easier if you just told me."

I take a breath, letting it out slowly. "I know you're gonna say I'm being silly, but I hate the way you behave around Vivian." There. I said it. Although I'm not sure it helped. Mac's frowning, his brow furrowing.

"Behave? You mean act, don't you?"

"They're the same thing."

"No, they're not. The way a person behaves is about how they conduct themselves. Acting is just pretense." He moves a little closer and reaches up, caressing my cheek with his fingertips, but I pull back slightly and his frown deepens. "Don't you get it, Ella? I might try to behave like the perfect gentleman around you, but I fail dismally every time and end up behaving like a perfect fool. That's what you do to me. You make me foolish and carefree… and so damn happy." He stretches out his hand again, and this time I let him touch me, closing my eyes at the moment of contact. "If you want me to put it another way," he says, and I open my eyes again and stare into his. "With Vivian I'm Blain, the TV presenter… the character I'm portraying. With you, I'm Mac. I'm me."

"But the way you were looking at her… it was like you believed the things you were saying."

He cups my face with his hand, shaking his head. "I didn't. I don't. It's just pretend." He leans in closer, gazing into my eyes. "I'm not pretending with you. I never have. This is real, Ella. Very real." I suck in a breath and he dusts his lips over mine in the gentlest of kisses. "Did that feel real?"

"Yes."

He kisses me again, a little harder.

"And that?" I nod my head. "Good. I don't think I'm capable of pretending with you."

"I don't think I like you pretending with other people."

"It's just a job."

"Have you ever had to kiss anyone, as part of a performance, I mean?"

"Yes."

"And sex?"

"Are you asking if I've ever acted in a sex scene? Because actors don't actually have sex when they're playing a part... you know that, don't you?"

"Even so... have you?"

"No. I've never been in a sex scene. Apart from making those commercials, which were all about bodybuilding, and nothing to do with sex at all, I've only ever acted on the stage. It's never been required."

"But you've kissed someone on stage before?"

"Yes, I have."

"What's it like?"

"It's part of the job. It's no different to shaking someone's hand, or passing them a cup of coffee. The foremost things in your mind are, am I standing in the correct place, are the angles right for the audience, and what the hell is my next line? It's nothing like a proper kiss. Especially not... not one where you actually care..."

He tilts his head, leaning in, and captures my lips with his. Within seconds, I'm on my back, and as he reaches between us, unfastening my jeans, I wonder... does that mean he cares?

"I never thought I liked goat's cheese, but served warm, with that dressing, it's absolutely delicious."

Vivian's reading of her lines is so awful it makes me cringe, although it's nothing like as bad as the way she keeps leaning over, showing off her cleavage to Mac, or the way she takes her time eating the food from the fork, and then licks her lips, slowly

and seductively. Nothing's changed about the way she behaves, but I don't feel as insecure as I did yesterday. Last night saw to that.

Mac might have rushed me out of my clothes, but once we were naked, he made love to me so slowly… so tenderly, I couldn't fail to be convinced by how real it all was… or how much he cared. I know he was hoping to set my mind to rest, and he did. And after dinner, he took me to bed and set it to rest all over again.

This morning, as we walked down the stairs together, hand-in-hand, he looked down at me and smiled. "Do you think we'll be able to come home tonight without any dramas?"

"I'm sorry. I don't mean to keep causing problems. It's just that this is all new to me."

He stopped then, and pushed me back against the wall, one hand behind my head, while the other rested on my waist. "You're not causing problems, and even if you were, I wouldn't be complaining. I love the fact that you're new to this… that you've never done any of it before, and I really don't care how much drama you bring to my door."

"You'd just like a break for one night?"

"I think this evening will be dramatic enough as it is."

"Oh?"

"We're watching the show… remember?"

I'd forgotten about that, what with worrying about Vivian, and I nodded my head. "It'll be fine, Mac."

"I hope so."

I could sense his nerves, and leaned up to kiss him before we continued on our way down the stairs again.

Fortunately, we've had a busy morning, so I'm not sure he's been able to worry too much about tonight's screening, but as everyone files out of the rehearsal room for lunch, I go over to him.

"Are you okay?" he asks, before I get the chance.

"I'm fine."

"Better than yesterday?" He pulls me into his arms, looking down at me.

"Much."

He seems more interested in me than tonight's events, and I decide to keep it that way... at least for now. There's no point in reminding him...

"Shall I make some coffee?" he says, and I nod my head, pulling my phone from my back pocket.

"Sure. I've just got to call Hunter."

He frowns. "Who's Hunter?"

"My big brother."

His frown clears in an instant, and I wonder if I'm not the only one who has moments of insecurity.

"I'll leave you to it."

He wanders off to the side kitchen and I sit at the table, connecting my call.

Hunter answers on the second ring, with a surprised, "Hello."

"Hi."

"Drew and I were only talking about you the other day," he says. "We were wondering if you'd emigrated."

"That's hilarious, Hunter. I've been busy, if you must know."

"Doing what?"

"Working."

"I see," he says. "And I guess you're not allowed to give me any details?"

"As it happens, that's why I called."

"Oh?" He sounds even more surprised now.

"Yeah. You see, the fruits of my labors are about to be shown on television."

"On television?"

"Yeah. The veil of secrecy has been lifted, and I'm allowed to tell you that I'm working on a TV show."

"Doing what?"

"My official job title is culinary consultant. It's a cookery show, and the first episode is going to air today at five." I avoid telling him the name of the show, because I know how amusing he'll find it, and how much he'll make me suffer as a result.

"Wow… text me the details and I'll forward them to Drew, if you like."

"Thanks. Where is he at the moment?"

"As far as I know, he's here in Boston. I'd suggest we all get together and watch your show at my place, but I can't."

"Neither can I. I'm under strict instructions to watch it here at the studio with the rest of the crew. What's your excuse?"

He hesitates for a second or two. "It's Livia," he says and I sit up straight.

"Is something wrong? Is she sick?"

"No. It's nothing like that. It's just that…" He pauses again. "I don't think I ever told you that before she and I got together, she was being stalked. It was when you were still in France, and she'd just come to work for me, and…" He stops talking and I wait. "And it was awful," he says. "She was so scared, and I felt powerless to do anything… except pay for a private investigator to look into it."

"Did they find out who was behind it?" I ask.

"They did. It was her former boss."

"Seriously?"

"Yeah. He was arrested and charged, and we found out today that he's been fined."

"Just fined? That's it? He won't serve any jail time?"

"No," he says. "Because he pleaded guilty and didn't threaten her, he only has to pay a fine."

"That's terrible, Hunter."

"I know. Although his life isn't exactly a bed of roses. His wife left him and he's lost his job... and I believe he's moving out of state."

"At least that's something."

"It is, although Livia can't see the positive side of it at the moment. Hearing the news has brought it all back to her, and she certainly doesn't feel like seeing anyone tonight."

"I can't stay I blame her."

"I'm sure she'll be fine in a day or two, so maybe we can all get together next week? It's been ages since we've seen you."

"I know, but it's gonna have to wait a while... until we've finished filming this season. It's exhausting."

"But you're enjoying it... right?" he asks.

"I am. I don't think I've ever been this happy."

There's a moment's silence and then he says, "There's more to this than job satisfaction. You've met someone, haven't you?"

I glance over at the side kitchen as Mac comes through the door, carrying two cups of coffee. He smiles at me, and I smile back. "I might have done."

"He's with you now, isn't he? I can hear it in your voice."

"Yes, he's here."

Mac puts the cups on the table and looks down at me, frowning, like he's confused.

"Who is he?" Hunter says in my ear, and I chuckle.

"Watch the show this evening, and you'll find out."

I hang up before he can ask anything else and twist my phone around in my hand.

"You told your brother about us?" Mac says, sitting down beside me.

"In a manner of speaking."

"So we're not keeping our relationship a secret anymore?"

"We are here, but…" He grabs me, his hands clasped around my face, and silences me with the deepest of kisses.

I guess that means he approves.

Kennedy is sitting at the head of the table, with Ruby to her left and Mac to her right. Luckily, because he and I came into the meeting room together, I was able to grab the seat beside him, although Vivian tried her best to get there before me. As it is, she's had to settle for sitting on the other side of Ruby and gazing across the table at Mac. At the opposite end of the room, the chairs have been turned around to face the TV screen, and because there isn't enough seating in here, people are standing around the edges of the room, waiting in anticipation.

I can feel the tension pouring off of Mac and I shift my chair just a little closer to his, then reach beneath the table, taking his hand in mine. He looks over and gives me a smile, and I squeeze his hand.

"Told you I'd find a way," I whisper under my breath and he chuckles, just quietly.

There's a general hum of excitement in the room, and Kennedy is looking very pleased with herself. Ruby told Mac and me this afternoon, that Kennedy and a few other people in here have already seen the show, and I guess the smile on Kennedy's face ought to give us confidence.

As the time ticks away to the top of the hour, a silence descends over the room, and you could hear a pin drop when the titles roll. To be honest, I don't like them. They're a little tacky for my tastes, focusing mostly on the 'Master' element of the 'Meal Master' name. But that's not my department, and now for the first time, I'm a little nervous myself… about the food.

We're all glued to the screen as the lights come up and the camera zooms in on Mac's perfect face. My God… he really is gorgeous, and there's a collective sigh from most of the women

in the room as they all focus on him, and the words he's saying, in his impeccable American accent. I suppose I ought to have realized it before now, but seeing the way he's dressed on the screen, and the way his muscles are shown off to great prominence in that super tight t-shirt, it's very clear the studio aren't even remotely interested in the dishes, or how they're cooked. The purpose of the show is to promote Mac as a sex symbol. Not that he needs any help; he looks incredible.

When the camera occasionally focuses on the food, rather than Mac's face or body, I take the time to check it looks okay… which it does. I also smile to myself when he's shown cutting up the vegetables to be roasted. He looks very proficient, and I can't help remembering the work that went into that first episode, and how annoyed I was at the time by Mac and his lack of culinary talents. Of course, what I hadn't realized at the time was that his talents lay elsewhere… and some of them are evident on the screen, not just in his looks, but also in his acting…

As the show draws to a close and Mac delivers his final lines, while the 'guest', who I remember was called Lyla, raises a forkful of roasted lamb to her lips, everyone in the room bursts into spontaneous applause.

The people around and behind us draw closer and I let go of Mac's hand, even though he tries to grab it back. Within moments, though, I'm shoved aside as someone steps between us.

"That was great, man… really great."

I don't even know who the man is, but he's clapping Mac on his shoulder, and once he steps back, his place is taken by someone else… and then another, and another, all heaping praise on Mac's performance.

After a moment or two, I get to my feet and step out of the way, moving to the edge of the room, and leaning against the wall, watching while Mac is swamped by well-wishers. I can't even see

him properly anymore, but I don't take my eyes from the crowd, which is why I jump with surprise when a voice beside me says, "Well done."

I turn to see Ruby standing next to me. "I don't think I can take very much credit," I say, nodding toward Mac, and she smiles.

"We wouldn't have a show if it wasn't for you. Kennedy knows that… and so does Blain, I'm sure."

I wonder if she thinks I'm jealous of the attention he's receiving. Nothing could be further from the truth. Not only am I thrilled by the response – for him, not me – but I'd hate to be where he is. I'd hate to be the center of attention. I'd much rather hide in the corner… like I am now.

Still, it wouldn't hurt to throw her off the scent a little, so I just shrug my shoulders and she gives me a sympathetic smile and wanders back to the table, into the throng.

It takes a good fifteen or twenty minutes for the fuss to die down, and Kennedy eventually takes control of the room, raising her voice above the chatter.

"I think we can all agree how great the show looks… especially Blain." She turns, smiling at him, her eyes sparkling. "Obviously, we've still got to see how well it goes over with the public, but I'll let you all know the viewing figures as soon as I have them. In the meantime, tomorrow is another day – as they say – and in our case, we're recording the next show, so I think it's time we all headed home and got a good night's sleep."

I push myself off of the wall, making my way back to Mac. Unfortunately, before I can get there, Vivian slides into the seat beside him… the one I was occupying. She leans in close, and as I come up behind her, I can just about hear her say, "My place is only around the corner. I've got some wine chilling and we could…"

I feel my blood boil, but before I can say anything, Mac turns to her. "I'm sorry, but you heard what Kennedy said. We're recording tomorrow, and I'm tired. It's been a crazy day."

She reaches out, as though to touch him, but he pulls away and gets to his feet, looking down at me.

"Ella… there you are. I—I'm just going back to the rehearsal studio to fetch my things."

I nod my head. "I'll come with you."

His lips twitch upward as he kicks his chair aside and waits for me to leave the room ahead of him. Once we're out in the hall, I lean in to him slightly

"I still wanna scratch her eyes out."

"Don't let me stop you."

I laugh and he joins in, and although we don't touch each other, I can feel the connection between us as we pick up our pace and head back to the rehearsal studio.

Once we're inside, Mac closes the door, leaning back against it, and lets out a long sigh.

"God… that was awful."

"The show wasn't. It was good."

"Hmm… I just hated all that fuss."

I move closer to him, resting my hands on his chest as he gazes down at me. "Would you like to come back to my place tonight?"

He frowns. "Don't you want to come back to mine?"

"Does it matter where we are, as long as we're together?"

His frown fades and his eyes light up in the most perfect of smiles. "When you put it like that, it doesn't matter in the slightest, but I'll need to go home first and pick up some clothes. Do you want to give me your address?"

"Why don't I drive you home? You can pack a bag, and then I'll take us back to my place."

He puts his arms around me, holding me hard against him. "That's not even remotely logical. If you're going to drive us to my place, we might as well stay there."

"It is logical."

"How?"

"Because I have food."

He chuckles, nodding his head, and bends to kiss me.

Mac

It only takes a few minutes to pack a bag. Like Ella, I've brought a couple of shirts and some spare black jeans, just in case I end up staying more than one night. I also grabbed two of the tight black t-shirts I need for work, which is enough to get me to the weekend. Ella waited in the car, telling me she was going to call her brother, and when I return to her, I can see she's still talking. She notices me coming, though, and pops the boot of her car, so I can dump my bag in there before I get in beside her.

"I don't know why they made us keep it a secret, but I'm glad you enjoyed it."

She looks over at me with a smile and I smile back, resting my hand on her thigh. Her brother's saying something and while she listens, I study her face. I'm still astounded by her beauty every time I look at her, but today there's something different. She seems more relaxed, more confident… happier, and I wonder if that's got anything to do with last night.

She had me scared for a while, when she was giving me the cold shoulder and refusing to talk. I don't take to fear very well, and rather than ignoring her obvious discomfort, I sat her on the couch and she explained her insecurities about the way I have to act around Vivian. I don't think it was me she had a problem

with, so much as Vivian, because although Ella asked about kissing and sex scenes, she didn't mention any of the other actresses I've had to perform with while making the show. She can't have forgotten last week, and the 'lie' I told Bonnie about being with someone else, when she asked me out. It wasn't so much a lie as an exaggeration, because in my head I was already with Ella, but her problem definitely seemed to be with Vivian. I got the feeling she needed reassurance… and I was happy to provide it.

I stopped short of telling her I loved her, in case she thought I was playing games, throwing 'love' into the mix to cover an indiscreet thought, or word, or deed, with Vivian. Instead, I told her I care… or I dropped a huge hint at it, anyway. And then I made love to her, like I've never made love to anyone in my life. That wasn't intentional or planned in any way. I'd practically ripped her clothes off in my desperation to be inside her. But when she was naked beneath me, it was like I was overwhelmed with love for her… and the need to express it in the only way I could.

I took it slowly, hoping she'd get my unspoken message… and I think she must have done. Why else would she have just said it doesn't matter where we are, as long as we're together?

"Like I told you earlier, it won't be before the end of the season," she says, shaking her head, still talking to her brother. "I know you want to meet him and as soon as we're done recording, I'll bring him down to Newport. Okay?"

I feel my heart swell. She wants me to meet her family?

"Of course we could meet in Boston, but our schedule is exhausting." She chuckles. "I'm not saying a word, Hunter." She laughs out loud and hangs up, turning to me. "Shall we go?"

"Okay."

She starts the engine, pulling out of the parking space. "Did you get everything you need?" she asks, glancing over.

"Yes. Did I gather your brother enjoyed the show?"

"He did. He's dying to meet you."

"So he can make sure I'm good enough for you?"

She takes her hand from the steering wheel, placing it on my leg. "I don't think there's any doubt about that, Mac."

I lay my hand over hers and sit back, letting out a sigh, as I allow my eyes to close…

I come to with a jolt as the car slows, and I look out of the window to see a classy apartment block.

"Sorry… did I fall asleep?"

"Yes, but don't worry. It's been a stressful day for you."

I'm about to reply when she pulls the car into the underground car park beneath the apartments, and I frown slightly. Is this where she lives? It has to be. She's got a code number to get past the barrier.

Should her car have given me a clue that she'd live somewhere like this?

Probably.

I don't say anything, though, and once she's parked, I go around to the back of the car and grab my bag from the boot, getting to Ella's side in time to help her to her feet.

"Thanks." She looks up at me with a smile, and takes my hand, leading me over to the elevator. I start to feel a little nervous when she presses the button, the doors open, and we step inside. My nerves have nothing to do with being in a confined space with her, but with the stylish interior of the lift. The two side walls are lined with wood… real wood, and the one ahead of us is mirrored, reflecting my pale face, as I turn around and Ella presses the button for the top floor. She looks up at me as the doors close, a smile lighting up her face. I know she's thinking over what I said about being in an elevator with her, but I'm

beyond confused right now, and can't think about anything other than where we are, and who she is... and why I didn't know any of this.

The lift stops with a smooth sigh, the doors slide open, and I look out onto a wide hallway, which is tiled with grey marble on the floor and the walls. I can see a single door, right at the end, and follow Ella towards it, watching as she pulls a key from her handbag. She lets us in, and I gasp as I accompany her into a large foyer, with closets on either side. She dumps her handbag on the floor, rolling her shoulders as she kicks off her shoes. I copy her, scared I might put a foot wrong, and place my bag behind the door, following her through into an enormous living room. It has pale grey walls, wood floors and white furniture. There are two separate seating areas; one around a fireplace and the other facing a huge television, in a separate part of the room, beyond which the windows overlook the city skyline. To my right, there's a formal dining area, with a table, surrounded by six chairs, and I stand for a moment, trying to take it all in.

"Do you want to come watch me cook?" she says, like it's the most natural thing in the world to live somewhere like this.

"Um... sure."

"I only bought this place because I fell in love with the kitchen," she says over her shoulder as she leads me through an archway behind the dining table, into a kitchen that's probably three times the size of the one we use at work. It has shiny grey cupboard doors, and granite work surfaces, a six-burner hob, double oven and an island unit, with four stools. There's also an informal dining table over by the floor-to-ceiling windows, with dark grey leather chairs surrounding it.

"Y—You bought it?"

"Yes."

"Y—You mean you own this place?"

"Yes." She smiles up at me, going around the other side of the island unit and pulling out a heavy-looking pan, which she places on the hob between us.

I watch as she grabs some onions, a chopping board and chef's knife, and puts some oil and butter into the pan before she looks up at me, her smile fading.

"Is everything okay?"

"I don't know… I guess I'm just a little bewildered, that's all."

"Bewildered?"

"Yes."

"Is this about what happened earlier?" she says, nodding her head as she starts to peel and slice the onions. "Are you thinking about how it felt to watch yourself on television?"

That's not it at all, but I don't know how to tell her I'm struggling to work out what someone like her is doing with someone like me. So, I nod my head.

"Well, I thought you were amazing."

I can't help smiling and even though I'm still nervous as hell, I decide to go with it. "Did I do okay with the cooking? I didn't make myself look a fool?"

"No. You were perfect." She stops, stares across at me and tilts her head, and then leans across, resting her hand on my arm. "In every way."

"As long as I didn't let you down."

She puts down her knife now and comes around to my side of the island unit, waiting until I turn to her, and then she wraps her arms around me, leaning up and kissing me. "Never," she whispers, and I deepen the kiss, hoping to find some reassurance in her lips.

She pulls back far too quickly. "Dinner…" she mutters, and returns to the other side of the island unit, lowering the heat under the pan before she picks up the knife and gets back to chopping.

"If you don't mind me asking… what on earth are you making that needs so many onions?"

She smiles up at me. "French onion soup."

"A recipe inspired by your time in Paris?"

"Of course. As I told you before, I cook a lot of French food… unless I'm in a hurry, in which case I'll usually fall back on pasta, or stir-fries. Besides, I like this recipe because all you have to do is slice up the onions and then leave them to caramelise for thirty minutes or so."

"Thirty minutes?"

Her eyes lock on mine, and she bites on her bottom lip. "Yes."

"So… we'll have some time to kill?"

"We will."

She sucks in a breath, and although I'm still nervous, my cock responds to the thought of how we could fill the next half an hour.

Ella finishes slicing, tips the onions into the pan of melted butter and oil, and stirs them briefly before she puts on the lid, and washes her hands. Then she turns back to me and I hold out my hand. She takes it across the island unit and I pull her around, and let her lead us back into the living room, where she takes us over to the three large sofas that surround the fireplace. It's not cold enough to light the fire, but we sit in the one facing it. She's in the corner, and although I go with my initial instincts and lean over to kiss her, I'm finding it hard to concentrate. Even as my lips touch hers, I can't focus, or feel comfortable, and after a few seconds, I pull back.

"Sorry… I can't do this."

She leans in to the sofa, staring up at me, confusion clouding her eyes. "Why? What's wrong?"

"I need to talk to you."

"What about?"

I wave my arm around. "This, Ella."

"My apartment, you mean?"

"This isn't an apartment. I live in an apartment. This is a palace… and I don't understand. You said working on the show was your first job."

"It is."

"In which case, how can you afford to buy somewhere like this? I can't believe they're paying you a lot more than they're paying me, and I just about get by paying a subsidised rent. So how can you make the mortgage payments?"

"I don't have a mortgage. I bought this place outright."

I struggle not to choke. "Right… because that makes it so much better."

She sighs, shaking her head. "Is this a problem, Mac?"

"How would I know? I don't even understand what this is."

"It's the result of me having inherited a lot of money from my father."

"Okay… before we go any further, can we define 'a lot'?"

"If you want to. My brothers and I inherited a little over fifteen million dollars each… plus the house in Newport, which we kind of share between us."

I shoot to my feet, unable to help myself. "D—Did you say fifteen million?"

"Yes." She sounds disappointed, and I sit back down again, taking her hands in mind.

"What's wrong, Ella?"

"You. You're gonna go all weird on me, aren't you?"

"I'm trying very hard not to, but it's an enormous shock, discovering that my girlfriend is a multi-millionaire."

Her eyes widen. "Y—Your girlfriend?"

I move closer. "Yes. Isn't that what you are?"

"Do you still want me to be?"

I put my arms around her, and she leans against me. "Of course I do. None of this changes how I feel about you. I'm just

a little embarrassed that I suggested you should feel at home staying at my place, when this is what you're used to."

She pulls back, looking up at me. "There's nothing to be embarrassed about. I love your place."

I look around the room. "Well... I love yours too, so we're even." She chuckles and leans against me again. "If it isn't a rude question, why do you work? You don't need to, surely?"

"No, I don't need to, but my brothers and I have never understood why our father left us his fortune, and I guess I wanted to prove I'm not just some rich kid who can buy her way into anything she wants. I didn't earn any of this, and it's important to me that people realise I'm more than just a bank balance. I'm pretty sure my brothers feel the same. That's why they're so driven, too."

"I see. Tell me about your father. What did he do?"

"He founded one of the biggest advertising agencies in the city... in the whole of America, I believe. At least, it was in its heyday. Hunter runs it now."

"You talk about its success as though it's a thing of the past."

She shakes her head. "Not necessarily. It's doing okay, but when Dad died, it hit a rocky patch. I think Hunter's pulled it back now... or he's getting there. The last time we talked about it, he said he'd picked up some new clients."

"When did your father die?" I ask, caressing her cheek with my fingertips.

"About eighteen months ago."

That's more recent than I'd expected, and I pull her a little closer. "I'm sorry, Ella."

"Don't be," she says, surprising me. "I barely knew him."

"Why not? You'd have been, what... twenty-two when he died?"

"Yeah, but he was too wrapped up in his business and his own life to care about his children." I can hear the hurt in her voice, and I pull her onto my lap, just so I can hug her tighter.

"What about your mum?"

"I don't remember her at all."

"I'm sorry… did she…?"

"She left us." Her interruption surprises me even more than her revelations about her father, and I lean back a little, gazing into her face.

"When?"

"When I was three."

Dear God. I pull her hard against my chest, and feel the sense of abandonment pouring off of her. My parents might have been taken from me, but at least I have a wealth of happy memories to look back on. She doesn't have any of that, and while I may not be able to say as much – yet – I make a silent vow to myself that I will never leave her.

I sense she'd like a change of subject, but I still have so many questions.

"Did you keep your wealth a secret from me on purpose?"

She pulls away, shaking her head. "No, of course not. It's just not something I feel the need to talk about."

"So you keep it from everyone?"

"Yes, I suppose so. No-one in London, or Madrid, or Paris had any idea."

"They didn't guess from the way you lived your life? From the lavish apartments and houses you lived in?"

"Very few people ever came to my apartments. But in any case, I didn't live anywhere lavish. In London, I rented a one-bedroom apartment in Belsize Park. It was only a quick ride on the underground to the cookery school, and it had the best kitchen of all the places that were available."

"What about Madrid?"

"Again, I rented a little one bedroom place. It was in the centre of the city, on the third floor, above a delicatessen. The kitchen

wasn't the best, but the delicatessen was fabulous." She smiles and I have to smile back.

"And Paris?"

"I struck gold there."

"Oh? You rented rooms in the Palace of Versailles?"

She slaps my arm. "No… you idiot. I rented a tiny apartment in Montmartre, near to the Sacré-Coeur. The living room had the loveliest arched windows that led out onto a balcony overlooking Paris. There was even a view of the Eiffel Tower."

"And the kitchen?"

"To be honest, with a view like that, for once in my life, I didn't care."

I chuckle, unable to help myself. "It sounds very romantic."

"It was, although I didn't see it that way at the time." She leans in, raising her face to mine, and waits for me to close the gap, kissing her. Our tongues meet, exploring, and she crushes her breasts to my chest… making me feel at home again… even in a palace. After a few minutes, she pulls away again. "Happy now?" she says.

I suddenly hate the thought that anyone else — especially someone at the studio — knows more about her than I do. "Does anyone at work know?"

"Just Kennedy."

"You told her?"

"No. She found out somehow and confronted me about it. Oddly enough, ever since then, she's been a lot nicer to me."

I roll my eyes. "Why am I not surprised by that?"

"Well, I guess she worked out she had no choice in the matter. Unlike you, I might be eminently replaceable…"

"Hey… you're irreplaceable to me."

She smiles, resting her forehead against mine. "Thank you for saying that."

"You know I'm not talking about work, don't you?"

"Yes, but I also know the show is about you, and not me. Even so, I don't think Kennedy wanted the hassle of trying to find someone else who'd do my job for the pittance of a salary they're paying. When she realised I don't actually need to work, and could walk out anytime I liked, I think she decided to play nice. Either that, or it was the thought that I could buy the studio and become her boss whenever I felt like it."

I laugh. "Now, that would be money well spent."

She leans back, looking me in the eye. "I wasn't deliberately keeping anything from you, Mac. It's just that it never came up… and we have been kinda busy."

I nod my head. "I know. And I can understand why you'd be wary. You probably have to be careful of men who are looking to take advantage."

"Advantage?"

I smile at her. God, she can be innocent at times. "Yes, of someone in your position."

She frowns. "It's not that at all. My brothers have said they've often worried about women doing that kind of thing to them… you know, trying to trap them. But I've never even thought about it. I've never been in a position to think about it. Like I said, I'd been waiting for the right man."

"And you still think that's me?"

"Yes, I do."

"So do I. Your money makes no difference to how I feel about you, Ella. I'd still feel the same, whether you had two cents to your name, or whether you were the richest woman in the world."

"I am."

"You are what?"

"The richest woman in the world… I've got you."

She captures my gasp with a kiss, and as I deepen it, holding the back of her head and crushing my lips to hers, I wonder if she already knows how much I love her.

We make it back into the kitchen just in time to stop the onions from burning, and while I sit up on one of the stools, Ella adds some flour to the pan, and then some stock, which she takes from a carton in the fridge, stirring it all around. She grinds in some pepper, and a little salt, tasting it, and then replaces the lid, looking up at me.

"We've got at least another twenty minutes," she says, and I get down from the stool and wander around to her, taking her in my arms. "Do you want to talk some more?"

"No."

I walk her backwards until she hits the work surface behind her, and I lift her onto it, pulling her forward so she's right on the edge. Then I put one hand behind her neck, and lean in, kissing her, while I reach between us, undoing her zipper. We break the kiss, both breathless, and she raises her backside off the work surface so I can pull down her jeans and underwear, and then she sits back down again, waiting while I tug them off and drop them to the floor. She's moved further back, so I pull her forward again, and bend down, parting her legs and flicking my tongue across her swollen clit. She moans, flexing her hips, and I look up at her.

"I thought you said clearing up was the only thing you did well in the kitchen?"

I smile, shaking my head as I stand between her legs. "Not anymore." She stares into my eyes and I don't take mine from hers as I unfasten my jeans...

Chapter Nine

Ella

"That's a wrap, everyone. Well done."

There's a collective sigh of relief that we've finally reached the end of recording. The season might only have been ten shows long, but sometimes it's felt like it would never end. The last two have been particularly difficult, because they're going to air in the run-up to Christmas, so they were themed around festive cooking... not for Christmas dinner itself, of course; Kennedy clearly felt that had been covered with the Thanksgiving show. For Christmas, the 'questions' related to 'easy meals to cook for busy moms', and 'party food', both of which required an enormous amount of work on my part. On top of that, the set had to be decorated, which caused some consternation when it had to be dismantled and then re-erected... and made to look *exactly* the same a week later, with not a fairy light out of place.

The decorations feel a little premature, considering we still haven't celebrated Thanksgiving yet, but I guess that's how it works in television, and as I look around the studio, everyone seems quite happy.

I'm happy, too... but that's because I'm so in love with Mac it's breathtaking.

We've spent every night together since that first one; sometimes at his place, and sometimes at mine, although it took him a while to get used to my apartment. I remember he laughed out loud when I first showed him into my bedroom, after we'd eaten the French onion soup, and cleaned up the kitchen.

"What's wrong?" I looked up at his sparkling eyes as they wandered around the room.

I'll admit, it's enormous, and is effectively divided into two halves. The main part of the room is taken up with my king-sized bed, the floor-to-ceiling windows covered by pale gray drapes. The other half of the room features a deep, white, cozy couch, which sits in front of a huge television screen.

"Nothing." He smiled and lifted me into his arms. "Except I think we could dispense with the rest of your apartment and just live in here, couldn't we?"

"We could. If there was a kitchen."

He chuckled and kissed me… like he meant it.

If the night before had been all about setting my mind at rest with gentle lovemaking, that night was definitely his way of showing me that my money didn't matter in the slightest… that he'd take me any way he could have me. And he did… repeatedly. Not just in the kitchen, while the onion soup was cooking, but also up against the wall in my bedroom, and on the cozy couch, and finally, in my bed.

The next night, after a long day of recording, we went to Mac's place again. That was my choice, because I wanted to show him I didn't need the trappings of wealth. I'd meant it when I said I loved his place… I do, and I wanted to go there and show him how much.

For the first time, we rode up in the elevator together. We might have done so at my apartment block, but he was otherwise occupied – or perhaps that should be overwhelmed – worrying

about how I came to live in such a place. That night, though, as we ascended to his apartment, I realized what he'd meant about being in a confined space. It was as though there was no air. I was certainly struggling to breathe, and almost as soon as the doors closed, our lips met in the most passionate of kisses. Our jackets were soon consigned to the floor, as was his t-shirt. He undid my blouse, pulling it from my jeans, and then startled when the elevator doors opened.

"Oh… God." I glanced outside, but there was no-one there. Why would there be? Mac has the top floor to himself, and he looked down at me, smiling as he bent to grab our clothes from the floor, then pulled my blouse closed and took my hand, dragging me out into the hall.

We ran to his apartment, and he fumbled with the keys, letting us in before he dropped everything and lifted me into his arms, carrying me to the stairs.

"What's wrong with the couch, Mac? Or the floor? Why are we wasting time going upstairs?" I was desperate for him, and didn't want to wait another minute.

"I don't have any condoms down here."

"But you keep some in your wallet."

He went up the stairs anyway, putting me down beside the bed. "I know… but I used them all last night and this morning, at your place."

"Oh." I looked up at him, smiling. "Maybe we should keep a supply at my apartment?"

"Sure, but can we discuss condoms another time?" He looked down at me, his eyes on fire. "I've got better things to be doing right now."

"You have?"

"Yeah." He put his fingers in the top of my jeans and pulled me closer.

I shuddered against him and clung to his shoulders as he peeled me out of the rest of my clothes…

Since that night, we've made sure there are condoms at both my place and his, and Mac always keeps some in his wallet, too… just in case.

We haven't exactly alternated between the two apartments, and I think we've probably spent more time at his than at mine… although we were at mine a couple of weeks ago, on the evening that my period started. It was my first one since we'd started seeing each other, and for some reason, I'd forgotten how awful they can be… and how unexpected. I've never really worked out whether it's a good thing, or a bad one, that I get no warning when my periods are due, but either way, I was glad to be at home that evening. Apart from anything else, I needed sanitary pads and a change of underwear.

We'd only just got in from work, after a hard Thursday of recording, and I'd gone to the bathroom, taking a lot longer than either of us had expected. When I came out again, Mac frowned, then got up from his place on the couch and came straight to me.

"Ella? What's wrong? You look really pale."

"Nothing's wrong. My period's just started, that's all."

"Oh. Are you okay?" He put his arms around me and I nestled against him.

"I'll be fine."

"You don't look fine." He turned me around and sat me down on the couch. "At the risk of bringing up my exes, they all had periods, but I can honestly say none of them ever looked quite this ill."

He sat beside me, and I took his hand in mine. "I'm not ill, Mac. And I'm used to it. The cramps will be horrendous for a couple of days, I'll feel washed out, and tired beyond words… and then I'll be okay again."

"That doesn't sound like something you should have to get used to."

"It's not optional, I'm afraid."

He smiled, although I could still see the worry in his eyes.

"How have I never noticed this before?" he asked.

"Noticed what?"

"How bad your periods are."

"This is the first one I've had since we've been together," I said, and he nodded his head.

"I know, but I've been paying fairly close attention to you since the moment we met. I would have thought I'd have noticed something like this."

I smiled and rested against him. "The last one started on a Friday, so by the time I got back to work on the Monday, I was over the worst of it."

"Oh… I see. I don't feel so bad now."

"Bad about what?" I asked.

"Being so incredibly unobservant."

"You're not."

He nodded. "Is there anything you want? Anything you need? I'd offer to cook us something, but I'm fairly sure that would only make you feel worse… so why don't I order in?"

"That sounds lovely."

It was, and although I think he was a little startled by the way my periods wipe me out, he couldn't have been more considerate. He did everything for me, held me when I needed him, and went out of his way to be attentive at work, while still not giving away our relationship – which was an achievement in itself.

I think that was when I first realized that, even though sex is important – to both of us – just being together means far more.

It means everything…

Kennedy comes into the studio, startling me back to reality, and I glance at Mac to find he's staring at me, with a smile on his lips. I know why that is… it's because, after today, we won't be working anymore. That might seem like a bad thing, but at least we can stop pretending. We can be ourselves all the time, and I think we're both looking forward to that.

Mac's been wondering what he's going to do now our contracts here are over, and I've been doing the same. So far, we haven't come up with any solutions, but there's no rush. Mac thinks there is, and I know why. It's because he has bills to pay… or he thinks he does. Obviously, I'd cover them for him, if he needed me to, but I've been thinking that it might be easier if he gave up his place and moved into mine. We haven't talked about it yet, because we haven't had time, and because I'm slightly wary he'll think I'm flaunting my money. But it just makes sense… or it does to me. Maybe I'll wait until we've had a few days away from the studio and then try to drop it into the conversation… somehow.

"Thank you, everybody… thank you." Kennedy is clapping her hands, trying to get us all to be quiet and give her our undivided attention, and eventually, it works. The hum of noise dies down, and she steps up onto the set, at the end of the island unit, and surveys her kingdom. "I wanted to come in and say 'well done' to you all." She's beaming with pride, like she's personally responsible for what's gone on in here over the last ten weeks. Mac is standing slightly behind her, and he rolls his eyes, which almost makes me laugh out loud, although I do my best to focus. "As you all know, the viewing figures started off a lot better than any of us had expected… and since then, they've soared." There's a general murmur of satisfaction, although Kennedy holds up her hands and everyone soon quietens down again. "As a result, the network have commissioned a second season." The

murmur becomes more of a roar, and the people around me burst into applause. I stare at them, and then turn to Mac, who seems pleased with the news. He's certainly smiling, anyway.

"When do we start recording?" Vivian asks.

"January. And this time they want twenty shows." Twenty? I feel my heart sink, although Kennedy turns her attention to me for some reason, and I force a smile onto my lips. "Those of you who were on a short-term contract will be sent a new one by email." She nods her head at me, although I can't believe I'm the only person in the room whose contract expired at the end of this season. There's Mac, apart from anything else… and the show is his, not mine.

I glance at Mac to see he's grinning. He's talking to Gavin and I can't blame him for being pleased. After all, this answers his problems about what to do next. As for me, I can't help feeling a little daunted. The schedule has been punishing, and I'm not sure about doubling it.

"Are you okay?" Ruby's voice makes me jump and I realize she's standing right beside me.

"Yes."

"It's the thought of doing this for twenty weeks, isn't it?" she says and I turn to look at her.

"How did you know?"

"Because I feel the same. I think we're due to get a break roughly halfway through, though, which is just as well. I don't doubt we'll all need to recharge our batteries by then."

"Neither do I." I guess that sounds better than working at this level for twenty weeks solid, although I'm still a little wary.

"Enjoy some time off now, and hopefully by January it won't feel so ominous."

I smile at her and she smiles back before she wanders off in Gavin's direction. The studio is clearing quite quickly. Kennedy

leaves without saying a word to me, which I guess makes sense. I'm not the star of the show, am I?

Eventually, Mac and I are alone, and he wanders over to me, pulling his red apron off over his head.

"That was good news, wasn't it?"

"I guess."

He frowns, dropping the apron and putting his hands on my waist. "Aren't you pleased?"

"Twenty weeks is a long time, Mac. It's tiring doing this."

"I know… but at least we'll be together."

I pull back, although he doesn't let me go. "Are you saying we wouldn't have stayed together if we weren't still doing the show?"

"No, of course not." He pulls me hard against him, even though I'm still trying to lean away. "What I'm saying is, this way we get to be together all the time. That wouldn't have been possible if I'd gone back to the theatre, or into some other TV show, or something."

He has a point, and I relax, nestling against him. "I see." He kisses the top of my head and I look up at him. "Are we still gonna be keeping our relationship a secret when we come back?"

"I don't see why we need to," he says. "But let's wait and see how we feel when the time comes, shall we? We can always just walk in on the first day, hand-in-hand, and shock the hell out of everyone."

"Okay." He bends his head, kissing me, just briefly. "I take it we can both stop looking for work now?"

His brow furrows. "Probably. I've just about got enough to cover the rent until January."

"You think you need to worry about money, do you?" I struggle not to smile.

"I don't know. I've got this really rich girlfriend, and…"

"And you're hoping she'll pay your rent for you?"

He shrugs. "No, but I don't think she'd let me starve, or allow my landlord to throw me out on the streets."

"No, she wouldn't… but she'd like to know what she's getting in return." I rest my hands on his chest, looking up into his eyes, and he flexes his hips, letting me feel his arousal.

"I'm gonna make her come… really hard… every single night."

I tilt my head back slightly. "That makes me sound like a prostitute… having sex for money."

"No, it doesn't. You've got it the wrong way around. If you were a prostitute, I'd be paying you."

"Oh… so you're the prostitute?"

"Of course I'm not. I don't have the legs for it."

I giggle, and he captures my lips with his. "Oh, Mac…" I whisper into him and he holds me closer, deepening the kiss, our tongues dancing, our bodies rocking and swaying in perfect harmony.

He breaks the kiss, pulling back, and looks down at me, breathless, his eyes sparkling.

"Do you like surprises?"

"Sometimes. It depends on the surprise."

He nods his head, and I wonder what he's got in mind and whether I'll want to do it here. "Do you remember this morning, when we left my place, I packed a bag?"

"Yes." Where's he going with this? It's no mystery. Last night, before we fell asleep, we discussed what we were going to do over the weekend. I suggested we go down to Newport, but Mac convinced me my brothers could wait another week to meet him, that it'd be better to go down there over Thanksgiving, anyway… and that we could spend a few days alone at my place. I wasn't about to say 'no'.

"Well, that's the surprise."

"That you packed a bag?" I frown up at him. "It's not a tremendous shock, Mac. I watched you do it."

He grins. "No, the bag itself isn't the surprise. It's what we're going to do with it… where we're going to go."

"You mean we're not going back to my place?"

"We are. But only so you can pack a bag, too."

"And then what?"

"If I told you, it wouldn't be a surprise, would it?"

"I suppose not. But if I'm driving to this place, then surely I'll need to know where I'm going, won't I?"

"Now you're just fishing…"

He's not wrong… but he's also clearly not going to tell me. Instead, he picks up his apron and leads me out of the studio. We can't hold hands as there are still too many people around, but we make our way back to the rehearsal studio, grab our things, and head for the elevators. I'm intrigued about what he's got planned for us, and judging by the glint in his eyes, he's enjoying this far more than he should.

"What should I pack?" I ask, looking over at Mac. He's standing in the doorway of my dressing room, having changed out of his too-tight t-shirt, into a white button-down shirt, and I'm staring at my open bag, wondering what to put inside.

"A toothbrush?"

"Be serious, Mac."

He steps closer. "I am being serious. But I guess if you insist on taking clothes as well, then warm ones would be best."

It's the middle of November, so I think I could have worked that out for myself.

"How long do I need to pack for?"

"We're coming back on Monday."

"Okay."

I grab a couple of pairs of jeans, four t-shirts, some sweaters, a thick cardigan and some socks, as well as underwear, and look up to see him smiling at me.

"What's wrong?"

"I meant this coming Monday… not the one after."

"Very funny."

He chuckles and I pack a few toiletries, adding them to my bag before I close it up. "Done?" he asks.

"Yes."

"Good… let's go."

He takes my bag, grabbing my hand at the same time, and leads me out of the apartment.

"Okay… so where are we going?" I ask as I start the car and look over at him.

"The grocery store."

"Excuse me?"

"We're gonna need a few supplies."

I shake my head and drive out of the parking garage, going a few blocks to a side road where there's a small grocery store.

"Will this do?"

"It'll be fine."

"Am I allowed to come in with you?"

"Of course." He smiles. "You think I know what to buy?"

I join him on the sidewalk and he takes my hand again, guiding me into the store, where he takes a small cart and starts pushing it around. "This place you're taking me to… we're going to have to cook?" I look up at him.

"Yeah. Sorry about that."

"Oh, I don't mind. I'm just wondering what to get."

"For tonight, I'd suggest something quick. It's gonna take us a couple of hours to get there."

"Okay."

I have to admit, I'm enjoying this myself now, and we walk around together, grabbing various things that take our fancy, as well as some basic essentials.

Mac insists on paying and we carry our bags out together, loading them into the trunk, before we set off again. He gives me directions, heading north onto the interstate, and once we've been on the road for a while, with music playing softly in the background, I turn to him.

"What was it like growing up in London?" I ask. We've got a long drive ahead of us, so I may as well find out a little more about him.

"I enjoyed it."

"Whereabouts did you live?"

"In Clapham."

I nod my head. "I think I went through it once on the train… Clapham Junction?"

"Yeah," he says. "Except Clapham Junction isn't actually in Clapham; it's in Battersea."

"Well, that's just silly."

"I know, but I don't make the rules."

"What did your parents do?"

"Dad was an artist and Mum was a musician."

"So they were both creative… like you?"

"Yeah, I guess. They certainly weren't at all fazed when I said I wanted to be a writer."

I look over at him, just briefly. "Tell me about your book."

He pauses for a second or two and then turns in his seat slightly, so even though I can't look at him, he's facing me, giving me his full attention. "It's set in a country house in Shropshire, in the depths of winter, and takes place over a long weekend."

"Is it historical?" I ask.

"Yes. It's set in the nineteen-twenties, when house-parties were all the rage."

"As were murder mysteries."

He chuckles, placing his hand on my thigh. "I know, but I've tried to make it different. My detective isn't a policeman… he's a doctor, who's staying at the house, and who solves the murder before the police can even get there."

"Why does it take the police so long?"

"Because there's a convenient snow-storm, which traps everyone at the house, including the murderer, of course."

"I see. And your agent doesn't like this?"

"I wouldn't go that far. She says she can't see it selling because it's been done before."

I shrug my shoulders. "Then change it."

"How?" he says. "I've been tweaking around with it over the last few weeks, but I still like the basic premise, and I can't see what I can do to make it different."

"Have you thought about changing your detective?"

"I can't, really. He needs to be a doctor in order to solve the crime. There's a medical element which only a doctor would understand."

"Okay. But does he have to be a man?"

He pulls his hand away and I glance over at him. I half expect him to be staring out the window, or frowning, insulted by my suggestion, but instead, he's sitting with his thumbnail in his mouth, staring into space.

"Do you know what? That might work," he says, sitting forward a little, so full of excitement it makes me giggle.

"Did they even have female doctors in the nineteen-twenties?" I ask, not wanting him to get carried away with my spur-of-the-moment idea.

"I don't know. They must have done, surely. Especially after the First World War."

He has a point. "I would imagine they were consigned to dealing with women's problems."

"Possibly, but I could always give her a rebellious nature… and I could introduce a little romance as well."

"You could?"

"Yes." He leans over, kissing my cheek. "This is perfect, Ella."

"Really?"

He pulls his phone from his pocket. "Just give me ten minutes to write all that down and I promise I won't talk about it anymore."

"I don't mind, Mac."

"You will. Trust me. Authors can be really boring. They talk about nothing other than their work in progress, and how it's going, or not going."

"Why did you say 'they', not 'we'? Don't you think of yourself as an author?"

"Not yet," he says and starts tapping away on his phone. I let him, continuing the drive in silence for a while, until he stops, sighing deeply and puts his phone away.

"Okay?" I ask.

"Absolutely."

He puts his hand on my thigh again. "Did you always want to write?"

"Yes, I think so. I can't remember wanting to do anything else. Not even when I was a child, when most little boys want to be a fireman or a train driver."

I chuckle. "Were you happy… as a child, I mean?"

"Yes." He gives my thigh a gentle and reassuring squeeze. "I was very lucky."

"Why do you say that?"

"Because I know you weren't so fortunate."

"Oh… I wasn't unhappy. I had my brothers, and Pat and Mick."

"Who are Pat and Mick?"

"After my mother left us, my father employed them to look after us and the house."

"The one in Newport?"

"Yes. We all lived there. Mick took care of the house, and Pat took care of us… like a surrogate mother, I suppose. Although I don't know why I'm talking in the past tense. Pat and Mick still live there."

"And they still look after you?"

I glance over at him, and even in the darkness, I can see he's staring at me. "Sometimes."

"You don't mind living with your brothers?" he asks, after a moment's silence.

"I don't live with them."

"Not most of the time, obviously, but when you go back there…?"

"I don't live with them, even then. Not anymore. I've got my own apartment down there now. You'll see it all for yourself, next weekend, when I take you down there… although I'm not sure it'll be as exciting as this."

"I don't know. Meeting your family sounds exciting."

He doesn't seem nervous at all, which surprises me. In his shoes, I would be.

We cross the state border into Vermont, and I frown over at him. "How much further is this place, Mac?"

"Not far. You're heading for Wilmington, so if you see a sign, take it."

I keep my eyes open, concentrating on the road and the signs, and after a short while I spot one that says 'Wilmington'.

"Okay… where now?"

"We need to go through the town."

I do as he says and once we come out the other side, onto a wide road with trees on either side, I turn to him again. "Do I just keep going?"

"Yes. Just a little further." He's staring out the windshield, and after about five minutes, he says, "Turn left… just here."

I indicate and take the turn, noticing the sign that says 'Mountain View Cabins'.

"Cabins?" I say, frowning at him.

"Yeah…" He sounds doubtful for the first time since we left the studio as I drive us carefully down a narrow track until we come out into a clearing with a long log cabin on one side. There are several parking bays out front, and I pull up in one close to the double doors. "Wait here," Mac says. "I won't be a minute."

I do as he says, looking out the windshield as he runs up the steps, disappearing in through the doors. Once he's gone, I glance around. There's only one other car here, and I feel a little lonely, turning up the music for company. I keep my eyes fixed on the doors and am relieved when they open again within a few minutes, and Mac comes back out, with a big smile on his face, and rushes back to the car.

"It's freezing out there," he says, settling in beside me.

"It's November. It's Vermont. What did you expect?" I select reverse gear and glance across at him. "I just hope, wherever we're staying, it's got heating."

"Oh, it's got heating, don't worry."

I'm not sure what that means, but I follow his directions down an even narrower track than the one that led us here. There are trees on either side of us, although every so often a lantern marks a turning to one side or the other.

"Where am I going?"

"Right to the very end."

On and on we go, the tall shadowy trees our only companions, until we come to the very last lantern at the end of the track. I turn left, our route becoming narrower still, the trees hemming us in.

"Are you sure this is right?"

"Yeah… the guy told me not to worry. He said it would look like we were going nowhere and then…" He stops speaking and I hit the brakes as we come to a gap in the trees, which opens up to reveal a tiny cabin. It's lit by two lamps on the porch and has smoke billowing from the chimney. The drapes might be closed, but there's a soft glow peeping through them, and I turn to Mac, smiling.

"Is this ours?"

"For the weekend, yes. I wish it could be longer, but…"

"No, don't." I don't want him to say anything to burst the bubble. "Two days of peace and quiet, just you and me… it's perfect."

He twists in his seat, looking right at me. "Yes, it is."

Mac

This place is everything I could have hoped for… and more.

It's rustic, but romantic, and as I open the door and let us in, I can't help smiling, because it just gets better and better.

We've walked right in to a living area which has a large sofa, facing a wood-burning stove that's already alight. There's a small kitchen along the left-hand wall, with a table for two, on top of which is a bottle of red wine, a bowl of fruit and what appears to be a loaf of home-baked bread. I'm guessing this is the 'welcome pack' that was advertised on the website for this place, and I'm certainly not complaining, although I'll admit my eyes are drawn to the rear of the cabin. It's divided from the front half

by a deep red curtain that hangs from a central beam, and is filled with an enormous wrought iron bed, covered with a patchwork quilt.

Ella's sigh brings me out of my momentary dream, and I wonder if she might be disappointed by the size of this place, or its simplicity. I look down at her just as she turns and throws her arms around my neck.

"Thank you," she whispers.

"Is it okay? Sorry the kitchen's so small. I didn't realise…"

"I don't care about the kitchen." She looks up into my eyes, and I bend my head, kissing her.

"Neither do I, really." She smiles and I hold her close, her head against my chest. "I—I don't want to share you this weekend."

"Share me?" She leans back, looking up at me, her brow furrowed.

"Yeah. Call me selfish, but I want you all to myself… no interruptions."

"Who's going to interrupt us out here?"

"I don't know, but just to be on the safe side, I think we should both turn our phones off."

She smiles again. "This wouldn't have anything to do with you not wanting to be distracted by your book, would it? Because I honestly don't mind, Mac."

"It's got nothing to do with that. I've made my notes, and I don't need to look at them again… but the only distraction I want for the next two days is you. No calls, no texts, nothing to get in the way of us enjoying each other."

She doesn't say a word, but pulls her phone from her back pocket and turns it off, watching me while I do the same, and once we've both replaced them, we just stare at each other for a moment or two. I don't know what Ella's thinking, but I'm struggling to believe this is real.

"Shall we bring our things in from the car?" she says eventually, breaking the spell.

"Don't worry. I'll do it." She opens her mouth to object, but I kiss her. "Get comfortable. It won't take me long to unload the boot."

"Or even the trunk."

"That too."

She hands me her keys and I go outside, bringing back the groceries first, surprised to find that, although Ella's taken off her jacket, she's standing in the kitchen, rather than sitting on the couch… but then I remember, the kitchen is where she feels most comfortable.

I dump everything on the table, and go back out for our bags, locking her car and coming back in. Ella's unpacking the food, and I take our bags through to the rear of the cabin, leaving them beside the bed. As I turn on the bedside lamps, I notice a door in the far corner, which I guess must be the bathroom. The website advertised 'luxury wet rooms' in all its cabins, and I wander over, opening the door, and switch on the light. Once again, I'm not disappointed. The room is quite narrow, running along the back of the cabin, and although there may not be a bath, the shower area, which is at the far end, more than makes up for it. There's an enormous waterfall shower head, above a stone bench, which currently has two fluffy white towels sitting on top of it, alongside a basket of soaps.

My imagination is already working overtime on all the things we can do in here, but we've got two whole days ahead of us, and for now, I'd rather just be with Ella.

"This is why you didn't want to go to Newport, isn't it?" she says, as I come back into the living area, shrugging off my jacket and leaving it over the back of the couch.

"Yes." I smile as I wander over to her. "You don't mind, do you?"

"Mind? How could I possibly mind?" She looks around the cabin and then gazes back at me. "Would you like to open the wine?"

"Sure."

She's clearly been busy in my brief absence and I notice a small pan bubbling on the back of the stove as she hands me one of the bottles we brought with us, rather than the one on the table. I find a corkscrew and some glasses, while she puts a larger pan on the stove, adding some oil. "What are we having for dinner?"

"Steak with chive butter and warm potato salad."

My stomach rumbles at the thought, and I smile over at her. "Why do I feel like I just read that off of a menu?"

She grins. "Because I'm a chef?"

"I guess so." I pour the wine, moving around the table to hand her a glass, and clink mine against it, gazing into her eyes.

"How long have you been planning this?" she asks, looking up at me.

"About two weeks. Our schedules have been really punishing, and I thought we could do with a break."

"And you kept it a secret all that time?"

"Yes. Although you nearly threw a spanner in the works, when you suggested we should go down to Newport this weekend."

She chuckles. "I can see why that might have caused you a problem."

"I thought I was going to have to tell you my plans, but you seemed to like the idea of us spending some time alone... even if I was only suggesting we spend it at your place."

"I love the idea of being alone with you... wherever we are." She looks around the cabin, her eyes sparkling. "But this is really..."

"Really what?"

"It's really special, Mac."

I can't help smiling and she leans up, kissing me just briefly before she puts down her wine, returning to the stove and swirling the oil in the hot pan, adding two thick steaks.

"Can I help with anything?" I ask.

"You can make the dressing, if you want."

"Okay. If you tell me how."

She hands me a small bowl, along with bottles of red wine vinegar, olive oil and mustard. "You're going to need to use the same three-to-one method we used before… remember?"

"Sure… so, I need to count to three when pouring out the oil?"

"No, in this instance, I'll need you to count to six."

"Oh?"

"The potatoes will soak up the dressing, so we need more of it."

"Ahh… I see."

I do as she says, mixing everything together in the bowl, and then Ella hands me a bunch of fresh herbs. "You need to chop up about half of those."

I remember her doing this, although it's not an art I've really mastered. Even so, I give it a go, and when I'm done, I show Ella my efforts. She nods her head and tells me to add the herbs to the dressing mixture. "Then you can set the table, if you like."

"Okay."

I clear away all the mess we've made, and find a home for the bread and fruit, discovering the cutlery in a drawer and laying it out, just as Ella dishes up our dinner, bringing the plates over. It looks amazing, so beautifully arranged, and we sit facing each other.

"Thank you," she says, raising her glass.

"You already thanked me once." I clink my glass against hers again.

"I know, but once isn't enough… not for all this."

We both put down our glasses and I take her hand in mine, raising it to my lips and kissing her palm. She keeps her eyes fixed on mine, and although I'm tempted to tell her I'm in love with her, it can wait. We've got all weekend, after all…

The steak was so tender, it melted in the mouth and I have to admit, the dressing was superb, but once we've finished, I offer to clear away and wash up.

"That's the one downside, I'm afraid… there's no dishwasher."

Ella smiles up at me as I get to my feet.

"Let me help."

"Absolutely not. You go sit down."

She doesn't argue, but having driven up here and cooked a delicious dinner, she's entitled to be tired, and she takes her wine and wanders over to the couch, sitting down on it and putting her feet up. She watches while I clear the table and even when I turn my back to wash the dishes, I can feel her eyes on me.

Fortunately, it doesn't take too long, and I'm soon wiping down the work surfaces and drying my hands. When I turn around again, she's still staring at me and I smile across at her.

"Do you want to sit up for a while?"

She shakes her head, biting on her bottom lip, and I walk over to the front door, turning off the main lights. The firelight and the lamps beside the bed are now the only sources of illumination, and I stride back to Ella, taking her hand in mine and pulling her to her feet. I lead her to the rear of the cabin, drawing the curtain closed behind us, and then lean down and kiss her. She comes alive in an instant, her tongue finding mine in the most erotic of dances as she tugs on my shirt, fumbling with the buttons. I yank her sweater over her head, only breaking our kiss for the briefest

of moments, before our lips clash again, and I go to work on her jeans. I shrug off my shirt, throwing it to the floor, while she kicks off her shoes and I push down her jeans, letting her shimmy out of them. She's in her underwear now, and I walk her backwards, until she hits the bed, then lower her onto it, her head resting on the pillows as I stare down at her perfect body, making quick work of removing my jeans and boxers, my shoes and socks following swiftly behind. She shifts to the centre of the bed and I crawl up her body, pulling down the cups of her bra as I dip my head to lick and bite her hardened nipples.

"Please, Mac… please…"

"Please what?" I lean up and look into her eyes.

"I need you."

She's not alone, and I reach between us, tearing through the thin lace of her knickers as I push her legs wide apart, entering her. Hard.

"Fuck… that feels good." I rock my head back, savouring the moment. In some ways, it feels like the first time, all over again, although I'm not sure why, and I take her hands in mine. Perhaps it's being here. Maybe there's something truly magical about this place. Whatever the reason, I hold her hands beside her head as I lean over, kissing her, and she parts her legs a little wider.

"More," she whispers into my mouth. "Give me more, Mac."

I release her hands, kneeling back slightly, and I bend her legs up, holding them there, my hands behind her knees as I pound into her. She grabs the iron railings above her head, and although I want to tell her to rub her clit, she doesn't need the added stimulation. Her body is on fire and within a few minutes, she lets out an almighty scream, succumbing to pleasure. I'd love to keep going, but there's something about this… about the way she feels, the way she's gripping me so tight. She's thrashing beneath me and it's too much. I can't hold back. I howl out her

name as I thrust deep inside her and let go, giving her everything I've got. There's nothing I can do to stop it. It's like I'm losing my mind, my body following close behind, as shocks of pleasure jolt through me, my body spasming into hers, over and over.

Eventually, my orgasm subsides. My fingers and toes are still tingling and I can barely breathe, but I release her legs, lowering them to the bed, and in that movement, I realise something's very different…

"Oh, shit." I pull out of her, even though it's far too late, and she winces, frowning up at me. "I'm sorry, Ella. I'm so sorry."

Her face clears, and she tilts her head slightly. "It's okay," she says. "It didn't hurt that much."

"What didn't?" What's she talking about?

"You pulling out like that." She frowns again, like she doesn't understand.

"Oh… in that case, I'm sorry for that, too. That wasn't what I was apologising for, but I didn't mean to hurt you."

"I'm sure you didn't, but what were you apologising for? And come to that, why did you pull out like that in the first place?"

"Because I've just realised, I forgot to use a condom."

Her face pales, her eyes widening. "But… but…" She can't seem to string a sentence together, although I can't blame her for that. It's my fault.

I pull her into my arms and turn us onto our sides, facing each other. "It's okay, Ella."

She leans back, although I keep hold of her. There's no way I'm letting her go. "You can't know that," she says. "My period started about two weeks ago, so I don't think the timing could be any worse, could it?"

"Probably not, but it'll be okay."

"Stop saying that, will you?"

"No, I won't… because it's true. Whatever happens, it will be okay. I promise. I'm not going anywhere."

"Even if I'm pregnant?"

"Especially if you're pregnant."

She stares up into my eyes, frowning, and I wonder if that's because she doesn't believe me, or whether my words just came out wrong. Does she think my loyalty is limited by what's just happened, and its possible consequences? I wonder if I should make it clearer for her… explain it better. I open my mouth, but she gets there first.

"Promise you'll stick around, no matter what?"

I smile. It seems I was right. "I'll stick around, Ella. No matter what."

"Even if I'm not pregnant?"

My smile widens. "Even if you're not pregnant."

She leans up, planting a tentative kiss on my lips and as I tilt my head and let my tongue find hers, she pushes me onto my back, straddling me and rolling her hips as she settles onto my cock.

I hold her steady, stopping her from moving. "We're compounding my felony, aren't we?"

She smiles, leaning down over me. "That horse seems to have already left the stable, so is there any point in bolting the door?" She takes my hands from her thighs, holding them as she rocks back and forth. "God… Mac, it feels so much better like this."

I pull my hands from hers and lean up, undoing her bra and throwing it aside, then I tweak her nipples, making her squeal, as I raise my hips to hers. "Yeah… it does."

She stops moving and looks down at me, resting her hands on my chest. "H—Have you done this before?"

"Made love without a condom, you mean?"

"Yes."

"No, I haven't."

"So this is a first for you?" I can hear the excitement in her voice.

"It is."

Her eyes twinkle, her face lighting up, and she rides me… harder and harder. I move my hands down, holding her backside and match her rhythm, so I'm as deep inside her as I can be, when she clamps around me, throwing her head back as she cries out my name, and I lose myself… all over again.

Chapter Ten

Ella

I don't want to go home.

I love it here, and we've had the best time… but we can't stay.

It's not that we've got anything in particular to go back to Boston for, but Mac only booked the cabin until this morning, and that means we have to leave.

Given the choice, I think he'd want to stay on longer, too… but as we said last night, when we were lying in bed, we've got nothing much to do for the next couple of months, and we can enjoy ourselves just as much at home and in Newport as we have here… well, nearly.

It won't be quite the same.

Here, it's been a perfect oasis, away from everything, and I've enjoyed every single moment.

Mac loads my bag into the trunk of the car and looks up at me as I take in a lungful of fresh, mountain air before he comes over and climbs up the steps, standing in front of me.

"Thank you," I murmur, looking up into his eyes.

"I told you, you don't have to keep thanking me."

"Yes, I do."

He smiles and reaches out, cupping my face. "No regrets?" he says, his face quite serious now, and I know he's thinking about what happened on Friday night. Forgetting to use a condom might have been a mistake, but it's one we've repeated over and over, every time we've made love since then. I didn't want the barrier between us... and to be honest, I couldn't see the point. I liked feeling him, and I know he liked feeling me, too. He said so on several occasions.

"None at all."

He smiles. "Good."

We haven't talked about the consequences of our actions, but we will... when we get home.

Once we're back at my apartment, I'm going to tell him why I was okay with throwing caution to the winds. I'm going to tell him I'm in love with him. And then I'm going to ask him to move in with me.

I could have said all that while we were here, but I want to say the words when we're in the real world, not in this small corner of heaven he's created for us.

"I guess we'd better get going." He sounds as disappointed to be leaving as I am.

"I guess so," I say, looking up at him as he takes my hand and helps me down the steps. "Do you want to come back to my place?" For some reason, if I'm going to bare my soul to him, I'd rather do so on my own territory. I feel a little nervous... not just about telling him I'm in love with him, but about asking him to move in. I think if we're at his place and I suggest moving to mine, he might wonder about my motives. He might assume I don't think his place is good enough... which isn't the case at all.

"Sure." He smiles. "I'll just need to go home first and get some more clothes."

"Why? You can wash the ones you've got with you."

He shakes his head. "I'd rather take care of you than take care of laundry," he says.

"When you put it like that, I'll take you home first."

Mac's been quiet all the way back to Boston, but so have I, I guess.

I've been trying to work out exactly how to phrase my invitation to move in with me. Oddly enough, I'm fairly sure how I'm going to tell him I'm in love with him, but the rest of it isn't so easy.

"Do you want to come up with me?" he asks as I park the car outside his apartment, and I turn to look at him. He never normally asks me to go in with him, and I usually wait in the car whenever he has to get clothes or check his mail. He's looking a little doubtful, though, so I nod my head.

"Okay."

He smiles and we both climb out of the car. He grabs his bag from the trunk and takes my hand, leading me to his apartment building. We both look at each other and I stifle a laugh when we see the sign on the elevator doors, which reads 'Out of Order'.

"So much for confined spaces," he says, and I chuckle, following him to the stairwell and climbing up to the top floor with him.

His apartment feels warm and I undo my jacket while he glances at his mail, throwing it down on the couch before he turns and takes me in his arms, kissing me deeply. I hadn't expected that, and as I feel his hands on my waist, pulling me closer, I moan into his mouth, my body crushed to his.

"Go pack your things," I murmur, breaking the kiss and leaning back.

"Why? Are you impatient to leave?"

"Yes."

A smile twitches at his lips. "Is there a reason for that?"

"What do you think?"

His smile widens and although I don't tell him that my reason isn't entirely physical, he lets me go and picks up his bag, heading for the stairs and climbing up them to his bedroom.

"Do you think we should turn our phones back on?" I call up to him.

"Probably." I pull mine from my pocket, switching it on. "I suppose there's a chance we might have heard from the studio. Kennedy said we'd be getting emails, didn't she?"

"Yes."

I can hear the excitement in his voice, although I find it hard to raise as much enthusiasm myself. The thought of twenty weeks of recordings is still too ominous to contemplate.

My phone sparks into life. I've got no calls or text messages, which is a relief. It seems I haven't missed anything important, and I quickly go onto my email app, just to check if I've heard anything from the studio. I haven't, and I'm just closing the app again, when I hear Mac's phone beep, and then beep again, and again, over and over.

"What the hell?" he says and I look up. He's at the top of the stairs, his packing clearly abandoned as he stares down at his phone, which is still beeping away.

"Someone obviously wanted to get hold of you."

"Yeah... Delilah. She's tried calling me twenty-three times since yesterday morning... and she's left fourteen messages."

Fourteen? I feel a shudder of fear creep up my spine.

"Who's Delilah?"

He comes down the stairs and walks straight over to me.

"She's my agent."

I sigh out my relief and he smiles, although his face clouds again as he looks back at his phone.

"What does she want?" I ask.

"I don't know."

"Maybe she's found someone who wants to publish your book."

He shakes his head. "I doubt it. She's not even looking… and besides, I've got a re-write to do now."

His phone seems to have stopped beeping. "Have you heard anything from the studio?" I ask, and he shrugs.

"God knows."

"I haven't. I checked my mail."

"In that case, I doubt I will have done. But it's early days. Kennedy only told us about the new season on Friday."

"Yeah… I guess." He looks down at his phone. "Are you going to listen to your messages?" I ask.

"No. I'm going to call Delilah. It'll be quicker."

"Would you like me to go wait in the car?"

He frowns. "No, of course not." He presses on the screen a few times and holds it out in front of him, making it clear he's taking the call on speaker. I'm surprised by that, but then I realize he's doing it because he wants to reassure me, and I move closer, nestling against him. He puts his arm around me just as the call connects.

"Blake? Where the hell are you?"

I notice her harsh New York accent, and that she doesn't get to call him Mac, which makes me smile.

"I'm at home. Why?"

"Where have you been all weekend?"

"In Vermont… and again… why?"

"Have you looked at the Internet in the last twenty-four hours?"

"For Christ's sake, Delilah…" He lets me go and steps away. "I think it's fairly bloody obvious I've had my phone switched off,

so will you stop asking me questions and tell me why you've been trying to get hold of me?"

"Because your name is all over the goddamn web... and in the tabloids."

"It is?"

"Yes."

"But that's good, isn't it? Kennedy told us the show was..."

"It's not good." She interrupts him. "It's bad... very bad."

I feel an icy chill creep over my skin and I look up at his face. He frowns, his eyes darkening. "What's it about?" he asks, his voice much quieter.

I hear Delilah sigh. "Someone's gotten hold of the fact that you're not who you claim to be. The headlines are that Blain — the supposed Meal Master — is a fraud, who can't even cook. The articles go into great detail about how you're... and I quote... 'nothing more than a second-rate actor, and would-be author'."

I see the pain on Mac's face, and reach out to him, although he pulls away, wandering over to the window. "Who'd do this to me?"

"I don't know," Delilah says. "The quotes are from someone close to the show, but there are no names attributed to them. Either way, you're through. Kennedy Black has made a statement this morning that the studio was tricked into hiring you. She hasn't mentioned my name, but she's implying that I was involved in the fraud you're being accused of."

"There is no fraud, Delilah," Mac says, pushing his fingers back through his hair. "I told Kennedy I couldn't cook. Hell... she was the one who hired me, after she'd seen me in that show."

"I know. It's also Kennedy who's fired you. Very publicly."

"She's fired me?"

Mac's as surprised as I am.

"Yes. I haven't heard anything from her personally, but she's given a statement to the press, saying that the studio have

terminated your contract and are considering legal action against you."

Mac staggers back slightly.

"Legal action?"

"Yeah. I'm not sure what they can do… if anything. She probably just said that because it sounds good."

"You think? It doesn't sound great to me. It also doesn't make sense. She came into the studio on Friday and told us the show had been recommissioned for a second series."

I walk over, standing beside him, and gasp at the worry etched on his face. "I know. The statement said they're bringing the show back in the new year, but with a different presenter."

"It did?" he says.

"Yeah. Someone called Ella is evidently lined up to take over from you, which I guess means they'll also be renaming the show… it can hardly be called Meal Master anymore, can it?"

Mac's staring at me, and I struggle to breathe, shaking my head.

"No… no, it can't," he mumbles.

"This all feels too well orchestrated to be a spur-of-the-moment thing," Delilah says. "If you ask me, someone planned it. Have you made any enemies at the studio? Anyone who'd want to ruin you?"

"Of course not."

I hear a rustle of papers on the end of the phone. "Your career is toast, Blake. My reputation won't be faring much better once word gets out that I'm your agent, so if we're gonna try to salvage something for either of us, we need to work out who's behind this. That way, we can discredit them. Let's think about it logically. Did everyone there know you couldn't cook?"

"Yes. The entire crew knew. It was obvious from the moment I stepped into the rehearsal studio."

"Right… in that case, who knew you were writing a novel? Had you told anyone?"

"Kennedy knew. I told her at my interview, and…" He stops talking and turns, looking down at me, his face like thunder. "I'll call you back Delilah."

He hangs up, even as she's shouting his name.

"What's wrong?" I ask, staring up into his face, but barely recognizing him as the man I love.

"You tell me." Even his voice seems strange and I step back. He moves forward, towering over me. "Tell you what?"

"Why you'd do this to me?"

"I haven't done anything, Mac."

"Really?"

"Yes, really."

"Only you and Kennedy knew about my book, so there's no point in denying you're the one behind this. All I want to know is why."

"How can I tell you that when I didn't do it?"

He takes a breath, looking up at the ceiling for a moment, and then lowers his eyes to me again, frowning slightly. "Okay. I'm not angry, I…"

"Yes, you are. You're furious."

"I just want to understand, Ella. I need to know why."

"I'd kinda like to know that myself." His frown deepens, like he doesn't understand. "I'd like to know why you're so quick to believe I'm the person responsible for all this."

"Because it's the only thing that makes any sense."

"Is it?"

"Yes. Think about it. No-one other than you and Kennedy knew about my novel, but unlike you, Kennedy had nothing to gain from selling a story like this to the press. Why would she sabotage her own show, for Christ's sake?"

"I don't know, but in case you've forgotten, I'm a multi-millionaire. Why would I need to sell you out for a few thousand dollars?"

"Is that the going rate for betrayal these days?" he says, his eyes darkening.

I stare up at him, shaking my head. "I didn't betray you."

"And yet, you're the one who comes out on top. You get your own show, with nothing to stand in the way of you becoming the next celebrity chef… and my career is over."

"I don't want the damn show, any more than I want to be a celebrity chef. That's never been my ambition."

"Then why did you do it?"

I don't know the man standing before me, and as he shakes his head at me, I realize I don't want to… not if this is what he thinks of me.

"I didn't. But you've clearly made up your mind about me, and you're not gonna listen to a word I have to say, are you?" I choke back my tears and although he steps forward, I move away, toward the door. "I thought I meant something to you, Mac, but I guess I got that wrong."

"Ella? What are you doing?" he asks, fear rather than anger lacing his voice now.

"What does it look like?"

"It looks like you're walking out on me."

"Well done. You might have been wrong about everything else, but you got that right."

He shakes his head, following me, as I get nearer the door. "No. No… don't do this."

"You seriously expect me to stay when you refuse to listen… to believe in me?"

"Okay… I'm sorry." He holds up his hands, palms out, like he's surrendering. "Let's sit down and talk."

"It's too late for talking."

"Ella… please."

"I—I thought I'd found the right man. But I was wrong about that, too, wasn't I?"

"No. I am the right man."

"Not for me. Not anymore."

I get to the door, yanking it open, and he stops. "Please, don't do this. Don't leave me."

"What choice do I have when you don't trust me?" A sob escapes my lips, tears falling onto my cheeks. "Damn you, Blake MacKenzie."

I run down the stairs.

Despite everything he's just said, he doesn't call after me, and I don't look back.

But I guess that's what happens when you both know it's over.

Mac

I stand outside the terminal building, looking up at the grey sky and wonder if I've done the right thing.

Should I turn around and go back?

What would I say to her if I did?

Would she even talk to me?

Do I want to talk to her?

I shake my head and pull my phone from my back pocket, turning it on and going to my contacts list. It only takes me a moment to scroll, although I pause at Ella's name, sucking in a

sharp breath before I move on to Henry's, connecting the call. I have no choice. I've got no-one else to turn to.

"Mac? How are you?" he says, sounding as cheerful as ever. "And why are you calling me in the middle of the night?"

"I'm not."

"Yes, you are. It must be four-thirty in the morning over there."

"I'm not over there, Henry. I'm here… at Heathrow."

There's just a moment's silence. "You're here?"

"Yes. I've come home."

"For a visit?"

"No, for good."

Another silence…

"Do you need somewhere to stay?"

I smile, even though it's an effort. I knew I could rely on Henry. "Would that be okay?"

"Of course," he says. "You know my basement flat is always yours whenever you need it. You jump in a taxi, and I'll make up the bed and put the kettle on."

I smile again, which feels like a miracle. "Thanks, Henry."

It's easy to find a taxi at Heathrow and the cabbie takes just over an hour to drive me into Clapham. Fortunately, he's not in a very talkative mood, which suits me just fine, and as he drops me outside Henry's four-storey town house, I look up and see my father's oldest friend, standing by the front door, waiting for me. I know I'm going to be staying in the basement, but after I've paid the taxi driver, I lug my cases up the steps and Henry greets me with a welcome hug.

"Come in out of the cold," he says, smiling up at me.

He moves aside and I follow him into the house, down the hall and into the kitchen, which overlooks the back garden. Considering the age of the property, the kitchen is very modern,

with dark grey units and stainless steel appliances, and I wonder what Ella would make of it… and how long it's going to be before she stops being the first thought that comes into my mind.

We sit at the table and Henry pours the tea from a bright yellow teapot, looking across at me in his usual, avuncular manner, his brown eyes sparkling behind his rimless glasses. Henry is a confirmed bachelor, in his early sixties, with steel grey hair, and a lean figure. He's the owner of a popular art gallery in Denmark Street, which is how he met my father… so many years ago.

He's also the kindest man I've ever met.

"So, you're back," he says, stating the obvious.

"Yes."

He frowns. "The last time you called, you said the show was going well."

"It was."

"Then what happened?"

I pick up my cup of tea, taking a sip. It tastes good, but then I haven't drunk tea in ages. Ella didn't like it, and because we were never apart, I got used to drinking coffee. I got used to a lot of things when I was with her… like being happy.

"I fell in love," I say and he nods his head.

"With someone who lives here? Is that why you've come home?"

"No. She's American. She lives in Boston… and in Newport."

"She's got two homes?" He raises his eyebrows.

"Yes. She's a multi-millionaire."

He leans back in his chair, staring at me for a full twenty seconds. "I don't understand. It seems like you had everything going for you. Love… success… happiness."

"I know. It sounds ideal, doesn't it? Until you add betrayal into the mix."

His shoulders drop. "She cheated on you?"

"No. Not in the way you mean."

"What did she do then?" he asks.

"She went to the press and told them I was a fraud. She told them I couldn't cook, that I was a second-rate actor, and would-be author."

"That's harsh."

"Which part?" I ask, and he smiles.

"All of it. But especially the would-be author thing."

"I know. But it's also how I know it was Ella who betrayed me. She's the only one, apart from the show's producer, who knew about my book. And there's no way the producer would have done this…"

"Of course she wouldn't," he says, frowning. "The show was a success. She'd be stupid to jeopardise that."

"Exactly. That's what I said." It's such a relief to have my suspicions confirmed. I've spent every minute of every hour since Ella left me, wondering if I made a mistake… even though I know I didn't.

"So, you broke up with her?" he says, sipping his tea.

"No. She broke up with me."

He shakes his head. "She did?"

"Yes. She denied talking to the press, even though the producers had announced they were going to keep the show going… with Ella taking over my role."

"In which case…"

"I know." I hold up my hand and stare down at my cup for a moment before looking back at him. "She denied it, Henry. All of it. And then she made it clear we were over, and… she left."

Memories flit through my mind… the tears on her cheeks, her calling me 'Blake', like she hated me… the sound of her footsteps on the stairs. I didn't want her to go. I wanted her to stay and talk;

to work things out… somehow. But my feet wouldn't move, and I guess that was when I realised… love isn't always enough.

"What are you going to do now?" Henry's voice brings me back to the here and now.

"I don't know. I'll have to do something, though. My bank balance took a hit, what with having to pay a month's rent in lieu of notice on my apartment… and booking a last-minute flight during Thanksgiving week."

"Hmm… the timing could have been better."

"I know. But I couldn't hang around over there any longer."

Once Ella had gone, I sat in my apartment for a while, just staring into space, until my phone rang. It was Delilah, and I knew I'd have to take the call. She wanted to know what had happened, so I explained, telling her everything.

"Forget about gunning for her," I said firmly as I finished my story.

"Your career's over." It sounded like she was still thinking of trying something.

"I don't care about my career," I yelled down the phone at her.

"Okay… okay." She paused for a second. "What are you gonna do now?"

"Go home." I hadn't even thought about it, but the idea flashed into my head, and it made perfect sense.

"To England?"

"Yes. There's nothing left for me here."

"She really got to you, didn't she?"

"Yes, she did."

"Well… stay in touch."

Her words held so little conviction, and she didn't even try to persuade me to stay, so I wondered if she was glad to see the back of me. My departure meant she could wash her hands of me…

publicly, at least. She could distance herself from any negative publicity surrounding the show and my role in it, and get on with representing more profitable clients.

Once the decision was made, it only took me a couple of days to organise everything, and even though I know I could have taken more time, or waited to see if something else came up over there, I didn't want to.

The adventure was over…

"Do you want to come and see the flat?" Henry says, and I look up to see he's smiling at me.

"Okay, but before I do, and while we're speaking of what I'm going to do and my lack of funds, I should probably warn you, I won't be able to pay you very much rent for the time being."

He leans across the table, his hand on my arm. "You don't have to pay me any rent at all. And you can stay here for as long as you want. You know that."

"Thank you, Henry."

He gets up. "Come on, then…"

I follow him to the front of the house, where I left my cases, and carry them outside and down to the basement. Henry pauses by the door, the key in his hand.

"I've had the whole place redecorated," he says, opening the door, and handing the key to me as we cross the threshold. "I hope it doesn't smell of paint."

I can't detect any smell at all, and follow him inside, closing the door behind me.

The hallway is narrow and quite dark, but Henry flicks on a light, revealing white walls and a pale grey carpet.

"The bathroom's just here." He opens the sliding door to our left, and I glance inside, looking at the smallest bathroom in the world… although there's no bath, just a shower, a tiny corner basin and a toilet. "And the bedroom is opposite." We turn and

he stands aside, pushing open the door. I go inside, looking around. The room has a small sash window, a double bed, which has been made up with white bedding, and two bedside tables. There's a built-in wardrobe, which takes up the whole of the wall to my left. It's got mirrored doors, which make the room seem bigger and lighter, and I nod my head as I dump my cases at the end of the bed.

"This is lovely," I say, turning back to him.

He smiles and I follow him out into the hall, and along to the kitchen, which is at the rear of the house. It's a galley style, with white units down one side, broken up by a built-in electric cooker and hob, and a washing machine at the end, underneath the draining board. The fridge/freezer is behind the door and on the right-hand wall is another sliding door which, this time, leads to the living room.

In here, against one wall, there's a large dark grey leather sofa, and against another, there's a small dining table with two chairs. The other two walls feature a fireplace, and a set of doors which lead out into a tiny courtyard. There are wrought-iron railings separating it from Henry's garden above, but at least it's an outside space… not that it's warm enough to sit out there at the moment.

"Is it okay?" Henry asks, and I turn to face him.

"It's perfect."

"You make yourself at home," Henry says. "And come up for dinner later on."

"Okay… thanks."

It's a relief not to have to think about food, or cooking… although thinking about Ella isn't optional. She's in my head every second of the day.

*

She's been there ever since, no matter how hard I've tried to distract myself.

On Friday, it'll be two weeks since I took her to the cabin in Vermont.

That means, on Monday, it'll be two weeks since Ella walked out of my apartment, and my life.

Not that I'm counting the days, of course.

I'm counting the hours… and the minutes.

I've relived that final scene in my head, over and over, wondering if I could have played it differently.

Except it wasn't a scene, and I wasn't playing.

And how else was I supposed to react? She'd ruined my career; she'd betrayed me and she was standing in front of me refusing to admit to any of it. As far as I was aware, we'd never lied to each other, but there she was, lying to my face.

How could I not be angry?

Okay, so I might not have been completely honest with Ella about my reasons for taking her to the cabin, but at least my intentions had been honourable. I wasn't lying when I said I wanted to get away from everything for a few days, but what I didn't explain was that I also wanted to take her somewhere quiet, so I could tell her I was in love with her. Of course, I hadn't anticipated that I'd get carried away with the atmosphere of the place, and forget to use a condom… but that and its consequences made saying those three little words absolutely impossible. She'd have doubted my motives and probably assumed I was only saying them because of what had just happened. I didn't want that. I didn't want her to doubt me.

So, I kept quiet, and looking back, I think that was a mistake.

I should have found a way to tell her, although how and when, I don't know.

The opportunity never really arose. We both got a little carried away with the situation... with where we'd found ourselves. Ella made it clear she didn't want to use a condom again, and neither did I. We both knew there were consequences to what we were doing, but we didn't talk about them, either... which was a definite mistake.

We should have discussed what we were doing, but we didn't. I reasoned to myself that we could talk it through when we got back to Boston... back to the real world. I told myself that when we got home, I'd explain to her how I felt, and suggest we move in together. It made sense, considering where we'd taken our relationship.

I mulled it over on the journey back from Vermont, trying to work out how to phrase my suggestion. After all, I was being kind of presumptuous. I was going to suggest that I move into her place, rather than the other way around, but I wasn't sure how to do that without it sounding like I was freeloading. I could hardly offer to pay rent, and any contribution I made towards our living expenses was always going to be a drop in the ocean as far as her wealth was concerned.

I still hadn't worked out what I was going to say by the time Ella parked her car outside my apartment... but in the end, it didn't matter.

She left me, regardless.

I suck in a breath.

Two weeks...

I know what that means.

It means, if there are any consequences to what happened in Vermont, she'll find out about them any day now. I've wondered whether to call her, but how can I? It'll seem like I'm only interested in the baby... assuming there is one. She doubted me at the time, and because of that, I have to wait.

I have to trust her.

That's not easy, when I know she's already betrayed me once, but if she's pregnant, she'll call. She'll tell me. I know she will. She wouldn't keep something like that from me. Ella couldn't do that.

Of course, if there is a baby, we'll have to work out what we're going to do about it. I told her I'd stick around, no matter what, and I haven't done that. I've flown three thousand miles, just to get away from the memory of her.

Not that it's helping.

She's everywhere. Even here, she's in everything I do, and say, and think.

But if she calls, I'll go back, in the blink of an eye. Not for the baby, but for her. It won't be easy – for either of us – but if I get the chance to try again, I'll take it, and I'll make it work. I'll make my love enough for her… for both of us.

For all three of us, I guess.

I think about that for a moment… about becoming a father… about having a child with Ella, and I feel a warm glow in my chest.

I tap on my phone, going to my contacts and finding her name. My finger hovers over the 'phone' symbol, but I can't do it, and I sit back, staring at the screen.

"Call me… please." My voice cracks and I turn, staring out into the courtyard, the view blurring as my eyes sting with unshed tears.

I don't just want her to phone because she's pregnant. I want her to phone because she needs me, and misses me, and loves me, like I love her.

If only…

It took me a while – and a cup of coffee – before I could focus on my laptop again, but when I did, I knuckled down and got on with re-writing my book.

I've been working on it every day since I got back, having discovered that there were, in fact, a few female doctors in the nineteen-twenties. I was relieved by that because it made it viable to change my central character from a man to a woman. At least I didn't have to change course yet again, and although it's taken a lot of work, as the grey daylight turns to dusk and then to darkness, my screen providing the only light in the room, I finally get to the end.

I liked my version, with Jonathan Hawkes, the male surgeon and part-time sleuth, but this new one is so much better. It now features Evelyn Harper, who prefers to be called Evie. She's very much a bright young thing, whose older brother was killed in the Great War, spurring her to follow in his footsteps and study medicine at university, defying tradition, and her father's wishes. I've moved the setting to the home counties and created both back and side stories to defy description, including a tentative love interest for Evie, in the form of the detective inspector who eventually arrives at the country house, just in time to arrest the villain. I wasn't in the mood for taking that too far, and because of the nature of the story, I didn't have to.

The good thing is, I think I might be able to write a sequel, pairing Evie and her detective inspector in another murder investigation. I've even got a few ideas for where to set it.

And it's all thanks to Ella...

I stand, stretching my arms above my head, and take a deep breath.

The question is, what to do with my novel now?

I could self-publish it, but I'm not sure I've got the know-how for that.

I could try to find another agent, although that's a notoriously long and laborious process, as I know from bitter experience.

Or I could swallow my pride and send it to Delilah.

I sit down again, clenching my fists a few times to relieve some of the stiffness from all the typing I've been doing, and then I go to my mail app…

'Hi Delilah,

I hope you're keeping well.

I'm not sure if you're still willing to represent me, but on the off-chance that you are, I'm attaching a revised version of my manuscript.

I've re-written it, in the hope it's now more to your liking.

Let me know what you think.

Best wishes,

Blake'

I re-read it, hoping it doesn't sound too obsequious, and then attach the file, and press 'send' before I can change my mind.

I didn't bother to explain to Delilah the ways in which I've changed my novel. I'm sure she'll work it out for herself soon enough.

I get up to fetch myself another coffee, just as my laptop pings and I sit down, surprised to see I've received a reply from Delilah… already.

'Blake,

It's good to hear from you. You had me worried when you bolted back to England, but I'm glad you've been busy.

I'll find the time to read through your manuscript in the next few weeks, but if you've made enough improvements, I've got someone in mind who I can send it to.

I think it's only fair to warn you, they're probably going to ask if it can be turned into a series. Standalone books are harder to pitch and sell, so is that feasible?

Let me know.

Best,

Delilah'

She didn't seem that worried when I told her I was coming home, so I wonder if she just feels sorry for me now, after

everything that happened. That said, I'm not sure pity is one of Delilah's strongest traits, and I fire off a quick reply, telling her I've got a few ideas for a second novel.

Now isn't the time to outline them to her, but as I wander into the kitchen, I let them percolate around my brain...

I like the idea of a limited number of suspects being involved. It keeps things simpler, and I'm contemplating setting the second story in a theatre. It's something I know a little about, and I rather like the idea of creating a strong female lead, and then having her killed off. I'd base her on Kennedy Black, I think, with Evie Harper in the audience and, therefore, on hand to interfere in the official investigation, which can be run by her love interest... the police inspector.

It's all coming together nicely in my head, and I grab a cup from the cupboard, wondering whether to have Kennedy whacked over the head with a piece of scenery, or stabbed with a prop dagger that turns out to be real. Either would do...

Chapter Eleven

Ella

I look up, startled by the sound of a car pulling up outside the house. I don't know why I'm surprised. It's Friday, after all… and that means Hunter and Livia will be here for the weekend.

Fortunately, they didn't come back last weekend. It might have been Thanksgiving, but Hunter called to say they were going to visit Livia's parents, and would that be okay?

"Of course it will." I struggled with my tears. Not because he wasn't coming home, but because I'd done nothing but cry for days.

"I know we said we'd meet your boyfriend, but we can do that next weekend, can't we?" I didn't reply, unable to say a word. "Are you okay, Ella?"

"Yeah, I'm fine. I'm just tired." That wasn't a lie. I was exhausted… and hurt, and confused.

"We'll be down next weekend, so we'll catch up then. Okay?"

"Sure."

Drew called the following day to let me know he'd been sent on an assignment to West Virginia.

That meant I was alone. And I wasn't sorry about that.

If they'd come home, they'd have found me in tears, just like I was when I got back here, after running out on Mac. I may have called him 'Blake' when I left him, but he'll always be 'Mac' as far as I'm concerned… even if we're not friends anymore.

I didn't even consider going back to my apartment, but just drove straight home, knowing I'd got some clothes here, plus the ones in the trunk of my car that I'd taken to Vermont with me.

"I'll manage," I muttered to myself, as I wiped away my tears and tried to focus on the road. I needed to be somewhere I could feel safe, and preferably with as few reminders of Mac as possible.

Pat was surprised to see me, but didn't comment on my red-rimmed, puffy eyes. She didn't ask any question at all… not even when I refused to join in Thanksgiving with her and Mick. I'm grateful for that, and I've buried myself in my apartment, ignoring the phone calls Kennedy made every day last week, and the text messages she's been sending twice a day since.

I've been ignoring everyone else, too… until now.

My apartment might be separate from the rest of the house, but I can easily imagine Pat and Hunter talking… and Pat telling my big brother about my sudden, tearful arrival. I know it won't be long before he knocks on my door, but even then I jump out of my skin when I hear the sharp tapping sound.

There's no point in trying to ignore him; he knows I'm in here. Pat will have told him I haven't moved from my apartment since I arrived.

I get up and wander to the door, opening it.

He stares down at me, his head tipped to one side, his eyes filled with pity.

"Where's Livia?" I ask, knowing I'll cry the moment he says anything.

"She's in the kitchen with Pat." He steps into the room, not giving me any choice in the matter, and closes the door behind

him, before he turns around to face me again. "Why didn't you tell me you were here? When I spoke to you before Thanksgiving, I assumed you were still in Boston with your boyfriend. I had…"

I burst into tears, much as I expected, and Hunter reaches out and pulls me into his arms.

"Hey, Sis… it's okay."

I shake my head, even though he's holding it against his chest. It isn't okay. Why can't he see that?

He holds me, letting me cry for a while, until eventually the tears subside. I think I'm running dry. For the first few days, I cried and cried and cried, but now ten minutes is about the most I can manage at a time. It's like I'm on a ration of tears, and that's my limit.

I pull back slightly and Hunter lets me go. "Is this something to do with Blain?"

"Yes, but that's not his real name. That's just the name they gave him for the show. His real name is Mac, or Blake." He stares at me, confused. "It's Blake Mackenzie, but everyone calls him Mac."

"I see," he says. "And did you break up?"

I nod my head, swallowing down the lump in my throat. "H—He accused me of betraying him."

Hunter frowns, his eyes darkening. "He accused you of cheating?"

"No. This was about work, not about… us."

It seems odd saying 'us' when there isn't one anymore.

"How did he think you'd betrayed him at work?"

"Someone at the studio told the press he can't cook."

His frown deepens. "He can't cook?"

"No."

"Then why is he presenting a cookery show?"

"The studio argued he didn't need to be able to cook… just to present. I was there to handle the cookery side of things, and to show him what to do and how to do it."

"Well… you did a good job. I'd never have guessed the guy couldn't cook."

"That was the plan. It made things really complicated to start off with, but we worked it out, and according to the producer, the ratings were going well. They were going so well, the network had commissioned a second season."

"In which case, why would someone at the studio tell the press that the star of their show was a fraud?"

I suck in a breath. "I don't know. Whoever it was knew that Mac had written a book, and according to him, the only two people he'd told were the producer and me. He couldn't think of a reason for the producer to shoot herself in the foot, and to be honest, neither can I…"

"So he accused you?"

"Yes. It probably didn't help that, according to Mac's agent, the studio were claiming they'd been duped by him, and that I was going to take over his role."

"You are?" He's as shocked as I was by that.

"No, of course I'm not. You know as well as I do that I could never appear in front of the cameras."

He shakes his head. "So, that part is a lie?" he says, frowning.

I shrug my shoulders. "I'm not sure. The producer has been either calling me or texting me every day since I got back here. I'm guessing she wants to discuss the situation."

"But you haven't taken her calls?"

"No. I'm not ready to talk to her yet, but when I do, I'm going to tell her I'm leaving the show. Not that I really need to. I had a contract for the first season, and that's ended now. They haven't sent me a new one for the second season, so I in reality, I can just ignore them."

"I think it's best if you make it official and tell her, even if you just send her an email."

He's probably right. "I—I know. I just need to get some strength back first. Kennedy's a tough woman to deal with."

"Do you want me to handle it for you?" he asks, and while I'm tempted to say yes, I shake my head.

"It's okay. I'll email her. I should have done it before now. She's been asking me to call, so I assumed I'd have to speak with her, but you're right, I can just send her a message, and keep it remote, can't I?"

"Yes, you can."

"Does Mac know you're leaving the show?" Hunter asks.

"No. We didn't get as far as discussing that. He'd already decided I was the guilty party. There didn't seem any point in talking things through."

"So you left him?"

"Yes."

"Just like that?"

"He tried to get me to stay. In fact…" I let my voice fade, remembering Mac's words.

"In fact, what?"

"He begged me not to leave him." The pained expression on Hunter's face makes my chest hurt. "What else could I do? He didn't trust me, Hunter."

He reaches out and puts his hand on my shoulder. "It's okay."

"No, it's not. We'd only just got back from Vermont. He'd taken us to a beautiful cabin up there, and we'd had the most perfect weekend. I was going to tell him I was in love with him. I was going to ask him to move in with me… and then we got back to Boston and it all…" My voice cracks and even though I thought I'd run the well dry, my tears fall again.

Hunter steps closer, putting his arms around me, and I sob against him.

My body aches. From the top of my head to the tips of my toes, I'm just a mass of pain, and I struggle against it, my fists clenched against Hunter's chest.

"Why? Why did he do this?"

He sucks in a breath. "Can I say something?"

I lean back, despite my tears, and look up at him. "What?"

"I remember, when I screwed up by jumping to conclusions about Livia, my little sister was the one telling me not to give up."

"I know, but I'm not the one who screwed up, am I? I didn't jump to conclusions. He did. That's why I left him. I've never… I've never…"

"You've never what? Never been in love before?"

"No, I haven't. But that's not what I'm trying to say." I look at his chest, at the button on his shirt. "H—He was my first." Hunter doesn't reply and after a few seconds, I raise my head to find him staring down at me, confusion written all over his face. "Is that a surprise?"

"Would you hate me if I said 'yes'?"

"No. I've always known how you and Drew lived your lives, and I guess you just assumed the same about me."

"Not exactly the same, no," he says, smiling, although I can't return the gesture.

"I—I was waiting for the right man, and I thought I'd found him. Mac said I had, but…"

He pulls me into a hug again. "Do you wanna come eat with us?" he says after a while, leaning back and looking down at me.

"No, thanks. I'm exhausted. I'm gonna go to bed."

He frowns, narrowing his eyes. "You've gotta eat something, Ella."

"I will, don't worry."

I'm not sure he's convinced, but he doesn't argue with me, and he leans forward, kissing my forehead. "I'll let you get some rest, but promise me you'll fix yourself something to eat?"

I nod my head and he smiles… but once he's gone, closing the door behind him, I switch off the lights and climb the stairs to my bedroom.

Inside, I undress, leaving my phone on the nightstand, and get into bed. Then I pull up the covers and wrap myself up in them, letting sleep claim me.

I've been awake since just after dawn. I didn't close the drapes last night, so I watched the sun rise through the picture window, staring out across the harbor, and trying not to cry. It'll be cold outside, but the sky is a perfect clear blue, and I wonder about maybe going for a walk later. I haven't stepped outside since I got back here, and I need to get some fresh air… and to reassure Hunter that I'm okay, even if I'm not.

My phone beeps. I know who it'll be. It's eight-thirty, and even though it's Saturday, it's time for Kennedy's first message of the day. I turn over, clutching up my phone and flip it around so I can read what she's got to say for herself.

— ***Ella, I'm sure you're aware of the situation here. We need to discuss your contract as soon as possible. Can you call me? Look forward to hearing from you. KB***

I don't know why I bother reading her messages anymore. They're all the same. She probably just copies and pastes them.

I'm not about to reply. I don't want to get into a long, drawn-out conversation with her, or give her a reason to call me… but I could send that email Hunter and I were talking about.

At least, I could, once I've been to the bathroom…

Leaping out of bed, I rush to my adjoining bathroom, wishing now that I'd eaten something last night. I feel a little lightheaded and I don't hang around. I'm just drying my hands when my phone rings, and I let out a curse. Does this mean Kennedy's going to start calling *and* texting? You would have thought my

silence alone would have made the message clear... at least, it would to most people. Just not to Kennedy, evidently.

I saunter back to my bed, where I left my phone, face-up on the mattress, and suck in a breath when I see the word 'Mac' on the screen.

My legs feel like they're going to give way beneath me, and I take the last two steps, collapsing onto the mattress and staring down at my phone. I reach out to pick it up, but pull my hand away.

Why is he phoning? He's had long enough to think up an apology, if that's what this is all about. Unless it's something else...

I guess there's only one way to find out, and I reach out again, my hand shaking, just as the ringing stops.

Why didn't I answer sooner?

For a split second, I wonder about calling him back, to ask what he wants... but I can't. I can't forget the way he looked at me when he accused me of betraying him.

My phone beeps, making me jump, and I glance at the screen again. He's left a message? Oh... God. Do I want to listen to it? Am I strong enough to hear his voice?

I guess I have to be, if I want to know why he called.

I pick up my phone, barely able to breathe.

'Hi, Ella. It's me. I... um... I don't know what to say. I've been trying to talk myself out of calling you, but... well, it's been two weeks since Vermont, and... and I guess what I'm trying to say is, if you need to talk, you only have to call. Things may not have ended well between us, but I'm here if you need me. Okay?'

His voice is quiet, and it cracks a little. My heart aches as I wait, wondering if he's going to say anything else... but then the automated voice asks if I want to save the message. I decide against it. Hearing his voice over again won't help... especially

when it brought back so many memories. How could I forget the way he used to whisper to me when we made love, or the way he'd implore me to come… just for him? But how can I forgive him for his false accusations… for his unfounded anger?

I throw my phone down on the bed.

Why did he call? And why does he think I'd need him? No woman needs a man who won't trust her.

We're over. Like he said, it ended badly.

The last thing I needed was for him to remind me it was two weeks since we were in Vermont? I know how long ago it was. I'm not likely to forget that it was two weeks ago today that we woke up in our perfect cabin, gazing into each other's eyes, knowing that what we'd done the night before had changed everything… knowing that making love without a condom…

"Oh… shit!"

I leap to my feet.

That's what he meant. That's why he made a point of saying it had been two weeks ago…

But why didn't I think about it?

I snatch up my phone again, going to my calendar to count back the days, trying to remember when my period started. It was the week when the show was all about brunches, and it was on the Thursday night, because we'd been recording all day. I remember, after I'd told Mac about my period starting, and he'd ordered in a pizza for us, I was grateful that at least the Friday would be easier for me…

"Twenty-eight, twenty-nine… oh, God… thirty."

I'm late.

Mac

She's not going to call.

That much is obvious.

It's been fifteen days since I finally broke and phoned her. I'm still counting them. I might have tried to convince myself that Ella would call if she needed me, but then as I paced around the flat on that Saturday morning, I reasoned, she might still think I was angry with her. What if she didn't feel she could contact me? She might have left me. She might have been the one to walk away, but putting it all on her to get in touch wasn't the most honourable way of going about things. And I had always tried to be honourable… at least until that last day.

That last moment at my flat wasn't the most honourable thing I've ever done… but I was hurt.

Like that's any excuse.

I had to wait for it to be a reasonable time of day in Boston, but by one-thirty, I couldn't take anymore. I knew that would only be eight-thirty in the morning for Ella, but I couldn't stop myself, no matter how hard I tried. Even as I was connecting the call, I kept telling myself it was a mistake… another one to add to my already substantial list, but what else could I do? I had to talk to her, although I was still worried she'd think I wasn't interested in her, but only in the baby we might have created… which was why I kept telling myself I couldn't mention it.

What I hadn't anticipated was that she wouldn't take my call… that she'd let it ring out and go to her voicemail. I don't know why I hadn't seen that coming. Maybe because it hadn't occurred to me that she might not be missing me, like I'm missing

her, but as the automated message finished, and I heard the beep, I knew I had to find some other way to get my point across, without actually saying the words 'pregnant', or 'baby'. Even if she wasn't willing to speak to me, I didn't want her to think I didn't care about her.

I was surprised by how hard it was to talk, though… even to a machine. My voice kept breaking up, and although I struggled to finish what I was saying, I'm pretty sure it made sense… and her silence can only lead me to one conclusion.

She's not pregnant.

She'd have called by now, if she was.

I sigh, trying not to think about that, and how it makes me feel, and I put the kettle on, reaching for the tea bags, to find the container is empty. There are some more in the cupboard and I empty the box into the container, turning around to discover my recycling bin is overflowing. It's cold and I've been putting off this task since yesterday morning… but I can't delay any longer, and I grab the bin, carrying it through to the front of the house, where I open the door.

"Good morning."

I look up, hearing Henry's voice, to find he's staring down at me from the steps above.

"Oh… hello."

"I haven't seen you for a while. Are you all right?"

"Yes, I'm fine."

He frowns. "You don't sound fine. Would you like to come up for a cup of tea?"

"I was just making one…"

"Shall I come down there, then?"

I can hardly say 'no', even though I'm not feeling very sociable. He's been so kind to me.

"Of course."

"I'll just get my keys."

He disappears for a moment, and I use the time to empty my recycling, leaving my front door open for Henry to come in, which he does a few minutes later.

"They're saying we're going to have a white Christmas," he says, closing the door and coming down the hall into the kitchen.

"I'll believe it when I see it. They say that every year, don't they?"

"Hmm… I think so."

I pour water over the tea bags, giving them a stir and turn to face him.

"How's work?" I get my question in before he can start quizzing me.

"It's fine. We're busier than usual for the time of year, so I'm not complaining, although I've got to go in later, just to catch up on paperwork."

"On a Sunday?"

He nods. "There's no peace for the wicked."

I fetch the milk from the fridge and finish making the tea, carrying both cups into the living room, where we sit on the sofa, gazing out of the doors onto the courtyard. It's so grey outside today, I wouldn't be at all surprised if it snowed, but I'm not about to start another discussion on the weather.

"You don't have a tree," Henry says, glancing around the room.

"No. I couldn't see the point when it's just me."

He frowns. "Really? I always enjoy decorating the Christmas tree." Somehow, that doesn't surprise me. He has a glorious beast of a tree that practically fills his front window.

"I noticed."

He turns slightly, so he's facing me. "Is everything okay, Mac? You seem very down in the dumps."

"I am down in the dumps."

"Is this to do with your young lady?" he asks.

"She's not my young lady. Not anymore."

"Okay… but it's to do with her?"

"Yes. I… um… I called her."

He seems surprised. "You did?"

"Yes."

"Can I take it the call didn't go well?"

"She didn't pick up. She let it ring, and then go to voicemail."

"Oh."

"Yeah. I left a message, but she hasn't called me back… and it's been two weeks now, so…" I leave my sentence hanging and he nods his head.

"I realise I'm just a crusty old bachelor, but can I say… I'm confused."

"Why?"

"Because after what she did, I assumed you'd be glad to see the back of her."

"No, not at all. I'm still in love with her, Henry. I didn't want her to leave. In fact, I begged her to stay… not that she paid a blind bit of attention."

"I'm sorry. I didn't understand. Is that why you called her? To work things out?"

"I called because I wanted her to know I'm still here for her… even if I'm three thousand miles away."

His brow furrows. "What does that mean?"

"It means there was an outside chance she could have been pregnant."

"Oh…" he says, pushing his glasses up onto the bridge of his nose. "Oh, I see. Can I take it she isn't?"

"I'm making that assumption, yes. She'd have told me, if she was… and she'd know by now."

He frowns. "Excuse me for asking this, but did you know when you left Boston that she might be pregnant?"

"Yes, I did."

"And yet you left, anyway?"

I shake my head, staring at my fingers, twisting them in my lap. "I know it doesn't sound great, but she broke my heart, Henry."

I hear him take a breath. "How do you feel now?"

I look up. His face has softened, and he's studying me with nothing but concern on his face. "What about?" I ask.

"About not hearing from her."

"Desolate." That doesn't even begin to cover it.

"And how do you feel about her not being pregnant?"

There's no point in trying to hide it. "Devastated."

"Because you saw it as a way to get her back?"

I think for a moment. "It would be easy to say 'yes' to that, but that's not how it is. I wanted Ella to be pregnant because I love her."

"And you want her back for the same reason?"

"Yes. That's why I didn't mention the pregnancy in my message. I just said I'm here if she needs me... because I—I thought she might have been as distressed as I was to find out she wasn't pregnant. I thought she might need someone to talk to, and that maybe I'd be the right man." Except it seems I'm not... not anymore.

"I'm sorry." Henry's voice cuts through me, and I turn away, unable to face him. I stare at the fireplace, which remains unlit for now. Its emptiness seems appropriate, and I struggle against the stinging behind my eyes and the lump in my throat. "How's the writing going?" he says at last, changing the subject... thank God.

"It's okay." I turn again, although I look over at my laptop, rather than at Henry. "I'm planning out the second book, and

doing my research for it, and I've already come up with outlines for a couple more."

"That sounds promising. We'll make an author of you yet. Have you heard anything back from your agent at all?"

"No, but I probably won't... not until after the New Year."

"Well... no news is good news, I suppose."

When it comes to Delilah, he's probably right. When it comes to Ella, nothing could be further from the truth.

Henry's been gone for a few hours, and although it's Sunday, I'm working on my book. I need to keep myself occupied, and figuring out how to kill off a back-stabbing leading lady in a way that my female doctor-cum-detective, and her admiring police inspector can solve within three hundred and fifty pages is giving me no end of headaches.

I gave up on the idea of her being hit over the head, or stabbed, and settled on poisoning as my chosen method of murder. It gives Evie more involvement in solving the crime. So, my problem now is not so much the 'how', as the 'why'. The most obvious answer is an affair, but that feels hackneyed, so I'm wondering about making the victim a blackmailer, and giving my leading man and murderer a murky secret that Evie can discover while he's flirting with her... much to the annoyance of the detective. This would, of course, make her even more invaluable to the plot, and help enhance the budding romance I've got going on in the background.

The problem is... what would the secret be?

I sit back, staring at the screen, wondering why I do this to myself, when my phone rings. It startles me because it hasn't rung since I've been back in London, and for a moment or two, I allow myself to hope it might be Ella...

I suck in a breath, and pick it up, surprised when I see the name 'Delilah' on the screen. I've rarely known her to call at the

weekend, and usually, she'd only do so if she had bad news, so with a shaking hand, I connect the call.

"Hi, Delilah."

"Blake… how are you?"

"I'm fine." I'm not, but she won't care in reality, so there's no point in explaining.

"Good. I'm sorry to disturb you on a Sunday, but I wanted to let you know, I've heard from that publisher I was telling you about."

"What publisher?"

"The one I said I was going to send your book to."

"I didn't even realise you'd finished reading the manuscript yourself, let alone sent it off to someone else."

"Oh… I finished it within a day. Once I'd started it, I couldn't put it down."

"Seriously?" I'm stunned.

"Yes. It's magnificent, Blake." I don't know what to say, and I sit with my mouth open. "The publisher thought so, too. He read it himself, and passed it to one of the other commissioning editors in the company, who sat up for the last two nights reading it. She called my contact this morning, and they've decided they want to offer you a contract."

"They did all this, even though it's the weekend?"

"Yes. They're that impressed with you." I fall silent again, unable to believe what I'm hearing. "Are you still there, Blake?"

"Yes… yes. What do I have to do?"

"Nothing. They're going to send through the contract in the morning, and I'll look over it before I forward it to you."

"Okay."

"There's just one thing…"

Oh… here it comes. The spanner in the works.

"What's that?"

"I was right. They want more. I know you said you had some ideas for a second novel, but what about a whole series? That's what they're looking for."

I nod my head, even though she can't see me. "I'm right in the middle of planning out the second novel, and I've jotted down ideas for two more."

"That's great. I'll let them know."

I sense she's about to hang up, but there's something I need to ask. "Delilah?"

"Yes?"

"Have you heard anything from the studio?"

"What about?"

"A—About Ella taking over from me, or the legal action they were threatening."

I don't care about the legal action, but I'm wondering if she might have heard anything on the grapevine about Ella.

"Are you still pining for her?"

"Yes." There's no point in lying.

She sighs. "They were never gonna tell me anything about her, Blake. I don't represent her, so why would they? As for the legal action, that was just a line they fed the press. They didn't have a case against you, so stop worrying. And stop pining, too. It's over, and you need to look forward." If only it was that easy. "Just think… in a few months' time, your book will be published, and all your dreams will come true."

That's not the case at all. My dream would be to have Ella back in my life, but getting my book published is now much more realistic than ever seeing her again, and I smile, unable to help myself.

"Yeah… you're right."

"Of course I am. Now keep writing. I'll be in touch."

She hangs up, and I put my phone down on the table, staring at the words on the screen in front of me, and letting the smile on

my lips widen to a grin. I can't help feeling happy about this. It's what I always wanted. I just wish Ella could be here to share it with me… I wish someone could be here…

I rush to the front door, grabbing my keys from the hook, and hurry out and up the steps to Henry's door. I hadn't realised how late it was, or that it's dark out here now, but I ring the bell anyway, and I wait… and wait, and then I remember, he said he was going to work.

"Damn," I mutter under my breath. I feel like celebrating, and I turn around, spying the pub on the corner of the road. "Why not?"

I'm wearing a thick sweater, and although it's cold, I don't feel the need for a coat. My wallet is in my back pocket, and I can live without my phone for the next half an hour or so. I cross the road, hurrying to the pub.

I'm hit by a blast of warm air as I enter, and I wander to the bar and order myself a large glass of red wine, taking it to an empty table, close to the roaring fire, where I sit and look around.

I never used to have a 'local' when I lived in London before, but I've been in here on many occasions when I've visited Henry, and I don't think it's changed since Queen Victoria's day. The wood panelling is dark, the floor worn and pitted, and the chairs and tables have seen better days, but there's a warm welcome, full of festive cheer. A tree decked with far too much tinsel fills one corner, and old Christmas songs play in the background.

I'm still smiling, taking my second sip from the glass, when I feel a pair of hands come around my face, clamping over my eyes, and I jump, trying to turn around, although there's a body right behind me, preventing me from moving. The body is definitely female, and all my muscles tighten against it.

"What the…" I reach up, grabbing the hands, and pull them away, twisting my head, so I can look up into a very familiar face. "Moira?"

She's changed her hair. It's shorter than it was, although it's still longer than Ella's, and is a shade or two lighter, but other than that, she looks exactly the same as she did when I left here… just as pretty… just as shapely.

She steps back slightly, her head tilted to one side as I stand and turn to face her.

"Hello, Mac," she says, like she's in a dream, her blue eyes sparkling and a smile tugging at her lips.

"Hi."

She leans in, planting a kiss on my cheek, and I feel obliged to return the gesture.

"When did you get back?" she asks.

"About a month ago."

"And how are you?"

"I'm fine." It's the answer I give to everyone… even though I'm not.

"Are you meeting someone?" She glances at the vacant chair opposite my own.

"No. I just came in to celebrate."

"Celebrate what?"

"My book's being published. My agent just called to tell me."

Her eyes light up. "But that's great. I knew you'd do it one day."

I can't recall her ever being this enthusiastic about my writing when we were together. In fact, as far as I can remember, she used to hate everything about it. She said I was obsessed with it, and I never had any time for her, but there's no point in worrying about that now.

"Thanks. Can I get you a drink? Or are you here with someone?"

"I am, but it's just some girls from my old office. We arranged to meet up for a Christmas drink, but they'll be fine without me for a while." She smiles up at me. "I'll have a vodka and tonic, please."

I nod my head and turn towards the bar as she sits down, clearly intent on staying, regardless of her friends. The distant tinkle of an alarm bell rings in my head, but I dismiss it. Moira and I are ancient history now. This is nothing more than a friendly drink. And besides, I'm not interested. Not any more.

I pay for her vodka and tonic and return to the table, sitting opposite her.

"Thanks," she says, holding out her glass and I clink mine against it.

"Cheers."

We both take a sip and put down our glasses. "So… why are you back from America?" she asks, leaning on the table. "I thought you were going for good."

"I was, but it didn't work out."

"Why not? Did the work dry up?"

"Not as such. After I'd finished the commercial contract, I did some theatre work, and then I got a job on a cookery show." And fell in love.

She grins. "What as? You can barely boil water."

"Yeah, well… that was the problem. The studio saw through me. They realised I was a fraud and fired me." I'm not about to mention Ella's role in any of that. It's none of Moira's business.

She reaches out, placing her hand on my arm, but I pull away, picking up my drink to put some distance between us.

"I'm sorry, Mac."

I shrug my shoulders. "It wasn't meant to be, and they probably did me a favour. Being unemployed gave me the impetus to re-write my book… and now it's going to be published."

"So, you're back for good?"

"It looks that way." Especially as I haven't heard from Ella. I'm not sure if this publishing contract will require me to go back to the States at all, but if it does, it'll probably be to New York,

where Delilah's based. That's a good thing, I think. Going back to Boston would remind me too much of what I've lost. I cough, swallowing down the lump in my throat. "So… what have you been doing?" I ask, changing the subject.

"Not very much. I changed jobs." I gathered as much when she said she was meeting some friends from her old office, and I nod my head, pretending an interest I don't feel.

"Where are you working now?"

"In the admin department at the local college."

As far as I know, Moira's jobs have always been administrative. When we were together, she worked in the office of a furniture outlet, and I believe, before that, she was employed at a printer's.

"Do you enjoy it?"

She shrugs. "It's okay."

I nod my head. "Where are you living now?"

She takes a sip of her drink. "After you left, I moved back in with Mum and Dad for a while, but I've just got myself a new flat." Her eyes sparkle, and she smiles. "You should come and see it sometime."

That alarm bell rings a little louder. "I don't think that's a good idea, do you?"

"Why not?" she asks.

"Because whatever we had is over, Moira. We can't—"

"God, you can be arrogant sometimes."

"I'm sorry?"

She leans back, staring at me. "Correct me if I'm wrong, but it sounds to me like you're assuming I only came over here because I clearly still find you absolutely irresistible, and I guess it follows that I must be trying to lure you to my flat to re-live our intimate past."

"Well… I…"

"Did it ever occur to you that I might be over you?"

I feel myself blush, knowing she's right. "Of course. I mean… sorry. I shouldn't have made any assumptions. It's just that there's someone else, you see, and…"

She frowns. "There's someone else? Already? You've only been back here for a month."

"I know, but she's not here. She's in America."

"So you left her behind too?" she says. "This is becoming habit-forming, Mac."

"It isn't. Not really. It's just… complicated." *A lot more complicated than when I left you.*

"I see. And does her existence on the other side of the Atlantic mean you and I can't meet up from time to time?"

"N——No. As long as you understand, we can't be more than friends."

"Like I said, I'm over you," she says. "So that's fine with me." She finishes her drink and gets to her feet, looking down at me and taking her phone from her handbag. "Why don't you give me your number and I'll call you? We can do this again. Or if you're feeling brave enough, you can come to my flat. I won't eat you."

I chuckle and give her my number. She doesn't offer hers, and I don't ask for it. But as I watch her walk away, returning to her friends, my mind drifts and I wonder what it must be like to be 'over' someone. It's not something I've had to contemplate before. I've never cared enough to worry. But will I ever be able to think of Ella as someone I used to love?

I think about that for a moment, shaking my head.

Of course I won't.

I don't even want to.

Chapter Twelve

Ella

Christmas seems like forever ago now.

So does the morning a few weeks beforehand, when I discovered I was pregnant. Having worked out I was late, I showered and drove into town, stopping at the drugstore for a pregnancy test. I was fairly sure it would be positive, but even so, reading the word 'pregnant' on that little screen still made me reel with shock, and I dropped the test into the basin, unable to even keep a hold of it. I stared at it for a while, but the word just stared back at me, so I went and sat on the edge of the bed, wondering what to do. Should I tell Mac? Should I tell Hunter? Or should I just stay in my room for the rest of my life?

In the end, I did nothing. I tried to forget about it in the short term, knowing both of my brothers would be home for the holidays. We could talk about it then… and we did.

I was free of the studio by that time, having emailed Kennedy a few days after I found out I was pregnant. I told her I didn't want to be involved with the show any more 'for personal reasons', and didn't go into any further detail. She replied with a very blank 'okay', and we left it at that. To be honest, I wished I'd done it sooner. It was a lot less trouble than I'd expected.

I just hoped Hunter and Drew would take my other news as well...

I waited until they all got here on Christmas Eve. Hunter and Livia had been frequent visitors in between, but Drew had been away, either on assignment, or in New York, visiting Lexi, and I wanted to tell them all together. For a while, I wondered if he might spend the holidays there, but he said she had plans. To be honest, I think spending so much time together was starting to make him feel like they were in the relationship neither of them had wanted in the first place. The thought of spending the holidays together was probably too much.

"Is she visiting her family?" I asked when he called to tell me he'd be coming home on Christmas Eve.

"I don't know. She didn't tell me. I don't think so, though. Her father hasn't reacted very well to the news about the pregnancy, and she told me her sister's working over Christmas."

"Working?"

"She's a nurse."

I couldn't remember if he'd told me that before, but my brain seemed to be malfunctioning. Just that morning, I'd found one of my favorite sweaters in the deep freeze. I still can't fathom how it got there, but I think that was when I knew the pregnancy was starting to affect me.

"What about her mom?"

"She died, I think. Don't ask me for details, though. It's not something we talk about."

"Seriously?"

"Yeah. We're not an item, and neither of us wants to be."

He had a point, and it was a reminder that his situation was difficult... maybe more difficult than my own was about to be.

"Has she met someone else?"

"She hasn't said so."

"Do you think she would? Say something, I mean… if she did?"

"I'd like to think so, considering she's carrying my child. But you never know."

"Does it worry you?"

"To be honest, everything worries me at the moment."

I felt sorry for him, but at least Lexi's plans meant we could all be together for the first time in ages, and I needed that. I knew it wouldn't be easy to break my news to them, but when I did, they were fabulous about it… especially Drew.

He's grown up a lot in the last few months, although I'm not always convinced that's a good thing. Sometimes I miss my carefree brother, and while I think it's great that he's taking responsibility for Lexi's pregnancy, I can see how broken-hearted he is that he'll never be with her sister now.

On the night I told them my news, even though it was Christmas Eve, he stayed with me for ages after Hunter and Livia had gone to bed, and we sat in the living room, just talking.

"I'm not telling Mac," I explained, because we hadn't really covered that.

"Excuse me?" He sat forward, staring at me. "You're not gonna tell him?"

"No."

"Why not?"

"You know how we broke up." Hunter had already explained everything to him, so I didn't have to, and he'd called me when he got back from West Virginia to make sure I was okay. I wasn't, of course. I'm still not. "You know he didn't trust me."

"This is different, Ella."

"Maybe, but I'm still not telling him."

"Give me a good reason."

"I can give you three."

"Go on then," he said, folding his arms across his chest.

"First… it's not his fault. It's mine."

"How do you work that out?"

"Because he didn't use a condom." I wondered if I was blushing. I felt like I was.

"And how is that your fault?" He tilted his head, frowning.

"Because I encouraged him." At least, I did after the first time, so I can hardly blame Mac for what happened.

He raised his eyebrows. "So, this is intentional?"

"I guess. Although breaking up with him wasn't. We were in Vermont when this happened…" I patted my flat stomach. "And when I made it clear I was happy with the consequences of not using condoms, I'd expected that we'd go back to Boston, and that I'd tell him I was in love with him and ask him to move in with me. I'd never expected it to end like this."

"Okay," he said, nodding his head, encouraging me to go on. "What's the second reason?"

"He called me."

"He did?"

"Yes. I didn't take the call, but it was his message that reminded me I could be pregnant."

"How? Did he ask about it?"

"Not in so many words. He just made me remember the dates."

"How?"

"He said it had been two weeks since we'd been in Vermont… and if I needed him, I should call."

"In which case, don't you think you should? He clearly hadn't forgotten his responsibilities. Regardless of what had gone on between you, he must have still cared, or he wouldn't have called."

"He didn't care about me, though."

"Why do you say that?" he asked

"Can't you see? He called about the baby, not me."

"I don't see how you can tell that from a message, but are you really not even gonna give him a chance?"

"No."

"I don't agree with you, but what's the third reason?"

"You."

He leaned back, his brow furrowed. "Me?"

"Yes. I can see what knowing about Lexi's baby is doing to you."

"Can you? What's it doing to me then?"

"It's ruining your life, Drew. It's changing you."

"Yeah... and so it should. I'm gonna be a father in a few months' time. I can't live my life the way I used to."

"But..."

"But nothing. Lexi and I may not be together, but she's carrying my child, and no matter what the personal consequences of that are to me, I'd still rather know about it. I decided to stand by her, so if anyone is ruining my life, it's me. I had a choice, because she told me, and you can't take that choice away from Mac. It's not fair, Ella."

I stared up at him, tears filling my eyes. "I—I love him so much, Drew, but it's over between us and I can't interfere in his life."

I could tell he wasn't convinced by my arguments, but he didn't pressure me, and he hasn't done since... not that I've had much time to think about it myself. In the intervening weeks, we've all been really busy organizing Hunter and Livia's wedding. We had precious little time as it was, but things were made even more complicated by a piece of news that stopped us all in our tracks. Hunter found out that Ken Bevan had been killed in a car accident just a few days after Christmas. His is a

name that's haunted our family for decades, and although Livia barely knew the man, he was her natural father, and she felt she should spend some time with her mom. It was understandable, and I agreed to take over the wedding plans while she was away.

Neither she nor her mom wanted to attend the funeral, but Hunter went on their behalf. He said it was poorly attended, which didn't surprise any of us, and once that was over, they returned to Newport. I think they both felt they could draw a line under that part of the past, and we got on with the plans for their future... together.

The wedding took place yesterday, and it was absolutely beautiful.

I know being pregnant makes you more emotional, but I barely stopped crying throughout the entire day. I was worse than Livia's mom. She sniffled a little, although that was understandable. Not only had her first husband just died, raking up some unhappy memories, but her daughter was getting married, and it had been a stressful week for her and Connor. Their house had only just been completed in time, so their move down here had been a little rushed, to put it mildly. The wedding helped her forget her problems for a while, I have no doubt.

Hunter was so happy, and so proud, and Livia was just bursting with joy. She looked beautiful, in the palest pink lace dress, and my brother has never looked better in a tux. Champagne flowed all day, although I couldn't partake myself, and the entire house was decorated with early spring flowers. Drew was the best man and his speech was hilarious, but even as I was laughing at his jokes, I couldn't help the feelings of regret from creeping up on me...

I startle at the knocking on my door, and go to answer it, surprised to find Drew standing there, looking down at me.

"I thought I'd invite myself for coffee."

I step aside. "You can invite yourself for a cup of tea. I'm still not up to drinking coffee."

"Even though the morning sickness has stopped?"

"Yeah. The smell of coffee still makes my stomach churn, and I'm not pushing my luck."

"Okay. Tea it is."

I let him in, closing the door, and we make our way through to the kitchen, where he sits at the island unit and I put the kettle onto the stove to boil.

"I take it you got Hunter and Livia to the airport okay?"

"Yes. I'm kinda jealous… two weeks at a secluded villa in the Seychelles sounds pretty damn perfect, doesn't it?" I nod my head and he tilts his. "Are you okay, Sis?"

"I—I just can't help wondering…"

"Wondering what?"

"If I've blown my chances."

He shakes his head. "Chances of what?"

"Don't be dense, Drew. Even if I wanted to be with anyone other than Mac, I'm going to have a baby in a few months' time. Do you honestly think it's going to be easy to find a man who'll want to take on someone else's child?"

"I don't know. Oddly enough, I talked that through with Lexi after the New Year. You'd made me wonder when you raised the idea at Christmas, and I wanted to know if she'd been with anyone."

"And?"

"She said she hadn't. She'd spent the holidays with some friends. I apologized for interfering, because that's how it felt, but we got talking in a more general way, and she said it doesn't feel right to date someone else while she's pregnant with my child, but that after the baby's born, she doesn't see it being a problem."

"And how will you feel about that if it happens?"

"As long as the baby knows who its father is, I'm okay with it. Lexi's a free agent, Ella." He sighs. "Although I don't know why you're worrying."

"Why not?"

"Because I'm pretty sure you've got a man already."

"Oh? Who?"

"Mac, of course." I shake my head as the kettle boils and I turn off the heat. "I wish you'd change your mind about telling him."

"Why?" He falls silent and I turn to face him, noticing the blush on his cheeks. "What's wrong, Drew?"

"I—I've been meaning to tell you for ages, but I didn't know how, especially when you were so upset… and pregnant."

"I'm still pregnant, in case you haven't noticed." I pat my slightly swollen stomach.

"I know, but I can't keep pretending."

"What about?"

He sighs, pushing his fingers back through his hair. "I met him."

"Who?"

"Mac."

"You did?"

"Yeah. I was hired by the studio to take his photograph."

I remember now and I nod my head. "Oh… so you took the publicity shots?"

"Yeah."

"And is that how you know Kennedy Black?"

"Yes, but I wasn't aware you knew I did."

"She made a point of telling me… and treating me differently once she'd worked out the connection."

"And you haven't brought this up before?"

"No. I—I wondered if you might have slept with her, and I didn't like to ask."

His eyes widen. "Slept with Kennedy Black? You're kidding, right? Aside from the fact that she'd eat me for breakfast, I've never slept with anyone who's old enough to be my mother."

I laugh, unable to help myself. "She's not that old."

"You think? Have you ever looked at her hands?"

"Not closely, no."

He nods his head. "She's had work done on her face, but if you study her hands, they'll tell you everything you need to know. Hands don't lie."

"How old is she, then?"

"I don't know exactly, but I'd guess at late fifties."

"Wow… I'd have thought she was in her early forties at most."

"That's what a good plastic surgeon can do."

I'm amazed, and take my time pouring hot water over the tea bags, bringing the cups to the island unit, along with a lemon, which I slice, adding some to each of our cups.

"How did you end up working at the studio?" I ask, sitting down beside him. "Did you already know Kennedy?"

"No. I heard they were looking for someone. Photographing Mac was my first job for them, but I had no idea you were connected with the show."

"You must have worked it out since, though."

"Yes, but I hadn't seen you… not until Christmas, and I wasn't sure about bringing it up then. You'd just announced your pregnancy… and made it clear you didn't want Mac to know. It felt inappropriate to tell you I'd met the guy."

"So, why are you telling me now?"

"Because I think you should know… he told me he liked you."

"Don't be ridiculous. The publicity shots were taken on our first day, weren't they?"

"Yes."

"In which case, he hated me then."

"He didn't hate you, Ella. On the contrary. We got talking, and he told me he was in danger of falling for you."

"But we fought... all the time."

"I know. He told me that, too, and then we had a conversation about Kennedy and how she kept flirting with him, and how uncomfortable he felt about it. He wondered if his behavior around you was so very different... and I reassured him that admiring from afar wasn't the same thing as forcing your attentions on someone. Of course, I didn't realize he was talking about my little sister at the time." I nudge into him and he chuckles. "He knew, right back then, Ella... he knew you were the one for him."

I feel a lump rising in my throat, and struggle to swallow it down. Can it be? Did he love me like I loved him? Does it even matter now, though... now it's all gone so wrong?

I jump at the sound of knocking on my door.

"I'll get it." Drew stands up, wandering to the front door. I hear him speaking and then he returns a few moments later, carrying a few envelopes. "That was Pat. The mailman has just been. There were some things for you."

He dumps everything onto the countertop. Most of it looks worthy of the trash, except for one cream-colored envelope, which I rip open, pulling a letter from inside, and reading it through quickly. "Oh, God..."

"What's wrong?" Drew says, sounding concerned, and I turn to look at him.

"It's the show. It's been nominated for an award."

"That's great, isn't it?"

"Not really. I'm supposed to attend the ceremony, which is being held at a hotel in Boston. This is my invitation." I wave the letter, then drop it down on the countertop.

"Do you have to go?" he asks.

"According to that letter, as part of the contract I signed, I agreed that, if the show was ever nominated, I'd attend."

"Well… don't complain. You damn well earned it."

"Maybe. But Mac will be there, won't he?"

Drew shakes his head. "I doubt it. The studio fired him. I can't imagine they're gonna want him to be there." He has a point, although I still feel reluctant to attend.

"Surely I could just refuse, couldn't I?"

"You could. But there's a risk they'd sue you."

"They wouldn't, would they?"

"They might. Otherwise, why bother telling you it was part of your contract? Besides, Kennedy's like that, from what I've heard. And while I know you can afford a court case, do you need the hassle… and the stress?" He nods at my baby bump and I suck in a breath, wondering what to do. "Would it help if I said I'd come with you?" he says, surprising me.

"Could you?"

"Sure. When is it?"

I check the letter, spinning it around, so it's the right way up. "April eighteenth. It's a Thursday, evidently." I glance up at him. "How does that tie in with Lexi's due date?"

"She's due on the twenty-fifth, so I can't see it making a difference. I'd either be here or in Boston anyway… and you never know, if you go, you might even find out who really leaked Mac's secret to the press."

"Oh, I've already got my suspicions about that."

"You have?"

"Hmm… the more I've thought about it, the more I've come to realize it had to be Vivian."

"And who's Vivian?"

"She was the production assistant, and she absolutely hated me, right from the beginning. She wanted Mac to herself, and I

guess she must have found out about us. I didn't realize she knew about his writing, and Mac didn't either, but she's the kind of person who'd have made it her business to find out about him."

"There's no-one else?"

I shake my head, then take a sip of tea. "Not that I can think of. No-one else had a motive. Mac was right about that. Kennedy had nothing to gain from telling the press about him, and I know I didn't do it, even if he didn't believe in me. The only thing that's never made sense to me is why Vivian hated me at first sight."

"Didn't you just say she wanted Mac? Isn't that a good enough reason for her to get her claws out?"

"It would be, but Mac and I didn't get together until halfway through the recordings. Vivian's dislike of me was instant, literally from the moment I first said my name."

Drew's face pales, and he clamps his hand across his mouth. "Oh… God."

His words are muffled, but I can make them out well enough. "What's wrong?"

He lets his hand fall and shakes his head. "I think this is my fault."

"What?"

"Vivian's dislike of you… and possibly her leaking of Mac's secret to the press, assuming she's responsible, of course."

"How can it be your fault?"

"Because I once dated someone called Vivian," he says. "And she was looking to get into either film or television production. Do you remember this woman's last name?"

I think for a moment. "Riley? No Reid. That was it… Reid."

"That's her. Vivian Reid."

"When did you date her?" I ask, pushing the invitation aside and leaning a little closer to him.

"I don't know… three, maybe four years ago."

"Why did you stop?"

"Why did I ever stop seeing women? She wanted more than I was willing to give, so I broke it off. She wasn't happy about it."

"Clearly." I narrow my eyes at him, and he holds up his hands, like he's surrendering.

"I'm sorry, Sis. I guess she must have heard your name and realized who you were."

"How, though? Ours isn't the most unusual last name in the world, so how would she have made the connection? Kennedy didn't. She had to ask me about it."

"I probably mentioned you," he says, biting on his bottom lip. He looks really contrite, but there's no point in him being sorry.

Not now.

Funnily enough, I think it was discovering Vivian's connection to Drew that made me determined to attend tonight's ceremony... if only to confront her. Drew's right, the studio won't want Mac to be there, and I'm damned if I'm going to let Vivian get away with ruining his career and our relationship, just because of something my brother did.

I don't think he was particularly keen to renew his acquaintance with her, but he'd said he'd come with me, and that's why he's sitting beside me in the car... although I'm driving, because he's staying on in Boston after the ceremony, while I'll be going straight back to Newport. In the end, our plans worked out even better than Drew expected, because when he told Lexi what was happening, she surprised him by announcing she was coming to Boston for a few days.

"She wants to spend some time with her sister before the baby's born," Drew said, when he called and told me. "Personally, I think she's insane, traveling here so soon before the baby's due, but she says she's bored, and I can't stop her."

"If she's spending time with her sister, does that mean you'll get to see her?"

"Lexi? Yeah. A friend of hers is bringing her here on the Thursday we're going to your award ceremony. She's got an interview, or something on the Friday morning – the friend, that is, not Lexi. And I've said I'll drive her home on the Sunday, to make things easier for her."

"And her sister? Will you see her, too?"

"Not if I can help it. I've avoided it so far… and I'll keep right on doing so, if I can."

"Forever?"

I heard him sigh. "I don't know. At the moment, I'm still in love with her. I can't face the thought of seeing her. It's too hard… especially as there's every chance she's got another man in her life by now. I think I'd rather live in ignorance of that."

I knew how he felt. I still do. It might have been months since I last saw Mac, but if I thought for one minute he was going to be at this ceremony tonight, I'd be speeding in the opposite direction.

There's only so much I can take…

And it seems the same thing applies to Drew.

"What's it like, knowing the sex of your baby?" he asks, out of the blue.

I glance over at him, smiling, and I shrug my shoulders, taking a hand from the steering wheel and gently rubbing my bump. "In one way, I suppose it spoils the surprise a bit, but in other ways, it's easier. I knew what color to decorate the nursery, and when I get around to buying clothes, I'll know what to get… I guess." I've bought a couple of things already. I got them on the day I first felt the baby move, when I was missing Mac even more than usual. Somehow, buying a few things for our baby made me feel like a normal mom in waiting, although my empty apartment

reminds me every day that there's nothing 'normal' about this at all.

He sighs. "Lexi didn't want to know what she's having…"

"But you did?"

"Yeah. I could hardly force her though, could I?"

"Not really."

"Have you thought of any names yet?" he asks.

"None whatsoever. What about you?"

"Lexi wants Xavier if it's a boy… and Maisie if it's a girl."

I frown at him. "Xavier?"

"Yeah."

"I take it you're hoping for a girl?"

He chuckles. "I always was, to be honest."

"You want a girl?"

"Yeah."

I smile, unable to help myself. "Would you be offended if I told you how proud I am of you?"

He twists in his seat slightly, but I don't turn to face him. We're coming into the city and I need to concentrate.

"No, but I can't see what I've done to make anyone proud. If I hadn't got Lexi pregnant…"

"It's easy to be wise after the event. The point is, you've done the right thing. You've changed your life. You've adjusted your work to fit in with Lexi."

I rest my hand on my bump for a moment, then indicate, taking a left-hand turn.

"Do you have any regrets?" he asks.

"About this? No. But I regret what happened between me and Mac."

"That it happened in the first place, or that it ended?"

"That it ended. I can't regret what we had. I still love him, Drew, and I think I always will."

He puts his hand on my knee, just for a second, and then withdraws it as we both stare out the windshield, sighing, and full of regret for things we can't change.

———~~———

Mac

I really don't want to be here.

I'm standing by the sign announcing the Daytime TV Awards, in the foyer of one of the most prestigious hotels in Boston, surrounded by too many people. My collar feels too stiff and my bow tie feels too tight around my neck, like between them, they're determined to choke me.

Or is that just nerves?

It must be, because I've been feeling like this ever since I landed at Logan International two days ago.

I'm staying with Calvin, and he's done his best to take my mind off tonight, and how awful it has the potential to be. The problem is, he's only been looking at it from the perspective of me having to meet the people who fired me. He has no idea that what's really troubling me is the thought of facing Ella for the first time in months.

She's going to be here… I know that.

When the invitation pinged into my inbox back in February, my initial instinct was to send back an immediate 'Hell, no'.

I didn't. Instead, I walked away from my computer and went upstairs to see Henry, in a state of shock.

"It's an honour," he said, once I'd explained my distress. "I know it wasn't your fault things ended the way they did with the studio, but at least they had the manners to invite you."

He had a point, although it wasn't one I wanted to consider.

"You don't think they might have an ulterior motive?" I asked.

He frowned. "Like what?"

"I don't know… showing me up in public, or something."

"No. Why would they want the negative publicity of doing something like that? It seems to me you're fishing for excuses not to go."

He was right about that, and no longer being the 'Meal Master' seemed like a reasonable one to me. Moira agreed.

"I don't think you should go," she said, when I mentioned it to her that evening. We'd met in the pub, which is something we've been doing since Christmas. It's not a regular thing, but she'll call every so often and if I'm not bogged down in a plot twist, I'll usually go along for an hour or two.

"Why not?" I stared across the table at her, hoping she'd come up with a valid reason for me to decline the invitation.

"They fired you, Mac. You don't owe them anything. Why should you go to their silly awards ceremony?"

I doubted they thought the awards were 'silly'. I knew how seriously they took these things, and that just to be nominated was a privilege.

Obviously, Moira didn't realise that Ella would be involved. I've never told her that Ella and I worked together. In fact, I've never discussed Ella with her at all, since that first night.

Even so, Moira's reasons made sense to me, and I mulled them over for a few days, trying to work out what to do.

In the end, the deciding factor and the reason I'm standing here, trying not to choke on my bow tie and my nerves, was Delilah.

She called a few days after I received the invitation to let me know that there's a production company interested in serialising my books, and I told her about the awards.

"You have to go." She put so much emphasis on the word 'have', I was quite taken aback.

"Have you forgotten what they did to me?"

"Of course not, but you need to be there. I seem to remember there being a clause about it in your contract, but more important than that, it'll look like sour grapes if you don't go, and no-one's gonna want to be associated with you if you behave like a diva."

"Do I sound like I care? I'm happy writing."

"Blake…" She sounded tetchy, and I braced myself for the hurricane I knew was about to hit me from three thousand miles away. "I'm working my ass off here, trying to get you a good deal with the production company. The last thing I need is for you to start pissing people off."

"I'm not even sure I want to get back into television."

"Don't be pathetic. If I can get the deal we want, this contract is gonna be worth a small fortune, and your involvement would be minimal."

I didn't particularly like the sound of either of those things. It had never been about the money for me, and while I was enjoying the security of the advance the publishers had paid me, I wasn't worried about earning 'a small fortune' at the expense of my sanity. As for having minimal involvement in my own stories…

"Delilah… I'm really not certain I want…"

"Just let me put the deal together, will you? Then you can come over and meet everyone involved, look at the ideas they've got in mind, and decide. Okay?"

I sucked in a breath, wondering what I was letting myself in for. "Okay."

"But in the meantime, book yourself a goddamn flight to Boston, and attend that award ceremony."

I did as I was told… not so much because I was worried about the contract, but because she was right; it would look like sour grapes if I didn't show up.

Ever since I booked the flight and spoke to Calvin about staying with him, I've been bracing myself for seeing Ella again.

I've done nothing but dream about her since I got back to London… not just when I'm asleep, but when I'm awake, too. I relive every moment; even the times before we got together, when we argued most of the time… when her attempted apologies led to insults. I wish more than anything that I could go back and do it all again. Except for her betrayal… obviously.

No, that's not true. The thing I wish for most is that we could just be together again. Regardless of her betrayal.

I know it won't happen, though.

She ignored my call and didn't respond to my message. She obviously has no need for me anymore, even if I need her, like I need to draw breath.

I can't put this off any longer and, with a heavy heart and a nervous tingle down my spine, I step forward, opening the doors into the main hall.

It's heaving with guests and I stop, looking around, hoping to see someone I'm familiar with. There are too many people here, though, and I shake my head, wondering what to do, just as I spot a seating plan, and wander over, taking a moment to find the table for 'Meal Masters', which is just to the left of centre, and two rows back.

Now I know where I'm going, I wend my way through the crowds of sycophants, patting each other on the back and making all the right noises about each other's success, until I see Gavin, in a tux, standing at the side of a table. He's with Kennedy and Ruby… and unfortunately, Vivian is there, too. I'd forgotten about her, and even as I'm taking in how different they

all look in long dresses, with their hair up, I steel myself for her reactions.

There's no sign of Ella, and for a moment, I wonder if maybe she's not here after all, until Kennedy moves aside and I see her sitting on the opposite side of the table...

My heart lurches to a stop in my chest, and I stand for a moment, just gazing at her perfect face. She looks divine, her hair still in that gorgeously messed-up style I love so much. She's talking to the man beside her. His face is obscured, tilted towards hers, engrossed in their conversation, both of them blissfully unaware of my presence.

I can't walk. My feet won't work, and as hard as I try to move, I'm stuck here... staring, watching as the man places his hand over hers, and my heart shatters. It was already broken, but now there's nothing left of it... just a hollow void in my chest, where it used to be.

This can't be happening.

She's here with another man?

How could she do that?

Even as I'm struggling to breathe, the man pulls his hand away and they both look up at the same time. I'm struck by how handsome he is, and that there's something vaguely familiar about him... but I don't dwell. My eyes are naturally drawn to Ella, and I struggle not to gasp as I notice how pale she is... and the look in her eyes.

It's shock, bordering on fear.

What's that about, Ella? What do you think I'm going to do?

"Blake... how lovely to see you." Kennedy's voice startles me and I drag my eyes from Ella, turning to greet my former boss. She holds out a hand, which I take, and she uses the opportunity to pull me closer. I'm feeling weak enough to let her, even if it means I'm standing right beside Vivian.

She looks up into my face, fluttering her eyelashes at me. "It's not the same since you left," she whispers.

"I'm sure it's a lot easier, working with someone who can actually cook." I glance across at Ella, but she's talking to the man beside her, and although I'm dying to ask how she's getting on in front of the cameras, I don't get the chance.

"Shall we all sit?" Kennedy says, taking charge, as usual.

She makes a point of seating me beside her, and fortunately Ruby is to my left, leaving Vivian on the other side of Kennedy, next to Gavin. I'm directly opposite Ella, but she's currently got her head bowed, staring at her lap.

"Where's Linus?" I ask to distract myself, and Kennedy blushes.

"He's up for two awards tonight, and he's chosen to sit with the other team."

"Oh." I can tell how much that hurts, and I almost want to smile.

"Still… I understand you're doing well for yourself," she says. "I've heard rumours about a possible TV show based on your books. Is that correct?"

"I leave all that to my agent."

She smiles. "Very diplomatic."

Ruby leans in to me and I turn to face her. "You're doing okay, though, aren't you?"

I smile. "Yes. For a second-rate actor and would-be author, I'm doing great, thanks." I know that was a cheap jibe, but I can't help it, and I glance over at Ella. She must have heard me, but she doesn't react. She doesn't even raise her head.

Kennedy coughs, and I turn around again. "I—I'm sorry about that," she says, confusing me.

"Sorry about what?"

"The press took some of my words out of context."

"Some of *your* words?" What's she talking about?

"Yes. I had to put some space between you and the show, but…"

I sit forward, clenching my hands together on the table in front of me. "What do you mean, Kennedy? It was Ella who spoke to the press."

She frowns, shaking her head. "Ella? Why would Ella have done that?"

Dear God… what have I done? My stomach feels like lead, and even though I know Ella's still there, I can't look at her now. I'm too ashamed of everything I said… everything I did. "W—Why would you?"

"Because when the network told me they were going to recommission the show, they also revealed that they wanted us to use real members of the public for the second season. There was no way I could keep you on… not when you couldn't cook and barely knew your way around the kitchen. They wanted us to let the guests ask questions during the show, too, instead of working to a script. It was going to be impossible with you at the helm, so rather than having someone else 'out' you during production, I did it myself."

"And painted the studio as the victims of my supposed fraud while destroying my reputation?" She didn't just destroy my reputation, she destroyed my life, but I can't say that here… and anyway, I'm the one to blame for what happened. I'm the one who jumped to conclusions.

"I had no choice."

Is she kidding? "What about coming to see me? What about talking it through with me? Did that ever occur to you?"

She shrugs her shoulders, shaking her head. "No. Not really. We needed a quick change of personnel… one the public would buy. There wasn't time for negotiations. And besides, that wasn't the only reason I had to let you go."

"Oh? What else had I done wrong?"

She places her hand over mine, but I pull them both away. "You'd become too damned popular."

"Seriously?"

"Yes. By the end of the first season, over ninety percent of the correspondence we were getting was about you. It had nothing to do with the recipes, or with future questions. It was just about you."

"Perhaps because you'd made me pose semi-naked in all the publicity material. You made it about me, Kennedy. I didn't. You made it about how I look, and I was never comfortable with that. But I'm not responsible for the way you marketed the show, or me."

"Maybe, but you're what made the show popular. So, I had no choice other than to drop you. The studio wanted to franchise 'Meal Masters' in other countries, and that meant the star couldn't be bigger than the show. The only way for a franchise to work is for the show to be the star. That's why we wanted Ella."

I always knew the woman was a bitch, but that takes the cake. I lean over slightly. "Didn't you get it?"

"Get what?"

"I was just a front… an actor playing a part. Ella was always the star, not me."

I hear a cry from the other side of the table and look up in time to see Ella leap from her seat, revealing the most beautiful dress. It's a dusky grey, with a sash around the waist, which draws my attention to the fact that where she once had a perfectly flat stomach, there's now a definite bump. I suck in a gasp, just as she places her hand over it, with all the protective instincts of a mother-to-be, and then she turns and runs.

My mouth drops open and I jump up, staring after her as she ducks between the tables.

I'm no expert, but that bump can only mean one thing. She's carrying my child. Except that can't be. She'd have told me. She'd never have kept something like that to herself...

"One of us needs to go after her." Ella's companion speaks and I turn at the sound of his voice. He's frowning up at me, and once again, I'm struck by a strange familiarity.

"Do I know you?" I ask.

"Yes. I took the photographs of you semi-naked, as you put it."

"Oh... of course." I guess that's how they met. Maybe he had to take Ella's photographs, too, when she started leading the show. "Are you and Ella...?" I can't bring myself to finish that question, but he smiles, shaking his head.

"I'm her brother."

My relief is overwhelming. "You're Hunter?"

"No, I'm Drew. Now, get after her, or I will. And I don't think that's what either of you really wants."

Chapter Thirteen

Ella

I'm surrounded by people, still filtering into the main hall. They're jostling me, nudging me out of their way, all desperate to get in before the ceremony starts, while I'm just desperate to escape.

The problem is, I can't leave without Drew. I'm supposed to be taking him back to his apartment in the city before I go home to Newport… and I can hardly abandon him.

I glance at the doors, wishing they'd open, and he'd come out. What on earth can he be doing in there? He won't be talking to Vivian, that's for sure. The look on her face when we arrived was an absolute picture.

"She's definitely the same Vivian," Drew murmured as we sat down, having greeted everyone.

They'd all seemed pleased to see me. To start with, Ruby just glanced at my bump a little pointedly, but then Kennedy offered her congratulations. I could hardly deny the fact that I'm pregnant, so I thanked her, and everyone else, who quickly joined in, although I could tell Kennedy was dying to ask who the father was. That was one of the reasons Drew and I sat down so

promptly, even though everyone else was still standing. It avoided awkward questions.

Vivian kept glancing at Drew with daggers in her eyes, and I was wondering whether I might have the opportunity – and the courage – to confront her during the evening, when I noticed Mac approaching the table.

Having convinced myself he wasn't going to attend, I could hardly breathe. He might have looked absolutely God-like in a tux, but I wanted nothing more than to run away. I couldn't, of course... not without revealing my ever so slightly obvious pregnancy. So, I stayed where I was and watched him, reliving all the times we'd been together, recalling his lips on mine, his fingers caressing my skin, his soft words. I could feel his eyes on me, but didn't dare raise my head.

I heard everything he said, though... and when Kennedy revealed she'd been responsible for what happened with the press, I so wanted to get up, to scream at him, "I told you so!" Except I hadn't told him so, had I? Because I'd never for one moment suspected Kennedy of betraying him.

I just knew it wasn't me.

And as she spouted her pathetic excuses for ruining his life – and mine – he realized the truth, too.

I think that was why he told her I'd been the star of the show. It was guilt talking. I know that. Mac was the star, through and through. But just hearing him compliment me, with that familiar softness in his voice... it was all too much, and regardless of my pregnancy, and my wish to keep it from him, I had to get out of there.

I look up as the doors open, Drew's name on my lips, and I gasp when I see Mac stride out. He looks straight at me, and although our eyes lock for an instant, I can't face him.

Drew will have to get back to his apartment by himself... I'm out of here.

I turn and run… again, heading for the main door, but have only gone a few paces, when Mac steps in front of me, blocking my path. There's too much of him to get around, and I stare at his broad chest, taking deep breaths.

"E—Excuse me, please."

"No."

I look up. He's frowning down at me. Is he gonna get mad? After everything he said and did? Is he gonna have the nerve…?

Seeing red, I raise my hand, jabbing him in the chest with my forefinger. "Don't you dare."

He doesn't flinch, but his brow furrows even more. "Dare what?"

"Get mad at me."

His face clears, and he tilts his head slightly. "Why would I get mad at you, Ella?"

I shouldn't have said that. I shouldn't have given him an opening to quiz me, and I cough to cover my mistake, lowering my hand again. "For running away?" It's the best I can come up with on the spur of the moment, and judging by the surprise on his face, he didn't expect that any more than I did.

"Which time? Tonight? Or when you ran out of my apartment last November?"

I can't believe this. Is he seriously trying to blame me for that? "I had every right to run. Both times, as it happens. But back then, you blamed me for something I hadn't done, even though I told you I was innocent. I chose not to hang around with a man who didn't trust me. I think it's better if we leave things that way, don't you?"

"No, I don't. Are you telling me you're happier like this? Because I'm not. I'm bloody miserable."

Oh… so am I.

I stare up into his face, forgetting my anger for a moment, and taking in the sadness behind his eyes. It's hard not to be drawn to him… but I pull back, shaking my head.

"I'd like to get to the door, please." I step aside, but he grabs my arm, turning me to face him.

"I meant to say… congratulations." He glances down at the bump, and I blush, unable to help myself as his frown returns. "You are pregnant, aren't you?"

"Yes." There's no point in denying it. "But don't get any ideas. It's not yours."

"Seriously?"

"Yes. You're not the only man in the…" He raises his hand, placing his fingers over my lips, and although my body ignites to his touch, I'm too angry to let the flames linger. I grab his wrist, pulling his hand away. "What are you doing?" I say, glaring up at him.

"Preventing you from hurling insults."

I narrow my eyes at him. "I'm sure you haven't forgotten, my insults only follow on from apologies… and I'm damned if I'm apologizing to you."

He shrugs his shoulders. "It's okay. You don't have to apologize to me. But you were going to insult yourself then, as well as me, and us, and what we had together. You were going to suggest you'd slept with someone else, weren't you?"

I raise my chin defiantly. "And? I can do what I like. We split up, if you remember."

"I'm not likely to forget, but I'm not going to let you suggest that you'd sleep around, either."

"Who says I did? How do you know I didn't meet someone else? How do you know I'm not in a relationship?"

He flinches, like that hurt. "I don't, I guess. Although I find it hard to believe you'd have met someone within days of us breaking up and had unprotected sex with him."

"That just goes to show what you know," I say, wondering why I started this, and didn't just tell him the truth.

"Okay…" He tilts his head, like he's thinking. "Assuming I believe you about this other guy and your relationship, why isn't he here with you tonight?"

"He's busy. He's…"

"Stop it!" He raises his voice, just slightly. "Stop pretending, will you? And stop lying to me. You're carrying my baby, and we both know it."

"You're as sure about that as you were about my role in ruining your career, are you?"

He pauses, sucking a breath. "I'm as sure about it as I am that I got it wrong with you." He moves closer, and it's like I'm wrapped up in him, even though he's not touching me. "I got it so wrong, Ella… and I'm sorry."

"You think 'sorry' is enough, after everything you put us through?" My eyes are stinging and I look down, struggling against my tears. I feel his finger beneath my chin, and the slight upward pressure as he raises my face to his. The pain in his eyes takes my breath away.

"No, it's not enough… for you, or for me. But can you stop pretending there's someone else? We both know I'm the right man for you. I always was. I always will be. Just like you're the only woman for me. Nothing you say is going to change that."

A tear hits my cheek and as he wipes it away with his thumb, I feel myself deflate. I can't deceive him any longer, and I place my hand between us, resting it on the bump.

"Okay… he's yours."

His eyes light up, a smile touching his lips. "He? I—It's a boy?"

"Yes. But, like I said before, don't you dare get mad at me."

"Mad at you for what?"

"Not telling you."

"I'm not mad at you. Although I'd like to know why you didn't get in touch. I called you. I left a message."

"I know. That was one of the reasons I didn't tell you."

His brow furrows. "Really?"

"Yes. I—I didn't want you to feel obligated."

"Obligated?"

"You know? Responsible... committed."

"I know what it means, Ella." He moves closer, lowering his head and his voice. "Did you listen to my message?"

"Yes."

"Then I don't understand. What did I say that made decide against telling me?"

"You reminded me it had been two weeks since Vermont, and you said you'd be there for me. It was about this, not about me," I say, rubbing my hand over the bump.

He shakes his head. "No, Ella. It was entirely about you. I didn't know if you were pregnant or not. All I knew was that the timing was probably right for you to find out. I thought, if you were, you'd tell me... and if you weren't, you might need someone to talk you. You'd seemed to like the idea of not using a condom, even though we never really talked it through... and I guess I let myself believe you kinda liked the idea of having my baby. I thought you might be upset if you found out you weren't, and I wanted to be there for you. For you, Ella. Pregnant or not. Just like I promised."

Another tear drops onto my cheek. "Oh..." I can't think what else to say. I misunderstood his message... spectacularly. Not that it really changes anything. He still didn't trust me.

"I don't deserve anything from you, after what I did, but..."

A group of people come through the door and a man barges into me from behind, pushing me into Mac's arms. He holds me close, protecting me, but the moment they've gone, I pull away, stepping back.

"Please, Ella," he says. "Hear me out."

"I—I'm tired, Mac." And I need to think. He wasn't supposed to be here. I hadn't expected any of this.

"Okay. I'm sorry. Can I come and see you… tomorrow, maybe? I'm due to fly back to London on Monday, but…"

My heart flounders, my stomach spinning, and I feel sick. All the time, I've imagined him in his lovely top-floor apartment, in that enormous living room, the windows overlooking the city… and he's been in London, thousands of miles away, in a place I can't even picture him. "Y—You went back to London? You don't live here anymore?"

He shakes his head. "No. I flew back home two days after you left me."

"Two days?" *That soon?* "Y—You didn't want to stay?"

"What did I have to stay for? You'd walked out on me, my apartment had too many memories of you, my career was over. I didn't think there was anything left for me here."

"And you're going back again? On Monday?"

He shakes his head. "Not anymore. That's what I was about to say. I'm gonna cancel my flight."

"Why? Like I said, there's no obligation. I didn't ask you…"

"You don't need to ask. I'm staying."

"If you think you need to stick around because of the baby, then think again. I can manage…"

"I'm sure you can. I don't doubt your ability to do anything. Believe it or not, I never did. But I just told you, this is about you… pregnant or not. It's about us. It has nothing to do with our son." He reaches out, placing a hand on my bump, and I stare up at him.

"Did I say you could touch?"

He pulls his hand away, hurt filling his eyes. "Do I need permission? He's mine, Ella."

"Yes, he is. But I'm not." He recoils, shrinking back, but I move closer, needing him to understand. "You can't just walk back into my life like nothing happened, Mac. You hurt me."

He bends his head, his mouth beside my ear. "I know, and I'm sorry. But I'm not walking away, either. If you think I'm gonna fly back to London, or let you leave me a second time, you're wrong. You're very wrong."

"Is everything okay?" I look up to see Drew staring down at me, concern etched on his face.

"Yes, it's fine," I say.

"No, it's not." I glance at Mac, surprised by his words, although he's looking at Drew. "Ella says she's feeling tired. I think she needs to go home."

Drew frowns at me, then turns to Mac. "Oh... okay."

"Can I come and see you?" Mac's talking to me now, but I don't know what to say. "At least let me call," he says, when I don't respond. "We need to talk."

He's not wrong, and I nod my head, although I'm not sure what we're going to say to each other.

I take Drew's arm, and after a moment's hesitation, he leads me out through the main doors and into the dusky evening. I suck in a lungful of air, my heart beating fast, my head spinning.

"I'll take you back to my place," he says. "You can drive yourself back to Newport tomorrow." I'm in no position to argue, and I hand him the keys, letting him escort me to my car, and help me into the passenger seat.

We've been on the road for about ten minutes, when he coughs rather obviously and I look over at him.

"What's wrong?" I ask.

"Nothing."

"Yes, there is. You want to say something. I can tell."

He sighs. "Okay. I'm just wondering why you didn't agree to meet up with Mac. I thought you still loved him."

"I do."

"So... you're playing hard to get?"

"No. I'm not playing at anything. This isn't a game. I'd love to be able to fall into his arms and pretend everything is okay. Except it's not, is it? Not when I know how easily he could hurt me."

"You're assuming he's gonna take that risk again? You're thinking the worst of him, without giving the guy a chance?"

"He assumed the worst of me."

"And? That gives you the right to do it back to him? To play with his feelings and hurt him? You're not twelve, Ella," he says, raising his voice. "You've got a chance to be with the man you love… to be a family. Don't blow it because you're too damn proud."

"I'm not!"

"Yeah, you are. Nobody's perfect, but you're punishing him for making a mistake."

"It was a damn big mistake."

"I get that… but are you gonna hold it against him for the rest of his life? Are you gonna punish yourself into the bargain?" I sit in silence, staring through the windshield, listening to Drew breathing hard, calming down. "Does he know the baby's his?"

"Yes."

"You told him?"

"He guessed."

He shakes his head. "How did he react? Was he angry?"

"No. Not really. I thought he would be but… I—I think I might have misunderstood his message."

"Really?" I can hear the sarcasm in his voice. "You mean it wasn't just about the baby, after all?"

"No. He said he'd realized the timing was right for me to find out if I was pregnant, and he called because he wanted to be there for me, in case I was upset at finding out I wasn't."

"So, he assumed you'd have told him if you were?"

"Yes."

"And this is the guy you're not sure about?" He pulls up at a set of lights and turns to look at me. "I can't be with the woman I love, Ella. I'll never be with her. It hurts like fuck, and I'm not sure I'll ever learn to learn to live with that. But I'd give everything I have for one chance... just one chink of light in all this darkness. Mac screwed up. He knows that. But please, don't let his mistake and your unfounded fears ruin your chance of happiness."

"Unfounded? I told you, he could hurt me again, so easily."

"I know, and I'm telling you, it'll never happen."

"You can't know that."

"Yeah, I can. He loves you, Ella. It's written all over his face. There's no way he's gonna risk losing you again."

The lights change, and he drives off, focusing on the road. I stare at him for a moment, wishing I could believe him... wishing it could be that easy...

Mac

"What the hell happened to you?"

I glance up as I enter Calvin's apartment, surprised to find him at home. He's standing in the kitchen, clutching a cup of coffee and looking like he needs it almost as much as I do.

"Don't ask." I'm sure I look a wreck. My tie is hanging loose around my neck, and I've pushed my fingers through my hair so many times on my cab ride back here, I'm sure I must look demented.

"Too late. I already did. Here… your need seems to be greater than mine."

He hands me the cup, fixing another for himself, and then leads me into the living room. Once we're seated at opposite ends of his dark grey couch, he turns to face me.

"So? What happened?"

"Ella."

"Your ex?" He knows a little about what happened… as much as I felt like telling, just before I left for London.

"She's not my ex."

"What is she then?"

"I'm not sure yet, but she's not my ex. She's going to be the mother of my son, though."

He's raising his cup to his lips and stops, almost comedically, poised like a statue. "She's what?"

"You heard me."

"She's pregnant?"

"Yes."

"And it's yours?"

I frown at him. "Don't go there."

He puts down his cup and holds up his hand. "Okay. But you went back to London in November, and it's now April…"

"I know. I can do the maths."

"Maybe. But what I mean is, why didn't she tell you?"

"Why didn't you?"

His brow creases. "Me? How could I have told you? I don't know Ella. I've never even met her."

"She's on TV every Wednesday night. You knew that."

"Maybe she is," he says. "But I'm in the theatre every evening. When do I get to watch TV?"

"Oh, yeah. Sorry."

His face clears. "And anyway, even if she is on TV, the shows are recorded in advance, aren't they? So I doubt her pregnancy would have been that obvious."

He has a point, and I nod my head, taking a sip of coffee. "Yeah… you're right." I feel like an idiot, but that's nothing compared to all the other emotions fighting for attention.

There's love… obviously. There's an overwhelming urge to protect her, which is tricky, when she doesn't seem to want to speak to me… and there's fear. Fear that she'll never be able to forgive me for what I've done. I suck in a breath, clenching my fist, struggling for control.

"Are you okay?" Calvin asks and I shake my head.

"Not in the slightest." I put down my cup and get to my feet, pacing the floor, as I push my fingers back through my hair, yet again. "I screwed up, Calvin."

"That much is obvious. Ella's pregnant."

I stop and look down at him. "That's not what I mean. I—I got it wrong… about the studio… about the press."

"You did?"

"Yeah. It wasn't Ella who spoke to them about me. It was Kennedy."

"How did you find that out?"

"She admitted it tonight, in front of everyone."

"Oh… shit."

"Yeah. I—I said some awful things to Ella when we broke up."

"But it was a misunderstanding," he says, trying to be reasonable, in the absence of reason.

"I don't think she sees it that way."

"Is that why she didn't tell you about the baby?"

"I think so… in part. She said it was because she didn't want me to feel obligated."

"And do you?"

I remember Ella's words. "Yes. I feel responsible… and committed, although I'm not sure exactly what it is I'm committed to. I asked if I could see her, and she didn't reply.

She's said I can call, but I don't know whether she wants me back."

"But you want her back?"

"God, yes. I always did. I wish I'd never left now," I say, looking down at him. "Speaking of which, would it be okay if I stayed here a little longer?"

"Sure. You can help me run my lines. If today's rehearsal was anything to go by, this show is never going to open on Saturday evening, and if it does, it'll be the first production of Uncle Vanya to be performed as a farce."

I sit beside him again. "Stop fretting. It always used to be like this before an opening night. You'll be fine."

He chuckles. "You didn't see the way Desmond was strutting around the stage. It was like a cross between the Ziegfeld Follies and Hamlet."

"I'm not sure that's possible, Calvin."

"You had to be there to believe it."

"Okay, I'll help where I can, and I'll certainly run lines with you."

"Thanks."

"I'm gonna head off to bed now."

"Yeah... you must be tired." He looks up, smiling. "It's not every day a guy discovers he's gonna be a father."

"No, it's not."

I don't remember when I last slept.

The night before the awards ceremony, I lay awake worrying about seeing Ella again. The night after, I lay awake thinking about how I was going to persuade her to give me a second chance... and last night, I lay awake fretting, because every time I've tried to call her, her phone goes straight to voicemail.

Is she avoiding me?

She must be.

But why?

She said I could call, but it seems she's turned her phone off… and I don't get it.

"Do you think I should go over to her apartment?" I look down at Calvin, who's reading through his lines again. We went over them yesterday, and he was word perfect, so I'm not sure what he hopes to gain by reading them again today.

"No. She said you could call. She didn't say you could turn up on her doorstep and harass her."

"I'm not harassing her."

"You've called her a dozen times."

"Yeah… and I can't get through. What if something's happened to her?"

"Her brother would've let you know."

He's right. I know he is.

"Look…" he says, sitting forward and putting down his script. "You've cancelled your flight, you're not in any hurry. Just give her time."

I let out a sigh. I wish it was that easy.

"I'm gonna call Henry."

I'm restless. I can't even think straight. It's lunchtime here, so it'll be early evening in London, and although it's a Saturday and the gallery will still be open, I doubt it will be busy.

Henry answers promptly, on the third ring, clearly surprised to hear from me… and even more surprised when I break the news that not only did I get it wrong with Ella, but I'm going to be a father… and I'm not coming home.

"Ever?" he says.

"I'll come back to visit, but Ella's here. Our son's going to be here in a few months' time, and that means I belong here, too… assuming she'll give me a second chance."

"She will. Just don't give up."

"I'm not going to."

"Good. If you need me to send your things over, just call, and I'll arrange it."

"Thanks, but I think you're getting ahead of yourself, don't you?"

"No. You shouldn't underestimate yourself, Mac."

His words are very comforting, and give me heart, even where I'm not sure there's much hope.

"I'll call you."

"Yes... please do."

We end our call, and I look up at Calvin. He's gone back to studying his script again, and I decide to take a chance and dial Ella's number... yet again.

It rings... it actually rings, and I leap to my feet.

"Mac?"

"Hi, Ella."

Calvin sits back, looking up, and then gets to his feet, vacating the room... bless him.

"Have you been calling me?" Ella asks.

"Yes, but I didn't leave any messages." *I couldn't think what to say, other than 'I love you', and I wasn't going to say that down the phone to your voicemail.*

"Sorry. My phone was turned off."

No kidding, "But I told you I'd call."

"I know, but I got back to Drew's place on Thursday and I had such a headache, I went straight to bed. It was still pretty bad yesterday, so I stayed with him again, resting, and I've only gotten home this morning. I'd forgotten I'd turned my phone off when we got to the ceremony... and I didn't switch it back on until about twenty minutes ago. I—I'm really sorry, Mac."

"Hey... don't be sorry. Are you okay?" She doesn't sound it.

"The headache's a lot better."

"That's not what I asked."

"I'll be fine."

That's still not what I asked. "Can I come over... please? I'm worried about you."

There's a brief pause and I hear her sigh. "Is this about the baby?"

"No. How many times do you need me to say this? I want to see you, Ella. I want you... I want us. Please? I miss you... so damn much." My voice cracks and I hear her gasp. At least I think it's a gasp and not a sigh. This is why I need to see her... so I can gauge her reactions, instead of guessing at them. "Please, let me come over? I can be there in about twenty minutes."

"No, you can't. I—I'm not in Boston."

"But I thought you said you went home."

"Yes... to Newport."

Shit. "Okay. I'll... I'll rent a car and drive down there."

There's another pause, which drags on for a little too long to be comfortable. "O—Okay."

She doesn't sound as enthusiastic as I'd like, but she gives me her address and after I've thanked her, we end our call, and I try to calm my nerves, wandering to Calvin's bedroom and knocking on the door. He calls out, "Come in," and when I do, I find him sitting on the edge of his bed, gazing down at his script.

"I need your help."

He looks up, raising his eyebrows. "What with?"

"I need to rent a car. Quickly."

The house has gates, although why that surprises me, I don't know.

I slow the Toyota Corolla that Calvin helped me to hire, and park in front of them, getting out and approaching the keypad on

the gatepost. I press the button at the base and wait, hearing a man's voice, which just says, "Come in," without asking who I am, and I dash back to the car as the gates open, keen to get through before they close again. This must mean I'm expected, which is a relief, although who the man is remains a mystery... one that nags at me as I drive forward.

The driveway stretches before me, with lawns on either side, so wide I can't see where the boundary of the property is, and I suck in a breath. This must be how multi-millionaires live, I guess, and I continue down the driveway until eventually an enormous house comes into sight.

"Jesus..."

I thought Ella's apartment was something else, but this is affluence on a whole different scale... demonstrated not only by the size of the property itself – which has a central section and two wings, around a forecourt – but also by the bright red Ferrari which is parked alongside Ella's Mercedes. It's like a stately home, or a country estate, and I park my hire car and get out, stretching my back, just as the front door of the house opens and I'm faced with a tall, dark-haired man. I'm guessing he's the man who just let me in, but what I'd really like to know is, what the hell is he doing here?

He looks relaxed enough, in jeans and a t-shirt, like he belongs, and he steps forward, holding out his hand to me.

"I'm Hunter Bennett... Ella's brother."

I relax and remind myself not to keep jumping to conclusions. It's cost me dearly in the past, and I need to learn from that before I screw up again. Now he's closer, I can see the similarities between Hunter and his brother, and I shake his hand. "Hi. I'm Mac."

He smiles. "I know. Ella asked me to be here. I hope that's okay?"

I sense it's not an option and nod my head. "If that's what she wants, sure."

I can't help feeling disappointed, but I swallow it down and follow him into the house.

He closes the door, and I just about have time to take in the vast hallway, the wide stairs leading up to the first floor, and the shining wooden floor. Hunter joins me and directs me to my left, through an archway, into an immense living room. The wall opposite is dominated by a fireplace, and there are four brown leather couches, on one of which Ella is sitting with her legs curled up beneath her. She goes to get up, but I move forward, holding up my hand.

"Stay where you are."

She does, looking up at me as I approach and then sit alongside her. She's wearing an oversized pale pink blouse and stonewashed jeans, which I'm guessing have some give in the waistband, to allow for the bump she's currently resting her hand on. Ignoring her brother, who I think has taken a seat on one of the other sofas, I reach out for her hand, holding it in mine, and gaze into her eyes.

"I'm so sorry, Ella. I made a mistake."

"I noticed." She leans forward slightly, although she doesn't pull her hand from mine… not that I'm about to let her. "You judged me."

"I know… but I also begged you to stay. I didn't want it to end. That was the last thing I wanted."

Anger flares in her eyes. "So you thought you could accuse me of ruining your career, and I'd just take it?"

"No, but try to understand… it was the only thing that made sense to me. I know I let you down, but why did you leave? Why didn't you stay and talk it through with me?"

She frowns. "Because you didn't seem to be in the mood for listening, and I couldn't see the point of staying."

"You couldn't see the point? Even when I was pleading with you not to go?"

She stares at me and blinks a few times, then looks down at our joined hands, although she still doesn't pull hers away. It's clear she's not going to answer, and I can't make her. I move a little closer.

"I'm sorry I judged you. It was wrong of me, and I'll never forgive myself for hurting you. I know you had your reasons for leaving, and that most of them were my fault, but can you explain why you didn't tell me about the baby?" Her eyes widen. "You told me the other night that my phone call was one of the reasons, so what were the others?"

"I did it for you."

Her brother shifts in his seat and I glance over at him, noticing the frown on his face, which I'm sure matches my own. "You kept our baby from me, for my benefit? How? Why?"

She rubs her swollen belly and lets out a sigh. "Because, if you must know, our brother's ex-girlfriend is pregnant with his baby, and I've seen what it's doing to him, having to live a double life. He's the father in waiting to a child he'll never get to live with properly, and because of that, he can't be the man he really wants to be. I decided I couldn't do that to you. This… this mistake isn't something you have to live with, Mac. The fact that I'm pregnant is my fault, just as much as it's yours, and you shouldn't have to give up anything or change your life because of it."

I hold her hand a little tighter. "Our situation is completely different."

"How?"

"To start with, you're not my ex-girlfriend."

"What am I then?"

"I—I don't know," I say, taking a breath. "But you're not my ex-girlfriend. I'll never be able to think of you as that. And

besides, what happened between us wasn't a mistake. It was intentional... or at least it was calculated. We both knew there were consequences to what we were doing, and I wanted to live with them. I still do. If I could be with you again, I wouldn't consider myself as giving up anything. I'd consider myself as gaining everything I ever wanted."

She shakes her head, seemingly unmoved. "There's no obligation, Mac."

I let go of her hand, pushing my fingers back through my hair, and she stares into my eyes. "Yes, there is. And in any case, it wasn't your decision to make. I told you when we were in Vermont that I wasn't going anywhere."

She leans forward, her eyes alight. "Yeah, you did. I remember it... and then you left."

"No. You left me. You walked out."

"Yes, I did. But what I mean is, you went back to London."

"Of course I did. What did I have to stay here for? I didn't know you were pregnant, and I decided I'd rather be fucking miserable in London than fucking miserable here. Jesus... we're going round in circles."

"I know, but the point is, this isn't your problem." She glances down at the bump, and then looks back at me, raising her chin defiantly. "If you've moved on..."

"Moved on?" I stand, staring down at her. "How the hell could you think I'd move on? I get that I let you down. I get that I hurt you... and I'm sorry for everything I did, for every cross word and false accusation. But move on? How was I supposed to do that when my heart was in pieces?"

"Y—Your heart?" she whispers.

"Yes. I love you, Ella. I've always loved you."

It's like time stops for a moment and then suddenly her face crumples and she bursts into tears.

"No… please don't cry." I sit again and pull her into my arms. She's a little stiff, but she leans against me and I hold her shaking body to mine. "Please, Ella…"

"W—Why did you have to say that now?"

I lean back, looking down into her tear-filled eyes. "Because it's the truth. I was gonna tell you when we were at the cabin, but then I forgot the condom, and I thought if I said it then, you'd think I was just making platitudes… just saying it because it was something you needed to hear. I wanted you to take me seriously, so I decided to wait until we got back to Boston."

"Oh, God. But… but I was going to say it then, too."

My heart stops beating, just for a second, and when it starts again, it's like the entire world begins anew. "Y—You mean you loved me?"

"Yes. I thought I'd tell you how I felt and then ask you to move in with me."

"I can't believe this."

"Why not?"

"Because I was going to do exactly the same thing… except I was going to ask if I could move in with you, rather than the other way around. I wasn't sure…"

I stop speaking as a phone rings, and I tear my eyes away from Ella and look over at her brother as he pulls his mobile from his pocket, looking at the screen.

"Sorry," he says. "I need to take this." He connects the call, holding the device to his ear. "Drew?" He listens, then sits forward in his seat. "Her waters have broken?" I feel Ella tense in my arms and she pulls away, focusing on her brother. "Do you want me to come to the hospital?" We both watch, while Hunter listens avidly, his face a picture of concern and concentration. "Okay. Call if you need me."

He hangs up, putting his phone down beside him, and turns to Ella. "Lexi?" she says, that one word obviously meaning

something to both of them as he simply nods his head in reply. Ella puts her hand on the bump again, her protective instincts coming to the fore, as I guess they're talking about her brother's ex-girlfriend, and the fact that she must have gone into labour.

"She's still in Boston, isn't she?" Ella asks. "Drew wasn't gonna take her home until tomorrow."

"No, she's still in Boston. He got a call from her sister."

"Oh, God... that must have been hard for him."

"It was. I think that's why he called. Lexi's sister is gonna be there at the birth, evidently."

Ella shakes her head and then turns to me. "I'm sorry. This probably doesn't make much sense to you. Our brother Drew was seeing Lexi for a while, and they split up shortly after he met her sister and fell in love with her."

"Was that the reason they split up?" I ask.

"No. It wasn't working out between them, anyway. Drew knew he couldn't ask Lexi's sister out straight away, so he was biding his time, and then Lexi got in touch and told him she was pregnant. That's what I meant when I said he couldn't be the man he wanted to be."

"Maybe not, but I can... can't I?"

Chapter Fourteen

Ella

He stares into my eyes and I swallow hard, wondering what he's going to say next. The last half hour has been a rollercoaster, and I'm not sure how much more I can take. I can't answer him and eventually he lets out a sigh. "Please, Ella… I don't want that to be me in a few months' time. I don't want to be the guy rushing to be by your side when you give birth to our son. I want to be with you… all the time." He reaches out, cupping my face and gazing into my eyes. "D—Do you think you could try loving me again?" His voice catches and the pieces of my broken heart somehow slot back into place, the pain of the last few months evaporating in his touch.

"I never stopped, Mac."

He sucks in a breath, his eyes glistening as he leans in and brushes his lips across mine. My body sparks to life, just like it did that very first time, and I bring my arms up around his neck as he deepens the kiss, our tongues meeting in the most familiar way. I'm home at last, and I moan into his mouth, just as I hear a cough from the other side of the room, and Mac pulls away.

We both glance over at Hunter, who's smiling from his place on the couch.

"Why don't you take this to your apartment?" he says, looking at me.

Mac frowns, but then turns back to me, raising his eyebrows. "I can drive us there, if you want?"

"Drive us there?"

"Yes. To Boston."

I shake my head. "I sold my apartment in Boston a week or so after... after what happened." I can't bring myself to say I left him... not now. "Hunter's talking about my apartment here."

"Of course. I remember you telling me about it now. But how could you have sold your place in Boston? I mean... what about the show? Surely you needed to be there for that, didn't you?"

"No. I left the show. I told you, I never wanted to be in front of the cameras and I wasn't interested in working on it with someone else. They hired another presenter... one who could cook. I—I only attended the awards ceremony because I was contractually obliged, and because I assumed it was Vivian who'd betrayed you to the press, and I wanted to confront her."

"Why did you think it was Vivian?" he asks, looking confused.

"Because I knew it wasn't me, and because I agreed with you that it didn't make sense for Kennedy to have done it. I'm not sure I understand why she did, even now. She could have just explained the situation to you, and told you they weren't going to renew your contract... but at the time, Vivian was the only other person whose involvement rang true. She was always flirting with you, and she never liked me... although that was because she'd slept with Drew and he'd dumped her, so..."

Hunter stands. "This is way too confusing for me," he says, smiling down at me.

"Can I assume you'd like us out from under your feet now?" I say, and he shakes his head.

"Not at all. You're welcome to stay wherever you want, but I'm gonna leave you to it. My wife's probably wondering where

I've got to." His smile widens, his eyes shining. "I really like saying that, you know?"

"What?" I frown up at him.

"That Livia's my wife."

I turn to Mac. "You'll have to forgive my brother. He and Livia have only been married a couple of months. He's still getting accustomed to the idea."

"No, I'm not," Hunter says, shaking his head again as he makes for the door. "I'm more than accustomed to it. But it's not something I'll ever take for granted."

"I can understand that." I look at Mac as he speaks, noting the smile on his lips and the way his eyes are fixed on mine.

"Shall… Shall we go to my apartment?"

"I'd like that."

Hunter's already disappeared, and Mac stands, holding out his hand. I take it, letting him help me to my feet and then I lead us out to the back of the lobby, where I open the door to my apartment.

We walk straight into my living room, and although it would be easy to stop and sit on one of my two couches, I take him over to the kitchen instead. It's the place where I'm most comfortable and Mac stops by the island unit, looking around.

"This is perfect for you," he says, smiling.

"Yes, it is. I love it here, although I spend a lot of time in the main house, too… especially when my brothers are here."

He turns, gazing down at me. "They look out for you, don't they?"

"Yes."

He nods his head. "Good."

"Why is that good?" I ask.

"Because I haven't been here to do it myself, so I'm relieved that someone has. It should have been me, I know, but…"

I shake my head, and he stops talking. "I'm sorry I didn't tell you about the baby."

"It's okay," he says. "I understand. If I hadn't jumped to conclusions and driven you away, none of this would have happened."

I pull my hand from his, desperate to change the subject. I'm done with apologies. There are so many more important things to talk about.

"Would you like a cup of tea?" That isn't one of them, but it's a starting point.

"Tea?" He frowns. "Since when did you drink tea?"

"Since coffee started making me feel sick."

"Oh. Is that a pregnancy thing?"

"Yes. At the beginning, it was horrendous. Just the slightest whiff had me rushing to the bathroom."

"But it's better now?" he asks, looking concerned.

"Better is a relative term. I'm not being sick anymore, but the smell makes me nauseous. So... is tea okay?"

"I'm British... what do you think?"

I chuckle and wander over to the stove, putting the kettle on to boil before I turn around and look across at him. "So... where have you been staying since you got back here? I assume you gave up your apartment?"

"Yes, I did. I've been staying with an old friend of mine."

I feel a shiver of jealousy, and fold my arms across my chest, just above the bump, sucking in a breath. "Oh?"

He comes around the island unit, putting his hands on my shoulders, and looks down into my eyes. "His name's Calvin. He used to be in the theatre company with me."

I step back slightly, his hands dropping to his sides again. "It's okay. I wasn't asking for details. We broke up. If you've been..."

He steps closer. "I haven't. I told you, I couldn't move on, not without you."

"Maybe. But if there's been someone… casual." I'm fishing now. I need to know.

He shakes his head. "There hasn't been anyone." I can't help smiling, and he smiles back. "What about you?"

"What about me?"

"Has there been anyone?"

"In my condition?" I say, patting the top of the bump.

His smile widens. "Pregnant or not, you're still the most beautiful woman I've ever seen… so yeah, in your condition…"

"No. There's been no-one."

"And has your condition been the only thing that's stopped you?"

He doesn't even blink or seem to breathe, waiting for my answer. "No."

He grabs me around my waist, pulling me close against him. His lips are barely an inch from mine and I can feel his breath, hot against my skin. "Am I forgiven?"

"Am I… for keeping this from you?"

"Yes. Now answer my question."

"You're forgiven. I love you, Mac. I can't not forgive you."

He closes the gap, his lips crushing mine, his tongue and mine swirling as he moans into my mouth, and I sigh in return.

"Whoa…" I pull back.

"What's wrong?" Mac keeps a hold of me, staring down into my eyes, his own filled with worry.

"The baby… he kicked."

Mac's face clears, and he smiles. "Really?"

"Yeah. You can't feel it on the outside yet, but every so often, I can feel him moving."

He reaches out, his hand hovering over the bump.

"May I?"

"Of course. I'm sorry about what I said the other night. You don't need my permission to touch. He's yours."

"And you? Are you mine, too?"

"Always."

He smiles and puts his hand on the bump, and even though I've told him he won't be able to feel anything, I adjust the position of his hand to where the movement was.

"What does it feel like?" he asks.

"It varies. Sometimes it's like being tickled from the inside… like butterflies. But I think he's been moving around a little more over the last few days. From time to time, like just now, I get a much more defined feeling of something… I don't know… stretching inside me. Like he's making his presence felt."

Mac rubs his hand over the bump, then brings it up, cupping my face. "I'm glad."

"What about?"

"That I didn't miss this… that I'm gonna be here for at least some of your pregnancy."

"Be grateful you missed the morning sickness. It wasn't pretty."

He shakes his head. "I'm not grateful I missed any of it. I—I wish I could turn back the clock."

I pull away slightly so I can see him properly. "To undo this?"

"No," he says, grabbing me and pulling me back. "No, Ella."

"It wasn't planned, Mac. I'd understand if you had doubts."

"I don't," he says, shaking his head and letting out a sigh. "I —I'll be honest with you, when I didn't hear from you, after I left you that message, I was devastated. Not just because I wanted you back, but because I wanted this… more than I would have thought possible."

"Really?"

"Yes. And whatever you say, I don't think either of us can claim it was entirely unplanned. I only forgot the condom once, but we both knew exactly what we were doing every time after

that. We understood the risks we were taking, and we went in with our eyes wide open, didn't we?" I nod my head. He's not saying anything I haven't thought myself. "I'd never want to undo this, but I'd love to turn back the clock and undo my mistakes and all the awful things I said to you, so I could have been here when you found out about this… so I could have been here right from the beginning."

"I should have told you."

"No. I shouldn't have left it for you to tell me. I should have followed through… made sure." He shakes his head. "Even if you didn't want me, I should've…"

"I—I wanted you, Mac," I say, resting my hands on his biceps, my body tingling at the memory of what it felt like to be safe in his arms. "I always wanted you."

He swallows my words in a bruising kiss. "I'm sorry, Ella."

I pull back, looking up into his glistening eyes. This has to stop. We can't keep looking back and apologizing all our lives.

The kettle is about to boil, but I turn off the stove and take his hand. "Can I show you something?"

"Sure."

I lead him to the bottom of the stairs, hoping as I put my foot on the first step, that what I'm about to show him will go some of the way to convincing him we've got better things to do than say sorry. We've got so much more to look forward to…

Mac

I follow Ella up the stairs, unable to stop myself from smiling.

She's in love with me... and all my fears, my worries, the months of loneliness and pain seem like distant memories now. I can feel her hand in mine. It's real. Like our love, which I can see in her eyes and feel in my heart.

I'm not sure where she's taking me. It could be her bedroom, I guess... although I've got no idea what she thinks she's going to 'show' me in there. I've seen it all already. Although I haven't seen her naked and pregnant... so maybe that's it.

We get to the top and she stops, staring up at me.

"I didn't realize you'd met Drew."

"Neither did I. At least, I didn't realize the photographer was Drew... and that Drew was your brother. When did you find out?"

"On the day the invitation arrived for the awards ceremony. He was here with me, and told me he'd met you."

"He hadn't realized the connection until then?"

She shakes her head. "He'd realized it," she says. "He'd just kept it to himself for a while."

"Did he have a reason?" I wonder if he'd decided I wasn't good enough for her. "Did he know about our argument?"

"Yes. Both of my brothers knew about that."

"So, did he think you'd be better off with someone else... or at least without me?"

"No. On the contrary. He kept it to himself because I was upset about us breaking up, and I was pregnant. He didn't think that was a good mix."

"He was probably right." Although I don't feel very good about hearing any of that. "What made him change his mind?" I ask. "About telling you, I mean?"

"He wanted me to know you'd liked me… even then."

I step back a little, although I don't let go of her hand. "Why did he want you to know that?"

She smiles. "I see you're not denying it?"

"No. Why would I deny it? It's true. I remember telling him I was in danger of falling for you."

"Even though we'd done nothing but argue?"

I nod my head. "I thought you were beautiful and sexy, and I wanted to spend some time with you… to get to know you. But stop changing the subject. Why did Drew tell you?"

"Because he wanted me to tell you about the baby. He said you had a right to know."

I'm not about to disagree or ask her why Drew's ploy didn't work. She's apologised, and that's enough for me. I'm the one who's in the wrong here, not Ella.

"I'm sorry you didn't feel you could tell me… even after Drew's efforts."

She shakes her head. "I don't want you to be sorry. I only told you about my conversation with him, because I wanted to explain that I was in love with you, too."

"Back then, you mean?"

She shrugs her shoulders. "Maybe not on the first day we met, but pretty soon afterwards."

"How soon? Before or after our first kiss? Before or after we first made love?"

She blushes. "I was most of the way there before, but it was making love that clinched it," she says and I can't help chuckling, as she leans in to me for a moment before she pulls back. "I brought you up here for a reason."

"Oh, yeah?"

I wiggle my eyebrows, and she smiles, shaking her head. I guess our presence upstairs has nothing to do with her bedroom, or me seeing her naked and pregnant, but as I'm about to ask her for an explanation, she turns and opens the door behind her.

"I wanted to show you this."

I follow her inside the room, my breath catching in my throat when I see the pale blue walls, the crib by the window and the dresser by the far wall. She releases my hand, and I let her go with some reluctance, watching as she wanders over to the dresser, pulling open the second drawer down.

"I—I haven't bought very much for him yet, but these rompers caught my eye, and…" She turns back, holding up two tiny garments, one in grey with white ducks on the front, and the other in white with grey ducks. I smile, going straight to her, and take the rompers, holding them in my hands.

"They're so small."

"Aren't they?" She leans in to me. "We can go out together and get some more things for him, if you like."

"I'd love to," I say, kissing the top of her head just as my phone rings. I pull it from my pocket, frowning when I see Moira's name on the screen, and I reject the call. "Have you thought of…" My phone rings again.

"I think you'd better take that, don't you?" Ella looks up at me and I nod my head, handing her back the rompers and connecting the call as I wander over to the crib, focusing on the mobile that's hanging above it.

"Hello?" I'm looking at a fox, a rabbit, a bear and a toadstool, all made of felt, and all hanging over what will be my son's crib. They're interspersed with green leaves and grey stars, and I can't help smiling, wondering what he'll make of it.

"Hi." Moira's voice brings me back to reality.

"I wasn't expecting to hear from you."

"I know… and before you ask, I've remembered you're still in America, but I wanted to see how it all went and ask if you need picking up from the airport on Monday."

I'm unsure how to answer the first part of her question, so I ignore it. "I'm not coming home on Monday."

"Oh? Is there a problem with the flights?"

"No, there's no problem. I'm just not coming home."

There's a brief silence. "Y—You mean you're staying there?"

"Yes."

"For good?"

"Yes."

"But why?" she asks, sounding doubtful. "I don't understand, Mac. I thought…"

I'm not sure I want to hear what she thought. That alarm bell is ringing in my head again, so I cut her off before she can elaborate. "Do you remember me telling you about someone I left behind in Boston?"

"Yes. Of course I do."

"Well…"

"You're staying for her?" she says, raising her voice, her doubt replaced by anger as she finishes my sentence for me.

"Yes, I am."

"But what about us?"

That alarm bell is deafening now. "There is no 'us'."

"There could be, though, couldn't there? Please, Mac. I want you back. Why do you think I've been making so much effort… spending so much time with you over the last few months?"

"I don't know. Because we're friends?"

"Friends? Don't kid yourself. This was never about friendship."

"It was for me," I say and she falls silent. "I told you that was all we could ever be."

"I know. But I didn't think you were serious."

"Then you should have said. I'm not a bloody mind-reader, and you told me you were over me. You called me arrogant for assuming otherwise."

"You led me on, Mac."

"No, I didn't. Whatever you thought was going on between us was only happening in your imagination." I hear a sniffle… or what sounds like one. "Look, I'm sorry if this isn't what you wanted to hear, but Ella's the only woman I've ever loved, and I'm staying here to make a life with her. I think it's best if you don't call me again. I won't risk my relationship with Ella… not for anyone."

I half expect her to start crying in earnest, but after a few seconds, she screams, "I hate you, Mac," and hangs up.

Well, that was different… and typically melodramatic.

Without giving it a second thought, I go to my contacts list and delete Moira's number. Then I turn to see Ella, still holding the baby's clothes, and looking at me, fear etched all over her face.

I pocket my phone and go straight to her, taking the rompers and putting them down, before I pull her into my arms. She's stiff, untrusting… but I hang on.

"Who was that?" she whispers.

"Moira."

She leans back and then pushes on my chest, trying to get away, although there's no way I'm letting her, and eventually she stops struggling and glares up at me. "Moira? As in your ex-girlfriend?"

"Yes."

"Have you and she been…?"

"No, we haven't. I told you, there's been no-one since we broke up, and I meant it," I say and she relaxes, just slightly.

"But you have been seeing her?"

"As a friend, yes. Nothing more. Looking back, I think that was a mistake, but it wasn't intentional. I only ran into her by accident when I went out to celebrate."

"Celebrate what?"

"My book was accepted by a publisher. I..."

"Really?" Her face lights up, all thoughts of Moira forgotten for a moment.

"Yeah. Didn't you hear Kennedy mention it the other night?"

She shakes her head. "No. I'm sorry. I wasn't paying attention. But how did Kennedy know?"

"Because Delilah's talking to a producer or someone about turning it into a TV show."

"Are you serious?"

"Delilah is. The producer seems to be."

"And you?"

"I'm not so sure, but I'm letting them run with it at the moment."

"But that's... that's so exciting."

I move my hand between us, caressing the bump. "Not compared to this, it's not."

She smiles and nestles in to me. "Tell me about Moira?"

I hold her close. "I went to the pub to celebrate the news of my publishing contract, and she was there."

"You went up to her?"

"No. She came up to me. I bought her a drink to be friendly."

"But she wanted more?"

"She said she didn't."

"And she called you arrogant?" she says, frowning, but making it clear she heard what I said to Moira.

"Yes. I was in the middle of giving her my best 'we can't be anything more than friends' speech when she delighted in telling me she was over me... and I believed her. More fool me."

She lets out a sigh and tips her head to one side. "Have you seen her since then?"

"Yes, from time to time. It wasn't a regular thing."

She looks up into my eyes. "Answer me one question?"

"Of course."

"Did you sleep with her?" she asks, surprising me. "Even if it was just for old time's sake. Please be honest with me. I won't mind if you did, but…"

"I didn't. I couldn't."

"We broke up, Mac. I left you."

"And? That doesn't mean I stopped loving you. It doesn't mean I stopped being yours. Even when we were three thousand miles apart, I was still yours. I always will be," I say, cupping her face in my hand. "It was a stupid idea to let Moira back into my life, and I'm sorry I did. I'm sorry for everything…"

She clamps her fingers over my mouth. "Please don't say sorry again."

I move her hand away, keeping it clasped between us. "Why not? I've got a lifetime of apologies to make."

"No… no, you haven't. That's why I brought you up here."

"Oh? So it wasn't to show me the nursery, and the baby's clothes?"

"Yes, in a way… but it was about more than that. I wanted to show you we need to stop looking back and thinking about all the hurt we caused each other… and start looking forward." She raises our hands, kissing mine. "I've missed you so much, Mac."

"I've missed you, too."

"We're going to be parents in a few months' time, and I'd rather we focused on building a future together than anything we've done in the past… other than this." She puts both of our hands onto the bump and I smile at her, nodding my head.

"I don't deserve you."

"Yes, you do. But if you want to come to my bedroom to prove it…"

I smile, and she bites her bottom lip. "If that's what you want?"

"It is."

She steps back and, keeping hold of my hand, leads me out of the nursery and across the hall to her bedroom. I barely notice the white walls and sheer curtains, and focus instead on the enormous bed, steering her towards it.

"Do you trust me?" I murmur, looking down into her upturned face.

"Why do you ask?"

"Because I've seen so much doubt in your eyes over the last hour or so, I need to know."

She sucks in a breath, moving closer. "I trust you, Mac. Do you trust me?"

"I always did."

She tilts her head, frowning. "Really?"

"Yes. I know you think I didn't. I know that's why you left, but believe me, even then I trusted you with everything that mattered…"

I capture her lips with mine, and she melts into me. She fumbles for a moment, then finds the hem of my t-shirt, pulling it up, as I unfasten her blouse, pushing it from her shoulders and yanking off my t-shirt at the same time. I quickly undo her bra, dropping it to the floor, and then I lower her carefully onto the mattress, kneeling up between her legs so I can look down at her.

"Do these undo like normal jeans?" I ask, taking in the elasticated panels at the sides.

"Yes." She nods her head, raising her hips so I can pull them down, along with her underwear. "Sorry about those."

"About what?"

"My panties. They're not the sexiest things in the world, but they're comfortable."

I lean over her, careful to keep my weight off of the bump. "Hey… I didn't notice. And anyway, you're not wearing them anymore." She chuckles and I kiss her, nudging her legs apart with mine, and kissing my way down her body, stopping when I get to her extended nipples. "Hmm… this is different."

"What is?"

"Your breasts. They're bigger."

"I know. They seem huge to me."

I cup them in my hands. "They are." I run my tongue over her nipples, one at a time, and she arches her back before I move lower, kissing the bump and then resting in the valley of her parted thighs. She's still shaved and I part her lips with my fingers, flicking my tongue across her exposed clit.

"Oh, Mac…" She bucks her hips off of the bed, grinding into me, her hand clamping down on the back of my head. She tastes so good, I can't get enough, and I suck her into my mouth, nipping at her with my teeth. Her body quivers, and although I need to feel her come, I need to be inside her more, and I pull back, kneeling up. "Mac…?"

I shake my head, unfastening my jeans and pushing them down, along with my boxers. "I—I can't wait any longer."

I lean over her, taking my weight on my arms and push inside her, letting out a sigh of satisfaction as I join us. She takes my length, raising her hips and parting her legs wide.

"Take me… please."

I nod my head, unable to speak, and pull almost all the way out, before I plunge back in, once… then twice before she screams, with pleasure not pain, her orgasm claiming her as she thrashes wildly beneath me. She's out of control, her head thrown back, her body convulsing, my name a constant cry on her lips… and all the while I hammer into her, harder and harder, until she finally calms, opens her eyes and smiles up at me.

"That was incredible," she says.

"I noticed." I keep moving, slowing the pace a little. "Did it feel different?"

"Yes. So much more intense… if that were possible."

I stop moving and lower myself down just a little, my lips poised above hers. "Is that the first time you've come since…?"

"Yes."

"You mean you haven't touched yourself in all these months?"

"No."

"Not once?"

She shakes her head. "I didn't want to… not without you."

I kiss her, my tongue finding hers, claiming her as mine again, and when I lean back up, she looks into my eyes.

"What about you?" she asks.

I shake my head. "It wouldn't have been the same."

She reaches up, her hands on my shoulders. "We can forget about that now. We're together again."

"Yeah… we are."

I pull out of her and she frowns. "Where are you going? I thought…"

"I'm not going anywhere… you are."

She opens her mouth, but only manages a squeal, as I flip her over onto her front, pulling her up onto her knees, so she's on all fours.

"I need to be deep inside you, Ella… as deep as I can go."

She parts her legs and I settle between them, slamming into her so hard I almost lift her off of the bed. She drops her shoulders to the mattress, grabbing a handful of the covers and yells out a strangled, "Yes!"

Beads of sweat form on my chest and back as I take her, harder and harder, and she urges me on.

"I'm so close, Mac… so close."

I can feel she is, and so am I. I grab her shoulders, pulling her up and onto me, her legs spread, so she's astride me as I kneel back.

"Ride me... ride my cock."

She raises herself up, slamming back down again, taking my entire length, and I reach around, one hand on the bump, the other below it, finding her clit and rubbing it... hard. She takes just a moment or two to clamp around my cock, her body tensing.

"I'm... I'm..."

She explodes, her body trembling, then spasming against mine. It's more than I can take, and as she rocks back into me, I hold her there and let go deep inside her, giving her everything I've got... months and months of pent-up emotions spilling out of me.

We both take some time to calm, and all the while we do, I hold her in my arms, supporting her, until she gets her breath back.

"Are you okay?" I ask eventually.

She sighs. "I'm absolutely fine."

I smile and she kneels up, parting us, which seems a shame, although she turns around to face me, putting her arms around my neck, and I lie us down gently, side-by-side, face-to-face. She's close enough to kiss, and she's in my arms, where she belongs.

"Stay," she whispers, and my smile widens.

I wrap a leg around her, pulling her closer. "For the night?" I'm teasing and she knows it.

"What do you think?"

"Well... I don't have a change of clothes, so I'm not sure I can."

She frowns up at me. "I didn't have any clothes the first time I stayed over with you... although I guess that was different. I only stayed for the weekend."

"No, you didn't." I shake my head and take her hand, kissing it and then placing it over my heart. "You stayed forever."

Epilogue

—⁓—

Ella

Why does the beginning of August have to be so damned hot?

I've never noticed it before, but I guess I've never been nine months pregnant before, either.

The last half of my pregnancy has been so much better than the first, but that's because Mac's been here, being oh, so solicitous.

He hasn't left my side since he said he'd always loved me. I knew then we had to put the past behind us; we had to move forward... and we had to do it together, because I've always loved him, too.

We've been living here in my apartment ever since. Mac helped me complete the nursery, and we had fun buying everything the baby could possibly need... and a few things he almost certainly won't.

We also converted the space that was once my formal dining area into a writing room, adding a wall and a door, where neither existed before. I never used it anyway, and we prefer eating in the kitchen.

Between supervising the alterations, looking after me, buying things for the baby, preparing the nursery, and attending all my

appointments with me, Mac has somehow found the time to finish the second book in his series and it went off to the publishers at the beginning of the summer. With luck, it'll be out before Christmas. He's started the third one now, and the fourth and fifth have already been planned. He doesn't tell me much about his plots while he's writing, but he doesn't make me wait to buy one either. Instead, I read the first one after he'd completed the last edit, and the second one before he sent it off to Delilah. I love them… especially the central character. She's strong and feisty, and funny, too… and in this second book, he's made much more of the love story between her and the police inspector, which is kinda cute.

We're meant to be together, and we share everything, which is why I was surprised when he suddenly announced a couple of months ago that he'd pulled out of the negotiations with the production company for the rights to his books.

"Really? Are you sure?"

He came and sat beside me on the couch. "Yeah. I've just spoken to Delilah."

"What did she say?"

"After she'd calmed down, she accepted my decision."

"But what made you change your mind?" We hadn't talked about it for a while, but the last time it had come up, he was still happy to let Delilah handle things.

He took my hands in his, looking into my eyes. "She sent me an email earlier, saying the producer wanted me to go to New York for four days."

"Why?"

"I don't know. She didn't explain. She just said it was important."

"I see."

"And then I realized that was just the beginning. They might only want four days now, but it could be longer next time, or they

might ask me to go further away... and I'm not doing it. I'm not leaving you."

"Y—You're doing this for me?"

"I'm doing this for us." He moved closer, letting go of my hand and pulling me into his arms.

"Because of the baby?"

"No. Because I love you. I need to be with you."

I needed him to be with me, too... and I kissed him. Deeply.

Since then, he's been a lot happier just writing. His first book is due out next month, and I have to admit, I'm almost as excited about that as I am about the impending birth of our baby.

I sit back in my chair, glancing across at him, and try to get comfortable. He seems oblivious of the heat, his head bent, his fingers flying across the keyboard, and I can't help smiling as I rub my hand across the bump. It's enormous now, and it's not just 'the bump' anymore. It has a name.

We decided on that the day after Mac came back.

As he'd rightly pointed out, he had no clothes, so the next morning, we drove into the city... him in his rental car and me in my Mercedes. He returned the Toyota to the rental company, and I drove him on to his friend's apartment, where he collected his things. Calvin seemed surprised to see us, and offered us coffee, which we both declined for obvious reasons. He and Mac discussed his opening night, which he said hadn't gone as badly as he'd expected, and then we went into Mac's room and I watched him pack his things.

Afterwards, we said goodbye to Calvin. Mac promised to stay in touch with him, and I drove us back to Newport. It all felt new and exciting, and I think we were both a little nervous. We might have found each other again, but we were still edgy... finding our way. We needed to make conversation, and it was Mac who got us started.

"Have you chosen a name for the baby?" he asked. I could hear the worry in his voice, and although I was negotiating traffic and couldn't look at him, I could tell he was fearful that he'd missed out on something else.

"No."

"You're not just saying that, so I'll feel better?"

"No, Mac. I haven't been able to think of anything."

He fell silent for a moment or two. "I'm guessing you don't want to name him after your father?"

"Hell, no."

He chuckled. "What about other male relatives… or friends?"

"I'm not naming my son after my brothers, if that's what you're suggesting. Aside from the fact that I'd have to choose one and offend the other, they'd never let me forget it."

"I wasn't thinking of your brothers. I meant other relatives. Don't you have any uncles?"

"No. Both of my parents were only children. What about you?"

"What about me?"

"Do you have any family names we could consider? I mean… what was your dad called?"

He paused and then said. "Blake."

I glanced over at him, although he was looking straight ahead and I couldn't read his face. "You shared the same name?"

"Yes. It's one of the reasons I prefer to be called Mac."

"But you and your father had a good relationship, didn't you?"

"We had a great relationship, but both of us having the same name was bloody confusing."

I laughed, and he joined in, which eased some of the tension. "I remember you saying you don't have any uncles, but is there anyone else?"

"I have a godfather," he said.

"Oh?" I vaguely remembered him saying something about leaving him behind when he came over here.

"Yeah. How do you feel about Henry? As a name, I mean."

I mulled it over for all of about two seconds, deciding I liked the sound of it. "Is that your godfather's name?"

"Yes."

"Have you told me that before?"

"I might have done. I can't remember now."

"Tell me about him," I said.

"He's always been there." Mac's voice was wistful, and I slowed the car so I could concentrate on what he was saying. "He was my dad's best friend, and when my parents were killed, he became... I don't know... a kind of surrogate dad."

"Someone you could turn to?"

"Yeah. When I... when I got back to London in November, I didn't know what to do. I was practically broke and had nothing to look forward to," he said and I reached over, putting my hand on his leg. He placed his on top, caressing my knuckles. "So, I called Henry, and he gave me somewhere to live... someone to talk to."

"Is that where you've been ever since?"

"Yes. In his basement flat. To be honest, I'd have been lost without him."

I was tempted to say 'sorry', but we'd agreed to stop apologizing, so instead I took his hand and placed it on the bump. "Say hello to Henry."

Mac shifted in his seat, twisting around so he was facing me. "You're happy with the name?"

"Yes."

"You're sure?"

"I'm positive."

He chuckled. "Henry's going to love this…"

We haven't told him yet. Mac had to call him when we got back to Newport, to ask if he'd arrange to ship all his things over, but didn't mention the baby's name. He'd decided to wait until after the baby's born. I think he was worried Henry would try to talk him out of it. I haven't met him yet, but I've seen him on FaceTime. Mac talks to him regularly, updating him on the baby's progress, and how his books are going. He says he'll come for a visit when the baby's born, and I can't wait to meet him… and thank him in person for being there when Mac needed him.

I focus on my laptop screen again, trying to concentrate. I've been working on a cookery book since Mac's return, and it's so nearly complete. Drew's taken the photographs for me, and they look fabulous. I've written all the recipes, having tried and tested them on Mac, Hunter and Livia, Pat and Mick, and even Livia's mom and dad, who've settled in well after the trauma of their move down here.

Now I've just got to finish the introduction, if I don't melt first. Delilah promised to look at it once it's done, so I just need to polish off this last paragraph…

"Is your brother coming down tomorrow?" Mac asks, just as I'm about to start typing again, and I look over at him. I love sharing our work space. We're good at it, and rarely interrupt each other, although neither of us minds when it happens.

"Which one?"

"Hunter."

"Yes, I imagine so. He hasn't said he won't be. Why?"

He turns in his seat, spinning it around so he's facing me, a smile etched on his lips. "If he and Livia are coming down early again, we should take advantage of having the pool to ourselves this afternoon… especially as Pat and Mick are away, too."

"We can use the pool when they're here, you know?"

He nods his head. "I know, but we have to wear swimming costumes."

I chuckle, and his smile widens. "In that case, I'd love to have a swim."

"Good. Why don't we stop in… say, half an hour?"

"Okay. I've just got the last paragraph of my introduction to write, and then I'm done."

"I won't hold you up any longer, then."

He spins back around again and focuses on his screen while I look back at mine, trying to decide what to write. I had an idea, but I can't remember what it was now…

I'm feeling distracted again. It seems to be easily done these days, and now I'm wondering why Hunter and Livia have taken to spending more time here. They used to arrive on Friday evenings and leave late on Sunday nights, but now they get here by Friday lunchtime and don't leave again until sometime on Monday afternoon. Don't get me wrong… I love seeing them, and we all get along really well. I just don't understand the change in their routine. I would have said it was because Livia wanted to spend more time with her parents, but her mom and dad have been living here for a while now, and this change has only been in the last few weeks. And besides, when they're here, they spend most of their time at the house… shut away.

As for Drew, he has absolutely no routine at all now. That's one of the reasons I want to get my book finished before our baby's born. I've seen the chaos Drew's life has become since the arrival of his daughter.

He was relieved Lexi had a girl… not just because that was what he wanted, but because he didn't like the name Xavier any more than I did. She's called Maisie, just like Lexi wanted, and she's absolutely adorable.

We don't see as much of her as I'd like, but he's brought them down here a few times, and they've stayed in the guest house

together. It's big enough that Lexi and Maisie can have their own space, and Drew converted one of the bedrooms into a nursery. It's easy to see that he loves spending time with his daughter, and he's so besotted that when they're not here, he's with them… whenever his work will allow.

"I feel like a weekend dad," he said the last time I spoke to him. "But what can I do?"

"You don't think Lexi would consider moving to Boston?"

"I doubt it. As far as I know, she's always lived in New York."

"You don't think she'd like to live nearer to her sister?"

"No. I'm reading between the lines, but I get the impression they're not that close."

"But I thought they were. I thought that was why Lexi wanted to spend some time in Boston before Maisie was born."

I heard him sigh. "Like I said at the time, I think a lot of that was to do with boredom, more than anything. I just wish I'd realized sooner that the tie between them isn't as strong as I thought it was."

"Would it have made a difference?" I'm not sure he'd have been able to date Lexi's sister, regardless of their relationship. Not when Lexi was expecting his child.

"I don't know… but it's too late now."

I could hear the regret in his voice, and my heart went out to him. I knew how it felt to lose the person you love. Except I'd been lucky. Mac had come back to me.

Drew wasn't so fortunate.

I stare at my screen, suddenly remembering what I wanted to say in this last paragraph. It was to offer my thanks to the people who helped me write the book… so that's Drew for taking the photographs, the rest of the family for being guinea pigs, and Mac… for everything.

I find a way of wording that, surprised by the tears that well up in my eyes, which is another thing that happens all the time at the

moment, and once I'm happy, I save the document and close my laptop. I can send it to Delilah another day. Right now, I need to get in the pool... before I spontaneously combust.

"I'm done. What about you?" I turn to face Mac.

"Just two more seconds."

He types furiously, his head bent, and I watch, loving his enthusiasm. Then he stops and spins around, smiling at me.

"Finished."

"Not the book?"

"No. Just that chapter."

I nod my head. "Can we go for a swim now?"

"Sure." He stands and comes across the room, leaning over me, his hands on the arms of my chair, his lips touching mine. "We need to get you naked."

My body shudders. "Hmm... I like the sound of that."

I heard somewhere that in the very late stages of pregnancy, women sometimes go off having sex. I guess that's probably because it's uncomfortable... and I can understand that. But, if anything, I seem to want Mac even more. We've had to be creative with positions, but I can't get enough of him, and regardless of my size, it seems he feels the same.

He offers his hand and I take it, letting him pull me up, just as a sharp pain rips through my abdomen and I let out a cry. The bump is harder than usual, and it feels tight, the pain searing through me. I struggle to breathe, and I cling to Mac for support.

"Ella? What's wrong? Tell me..."

I look up at him, the pain subsiding. "I—I don't know."

"Was that a contraction?"

"I'm not sure. I—I mean, there's no guidebook for this, is there?"

He smiles. "No. Do you want to sit down again?"

"I don't think so."

I take a step closer to him, then feel a trickle of water running down my leg. It's followed by a gush, and we both look down at the puddle on the wooden floor before our eyes meet again.

"I think that tells us everything we need to know." Mac sounds very calm, even though my heart is racing. He smiles and leans in, kissing me briefly. "Stay here. I'll go fetch your bag."

I nod and he disappears, although he returns a second later, empty-handed, and comes up, taking me in his arms, his lips meeting mine in a hard, fast kiss.

"I love you, Ella."

"I love you, too."

He smiles and turns away again, and even though I'm a little nervous about what's to come, I know I'll be okay. I'll be safe, because Mac's with me.

And he always will be.

Mac

I'm doing my best to stay calm, or to give the appearance of being calm, anyway.

We've been waiting so long for this moment, and now it's here, it feels unreal. But there's no time to think, and I run upstairs, grabbing Ella's bag from the bedroom, before I rush back down and re-join her in the writing room.

She's leaning over the desk, clutching the bump with one hand and her phone with the other.

"What are you doing?" I ask as I stop in the doorway, looking at her.

"I'm calling the birthing centre." It's not the most logical thing to be doing right now, but I guess if it makes her happy…

She suddenly yelps, and I drop the bag, going straight to her as she turns her head, looking up at me.

"This really hurts, Mac," she says, her face creased with pain.

I feel so helpless, wanting to do something, but knowing I can't… not really.

"What do you need?"

"I need someone at the hospital to answer the goddamn phone."

"Forget about it. Let's just go." It makes more sense to me, anyway.

She nods her head, hanging up the call, and I take her hand, grabbing the bag with my free one, and help her outside.

We changed Ella's convertible for a more sensible SUV about a month ago, although it's still a Mercedes, and once I've helped her into the passenger seat, I leap in behind the wheel.

"Are you o—"

Her cry interrupts my question and I watch her face crumple in agony as she clutches the bump. For a second I wonder if we're even going to make it to the hospital, but after a short while, she relaxes and looks over at me.

"Just go, Mac."

I start the engine and put my foot down.

Fortunately, the hospital is only ten minutes away, but by the time we arrive, Ella's already panting hard, and I'm struggling not to panic. I get her inside the building and a nurse comes straight over, taking charge and ushering us into a delivery room.

I'm nudged aside, while it seems all hell breaks loose. Ella's contractions are really close together now, and several people come into the room, examining her, wiring her up to a monitor and writing things down on charts… and although Ella's only a few feet away, she's not close enough for me.

That's one thing I've learned over the last few months… that having Ella close to me is everything I need. That's why I walked away from the negotiations with the TV company. Delilah didn't understand, but I was adamant. If it meant spending even an hour away from Ella, I wasn't going to do it.

That was the best decision I've made – apart from coming back here – and I have no regrets about any of it.

Ella's taught me that looking back and harbouring regrets is a waste of time. We have so many more positive things we could be doing, and we spend a lot of time doing them.

If we're not working together, we're cooking together, and I've surprised myself – and Ella – by becoming quite adept in the kitchen. I'm nowhere near as proficient as she is, but I could survive by myself, without relying on take-aways… although I hope I never have to.

When we're not working or cooking, we've been relaxing, enjoying each other and making love as often as possible… making the most of the time before the baby comes and relaxing becomes a thing of the past.

Making love won't become a thing of the past. I'm sure of that. We both want each other too much for that to happen.

"Mac?" I look up at the sound of Ella's voice and notice that the initial chaos seems to have died down. Everyone else has gone, except the midwife, who's moved to the other side of the bed and is studying the monitor. That means there's space enough for me to step forward, taking Ella's hand in mine. She gives me a squeeze, her eyes filled with a mixture of fear and excitement. I feel the same, but I do my best to bury my emotions and focus on hers, leaning in, so my lips are beside her ear.

"I love you so much."

"I love… oh, crap…" She's seized by yet another contraction, her grip tightening on my hand, crushing my fingers. In an ideal

world, I'd pull my hand away, but I know this is nothing compared to what she's going through, and I clench my teeth, pretending it doesn't hurt.

The midwife turns, focusing on Ella, although she seems remarkably unfazed. She's young… probably only around Ella's age, and she smiles as she pats Ella's leg.

"Keep going. You're doing great."

Ella glares at her but stays silent, other than a mild groaning noise that seems to accompany every contraction now.

"When can I push?" she says, once the pain has subsided enough for her to speak coherently.

"Whenever you're ready. You're fully dilated."

"I am? That was quick."

The midwife smiles and nods her head, and Ella glances up at me, taking a deep breath, like she's preparing herself…

I wait, flexing my hand as far as her grip will allow, and although we both know what's coming, it seems to take forever. The midwife changes position, settling at the end of the bed, but still nothing happens. I'm just wondering if this is a cruel false alarm, whether it's all going to stop for a while, when Ella grasps my hand again, tipping her head forward onto her chest as a new contraction seizes her and I see the effort in her face as she pushes with everything she's got.

The contraction passes, and she settles her head on the pillow, looking up at me. "Never again," she whispers. "I'm never doing this again."

"Okay. Whatever you say."

"Can I have some water?"

I pull my hand from hers, taking the opportunity to clench my fist a few times, and reach for the beaker on the nightstand, helping her to take a few sips. I've only just replaced it and put my hand back in hers when the next contraction hits. She repeats

the same process, only this time with even more effort, wanting it to be over, I guess.

"Keep pushing… keep pushing…" The midwife urges, but Ella flops onto the pillow, spent, and I lean over, kissing her forehead.

"You're doing so well."

"Shut up."

I try not to smile.

"If you can give me one more big push like that, I think we'll be there," the midwife says, and I turn to look at her. She gives me a slight wink and I nod my head. I guess she's heard it all before.

"How do women do this for hours on end?" I ask. I can't believe anyone can, but the midwife just smiles at me.

"It's not really optional by this stage."

I guess not, and I return my attention to Ella, who's closed her eyes, presumably to make the most of a few moments' peace. They shoot open again within seconds and she grabs my hand even tighter than ever, a throaty cry coming from deep inside her.

"That's great, Ella… keep going… keep…" The midwife stops talking and Ella suddenly slumps… and after just a couple of seconds, I hear our baby's first cry, and my heart bursts.

"I think I could look at you like that forever."

Ella's sitting up in bed, Henry cradled in her arms, and I can't stop staring.

"Don't," she says. "I'm a mess."

"You're beautiful." I lean in and kiss her for the hundredth time today. "You're the bravest woman I know."

We've been sitting here by ourselves for about an hour now, the midwife having left us to get to know our son, and I still can't

stop looking at him. He has a shock of dark hair, and the bluest of blue eyes, and he keeps gazing at Ella, like she's the most precious thing in the world… which, of course, she is.

"Can you do something for me?" she says.

"Of course. Anything."

She smiles. "Can you call my brothers?"

I nod my head and pull my phone from my back pocket. Hunter gave me his and Drew's numbers a couple of weeks ago, just in case, and I look up his details first. He answers promptly.

"Mac? Is it Ella?"

"Yes… well, Ella and the baby."

"She's had it? Him, I mean?"

"Yes. About an hour ago."

"And they're both okay?"

"They're both perfect."

I hear him sigh, knowing how relieved he'll be. "Livia and I are gonna come down tomorrow. Do you think Ella will be home by then?"

"Yeah. They said she can go home in the morning, so I guess she'll be back by the time you arrive."

"Great. We'll see you all tomorrow. Give Ella a kiss from me, will you?"

"I will."

"And congratulations."

"Thanks."

We end our call and I glance at Ella, who's gazing at Henry, her eyes filled with love, a smile twitching at her lips. I love her more than ever, and I need to tell her that… and a few other things besides. But first I need to call Drew.

He takes a little longer to respond, and I half expect the call to go to voicemail, just as he picks up.

"Sorry I took so long. I'm at the airport."

It's a strange greeting, but nothing about Drew's life surprises me. He rarely even sits down these days.

"Which airport?"

"Logan. I'm flying to Rome."

"You are?"

"Yeah." He doesn't sound entirely thrilled about it. "I've been trying not to travel too much since Maisie was born, but the client insisted... although, on the bright side, at least it's not a fashion shoot, so I don't have to take too much kit with me."

"How long will you be away?"

"Ten days. I'm gonna miss Maisie so much." I can hear it in his voice, and understand it so much better now. "Anyway, why did you call?"

"To let you know Ella's had the baby."

"Oh, my God. Is she okay?"

"She's fine. Things were a little different about an hour ago. I think she'd have happily killed me then."

He laughs. "I remember that feeling. Lexi and I weren't even together, and she threatened to castrate me, just so I couldn't inflict the pain of having to give birth on any other woman." He pauses. "It's a great feeling, isn't it? Not the threats against your manhood, but becoming a father?"

"It is." I glance over at Ella again. She's looking up at me now, and I blow her a kiss. She returns the gesture, and focuses back on our son again.

"Don't miss a second of it," Drew says in my ear.

"I won't."

"And tell Ella I'll come visit the moment I get back from Rome."

"Okay. Take care of yourself."

"I'll do my best."

He hangs up, and I turn to Ella. "I just need to call Henry. Is that okay?" She nods her head and I find Henry's details, placing the call.

"Mac?"

"Henry. I'm just calling to let you know I'm a father."

"Oh... oh, my dear boy. That marvellous news."

"I also wanted to tell you, we've named the baby Henry."

There's a slight pause and then he says, "I—I don't know what to say." I can hear the emotion in his voice, though, and I wish he could be here, so I could hug him.

"You don't have to say anything. Just promise you'll come over for a visit."

"I will, although I'll give you a while to get used to being parents first."

"Not too long."

"No, not too long." He coughs. "Give my love to Ella, won't you?"

"I will."

"And give little Henry a kiss."

"Of course."

I can't help smiling as we end our call, and I pocket my phone, wandering back to Ella. Henry's asleep now, and I lean over, kissing his forehead. He wrinkles his nose, but doesn't stir, and I whisper, "That's from Uncle Henry."

Ella looks up at me. "How was he? Did he mind us naming Henry after him?"

"Not at all. I think he was very moved by it, actually."

She nods her head. "And my brothers?"

"They're thrilled. Hunter says he and Livia will see us tomorrow, when they come down."

"And Drew?"

"He's on his way to Rome."

"Rome?" she says, as surprised by that news as I was.

"Yeah. It's an assignment. He's not happy about it, but he said he'll come and visit when he gets back."

She nods her head. "Okay."

"You look tired."

"I feel tired."

I take Henry from her, being careful of his head, and place him in his crib, gazing down into his perfect face before I turn back to Ella. She's moved down the bed a little, but I perch beside her.

"I've been waiting for the right moment to do this… and I can't think of a better one, even if I don't have the ring with me."

Her eyes widen. "Ring?"

"Yes." I smile at her. "It's at home, in my bedside table, where it's been for the last three months or so."

"What ring are we talking about?"

"The one I hope you'll allow me to put on your finger." I take her left hand, caressing her ring finger. "I—I guess a lot of men would have proposed before now. It's considered the decent thing, when you get your girlfriend pregnant. But I didn't want you to think I was asking you to marry me just because you were carrying our child. I knew I had to wait until you weren't pregnant anymore, and now you're not, I don't want to wait another second to ask you to be my wife."

She blinks hard a couple of times, trying not to cry, I think. "Y—You want to marry me?"

"God, yes. I'd have asked before now, but like I say, I didn't want you to have any doubts about me or my motives."

"I could never doubt you, Mac."

"Then say yes."

She nods her head, a tear falling onto her cheek. I lean in and kiss it away, and she smiles up at me, sighing her happiness. I kiss her lips and she responds, our tongues meeting in a gentle caress, although we both chuckle when Henry starts to cry.

"Is this how it's gonna be?" I ask, leaning back.

"I hope so," she says, her eyes never leaving mine as I get up to fetch our son, and I nod my head... because there's nothing I want more than my family, and our life.

The End

Thank you for reading *Mistaken Impression*. I hope you enjoyed it, and if you did, I hope you'll take the time to leave a short review.

Dedication

For S.

ISBN 978-1-915109-33-0 Paperback Edition

GWL Publishing
Chichester, United Kingdom
www.gwlpublishing.co.uk

Mistaken Impression

BIG MISTAKES SERIES - BOOK TWO

by

SUZIE PETERS

GWL
PUBLISHING

nickname, but secretly, I think she loves it.

Being friends with Lark is both the easiest, most natural thing in my life, and the most heartbreaking. Have you ever tried to convince yourself *not* to love the one woman who's ever caught your attention? And I do mean *ever?*

Nothing could keep me from wanting to be near Lark. She's a shining star and I'm a planetary body caught up in her gravitational pull. Our friendship formed quickly once we discovered our mutual love of all things *Star Wars*, chips and salsa, and of course, fancy coffee.

But being Lark's friend comes with a steep price. At times, it's mentally and emotionally exhausting being around her. Having to hide my attraction to her, feelings that from the start were new and unfamiliar, but exciting at the same time. But I keep all of that stuffed down, deep inside, working hard not to let her see it.

Because her happiness is the most important thing.

And she has a boyfriend. And if he can make her happy, then no way will I ever come between them.

We round the corner, the famous hollow tree in sight. I put on a burst of speed, reaching it seconds before her. Naturally, my only response is to pump my arms in the air and let out a *whoop*. "That's right, Dan Montgomery wins again!"

"Cocky much?" Lark huffs when she comes to a stop herself, treating me to a big eye roll.

"Don't be a sore loser, Birdie." I grin, but then I, too, slow to a stop, bringing my hands to rest on my hips as I regulate my breathing.

"What time are you going to the stadium?" Lark asks after

the two of us focus on breathing and stretching for a couple of minutes.

"Around eleven, I think. Yami and I want to get in some extra practice."

The connection between pitcher and catcher is sacred on the Tridents. Up until last season, our lead pitcher, Rafe Montego, was my number one guy. Nicknamed "Pops" because he was the oldest on the team, and acted like a dad to all of us, I still miss the guy. But Kai Yamaki or Yami as we call him most of the time, is a solid pitcher. We get along well enough. It's just been rocky at times, finding our groove. There's plenty of other pitchers on the team, and I can work with all of them, but if Yami wants to take the lead pitcher spot, he and I need to iron out a few kinks before next season.

And with next year being the last season on my current contract, it's extra important to make sure we have a great one.

"So..." Lark starts, and I look over to see her twisting her hands together nervously. Her eyes keep darting between the tree and me.

"So?" I parrot back, confused as to what has her acting so strangely.

"Dan, this is so weird." She exhales. I can't handle seeing her distressed, and close the distance between us, pulling her in for a hug.

"Hey, whatever it is, it's okay." I feel her nod against my chest, and release her, taking a step back.

"BaronaskedmetomarryhimandIsaidyes."

It takes me a few seconds to catch up to the rapidly blurted out words. And when I do, my stomach flip-flops. Guess that peanut butter sandwich I had before I left wasn't such a good idea. Then again, I didn't know this was going to happen.

"Oh," I say, hoping like hell she can't tell a part of me is dying inside. I bend over and pretend to tie my shoelace, when in reality, I'm trying to pull myself back together. Because right now, I feel completely torn apart.

Apparently, Lark is unaware of how she's just destroyed me, as she keeps talking. And I force myself to listen.

"I mean, we've been together for so long. And I think our families expected it to happen sooner. I don't know. It's crazy, and it's happening fast. Like, New Year's Eve fast. And okay, Dan, I need you to say something, please."

The panic in her voice snaps me out of my bleak thoughts. I might still feel broken, but my friend is spiraling. And if there's one thing I've become good at these last few years, it's putting her needs before my own.

"Hey. Breathe, Birdie. This is meant to be a good thing, right?" I straighten, forcing a grin, and rub my hands up and down her shoulders until she finally nods. "New Year's Eve will be good. You'll never forget your anniversary." I tease.

She lets out a shaky laugh, but her shoulders relax somewhat. "Yeah, I guess."

If I had to guess, I'd say she's feeling pretty damn overwhelmed. Which, to me, as someone who knows the woman pretty fucking well makes sense. Lark's not one to love having a lot of attention on her, and a wedding is pretty focused on the bride from what little I know.

But she's doing this, I guess, overwhelmed or not. Which means there's only one thing for me to say. "Congratulations,

Lark. I'm happy for you. And I look mighty fine in a tux, so no worries there."

The look of relief she gives me says she believes those words.

Guess I've also become good at lying to her.

I offer to take Lark out for breakfast to "celebrate" her news. Even though celebrating is the last fucking thing I want to do.

I'll do anything to see her smile, and when we pull up to the café, the same one I got coffee from earlier this morning, that smile is back where it belongs.

"Mmm, I can't wait for pancakes." She moans, rubbing her stomach as we walk inside.

I tuck my ball cap down low, and we head for a booth in the back corner where I can sit facing the wall and hopefully not be recognized.

"Blueberry or strawberry today?" I ask, and she taps her chin, pretending to think seriously about it.

"Blueberry. With a chocolate shake. Let me guess, eggs Benedict for you?" She winks. A part of me rages inside my head, still angry at the fact that I let this woman, who knows me better than anyone, slip through my fingers.

"Yeah, but I might mix it up and try the salmon benny today." It takes a lot of effort to keep my voice casual as she smiles at me from across the booth. This is the Lark I love. This light, happy, fun-loving woman with a heart of gold.

"Oh, really? Gettin' fancy on me, Montgomery?" she teases.

Lark is the one person who doesn't call me Monty. Aside

from my parents and a few folks back home, of course. I don't know why, I've never asked her. I like it, though. But it means when she calls me by my last name, it's a special thrill.

Pathetic as that may sound.

"Well, only the best for you," I quip right back and her eyes dance with amusement.

"How is you choosing salmon instead of ham best for me?"

I lean back against the booth and fold my hands together on the table. "Simple..." I pause, and Lark sees right through me.

Snorting, she shakes her head. "You've got nothing."

My own head shakes from side to side ruefully. "I really don't."

She reaches out and pats my hands. "That's okay, I still like you."

Yeah, I like you, too. That's the problem.

The waitress comes over and we place our order. After she leaves, I lean forward. "When is your application for the internship due?"

Lark chews on her lower lip. "I sent it in yesterday. I'm so nervous. What if they don't choose me?"

I know how nervous she's been, how much she hopes to get a spot on the department of kinesiology research team at the local university. Even though the position won't start until sometime next year, the application process starts early. I wave my hand dismissively. "Don't be crazy, they will. Who better to study ways to prevent muscle decline in athletes than a trainer who has spent years working directly with a team of professional baseball players."

She gives me a half smile. "Their research will be ground-breaking. I could learn so much in just a few months and bring it all back to the Tridents to make the team even stronger."

"You'll get the spot," I say confidently, and am rewarded with a nudge of her foot against mine.

"How are you always so positive?"

My shoulders lift in a shrug. "I just believe good things happen to good people. And you're good people, Birdie."

Her hand reaches out again and squeezes mine. "So are you."

Just not good enough for her.

Chapter Two

Lark

I can't possibly be the first bride-to-be that dreads having to spend time with her fiancé's parents.

Honestly, it's not just them. It's their lifestyle, their home, and everything they represent. I may have been raised in a similarly-wealthy family, but the Hazelwoods have the stuffy, conservative, rich-and-we-know-it attitude down pat.

Thank God Baron doesn't act the same way as his parents. At least, not all the time. There's no way I could marry a man so consumed with wealth and status like his father.

I've never been comfortable with the money and privilege my family and Baron's have. It has always felt like a scratchy sweater I can't take off. That's probably why I threw myself into sports as soon as my parents relented and allowed me to join some teams. Anything to get away from their world, the one where I never felt like I belonged.

The only thing in that world I have ever wanted a part of was Baron.

It's why he ended up being my first kiss, my first everything. My *only* everything.

When he proposed a few weeks ago, it was a bit of a relief, to be honest. Finally, it was done. We both knew it was inevitable, and waiting for him to pop the question was making me anxious.

Now, I'm starting to wonder if that anxiety wasn't trying to tell me something...

Over the last year or so, Baron has changed. He stopped agreeing with me when I would rant about how much good our families could do if they chose to use their wealth to help others. He joined a golf club and has been gone most weekends — for business, he claims. His car needed to be "upgraded," despite being only a year old.

Small things, but noticeable. I used to feel like we were a team, united in our desire to live life differently from our parents. Nowadays, he seems quite content in their world.

It's left me feeling as though I'm on the outside of our relationship at times, and I'm not entirely sure what to do about it.

Coming around to my side of the car, Baron takes my hand in his. The TAG Heuer watch his father gifted him last year peeks out of the sleeve of his dress shirt. Together we walk up the paved circular driveway to his imposing family home. Tall white pillars loom in front of us with ostentatious planters on either side, each holding a perfectly shaped hedge plant.

The amount of money they must pay just to have their home look like a museum...

"Smile, Lark. You look like I'm taking you to your last supper or something."

Baron's attempt at a joke falls flat for me, but I paste on a smile and give his hand a squeeze. "Sorry, just preoccupied, I guess."

"With what? Isn't the season over? All you have to worry about is planning the wedding of your dreams."

Once again, his words don't land the way I assume he means them to. My defenses go up. "I still have to work in the offseason, you know that. And planning a wedding in three months isn't exactly easy."

He pats the hand he's holding with his other one and smiles, but it doesn't reach his eyes, and it certainly doesn't make me feel any better. "Then just let my mother take care of it. You know she'll be happy to."

Yeah. I know Cordelia Hazelwood would love nothing more than to swoop in and take over planning the wedding. I just don't know if I would be happy with a single aspect of it if she did.

As my fiancé, shouldn't he want *me* to be happy, not his mom?

I'm saved from having to reply by the door opening and the appearance of an older gentlemen wearing a crisp white shirt tucked into white pants with a black bow tie.

"Hey, Jefferson," Baron says, stepping inside as the man gives us a small bow. I give him a smile and am given a slight one in return.

Even though my parents are not exactly what you'd call casual, they don't have a freaking butler greeting guests.

The older Hazelwoods always like to appear to be a level above everyone else.

I hand Jefferson my coat and follow Baron down the hall, trying not to fidget with the high-waisted dress pants I wore for dinner. I hate dressing up. I have ever since I was a child and my mother chose my clothing every day, forcing me into frilly dresses and uncomfortable shoes. Give me leggings and a T-shirt, or my work uniform of joggers and a Tridents polo any day. But Cordelia insists on a dress code for family dinner, and since I refuse to wear dresses unless absolutely necessary, outfits like the silk blouse and dress pants I have on today are the only acceptable alternative.

I ache to toe off the pointy shoes I stuffed my feet into, but that's another no-no here. Shoes stay on. And heaven forbid I show up in sneakers. I made that mistake once, early on in our relationship, and the look of horror on Cordelia's face is not one I'll ever forget.

Baron's parents are waiting in the lounge, as they call it. A stuffy room with uncomfortable furniture and a creepy family portrait hanging above the fireplace. Baron squeezes my hand again and gives me a small smile, his eyes glinting. I know exactly what he's thinking because the memory comes to me every time I see that portrait as well.

It was a Canada Day party two years ago, and we ended up far too drunk, making out in this very room, trying to escape our parents and their friends. Back then, we couldn't keep our hands off each other.

Unlike now. We might be holding hands, but that's about as much affection as I can expect from him these days.

But that late afternoon years ago, tipsy on mojitos, we came up with a ridiculous plan to deface the portrait together. His mother really would be improved with a mustache, and his father could really rock a monocle.

Too bad we never went through with the plan.

Too bad we never drank mojitos again.

"Ah, Baron. Lark. There you are, we were wondering if we'd have to tell the staff to delay dinner." The chiding tone is clear, even as Cordelia sweeps forward with a tight smile.

He gets a hug and an obligatory air-kiss toward his cheek. I get a once-over and then an even more perfunctory air-kiss. Baron Senior shakes his son's hand and gives me a nod before pulling Baron into a conversation about work. Now that Baron's head of the finance department at the property development firm our fathers run, it seems all they do is talk shop.

Jefferson enters the room with a silver tray, with two flutes filled with effervescent liquid. Champagne. Not my favourite, but I resign myself to drinking it every time we're here.

Lately it's becoming harder to accept just how many things I give in and take, despite being the opposite of my preference. Maybe it's watching my friends fall in love, I don't know. But ever since Baron proposed to me, I've had this weird feeling in the middle of my chest. This knot of discontent poking at me. Asking questions I'm steadfastly ignoring.

I hear my name and focus on the conversation. Cordelia is looking at me and her displeasure is poorly hidden.

"I'm sorry, what did I miss?" I say, sipping the overly sweet champagne.

"I was informing Baron of our schedule while he's on his business trip. We don't have much time to solidify wedding plans, you know. With just over two months until New Year's Eve, there's a lot to do. We have a dress-fitting appointment at the Terrence Bovier salon on Saturday, then I've set up some time for us to tour the Devereaux Hotel downtown Tuesday night, and cake tasting on Friday. You'll attend that without me, I'm afraid. I have a ladies' luncheon at the club."

It's a fight not to let my mouth fall open. "I...I had no idea about any of that."

"Well, of course, you didn't. I took it upon myself to arrange everything, as Baron told me you were occupied with work." Her little sniff at the end says everything about how Cordelia feels when it comes to my job with the Tridents. Working for a sports team, even a professional one, is not the career path they would have chosen for a daughter-in-law. If it weren't for my father and Baron's father having such a long-standing history, there's not a chance they'd support our relationship.

Then again, if it weren't for our family's connection, there probably wouldn't *be* a relationship.

"Wow," I say, only to have Baron's hand land on mine, squeezing it tightly.

"What Lark means to say is, wow, Mother, that's very generous of you to give us your time and energy into wedding planning. I'm sure I speak for us both when I say we appreciate the assistance. What with my trip taking up the next couple of weeks, I was worried about Lark managing it all. It's great she'll have your help."

My teeth grind together. Yeah, *great* is *not* the word I'd use. But I know there's no stopping Cordelia Hazelwood once she starts, which means I'm simply along for the ride.

"Right." I exhale slowly. "I'll check with my mother and my maid of honour to make sure they can be there on Saturday."

"I already discussed the plans with your mother over lunch

earlier this week," Cordelia says calmly, with no acknowledgment of how much she's overstepping. "Unfortunately, she's occupied at that time with a commitment with your father, but she wishes us well."

And that, folks, is my relationship with my mother perfectly summed up. *She can't come wedding dress shopping for her only child, but she wishes me well.*

"Oh."

Baron's thumb strokes across the back of my hand. A kind, affectionate gesture. He can tell how much that news affects me. I've had my entire life to get over the fact that I'll never be close to my parents, but even so, it hurts to be dismissed like that.

Jefferson announces dinner, and we move into the formal dining room. I'm distracted throughout the meal, something Cordelia definitely notices. But I can't help it. I've felt like I'm on a runaway train for a while now. Like my life is not entirely my own. I'm living it for someone else, not me. And planning this wedding, to this man, has turned up the speed on the train to dizzying levels.

Thankfully, we leave shortly after dessert is cleared away. Baron has a car arriving here to take him straight to the airport for a trip to Ontario to work on some merger or something.

After saying goodbye to his parents, we move outside. He walks me to his car since he insisted on picking me up tonight, despite the fact that he wouldn't be driving me home. Which wouldn't be so bad, except he lives a lot closer to his parents than I do. So now I have to drive back to his house, drop off his car, then make my way home.

"If you'd moved in with me already, this wouldn't be an

issue," he reminded me earlier when I questioned him about coming to pick me up. And he's not wrong. I've been dragging my heels on moving in with him for several reasons.

None of which I wanted to get into with him tonight, especially right before dinner with his parents.

At his car, he leans down and pecks my cheek. "Have fun with Mother. I'm sure everything will be great."

I stare at him, debating whether or not to point out the obvious — that everything will absolutely *not* be great.

His mother is going to take over completely and plan the wedding she wants us to have with no consideration for what either of us might want. How he can't see that is beyond me. But as always, he's oblivious.

"Baron, I really don't think —"

"Listen, babe, can this wait? I gotta go, I'm meeting the guys from the office for a preflight drink and I don't want to be late."

I bite down on my tongue so hard I worry I'll draw blood. Drinks with his coworkers apparently trumps my attempt to have a conversation about our freaking wedding.

"Yeah. Sure. I hope your trip goes well." My voice sounds hollow to my ears, but Baron doesn't seem to notice.

Instead, all I get is a brief nod as a car pulls up. "Great. We'll talk soon. I'll email once I land in Toronto."

He'll email. Wonderful. Guess the days of phone sex and constant text messages are over. Oh, who am I kidding? They have been for a while.

He slides into the back seat without another word. No kiss, no hug, nothing.

For a woman who's meant to be in love, meant to be committing her life to the man driving away from her, I can't help but feel very, very alone.

CHAPTER THREE

Monty

The drive out to Meadowvale, the small town I grew up in, takes just over an hour. Tucked away in a small pocket of the valley outside of Vancouver, it's a beautiful place to live, even if, as a kid, I resented how far away from everything it seemed.

Now, I love coming here. The quiet streets and slow pace of this sleepy little town instantly make me feel peaceful. I pull up outside of the store my parents have owned for decades. The closest thing to a grocery store in these parts, they sell a little bit of everything. As soon as I was old enough, I was helping out, sweeping floors, stocking shelves, packing bags. The bell over the door that jingles when I walk in brings a wave of nostalgia, but it's the grey-haired woman walking over with her arms wide open that has me grinning.

"Hey, Mom," I say, gently folding her much-smaller frame into mine for a hug.

"Twenty seconds, young man." She says the same thing every time we hug. Gotta hold on for twenty seconds to get the maximum mood boost. As a teenager, I cringed, and insisted on only hugging her in private. But now, as a grown-ass man, I love hugging. Not just my mom, even though hers are the best, but everyone.

Hey, I'm an affectionate dude, and hugs are awesome.

When we eventually let go, she holds onto my arms with a grip that hasn't weakened one bit since I was a kid.

"Now. Your dad is in the back unloading the produce order. Have you had lunch?"

"Mom, it's 10 am. I don't need lunch." I glance to the back of the store. "Should I go help Dad? Those apple boxes get heavy."

"Honey, your father might be seventy-two, but he's not dead yet. He can handle some apple boxes. If you don't want lunch, how about a snack? We got some new treats from Delores for the bakery case. She made these croissant-donut things. Cronuts, she called them."

I chuckle. "Yeah, I've heard of a cronut. I'm surprised Delores branched out from scones and coffee cake."

"Listen, young man, we're hip, we can keep up with things."

I don't have the heart to tell her cronuts were a thing a couple of years ago. I love my parents, but they struggled to conceive and didn't have me until my dad was in his forties and Mom was close to it. Having parents that much older means there's always been a much bigger generational divide between us.

But it didn't stop my dad from teaching me to hit a ball at three or my mom from lecturing me about safe sex at sixteen.

She could've saved herself the trouble of that awkward conversation... I was a scrawny kid, a total goofball, and a science geek, and even being the captain of my high school baseball team wasn't enough to save my reputation at school. I was always solidly placed in the friend zone with every girl.

Dad chooses that minute to push through the swinging doors at the back of their shop, struggling under not one but two large boxes of apples.

"Jesus, Dad, what are you doing, trying to throw your back out?" I jog down the aisle and grab the boxes from him.

"Hello to you, too, son, and I could've managed them." He pats my shoulder and follows me over to the produce section where I set the boxes down and start unpacking apples.

It bugs me that my parents still work in the store seven days a week. Sure, they've hired help, teenagers like I was back in the day that stock shelves and clean up. But they're still here doing the brunt of it, running the store full time. Getting them to take vacations is almost impossible. And as much as we all might want to ignore it, they're getting older.

My dream is to be able to support them so they can sell the store and retire. But being so far out from the city, they won't make a lot from the sale, certainly not enough for Mom's dream of buying a luxury RV and traveling the continent.

I could buy the RV for them, even now, but they won't accept it. Dad made it clear when I signed with the Tridents four years ago that my priority had to be on making smart decisions with my money to set myself up for my own future. He knew, just as I did, that being a catcher in the major leagues meant my career wouldn't be a long one. The wear and tear on my body is just too much. And since I was recruited before I could finish college, I don't have a lot to fall back on outside of baseball. Unless I want to run this store...which I don't.

Thankfully, my parents don't pressure me on that one bit. They just want to see me happy. The problem is, I want the same for them. And that means I need to secure a second contract with the Tridents after this season, so I can use the signing bonus I'll hopefully get to set my parents up.

It's easy to fall back into the rhythm of working in the store. Customers come and go, some of them greeting me, but no one making a fuss. That's the benefit of a small town. These people have known me since I was in diapers; they couldn't care less that I'm now a somewhat famous athlete.

I mean, I'm no Maverick King, who used to grace the tabloids on a regular basis, but I do okay.

"Is that Daniel? How lovely to see you."

I turn at the shaky old voice, a smile already on my face. "Mrs. Chen, look at you, beautiful as always. Can I help you find something?"

My former elementary school teacher frowns up at me. "When are you going to bring a girl around here, Daniel? Or a boy, I suppose, it doesn't matter. But your mother's not getting any younger and she deserves grandchildren."

"Mrs. Chen," I gently chide. "You say the same thing every time I come to visit. I'll bring a girl back home when I find the right one."

The old lady harrumphs, but her face softens into a wrinkled smile. She reaches up to pat my cheek. "You're a good boy, Daniel. Any woman would be lucky to have you."

"Thanks, Mrs. Chen. Now, have you tried a cronut? Mom says Delores dropped off a batch and they're delicious."

I escort her over to the bakery section and help her put one in a bag before waving goodbye.

A *good boy*. Yeah. I am, and I don't mind people knowing it.

I'm a happy dude with not much to complain about in life. But one thing Mrs. Chen said is sticking in my stomach, churning up the breakfast I had before I left to drive out here.

Any woman would be lucky to have you.

Except the only woman I want, the only one I've *ever* wanted, is marrying some other man.

And that fucking sucks.

It's not hard for my mom to convince me to come upstairs to the apartment above the store where I grew up and stay for dinner after I help them all day. With the season over, I've got all the time in the world. And there's nowhere I'd rather be than here with my parents.

After packing away more of my mom's lasagna than I should admit to, because no one makes lasagna like Edith Montgomery, I shoo them both out of the kitchen and take care of the dishes. At some point, my phone vibrates, but I ignore it until later, when Mom and Dad have gone off to watch some nature documentary, and I'm nursing a beer out on their back deck, huddled around the firepit I bought them last year.

I see a missed text from Rafe and dial his number.

"Hey, Pops." I smile when I hear his gruff *hello*. "You missin' me or something?"

His low chuckle echoes my own. "Monty, my man, if there's anything I miss about playing ball, it's the paycheque, not you."

I clutch my chest even though I know he can't see me. "Ouch, and here I thought we were friends."

I hear his loud exhale. "Fine, we're friends. I miss you and your creepy long hugs."

"That's more like it," I say, smirking. "What's up? How's

Imogen and Taylor?"

"They're great. This whole retirement thing is fucking awesome."

I can hear the truth behind his words. We worked together for three years, and in that time, he became the older brother I always wanted. He knows me and I know him, and I've never heard the man sound so peaceful and happy as he does now with his fiancée and kid by his side. "That's good. I'm happy for you."

"Thanks. So, season's over. What's the plan? Heading back east?"

I consider his question. Other than my parents, the rest of our family is in Ontario, including some cousins I'm sort of close to. "Nah, sticking closer to home this year, I think. Spend some time with the folks, help them out. That kind of thing."

"And that decision wouldn't have anything to do with a certain trainer getting hitched, now, would it?"

"How did you hear?" I say nervously. All the guys on the team know I've got a thing for Lark, but Rafe's the only one who knows just how much of a thing it really is. He was there that day when I was going to ask her out. He's the one who explained she was with Baron and had been for a while.

"I might have retired from the team but that doesn't mean I don't hear things." He pauses for a second. "How're you doing, Monty?"

I'm silent for a second. Maybe two. "I mean, I don't know. Nothing's changed, not really. If she's happy, that's all that matters."

"Does that mean you're finally gonna move on?"

"I date."

Rafe scoffs. "You've gone on a handful of first dates that somehow never turn into a second. You've never brought a girl to a team event or a game. You've never even talked about a girl. And hey, it's your life, you live it however you want. But at some point, you gotta get over her."

"Yeah. I know." I lean forward in my chair and let my head hang low. "But what if she was it for me, Pops? What if Lark is the only woman out there for me, and I never get a chance?"

"Monty, there's no good answer for that. I'm sorry, man."

It's my turn to exhale. "Thanks."

"What are you gonna do if she asks you to be in the wedding?"

I snort. "What, like as a best man? She won't, she's got Willow and Sadie, and Baron's got a sister, I think."

"Yeah, but you guys are close. She might want you involved."

I swallow around the lump in my throat. "Then I'll be her friend and whatever else she needs me to be. Just like always."

CHAPTER FOUR

Lark

"I want to see her in the ball gown next." Cordelia's imperious command reaches me in the changing room and I don't bother hiding my grimace. It's not like the salesgirl who has been helping me in and out of dress after dress cares that I have yet to try on one that I actually like. She only cares about the hefty commission she sees coming her way.

I take in a full breath when she finally gets the last button undone on the current monstrosity I'm wearing. Any sense of modesty is gone as I place my hands on my hips and breathe in and out slowly. I'm wearing a strapless bra and a thong and have already been informed by my future mother-in-law that it is unbecoming to wear that style of underwear. How did she know? Apparently, the line of my underwear was visible underneath the first dress I tried on, a satin sheath that clung in all the wrong places, and hung off me like a sack in others.

The salesgirl steps out and I take a second to text Monty a quick photo of the last dress with a one-liner from *Star Wars*.

LARK: I've got a bad feeling about this...

The man knows those movies inside and out, and I know he'll appreciate the joke.

The four laughing emojis he immediately sends back fortify me just enough. I can get through this.

I think.

I'll give Cordelia one thing, she at least let me try a wide variety of styles. But every single one has earned a sneer or a grimace of distaste and a hand wave. Baron's sister Felicity has had her nose glued to her phone, and Willow, who arrived late, has been turning more red by the minute. Our other friend, Sadie, who's dating another Tridents player, couldn't make it because of a family commitment. Too bad, because I could really use the backup right about now.

A knock on the door has the salesgirl opening it, and I assume it's the next dress. Instead, I hear Willow's voice. "Give us a minute, please."

I sink down on the small tufted stool in the corner and let my head fall into my hands. That fortification from Dan's text is gone. With Willow, I can show how I truly feel. "This is torture."

Willow lets out an indelicate snort. "What, the horrible dresses you keep coming out in, or the vile energy Cordelia's putting out."

I look up and Willow, noticing my misery, drops down into a crouch in front of me. "Babe, why are you doing this? Why are you letting her dictate everything? Buying your wedding dress should be fun and exciting, not the worst day of your life."

"She's impossible to say no to."

"I'll do it for you. Say the word, and I'll kick her ass out of here."

I laugh and sniff back a tear. "You're the best, but that would only make it worse."

"You're only saying that because you haven't seen the next dress she wants you to try on." Willow shudders. "Trust me. It's by far the worst one yet. And I'm willing to bet she loves it."

"It's just a dress, right? If it makes her happy..." I trail off, fully aware of how crazy I sound. Willow's already shaking her head.

"Lark, *you* should be happy on your wedding day. It's not about her, it's about you and Baron." She glances down for a second, and when she meets my eyes again, her expression is concerned. "Are you sure this is all worth it? I thought maybe...after what you said..."

I know what she's referring to without her even finishing her thought. The night I told the girls I was engaged, I also admitted it may have been a mistake, and that I didn't want to marry Baron.

"I don't know what to do, Willow," I whisper. "Is he the man of my dreams? No. But is he a good man who wants to marry me? Yeah. What if this is as good as it gets for me?"

"That is the biggest pile of bullshit I've ever heard come out of your mouth, Lark Miller." Willow squeezes my knees. "You are a phenomenal woman. Gorgeous, smart, athletic, funny, kind. You're a hell of a catch and you can abso-freaking-lutely do better than Baron and his horrendous family. If you're marrying him because you honestly don't see that, then I need to kidnap you right the heck now and hold you hostage until I get you to see it."

I give her a watery smile. "Like I said, you're the best." I inhale and exhale slowly once again. "I know I need to decide what to do, and soon. It's just not exactly an easy decision, you know?"

Willow nods. "I know." She stands up and places her hands on her hips. "Now, let's get this last dress over with so we can go and get lunch. The wine's on me."

I nod and paste a large smile on my face. "Sounds good."

When I come out of the changing room a little while later, feeling like a cupcake in the ridiculously large ball gown, sure enough, Willow's prediction comes true. Cordelia stands up, smiling for once.

"Now *this* is a dress fit for a Hazelwood wedding."

I bite my tongue as she walks slowly around me, tugging at parts, talking to the salesgirl, and completely ignoring me.

Probably a good thing since it might be written all over my face that I can't shake the image of Julia Roberts in the opening scenes of *Runaway Bride*. This dress bears an eerie resemblance to hers...which is kind of a bad omen, isn't it?

"Yes. This is the one."

I turn to Cordelia at her imperious announcement. "This one?" I ask, hoping she'll hear the hesitation in my voice and at least ask my opinion. But she simply nods.

"Yes. Trust me, Lark. This is the dress."

Trust her. More like relinquish all control to her. I'd say something, but what's the point? It's not like she'd hear me, anyway. And I meant what I said to Willow earlier. It's just a dress. I've always believed when I got married, the only thing that would truly matter would be the love I had for the person standing in front of me. Not the dress, or the party, or the cake, nothing but the person I was promising my life to.

I step back into the changeroom and let the salesgirl help me out of the hideous dress. Once I'm dressed, I rejoin Felicity and Cordelia at the front of the store. Willow is outside on a call from work. Cordelia is also looking down at her phone, and when she glances back up, there's a light in her eyes that I don't like the look of.

"Wonderful news, Lark. That was Helen over at Green Briar. I had reached out to her to see how long their current wait list is. It's never too soon, you know. We must be prepared."

My brow furrows in confusion. "What's Green Briar? A wedding venue?"

Cordelia lets out a brittle laugh. "Heavens, no. It's the boarding school Baron and Felicity went to. They've recently opened an elementary-aged program. Your children can start attending when they're eight. Helen informed me that as soon as we have your anticipated due date, we should be in touch to secure a placement."

What. Did. She. Just. Say?

"I'm sorry, boarding school?" I ask, not bothering to hide the shock in my tone.

"Yes. Of course. The last three generations of Hazelwoods have gone to Green Briar, it's the leading coed boarding school in the country. Hasn't Baron told you about his time there? He looks back on it fondly, I know."

Thank God Willow's outside on her phone, or I know she would have bust out laughing at the absurdity of this.

I grew up with distant, disconnected parents. Heck, Rose, my childhood nanny, was more of an influence on me than they were. And I swore that if I ever had children, they would know nothing but unconditional love from me.

Boarding school is not an option.

To say nothing of the fact that I'm not planning on becoming pregnant any time soon. The very idea of going on a list for some hypothetical child that will exist some time in the future is absolutely insane.

"Baron and I have not discussed his time there," I say stiffly, meeting her gaze head-on. Her eyes narrow, as if she senses the fight that's coming. "But I can assure you, I do not agree to my future children attending boarding school."

Cordelia doesn't rise to my statement. She simply sniffs, turns away without another word, and walks out of the boutique.

Honestly, I'm counting that as a win.

After the horrifying dress shopping experience, Willow and I went to lunch. When I told her about the boarding school bomb, she was suitably horrified on my behalf.

And even now, hours later, as I head to Dan's house to watch a movie with him, I can't stop fuming about the entire situation.

It's one thing to take over my wedding. But to try and control the way I will raise my future children is too far. *Boarding school.* I realize, for some families, that's the best option. But that's not even up for consideration in my mind. And the next time I talk to Baron on the phone, it won't matter if he's on the other side of the country doing who-knows-what for the firm. I'll be telling him that it will never happen. Ever.

I knock on Dan's front door, then turn the knob. He never leaves it locked when he knows I'm coming over.

But I guess I'm early tonight, either that or he's running late. Because I come to an abrupt halt just inside when he walks into the living room shirtless. His trim, muscular body is on full display, right down to the trail of dark hair running from his belly button down...

"Lark!" he says, his eyes widening. He's holding a shirt in one hand, and his shaggy dark hair looks wet. "You're...you're here. Shit. What time is it?"

I can feel my cheeks growing red, which is ridiculous. It's not as if I haven't seen him without a shirt before. Heck, most of my workdays are spent surrounded by muscular baseball players in various stages of undress.

There's something about this moment, in his home, just the two of us, that feels different, however. Intimate, in a way.

"Sorry, I guess I'm early?" I say, casting my eyes to the side. He pulls the shirt in his hand over his head and moves toward me.

"It's fine, you just surprised me." He sounds a lot calmer than before, and certainly more than I feel. But I glance over to see he's heading toward the kitchen. "Pizza will be here in half an hour. Want a beer?"

I follow him, grateful to have moved past that awkward moment, whatever it was. "I'm not sure that's going to be strong enough, but yeah."

Dan looks at me with a half smile. "That bad, huh?"

"Death by tulle was a definite possibility."

His deep chuckle has me relaxing for the first time all day. It's always like this with him, easy and fun.

"Tulle? Really? I would have thought sequins would be more of a risk to your well-being."

"It was all dangerous." I take a long pull from the bottle of beer he gives me. "But you want to know the worst part? It wasn't even the uncomfortable dresses that made me struggle to breathe. Oh no." I stand up, unable to stay seated for this tirade. I pace Dan's kitchen, clutching my bottle of beer in two hands. "Baron's mother had the freaking audacity to tell me she's already got my nonexistent future children on some wait list for a boarding school. Boarding school! Who the hell even goes to boarding school aside from, like, politician's kids or whatever? Good Lord, as if I would want my kids raised anywhere but at home with their parents. No, thank you, not happening. I mean, my childhood sucked, but at least I saw my parents at dinnertime and lived under the same roof as them. And come on! I'm not even married, and she's already planning my child's future? There's control freak, and then there's Cordelia Hazelwood."

I stop, breathing heavily, and turn to see Dan leaning against the counter, his brown eyes wide. "Say something. Please tell me you agree that she's nuts."

His head slowly starts to move side to side. "Nuts isn't even strong enough, but I don't want to be offensive to people who struggle with their mental health. She stepped so far over every single fucking line, it's not even funny. I'm sorry, Lark." He frowns. "Boarding schools might be a good option for some families, but I can't imagine not having my kids at home. If I ever have them."

I tilt my beer bottle toward him. "Exactly."

"Mother-in-law drama aside, did you find a dress?"

I groan, letting my head fall forward. "No, but Cordelia did."

Dan coughs on his sip of beer, wiping a hand over his mouth before answering. "What does *that* mean?"

"It means she wants me to wear the most ostentatious, uncomfortable, gaudy dress I've ever seen in my life."

His brows furrow. "Um, Lark, I'm no expert, but isn't the bride meant to choose her own dress?"

"Not when you've got someone like Cordelia in charge." I grimace. "Honestly, it was easier to just let her get her way."

"Listen, I don't want to be rude or anything, but that doesn't sound like the greatest attitude to have about planning your wedding," he says, wincing. "Sorry."

My sigh is long and drawn out. "You're not wrong." My laugh comes out a lot harsher than it probably should, but Dan doesn't say anything.

He's never come out and said he thinks I shouldn't be with Baron, not like Willow has. Part of me wishes he would, because in the back of my mind, there's always been a quiet voice questioning what if... What if I was single when I met Dan? Would something have happened? Even though he's never once made a move outside of friendship, we've been mistaken for a couple before when we've gone out just the two of us for some reason.

He's a catch, and I've always wondered why he's single but never been brave enough to ask. I told myself I had no business asking since I was in a relationship.

And now? Now, I'm trying to figure out how I ended up here, engaged to a man I don't actually love. Feeling trapped and knowing I let myself get to this point.

Torn between wanting to walk away from it all and being terrified of disappointing everyone if I do.

And beneath all of that, the voice continues to whisper. What if I walked away from it all...

Chapter Five

Monty

"And then, Marcus said girls suck at baseball, and Sydney punched him the stomach. It was awesome." Grayson pumps his fist in the air as he bounces beside me on the bench outside of the ice cream shop we stopped at after playing catch for an hour.

Whoever says you shouldn't eat ice cream in November is wrong. There's never a bad time for bubble gum ice cream. Yeah, I said bubble gum.

"You know he's totally wrong, right?" I say seriously. "Girls are just as good at baseball as boys. Sometimes they play the game differently, and they call it softball, but that doesn't mean it's easier. They pitch fast and hit hard."

"Yeah, I know. We had a girl on my team last season, and she hit a home run." He slurps at his rocky road ice cream cone as I silently beam with pride. In the three years I've spent as Grayson's Big Brother, he's come a long way from the sullen boy he was at nine years old.

Growing up as an only child, all I ever wanted was a sibling. Someone to play with, to teach and help grow. I was overflowing with affection and a desire to be friends with everyone around me. Sure, it made me popular in school, being the class clown, the fun guy to have around, but it wasn't the same.

Which is why, as soon as I could, I signed up for the Big Brother program. It took a while to find a match, and even once Grayson and I connected, it took some time for us to actually bond. But now, my time every other week with him is something I look forward to.

It helps that he's developed a love of baseball, and his mom doesn't try to take advantage of my fame in any way. She's just a single mom trying to do right by her kid, struggling with a low income in an expensive city.

It's why I break the rules occasionally and hook them up with gear I can get from my sponsors. It's also why I anonymously donate equipment to his baseball league. Because I know how powerful sports can be for kids.

"Can you come to my game this weekend? It's the last one for the fall season." Grayson turns his hopeful gaze on me. "Coach said you could help me warm up if you wanted."

I hide my smile. I'm sure his coach would be more than happy to have a major league catcher warm up his pitcher. Truthfully, I don't mind. I like hanging with Grayson, and being around other kids that love baseball is fun. Even if the coaches and parents get a little much sometimes.

"I'll be there. You been working on those shoulder mobility exercises I showed you? Lark wanted to know how it's going."

"Yeah, I do them every night. I think it's helping. Hey, can she come to the game, too?" Grayson's voice cracks slightly, and once again, I'm biting back my grin. Dude's got a little crush on

Lark. Not that I blame him, of course.

"I'll ask her."

"Cool." His head tilts down as he stares at his ice cream. "Hey, Monty. Can I ask you something?"

"Of course. Anything, you know that. Open book, man." I turn on the bench to face him slightly. "What's up?"

"So, um. Like, there's this girl at school." He shifts in his seat, eats some ice cream, and darts his gaze up to me, then back down, his cheeks starting to colour.

Meanwhile, my palms start to feel sweaty. And for a guy that relies on steady hands and quick reflexes, sweaty palms are a rare occurrence. But he wants to talk about girls? Oh shit.

"Oh yeah?" I say, clearing my throat. Do I want him to feel comfortable talking to me or not? I honestly can't decide. In three years, he's never once brought up girls in this way. I am most definitely not prepared.

"She's cool. I mean, like, smart. And really good at volleyball. And nice. We talk sometimes, and she likes my jokes." He takes another bite of ice cream, and then his shoulders slump. "Our first school dance is coming up and I want to ask her to dance. But I'm scared she'll say no. What do I do?"

Finally, he looks up at me, and the mixture of hope and dread is one I'm sure was on my face a time or two back in middle school. Wanting to be cool enough but also terrified.

I take a minute to try to figure out how the hell I'm gonna handle this. I can't exactly come out and tell him that I'm a twenty-nine-year-old virgin who's only been on a few dates, kissed three girls, and who got stood up at his prom the one and only time he was brave enough to ask a girl out in high school.

Yeah. That would scar him for life. Kinda like it did me.

"Well," I start, then pause. "I mean, you gotta be bold, dude. If you want something, or someone, you gotta shoot your shot. Just remember, if she says no, that's a final answer."

There. That's some good advice, right? Teaching confidence and consent? Fuck, I am the wrong man for this conversation. I rub my palms on my pants, hoping he doesn't notice.

"If she says no, I'm gonna be so embarrassed," Grayson says morosely. "Maybe I just shouldn't ask. I mean, everyone would see her shoot me down and that would suck."

"*Or* everyone would see her say yes." I lean over and nudge him with my shoulder. "Don't sell yourself short. You're cool. She'd be lucky to dance with you."

Grayson just huffs. "You have to say that."

"I don't have to do anything. Didn't I promise you in the beginning I'd never lie to you?"

Maybe I don't tell him everything, but I don't lie.

He looks up at me. "Yeah."

"Well, then, trust me. I don't know who this girl is, but if you think she's cool, then I'm sure she is. The thing is, so are you. And you'll never know what could happen if you don't put yourself out there."

It's not lost on me that I should have taken my own advice years ago. Before Lark ended up engaged. But coming between her and her boyfriend felt wrong, even if every instinct has always told me she's not meant to be with him.

Out of the corner of my eye, I watch Grayson take a deep breath in, then relax against the bench with his exhale. He slowly nods. "Yeah. Okay. I'll ask her. You're right, she's probably not gonna say no. We have a good time when we hang out, and it's just a dance. No big deal." He sounds more confident, but still nervous. I'm proud of him, and I give him a smile, even as I inwardly give myself a slap across the head. A freaking twelve-year-old has more game than I do.

This is why I'm still a virgin.

Dammit.

Chapter Six

Lark

"So you're not coming?" I try to keep the disappointment from my voice. It's not as if I *enjoy* spending time with my mother, but her apparent lack of interest in doing anything with me for this wedding still hurts.

"No, Lark." She sounds distant and exasperated. Like always. "Your father and I have had plans with the Riordans for weeks. I can't be expected to drop everything just to sample cake."

I could fight back and tell her that most mothers would absolutely drop everything to help their only child plan their wedding. But then again, this is exactly what it's always been like. I'm the lowest priority for my parents.

"Fine."

"We'll talk soon."

That's all I get before she hangs up, leaving me staring at the phone. I push off my couch and go to the kitchen to pour a glass of water. Now what? I don't exactly want to go cake tasting alone.

I consider asking Willow if she wants to join me, but then I remember her mentioning she has plans with her boyfriend

Ronan and his daughter Peyton.

Before I can overthink it, I type out a text to someone I at least know I'll have a good time with.

> **LARK: How do you feel about free cake?**

> **DAN: How is that even a question...**

> **LARK: Right. Well, are you doing anything in an hour?**

> **DAN: Other than eating free cake? Nope.**

An hour later, I'm biting back my grin as Dan comes swaggering up to me, a big, goofy smile of his own stretched across his face.

"What the heck are you wearing?" I fold my arms across my chest. He looks down, spreading his hands wide.

"This old thing? Just a shirt I had lying around."

The bright blue shirt with a huge cartoon slice of cake and the words "My Favourite Flavour of Cake is More" is stretched across his muscular chest.

"That is ridiculous." My smile breaks free. It's nice to be around someone who doesn't care about appearances or status, just about having fun and enjoying life. That's always how I feel with Dan. Carefree, light, and happy.

He shrugs, giving me a grin. "Yep, it is. Also, appropriate."

I bite my lip to not laugh, but he's right.

"Hey, any word from the university?" Dan asks as we near the coffee shop we decided to meet at before the tasting.

His question makes my mood drop slightly. I shake my head. "No, still nothing. I don't think I'll hear for a while. The placement wouldn't even start until next fall."

He nudges me with his shoulder. "They'd be stupid not to take you."

Here's hoping the people running the research project at the university agree with him.

Inside the coffee shop, the line isn't too long and there's an open table by the front. Dan gestures to it and says, "You grab us a seat, I'll get drinks."

I go and sit down, and a few minutes later he joins me, setting two mugs down. "Vanilla cappuccino, half caff with oat milk for the lady, and a mocha with extra whip for myself."

For a few seconds, I stare at the steaming mug in front of me, more uncomfortable truths hitting me, this time strong enough that I can't ignore them the way I normally do. In all the years I've been with Baron, I don't think he has even once ordered my coffee the way I like it. I'll drink coffee with regular milk, without flavouring, whatever. But my favourite? It's right here in front of me, courtesy of a man who is so good a friend, he always gets my coffee order right.

I lift it to my lips and take a sip, my mind spinning. I've always known Dan is a special kind of guy. A good man with a heart of gold. He's the one who always makes everyone around him smile, and nothing ever seems to get him down.

He's silly, and kind, and giving, and smart. And I count myself incredibly lucky to have him as a friend.

And as I look at him smiling around the coffee shop, sipping on his mocha, not caring that a smudge of whipped cream is on the corner of his lip, my heart flip-flops in my chest.

Because someday, a woman is going to be even luckier than I am and have Dan Montgomery as her partner.

Leaning forward before I can think about what I'm doing, I lift my thumb and wipe away the whipped cream, stilling when he quickly turns and his piercing brown eyes fix on me.

"You had a little..." I show him my thumb, still frozen. His gaze bounces down, then back up. Slowly, I move my thumb to my mouth. He follows my movement, and there's no mistaking the clenching of his jaw when my tongue darts out to lick it up.

All of a sudden, I feel hot and squirmy.

Pushing back from the table, I pick up my coffee cup and drain it, letting the still-hot liquid run down my throat. "We should go," I say when I'm done, moving to the counter where a bin holds dirty mugs. I don't meet his gaze as I walk out the door of the coffee shop, still trying to figure out what exactly was that reaction I just had.

I don't get hot and squirmy around Dan.

Then again, there was that moment at his house the other night when I walked in on him shirtless. If this is going to be happening every time I see him, if I'm going to start feeling things I have no business feeling, things are going to get awkward really fast.

And the thought of things changing between us, of me somehow ruining our friendship, has me filled with dread.

But he seems oblivious to my internal freak-out as he chatters to me about the Little League team his Little Brother is on. Grayson's a good kid, and I smile and nod as necessary, even though my head is a million miles away.

We reach the bakery in a few minutes, and Dan holds open the door with a little bow. "After you." He's always doing cute things like that, and I can't help but compare him to Baron, who hasn't held a door open for me in years.

"You must be the Hazelwood couple, welcome. I'm Joanne." An older woman wearing a pristine white chef's coat comes out from behind the counter.

"Oh, actually —"

"Yes, lovely to meet you."

I turn wide eyes on Dan, who just winks as he shakes the woman's hand. What the heck is he doing?

"I've taken the time to pull the designs Mrs. Hazelwood pre-selected, and we have an array of flavours for you to try."

"I'm sorry, what was that about the designs?" I ask, interrupting Joanne. She looks confused as we take a seat at a small table where a thin folder awaits us.

She turns to Dan. "Your mother was in here earlier this week and selected half a dozen designs she felt would match your aesthetic. She informed me you would choose from those."

Once again, Cordelia takes over. I shouldn't be surprised by now, yet somehow, I am.

"Why don't we focus on flavours first." Dan's hand lands on my knee, squeezing it gently. I look at him and see the concern etched on his face. Pasting on a smile, I cover his hand with mine for a second, then turn to Joanne.

"Yes. Let's start with flavours. Should we give you a list of what we'd like to try?"

Joanne blinks, and it's such a small gesture that it shouldn't feel so ominous. But I know what she's about to say before she even opens her mouth. "Mrs. Hazelwood already notified me which flavours you wish to sample."

"Of course, she did," I mumble under my breath.

"As long as one of them is carrot cake, we're good."

I turn sharply at Dan's words. "Carrot cake?"

He gives me a wink and a shameless grin. "Your favourite."

"How did you know that?"

Now his eyebrow lifts. "Come on, Birdie. Do you really gotta ask me that?"

I blink slowly. "I...I guess not."

He turns to Joanne, that wide smile now directed at her. "So, carrot cake. With cream cheese frosting. That's gotta be an option for my girl. She loves to bake, but no way is she making her own wedding cake."

There's no hope in trying to ignore the shiver I get hearing him say *my girl,* even if I know he means nothing by it. We're playing along with the assumption we're a couple, and maybe the guilt over that deception will hit me later, but for now, I'm glad he's here. I don't think Baron would have thought to ask for carrot cake.

As Joanne wheels out a cart covered in plates, each one with an admittedly gorgeous-looking slice of very fancy cake on it, I force myself to relax. As Dan said on the phone when I asked him to come with me, who doesn't like free cake?

"Okay, we have to start with this one." Dan gestures to a slice of light-coloured cake covered in pristine white icing with some sort of orange filling. "What's that flavour, Joanne?"

"That would be a cardamom cake with a citrus curd filling."

Dan dishes some onto a fork and hands it to me before scooping up his own bite. He raises his utensil, and I can't help but smile as we clink them together, then bring them to our mouths.

But my smile quickly falls. I try to school my reaction as I quickly chew and swallow, but one glance at Dan tells me I'm not alone in the struggle.

He ducks his head and whispers under his breath, "Say nothing, it's a trap!"

I have to muffle my laugh at the *Star Wars* reference, turning to Joanne with a hopefully believable neutral expression. "That one is not my preference," I say politely after wiping my mouth. "Sorry."

"No need to apologize," Joanne says breezily. "I'll leave you two lovebirds to your tasting. And once you have your top few choices, we can discuss design plans."

I nod in thanks and wait until she walks back into the kitchen before leaning over the table. "Oh my God, that was repulsive."

Dan lets out a quiet chuckle. "Thank fuck you agree. I don't know if I've ever met a piece of cake I didn't like, until now."

Eyeing the rest of the selections, I feel my worry mounting. "What if they're all weird like that? She didn't leave us a list or anything. Is it meant to be cake roulette?"

"We can do this. And after, we'll go for burgers and brews."

His confidence is cute, but I'm not buying it. "Ugh, what's so wrong with simple? Vanilla, chocolate, that's good enough."

"How about a carrot cake slab from the grocery store?" Dan winks. "That simple enough for you?"

"Honestly, yes," I answer, leaning back in my seat. Waving my hand at the tray of small plates, I mutter, "All of this is just too much."

He opens his mouth, then closes it, as if thinking better of what he was about to say. I wish he wouldn't. I wish he would be honest and tell me his opinion. Because the doubts I have about this wedding are growing bigger and bigger with every day that passes, and I need someone to tell me I'm not crazy for questioning if I should be going through with the marriage at all.

And I know every one of my friends would support me if I said I wanted to cancel everything. Heck, Willow already did when I told them I was engaged but I was worried it was a mistake.

Yet somehow, despite my doubts and misgivings, I'm still here, going through the motions. All the while wondering if this is going to turn out to be the biggest mistake of my life.

CHAPTER SEVEN

Lark

Do I have to answer?

It's sad that's the first thought that crosses my mind when my phone rings and I see who's calling.

But a lifetime of craving my mother's approval means I answer.

"Hi, Mom." I swirl the peppermint tea bag around in my glass cup, watching the water slowly darken.

"Lark, I heard from Ellen at the club that the Devereaux Hotel downtown has an opening for their larger ballroom. I took the liberty of contacting them and reserving it."

My hand comes to a stop as I take a deep breath in. "We don't need a larger room, Mom."

"Nonsense. The guest list Cordelia and I approved won't fit in anything less."

She continues to prattle on about something someone at the club said, and I completely tune her out. Reaching for a bag of licorice, I pull out a few pieces, then pick up my cup of tea and settle into a large chair by the window in my living room. Nestling the phone between my shoulder and ear, I light one of the many candles I have throughout my house. There's something about the flickering warmth that soothes me. And Lord knows I need soothing right now.

Honestly, it's no wonder my mother and Cordelia get along, they both enjoy ignoring anyone's opinions but their own and deciding things for other people.

The difference is, I've spent most of my life letting my mother be this way. It seemed easier than the alternative, which came with never-ending guilt trips and reminders of how much my parents have done for me.

Tuning out her lectures has become a survival strategy. A carefully honed technique made up of sounds of acknowledgments, never fully agreeing or disagreeing to anything, and trying to avoid commitments whenever possible.

Letting her drone on might be time consuming and draining, but it became second nature for a child born to parents who never wanted kids for any reason other than status. A child like me.

"Lark? Lark! Honestly, are you even listening?"

My mother's annoyed tone startles me back to attention. "Sorry, Mom. Could you repeat your question?" I wince, waiting for the huff. Yup, there it is.

"I said, I've decided to wear a navy blue dress, so please ensure your bridal party coordinates so there's no clashing in photos."

"Oh. Yeah, sure." I'm mentally rolling my eyes. Forget bridezilla, I've got two mothers-of-the-bride-and-groom-zilla.

"Alright. I need to go, we've got a dinner at the club tonight to celebrate Howard's promotion."

I make a noise, as if I know who the hell Howard is, or even care about his job status. "Okay. Bye, Mom."

Tossing my phone down on the table beside me, I let my head fall back against the chair and close my eyes. I know not all parents are as exhausting as mine and Baron's. I know not all families are more obsessed with appearances than anything else. I know normal families are capable of showing love and respect for one another.

I just don't know what any of that feels like, having never experienced it myself.

Twenty-four hours later, I push open the door to the restaurant I'm meeting the girls at for dinner, my head still full of spiraling thoughts. I honestly don't see how I can marry Baron, but I also don't see a way out of it without having to face not only two very disappointed families but also a lifetime alone.

But I'm not so pathetic as to believe that's a good enough reason to marry a man I don't love.

All of my anxiety spirals are leading to the same conclusion. I need to end my engagement.

I drop down into an open chair with a thump.

"Well, hello to you, too," Willow says, pushing a glass of wine over toward me. "Drink?"

"God, yes." I pick it up and take a long swallow.

Sadie leans forward, a concerned expression clear behind her glasses. "Are you okay?"

"If by okay, you mean exhausted from trying to keep up with the overbearing planning my mother and Cordelia are forcing me to be a part of? I honestly don't know why they bother telling me anything when they're just making decisions without my input, anyway."

"They sound awful," Sadie says, reaching out and covering my hand with hers, giving it a soft squeeze. "I'm sorry. Has there been any part of it you've enjoyed?"

"Cake tasting with Dan yesterday was fun," I reply honestly. Then I catch Willow's expression, eyebrows raised, questioning. "What?"

"Monty went cake tasting? Where was Baron?"

"He's still on his work trip out east, and you couldn't come. I didn't want to go alone," I reply defensively, taking another sip of wine.

"Mm-hmm."

Her reply, and the small smirk, has me sagging against my chair in defeat. "What am I doing?"

"Besides marrying the wrong guy?" Willow fires back, earning a gasp from Sadie. "Hey, I'm not saying anything none of us aren't already thinking. Right? You're the one who said to us the night you told us you were engaged that you thought it was a mistake. So why the hell are you still going through with it?"

I drain my glass before answering. "If I could explain it in a way that doesn't make me sound like a loser, I would. But I can't. And yes, I know that only highlights the fact that I shouldn't go through with it. I mean, who marries a guy just because he's the only one to ever show interest?"

"But Monty..." Sadie starts, then abruptly stops. My brows furrow. I swear it looked like she got kicked. But why would Willow shut her up like that?

"There is no me and Monty. Dan is my friend and that's it. He's never once made a move for anything else."

Willow reaches over casually to refill my glass before shooting her verbal arrow. A direct hit, straight to my heart. "Could that be because you've always been with Baron, and Monty's a good man who doesn't want to come between you two?"

I stare down at the ruby red liquid in my glass, uncomfortable with the raw truth of what Willow's pointed out. Monty is a good man. The best. And he absolutely is the kind of man that would respect someone's relationship, one hundred percent. But at the same time, if he truly had feelings beyond friendship for me, wouldn't I have sensed, I don't know, something?

"How did you and Baron get together?" Sadie asks quietly. I continue to stare into my glass, my mind tripping back in time to when Baron and I first became romantically involved.

"Through our parents, I guess you could say. Our fathers partnered to start their company when I was seventeen. He was two years older, and already in university, so we didn't see much of each other for a few years. We didn't have much in common, and despite our families' connection, we didn't exactly run in the same circles." I laugh, remembering how I used to look at him and Felicity with disdain, in their perfectly pressed clothes, while I was covered in grass stains from playing soccer. "But when I was in university, things started to change. My mom and his started making comments about the two of us. About us being meant for each other, and how serendipitous it was that we were near the same age and our families were so close."

"That sounds like a bad movie plot," Willow remarks, and I look up with a wry smile.

"No kidding. I wish I was joking." I let out a sigh, running my finger around the base of my wine glass as my smile softens. "But he was handsome, kind, and smart. When every other guy I met treated me like a friend, Baron was the only one to show interest in me as a woman. And at least, in the beginning, I was happy. I did fall for him, kinda quickly, if I'm honest. He was my first boyfriend, the guy I gave my virginity to. I started to buy into the idea of us being meant for each other, especially when I saw how happy my mother was to see us dating."

"So what happened?" Sadie's gentle voice prods me to continue.

I shrug. "I wish I knew. Things change, people change. The guy I fell for when I was younger became someone I didn't love as much. We drifted apart, I guess. The intimacy stopped along with the affection. But you know, isn't that how it goes with long-term relationships? The honeymoon phase doesn't last forever."

Willow snorts. "Speak for yourself. I don't plan on letting the intimacy die off one bit with Ronan."

I just barely stop myself from rolling my eyes. "Yeah, well, you two found unicorns with your men. Most of us have to make do with normal horses. No magical horns."

We all break into giggles at my unplanned innuendo. But things quickly turn serious when Willow reaches one hand over to cover mine.

"Babe, we love you and respect your decision, no matter what," Willow says, more gently now. "But I, for one, feel like I've kept my mouth shut for too long. And I regret that choice, because maybe if I had said something sooner, you wouldn't be in this shitty position. You're settling for Baron, maybe because of your parents, but I think it's because for some messed up reason, you don't see how amazing you are, and how any man would be lucky to love you. You don't need to marry him because you think you'll never find someone else. You don't need to marry him because it's what everyone expects you to do. You don't need to marry him, or anyone, unless you absolutely, without a doubt, love them and can't imagine a life without them."

Tears are forming in my eyes as she speaks, and when she finishes, they spill over, running down my cheeks. Everything she just said are words I wish I had convinced myself were true ages ago. But maybe it took getting to this point for them to truly sink in.

"I don't love him. And I don't want to marry him."

"Then don't."

It can't be that simple.

Can it?

In the silence that follows Willow's words, I finally give in to what I've wanted to say and do for so long.

"I'm breaking up with Baron."

"Thank fuck for that," Willow says, leaning back in her chair and flinging her hands in the air dramatically.

I manage to laugh, even as I'm crying. They're happy tears. Relieved tears. Nervous, but finally excited-for-the-future tears.

Sadie lifts her glass. "To making the right decision."

I swipe away my tears, then with a tremulous smile that grows stronger with every second, I pick up my glass. "To making the right decision. *Finally*"

I drink, feeling completely at peace with my choice. It's not going to be easy, ending a relationship that has defined me for so many years, but it has to happen. It will happen. For once, I'm standing up for what I need, instead of letting others decide what should happen.

And no matter what, I know I've got my friends to support me through it all.

As for Dan? Well, maybe what Willow said is true, and all that was stopping him was me being in a relationship. The thought of that is both exhilarating and terrifying all at the same time. Especially since I know the only way to find out is to make the first move.

CHAPTER EIGHT

Monty

"Hiiiii, Dan. You're amazing, you know that, right? Like, super-cool-fantastic-awesome-amazing. And like, a great guy. And a great friend. And you have a great butt. Oh my God, pretend I didn't just say that. Okay. Wow. So, um, anyway. I'm out with Willow and Sadie and they just bought a bottle of champagne to help me celebrate. Oh! Wait. I'm not celebrating getting married. I'm celebrating not getting married! Yeah. I have finally decided to stop being stupid. I'm ending it with Baron. Oh man, I think I gotta go drink champagne. Champaaaaaaaaaaaagne. That's a funny word to say. Okay, anyway, ummm, I don't know what else to say, except you're amazing! Okay. Bye!"

I listen to Lark's drunken, giggly message for a third time as I drive through the city toward the restaurant Willow texted me they were at. The first time I listened, I almost dropped my phone. The second time, I paced around my apartment, alternating between shaking my head in disbelief and grinning. This time, I'm coaching myself not to get too excited.

Just because she's ending it with the asshole doesn't mean there's anything there for me. She might say I'm amazing, and have a great butt, but she also said I'm a great *friend*. Goddamn friend zone. I hate it here. Can I give up my lifetime membership? Please?

At Grayson's game last week, so many people were looking at the two of us. Probably taking notice of how Lark would lean against me or steal my water to take a drink. Things couples do.

Oh, how wrong they were to assume that.

I'm a great friend. So great, I'll press pause right at my favourite scene in *The Empire Strikes Back* to pick her up.

Luke's freak-out over the identity of his father? Classic.

I pull up outside the restaurant and thankfully find a parking spot. It's a fancy place from the looks of the people coming out the door. I glance down at my grey sweats and hoodie, complete with a pizza stain in the middle of my chest, briefly second-guessing my decision to not bother changing before coming. But Willow made it sound like Lark was too drunk to just take an Uber home. So here I am, dressed like a schlub, ready to make sure she gets home safe.

The second I get out of my car, I hear someone call my name. Looking over, I see Ronan Sinclair, the first baseman for the Tridents, walking up. "Hey Monty, you here for Lark? We could have driven her home."

That makes me pause, because yeah, he could have. "Willow just said I should come and get Lark."

Ronan does a terrible job of hiding his smirk. "She did, did she. I see."

I pointedly ignore him. Just then, the door to the restaurant opens, and three women stumble out, holding onto each other and giggling.

We start toward them, Willow spotting us first. "There you are, our knights in shining" — her gaze drops down, then back up with a giggle — "sweatpants." She waltzes over to Ronan, wrapping her arms around him and plastering a kiss on his face. "Hi."

Turning my attention from them, I see Sadie, standing to the side, typing something on her phone, and Lark, looking at me.

"Why are you here?" she asks, then hiccups, slapping a hand over her mouth.

"Willow said you needed a ride home." I stuff my hands in my pockets. Does she not want me here? Then she starts to sway, and I step forward, wrapping my arm around her shoulders to support her. "And it looks like you had a good time."

Her head falls onto my shoulder as she lets out a soft giggle. "I did. I feel good, Dan. Really good. For the first time in a long time."

I want so badly to ask her if that's because she's ending it with Baron, but now's not the time. Not when she can barely stand up on her own. "Okay, Birdie. Let's get you home."

I steer her over toward my car, waving goodbye to Ronan who's loading the other two into his car.

As I pull out of the parking lot, I make a snap decision to take her back to my place. It's closer than hers, and if she's had as much to drink as I think she has, the sooner I get some water into her and get her horizontal, the better. "Hey, Lark, we're gonna go to my place, okay? You can sleep it off there, so I can keep an eye on you."

"Mm-hmm," is her only reply, and I glance over to see her leaning against the window, her eyes closed.

A couple of minutes later, soft snores fill the car.

When I pull into my parking stall, Lark is still asleep, her head against the headrest. I sit there for a couple of minutes, watching her. Is it creepy to watch her sleep? Maybe, but I can't help it. She's so damn pretty, and seeing her so relaxed and peaceful with me, knowing she trusts me enough to get her home safely, to fall asleep in my presence, it does something to me. I like being the guy she can rely on. No, I love it. I've witnessed my parents' love over the years, and this is what it's like for them. They know, without a doubt, they're safe with each other. I've seen my dad climb a ladder with my mom holding the bottom. I've watched my mom care for my dad when he's sick, and my dad do everything for my mom after she had surgery a few years ago. Their love, their support, their trust. That's what I want for myself.

That's what I want *with Lark*.

Quietly, I open my door, closing it just as softly before going around to her side. This part will be a bit more tricky, but I manage to open the door, reaching in to unbuckle her. Then, using the muscles honed over years of being a catcher, I squat down and scoop her into my arms, lifting her out of the car.

"Dan?" she mumbles, her head lifting.

"Shh, it's okay, Birdie. I got you," I whisper back. And her head falls against my shoulder, her arms winding around my neck.

"Always," she whispers against my skin, and my goddamn heart stutters in my chest.

"Yeah, always."

Somehow, I manage to lock my car, and then I carry her over

to the elevator. Thank God for automatic opening doors. The elevator is empty the whole way up to my apartment. But that's where it gets tricky. My keys are in my hand, and even though my arms are starting to feel the strain of carrying her for this long, I get the door unlocked and open without smacking her head against it.

Go me.

Once inside, I carry her straight down the hall to my bedroom and set her down on my bed. Good thing I never bother to make it in the morning, so the blankets are already pulled down. Eyeing her outfit, I decide against trying to get her into something else. Until, that is, her eyes blink open, and she pushes her way to sitting.

"Where are we?"

"My place," I say, walking over to my dresser and pulling out a T-shirt and some shorts. "If you want to change, here you go. Sleep it off and I'll take you home in the morning."

She rubs her face and gives me a small smile. "Thanks." Her mouth opens in an adorable yawn that morphs into a hiccup. "Oh my God." She moans. "Too much wine."

I chuckle and move into my kitchen to fill a glass with water and grab her some painkillers. When I get back to my bedroom, I freeze in the doorway. Her back is to me, but she's taken off her clothes, leaving her in nothing but a pair of black panties.

Whipping around, I clear my throat. "I've got some water for you."

"Oh!" I hear her soft sound of surprise, then the rustle of fabric. "I'm decent."

Turning around slowly, I swallow, my mouth suddenly dry.

Decent? She's wearing my shirt, and the shorts are still on the bed beside her. Which means she has nothing else on underneath except those black panties.

I don't dare step any closer, simply extend my arm with the glass of water. She closes the distance and takes it.

"Thanks."

"No problem. I'll be on the couch."

Her head slowly nods. "You're a good friend, Dan Montgomery."

"Yeah," I say, the word coming out hoarse. "Sure."

As I turn to go lick my wounds over that goddamn word *friend*, her hand darts out and grabs my wrist. I twist back around, and she lifts up onto her toes, her lips brushing my cheek gently, too fast for me to register what she's doing until she's stepping back with a soft smile.

"Goodnight."

I'm too dumbfounded to say anything, my head bobbing up and down as my only response. Then I turn and stagger to my living room before collapsing on the couch. Only then do I exhale slowly, my hand running through my hair.

It figures. The first time I feel Lark's lips on my skin, she's so drunk she probably won't remember it in the morning.

But I sure as shit will.

Chapter Nine

Lark

Oh my God. My head feels like tiny elephants are stampeding through it. There's a blinding light burning the backs of my eyes. My mouth is drier than the desert and feels like it's full of fluff.

Hangovers are so stupid.

Forcing myself to blink my eyes open, for a minute, I'm confused. Where the heck am I? Then I inhale slowly, the scent of fresh laundry blowing in the breeze as familiar to me as anything.

Dan.

The guys on the team tease him about his obsession with making sure his laundry smells good, but I secretly love it. I don't need musky, woodsy, whatever. Give me clean laundry smell any day.

I burrow my head in his pillow as bits and pieces of last night come back to me. Drinking with Willow and Sadie, deciding to end my engagement, and then Dan showing up like a white knight to take me home.

Wait.

Did I...

Oh God.

With a muffled groan, I roll over, and spy my phone on the bedside table. Opening it, I check my call log. Yup, there it is, a two-minute call to Dan's phone. Except, I don't remember him answering. No, I left him a rambling voice message. And I can't remember what I said.

Dropping my phone, I yank the covers over my head. Except, all that does is flood my senses with his smell.

Tossing off the covers, I glance down. Crap, I'm wearing his clothes? This is…this is too much. I need to get out of here, get rid of this hangover, and get my head thinking clearly.

Because the one thing my traitorous brain keeps imagining? Is waking up in this bed…

With Dan next to me.

I'm not proud of sneaking out of Dan's apartment, still wearing his T-shirt, no less. But when I gathered my stuff and walked out to his living room, he looked so peaceful, asleep on his couch. I didn't have it in me to wake him up.

Not to mention, I wasn't ready to face him. Not until I figure out what to do about everything.

As soon as I'm home, having taken a taxi back to the restaurant to collect my car, I get in the shower, turning it on as hot as it can go.

That, along with some eucalyptus-scented body wash, helps to clear some of the hangover. And when I step out, I roll on some peppermint and lavender essential oil to deal with the pounding in my head as I get dressed.

First things first. I need to talk to Baron. I don't feel good about having this conversation while he's still away, but there's no way I can wait any longer to end this. It has to happen, and it has to happen *now*.

I make a cup of coffee and a bagel, then settle in on my couch. Even though it's still very early here in Vancouver, Baron's work trip has him on the East Coast, meaning it's a reasonable hour there.

Sure enough, he answers my video call immediately.

"Hey Lark, what's up?"

I look at him for a second, trying to find any love in the way he looks at me or in the way he greets me. But there's nothing there. I suppose the fact that we haven't spoken — not even a text — in several days is proof that I'm making the right decision. I deserve someone who wants to talk to me every day, who cares about me, my life, my heart. I deserve more than a "What's up?"

"Hi. How's your trip so far?"

"Fine. I'm about to head into the office for a meeting, so I only have a few minutes. What can I do for you?"

"Baron, do you still love me?" I ask, ripping off the Band-Aid. I watch him closely to see his reaction. All he does is raise his eyebrows.

"What kind of a question is that?"

"A perfectly reasonable one if we're meant to be getting married in a few weeks," I fire back.

His gaze drops away from the phone, and I hear him exhale a long, slow sigh. "Lark, I really don't have time for this."

Stubbornly, I ignore him. "It shouldn't be that hard to answer me. Unless you don't, in which case, we're making a big mistake."

"We've been together for so long, and our families —"

"Forget our families, Baron. I don't want to marry someone I don't love with my entire heart and soul. And I deserve to marry someone who loves me that way in return." I pause, staring at him until he finally looks up. "And so do you."

Emotions play across his usually placid face, eventually settling on relief. And that sentiment is echoed in myself. Baron's not a bad guy, he's just not right for me. And I'm not going to settle for *not right* any longer.

"I did love you."

I finally give him a small smile, because I get it. "I know. It was good for a while. But we changed."

He nods slowly. "We did. And I'm sorry for that." He glances to the side, then back to the phone as he stands up. "Look, can we continue this later, I really do need to go."

And just like that, any goodwill I was feeling for him based on how this conversation was going dissipates. How can this not take priority?

"No, your meeting can wait a couple more minutes."

I guess my annoyance comes through because he stops. "Okay..."

Taking a deep breath, I finally say it. "I don't think we should get married."

I see his lips purse as he blows out his breath. "No, I don't suppose we should." There's a slight tinge of regret to his voice, but mostly it's acceptance.

Which gives me the courage to forge on, all the words that

have been swirling around in my head for weeks pouring out of me. Being this honest, this raw, feels uncomfortable, there's no doubt. Especially since we've never been this way with each other. But instinctively, I know there's no other option right now. Not if we want a clean break.

"And I think it's best if we go our separate ways. Amicably. I don't hate you or anything, but I don't love you, and I don't want to be with you anymore. You're a good man, and at one point, we were happy together. But that doesn't mean we're meant to be together forever. No matter what everyone else thinks. We want different things, have different goals and ideas for the future. And we probably should have talked about all of that before we got engaged, but I think we both got caught up in what we believed we *should* do instead of what we *wanted* to do."

He nods again.

"So this is me saying it's time to do what we want, what will make us happy. Instead of worrying about everyone else."

A small, somewhat sad smile twitches at his lips. "You're a smart woman, Lark. Kind and beautiful. You would have made an excellent wife. But you're right. We changed. As individuals and as a couple. And for what it's worth, I'm sorry I let it get this far."

Hearing him apologize, hearing him be honest and admit his feelings in return, is exactly what I needed. The last chain around me falls away. I didn't realize I was harbouring some guilt over my decision to end our relationship, but given how good I feel right now, I guess I did. And now, knowing he doesn't want to go through with it either, that guilt dissipates leaving me feeling nothing but relief.

We talk for a few minutes longer, sorting out the details of how and when we'll tell our families. In the end, we decide to handle it separately, for which I'm eternally grateful. Not having to face Cordelia Hazelwood and tell her that her wedding plans were for nothing? Sounds great to me.

I hang up with Baron after agreeing we'll meet up when he's back in town for us to return anything we have of each other's and for me to give the ring back. Then I slide it off my finger and set it on my dresser. Staring down at the band, the diamond sparkling up at me, I feel an overwhelming sense of lightness. As if removing that ring removed a weight from me.

I still have to deal with my own family, but after that? I'm free.

And I know exactly what I'm going to do first.

CHAPTER TEN

Monty

I woke up to an empty apartment and a sore neck from sleeping on the couch. Not the best start to my day.

She left without a note, no sign she had even been here except for the folded-up pair of shorts I guess she never put on and the water glass beside the bed. That and the pillow I normally use was lying lengthwise as if someone was hugging it in their sleep.

That makes me smile.

I make a quick protein shake and shoot a text to Darling and Yami.

> **MONTY: My dudes. Who's up for a run this morning?**

> **YAMI: Seriously? Damn, it's 7 am.**

> **MONTY: Okay T Swift, if you're too lazy just say so...**

YAMI: Don't bring my imaginary girl-friend into this.

YAMI: Meet at the usual spot?

DARLING: Y'all are lazy. I've been up since 6. Already done my yoga. See you there in thirty?

MONTY: It's on like donkey kong. And Yami, I'll treat you to donuts after.

YAMI: Fine. But I want TWO donuts.

With just a few minutes to get ready before I need to leave and meet the guys, I briefly debate texting Lark. In the end, my self-doubt wins and I don't. She probably doesn't remember much from last night. Heck, she might even be embarrassed that I had to carry her inside. Not that I care; any excuse to hold her. Besides, she was a cute drunk, with those little hiccups and giggles. And seeing her in my shirt, in my bed?

Goddamn, that was as close to heaven as I've ever been.

I get dressed in compression tights, shorts, and a Tridents long sleeve thermal shirt, grab a toque, my keys and a water bottle, and I'm out the door. When I pull into the parking lot in Stanley Park where the guys and I like to meet, I can't help but remember the last time I went for a run here.

With Lark.

The day she told me she was engaged.

I've avoided this spot since then and didn't realize it until now.

Darling's already waiting, but there's no sign of Yami as I get out of my car.

"Mornin', how long are we gonna wait for him?" Darling says as I walk over.

I shrug. "We'll give him a few, we're early." I start to do some warm-up stretches, letting the crisp November air fill my lungs. If the skies stay clear all day like they're meant to, I'm going to head up to one of the local mountains with my telescope.

It wasn't easy being a science geek in a small town. And even being on a sports team, helping them hit the championships, didn't outweigh the social suicide I brought on myself with my *Star Wars* T-shirts and space puns. Yeah, I was the nerd in school who wanted to study the stars.

At least now as an adult, I can embrace my nerdy side openly, and not fear the backlash. If anything, people love me even more for it — now.

I've always said that if I hadn't gone on to play ball professionally, I would have considered getting a degree in astrophysics. Visiting NASA is a bucket list dream of mine.

A low black sports car speeds into the parking lot, the music thumping from inside.

"Always gotta make an entrance," Darling says, a wry smile on his face.

We've all got our roles to play. Where I'm the friendly one, Darling's the southern gentleman, Maverick's the bad boy, Sin's the father figure, and Yami? He's the drama queen.

We're finding our groove as a duo, and most of the time, our energies compliment each other. We're both outgoing and love to have fun. But where I try to put everyone else first, Yami can be a bit more selfish sometimes. Not malicious, though. Nah, the guy doesn't have a mean bone in his body. But it's the little things like this — blaring loud music early in the morning, not caring who he might disturb as he drives through town.

When he cuts his engine and the music stops, the silence feels abrupt. He climbs out of his car and immediately stretches his arms overhead with a yawn.

"It is so fucking early."

"Okay, you big baby, stretch and let's go. I want some donuts." Darling starts to bounce side to side.

We set off, the pace nice and easy, the only sound our breathing. But as always happens when us guys get together, the competition soon starts. And the next thing I know, I'm sprinting against Yami, proving catchers can do more than just squat.

Once again, I'm reminded of racing Lark that day. I guess it's not one I'll soon forget, seeing as it felt like the end of something that never even had the opportunity to start.

Except now? Now I might have a second chance with her. Maybe being here in the same place where she broke my heart without ever knowing it, the day after she tells me she's ending things with Baron, is a sign. A sign my time is coming.

After finishing our run, I make good on my offer and we head to a local bakery that specializes in gourmet donuts.

We sit down at a table, each with a donut and coffee in front of us, and dive in. This is why I love the offseason. I can eat donuts after a run and not worry the team nutritionist is gonna give me shit.

Not that it would stop me from having one during the season, but still. Guilt-free donut? Yes, please and thank you.

"Excuse me, hi, um, are you guys from the Tridents?"

We all turn at the high-pitched, feminine voice. I gotta be honest, it's way more common for dudes or kids to come up to us, but every now and then, women will approach us. Like the pair standing next to our table right now.

"Yes, we are, pretty lady." Darling turns on the charm, his accent somehow more pronounced as he gives the women a grin. I just internally roll my eyes. He knows being the good old southern boy gets them every time.

"Oh my God, we love the Tridents!" One of them giggles, and without being asked, the two of them start to pull over chairs and sit down.

A brunette squeezes in between me and Yami, the space so narrow her thigh is pressed against mine. I give her a small smile and try to subtly put some space between us, which proves impossible. "Hey. I'm Monty."

"Hi, I'm Leia," she says in return.

"Like from *Star Wars*?" I blurt out, and she nods, giggling again. Not sure how my question was funny, but okay. Or wait, do I have something stuck in my teeth? I run my tongue over them to check but can't feel anything.

A hand lands on my arm, startling me. "So, what position do you play, Monty?" she asks coyly.

"I thought you said you love the Tridents?" I ask without thinking about how it might sound. "I'm one of the catchers." And seeing as there's only three of us, a fan would know who I am.

Her face falls slightly, but she recovers quickly. "Right, of course." She giggles again. Okay, now that sound is getting annoying. And I'm not easily annoyed. Leia leans in and presses her chest into my arm. Woah, that's not cool. I try to shift away but Yami's on my other side and there's nowhere to go.

"Uh, yeah. So." I push away from the table, my chair scraping across the floor and stand up, dislodging her. "I gotta take a leak."

I escape to the back of the bakery, not even sure if there is a washroom back here. But I don't know how to act around women like Leia. Women who are bold and forward. It's cool, I mean, all power to them. I just don't have a fucking clue what to do when I'm not interested in that at all.

At least, not with them.

After a couple of minutes, I peer around the corner, and to my relief, the girls are gone. I make my way back to the table and sink down in my chair.

"Monty. Dude. What the fuck?" Yami punches my shoulder. "She was into you."

"Yeah, but I wasn't into her," I reply lightly. "I'm here for donuts, not girls."

"Who says you can't have both?"

"Give our boy a break, Yami," Darling says, leaning forward. "Everyone knows he's only got eyes for one woman. He has since the day he joined the team, ain't that right?" He looks at me, sympathy clear on his face. "But Monty, you gotta figure out how to move on. She's gettin' hitched."

I want to tell them she's not. But it's not my news to share, so I keep my mouth shut, and just incline my head to show I heard him. He *is* right, I've had eyes for Lark since the very beginning, and unfortunately, these guys know the story all too well.

They helped me work up the courage to ask her out, witnessed me show up at the stadium with flowers, only to find her kissing some dude in khaki shorts and a polo shirt.

She introduced him as Baron, her boyfriend. Of course, the guy wearing fucking khakis and a polo shirt had a name like Baron. There was no mistaking the arrogance as he looked me over. I can still remember how his chin lifted, likely taking in my clothes — athletic wear for the workout I had to go and do — and clearly finding me lacking. I knew right then, there was no hope for me. If she was with a guy like him, she'd never want a guy like me.

"Who's up for some batting practice this afternoon?" I ask as a way to try and redirect the conversation. It works, and talk turns to what time we want to meet up at the stadium to get some hits in.

Thank fuck. Talking about women with my teammates is one thing I work hard to avoid. I don't want to deal with the questions that might come up. It's been easier to let them believe I'm pining over Lark and that's why I've never had a girlfriend.

And I mean, let's be real. That's basically the truth.

They just don't need to know exactly how *true* it is. It's not only the last few years that have seen me single as single can be. It's my entire damn life.

Hours later, after meeting the guys for BP, then joining some of them for dinner at a local pub, night has fallen and I still haven't heard from Lark. She wasn't at the stadium either, at least not that I could see.

But the skies are still clear, which means, regardless of how I'm feeling about the lack of communication from her, my mission is a go.

I grab an old hoodie from my closet and the large case that holds my baby. My pride and joy. The second most important item I own, next to my very first catcher's mitt.

Once my astronomy gear is loaded in the car, I drive out of the city, and up the winding road that climbs one of the mountains in North Vancouver. When I reach the lookout I'm headed for, it's empty.

Perfect.

It takes no time at all to set up my telescope, the hardest part being leveling the tripod on the rocky ground. But I've set up here many times before, so it's doable. The air is cold tonight, with a bit of wind that's biting against my skin. I grab the jacket I'm grateful I tossed in at the last minute and zip it up tight. There's no snow up here yet, but it's coming soon, I would guess. Then I won't be able to come up here so easily, since setting up my equipment in the snow is a pain.

I take out my phone and open my favourite star chart to double-check the location of what I want to see, then set the telescope in that direction. It takes a bit to align everything and get it into focus but then, there it is.

It's not the best time of year to view this particular star; in the spring, it's much brighter. But there she is. The star I bought two years ago as a birthday present. A present I never gave to the person I purchased it for, worried it would be seen as too much.

The star I named Birdie.

Chapter Eleven

Monty

I love sleep. Sleep is awesome. Babies have it so good, all they have to do is eat, sleep, poop, and cry whenever they want. And take toddlers. Some of them actually protest nap time! Come on, kid, don't you realize sleep is fucking amazing?

Mom said since the day I was born, I loved to sleep. She actually worried about me as a newborn because all I wanted to do was eat and be cuddled while I slept.

All of that is to say, when it's the one morning this week I'm allowing myself to sleep in as late as I want, and someone won't stop knocking on my door, I'm not pleased.

Security in my building is pretty tight, which means there's only a few people it could be. The guys on the team are on my approved entry list. Hell, Darling lives two floors below me. Lark and my parents have access, but that's about it.

Normally, none of those people are ones I'd be grumpy toward, but I was really looking forward to that sleep in. Which is why there's a frown on my face when I drag my feet over to the front door.

"Okay, okay. Geez. Give a guy a chance to wake up," I grumble. But when I wrench open the door, ready to give whoever it is a hard time for waking me up, the grumpy, tired feeling fades away in an instant. Lark is standing there, her hands clasped tightly in front of her, and a nervous expression on her face I've never seen before.

"Hi." Her voice is soft, just above a whisper.

"Hey," I say, the word catching in my throat, my voice cracking like a fucking teenager going through puberty. I clear it, and try again, attempting to look cool and casual as I stand in the doorway. But given the fact that I'm still in my pajamas with Wookiees all over the pants and holes in my T-shirt, I'm guessing I fail.

"I mean, hi, Lark. How's it going this fine morning?"

Jesus Christ. Now I sound like a dork. And seeing as she's fighting not to smile, she thinks so, too.

I push off the door and step back. "Wanna come in?"

She nods, biting her lip, and brushes past me. Heading straight to the kitchen, I watch with some bemusement as she just makes herself at home, turning on the coffee maker and pulling down two of my *Star Wars*-themed mugs. The one she always uses is black and reads "This Is Not The Coffee You Are Looking For." The other is one of my favourites and reads "May The Caffeine Be With You." It's not like this is the first time she's made coffee in my apartment, but something seems off. Her hand trembles slightly when she sets the mugs down, and her movements are jerky as she goes to the fridge to pull out the vanilla flavoured creamer I keep there for her.

"Lark, what's going on?" I ask, starting to get concerned. "Is this about the other night? Because I swear, I don't care that you were drunk. It was no big deal helping out. You didn't puke or anything. And I slept on the couch the whole time, promise."

"I broke up with Baron."

The silence that falls after she says the five words I've wanted to hear for years is deafening.

Then, like a total idiot, I open my big mouth. "Oh. That's cool."

Lark makes some weird sound, something between a hysterical laugh and a snort, immediately clapping her hand over her mouth. I reach my hand up and scrub it across my face, partly wishing I could rewind time by ten minutes or so and not make a fool out of myself in front of my female best friend.

"Let me try again," I rasp. "How are you feeling about that?"

There, that sounds better. More appropriate of a response. But when I force myself to meet Lark's gaze, I am very much unprepared for what happens next.

Like a tiny blond tornado, she flings herself across the kitchen, my arms opening just in time to catch her. But when I go to hold her away from my body, she presses in. My eyes widen as she fumbles her hands up to cup my cheeks, fiery determination clear in her gaze.

She pauses, her eyes searching my face.

I hear her mutter under her breath, "Fuck it."

Then.

Holy shit.

Then, she kisses me.

CHAPTER TWELVE

Lark

Somehow, I keep it together until I pull my car into the parking lot of the Tridents stadium. Then, and only after making sure there's no one around to witness my impending freak-out, I drop my head to the steering wheel, thunking it over and over again as I mutter under my breath, "What. Was. I. Thinking."

Once my forehead starts to hurt, I stop beating myself up, physically, at least. Slumping back in my seat, I let my eyes fall closed, my mind instantly bringing up the image of Dan's face after I pulled back from our kiss. Shock was written all over his features, from the rigid stance of his body to his blank expression.

It wasn't the reaction of a man with romantic feelings. It was the reaction of a man stunned by what I did. And not necessarily in a good way.

I didn't wait around to discuss what happened. Instead, I bolted from his apartment as if I was trying to outrun the devil. And maybe I was, if the devil is my impulsive decision to kiss my best guy friend just a few hours after breaking off my engagement.

I guess I drove on autopilot, coming to the stadium like this. I do have some work to do, a couple guys coming in for treatment, but not until later on.

But I climb out of my car anyway and slowly make my way into the facility. It's drizzling, cold, and wet. Kind of fitting, given the way I feel. Like there's a very real possibility I messed everything up.

Inside, the stadium is fairly quiet. Most of the offseason work happens up in the administrative offices. The lower level where the gym, locker rooms, and training facilities are located tends to be mostly empty with so many of the players not in the city right now. When I push open the doors to the therapy wing where we do all medical and rehab assessments and treatments, the Tridents' head trainer Mattias is there, walking out with one of the second basemen, Ben.

"See you next week and remember to take it easy on that knee."

"Will do." Ben gives Mattias a nod and turns toward the door. "Oh, hey, Lark. How's it going?"

I muster up what I hope is a believably calm smile. "Great, thanks. Have a good one, Ben."

He leaves and Mattias turns to look at me over his shoulder as he types some notes into one of the tablets we use to keep track of treatment plans and progress. "Yo, Lark, you're here early."

I set my bag down and move to the coffee machine we installed last year to save us having to go to the cafeteria all the time. "Yeah, I figured I'd get a workout in, catch up on some notes."

Lies. All lies.

But Mattias just nods. "Cool. Any word from the university yet?"

He submitted a reference on my behalf to the research team, but honestly? That is the *last* thing on my mind right now.

"No, nothing yet."

"It'll come soon," he says. "Hey, I'm heading to Maura's for lunch, want me to grab you a sandwich when I go?"

"Sure, that would be great, thanks."

The mundane conversation does the trick of settling some of my freak-out nerves. Coffee in hand, I move into the smaller room where I have a table for when I need to do manual treatments. Setting my water bottle and coffee down on the small desk, I fire up my computer and check my emails and calendar for the day. Nothing new has cropped up, which means I've got some time. I could do what I told Mattias and go to the gym, but I need to talk to someone first, before I explode.

A few minutes later, I'm knocking on Willow's office door.

"Hey girl, come on in."

I walk in, close her door, and sink down onto a chair. "I did it. I ended things with Baron."

The pen Willow was holding clatters to the desk. "Holy fuck, really?" She stands up, moving quickly around the desk to sit in the chair next to me, taking my hand. "That's great, I'm so happy. Do you feel good about it? Relieved? Was it easy, or did he give you shit? Do we need to go beat him up?"

I choke out a laugh. "Yes, yes, sort of, no, and definitely not. He agreed, we weren't doing it for the right reasons, and there was no real love between us. Honestly? The worst part was telling my parents. Did you know disappointment has a sound?

It's the huff-sigh combo my mother does that makes it clear she disapproves of my decisions."

Willow winces. "Yeah, I'm familiar with the sound. Lydia had it down pat." Her reference to her former boss makes a small smile break free.

"Lydia would have gotten along great with my mom and Baron's."

"Okay, so, he took it well and it's done now. Why do you look so freaked out?"

I choke down a sip of coffee, feeling it burn my throat. "Um, well, see, I couldn't get what you said at dinner the other night out of my head."

Her eyebrows raise, and I drop my gaze to my lap.

"About what, exactly?"

"You know what."

"About Monty? Oh Lark, what did you do?"

To her credit, she doesn't sound worried or upset, just curious.

"I...kissed him."

"Oh."

My head slowly nods up and down. "Yup."

"Well, what happened next?"

I force myself to lift my gaze and look morosely at Willow. "He was shocked, frozen. And I bolted."

"Oh, Lark." Willow leans forward, pulling me into a hug. "You just took him by surprise. Don't think anything of it. The poor guy probably thought he was dreaming."

"Or living a nightmare," I say miserably, letting my fear come to light. "What if we've been reading him all wrong? What if there's nothing there but friendship, and I just messed it all up with one stupid kiss?"

Willow pushes me away, holding my shoulders and shaking them gently. "Stop it right now, Lark Miller. Believe me when I say, Monty is in love with you. I think he has been for a long time, but he had no choice but to bury those feelings out of his respect for you. Now that things are different, you need to give him a chance to realize that. Did he know you had broken up with Baron before you kissed him?"

"Yes," I say, then drop my gaze. "I told him right before I did it."

Willow's quiet laugh isn't mocking in any way. "So he had zero time to adjust before you gave him the shock of his lifetime and made all of his dreams come true."

I try to think of what happened from that perspective, and it's easy to see how Willow could be right. I really did kind of blindside him, especially considering my radio silence between the night he brought me home from the restaurant and today.

"Okay." I exhale. "I need to go and talk to him, don't I?"

Willow stands up, moves back around her desk, and opens a drawer, pulling out the jar of Skittles Ronan keeps stocked for her. She offers it to me, and I take a handful.

"Yes, you do," she says simply, tossing a few Skittles into her mouth. When she finishes chewing, she leans forward, and looks me straight in the eye. "But what are you going to say?"

My shoulders lift and fall, because ain't that the question of the day. "Honestly? I have no idea. I just got out of a long-term relationship with a man I mistakenly thought I was going to marry. I'm hardly looking to jump straight into another relationship, if that's even what Dan wants."

Willow lets out a small laugh. "Trust me, that's what he wants. But he won't push you into something you're not ready for. He's not like that."

"And that's just it. It's Dan. He's the best man I know, no offense to Sin."

Willow gives me a smile and nods her head. "None taken."

I pop another Skittle into my mouth and continue. "But the idea of being with Dan doesn't feel weird. Shouldn't it feel weird this soon? Or is it just because I'm ridiculously horny and haven't had sex in months?" I end with a groan, shifting forward to drop my head into my hands. "Willow, I'm a mess. I don't know what I want or what to do or say or anything. Help."

"Alright, girlfriend, let's figure this out." Willow adopts her take-charge voice, the one that can corral a locker room full of jocks that need to do press interviews. "First of all, do you have feelings for Monty that go beyond friendship?"

"I don't know. I haven't let myself ever really consider that," I answer quietly, still looking at my hands. "Maybe? Probably? I think I could."

"We'll take that as a yes for now. But I think you're right to not move quickly. Monty's a special kind of guy, and I don't think he would want you to jump into anything right away, either. So really, nothing has to change. You're still friends, it's just that now you're friends who are free to explore whether there's something more. Just..." She trails off, and I look up.

"Just what?"

Willow looks torn. "I love you, you're one of my closest friends. But I care about him, too. So I'm sorry, but I have to say this, just know it doesn't mean I'm picking sides or anything."

I nod quickly. "Okay, what?"

"Be careful with his heart. We all know he's a fun guy, friendly and outgoing and not afraid to be silly. But there's more to him. You know that probably better than I do. His heart's on the line just as much as yours is, so you have to be really clear and honest with each other about what's going on. Which you can't do unless you're clear and honest with yourself. So figure out your feelings first, then go and talk to him. And maybe this time, hold off on the kissing until you've sorted out your head *and* your heart."

Chapter Thirteen

Lark

For the second time in less than twelve hours, I find myself standing outside Dan's apartment, nervous as heck. I lift my hand to knock and drop it back down at least three times. When my phone vibrates in my pocket, it startles me enough that I take a step back, grateful for the reprieve from the anxiety of what I'm about to do.

Until I read the message.

> **DAN: Are you planning on coming in any time soon, or should I go take a nap?**

"Shit," I mumble under my breath as his door opens, and the man in question is there, leaning against the door frame. With his arm over his head, his Mandalorian T-shirt has ridden up, revealing a sliver of skin above the waist of his jeans. My tongue darts out to moisten my lips, and of course, he catches me staring.

"Hey, Birdie."

"Hi," I whisper back, unable to stop staring at him. He looks different, somehow. More confident, maybe? Or perhaps I'm just seeing him differently now that Baron's not in my life.

Dan pushes off the door frame and takes a step back, inclining his head inside. "I just ordered some pizza, are you gonna stay for dinner?"

How he's able to act so casual when I'm tied up in knots, I do not know. And honestly, it leaves me even more confused as to how he feels about what happened this morning. Not that I was expecting him to grab me and pin me against the door to ravish me — although I'm not sure I'd stop him if he did — but this nonchalance is disconcerting.

I walk past him, just like I did this morning, only this time, he catches my hand as I go by. Turning to face him, I take in the raw, vulnerable hope written on his face.

"You're not gonna run away again this time, are you?" he asks quietly, and I shake my head. He squeezes my hand, giving me a small smile, then drops it to head into the kitchen. Opening the fridge, he pulls out two beers, a lager for him and a fruity ale for me. Cracking the tops, he moves to the glass sliding doors that lead to his large heated patio. I trail after him, finding some comfort in these familiar actions.

We've had pizza and beer on this patio many times. But this time, everything's changed.

I take the beer he hands me and settle down on one of the lounge chairs. I expect him to take the other, but he doesn't. Instead, he sets his beer down on the same table as mine and crouches down next to me.

"Promise you're not gonna run, no matter what happens next?"

My head is already moving from side to side as I open my mouth to respond, but he doesn't give me a chance to say a word.

His lips land on mine, soft and tentative at first, but quickly becoming more firm and sure. It's a chaste kiss, sweet, even, but I feel it reverberate throughout my body, unlocking parts of me that were forced to stay quiet for too long.

He backs off too soon, and a whimper escapes me. But the look of pure satisfaction on Dan's face soothes my disappointment.

"I've wanted to do that for years," he says, his voice all gravelly and deep.

He straightens up and moves to the other chair, stretching out on it with a sigh. All I can do is watch him, shocked, curious, and more than a little turned on. But to my surprise, Dan leans back, closes his eyes, and just lies there with a smile.

"What —" I start to say, but he holds his hand up to stop me.

"Nope, we're gonna talk, Birdie, but first, just give me a minute to soak this all in."

His smug tone of voice is tinged with so much joy, I can't help but smile in return. Settling back into my chair, I make myself relax under the warmth of the patio heater.

A hand brushes against the back of mine, fingers lightly grazing. I look over, but his eyes are still closed, and he's just smiling up at the evening sky. But he keeps brushing his fingers back and forth across my hand.

I'm here, his action seems to say. *I've always been here, waiting for you.*

On his next pass, my hand reaches out and takes hold of his. I weave our fingers together for the first time, holding hands with him as maybe something more than just friends.

His eyes flutter open and he looks over at me, that little smile deepening. "So," he says. "What was that all about this morning? Not that I'm complaining, in case that wasn't clear, but I feel like I need to hear you tell me what it meant." His hand tightens on mine ever so slightly. "You kissed me, Lark."

I swallow down a sip of beer, reaching for the courage to vocalize what I need to say. Not that I feel like I need it, not anymore. I'm pretty sure I know how this is going to go. But that doesn't fully erase the tiny kernel of fear deep inside me. Is this going to change everything? For the better or for the worse?

"Yeah, I did. And I'm sorry that I disappeared right after, but I didn't come over this morning expecting to kiss you. It was... I don't even know how to explain it. Something came over me, something instinctual and a little bit impulsive. I just knew in that second, I had to kiss you."

He sits up and pivots, his feet coming to the floor. He braces his elbows on his knees, and leans over into my space, closing the distance between our two chairs. "I can understand that," he says in a low voice. "I've been fighting that impulse for years."

Dan's confession warms me from the inside. Hearing him finally put it into words that he *wants me.*

"I know I was kind of oblivious, but I truly had no idea how you felt," I say honestly, looking down at the amber bottle of beer in my hand. Beer that Dan keeps in his fridge just for me. The same way I know he has tampons under his bathroom sink and my favourite brand of licorice in his pantry. He's been showing me how he feels in little ways since day one, and I missed it. "I think I had blinders on because of Baron. It seems everyone else knew how you felt about me, except for me." I pick at the label on my beer and decide I need to ask the one thing I really want to know. "Why didn't you say something sooner?"

His laugh is not a light one, and it's not an amused one. It's tinged with pain and regret, and I hate it.

"Come on, Birdie, what was I meant to do? Tell you that you should break up with the guy you had been with for years, long before you ever met me, and go out with me instead? Why the heck would I do that? You seemed happy, and I wasn't about to break up something that was making you happy."

Except I wasn't happy. But I don't tell him that. There's no sense in adding to his regret.

"But now," he says, his voice growing stronger. "Now, there's nothing in my way. There's nothing to come between us. You kissed me, and tonight, I kissed you. Does that mean as much to you as it does to me?"

I nod slowly, my lips curving up at the corners "It does. It means everything. But I have to be honest, Dan. I'm scared. You're one of my closest friends, and I don't know what I would ever do if I lost you. As much as I want to explore whatever this is going on between us, I can't help but worry. What if it doesn't work out? Not only do we work together, but..." I trail off. Of everything I've said tonight, what I'm about to say might be the hardest words to get out. My voice drops to a whisper, but I force myself to look him in the eye. "You could break my heart more than anybody else in this world."

His hand lets go of mine, only to cup my cheek. Those beautiful brown eyes stare straight into mine and I feel like I can see to the depths of his soul. Everything he is, is laid bare.

"Lark, I swear to you, if you give me your heart, I will never do anything intentionally to hurt it. You mean more to me than anything, almost more than baseball." He chuckles. "And I'll do everything in my power to make sure we don't regret it if we take things to the next level. I was prepared to only ever be your friend, and just because there's now a chance of more doesn't mean I'm going to risk losing you."

I lean into his hand, turning slightly to press a kiss to his palm. His confident reassurance is like a soft blanket, soothing and settling my fears. Feeling brave, I push up from my lounge chair, and stand in front of him. For a moment, he just looks up at me, confused, until I give him a gentle smile. Realization dawns on him and he lies back on his chair, widening his legs, making room for me to sit and lean back against his chest.

His arms slowly move to circle me. "Is this okay?" he asks, sounding oddly tentative. I nod, and his hands settle on my body.

"You can breathe, Dan," I say teasingly, and his chest rapidly rises and falls under me as he laughs.

"Right. Sorry."

We lie like that for a minute, and I catalogue every sensation. His hard chest underneath me, the strength of his arms holding me, and something else growing firmer against the base of my spine.

I shift slightly, and he grunts.

"Sorry," I whisper, secretly grinning to myself. It's been a very, *very* long time since Baron and I had sex, and from the feel of things, Dan has got some fun equipment hiding under those jeans.

"No, I am. I can't...I can't control it around you." Embarrassment tinges his tone and I shift, twisting slightly so I can look up at him.

"It's okay," I say quietly, covering his hands with mine. "I mean, I think I'd be more worried if you didn't have some kind of a reaction." I laugh nervously. "It's been a long time since I...you know. And um, well, you're not the only one whose body is thinking of moving faster than we probably should."

Dan chokes out a pained laugh, and I frown. "What? Was that funny?"

"No, no." He moves under me, and yeah, he's packing. "It's just, you say it's been a long time." I feel and hear his long, quiet exhale. "But I can promise you, it's been longer for me."

Confused, I don't respond right away. "Long as in, a few months?" I eventually ask, laughing self-deprecatingly. "Because sad as it may sound, it's been at least that long for me. Baron wasn't exactly an enthusiastic guy in bed. And *that* is the last I'll say about that."

Dan makes a noise, a strange one, and when I once again twist to look at him, his cheeks are flushed and his gaze is darting all over the place. Everywhere but toward me.

"Dan?"

"Lark, I...I'm... Well, I've never..." His head falls back against the chair. "Shit."

My brain struggles to comprehend, but then it clicks. Does he mean...

"Never?" I whisper.

He slowly shakes his head back and forth. "Nope."

"So you're a…"

"I'm a virgin, Birdie."

He says it quietly, calmly, and somewhat resignedly. Is he expecting me to be upset? I pull out of his arms and turn around to face him fully, crossing my legs so I can cup his face in my hands.

"Dan, there's nothing wrong with that. Nothing. And I'm honoured you told me. Thank you for trusting me with that."

His entire body seems to deflate with relief, and the sweetest little smile breaks free on his face. "That's really fucking good to hear you say. And I trust you with my life, Lark."

"Can I ask why?" I say, unable to hold the question back.

Dan just shrugs. "A bunch of reasons, but mostly, I never found anyone that I wanted to go there with."

My stomach starts to sink until he reaches out and tucks my hair behind my ear, that sweet smile growing wider.

"Until I found you."

Shock, warmth, anticipation, happiness, and instant lust all combine within me, until I feel like a puddle of emotion.

Me. I'm the *one person* this beautiful, strong, kind man wants. I've never felt this before.

Wanted.

Desired.

It's almost enough to make me want to rip our clothes off and give myself to him. But no matter how amazing it is to know that's how Dan feels, I won't let us rush this.

But surely…another kiss or two isn't rushing it?

I'm leaning forward when I hear him groan.

"Lark, we can't."

I freeze. "Wh-what?"

His pained expression is the only thing that makes him stopping me any easier to accept. "You just, and I mean *just* ended a long-term, serious relationship. As much as I'm jumping up and down like a little kid on Christmas morning inside, I need to pump the brakes on this. I need you to be sure, really sure, that I'm who you want to be with. Because you say I could break your heart, well, same. You've had my heart for years, and you're the only person who could destroy it."

He's right. I hate that he's right, but he is. Moving too fast would be the worst idea.

"Okay, so friends."

He nods. "Yeah, friends."

I bite my lip, not sure if I should say the rest of what I'm thinking. But tonight has shown me I owe Dan honesty, above all else.

"Can we be friends who cuddle?"

This time the smile on his face is so big, it's almost overwhelming. He grabs me, turns me around, and tucks me right back against his body. "Damn right we can be."

Chapter Fourteen

Monty

"Let me get this straight," Rafe huffs out as we run along the gravel path that circles Burnaby Lake, an urban park just outside of Vancouver. "She's broken up with the idiot, kissed you, made it clear she's interested in being more than friends, and you put the brakes on? Monty, you've got balls of steel."

"It's got nothing to do with that," I say indignantly. "I've waited this long, what's a little longer? I love her, like, really love her. And if I've finally got a shot at being with her, the last thing I want to do is rush it. She deserves the fucking world. You know that. And part of that is me giving her time to settle into a life without her ex in it."

Rafe slows to a stop, his chest heaving with exertion. His hands go to his hips as he shakes his head at me. "You are one in a million, Dan Montgomery. Seriously."

I duck my head, hoping I'm not blushing. He's a good friend, someone I respect and just like as a person. I mean, you don't spend as long as we did as a catcher-pitcher duo without bonding. So for him to say that? Means a lot.

"Thanks, old man. Now, are we running or are we out for a

light jog?"

His eyes narrow, and I grin. I'm in for it. Sure enough, he puts on a burst of speed all of a sudden, passing me, and shouting "See ya, sucker" as he sprints away. I shake my head, content to let him think he's got me for a few seconds.

But I can't let him get too far ahead. Picking up my pace, I close the distance between us. Rafe hasn't played for the Tridents in over a year, and while I know he keeps up a certain level of conditioning, he's got nothing on those of us still actively playing.

Within a couple of minutes, I'm drawing up alongside him, and flash him another wide grin.

"What was that, Pops?"

He grunts, and I can tell he's pushing himself to his limits to try and keep up. Taking pity on the old guy, I moderate my pace so we're running more comfortably, side by side.

"Is this what I have to look forward to when I retire? What happened to the guy who could sprint the bases like the devil was chasing him?"

"He traded in multiple workouts a day for beer, sleeping in, and a good woman," Rafe retorts.

His words hit the mark, whether he intended them to or not. I hold deep respect for Rafe's choice. A couple of years ago, he found out he had a kid with a woman he'd loved a long time ago. They reunited, reconciled, and he chose to retire to spend time with his family.

Someday, I want to be where he is. Happy, in love, surrounded by family, and living the good life after many years of sacrificing for his career.

But not right now. I'm nowhere near retirement. If anything, my career is my number one focus, for a lot of reasons. And I'm not talking about my deep-rooted desire to see my team take the championship one day, even if that is a big one. I've got goals that can only be achieved by putting all of my energy and effort into being the best goddamn player I can be.

Which is a troubling thought alongside the possibility of a relationship with Lark.

I never bothered to think about whether or not I could juggle both. It seemed like it would never happen, so I didn't let myself consider it.

Except now? It's a very real possibility. And it's overwhelming.

"Do you think you could have juggled your relationship with Imogen and Taylor, as well as your career, if you had wanted to keep playing?" I blurt out as we slow our pace, nearing the end of the ten-kilometer loop around the lake.

Rafe's head turns my way for a second before he looks forward again. "You mean if I wasn't already getting old and at the end of my career?"

"Yeah. Like, if you knew you had a bunch of good years playing ball left, do you think it's possible to balance that with a relationship?"

"Lots of guys do."

My mind darts back to last season, when one of our outfielders found out his wife wanted a divorce while we were on a stretch of away games. "Yeah, and lots of guys have relationships fall apart."

"If you go into any relationship already thinking it could end, you're fucked."

He's right, and I'm not a glass-half-empty kinda guy. Never have been. But I am trying to be realistic. I know my feelings for Lark are huge and could easily be all-consuming. I can't imagine my life without her in it, and if I'm being honest, there's not a chance in hell of me staying away from her if she truly wants to be with me as more than friends.

Which means, no matter what, I'll find a way to balance it. Baseball and my career goals might be number one, but Lark has always been tied with my family for number two. And if there's a chance I can have it all?

Game fucking on.

Back at my apartment after my run, I shower, get changed, and chug a protein shake. I missed a call from my mom, so after sitting down on my couch, I pull up their number to call her back.

"Hi, honey." Mom's voice makes me smile.

"Hey, Mom, sorry I missed you earlier. Rafe and I were out for a run."

"I figured you might be. Hang on, let me just finish making my tea." The phone clatters, and I know she's put it on the counter. I can hear muffled sounds coming through, and in my mind, I picture Mom bustling around their kitchen that desperately needs updating, getting the milk and sugar out, and fixing her tea in the china cups she prefers.

I've tried to convince my parents to let me pay for renovations ever since I signed my first contract with the Tridents, but they've always refused, telling me to save my money for a rainy day.

It's Vancouver. It's always raining.

I don't know how to get them to see that taking care of them would be the best way for me to say thank you for everything they've done for me. I might be biased, but I swear, Howard and Edith Montgomery are the best parents on the entire planet. And the most annoying for refusing any help from me beyond physical labour when I go to visit.

Even that takes some convincing.

"Alright, I'm here now. How are you doing?" Mom's voice returns.

"Good. Taking it easy, enjoying some slower days," I say in return, settling back against the couch cushions. "How's Dad? Did you get him in for his physical yet?"

Mom laughs. "Oh, Daniel, you know your father. Getting him to take time out for things like that is almost impossible. But yes, I made the appointment, and didn't tell him until that morning, so it was too late to cancel. He saw the doctor and got a clean bill of health."

That's a relief. The biggest downside to having older parents is being all too aware of their declining health and rapidly approaching mortality. It's a fact of life we all have to face, and growing old is a privilege. But watching my parents age has become more and more difficult over recent years.

"Did the doctor convince him to slow down at the store at all?"

Mom snorts. "Of course not."

My head moves slowly back and forth, even though she can't see it. I pinch the bridge of my nose and decide to shoot my shot. "You know I'd help cover the cost of you hiring more staff. A manager, even. Anything to take some of the workload."

"And you know that when your father and I reach that point, we'll talk." Her tone is firm and leaves no room for discussion.

Even if I highly doubt that point will never come.

"Okay. What else is new?" I ask. There's nothing to be gained by pushing her, which means changing topics is the best option.

"Well, let me tell you something I heard from Linda..."

I get off the phone with her a half hour later, after promising to come back out for dinner later in the week. When I said I was going to bring Lark with me, I could hear the curiosity in her voice. They've met a couple of times, but I've never brought her to my childhood home.

When it starts vibrating a couple of minutes later with a call from my agent, I get right back on the phone. He was Rafe's agent, as well, and a good dude. Total shark, but one that gives a shit about his players.

"Hey, Rocky," I say, wandering into the kitchen and filling a glass with water. "What's shakin'?"

"Monty, my man, how's it going? Keeping up with conditioning?" Rocky says by way of greeting. It's always business first with him, but I can't resist having some fun.

"You know it, can't let my ass get flabby or I won't bring in the big bucks. Who wants a catcher without a great butt?"

He snorts, which is exactly the response I wanted. "Right, I don't exactly want to talk about your ass, Monty. But good to know you're keeping in shape. Let's talk next season. Last one on this contract, you know what that means?"

Yeah, it means the pressure's on and dialed up to a hundred.

But I don't say that to Rocky. "Of course. It means I play the same way I always do. With a smile on my face and my eye on the ball."

"That's my boy. Okay, are you still set on wanting to stay in Vancouver? Is that what we're working toward? Because even though you've got a year left, there's some chatter about Arizona wanting you."

"No." My response is swift and firm. "I'm not going anywhere, Rocky. Vancouver or nothing. And it better not fucking be nothing."

"Heard, loud and clear. Just wanted to make sure that was still your opinion. Because they could be willing to offer you big bucks."

"I want the big bucks from Vancouver. This is my home, and I don't want to play anywhere else."

"Then you really need to pull out all the stops. Be a fucking wall behind the plate. Show them you're the best goddamn catcher out there and worth every penny you want from them."

"That's the plan," I say, realizing I'm clenching the water glass so tightly my hand is starting to tremble. I set it down, opening and closing my fist a few times. "I'll do my job on the field; you do your job in the board room."

"Deal. Now, let's talk sponsorships."

CHAPTER FIFTEEN

Lark

Over the next week, two things happen. Winter fully sets into Vancouver, bringing freezing cold rain and wind, but of course, no snow. And Dan seems to unconsciously make it his mission in life to drive me crazy. Crazy horny, that is.

Which is amusing, considering his confession. I'm still stunned by that. How is a sexy pro baseball player still a virgin in his late twenties? He's like a unicorn, I guess. I know there must be more to his reason why he hasn't had sex, and someday, I hope he'll tell me. But for now, I can't help but feel special to be the one he confided in.

But at the same time, knowing that brings with it some nerves. Could I really act as just his friend, knowing what I do now, feeling the way I do?

But outwardly, at least, nothing seems all that different. We still meet for early morning runs, have dinner together, watch our favourite *Star Wars* movies — the original ones, of course — and talk about everything and anything.

Everything except what's happening between the two of us. That subject is off-limits.

And despite the seemingly normal interactions, there's been a thread of anticipation lying just under the surface. I don't know if that's all in my head or if Dan notices it, too, but it feels like a steady stream of low intensity static electricity running through my body. Making me feel as if every cell is buzzing, more alive than normal, with occasional shocks when his hand brushes against mine, or he gives me that goofy smile that suddenly means so much more.

Or like tonight, when he seems to be sensing my every move.

"I'm thirsty, you want anything?" He jumps up from the couch as soon as I start to shift. How did he know I was about to stand up and go get some water?

I blink up at him. "Sure, some water would be great."

He hurries into my kitchen, and I hear him take down two glasses and the tap running. I open my mouth to ask him to bring back some snacks when I hear another cupboard open. When I swivel my head to look, he's taking out the very bag of corn chips I was going to ask for.

How. Does. He. Know?

When he returns to the couch with the bag of chips as well as a jar of salsa tucked under his arm and two glasses of water in hand, he sets everything down before settling back beside me.

"Chips and salsa?" I ask, belatedly realizing there's no context to my question. But Dan just shrugs, popping the top off the jar of salsa and dunking a chip in before holding it out to me.

I lean forward and let him pop it into my mouth, relishing the way his eyes grow a teeny-tiny bit darker when my lips lightly touch his fingers.

"You always want chips and salsa for a late-night snack. That or licorice."

I'm pretty sure my eyes are bugging out of my head. He turns and gives me a gentle smile, so at odds with the goofy, fun-loving man he normally is. This smile, this version of him, is softer, more vulnerable. And I know, without a doubt, I am one of the lucky few who get to see it.

"I think you know me better than anyone," I say in a whisper, tentatively reaching my hand across the couch to pick up his. My eyes cast down as I clasp his fingers in mine, feeling his steady warmth. "And I'm really happy I'm finally realizing that."

Dan gives a slight tug and lifts his other arm up, beckoning me in. With a happy sigh, I tuck in against his side. His lips land on the top of my head, and I feel him press them lightly in a kiss.

It feels so good to just be held by someone in an affectionate embrace, even though I know it won't go any further. It makes me try to remember the last time Baron held me like this, and I honestly can't.

At some point, I guess I drift off, I'm so damn comfortable and secure in Dan's arms. Because when my eyes flutter open, it's because I'm being lifted into the air, tucked against his chest.

"I'm sorry, I fell asleep," I murmur, deciding not to protest him carrying me and just enjoy it this once. I feel his low chuckle reverberate through his chest, and my lips curve up in a smile.

He sets me down on my bed and pulls the blanket up to my chin. "Night, Birdie. I'll lock up."

I don't stop to think about what I'm suggesting when my hand darts out and wraps around his wrist. "Stay?" That one word lands in the dimly lit silence. It's broken only by a sharp intake of breath before Dan answers.

"Are you sure?"

My tongue darts out to moisten my lips. I know nothing's going to happen. I trust him. Especially knowing he's never had sex. Heck, I get a secret thrill out of the idea of being his first some day. But not tonight.

"Yeah. I am. If you want to. Friends who cuddle, right?" I quip, trying to inject some lightness.

It works as I hear him huff out a chuckle. "Okay. I'm gonna go brush my teeth."

He moves toward the bathroom and I throw off the blanket to join him, my recent tiredness fading. Dan turns with a frown when he sees me behind him.

"What was the point to me carrying you to bed?"

I smirk and step up beside him at my bathroom sink, opening a drawer and handing him a new toothbrush. "It was very sweet and very chivalrous. But if we're having a sleepover, I don't want to poison you with salsa breath."

I bump his hip with mine to break his stare, and he turns forward with a grunt. We go through the motions of brushing our teeth, then he steps out to give me privacy, and then I do the same. While he's in there, I quickly change into a very basic pair of pajama shorts and a T-shirt.

The bathroom door opens and Dan steps out, his gaze immediately traveling up and down my body where I stand at the side of the bed.

"That's my shirt."

I glance down and realize it's the one he gave me that night he took me home from the bar. I toy with the hem and look at him. "Yeah. You want it back?"

His head moves slowly side to side. "Keep it. Looks better on you."

My thighs clench together as another wave of pure want crashes over me. I don't know how much longer I can resist this sweet man.

He clears his throat and moves to the other side. "Are you okay with me taking off my jeans?"

I nod silently.

Hell yeah, I'm okay with that. I'm more than okay. I'm flustered, hot all over, and suddenly wishing I had a bigger bed.

No, a smaller one.

Gah. Maybe this was a mistake. I'm not sure I trust my unconscious self to keep her hands off him.

Especially once he peels off his shirt and tugs his jeans down, leaving him in nothing but a navy blue pair of boxers with...

"Are those wiener dogs?" I blurt out with a giggle. Dan glances down, then back up, shrugging his shoulders with an impish smirk.

"I like wieners."

An indelicate snort escapes me. "Okay, then."

Dan peels back the blanket and slides into my bed, folding his arms behind his head. He looks over at me, catching me staring at his delicious upper body currently on display.

To my surprise, his cheeks darken with a blush. I quickly look away and climb into bed, turning off the lamp.

The only light coming in is from the street outside. But despite the dark, I can *feel* him close to me. Knowing there's barely any space and even less clothing separating us has me on edge, but in a good way.

"I've never shared a bed with anyone," he says quietly, and I turn onto my side, propping my head on my hand.

"As long as you don't snore, we'll be fine," I say with a smile. Dan snorts, rolling onto his side to face me.

"I do not snore."

"How would you know if you've never slept with anyone?" I quip, earning a scowl.

"I've shared hotel rooms with teammates and no one has ever complained."

I can't help but smile at his haughty tone. "Good. Well, g'night." I flip over before I do something stupid like kiss his handsome, all too tempting face.

To my surprise, I manage to fall asleep fairly quickly. The next thing I'm aware of is waking up while it's still dark out, a heavy weight draped over me. Blearily, I blink my eyes open, and it still takes a second to realize what's going on.

I'm in the same spot I was earlier, on my side, at the edge of the bed.

But Dan is no longer on his side of the bed.

He most definitely is not.

His hard body is wrapped around mine, his bare chest pressed against my back, his arm holding me snug, and his head buried in my hair.

Sleep is pulling me back under. But before it overtakes me, I lift his hand carefully to my lips and kiss his knuckles before tucking it back into place against my chest.

Friends who snuggle is kind of amazing.

Chapter Sixteen

Monty

"I swear to fucking God, if you don't stop whistling, I'm gonna tape your goddamn mouth shut."

I purse my lips in Mav's direction and let out a trill. "You love me, Maverick King, and you know it. Tell Sadie she needs to help you to lighten up some more. Let us see that big, beautiful smile of yours."

My teammate glowers. But that's basically his normal face, so I take no offense. Slapping him on the shoulder, I strut past him, taking my position in front of the pitching machine. I nod at Sin, who's manning the machine, and the first ball comes flying at me.

CRACK.

"That's how you do it, boys!" I crow, flipping my bat in the air before taking my stance again. Another ball comes at me and I swing.

CRACK.

"Oh yeah, baby." I give my backside a little wiggle, too high on life to care how much of a fool I look. "More than just a pretty face with a good butt."

"I know it's Monty, but don't you think he's a little *extra* today?" Ben Wilson mutters from outside the cage.

I hear Maverick's grunt just before connecting with another pitch. "Woo! Watch and learn."

"Maybe he's gettin' laid," Darling jeers from next to him, and goddamn it, his comment makes me miss the next pitch. "Oh, damn! He is!"

I turn and glare at my teammates. "Would you please shut up? I'm trying to focus."

"And your fucking whistling was preventing the rest of us from doing just that. Fair's fair, Monty." Maverick folds his arms across his chest with a smirk.

I finish my round with the machine and exit the cage, frowning at each of them in turn. "Just for that, I'm gonna *sing* next time. Any requests?"

Darling takes a ball I didn't even realize he was holding and whips it at me, and it's only thanks to my finely honed catcher reflexes that it doesn't hit me in the head. Instead, it stings my bare hand.

The thing is, their teasing? It isn't getting to me. Not at all. Because nothing can touch me right now. The girl of my dreams is within reach. And tomorrow, I'm taking her to my parents' place. They've met a couple of times, but only briefly and only in professional situations. Now, I get to introduce her as my...something.

Maybe I gotta figure out what that is first. Friend? Almost girlfriend? Future wife?

All of the above?

Yeah, I'm on top of the fucking world, and it's only gonna get better as Lark and I find our way together.

The guys and I wrap up our practice and head over to the diner next to the stadium for some lunch. Pushing open the door to the fifties-style diner is like pulling on your favourite pair of sweats. Comfortable and relaxed. The vinyl booths are bright teal to match our team colours, there's always oldies music playing, and Maura, the owner, makes damn sure no one bothers us when we're eating there.

"Hey boys, want your usuals?" the woman in question says as she bustles over with a tray of water.

"You're an angel, Maura, thank you." I give her my winningest smile. "If some fries landed on my plate with that burger and salad, I wouldn't be mad."

"You got it, honey."

The rest of the guys confirm their orders, and she heads off to the kitchen.

"Okay, are we just not gonna talk about the elephant in the room?" Sin leans forward, folding his arms on the table in front of him.

Darling chokes out a laugh as Mav rolls his eyes.

"What elephant?" I ask stupidly.

"You and Lark," Sin says, his gaze bouncing between the other two guys. "Willow said she broke up with what's-his-fuck, so..."

"Oh shit, I was right? You *are* gettin' some? And with Lark?" Darling sits forward, his eyes wide. "Fuck yeah, brother! And to think I was jokin'."

My head is whipping back and forth. "No guys, stop. I'm not sleeping with Lark."

"Why the fuck not?" Mav barks out. "You're fucking in love with her."

"Exactly!" I throw my hands up in exasperation. These guys don't know my secret, and I'm certainly not about to spill the beans right here and now. But I know I have to explain myself somehow. "I care about her —" Mav snorts, and I narrow my eyes at him. "Fine, I love her. And because of that, I don't want to rush things. She was with that guy for years. And only just ended things. What kind of a dick move would it be to rush her into something before she's ready?"

"Look at you, bein' all gentlemanly like," Darling teases, punching my arm. "I'm proud of you, Monty."

I roll my eyes. "For what? Doing the bare minimum of being a decent human being and respecting a woman?"

"Fair point." He inclines his head toward me. "Well, we're all rootin' for ya. Hopefully, our Lark sees the light and puts you out of your misery soon."

I'm saved by the arrival of our food, and the conversation drops off as we all devour our meals. We make quick work of it, what with being professional athletes who just worked our asses off in the gym and batting cages. And then, everyone heads their separate ways. But I should have known I wouldn't get off that easy.

In the parking lot of the stadium, Sin follows me to my truck.

"I'm sorry if I overstepped back there, asking about Lark."

I give him a small smile. "Nah, it's fine. Everyone knows how I feel about Lark. Everyone except Lark, it seems."

His eyes widen. "She doesn't know?"

"Oh, she does now," I quickly clarify, then instantly feel my cheeks start to heat up. "We, ahh, we've talked about it."

Sin's eyebrows raise as a smile breaks free. "Oh really. Talked about it, hmm?"

I unlock my truck and open the door. "Yeah. Talked. Okay, gotta go. Bye."

Getting in, I close the door and turn on the engine without looking out the window. When I finally do lift my head, thankfully, Sin's walking away. *Phew*, dodged that bullet.

Now, to get through tomorrow without Mom embarrassing me.

"Seriously?" I groan as I walk into the living room and see Mom and Lark pouring over an old photo album. "Baby pictures? Mom, come on." My voice takes on a slight whine, but this is exactly what I was afraid of.

It's not the fact that Mom and Lark are getting along so well. I expected that, Mom's awesome and so is Lark. It was a given they'd love each other. But I was really trying to avoid the naked bath time photos a little while longer.

I set down the cups of coffee I just finished making and sit beside Lark, leaning over to see exactly where they're at in the mortification process.

"Oh great. My shining moment as a sunflower in the grade one class play."

Lark giggles. "You were an adorable sunflower."

"Wait until you see his costume for *Star Wars* day the year he turned eight. He wanted to be a Wookiee! I spent hours gluing fake fur onto a brown sweater."

I slump back against the couch with another groan. But Lark's hand lands on my thigh, squeezing it gently, and my gaze darts over to her.

"Well, Chewie was the best character, so I support his decision."

Goddamn, she's perfect for me.

My hand covers hers, but only for a second so Mom doesn't see. Baby photos are one thing. Meddling mothers are another. And from what I know, Lark had enough of that with Baron's mom to last a lifetime.

I listen to the two of them chatter on for a while longer, content to just be here next to her. It's familiar and yet so different all at the same time. Because now, when her leg presses against mine, I don't have to pull away. And when she smiles at me, I can let myself believe it means something. And when she and my mom laugh over some crazy photo of me as a kid, I can imagine the future when she's really mine.

Eventually, they take a break from looking at photos, and my mom shows Lark her quilting room, aka, my old bedroom. They're gone for a while but given my mom's a fucking genius at making quilts, I'm not worried. I wander downstairs to the store to check on my dad instead.

He's just finished ringing up a customer, and I glance at the clock to see it's closing time. "Want some help shutting up shop?" I ask, already moving to the front to get the signs from outside.

"Sure, son, thanks."

We work in an easy silence for a while, going through the

steps of locking up. It's only when we're done, and heading back upstairs for dinner, that I see him wince.

"You okay, old man?" I ask.

"Fine, fine. Just the sciatica," he answers dismissively, and I know he's minimizing things, like always.

I keep my mouth shut. Now's not the time to push. But someday soon, I'm gonna sit my parents down and tell them they have to let me help.

Maybe once I secure my next contract, they'll see I can take care of them *and* be secure in my own future. And who knows. Maybe by then, Lark will be by my side to help convince them.

A guy can always dream.

Chapter Seventeen

Lark

The thing about working with professional athletes, in particular, *male* professional athletes, is that you very quickly have to be okay with seeing the nude or nearly nude male form.

I'm talking day one on the job, I walked into the locker room when my supervisor was taking me on a tour of the stadium to find four of the players in various stages of undress, walking out of the showers, laughing and joking with each other.

They don't care, and why should they? Their bodies are finely honed machines. And to them, the training staff are just the medical professionals whose job it is to keep those machines running in peak condition.

Once I got over the initial surprise that yes, I would be seeing bare butts — and more — at my job, I didn't let it bother me. Heck, I've had to treat those bare butts on more than one occasion when glute muscles get cramped or injured.

Besides, I was in a relationship, so ogling another man's body felt wrong. I maintained a strictly professional approach to my work.

But even so, there are moments when it stings a little, never being seen as a woman, only ever as staff, or worse, as one of the guys.

"Mornin' Lark," Rhett Darlington says, strutting out of the showers with a towel wrapped around his waist and another draped around his neck. "How's it goin'? You here for me?"

There's a reason the team nicknamed him Darling. He says he can't help but be polite, because his mama raised him right. That, and his habit of calling every single female he comes across, darlin. But somehow, when he talks to me, there's none of the flirtatious southern boy charm he's famous for. Just friendly, polite manners.

I nod, averting my eyes when he turns to his locker and pulls on a pair of underwear. At least he does it before dropping the towel. "Yes. Time for your yearly assessment."

Every offseason we work our way through the active player roster and run them through a full assessment. Not just for fitness, but overall physical and mental health. It's something the team owner, Mike Cartwright, instituted years ago, making it clear he cared about his players, not just during the season, but all the time. And not only as players, but as human beings.

My job is to put them through part of the fitness evaluation. It's simple enough, an hour in the gym with some sensors strapped to their body to measure heart rate, oxygenation, and a couple of other things. We spread out the assessments, working around the guys' schedules and offseason plans. Another way Mr. Cartwright makes sure players know he values them.

It's things like this that inspired me to apply for the internship. If I can contribute to the research, and maybe learn a few things to bring back to the team, all the better.

Rhett pulls a shirt on, and I see he's now wearing some athletic shorts. He grabs a pair of shoes out of his locker and holds them up to sniff before scrunching up his nose. "Damn, time for a new pair. Give these a whiff." He shoves the shoes in my face, and I recoil in horror.

"Why the hell would I want to smell your shoes, Rhett? That's disgusting."

He just shrugs. "Eh, I dunno. Guess ya wouldn't now, would ya?"

Kai and Ronan walk in just then, all sweaty from the gym. Ronan gives me a nod and a smile, heading toward the showers. Kai, on the other hand, starts to strip down right in front of me.

"Dude. You shoulda seen the bomber Sin hit off my curveball. Holy shit, it was amazing, straight shot out to center field, homer for sure. It was a thing of beauty." He keeps yammering on as more clothes come off. "Someday, Lark, I'm gonna get you in front of my balls. I bet you'd hit a slammer." He snorts, realizing what he just said as I turn bright red. "Shit, that sounded bad. Sorry, Lark. You know I don't mean it that way, right?"

Of course, he doesn't, and while I know that's because Kai's a decent guy, I guess I'm feeling sensitive or something, especially coming right after Rhett and his gross shoes, because I don't say that. Instead, I say, "Of course, you don't. Because I'm just one of the guys, right? Fine to joke and tease with."

I guess the guys hear the bite in my voice, because the locker room falls silent.

"Everythin' okay, darlin'?" Rhett says cautiously, and I close my eyes for a second to gather myself. I don't do this, get all sensitive and crap. It's not *professional.*

"Yep. Fine," I say, the words sounding forced.

"Okay, because you know Yami's harmless. He's just bein' an idiot."

"Mm-hmm. I know. We should go get your assessment done." I turn on my heel and walk out of the locker room, not giving any of them a chance to say anything else.

I should've known he wouldn't let it go. As soon as we're in the gym, empty of anyone but the two of us, he crosses his arms over his chest and stares at me.

"Talk, woman."

I pretend to be very much occupied with pulling up Rhett's file on my tablet, not meeting his gaze.

"Fine, you wanna do this the hard way? I'm gonna have to guess at what's eatin' ya."

I swallow, my mouth suddenly dry. In all the time I've worked for the team, I've never once let it slip how it sometimes bothers me to be treated like one of the guys. After all, shouldn't I be happy sexism has no place on the team? That I'm treated with professionalism and respect above all else?

But sometimes, a girl just wants to be seen as a girl, damn it. I see how the guys treat Willow, still with respect but also charm and the occasional flirty words. At least before Ronan showed up. Me? Nothing.

"I'm thinkin' it had something to do with Yami being a dumbass. What I can't quite figure out is what he said that made you react. Especially since he apologized for his ridiculous comment about his balls."

I whirl around, ready to lash out. "That's just it. He was a dumbass around me, you all are dumbasses around me. And that's fine, because that's the way you are with each other, so why be any different around me? I can handle the dumbass behaviour just like one of the guys, right? That's what he meant by his *apology*." I bite out the last word, fully aware I sound like a lunatic. But now that I've started, there's no stopping the crazy train. "But maybe it's okay to say something dirty or flirty to me. Because I'm *not* one of the guys, I'm a woman. A red-blooded woman, fully capable of handling a baseball player making a flirty comment. But you guys don't seem to remember that I. Am. A. Woman, and while I want to be respected, I'd also like to be seen as who I am, not just a buddy, or worse, a nobody. Which means, stop shoving stinky shoes in my face, talking like dumbasses, or dropping towels and waving your dicks around."

When I finally stop ranting, Rhett stares at me, his mouth half open, arms hanging by his sides. I heave out a sigh, and he lifts one hand to rub his jaw.

"Damn, Lark." He shakes his head, those big brown eyes I've witnessed make many a woman swoon filling with understanding and compassion. "I hear ya. And I'm sorry we made you feel that way. Can I explain somethin' that might help?"

I gesture over to the treadmill stiffly. "Only if you can do it while you run."

He gives me a smirk. "'Course I can."

He doesn't say anything more until he's hooked up to the sensor, on the machine, and at his warm-up pace. In those few moments, I run the gamut of emotions, from mortification to vindication. I finally said my piece, crazy as it may have sounded to him. And if he really does have an explanation, I'll listen.

"Alright, darlin', you listenin'?" he says, turning his head slightly to me. I nod, and he continues.

"Good. Here's the thing, when I joined the team, you were already workin' here. And I was pulled aside by Pops and Gomez on my second or third day and told a few things. Not just about you, but about every woman who works here. Pops made it clear that Mike ran an organization that put equality and respect first and foremost among players and staff. It was drilled into me, and every player, that everyone from the trainin' staff to the janitors deserved as much respect as the players. Your job puts you in close proximity to us every day. Hell, half the time, we're near-to-naked around you. Makin' sure you and all your female colleagues felt comfortable was a priority."

He's saying all the right things. Statements that women working in male dominated fields dream of hearing. And yet...I feel like there's more. That feeling is confirmed after I increase his pace to begin his cardio fitness assessment, nodding at him to continue.

"But with you, there's a second reason." He huffs out the words, and I can't lie, internally, I gloat a little at making him suffer through his workout while he tries to explain things to me.

"And that is?" I say acerbically.

He gives me an incredulous look. "You really can't figure it out?"

My brows draw together and I frown. "No, Rhett. If I could, do you think I would have gone off on you like that?"

He chokes out a laugh. "Damn. I thought men were the oblivious ones." He sees my frown turn to a glare and holds up his hands. "Come on, Lark. Just about every single person in this building knows that Monty is obsessed with you and has been since day one. And we all love, and more importantly, respect the guy, just as much as we love and respect you. This part was never said out loud, but there's been an unspoken rule in place to never cross any lines with you, out of respect for his feelings. That meant no flirting, nothin'."

"Are you freaking serious?" I shriek, making him stumble. He recovers quickly, of course, and continues running, shooting me nervous glances as I start to pace in front of the treadmill. "You're saying Dan Montgomery has had feelings for me for years and everyone *but me* has known that, and *that* is the reason you've all been treating me like one of the guys this entire time?" I come to a stop, crossing my arms across my chest, and stare at him. "That's...that's...ridiculous."

Rhett lifts his eyebrows. "Is it?"

I deflate. "No," I say quietly. "I...thank you. For explaining. And for, well, yeah."

He gives me a knowing smile. "You both deserve to be happy. And I know we're all rootin' for team Mork."

"W-what?" I splutter. "Absolutely not, no way."

Rhett just laughs, and I know it's a done deal. "Take it up with Monty. He came up with it on the last night of spring training two years ago, after one too many shots of tequila."

"Don't worry, I'll have words with him," I grumble. "Can we finish this damn assessment now?"

He gives an exaggerated groan and steps off the treadmill, onto the side boards, as he punches down the speed. "Fuck, yeah. I hate runnin'."

"Then you shouldn't have become a baseball player," I reply

sarcastically as we move over to the mats where I'll be testing his strength and flexibility.

Rhett turns his full force southern boy charm my way, and I can finally confirm it's just as potent as expected.

"But darlin', if I didn't play ball, I'd be back home in Tennessee, workin' on the family ranch, and then you'd miss me."

I roll my eyes at his cocky — yet true — statement. "Okay, okay. Let's get this over with so you can go and charm someone who cares."

His hand goes to his chest, and Rhett tries to look wounded. "First, you want me to flirt with you, then you deny me when I do? There's just no pleasin' ya, Lark Miller." He winks and my answering grin is automatic.

"You want to please me? Get going on your mobility assessment, and for the love of God, never repeat that nickname for me and Dan again."

CHAPTER EIGHTEEN

Monty

"What do you mean, you've *never* cut down your own Christmas tree?" Okay, fine, maybe I'm exaggerating the look of shock on my face just a little, but really? How has she been deprived of this experience for so long?

Lark just shrugs, her eyes wide with wonder as she takes in the cheesy decorations, the crackling fires, and everyone wandering around with smiles on their faces and handsaws under their arms.

Fuck, I love Christmas tree farms.

"We always had artificial trees. Three of them. Mom didn't want the mess of a real tree."

"The way you say that, so matter-of-fact, it makes me question your sanity, Birdie. Like a few pine needles on the floor was a good enough reason to never let your kid feel the joy of running through rows of Christmas trees, the thrill of hunting for the perfect one, and experience the flawless aroma of a fresh cut fir."

If her eyes could roll any harder, I'm sure they would. "You're the one who's insane, Dan. There's nothing wrong with artificial trees."

My hands clutch my chest. "You wound me."

Lark ignores my antics, but she's smiling. And that's all I need. She lets me take her hand and lead her toward the wooden stall where we check in and get our dull handsaw. I take it in one hand from the young kid working. There's no chance in hell I'm letting go of Lark. Not when it feels like fucking heaven just holding her hand.

It makes today feel like more than just two friends having fun together. It makes it feel like...a date.

How long have I fantasized about simple moments like this? Honestly, it probably makes me sound kinda creepy, imagining all the ways I wanted to be with Lark. Except, thanks to my complete lack of experience, very few of those ways were sexual. Most of them were things like this. Going through life, having fun together, the way we did as friends but *more.*

And now that *more* is reality. Holy fucking shit.

I guess I'm squeezing her hand kinda tightly because Lark leans into me with her shoulder. "Everything okay?"

I look down at her with a grin. "Everything is peachy keen, Birdie."

She smiles back at me, and I start to loosen my grip, but then she tightens hers. "Good."

Fuck, I love this woman.

I want to shout it out to everyone around me. The girl of my dreams, the only woman I've ever felt any sort of anything for is here with me. Holding my hand. Making me feel like the king of the entire goddamn universe.

We wander through the trees, kids darting around us, hollering for their parents. Lark hasn't stopped smiling and my own cheeks are starting to hurt because I haven't, either. Then she pulls me to a stop.

"What about that one?"

I look to where she's pointing. It's a small tree, maybe six feet, but that's being generous. A little lopsided, since it's still got its natural shape and hasn't been trimmed to perfection like most of the trees here. But when I glance at Lark, her face is glowing with excitement, and I know I'll do just about anything to keep that look on her face.

"That one? It's perfect."

We walk over to it, and despite not wanting to let go of her hand, I do. And just to play up the cheesy moment, I make a show out of walking all the way around, examining the tree, and making random noises of approval.

Lark's eyes are dancing, her hands clasped together as I come back to stand in front of her.

"You ready, Birdie?"

"For what?"

I hold out the saw. "You're doin' it."

She takes it from me, holding it gingerly. "I've never done anything like this, Dan."

I can hear the nerves in her voice, so I crouch down, and beckon for her to join me. Once she's next to me, I wrap my arm around her, still kind of in awe that I can do this. "I'll help you get it started."

Together, we place the saw against the trunk. Covering her hands with mine, I exert enough pressure to show her how to move it back and forth, and we slowly start cutting into the tree.

It's not a sensual action, not at all. But being like this, wrapped around her, our bodies moving in unison, is making me hard.

Guess I really am a fucking teenager again, getting hard at the slightest breeze.

"This is harder than I thought it would be," Lark comments, and I don't have the heart to tell her I could have done it in five seconds.

"But are you having fun?"

She nods, turning her head over her shoulder to smile at me. "So much fun."

I can't help it, I lean in and peck a kiss to the tip of her nose, red from the cold. Once again, I'm filled with so much goddamn wonder that I can do shit like this.

Her cheeks, already pink, darken.

"Focus on the saw, Birdie," I say roughly, my eyes not leaving hers, despite my instruction.

"Kind of hard to do when you're right there, looking so hot in that toque."

I chuckle. "That's what does it for you? My toque? It's the pom-pom, isn't it?"

Her giggle is adorable. Light and so damn happy. "Definitely the pom-pom."

I tilt my head toward the tree, where we've completely abandoned sawing the trunk. "C'mon, let's finish this, and then I'll treat you to some hot chocolate."

That gorgeous smile of hers grows impossibly wider. "With marshmallows?"

I lean back and pretend to be outraged. "Of course, with marshmallows. How could you even ask that? What kind of monster would I be to get you hot chocolate without marshmallows?"

We turn our attention back to the tree, Lark seeming invigorated by the promise of hot chocolate. A few minutes later, I hear the telltale creak that we've cut most of the way through the trunk and pull Lark to stand. Then, putting my hand on the tree, I give her a wink and push it just enough to allow it to fall over.

She claps her hands in delight, and it's so goddamn cute I might keel over from it. "Alright, let's get this beauty paid for and loaded up." My voice is rough, and I hope she doesn't ask why. I'm not ready to tell her how overwhelmed with happiness I am.

Once the tree is in the back of my truck, Lark automatically takes my hand in hers again. And for the billionth time today, I feel my heart swell at her easy affection. I've wanted this with her for so damn long, it feels like I'm living a dream. We wander around the farm, standing by the bonfire for a few minutes, sipping our hot chocolate.

But this place has one more surprise for Lark, and I can't wait to show it to her. Taking her empty hot chocolate cup, I toss it in the trash can and gesture to the barn. "You have to see something before we go."

She lets me lead her over to the large red building, and we step inside.

"Oh my God," she half whispers, half squeals, dropping my hand and darting over to the pen. "Look at them!"

We lean over and stare at the adorable baby goats wandering around the pen.

"These babies were just born a week ago. We named them after Santa's reindeer." Someone wearing a hoodie with the farm's logo on it comes over and opens the latch on the pen. "Have you ever cuddled a baby goat?"

Lark's mouth falls open. "No."

I nudge her with my hip. "Go on, Birdie."

She stumbles into the pen after the farm worker and holds out her arms as they place a brown and white baby goat in her embrace. Turning slowly, she gives me a tremulous smile, her eyes shining with joy. "Dan. I'm holding a baby goat," she whispers.

I lift my phone up and snap a few photos before answering. "Lucky goat."

She giggles and brings the goat closer so I can give its head a scratch. "This is the most amazing day ever."

Yep, that fills me with pride. I might have no dating experience, but that doesn't matter as long as I can make one woman happy. *This* woman.

After a few more minutes, Lark sets the baby down and leaves the pen. We wander around looking at the other animals — bunnies, pigs, chickens, and sheep. And at the very end, in a large indoor paddock, stands a massive horse.

"Holy crap."

"He used to pull the carriages around Stanley Park," I tell her, familiar with the horse's history from years of coming here with my parents. "The farm bought him when he retired, to let him live out his years being loved on by everyone who comes to visit."

Lark reaches out her hand and strokes the long nose of the giant who has ambled over to greet us.

"He's gorgeous."

It does something to me, seeing Lark fall in love with the place I've come to for so long with my family. My memories of coming here are nothing but happy, and if I can give her that, then my work here is done.

When the horse wanders off to greet some kids who have approached his paddock, we take that as our cue to leave. The water at the handwashing station outside the barn is freezing cold, and after using it, Lark starts to rub her hands together to try and warm them up.

I lead her over to one of the bonfires and take her hands in mine. "Let me." I rub them briskly. Lark steps in close, her body almost touching mine. She pulls our hands into her chest and rises up on her toes.

"Thank you, Dan."

That's all she says before her lips land on mine. Tasting faintly of hot chocolate, and a sweetness that is all her own, Lark Miller kisses me.

I release her hands so I can cup the back of her neck, holding her to me as I take a chance, teasing her lips with my tongue. Conscious of the fact that there are a lot of kids around, and the fact that I don't really know what I'm doing, I keep it light, taking things only slightly deeper. But the feel of her body pressed against me, her soft lips under mine, the fucking magic of this entire day has my dick starting to harden, yet again. And I know she feels it when she pulls her head back and gives me a coy smile.

She opens her mouth to say something just as a big white snowflake lands on her nose.

"Oh my God, it's snowing," she says, casting her gaze upward in delight. She might be staring at the snow starting to fall, but I can't stop staring at her.

And when her head tilts back down, and she beams that smile my way, I know there will never be another woman for me.

Lark is my lobster. My swan. My penguin.

I lean down and kiss her again as snow falls around us. And the only reason I manage to eventually tear myself away from her is the knowledge that this isn't a dream, and there will be more chances to kiss her.

That and the fact that my toes are going numb.

Chapter Nineteen

Lark

If everyone in the world could see Dan Montgomery dancing around his living room, Christmas music playing as he drapes lights across his mantle, they would fall even more in love with him than they are already.

He's known as the golden boy of the team. Always smiling, always having a good time. But that happiness feels dialed up to a thousand today, and I feel like the luckiest woman on earth to get to see it.

"Can you hand me that garland, Birdie?" he calls out over his shoulder as I carry two plates laden with sushi, Dan's favourite light saber chopsticks pinched between my fingers. I'm starving, and can't wait to dig in, so I have to pause a second to think about what he's asking for.

It's not only the food distracting me. It's also the gorgeous man in a ridiculously cheesy sweater with Yoda wearing a Santa hat and the words "The Season, Jolly It Is" on it. The man who hasn't stopped smiling, except when he's singing along to the music or when he's kissing me.

He hasn't stopped kissing me.

Just short little pecks, each one sweet and chaste, and each one leaving his face full of such amazement, as if he can't quite believe it's happening.

I know the feeling.

Part of me keeps thinking this can't be real. I can't actually be here, with my friend Dan, decorating his place for Christmas. I should be with Baron at some stuffy office party somewhere, or worse, I should be home, bored and lonely. But I *am* here. With a man I can't stop smiling around. Who seems so dang happy to just be with me.

It feels a little crazy, a little too good to be true. And if it were anyone other than Dan, I would definitely be questioning my hold on reality.

But it *is* Dan. I know him, probably better than most people in my life, Baron included. I know what he eats on his pizza and that he's terrified of lizards. I know he thinks the Ewoks are the most underrated characters in the entire *Star Wars* franchise. I know he has two pairs of lucky socks, one for home games and one for away games. I know his parents are the most important people in his life, and that everything he does is for them. I know he's the best man I have ever met, with a heart of gold as big as the Pacific Ocean.

And now I know he likes me. Really likes me. Maybe even more than likes me. He doesn't want me to be anything other than what I am, doesn't see me as just a friend or one of the guys. He doesn't want me to change, to act differently, or be someone I'm not.

He wants *me*. And he's never wanted anyone that way before.

If this is a too-good-to-be-true dream, I don't ever want to wake up.

Setting the plates and chopsticks down, I pick up the green garland and carry it over to him. He takes it, leaning in to kiss my forehead. "Thanks. Go ahead and start eating, I just wanna get this up."

I ignore him, instead taking the other end of the garland and working to fasten it to the hooks he attached to the mantle earlier. "We'll finish this, then eat."

The happy smile he unleashes warms me on the inside. We make quick work of finishing the garland and then sit down next to each other on the couch with our dinner. He sits right next to me, our thighs touching. It's the little things like this that tell me just how much things have shifted in our relationship. A month ago, we would have been at opposite ends of the couch. Still comfortable, still having a good time together, but with a necessary distance. Dan was never anything but respectful of my relationship with Baron, keeping things strictly platonic. And I had no clue how hard that must have been, being close to me as a friend but not allowed to even consider anything more.

It makes me fall for him a little harder, thinking about how he set aside his feelings, never breathing a word of them to me out of consideration. It also makes my heart break just a bit, thinking about the wasted years, the time we could have been together, if only I had wised up sooner to how unhappy I was.

"Everything okay? You haven't tried your food." Dan's knee nudges mine and I startle back to reality.

"Yeah, fine. Sorry, just thinking about things."

He sets his plate down and turns his body toward me. "About what?"

I study him for a second, taking in how genuinely interested he is in listening to me. How much he truly wants to know my thoughts, my feelings, my opinions.

It's a unique experience. Which is a very sad realization to have.

"I wish I hadn't wasted so much time with Baron, trying to convince myself I was happy."

Dan's face shows his confusion for a couple of seconds before he grasps what I mean. Then he takes my plate, setting it down beside his, before gathering my hands and lifting them to his mouth to kiss my knuckles.

"Don't think of it that way, Birdie. That wasn't wasted time. That was necessary for you, for us, to figure out exactly what we wanted. Who we are. Besides, there's no good to be found in looking back. Only forward."

I slowly shake my head from side to side. "How did you get so wise?"

His shoulders lift in a bashful shrug. "My dad. He's always got some random phrase that works for any situation."

I lean in and kiss his cheek. "Well, I'll have to thank him for raising such a smart man."

Dan turns his face slightly and places a light kiss on my lips. Not satisfied with that, I tug my hands free and run them through his hair, holding his face close to mine so I can kiss him again, deeper.

He lets out a low groan, and his strong arms band around my body, pulling me into his lap. We haven't gone further than kissing yet, but God, do I want to. I don't want to rush him, however. Knowing he's never done this with anyone makes me acutely aware of every move I make.

And makes me wonder if I'll have to be the one to move things along...

Deciding to test that theory, I bring one hand between us and push on his chest. He takes the hint, falling backward on the couch until I'm stretched out on top of him. We've never been in this position with each other.

Ever.

I can feel every line of muscle bunching and tensing under me. I can feel the hard ridge of his cock between my legs. I can feel his hands tentatively roaming across my back. And I can feel his heart racing beneath my chest.

Feeling bold, and more than a little horny, I press my pelvis to his, grinding slightly against him.

He groans. "Jesus, Lark."

I hum in response, trailing kisses down the scruff of his jaw and neck. My hands start to move, and I drag my fingers lightly up and down the side of his chest, stopping at the hem of his shirt before lifting myself up enough to look at his face.

He's turned on. That's obvious. But is he nervous? Is this too fast? I'm suddenly filled with hesitation, unsure of what to do.

Dan doesn't seem to feel that same hesitation. He reads my mind, replacing my hands with his and whipping his shirt off.

I've seen the man shirtless many times before.

But I've never had him laid out underneath me quite like this.

His thumb grazes my lip, and my gaze flies to his. He smirks. "You had a little bit of drool there, Birdie."

I slap at his chest indignantly. "I did not."

His chuckle vibrates through him and I struggle not to be too obvious while clenching my thighs together.

"Can we make this even or do you get to be the only one who can ogle."

My eyes widen. "I..."

Once again, Dan somehow knows what I'm thinking before I even really do.

"Just because I haven't had sex before doesn't mean I haven't thought about all the things I want to do to you, Lark. I've thought about getting you naked, running my hands over your curves, and discovering every inch of you with my tongue. I know we're taking it slow, but I just want to feel your skin against mine."

Oh, come on. I didn't know words could make me melt, but I'm pretty sure I am no longer a human, and am instead a pile of goo.

"That's the sweetest dirty talk I've ever heard, Dan Montgomery," I tease as I sit up and slowly inch my sweater off. When I finally pull it over my head and meet his gaze, the fire burning in his brown eyes takes my breath away. He slowly sweeps his eyes up and down my body before lifting his hands and placing them on my hips. His tongue darts out to moisten his lips and he glances up at me.

"Can I..."

I shiver at that loaded question. And even though he doesn't specify, I know I would let this man do absolutely anything to me. My head moves up and down. I don't need to know what he wants to do, because I want it all.

Slowly, he slides his hands up my rib cage, drawing them in until his thumbs are dragging along the underside of my bra.

His stare never falters, his focus intense.

Something dawns on me. A small clarification that doesn't matter but has me curious. "You said you've never had sex but have you ever...done anything with a woman?"

I watch his throat move as he swallows, and some of that heat in his eyes dies. I instantly want to take back my question and restore his desire. But before I can try to salvage it, he answers.

"Before you showed up at my apartment, I had kissed just one woman other than my mom. And that was only because of a dare in eighth grade. I've gone on a few dates, but never done any more than a kiss on the cheek. I've never been intimate with anyone before you, Lark. I want to say I'm sorry for that, because it means I have no fucking clue what I'm doing. But I can't be too sorry, because I know no one would have ever come close to making me feel what you do with nothing more than your hands on my body and your lips on mine."

I stare down at him, at the honest, vulnerable, beautiful man beneath me. How the hell did I get so lucky to be with him?

I reach behind my back and unhook my bra, sliding it off my shoulders as Dan's eyes widen.

"What are you doing?" he says, his voice raspy.

I toss my bra to the side, leaving me as bare as he is. "You said I shouldn't be the only one allowed to ogle," I say impishly, leaning forward so my small breasts brush his skin. "And you wanted to feel your skin on mine."

One large hand tangles in my hair while the other comes to the middle of my back, holding me against him as he attacks my mouth. There might not be any finesse, but what he lacks in experience, Dan makes up for with enthusiasm and passion.

We're pressed together, the heat building between us. Dan's hips start to move under mine in jerky movements, a sort of thrusting and grinding combined.

Pushing up on his chest, I take his hands and lift them to my breasts. His hips still as I look down at him.

"Follow my lead," I say, then slowly, I start to roll my hips, swiveling around on him. For a moment, he's frozen, his eyes staring at his hands that are now covering my breasts. But for a guy with no experience, he catches on fast. When he squeezes me, I nod, encouraging him. He pinches my nipples and I can't hold back my moan. Cautiously, he starts to move beneath me, much smoother this time, picking up the rhythm.

"Oh God," I gasp as his dick rubs against me. Even through layers of clothing, I'm so turned on by him, by everything, that I realize with some surprise, I'm close to coming.

"Keep going," I moan, my eyes fluttering closed. I cover Dan's hands with mine, showing him how to twist and pluck at my nipples the way I do when I'm playing with myself.

Again, he proves to be a quick learner, and I bring my hands to his chest, leaning forward so I can rock back and forth along him, rubbing my clit, listening to his pants and grunts and echoing them with my own sounds of pleasure.

"Shit, Lark," he grinds out, dropping his grip down to my hips, holding me in place. He grunts, driving his hips up. "Fuck. Oh fuck." Once, twice, three more times he grunts and thrusts before I feel him shudder through his release.

Mine is right there, but I don't actually care about it anymore as I look down at him, his eyes closed, lips slightly parted, and pure ecstasy written across his face. I trace my fingers along his cheek, marveling at how right it feels to be with him this way.

But his eyes flutter open, and they're filled with determination.

"Teach me how to get you off, Birdie."

I'm moving before I can respond as he flips our positions. Once he's stretched out on the deep couch beside me, he rests his palm on my stomach, his other arm propping up his head.

"I want to make you come."

I nod vigorously. I want that, too. Very much. I take his hand and slide it down my body, dipping below the waist of my leggings. His fingers graze the dampness between my legs and his eyes grow dark. "Damn. Is that...is that because of me?"

A giggle escapes me. "Is there another deliciously sexy baseball player charming me with dirty sweet talk?"

He growls, bending down and kissing me before tugging my lower lip between his teeth. "There better not be."

His fingers dip in and out, lightly circling, teasing. My hips start to shift as I fight not to grab his hand and put it exactly where I want him. If he wants to explore, who am I to say no?

But all too soon, that teasing becomes too much to bear.

"My clit, please," I beg, my back arching as I clutch at his arms. "Your hand, anything. Please."

All I can do is hope he can figure it out, because I'm too close to give him any more instruction than that. He fumbles at first, but then he proves, yet again, that he's very in tune with me and my body. Because after a couple of minutes, I'm keening and crying out his name as the sweetest orgasm washes through my body.

When I drift back to reality and drag open my eyes, he's

looking down at me with such wonder and amazement. I cup his cheek and smile. "That was incredible."

Slowly, he pulls his hand free and brings it in front of him. His fingers are shiny with my release, and I flush at the sight of it.

I don't know what I expect him to do, but it certainly isn't to lift it to his mouth and lick off the moisture.

"Delicious," he says in a low voice. "Next time you need to teach me how to make that happen with my mouth so I can taste your sweetness."

"Oh," I gasp as he sucks another finger clean. "Well, um, okay. If you insist," I stammer, feeling another wave of heat wash over me.

Dan looks down at me with a wicked smirk that promises all kinds of pleasure.

"Oh, I very much insist, Birdie. I'm gonna want to see you let go like that again, and again, and again."

He pulls me up to sit, and tugs his shirt over my head, before picking up his lightsaber chopsticks, still glowing red from when he turned on the LED lights earlier. He lifts a piece of sashimi and holds it to my mouth.

"Eat."

I chew and swallow before answering. "That was your dinner. Aren't you hungry?"

"Oh, I am. But not for sushi."

CHAPTER TWENTY

Lark

As I stare around the disaster formerly known as my kitchen, my mood drops lower and lower. What the heck was I thinking, agreeing to bake eight dozen cookies for the Tridents' staff holiday party?

When Candice, the administrator in charge of the party, called me in a panic saying their vendor fell through and she needed cookies at the last minute for the staff party tomorrow, I should have said no.

But everyone knows I love to bake, seeing as I often bring in extra to share. And Candice was so stressed about the kids not having cookies, who was I to deny children their treats?

So I said yes.

And now, less than twelve hours later, my kitchen is covered in flour and sugar, and my overwhelm is at an all-time high. I foolishly thought I could get this done and still go with Dan to the Christmas market tonight, but there's not a chance of that happening.

Lifting my now-cold coffee to my lips, I take a sip and grimace. I hate having to cancel, but I don't have a choice.

Pulling out my phone, I open our text thread.

> **LARK: I'm so sorry to do this, but I can't go to the market. I've got a million cookies to bake for the staff party tomorrow, and there's no way I'll finish in time. Especially not since I discovered I'm out of kisses.**

I drop the phone back on the counter and pick up my recipes, wanting to double-check I'm not missing anything else. When I went to the store last night, I was certain my list was accurate, and I could get started bright and early today. Instead, I pulled everything out this morning only to realize I was missing the key ingredient for my Grinch Kiss cookies.

Finally satisfied I only need the one thing, I pick up my phone and head to the front door just as it vibrates in my hand.

> **DAN: Don't apologize, it's all good. Except for the out of kisses part. That's unacceptable. I'll be there as soon as I can to rectify the situation.**

His response makes me smile, breaking through the stress of my morning.

> **LARK: You're sweet, but you don't have to come. I meant chocolate kisses. ;)**

> **DAN: Who says I can't bring you both?**

> **DAN: I'm on my way.**

Sure enough, half an hour later, there's a knock at my door. I turn off the mixer where I've started working on the peanut butter dough and dust off my hands before going to open it.

There's no way to prepare for what awaits me. I burst out laughing as I take in the sight of Dan wearing a Santa hat and an elf costume apron. He's holding a cloth bag in one hand, and in the other...

"Is that for me?" I ask delightedly. He grins and drapes the matching apron over my head.

"Sure is."

I tie the red strings behind my back and model the apron for him.

"Cutest elf I've ever seen," he says, leaning in and kissing me softly. "There. You're officially no longer out of kisses." He kisses me again, then holds up the bag. "I wasn't sure which ones you wanted, so I bought them all."

My eyes widen when I take the surprisingly heavy bag. Opening it, I see a *lot* of packages.

"Oh my God."

Dan takes the bag from me and heads into the kitchen. I trail after him, finding him at the sink, washing his hands.

"Wanna turn on some tunes? Let's get baking."

His easygoing nature is such a welcome balm from the stress I was feeling just an hour ago. And so at odds with what I had grown used to with Baron and his family. Heaven forbid I change or cancel plans or need assistance of any kind. No, I needed to be independent, yet accommodating, all the time. Being with someone who cares about me and doesn't make me feel like a burden when something comes up or I dare to have an opinion that goes against theirs is a refreshing change.

Dan looks over, catching me in my mental reflection.

"Everything okay?" He moves toward me, his hands coming to either side, resting on the counter at my back. I'm caged between his arms, and my own hands automatically lift to his shoulders before sliding around to toy with the hair at the nape of his neck. His eyes flutter closed, a small smile of pure delight creasing his features.

"Yeah, everything's great," I reply softly, leaning in to kiss the scruff on his jaw. "I was just thinking about how different it is with you than it was with Baron."

His eyes open, flooding with concern. "Different in a good way, I hope?"

A laugh breaks free. "Oh my God, yes. So good, I promise." I kiss his lips, once, twice, three times before continuing. "You make me happy. You care about me, just as I am. And you don't make me feel bad for anything."

The concern turns into something darker, and I draw back slightly, impeded by the counter behind me. But Dan's anger isn't directed at me. I know this instinctively.

"I'm sorry, Birdie. If I had realized how unhappy you were, I never would have kept quiet. Fuck. I know I'm the one who said we need to look forward, not back, but hearing you say stuff like that makes me so angry at myself for not fighting for you."

I fling my arms back around his neck and squeeze him tight. It's still not enough, and obviously he feels the same way because his hands come to my ass, lifting me onto the counter. My legs wrap around him, and we're as close as possible, and something in me settles with a happy sigh.

We stay like this, me wrapped around him, our breathing synchronized, for several moments. It feels so good, so right, being with him. As much as we both know we can't dwell on the time we lost, it's hard not to feel frustrated that we could have felt this happiness so much sooner, if only...

If only I hadn't been so consumed with doing what I thought I should, trying to be who my family wanted me to be, and settling for so much less than I deserved.

After a while, Dan's hold on me loosens. "Should we get those cookies baked?" he asks.

I nod, and when he steps back, I hop off the counter. "Okay. The dough is almost ready to be coloured green, then we just have to roll them into a ball and press the kisses on top."

Dan goes to the bag he brought and pulls out several packages of chocolate. "Which ones should we use?"

I point to the red and white striped ones, and he gets to work opening all the chocolate. For a while, we work together in silence, having forgotten about putting on any music. I already feel less stressed about the job at hand, simply having him with me. Between the two of us, I know we'll get all the cookies made and packaged in time.

Sure enough, several hours later, the kitchen is even more of a mess than it was this morning, but Dan is pulling the final tray of cookies out of the oven. He sets it down on the counter with a flourish before walking over to me with his hands in the air.

"Go, Team Cookie!"

I slap my hands against his, only for him to lace our fingers together and pull me in for a kiss. I let him because no way am I saying no to a kiss, but I wrinkle my nose when we separate.

"I'm covered in flour."

He lets out a deep chuckle, looking down at his own dirty apron with a smile. "Yeah, same. Guess I should have brought some extra clothes."

A little devil and angel appear on my shoulders as I consider my options. Do I say what I'm thinking, or not...

The devil wins.

"We could put your clothes in the laundry here."

Dan gives me a confused look, and his innocence is so adorable I struggle to keep a straight face. "I don't have anything else..." He trails off, his eyes widening as comprehension dawns.

I step forward, slowly sliding my hands around his waist to untie his apron. "We don't have to do anything. I'm sure your underwear isn't covered in flour." With a wink, I lift the apron over his head and let it slip to the floor. "Washing your clothes feels like the least I could do to thank you for your help."

I pull his T-shirt up, and he lifts his arms automatically, letting me remove it, baring his upper body.

"Or there are other ways I could thank you." My hands go to his belt and pause. "If you want."

His head bobs up and down eagerly as I slip his belt free of the buckle. "Lark," he groans, dropping his forehead to mine. "I'm scared I'm gonna embarrass myself."

The quiet statement is full of so much vulnerability, I freeze, moving my hands up to his chest before wrapping them around his body so I can hug him close. His arms squeeze me tightly, and his heart races beneath my ear.

"Please don't feel like that," I whisper. "You have no reason to be embarrassed. We go at your pace. I don't want to pressure you."

"You don't understand." His voice turns rough. "Me being embarrassed has nothing to do with us moving too quickly and everything to do with how desperately I want you."

I barely get out my gasp before his lips are crushed to mine, his hands moving to grip my hair tightly as he plunders my mouth. His confidence in kissing me has grown rapidly, and he takes control, infusing our kiss with all of his built-up desire.

Which only makes that devil on my shoulder even louder. As much as I don't want to end our kiss, I do. Because something better awaits. And then I take his hand and lead him down the hall to my bedroom. He lets me push him to sit on the edge of the bed, and then I take a step back. I untie my own apron and take it off before lifting my sweater over my head.

His hands fist at his sides, his eyes not leaving me as I slowly wriggle my leggings down, kicking them off to the side along with my socks. Watching him devour me with his gaze, I'm incredibly glad I put on a cute set of blue panties and a matching bra this morning.

"You're so fucking beautiful."

I beam at him, closing the distance, stepping in between his legs. "So are you, Dan." I slide my fingers through his hair, tipping his head back so I can kiss him. "You're a beautiful man, inside and out. I wouldn't change a thing about you."

His head falls forward, landing on my chest as his arms wrap around me again. This man loves his hugs. "How do you know just what to say?"

I bend down and kiss his head, inhaling the fresh scent of his shampoo. "The same way you do. I know you, and you know me. It's that simple."

"It's that incredible."

I smile against his hair, feeling his lips press against my skin. But when his hands start to travel, I draw back. "This is meant to be me thanking you for your help."

His pout is adorable, but I don't give in. Dropping to my knees, I raise my eyebrows as my hands land on the waist of his jeans. "Lift."

"Oh. What? You don't have to..." He stammers out, even as he lifts his hips so I can tug his jeans down.

"Trust me, I know I don't have to. But I really want to, if you do." He nods quickly, and that's all I need to see. I toss his jeans behind me and run my hands up his muscled thighs. The large outline of his cock pressing against his boxer briefs has me licking my lips, even as I want to giggle at the bananas that are printed on his underwear.

"Bananas?" I ask, giving him a grin.

"I like fun underwear. Wasn't expecting anyone to see them today, I must admit."

"I like them, too. But I want to take them off. Can I do that?"

He chokes out a laugh. "Let me make one thing clear. You can do whatever the fuck you want with me. I want it all, Birdie. Every fucking thing. I might be terrified I'll make a fool of myself, but that's not enough to stop me from taking anything you'll give me. I feel as if I've waited a lifetime for this. For you."

I surge up to my knees and kiss him, surprising him at first but he recovers quickly, holding me in place as I pour everything I can into the kiss, trying to tell him without words just how much it means to me that he wants this. With me. And only me.

Settling back on my knees, I slowly tug his boxers down his legs, trying not to be too eager when his dick pops free. But dang, it's beautiful. Long and not too thick, already shiny with a drop of precum at the tip.

I force myself to look up at his face, not wanting to miss a second of his reaction. When I slowly wrap my hand around the base, his eyes close and he lets out a small groan. I slowly drag my hand up and back down, fully aware that with no moisture to lubricate the movement, the friction might be too much for him.

But apparently not. His eyes fly open, burning with intensity now. His hands are gripping fistfuls of my blanket, and his shoulders are heaving with every breath.

Tilting my head down, I circle his tip with my tongue.

"Lark," he breathes, that one word a benediction. And all the encouragement I need.

Opening wider, I slip my mouth around him

"Holy shit," he curses.

I look up and see him still staring at me. Slowly, I start to bob up and down, applying some light suction, and moving my hand in time with my mouth. His musky taste isn't so bad, and I find myself actually enjoying the act. Knowing I'm bringing him pleasure he's never experienced before makes this less of a chore, like it used to feel in the past, and more of a privilege.

"Birdie," he gasps, one hand moving to my shoulder. "Holy shit, I'm gonna...I'm gonna come. Oh my God."

I don't have time to decide what I want to do, much less think about what he might want, before warm jets of come are hitting the back of my throat. I quickly swallow, not stopping until I feel him shudder, and the tense muscles of his legs relax around me.

Only then do I draw back, releasing him from my mouth. Strong hands are under my arms, lifting me up and onto the bed where Dan cuddles me against his chest.

"That was... Fuck, I don't even know what to say." He lifts his head. "Was that okay? Are you okay?"

I kiss him lightly. "I'm more than okay. Thank you for your help with the cookies and for letting me do that."

His head flops back down as he laughs again. "Woman, I will do just about anything for you. And I'll do it all twice if you do that again sometime."

I burst into giggles as well and nuzzle into his chest. "Deal."

"But first, you have to teach me how to do that to you."

"Well, if I must."

Chapter Twenty-One

Monty

"I can't believe you turned down Barbados for this." I peer out the windshield at the slushy rain pouring down. But even the dreary weather can't fully get me down. No, my hands are holding the steering wheel tightly, partly to keep us safe but also so I don't get distracted by wanting to touch Lark. I don't dare even look at her or the excitement bubbling inside of me might spill over.

It's Christmas Eve and we're driving out to my parents' place. I love the holidays, always have. What's not to love about Christmas jammies, spending time with your family, and eating your body weight in cookies?

And getting to do all of that with Lark by my side? Holy shit, I might explode from happiness. But even knowing how weird and toxic her family can be, there's a part of me that wonders if she's going to feel like she missed out on something by not being with them over Christmas.

"Trust me, Dan. I'm not missing anything or anyone I truly care about. My parents haven't done Christmas in Vancouver in years and being stuck somewhere with them? No thanks."

"What did you do last year?" I ask with some curiosity. We've never discussed holiday plans; I always just assumed she was with Baron or her parents.

She huffs. "Spent it at the Hazelwood museum with Baron and his family."

My eyebrows raise at her words. "Museum?"

"That's what I call their house in my head. Imagine the most imposing, formal building, and then call it a home." Another forced laugh. "So, yeah, even with the rain, I'd much rather be here with you." She gives me a warm look, and her hand lands on the back of my neck, toying with the hair that sticks out from underneath my ball cap. I don't think I'll ever get used to these small touches, the affection that comes so easily after so many years of just dreaming of it.

God, I sound like a fucking putz, and I love it.

Lark shifts in her seat, twisting to get something out of the back, and of course, the second I look over, my eyes go straight to the gap in her shirt, giving me a clear view straight at those perfect tits.

Tits that I, apparently, am now free to look at and even touch. Fuck, that's weird to think about. And getting a boner while I'm driving down the highway is not something I ever expected to deal with.

This is why I kept my feelings for her repressed for all those years...

She settles back into her seat, now with a bag of chocolate kisses in hand. One of the many leftovers from our baking day last week, seeing as I kind of went overboard at the store. Did I empty the entire shelf of kisses into my basket? Maybe. But

I didn't want to disappoint her by bringing the wrong ones or not enough.

Besides, is there such a thing as too much chocolate? I think not.

Lark unwraps one and holds it up to my mouth. Sweetness bursts on my tongue from the creamy chocolate, but it's when I glance over and see her looking at me with a soft, open expression that I melt, just like the damn chocolate.

Is this real life?

And if it is, how the hell do I make sure I don't fuck it all up?

My inhale almost sends the chocolate kiss down my throat, which would be really bad as we speed toward my parents' place. Coughing lightly, I recover. Another quick glance and I see she's looking out her window at the farmland we're passing through.

I want to touch her. No, I want her to touch me. To play with my hair like she was before. But I'm pretty sure it would be weird if I asked her to do that. Which means I'm gonna have to initiate something. Hoo boy.

I slowly unclench my right hand from the steering wheel and flex my fingers a couple of times. Then I set it on the center console between us. Maybe she'll get the hint and take over?

Nope. She's still staring out the window. Okay, Monty, you can fucking do this. You've touched her a hundred times before. Hell, she had her mouth on your dick a few days ago. Resting your hand on her leg is no big fucking deal.

Except, it really is. Because the feelings I have for this woman are like nothing else. And finally being free to express those feelings, to act on them, has me all kinds of fucked up — mostly in a good way, but with a healthy layer of anxiety on top.

I want to be good for her. I want to be everything she deserves. And I'm terrified I won't be.

Taking a deep breath, I move my hand over and place it on her thigh. Her head doesn't move, but she covers my hand with hers and squeezes gently.

And I exhale.

Waking up in the middle of the night in the spare bedroom — the one not taken over by my mom's quilting supplies — at my parents' house, with Lark draped over my bare torso, is a very odd experience.

Not a bad one, just...not one I ever really thought I'd have. Honestly? It's not even something I let myself imagine. Partly because it always felt out of reach and partly because being in bed with the woman of my dreams with my parents right down the hall isn't exactly the most romantic concept.

I'm pretty sure you could see my cheeks turn red all the way from the fucking moon when Mom casually said the two of us would be staying in one bedroom together.

But when Lark nuzzles into my chest, letting out a contended hum, I tell my overthinking brain to shut the fuck up and let me enjoy this Christmas miracle.

I guess I drift back to sleep because the next thing I'm aware of is something rubbing against my dick, making it uncomfortably hard. My eyes blink open, and I look down to see Lark shifting against me. Her eyes are closed, but it's hard to tell if she's asleep or not. When she makes a cute little mumbling sound, it becomes clear she's not awake. Which means her rubbing against me is not a conscious choice.

I stifle my groan when her bare thigh presses down on my dick. It hurts, but in a good way. And if I don't want to embarrass myself and have to do laundry later, unfortunately, I need to extricate myself from the situation.

But when I go to move out from underneath her, Lark's hold on me tightens and she lets out a small whimper.

Well, fuck.

"Dan," she whispers. "See me."

Oh, Birdie. My heart fucking swells. *I do see you*. I always have.

There's not a chance I'm going anywhere until she's awake, so I try reciting my Little League stats to get my mind off how fucking amazing it feels to have her body against mine. To know that she feels the same way for me as I do for her.

Because all I've ever wanted is to find someone who sees me for me. Who loves all the things that make up who I am. And Lark is the one person I want to let in, to show all the sides of Dan Montgomery.

Her breathing changes, and when I glance down from the ceiling where I've made it to my fourth year of baseball in statistics, she's blinking sleepy eyes open. I give her a nervous smile, not sure how she'll react to what's going on down below.

I watch her face shift from soft and relaxed to something else as our physical position becomes apparent.

"Um, good morning?" she says, phrasing it as more of a question than a statement. She drops her face into my chest as she removes her thigh from pressing on my dick. "Sorry about that."

I clear my throat. "It's fine." Yeah, given how my voice just squeaked, it's obviously not fine. "I'm just gonna..." I don't finish the statement before rolling out from under her, throwing off the covers and dashing across the hall into the bathroom after making sure the coast is clear.

After I brush my teeth and get things under control, I return to the bedroom. It's still early enough that Mom and Dad aren't up yet, but I know they will be soon. Dad will get up first, as he does every morning, and make a cup of tea to take to Mom in bed.

Lark is sitting up on the bed, her hands playing with the Christmas quilt Mom pulls out every year. I settle in beside her, picking up on the uncomfortable vibes but unsure what the fuck to do or say.

"I really am sorry for whatever *asleep me* did to you," Lark blurts out. "I didn't mean to make you feel weird."

Well, fuck. Rolling onto my side, I prop my head up on one arm and reach out to her with the other, pulling her into me. My own nerves don't mean shit, not when Lark obviously needs some reassurance. It's funny how I can get lost in my own brain, overthinking everything, but all it takes to calm me is realizing Lark needs my protective side to take over.

Her soft sigh as she settles into my embrace soothes me even further. And it gives me the courage to explain things as best I can.

"Don't apologize, Birdie. You did nothing wrong. I'm the one who has to wrap my head around everything. You gotta remember, for the last few years, I've had to keep my hands and my thoughts to myself. I wouldn't even let myself dream of mornings like this too often, because when I did, I felt so guilty and messed up about it. Dreaming about my best friend while she was supposedly in love with someone else? It felt so fucking wrong, and I hated myself for it. But now that you're here, that *we're* here, I don't have to feel guilty about it, and I don't have to hold back my physical reactions. It's just taking my brain a minute to catch up to that new reality."

"Oh." That one word is filled with understanding, and the very fact that she gets me so easily feels like further proof that this was meant to be all along.

She was always meant to be mine, we just had to take a long and windy road to get here.

"I just need you to know, when I have a moment like I did just now, it's not about you. Not at all. I just need you to be patient with me." It's hard to keep the pleading from my voice, and I wish I could be more confident and secure. But you don't spend your entire life *not* feeling romantic things for anyone else, only to suddenly have the one person you *do* feel those things for become available — and wanting those same things — without needing an adjustment period.

"I'm not going anywhere, Dan. You've shown me in so many ways over the years that you're a man who's worth waiting for. You're the man I deserve, who will love me the way I should be loved. I was feeling guilty for how easy it was to move on from Baron until I realized it's only easy because I never loved him the way I should have. I honestly don't know if I ever truly loved him at all. But you..." Her voice trails off, her finger drawing light circles over my chest.

No, wait. Those aren't circles. Those are hearts.

I swear to God, if she doesn't start talking again, *my* heart might stop completely.

"I'm falling in love with you."

Holy. Shit.

I'm not saying I expect the heavens to open up and choirs of angels to sing, but this does feel kind of like a Christmas miracle. Like, what is even happening right now? Am I dreaming? Is this my brain cruelly torturing me by dangling the one thing I want more than anything, more than a championship, more than a contract that can retire my parents, more than a Bugatti in my driveway...

"Dan?"

Her tentative question snaps me back to reality. Back to the woman that just made my dreams come true. I lean in and kiss the tip of her nose before resting my forehead to hers.

"Lark, I've loved you for so long, it feels as natural as breathing. I've never felt like this about anyone else. And all I want is to be worthy of your love in return."

Her hand lifts to cup my cheek. And what she says next goes a long way to erasing all the nerves I've had about being enough for her.

"You already are."

CHAPTER TWENTY-TWO

Lark

"Why am I nervous?" Dan mumbles under his breath as he takes my hand. I lean into his side reassuringly and we walk to the front of Ronan and Willow's house.

"Good question. If you figure it out, let me know."

He lets out a strained laugh, but his shoulders drop a little bit.

Tonight is the team's holiday dinner. It'll be just the players and their significant others. I've never been to it before, but I've heard the stories. The gifts the players get each other, the elaborate feasts, and the drinking that invariably leads to shenanigans.

Dan arranged an Uber for us so we don't have to worry about driving home, but even so, I don't plan on having too much to drink. I'm too anxious about our first time being together in front of his teammates.

They might all know how he's always felt about me, but how do *they* feel? Are any of them mad that I was so oblivious? Do they think I strung him along? Do they think we're moving too fast?

I can't voice any of this to Dan. I'm sure he'd tell me I'm being silly, but on the off chance that he doesn't, the last thing I need to do is add to his own nervousness. Nor do I want to know what *he's* nervous about.

We reach the front door of a house I've been to many times. Subtle sounds of voices and laughter float out. The party is already underway, and we would have been here sooner, except when I opened the door and Dan saw me in this dress, I suddenly found myself against the wall, engaged in a very intense make out session that surprised even me.

For all that he claims to be awkward and nervous, and needing to take things slow, Dan also very much enjoys kissing. Lots and lots of kissing.

By the time we broke apart, I needed a few minutes to fix my hair and makeup. All of which made our Uber driver leave without us, so then we had to request another one and wait for it to arrive.

Dan looks at me one more time, a slightly shaky smile on his face, then he pushes the front door open. The volume rises considerably as we enter the house. I know my way better than he does, so I take over, leading him into the large, open space near the back of the house.

Sure enough, most of the team is already here. Rhett and Kai are in the corner talking with one of the outfielders, Ronan's in the kitchen doing something, and I can see Willow chatting with Mav's girlfriend Sadie. A few of the other guys are outside on the heated patio, and some more of the wives and girlfriends are with them.

My nightmare does not come true, and all conversation does not stop the second we walk into the room. In fact, no one seems to even notice us arriving together until Willow glances over.

"You're here!" she cries out, walking over quickly and pulling me in for a hug, forcing me to drop Dan's hand. "Hi Monty." She releases me and moves to hug him and I take a step to the side, against the wall of the living room. Her exuberant greeting has drawn some attention, and a few of the other players move over to say hi. I hang back and watch Dan greet everyone, smiling and hugging his teammates.

"Monty, my brother!" Kai booms, pulling Dan in and slapping his back as they hug. It's true that a pitcher and a catcher often develop a unique bond. And I've watched Dan and Kai grow their connection over the last year. But hearing Kai greet him, I suddenly realize I've never once asked Dan in all the time I've known him if he would rather I call him Monty like everyone else on the team.

Why my brain chooses this exact moment to fixate on that, I don't know, but now I can't seem to let it go, my eyes going to him as if I might find the answer somewhere on his face.

Of course, I don't. All I see is him smiling, having a good time, completely unaware my brain has hijacked my logical self, and I'm semi-spiraling over something as random as his nickname.

Then again, maybe it's not so random. When Rhett walks over to me, his big arms wide open, I realize with a start that focusing on the name I call Dan has distracted me from my worries over how the team will react to my being here with him.

"Lark! Happy holidays, it's great to see you, darlin'."

I hug him back, hoping his reaction is a sign that my nerves are unfounded. "Thanks, Rhett. How was your Christmas?"

He shrugs, looking a little disappointed. "Not the best, if I'm bein' honest. I was goin' to head home to see my mama, but shegot a last-minute deal for some trip to the coast to visit my aunt. Turkey and mashed potatoes ain't the same when you're by yourself."

He sounds so morose, my heart breaks for the big guy. "I'm sorry, Rhett. You should have let one of us know."

He shakes his head, glancing from me to Dan. "Nah, don't worry about me. I knew Monty wanted to take ya to meet his folks. No way was I gonna get in the middle of that."

Kai joins us then, draping his arm across my shoulders. "Lark, Lark, Lark. You finally saw the light and put our boy out of his misery."

My cheeks heat. But before I can say anything, Kai is shoved to the side, and Dan takes his place, pulling me into his arms, my back to his front. "What did I say, Yami? Don't be a dumbass."

"I wasn't!" Kai protests, and I feel Dan's lips land on my bare shoulder, making me shiver.

"Aww, look at you two. Freaking finally."

That comes from Willow, who walks over with Sadie, Maverick, and Ronan. I feel Dan inhale, and his arms tighten around me.

"Okay, let's get this over with. Lark and I are together. Yes, finally. Yes, it's real, and amazing, and everything I've ever wanted. No, you cannot give her a hard time about taking so long to realize Baron was a fucking douche canoe. No, you cannot give me a hard time about being too chicken to tell her how I felt. Yes, you can be happy for both of us. Got it?"

Mav starts a slow clap, a rare smile just barely crossing his lips. Pretty soon, the others join in. While I can tell my face is flaming with embarrassment, it also feels pretty great, finally having everything out in the open. Knowing the team is aware of our change in relationship status and are seemingly on board with it is a relief.

And hearing Dan sound so calm, confident, and most of all, happy when he made that declaration to everyone?

Well, that might be the best feeling of all.

CHAPTER TWENTY-THREE

Monty

"Why are you so nervous?" Yami punches my arm as we walk up to the cashier at the grocery store. "Big plans for tonight?"

Yeah...like having the woman of my dreams in my bed, making me no longer the oldest virgin in the major leagues.

"Dinner with Lark," I answer instead, dumping the items in my arms onto the conveyor belt. I mentally review my list, double-checking I've got everything.

Sparkling wine...ingredients for my mom's famous pasta primavera...two chocolate cupcakes...and licorice.

I got the condoms in an online order that arrived yesterday, saving me from explaining that purchase to Yami. Granted, he probably wouldn't bat an eye at me buying them, likely assuming I'm restocking, rather than purchasing for the first time.

"Things are goin' good with you two?" he asks, leaning against the checkout counter. I'm starting to regret agreeing to hang out today. I'm not exactly interested in casual conversation right now. Not while my stomach is churning and my mind keeps running through my plans for tonight.

"Yeah. Fine."

"Great chat, pal," he says sarcastically, and I return his earlier arm punch with one of my own.

"Listen, I agreed to go to the gym with you. You chose to invite yourself along for my errands, so don't give me shit when I'm distracted, thinking of everything I need to do."

My words come out sharper than I intended, earning the raised eyebrows Yami gives me. Normally, we're pretty well in sync. Pitchers and catchers have to be. The good ones, at least. Rafe and I had it, the magical dynamic that allowed us to read each other like an open book. Yami and I are getting close, but we're not quite there yet.

And thank fuck for that, because if he knew about my internal panic, I'd never hear the end of it.

We finally reach the cashier, and I quickly pay for my groceries, throwing them into a bag that I snatch up before walking swiftly to the exit. Outside, it's freezing and overcast, and I turn up the collar of my coat as we hustle to my truck.

"Jesus, it's colder than Satan's balls out here."

"Does Satan have cold balls? Wouldn't they be hot?"

I huff out a laugh. "Good point."

"Seriously, Monty. What's going on? You're not yourself. Is it Lark? You sure you guys are good?"

The genuine concern in his voice makes me pause. Maybe we're not as far from the magic as I thought.

I lean back against my seat, the truck slowly warming up with the engine running. I consider the guys on the team my friends, hell, my family. But other than Pops, none of them ever knew my secret. It's not exactly something that comes up easily in conversation.

Yeah, I'm a twenty-eight-year-old virgin. Nah, not for some religious reason, just because my entire life has been ruled by baseball, and when I wasn't on the field shagging balls, I was a science geek with zero game.

Nope. Not something I have ever been open about with a group of professional athletes who have enjoyed more than their fair share of cleat chasers.

But Yami, he's different. Sure, I've witnessed him flirt with countless women, even taking a few of them home. But he's never been in a relationship as long as I've known him, and for the most part, he seems like a respectful guy. Maybe he won't give me too much shit.

"Me and Lark. We haven't…" Shit, this is harder than I thought. I swallow. "We, ah, we haven't gone all the way yet."

"What is this, high school? You haven't fucked. Is that what you mean?"

I frown, even as I nod. "Yeah. Fine. We haven't…done that."

"Jesus, Monty, I know you're a grown-ass man who can use the word fuck."

Maybe I was wrong and telling Yami was a mistake. I'm sure as shit not telling him the whole story now. I clench my jaw, staring forward.

"I think it's cool. You care about each other, and you're treating her the way a woman should be treated."

My head turns to stare at him, but he's not done surprising me.

"Casual sex is fine, but when there's feelings involved, waiting till it's right is a good idea. That's all I'm saying. So is tonight the night?"

I nod again. He gives me one in response. "Cool. Let's get going then, so you can manscape."

That makes me snort, then my eyes widen. *Manscape?*

Three hours and two disturbing articles from the internet later, I'm in the world's most awkward position in my bathroom, one leg up on the counter as I peer down at my junk. Thank fuck, I'm flexible. When the hell did manscaping become a thing? I mean, I've always kept it trimmed; no one needs a bush hiding their dick. But this is next-level.

I'm rereading part of the article that talks about waxing your goddamn ass cheeks, *no thanks,* when there's a knock at my door.

"Shit."

How the hell is it eight already? In my surprise, I lose my balance, which is embarrassing for a top-tier catcher. What's even worse is the horrifying realization that I didn't lock the front door, apparent when I hear Lark's voice call out from the front.

"Dan? Are you here?"

I stumble, knocking my hip into the towel rail, hard enough to leave a bruise. "God-fucking-damn it."

I can hear her footsteps, and here I am naked from the waist down with my very limp dick only half-scaped. Is that the term? Who fucking knows. All I know is this is not exactly how I wanted tonight to start.

"Hang on," I holler back, hoping she'll wait for me in the

living room.

No such luck.

"Shoot, I'm sorry!"

I straighten up from grabbing my underwear off the bathroom floor and catch her staring at me in the mirror, her cheeks flaming red.

"Hey, Birdie." I laugh nervously, clutching my boxers in front of myself. Her eyes slowly drag down my body, only to freeze and then widen.

"Dan, when did you get a tattoo?" she whispers, and I frown in confusion for a second before understanding dawns on me. Ah, crap. I guess I forgot she's never seen it. Somehow, the other night when she gave me the blow job that made my world stand still, she didn't notice it. I panic, not sure how to answer. Is she happy about it? Does she know what it means?

"Um, I dunno." Lame, Monty. Real lame.

She looks back up at me and steps in closer, her fingers coming to my hip, resting right over the small tattoo. "Dan. What kind of bird is this?"

Ohshitohshitohshitohshit.

My brain is no longer functioning. I can't possibly think clearly when she's this close to me and I'm half naked with my cock waking up to her proximity.

"Uhhh..."

Her pink tongue darts out and moistens her lips as her gaze drops down again, then back up to my face. Well, fuck. Here we go.

"It's a skylark." My whisper is hoarse, but her mouth slowly turns upward. "I got it two years ago."

"Why then?" she whispers back.

There's no option but to tell her. As Yoda would say, *"Do or do not, there is no try."* And this has to be a *do* moment.

"Because that was when I realized I love you."

Chapter Twenty-Four

Lark

"Dan," I whisper seconds before crashing my lips onto his. I'm overcome with emotion, floating on an endless sea. He's loved me for so long. He carries me with him, every day of his life, and has for years.

And what have I done?

I've allowed myself to believe that doing what I thought was expected of me was the right choice. I believed so little of myself, I was able to overlook this beautiful man and his love.

It would be so simple to spiral into self-flagellation and guilt over how much time I wasted. Time I could have spent with Dan. But now, when those thoughts creep in, it's easier to push them away. To center myself in his kiss, in his arms around me, and in the deep sense of knowing this is exactly how it should be.

Eventually, we break apart, and I remember my curiosity when I found him in the bathroom, bare from the waist down.

"What exactly are you doing?" I don't bother trying to hide the way my gaze travels down his body, landing on that beautiful cock of his that's so hard, it's pointing at me. But something's different. I lean forward slightly, squinting. "Um, Dan, why is your —"

"It's all Yami's fault!" he blurts out, attempting to cover himself with his hands.

"I'm sorry, what?"

Dan groans, his head falling forward. "He was with me when I was grabbing groceries for tonight and you know how he can't shut up. I swear, I didn't tell him anything. And I'm definitely not presuming something's gonna happen, but just in case, he said something about manscaping, and I started googling, and then you showed up, and *fuck*."

I'm openly laughing now, and Dan's cheeks are bright red. I'm starting to understand the bizarre sight I walked in on. My laughter dies as I comprehend more of what he's saying.

"Are you saying you want to..."

His eyes flash with something indescribable, and his head moves in the barest of nods. "I do. With you. I want you, Lark. In every possible way. It doesn't have to be tonight, not if you don't feel ready yet. But when you are, just know, so am I."

How do I tell him I've been ready for this, for him, ever since I realized my feelings went way beyond friendship?

How do I tell him it's been many, many months since I had sex, and my body is already aching for relief?

How do I tell him I feel so incredibly honoured that he wants *me* for his first time?

I register the downturn of Dan's face a second later and realize I've been so caught up in my own feelings, I didn't actually respond to him.

I lean in and press my lips to his jawline, peppering kisses down the column of his throat. Then, knowing I have to be brave and bold, I take his hand and slide it down the front of my leggings.

His fingers brush over my damp panties and his head falls to my shoulder with a groan.

"In case that isn't clear enough, I'm very much ready."

With a deep rumbling sound, Dan lifts me up and throws me over his shoulder, bringing me almost eye level with his bare ass. "Oh my God!" I shriek, closing my eyes and giggling. Wait. Why am I closing my eyes? I open them and take a good look at the round, tight bubble butt on my favourite catcher.

When my hand just so happens to pinch it, Dan yelps, and then I'm tossed down, bouncing on his mattress. "Did you just pinch my ass, Birdie?"

He sounds so outraged, my giggle turns into a full body laugh. Which grows even more when I look at him standing there, his arms folded across his chest, his dick jutting out at me. It's clear he's also barely holding back his laughter, and a second later, it breaks free. He jumps on the bed, making me bounce and shriek again. But this time he muffles the sound with his lips on mine as he lowers his large body between my legs.

My hands wrap around his back and find the hem of his shirt. Tugging, I lift it up. Dan raises his upper body and quickly pulls it the rest of the way off until he's completely nude.

"You look way too damn satisfied for a woman who hasn't even had an orgasm yet."

I can feel my smile grow even wider. "With a view like this, who wouldn't be satisfied?"

He sits back on his heels and pulls me up. "No fair. I wanna be satisfied with my view, too."

I let him strip off my shirt, but when he goes to unclasp my bra, I stop him with a mock frown. "Are you saying the view isn't any good unless I'm naked?"

The look of horror on his face is comical, and I bust out laughing. "Oh my God, I'm joking. I promise, I'm not that insecure!"

Dan recovers quickly, wrapping his arms around me and pulling me into his chest, nuzzling my neck. "Lark, you're the most beautiful woman in the entire goddamn world. You could be wearing a unicorn costume and I'd still find you sexy as hell."

"I think you'd prefer me to wear an Ewok outfit."

He draws back, sees my grin, and narrows his eyes. "Woman, you need to stop mocking me."

"Or?"

"Or..."

I get no other warning before his fingers dig into my side, instantly finding the ticklish spots. "Dan!" I scream, squirming and trying to get away. But he's got me pinned between his strong thighs, and there's no escape. Then he stops, with one hand holding both of mine above my head, and the other wrapped around my rib cage just below my breasts.

"You're so fucking amazing, Lark," he says, his voice hoarse. "If this is a dream, I hope I never wake up."

"It's not a dream," I whisper back. "It's real. And I'm here. Yours."

"Mine."

The rest of my clothes come off in a matter of seconds. And then our naked bodies are slipping against each other as we lose ourselves in a kiss so full of passion and love, it would take my breath away if Dan wasn't already stealing it.

He lifts his head just enough to look down at me, releasing my hands so he can stroke my cheek. There's a vulnerable expression on his face that I ache to ease.

"I don't know if I'll be any good at this, Birdie. There's only so much you can learn from locker room chatter and porn. But I want to be good for you."

I slide my hands up and down his strong back, feeling the ripple of muscles. "You will be."

"Teach me? Teach me what you like, what feels good."

My cheeks burn with a mixture of desire and embarrassment. Proving how in tune he is with me, Dan pulls back.

"What's wrong. What did I say?"

I shake my head and cup his cheek. "It's not you, it's me. I...I don't know if I can teach you, because I don't know if I even know what feels good."

His confused frown is adorable, lightening the mood. "What the hell does that mean?" It doesn't take long before he realizes exactly what I meant. "Hold on a fucking second. Are you telling me Baron didn't..."

My gaze slides to the side, but Dan takes my chin and turns my head so I'm looking at him.

"Did he not know how to make you come?"

I clear my throat. "I mean, he did, like, once or twice, but the rest of the time I either faked it or got myself there with toys after."

His eyes narrow thoughtfully, and then he leans down and kisses my forehead, then the tip of my nose, then finally, my lips.

"I have learned a couple of things from listening to the guys. First, toys can be fun, and I definitely want to play with them with you at some point. But second, and most important is that you come first. No matter what. So I need you to promise me something, Birdie. Never fake it. Not with me. Because your pleasure, your happiness, means more to me than anything else. Certainly more than my own." He pauses, kissing me again, keeping his eyes open and trained on me. Then he grins. "And if it takes a lot of practice to get there, well, Coach always did say I had a good work ethic."

CHAPTER TWENTY-FIVE

Monty

Is cracking jokes and being a wiseass the best idea for foreplay the first time you have sex — or are about to?

Possibly not...

But it is on-brand for me, I guess. Making Lark smile sure as fuck is an aphrodisiac for me. Underneath the jokes, however, I'm scared shitless. I want this to go well, and I certainly don't want to hurt her. I know, it's not her first time, only mine. But still.

I just keep reminding myself, I trust her with my life. So I can trust her with this.

Shifting so I'm lying beside her, propped up on one arm, I keep my gaze trained on hers as my fingers slowly start to trail lightly over her body. I come to rest my hand between her breasts and lean in to kiss her slow and sweet. Truthfully? Even if nothing else happened tonight, a part of me would be in fucking heaven just being here with her.

But a bigger part of me wants to feel this woman's body clench around my dick.

Which is why I'll do slow and sweet now. Because I know as

soon as I get inside of her, it's game on, and game over, probably in less time than it takes me to round the bases.

I move my lips down the smooth column of her throat, along her collar bone, and down farther. My hand precedes my mouth, grazing the soft swell of her stomach and over her hips. I can feel her move restlessly under me, seeking more touch, more pressure, just *more*.

I'll give it to her. But I want to explore first.

My mouth covers one of her breasts, sucking gently until her nipple is a stiff peak under my tongue.

"Oh my God," Lark moans, her fingers raking through my hair. Her back arches into my touch and I move to the other side, lavishing attention on that breast. I take my time, licking, sucking, even biting down gently, listening to her cues to see what drives her wild.

"I can't decide which one I like best," I say, popping off and cupping them both in my hands.

Lark sputters, and I glance up to see her looking at me with a wild expression. I nod to her tits. "Left one feels rounder, but the right gets so stiff in my mouth. And they both cause you to make the most delicious sounds."

She whimpers as I squeeze them, and I give her a wolfish smile. "I guess I don't have to choose favourites. I can take my time and enjoy them both."

"Don't take too long," she says, and I'm guessing she meant it to sound sultry but the thread of need in her voice makes me feel like a goddamn king. I'm the one driving her crazy with lust. Me. The oldest virgin in the entire goddamn league is making Lark Miller come undone with nothing but my hand and my mouth on her tits.

Fuckin' right.

I suck a nipple into my mouth once more, just because I can. Then I move my way down. I don't know what to expect, I've never done this before. But I damn well want to.

Lark spreads her legs, giving me space. I kiss my way down one thigh. Do all women taste this good? Like, her skin is somehow sweet. Jesus, it's addicting.

She's addicting.

My hand runs all the way down to her ankle, and I lift it up to drape over my shoulder, pressing one final kiss to the inside of her knee. Then I do the same on the other side, all while listening to Lark's soft sighs and hums of pleasure.

Thanks, porn, for the inspiration.

But no video, no locker room chatter, *nothing* could have prepared me for the way I'm stunned speechless by the pink folds of Lark's pussy staring me in the face. I didn't know what the guys meant when they said a pussy could be beautiful until now. Like, weirdly mysterious, totally delectable, and holy shit, *I want it.*

Looking up the expanse of her body, I see Lark's head lifted from the pillow, staring down at me. I don't want to fuck this up. I *really* don't want to fuck this up.

"I want to be good for you, Lark. Teach me."

She swallows, and it kills me, waiting for her to say something. Then she says, "I'll try."

Maintaining eye contact right now starts to feel like too much pressure, so I close my eyes and lean down, aiming to press a kiss to her clit.

I miss.

"Shit. Hang on," I mutter, opening my eyes.

Lark slides her fingers down, making a vee on either side of her pussy. "Right there," she murmurs.

I'm not going to ignore the instruction, not when I'm well aware of my shortcomings in this situation. This time when I lean down, I keep my eyes open and kiss the peak framed by her fingers.

"Dan," she whispers. And mentally, I cheer. Target acquired.

I do it again, this time, snaking my tongue out to lap at her softly. She hums, a soft, contented sound, so I stay there, licking her pussy, exploring it with my tongue. She tastes just as good as when I licked her off my fingers. Speaking of which...

I pull her hand off, kissing her fingers before placing them on her stomach. "I got this now, Birdie." I smirk, then move one hand between us and stroke her entrance before slowly sliding a finger inside her heat.

She answers with a moan, and I can't hold back my reaction.

"Jesus, Lark," I groan when I instantly feel her muscles tighten around me. My eyes are open now, because I don't want to miss a second of this. I watch, fascinated, as my finger moves in and out, glistening with her arousal.

"More," Lark whimpers, her hand gripping my shoulder. I add a second finger, watching her stretch around me. God, that's gonna feel good on my cock. I rotate my fingers, exploring her body for several minutes, just listening to the little sounds she makes.

"Curl them over," she gasps. "Oh my God, Dan!"

No way. Is she? I stare up at her face, entranced as her head goes back. Her eyes are closed and she's quietly keening as I do exactly as she asked, curling my fingers one at a time and pressing against a soft, fleshy part of her pussy.

Yeah, she's definitely coming. Her hold on my shoulders borderlines on painful, but I don't give a fuck as Lark starts to moan my name, and I feel her squeeze my fingers like a vice. There's a rush of warmth and moisture, and I bend over and lap at it, licking around my fingers, not stopping until her hips sag onto the bed.

Her arm drapes over her face as I slowly withdraw my fingers. But I see her peeking out from underneath as I slowly suck off each one.

"That was fun, Birdie," I say with a smirk. "We're doing that again."

She lets out a breathless laugh and reaches for my arms with grabby hands. "I won't say no to that. You're sure you've never done that? I've never come that quickly."

I let her pull me over top of her, and when I'm level with her face, I push back some sweaty strands of hair. My smirk falls, and my voice turns serious. "Remember the whole virgin thing? Seriously, though, was that okay? Like, honestly?"

Lark blinks up at me with a sweet smile. "If that was any more *okay*, you'd be peeling me off the ceiling. That was amazing. Ten stars. Would recommend."

I snort, dropping my face into her shoulder. But inside? Inside, I'm strutting like a goddamn peacock.

"I know we've talked about it a little bit, but I still don't understand. How? How have you never been with anyone?"

I roll onto my side, keeping one arm and leg draped over her.

"Honestly, it was a combination of things. Baseball was my life, and when I realized I had a shot at making a career of it, I knew I would have to sacrifice a lot of other stuff." I let out a small laugh. "Granted, I never *planned* on sacrificing my social life. But I also wasn't about to throw away my future if it didn't feel right, and no one ever felt right."

"No one? Not a girl in high school you wanted to take to prom or anything?"

I guess I don't do a good job of hiding my wince, because Lark points at me, leaning back slightly. "Ah-ha! There was someone."

"Cool your jets, Detective Miller. Yeah, there was one girl I sort of liked. But you gotta remember, not only was I fully focused on baseball, but I was also a major nerd. In the very little spare time I had, I was obsessed with space, NASA, all that shit. Not exactly cool guy material. When I asked Jessica to prom, she laughed in my face."

Lark snuggles in close, pressing a kiss to my sternum. "Nerds are hot, Dan. I wouldn't have laughed if you'd asked me. She was an idiot."

I smile. "Thanks, Birdie."

Her hand comes up and pushes on my chest. I roll over willingly but keep hold of her, so she's straddling me.

"We've got two options," she says, her tone almost conversational now. I quirk a smile, lacing my fingers together behind my head. Her body is still flushed, and I'm still feeling damn good about myself.

"Yes."

Lark laughs. "You haven't heard the options!"

"Doesn't matter, the answer is still yes."

She slaps my chest and rolls her eyes. I cover her hands with mine and lift them to my mouth for a kiss. "Sorry, Birdie. What are my options?" I try to sound contrite, but I'm too damn happy.

Her smile tells me she is, too. And that's honestly all that matters.

"Well," she starts, pulling her hands free so she can plant them beside my head. Her hips roll against mine, reminding me there's so much more to come. "I could repay you for that excellent orgasm you just gave me by sucking your cock into my mouth until you explode on my tongue."

"Oh fuck," I whisper, grabbing her ass and holding her still. I'm pretty sure my dick is starting to leak just listening to her.

"Or we could take things further." She bites her lower lip, and I surge upward, covering her mouth with mine and teasing her lip free with my tongue.

"I was right," I mumble against her mouth. "The answer is yes."

She giggles as I stretch to the side, fumbling to open the bedside drawer where I stashed the brand-new box of condoms. Grabbing the strip, I move back underneath her and brandish it.

"But for now, I choose option two."

Chapter Twenty-Six

Monty

My heart is thundering in my chest as Lark sits up and takes the strip of condoms from me. She tears one off and looks down at me.

"May I do the honours?"

I nod rapidly. She opens it and takes my cock in her hand, sliding up and down my length a few times. It's not necessary, I've been rock-hard ever since she walked in on me in the bathroom. But it feels good, so I'm sure as shit not stopping her.

Once the rubber is rolled over my dick, she pauses. But with her hand wrapped around me, my brain is a scrambled mess.

"Dan, are you sure?"

I must resemble a fish with how my mouth flaps open and shut. Is she serious? It's sweet she's checking in, I guess, but good God, woman.

"Birdie, if you don't put my dick in your sweet pussy immediately, I'm gonna embarrass myself and start begging. Please, don't make a grown man beg."

Her only response is to lift her hips, and holding my dick, she lines herself up. Then, achingly slow, she slides down me.

"Holy fucking shit," I groan, gripping her hips tightly. The sensation overload washes over me like a goddamn tidal wave. This is so much better than my hand, even better than Lark's mouth. Why the fucking hell did I wait so long to do this?

Oh yeah. Because I was waiting for her, even when I didn't know I was.

When I crack my eyes open again, Lark's looking down at me, awestruck. "You...I...Ohmygod," she sighs.

"Ditto," is all I manage to get out because now, she's moving, slowly rocking her hips back and forth. All I'm doing is lying here like a useless idiot. Get control man, figure out how to use your fucking body again. This feels good, but I'm willing to bet I can figure out how to make it feel even better.

Pep talk to myself over, I begin to thrust up. It takes a few minutes to figure out the rhythm, but then we're moving together. Lark's hands land on my chest, her hair falling around her face as she starts to breathe heavily.

Yeah, this is good. *Holy shit* good. I draw my feet up and push up even faster, and Lark almost topples off. "Oops."

She just giggles, thank fuck, and we readjust.

"Maybe not quite that enthusiastic?" Lark teases, dragging her fingers over my nipples. "Slow is fine to start with, you know."

I nod eagerly and focus again on matching her pace. Her smile is all the encouragement I need. Then she does something with her hips, rotating them somehow.

"Good God," I groan, my mouth falling open. Oh shit, this is gonna get embarrassing. "Stopstopstop."

Lark freezes, and I focus on my breathing, trying to regain

some control.

"Are you okay?" she asks softly, and I can hear the worry in her voice. Opening my eyes, I force out a nod.

"Yeah," I croak. "Just trying not to be a two-pump chump."

Her laugh has me smiling in response. "It's fine, Dan. Our first time doesn't have to be perfect. Remember what you said about practice?" She gives another swivel of her hips and I groan.

"You're killing me, woman."

"They do call it *la petite mort*."

"I'll die a happy man."

Her lips land on mine, and we start to move in tandem again. "I'd rather you didn't die. I'm nowhere near done with you, Dan Montgomery."

Something in her voice wraps around my heart, holding it tight. And just like that, things start to move quickly again. Lark rocks up and down on my dick, and I'm content to let her lead — this time, at least.

Within a minute or two, I have to start listing off all the teams in the major leagues, trying to distract myself. Because the orgasm I can feel building? Is gonna be intense. And I'll be damned if I let it happen too soon.

But this feels fucking incredible. I was already obsessed with Lark, but now? Being with her like this, as close as two people can get? Jesus, I don't ever want to stop.

"So good," she whines, and I reach one hand up to cup the back of her neck, needing to kiss her.

"You feel like heaven, Birdie. I had no idea," I growl against her lips, kissing her messily. "Fuck."

"Don't stop," Lark pants, her hips starting to move faster. "Oh God, my clit. I need..."

Some primal instinct kicks in, and my hand immediately reaches between us, my thumb finding her clit. I don't know how I know what she needs, but I do. And seconds after, I start to circle around the hood of her pussy, her short nails dig into my chest, and she flings her head back.

"Yes, yes, yes!"

When I feel her pussy gripping me like a fucking vice, all bets are off on trying to control my own release. My thrusts are erratic and wild, probably uncoordinated as fuck. And all of a sudden, the sensations change, becoming way more intense. My dick is surrounded by warmth, and I swear to God, I can feel her pulsating around me. The noises coming out of me sound animalistic, and all too soon, I feel myself emptying into the condom.

"Fucking hell," I breathe when I'm finally done. Lark is draped over my chest, and I can feel her heart racing with mine. I'm starting to soften inside of her, but I'll be damned if I want to move.

Unfortunately, Lark does that for me. "Hold the condom?" she instructs, and I grip my base as she slowly lifts off me.

She stills, looking down at my dick. I lift my head to see what she's staring at. "What?"

"Um. Well, the condom. It broke."

"Oh."

"Hold on." She doesn't look at me, climbing off the bed and disappearing into the bathroom. A minute later, she returns with a small towel. After she hands it to me, I wrap it around the base of my cock and pull off the condom. It's a lot messier than I expected, but I guess that's what happens when it breaks. I wrap it in a ball and drop it to the floor.

My mind is racing, trying to figure out what to say. It's clear Lark's nervous about this, and I need to reassure her somehow.

"I guess I don't need to tell you, I've got a clean bill of health." I say, trying to make light of it. A tiny flash of a smile crosses her face but it's gone too soon.

"Lark, I'm sorry."

That seems to break whatever spell she was under, and she reaches a hand out to rest it on my arm. "No, don't apologize. I'm sorry I freaked out for a minute there." She manages to muster a smile, but it doesn't reach her eyes. "It's fine, really. I'm on the pill, so you know, we'll be okay."

Her nervous laugh doesn't convince me that she's truly fine. But I'm at a loss for what else to say. I wish I could go back in time and recapture the fucking *magic* from a few minutes ago.

"We'll be okay no matter what, Birdie. It's me and you."

Her shoulders sag at last, the tension receding. I take the chance and reach for her, pulling her to lie back down in my arms. Thank fuck, she comes easily, nestling back in to snuggle.

"That's better," I say, nuzzling into her hair.

Her arms squeeze tight around me for a second before relaxing. "Sorry I ruined your first time with my panic."

My hand finds her ass, or at least the side of it, and I smack lightly. "Stop apologizing. You didn't ruin anything. That was a goddamn experience. I'm talking angels singing from on high, fireworks exploding, World Series championship, top-ten moments of all-time, experience."

This time, her giggle sounds more like my Lark. "Top ten, huh? What needs to improve to make it into the top five?"

"For starters, me not bucking you off."

An adorable snort escapes her, and now we're both laughing.

"Rookie mistake," she says, her lips finding my jawline. "You'll do better next time."

"Practice makes perfect," I say conversationally, not bothering to hold back my grin.

"Hmm. So it does," she replies, and I can tell she's smiling, too.

"And I do pride myself on being the very best I can be."

"That work ethic of yours."

"Exactly."

"So."

"So." I move suddenly, rolling on top of her, pinning her between my arms, and letting my already-starting-to-stiffen dick settle between her legs. "Clearly, I need to continue my lessons."

"Lessons?" Lark snort-laughs again, clapping her hand over her mouth. I peel it away and kiss her lips.

"Yeah. Sex ed." I rock my hips against her. "I want an A plus."

She gasps softly as my dick rubs against her clit. "You're a good student, Dan. But maybe some study sessions would help." Her hand moves blindly to the side, patting the mattress for the other condom packets. I reach over and grab them, settling back on my heels.

I might not have had sex until tonight, but I do know how to put on a condom. As soon as it's rolled over me for a second time, I move back over top of her. And gripping the base of my dick, I slide right back into her fucking incredible pussy.

"Class is officially back in session."

CHAPTER TWENTY-SEVEN

Lark

Blinking my eyes open slowly, I become aware of the heavy weight of Dan's arm over my waist, his hand cupped lovingly over my breast. I can feel his breath, slow and even against my neck, and the solid point of his cock nudging against me between my legs.

The man is insatiable. After the fumbles of our first time, he rallied impressively, bringing me no less than five orgasms.

How he got so talented with his tongue with zero experience, I do *not* know. Maybe he's just a quick learner, or maybe he takes direction well, or maybe Dan Montgomery is simply the perfect man for me.

Whatever it is, I don't think I've ever felt this happy, this satisfied, or this deliciously sore in all the right places.

I shift slowly, trying not to wake him. At least one of us should get some sleep after how busy we were last night.

Last night...when I was supposed to marry Baron but spent it in bed with Dan instead. Today being New Year's Day feels especially poignant. It's the start of a new day, a new year, and a new life for me. Guess Michael Bublé was right. Because I am definitely *feeling good*.

"Mmm. Why are you awake?" Dan grumbles into my hair, and I feel him nuzzle in closer. He's so affectionate, and I freaking love how he can't seem to get enough of touching me, always wanting to be as close as possible.

Maybe other people would feel smothered, but not me. After a lifetime of chasing affection and constantly being denied, I'm loving every second of it.

"Well, it's kind of hard to sleep when I'm being poked in the behind," I tease, pushing my butt back slightly, nudging him.

Of course, all Dan does is squeeze my breast before moving that hand down to my hip and thrusting against me a few times.

"Not my fault. I can't control what my body does when I'm asleep."

"Uh-huh, sure. That's a great argument." I roll over to face him. "For the record, I'm not complaining. Waking up in your arms is no hardship."

His sleepy smile is just too freaking cute.

"But I need coffee." To punctuate my statement, I yawn, covering my mouth and turning my head to save him from morning breath.

"I got it." With a surprising display of energy for a man who was just asleep, Dan throws off the blankets and hops out of bed. I watch him unabashedly as he struts bare-ass naked into the bathroom. He emerges a few minutes later, still naked, only to swipe up his boxers from the floor, this pair covered in Santa hats.

"Christmas is over, you know," I call out as he walks from the room, unable to resist another tease.

He doesn't respond, at least not verbally. But as I'm sitting up, the Santa hat boxers come flying through the doorway, and I burst out laughing.

I go to his closet and pull down an old Tridents T-shirt that looks soft and well-loved. Pulling it over my head, it barely covers my ass, but I was right. It smells like him and is extremely soft. Padding out of the bedroom, I find Dan in the kitchen, once again naked.

This time, he's shaking his ass and humming under his breath, something that sounds like "Jingle Bell Rock" but not quite in tune.

I walk up behind him and grab both of his butt cheeks in my hands, squeezing them.

"Hands off woman, or no coffee for you," he admonishes, pushing me away.

I back off, laughing. "Hey, you can't parade that naked baseball booty around and not expect me to grab it. That's just mean."

He looks over his shoulder at me with a wicked smirk. "I knew you liked my ass."

"Of course, I do. Have you *seen* your ass?"

He pretends to dust off his shoulders. "I mean, I do spend a lot of time squatting."

Turning back to the coffee machine, he pours two mugs before turning and setting them on the counter next to me. Completely nonchalant, as if his nudity is perfectly normal, he moves to the fridge and pulls out two creamers. One vanilla for me, and one...

"Is that sugar cookie creamer?" I ask, partly fascinated and partly disgusted.

Dan pours a liberal amount into his mug and nods. "Hell, yeah. Yami convinced me to try it, and it's delicious." He passes it to me, and I take a tentative sip.

My eyes widen. "Woah." He holds out his hand for his coffee, but I turn and pull it into my chest. "No. Mine."

He just chuckles and gives me a wink as he doctors up the other cup the same way before putting both creamers away.

I take another sip of the sweetened coffee and close my eyes with a contented hum. "That's so good."

"I'll stock up for us before they stop selling it."

Us.

We're an *us.* I love that.

My eyes flutter open to see him staring at me so intently, his eyes so full of love, I'm not sure how I missed it for so long.

"God, you're so beautiful. I've dreamed of this. Of mornings spent with you wearing my clothes, drinking my coffee. It's perfect."

I set my mug down and step forward, sliding my hands up and around his neck. He meets me half way for a kiss, and I can taste the coffee creamer on him. I hear him set his cup down as well, and then his hands are on my ass and I'm lifted in the air. He starts to walk away, and I make a sound of protest.

"No, my coffee!"

Dan shakes his head, his stare intense, almost feral with desire. "Coffee later. I need to fuck you right now while you're wearing my shirt."

Well. Okay, then.

We spend the day being lazy. But when evening approaches and I start to feel antsy, I drag Dan out of his apartment for a walk. It gets cut short once we realize how many people are out for possibly the same reason.

After barely half an hour, we turn around and head swiftly back to his building.

"That was too people-y," he says, leaning back against the elevator wall dramatically. "I don't want to deal with people today."

I giggle. "Aren't I people? Are you saying you don't want to deal with me?"

"Oh, I'll deal with you. Don't you worry." He gives me a smirk.

I respond by stepping in close and sliding my cold hands under his sweater. He gasps in shock. "Damn it woman, warn a guy, would ya?"

"Nah, this is more fun."

He groans but covers my hands with his over the top of his sweater. "You're lucky I love you, Birdie."

He might be meaning it in a teasing way right now, but those words make me melt. "Yeah, I am."

His smile softens into something sweeter, and he presses a gentle kiss to my lips. The elevator opens and we step out. I slide my hands from under his sweater and lace our fingers together instead. We walk in silence to his apartment, and Dan holds the door open for me.

"So. Bubble bath, then dinner?"

"Sounds lovely." I smile, hanging our coats up. "But after dinner, I want you to show me your telescope."

He lifts his hand, squeezing the back of his neck. "You really want to?"

I nod. "I can't believe you haven't told me about it before last night." His fascination with space was something I knew, but the fact that he has a telescope? I didn't know until now. And I'm ridiculously excited to view what he sees when he looks into the night sky.

"We'll have to drive a bit to get away from the city lights."

"Then let's skip the bath and eat quickly. I want to see the stars."

"Oh, I'll show you stars," he mockingly growls, dropping his hand and strutting over to me. "All the stars, baby."

I burst out laughing. "Oh God, no. You are definitely not cut out for slimy flirting. Please, just stop."

"I thought that was a good line." He pouts, but it quickly turns into a grin.

I pat his arm, shaking my head. "Not even a little."

"Fine." He huffs, turning to open the fridge. "Okay, dinner options. We've got leftover Thai from last night, or I can whip up some chicken and pasta."

"Leftovers are fine."

We move around each other in an easy silence, getting down plates, reheating food, and eating as if we've shared a thousand meals before. And I suppose, in a way, we have. When we were just friends we would eat together. But it's so much more now. *We* are so much more.

And later, when we reach the lookout high up on one of the

local mountains, Dan cements his place in my heart.

"What am I looking at?" I ask, peering through the eyepiece of the telescope. He spent forever getting it lined up on something in particular but wouldn't tell me what it was.

He clears his throat, and I glance up at him. "That's, ah, that's my star."

"What do you mean, your star?" I ask. He looks up at the sky, then back at me, a soft smile on his face.

"You can buy and name your own star. I bought that one two years ago."

"What did you name it?"

His eyes move down to the ground, and he shifts from side to side as if he's nervous.

"Um."

I tilt my head to the side. "Dan?"

"I named it Birdie." He says it so quietly, at first, I think I heard wrong. Then he lifts his head, and I see the truth shining in his eyes.

"Birdie, because I bought it for you."

Chapter Twenty-Eight

Monty

"I swear to God, Dan Montgomery, if you throw that snowball, you're not getting sex for a week!"

"It's cute you think that you sound threatening, Birdie. We both know you wouldn't last a day without needing some double D." I throw in a wink for good measure and continue to smooth the snow I'm holding into a ball.

"Double D? Are you serious?"

"Dan's Dick. It's got a nice ring to it, doesn't it?" I cock my head to the side and move my arm back into a throwing position. "Now, hold still so I don't miss."

She shrieks as I let the snow fly, but I purposefully aim for the ground in front of her. I burst out laughing as she glares at me, then... "Oh shit."

I duck into the trees as a snowball is fired my way but goes wild. "We gotta work on your arm, babe," I call out, gathering up more snow. I peek around the tree, only to get hit in the face with cold, wet snow. "Damn it."

Lark's laughter is a lot closer than I anticipated. "How the hell did you sneak up on me, woman?"

"Revenge is sweet," she answers, reaching up to brush snow off my chest. "Truce? I'm cold."

Nodding, I return the favour, dusting snow off her toque. "Truce. Want to head back and warm up?"

When Lark suggested we head up one of the local mountains to go snowshoeing, it was an immediate yes. The best part of living in Vancouver is the proximity to activities like this. My mind has already jumped ahead to next fall, when we can come back and hike this mountain.

After the Tridents win the championship, of course.

It's called manifesting.

We turn and make our way back along the snowshoe trail that leads to the ski lodge. It's nice and quiet on the mountain today, with most people already back to work and not out enjoying the winter weather. For most of the trek, the trail is wide enough for us to walk side by side, and I love holding Lark's hand, even through winter gloves. This shit never gets old. Having her with me, free to be affectionate, not needing to hide my feelings. It's almost — *almost* — better than sex.

Nah, who am I kidding? It's nowhere close. Sex with Lark is fucking life-changing. Earth shattering. Best. Feeling. Ever.

The first few days after popping my cherry, we were insatiable. Thankfully, Lark's desire was just as intense as mine, or I might have felt a little guilty for how often I wanted her. Then again, I made damn sure she got off every fucking time, so maybe the guilt is misplaced.

Even now, over two weeks later, I can't stop wanting her. But moments like this, when we can just *be*, help ease the ache.

We reach the lodge, and I bend down to help unstrap her

snowshoes. Glancing up from my crouch, I catch her staring back at me, love shining from her eyes.

"You're a goner for me, Lark Miller." I wink, loving the way she blushes.

"Pointing out the obvious isn't all that charming, you know."

I stand up, her snowshoes in hand, and arch my brow. "Excuse you, I'm exceedingly charming."

All that gets me is an eye roll. "When you're not making obnoxious jokes about your double D, maybe." She's fighting back a smile.

Leaning in, I kiss her nose, which is red and icy cold under my lips. "Good thing you love me anyway."

Her arms are around me in an instant, pulling me tight. "I do, I really do."

We stay there, right in front of the ski lodge, for a minute or two. Until the cold air seeps in, making us all the more freezing now that we aren't moving.

Reluctantly, I pull back and drape my arm over her shoulders to steer her toward the door. "Come on, Birdie. Let me buy you a fancy hot chocolate."

The interior of the lodge is impressive, with vaulted ceilings, lots of windows, and plenty of comfortable seating. We find a couch near a large fireplace, surrounded by rocks that go all the way to the top of the building. There's a nice fire crackling away, giving off some welcome heat.

We discard our coats, and I gesture to the nearby café. "I'll be right back with drinks." Lark nods and sits down, removing her boots so she can tuck her feet underneath.

While I wait at the counter, I can't stop looking back at her.

She's so damn pretty, but it's more than that. She's had my heart for years, without even knowing it.

The guys all gave me shit when I got my tattoo, but I didn't care. Because somewhere along the way, Lark became more than just the woman who stole my heart. She became my best friend.

The barista sets the hot chocolates down on the counter, and I take them with a smile after dropping a bill in the tip jar. Picking up the two mugs, I turn and find Lark looking at me.

Closing the distance between us quickly, I bend down and meet her upturned lips with a kiss. "Good, you're not an icicle anymore." I sit down and hand her one of the mugs. "I asked for extra marshmallows."

Lark lets out a happy hum and inhales the sweet aroma coming from the mug. "Perfect."

Draping one of my arms along the back of the couch, I toy with the end of Lark's blond hair, tied back in a braid. "Do you know how to ski?" I ask as I watch a couple walk in with ski helmets under their arms.

She shakes her head. "No, I always wanted to learn, but it wasn't an approved activity in my house."

"That's some bullshit." I snort. "What was considered appropriate for the Miller family?"

Lark looks up at the ceiling and shifts closer to me. "Ballet, which I hated. Swimming, which was okay, but not my favourite. I begged my parents to let me try gymnastics, did that for a couple of years, but I wasn't very good. It was one of my nannies that helped convince Mom and Dad to let me try out for a soccer team, and that's where I found my passion."

I lean forward, fascinated. "How did I not know you played

soccer?"

She shrugs, looking down at her hot chocolate, now empty. "I don't talk about it a lot. But yeah, I played all the way through high school. Even got scouted by a university down in California, but Mom and Dad said no."

I scoff. "Seriously?"

"It wouldn't have mattered anyway. I blew out my knee in a spring training camp my senior year. That ended my soccer career pretty quick."

"Damn, Birdie. I'm sorry." I pull her into my chest, pressing a kiss to the top of her head. "That's shitty."

She nods, and I hear her sniff. "Yeah, it was. But my high school coach is the one who convinced me to get my kinesiology degree, so I guess it wasn't a complete loss. After all, if I had kept playing soccer, I might not be here."

My arms tighten around her. "In that case, is it bad for me to say I'm glad you injured your knee?"

Her laugh reassures me the conversation hasn't been a total downer.

"Nah, it's okay. You can say that."

"So how did your parents handle the end of your soccer stardom?"

"They couldn't have cared less."

I push back, tilting her chin up so I can look her in the eye. "Excuse me, what?"

Lark's cheeks darken, and I hate the idea she might be embarrassed, but I have to know what she means.

"I think they only ever came to maybe two or three games. The championships, mostly. They didn't have the time, and heaven forbid if it was raining." Sarcasm drips from her voice.

"That is complete bullshit." I'm outraged on her behalf. "I'm sorry, Birdie. I would have come to every single fucking game and cheered you on so loud."

Her smile doesn't quite reach her eyes, but it's a start. "I know you would have. You'll be a great dad someday."

Dad.

That's something I rarely think about. Having kids someday. Kind of hard to do when you aren't having sex, after all.

But now? The idea of having a family with Lark one day doesn't freak me out. Quite the opposite.

"Our kids would be badasses. They'd dominate the sports field." The words fall out of my mouth before I can think about how it might sound to say *our kids.*

"Oh really?" Lark laughs. "And what if they don't like sports? What if they'd rather read or draw."

"That's totally cool, too," I reply, warming up to the conversation. I can see little blond girls racing around and brown-haired boys hugging their mom as tightly as I do. "I don't care what my future kids want to do with their lives as long as they're happy."

"Same," she says with a happy sigh. "Do you want a lot of kids?"

"Honestly? I've never thought about it. But yeah, I think a big family would be cool. Just not until I'm done playing ball," I say firmly.

"Why's that?" Lark asks, without a hint of judgment.

I pause, considering my answer.

"Reality is, as a catcher, I have maybe five or six more years before my knees start to give me trouble. And if I want to be an involved dad who can run around with his kids and do fun stuff with them, I don't want to be a cripple from more than a decade of catching in the big leagues. Plus, if I wait till I'm retired, I'll have time. And I won't be gone half the year. My mom and dad were always there for me, and I want to give the same to my kids."

I sense her move her head, and when I glance down, she's looking back up at me.

"That's incredibly thoughtful for something you haven't considered before."

I give her a bashful grin. "Well, if I'm lucky enough to have kids with a woman I love, I want to do it right."

Lark stretches up and kisses my chin. "She'd be a lucky woman."

I adjust and kiss her lips. "Yeah? Know anyone who might want the job?"

She giggles against my lips. "Maybe. Ask me in five years when you retire."

I grin at the thought of Lark and I still together in five years. "Deal."

Chapter Twenty-Nine

Monty

"Didn't your mama teach you that your face is gonna get stuck like that if you keep smilin' so hard?"

I turn to see Darling jogging up to me in the parking lot and shrug. "Life's good, man, gotta smile."

He drapes his arm over my shoulder and we head into the indoor sports facility where Grayson's baseball league runs some winter clinics. During our last afternoon together, the kid turned on the most epic set of puppy dog eyes and practically begged me to see if I could get a couple of the guys together to attend one of the workshop days.

Listen, I'm a sucker for puppy dog eyes. Been known to use them a time or two myself. They're a powerful weapon.

Luckily, Darling and Yami were both free this afternoon and happy to help out.

When we get inside, Yami's already there, chatting with a couple of the coaches who are staring at him with stars in their eyes. It's still weird to me, the fact that people see us as celebrities.

We're just dudes who like to play ball and happen to get paid a boatload of money to do so.

With Darling's and my arrival, the excitement ratchets up even higher. I spot Grayson standing with some other boys, and the second he sees me, a goofy grin crosses his face. I give him a head nod, letting him decide how to play it. Sometimes he's fine with kids knowing I'm his Big Brother, sometimes he isn't.

"Hey, Monty! You're here. Cool. Think Yami will help me with my slider? Oh, and Marcus wants to be our catcher next season, so maybe you could help him out?"

"Dude, slow down. We'll do whatever your coaches want us to, okay?" I hold back my chuckle at his eager greeting. His face falls, but only slightly, before brightening again.

"Sure. Cool. Hey, did you see we got new team bats?"

Yeah, I saw, because I donated them... But I don't tell him that. Instead, I let him lead me over and pretend to be super impressed by the bats.

Eventually, the coaches call everyone over, introduce us — which really isn't necessary with this crowd — and we split into groups. Yami and I are paired up, of course, and that's when the fun begins.

"You better call some good pitches today or I'm throwing nothing but knuckleballs," Yami calls out as he walks to the middle of the space we've taken over. The kids all titter with laughter as I tilt my mask up and glare at my pitcher.

"Listen, buddy, it's not my fault you can't see far enough to catch my signals. Better get your eyes checked before spring training."

Yami grins. I drop my mask and crouch down, smacking my glove with a fist.

"Okay, boys. Let's start things off nice and easy." He holds up the ball, demonstrating his finger placement. "When you want to throw a slider, it's important you remember three things: two seam grip, pressure from the middle finger, and karate chop."

He lets the ball fly and it lands straight in my glove.

"But sometimes, you plan a slider, and it turns into a curve. Which, if your catcher isn't ready, can be a disaster." He leans back and throws, and fucking hell, I'm not ready. But I still make the catch.

"Thought we agreed you'd leave the bad pitches at home," I call out as I throw the ball back to him.

"I did, but they missed me. Guess they followed me here."

Our banter has the kids laughing, but also paying close attention. I see Grayson's gaze locked on Yami, his intense focus mixing with open admiration.

After showing them a few more pitches, Yami and I split up and each take half of our group to work on specific skills. I love working with kids, they're so eager to learn, and goofy with their enthusiasm. Pretty soon, I've got them practicing their pop-ups from a squat position to throw position, seeing who can go the fastest. Then we pull out some irregular-shaped balls that bounce all over the place so they can practice catching unpredictable throws.

The two-hour clinic is over way too soon. Even after lingering for another half hour signing hats, shirts, and taking photographs, it's clear none of us want to leave. It's been too much fun.

But Lark's waiting for me at home and fuck, do I ever want to get back to her.

I walk Grayson out to his mom's car, and he surprises me by wrapping his arms around me for a hug, even with some of his teammates still walking by.

"Thanks, Monty," he mumbles into my shirt. I can see his mom smiling at us from inside her car as I hug him back.

"Hey, anytime, buddy. You know that. If I'm available, I love helping out."

He looks up at me, nervous hope written all over his face. "Do you think I might make it to the major leagues someday?"

Oh, my little dude. His question wrenches at my heart. Surprisingly, it's the first time he's ever asked. And I don't know what to say. So I fall back on what my Little League coach said to me when I was a little bit older than Grayson.

"I think if you keep focused and try your hardest to always improve your game, physically and mentally, you can do anything. But I also think it's important to have something else in your life that you love, not just baseball. Because sometimes, no matter how hard you work, it just isn't meant to be. And that's okay, too."

"You had your space stuff, right? You were gonna go work for NASA?"

I chuckle, remembering how naive I was as a teenager, thinking it would be that simple. To simply want to work for NASA. "Yeah, I had my space stuff."

He nods slowly. "Cool. I like biology, learning about the inside of our bodies and stuff. It's gross, but cool."

"Totally gross but totally cool," I agree. "And a great thing to continue learning about. It'll help your game, too, if you understand muscles and bones and how our bodies work."

"'Kay. I gotta go. See you next week?"

I lift my hand up and he slaps it with his. "You bet. Bye, Gray."

A few minutes later, I'm driving home, drumming my hands on the steering wheel in time to the music pumping through my speakers. But just as it gets to the good part, the song is interrupted with an incoming call from Rocky.

"Monty, my man. How's it goin'?" His voice booms out, and I wince, turning down the volume.

"Can't complain," I say cheerfully. "What's up?"

"Listen. You should know there's some chatter in a few gossip rags about you and the trainer. Nothing bad, just speculation about the two of you, how it'll affect your game. You know not to read anything into it, but I gotta do my job and check in. This thing with her. It's serious?"

I clench the steering wheel and my jaw, my previous good mood evaporating just like that. Fuck. I don't know how I didn't anticipate this. Of course, somehow, the media would find out about me and Lark and put a shitty spin on it. Just because I've never had any negative issues with the press before doesn't mean I'm immune to it.

"What are they saying, Rocky?" I grind out.

"Nothing that matters," he says, and I know he's trying to calm me down. "Seriously. I'd tell you if I thought it was something we had to address, but it isn't and we don't. But in all the years we've been working together, you've never once been seen with a woman." There's a pause. "Honestly? Not that it matters, but I was kind of thinking you weren't into women. Which is sorta something I should know as your agent, but also, at the same time, is none of my — or the world's — goddamn business. But I digress. You and this woman."

"Lark. Her name is Lark," I interject, still holding the steering wheel in a death grip. "And yes, it's serious."

Rocky's silent for a second. "Okay, noted. All I'm gonna say is, remember your goals. Unless you're really fucking good at keeping secrets, this is the first relationship you've juggled along with playing in the big leagues. The pressure of managing both can be a lot. And the last thing I want is for you to lose focus this upcoming season when you've got so much on the line."

He means well. I know he does. But that does nothing to quell the anger building inside of me at the very thought that being with Lark could be anything but amazing.

"I'll be fine."

"Okay. If you say so. That's all I wanted to check in on. I'm off to Santa Barbara for a few days to scout out some new kid. Talk later."

We hang up, and I stew in my thoughts the rest of the drive home.

Of course, everything will be fine. If I managed to stay focused on my career this long, finally getting the woman of my dreams isn't going to knock me off course.

I was able to rise to the top, all while pining after someone I thought I would never have. Surely, now that she's mine, if anything, it'll be easier to concentrate.

Right?

Chapter Thirty

Lark

"You're gonna give your mail carrier a complex if you keep looking so depressed every time you see them." Willow hands me a glass of wine, and despite her teasing, there's a sympathetic smile on her face.

I groan. "I know, I just can't believe it's taking this long."

My acceptance letter for the internship at the university still has not arrived. It's hard to stay optimistic when I had expected to hear just after Christmas, and it's now the end of January. Spring training is right around the corner, and then the season will begin. If I'm going to be asking for time off next fall, I need to be letting the team know soon so they can find a temporary replacement for me. Just because it'll be the offseason doesn't mean there won't be players needing treatment, to say nothing of us making the playoffs. Then I'll be trying to juggle the internship and my job. Which isn't ideal, but Mattias said he would help make it work.

"They'd be fools not to take you on. Remind me what it's for?"

"It's a three-month internship working in the sports rehab

lab at the University of Vancouver. They have a research project going on right now looking to map muscle health in professional athletes, to try and determine how to best prevent and treat muscle decline. The hope is to be better able to prevent joint injuries by understanding why our muscles age and decline the way they do, even in professional athletes." I rattle off the explanation with ease, having studied the research project's material a thousand times.

But when I look at Willow, she's got a blank expression on her face.

I sigh and try again. "It's a research project to help find a way to prevent injuries by studying the muscles of athletes."

"Oh. Well, why didn't you say that the first time?" She nudges me with a smile.

"You work in the pro sports field. Shouldn't you be able to understand the rehab side of it a bit better?" I tease.

"Nah, all I need to know for my job is what they injured and how long they're out."

I shake my head and take a sip of wine. "Fair enough."

"So." Willow looks at me expectantly. I know exactly what she wants to talk about but I pretend not to.

"What?"

Her eyes couldn't possibly roll back any farther. "Oh my God, don't be a tease. You know what! You and Monty. How's it going? I need details, woman."

I take another sip, and try to look cool, calm, and collected. "A lady never kisses and tells."

Willow knows me too well and just snorts. "You're not a lady, you're Lark. So spill."

"Fine, fine. He's amazing, and I had no idea I could be this happy."

I watch closely as Willow sets down her wine glass far too calmly. I hurry to set mine down, too, fully aware she's not going to accept that. Sure enough, out of nowhere she grabs a throw pillow and whips it at my head.

I shriek, blocking the pillow. "Okay, geez!" When I look at her again, she's got a far too pleased expression on her face. "You're relentless."

"I know. Now, go on."

Here's the thing. I'd love to tell Willow everything. She's my closest female friend, and we don't keep secrets. I knew about her and Ronan before anyone else. But telling her about Dan being a virgin up until being with me feels like I'd be betraying his secrets, not my own. Which means, I've got to tread carefully.

"He really is amazing, Wills. It's like all the goodness in him is amplified by a thousand now. His hugs are magic, and when I'm with him, I feel so cherished. Did you know he has a tattoo on his hip? Of a skylark?"

Willow swoons against the couch. "No way. That's the most adorably cheesy romantic thing ever." She bolts back upright. "And so perfectly Monty. I love it." She grabs my hands. "You deserve that kind of love, Lark. He truly adores you."

I nod. "He does, and I love him."

"Gah, I'm so happy for you." Willow drains her glass and gestures to mine. "Want a refill?"

My nose wrinkles. "Nah, I'm not even sure I'll finish this. My stomach hasn't been feeling great lately."

"Okay." She stands up and goes to the kitchen, coming back with a fresh glass of wine for herself. "How's the sex?"

"Really, really good." I smile, because it's the truth. What he lacks in experience, Dan makes up for with enthusiasm and a willingness to learn. He listens to me and pays such close attention to my body, I swear, he already knows it better than Baron ever did, even after several years together.

"That's not a surprise." Willow waggles her eyebrows. "All that cinnamon roll, golden retriever energy? He's gotta be fun in bed."

The sound of my front door opening has both of us turning. Dan walks in, wearing a Tridents hoodie and dark grey sweatpants. My gaze drops immediately to the front of his pants.

"And that's my cue to leave."

I blink and look over at Willow to see her amused grin. "What? Why?"

"Because he's here and you're drooling." She stands up and walks over to Dan, giving him a quick hug. "See ya later, Monty. Take care of her."

His gaze is trained on me, and I can already see the lust burning in his eyes. "Don't worry, I will."

He breaks our stare to walk Willow to the door, closing and locking it behind her.

"What were you two talking about, Birdie? You look a little flushed."

My tongue darts out to lick my lips as he prowls around the couch and squats down in front of me, his hands coming to my knees. "Oh, just girl stuff," I say faintly, my focus zeroing in on his thumbs that are drawing lazy circles on my inner thighs.

"Hmm. Girl stuff. Right."

He surges upward, kissing me and pressing me against the couch, his hands bracing on either side of me.

"You were talking about me, weren't you Birdie."

The words are conversational, casual even. But his voice is anything but. Rich, sultry, and promising a hell of a lot of pleasure. I bite my lower lip, trying to look coy, but I don't know if I pull it off. Given the smirk Dan shoots me, I probably don't.

"Maybe I was. Is that a problem?"

His head moves slowly from side to side. "Not at all, as long as you're saying good stuff." A thread of vulnerability pokes through his sexy bravado, and I bring my hand up to cup his cheek.

"*Very* good stuff." I lean in and kiss him. With a groan, he wraps one arm around me, pulling me almost off the couch.

"Jesus, am I ever gonna stop wanting you?" he rasps before kissing his way down my throat. "I can't stop thinking about you, about us, about how fucking good you make me feel."

"You say that like it's a bad thing," I say, tipping my head to the side. He chuckles against my skin, then lifts his head, fixing me with his molten chocolate stare.

"Right now, it's not. But when the season starts, you know I'll have to be focused on the game, right?"

Again, that tiny bit of vulnerability shows through. I love that he's comfortable enough with me not to hide it. I nod and kiss his cheek.

"I know what your job needs from you, Dan, and you know I'll be there supporting you the whole time."

"You're fucking perfect," he whispers. "But you'll be even

more perfect once you're naked."

He stands up and strips out of his own clothes so quickly I feel like I barely blink and then, there he is, in all his naked glory. His cock is already leaking precum, and I lean forward and lap at it with my tongue.

That makes him groan as he wraps one hand around the base and threads the other in my hair. "Baby, as much as I want your mouth on my dick literally all the fucking time, right now, I need to be inside of you."

Despite being insanely turned on, I can't quite stifle a yawn. Dan catches it and frowns. "Hey, we don't have to do this. You want to just go to bed and snuggle?"

"Absolutely not," I say in mock outrage. Then I lift my sweater up and over my head, tossing it to the ground before reaching behind my back and unclasping my bra. I let it dangle from my hand for a second before dropping it to the ground as well.

Dan drops to his knees and grips the waist of my joggers before slowly easing them down. I lift my ass off the couch to help, and he peels them off my legs before running his hands back up, raising goose bumps everywhere he touches.

"You're so soft," he murmurs. "Like, everywhere. It sounds dumb, but I didn't realize you'd be so soft."

These little reminders of his previous innocence make me melt.

"And you're hard," I say, leaning forward to kiss him as I reach down for his cock. "It's the perfect combination," I whisper against his lips, feeling them turn up in a smile.

"It really is." His fingers find my pussy, flicking lightly at my clit before slowly dragging between my wet lips. "Mmm. You're soaked, Birdie."

I nod, biting back a whine. His confidence in taking the lead has grown incredibly quickly, but there are times when I wish he'd stop taking his time and just fuck me. I haven't come out and said that yet, not wanting him to think I don't love it when he wants to play first.

Thank God, today isn't one of those times. Dan steps up and pulls me to stand before spinning me around. "Put your knees on the couch. That's it, grab the back, baby. Fuck, yes." I move the way he tells me to until I'm on my knees, pushing my ass out toward him.

Hands grip me firmly, kneading the flesh just before I feel him take a bite.

"Dan!" I yelp, twisting to look at him. "Did you just bite me?"

His grin is unrepentant. "Sure did. Delicious and juicy."

I shake with laughter that dies instantly when his fingers find my pussy again, and he thrusts two of them in with no further warning. "Ohhh," I moan, arching back into his touch. "Yes."

Lips land on my spine, and I feel him press against me. Then his mouth pauses. "Shit. Condom."

This time, my whimper breaks free. "Bedroom. Hurry."

There's a cold draft as he leaves, and my hand drifts down between my legs.

"Oh really?" His amused voice has me lifting my head to see him staring intently at my fingers, his long cock now covered in a condom. "You think you get to play with what's mine?"

"Well, you weren't here to do it," I reply saucily.

He raises one brow and circles around behind me. Then my

hand is pushed away and replaced by his mouth. He sucks my clit into his mouth, his tongue snaking out to play with it. But just as I feel my release cresting, he lets go, and I cry out. "What? No! Go back!"

Dan just chuckles. "Don't worry, Birdie. I've got you."

I feel his blunt tip nudge my entrance, and then he slides it back and forth, collecting moisture before slowly pushing inside.

"Oh yes," I moan, my eyes closing as I lean my head down on the back of the couch. Dan sets a slow and steady rhythm, rocking me back and forth. His hand gathers my hair, and he gently tugs my head, making me lift it so he can lean down and kiss me. It's messy, sloppy, and so damn hot.

"Fuck," he grinds out, dragging his dick out slowly before slamming it back in. "So good, baby. So fucking good."

It is good. But I need more. My hand moves to reach back down to play with my clit, and he pauses.

"What are you doing?" he growls.

"I need...I need to...my clit," I gasp.

"Let me."

Instead of thumbing my clit, I reach my hand behind me to run along his strong thighs. He curls over me, and his hand finds where we're joined. When he pinches my hood, I wince.

"Too strong."

"Sorry," he mumbles, kissing my back. "Better?"

I nod dreamily as he eases off into steady circles. "Oh yeah."

"Fuck, I need to see you." Dan pulls out and drops down onto the couch before grabbing me by my waist and lifting me onto his lap. I reach down and take his cock, lining it up and sinking down with a satisfied groan.

"That's better. Look at you. So fucking gorgeous."

I smile and take his hand, leading it back down between us. He gets the message and returns to playing with my clit as we kiss, our hips moving in perfect sync.

"Fuck, Dan," I pant as I feel my climax building. "Faster. Please."

"I'm there, baby," he grunts, letting go of my clit to grip my hips and rock us faster. But I need that stimulation. This time when I reach down myself he doesn't stop me.

Our eyes lock and my mouth falls open just as I feel his hips shudder. "Yes," I cry out as my orgasm washes over me. Dan follows, groaning out my name as he thrusts up into me shakily.

I collapse onto his chest, feeling incredibly satisfied and incredibly sleepy. Lips press to my forehead.

"I'm gonna go deal with the condom."

I nod, my eyes still closed, perfectly content to let him lift me off his lap and set me down on the couch.

"Mmmkay."

"You gonna fall asleep on me, Birdie?" he says with a chuckle, and I smile.

"Nah. We're gonna snuggle."

The last thing I remember before waking up in my bed the next morning, Dan wrapped around me from behind, is hearing that chuckle again and feeling lips pressing a soft, loving kiss to my forehead.

Chapter Thirty-One

Monty

I stroke Lark's hair away from her face, unable to ignore how worried I am any longer. We should be heading to the airport together this morning, bound for Arizona and spring training. But Lark's been feeling under the weather for a week or so and threw up a couple of times yesterday. So she's staying home and going to the doctor later this week instead. The plan is for her to fly out with the rest of the team that starts training next week. This week it's just pitchers and catchers.

I'm hoping she'll feel better and can make the trip down south. Because the idea of being away from her, even for a short while, physically hurts my chest.

"Hey, Birdie, I gotta go," I say softly, bending down to kiss her forehead. Her eyes slowly flutter open, but it's the dark circles underneath those beautiful baby blues that have me concerned. She's been sleeping like the dead, barely making it to nine most nights before I'm tucking her in bed. Something's not right, and it's freaking me out.

"Do you want me to drive you to the airport?" she asks sleepily, covering her yawn with her hand.

"Nah, stay here and rest. I'll get one of the guys to pick me up. You see the doctor on Thursday, right? I know we'll be talking before then, but you better let me know what they say as soon as you can."

She nods. "I will, but it's just a virus, I'm sure. I hope you don't come down with it."

I thump my chest lightly with my fist. "My immune system is strong. I'll be fine." I don't tell her that if it were a virus, she'd be getting better by now. "Can I get you anything? Coffee, water, a milkshake?"

She gives me a small smile. "Some coffee would be amazing."

I lean down again and kiss the tip of her nose. "Coming right up."

Out in the kitchen, I shoot off a message to Yami asking for a lift to the airport, then busy myself making Lark some coffee. Grabbing the stack of sticky notes on the counter, I scribble out a message and hide it in the cupboard that holds the mugs. When her coffee is ready, I carry it back into the bedroom to find her curled up on her side, holding her stomach protectively.

"Baby, are you okay?" I set the coffee down and crouch beside her.

Her face is so pale and drawn, but she manages a nod. "Yeah, I tried to get up and my stomach revolted on me. I'm better now that I'm lying down."

I blow out a long sigh. "Fuck, I hate that I have to leave you like this."

She reaches out a hand and pats my shoulder lightly, mustering a tiny smile. "I'll be okay, Dan. It's not the first time I've been sick."

"Maybe so, but it's the first time you've been sick when I've been the one who gets to take care of you, and here I am, failing that job by abandoning you." I give her an exaggerated pout, and it earns me a slightly bigger smile.

"Daniel Montgomery, you're not abandoning me, you have to go to spring training. Besides, I'm sure I'll be fine in a few days. The doctor will clear me, and I'll be on the plane to Arizona with the rest of the team to join you."

I press a gentle kiss to her lips. "I'm holding you to that, Birdie." My pocket vibrates with a text, probably Yami letting me know he's on his way. "Shit, I gotta go." I drop my forehead to meet hers, and her hand snakes around the back of my neck, holding me there. "I love you."

"I know."

The *Star Wars* reference makes me grin, just as it does every time. But her answering smile is way too small and pathetic looking. I smooth her hair back, worry filling my head and heart.

Another buzz from my phone means my time is up. Somehow, I drag myself away, looking back at her when I reach the doorway. Fuck, I really hate leaving her like this. But I don't have a choice. Turning, I move into her living room, grab my bag and the handle of my suitcase and leave, locking the door behind me.

Yami's waiting downstairs, his low-slung sports car idling at the curb. I load my stuff in the trunk and then get in.

"Hey, thanks for the ride."

"No prob. Lark's still not feeling great?" he asks, concern clear on his face as well. All the guys like Lark, and strangely, it makes me feel better knowing I'm not the only one worried. She doesn't get sick. At least, she hasn't in the years I've known her.

"Yeah, she's seeing her doctor later this week. It's weird, she's just so tired all the time, and her stomach is upset. I dunno, I just don't like seeing her sick." I slump against the seat of the car. We're stopped at a red light, and I can feel him looking at me. Glancing over, I see a weird look on his face.

"What's that look for?"

His head turns forward. "What look?"

"The one where you look like you just swallowed pickle juice."

"Nothing, nothing. Hey, did you hear about one of the rookie's superstitions? He doesn't change socks all fucking season. We're gonna need some heavy-duty air freshener in the locker room." He wrinkles his nose.

"That's nasty."

"No shit. Anyway, hopefully, Lark can head south soon. My shoulder's gonna need her magic hands." He waves one of his in my face and I slap it away.

"Just keep your hands to yourself," I say, probably more harshly than I need to. Yami immediately sobers and cuts me a look.

"Monty. Dude. You know I'd never do that. She's your girl, always has been. No matter what happens."

The weird defensive tension in my shoulders recedes. I've never felt this kind of possessiveness, not even in the past over Lark. I mean, I guess I had no right to, back when she belonged to someone else. But now, everything's changed. She's mine, and despite knowing the guys all respect that, some instinct has me on edge.

It's not fair to take that out on my teammate, though. We're partners, and the next few weeks in Arizona will be pivotal. We're heading down a week before the rest of the team to get in some dedicated time on the mound.

"Sorry, man. Guess I'm just feeling a bit stressed leaving her when she's not feeling great."

He gives a tight nod but doesn't say anything.

The rest of the drive to the airport is spent talking about the new prospects that will be at spring training. Our roster is solid, but some fresh players can be a good thing. As long as they don't mess with my game. I need this season to be my best one yet.

As worried as I am about Lark, I know I can't let anything distract me. As soon as I get on that plane, it's go time.

My future depends on my focus being locked in tight on playing the best damn game I can.

Chapter Thirty-Two

Lark

You are my penguin
— Love DM
I love you more than I love spaghetti. And I love spaghetti a lot
— Love DM
You're just like bacon. You make everything better.
— Love DM
Being normal is overrated. I'd rather be crazy over you.
— Love DM
I've fallen for you and I don't want to get up.
— Love DM

The collection of sticky notes, each with a silly, sweet message from Dan, grows each day as I discover them around my apartment. I don't know when he found the time to hide them, but each one has made me smile, despite still feeling unwell.

We've talked every day since he left on Sunday, and so far, it sounds like spring training is going well. He and Kai are in a good rhythm, and Dan sounds excited about what's to come.

I wish I was there.

Hopefully today, my doctor can explain why I've felt so

run-down and nauseous all the time. In the back of my mind, one explanation keeps popping up, but I don't — can't — let myself dwell on that possibility.

When my phone rings, I reach for it, eager for the distraction. Anything to fill the next hour before I leave for my appointment. But that eagerness fades when I see who it is.

"Hello, Mother."

"Lark, are you coming for dinner this weekend?"

No hi? How are you? I miss you? *Nah, of course not.* That would imply caring and emotions my parents just don't seem to have.

I swallow against a wave of nausea and lean against my kitchen counter. "I'm not sure. I was meant to be in Arizona already, but I needed to stay back for a doctor's appointment."

There's a pause before she speaks, and to my shock, she actually sounds mildly concerned. "Is everything alright?"

My mind battles with my heart. A small part of me wants to tell her, about Dan, about feeling sick, and about the scary possibility the doctor is going to tell me something life-changing. But I don't have that sort of relationship with her, and quite honestly, I don't trust that she'll respond with compassion.

"Just need to get some stuff checked out," I say lightly, pushing off from the counter. "Actually, I need to get going soon. I'll let you know if I'm in town for dinner. Was there anything else?"

Another pause, this one longer than the last. "No, I suppose not. I hope your appointment goes well."

"Thanks, Mom," I say, feeling kind of uncomfortable with this ever so slightly softer side of my mother. "I'll talk to you soon."

"Goodbye, Lark."

We hang up and I stare at my phone for a second, processing what just happened. She actually showed some sort of something emotional toward me. Unexpected, yes, and somewhat touching.

Shaking my head, I move into my bathroom to finish getting ready. When I pull open a drawer to take out a hair elastic, I find another sticky note.

There's nothing better than waking up with you in my arms.
— Love DM

I love that he's made it so he's here with me, even when he's so far away. I go to pick up my phone and text him when another wave of nausea hits, this one stronger. Thank God, I'm already in the bathroom because I'm bent over the toilet retching seconds later.

When it finally subsides, I'm panting on the bathroom floor, feeling even more miserable. This is awful, whatever it is.

I drag myself up, brush my teeth, and braid my hair. Time to get some answers. Grabbing my water bottle, keys, purse, and a package of crackers, I lock up and head to my car.

At the doctor's office, they sign me in, then a nurse takes me to the back and hands me a small cup.

"We're going to get a quick urine sample and then Dr. Rhodes will be in soon." She gives me a reassuring smile, but as I stare at that plastic container, I feel anything but reassured.

She directs me to the bathroom, and I move on autopilot. There's no more denying my fear. Nausea and exhaustion that won't go away? There's one very real possibility for what's causing it.

And a few minutes later, Dr. Rhodes confirms it.

"Lark, you're pregnant."

An hour later, I'm back home, staring at the pamphlets the doctor gave me after dropping the bomb on me that I'm pregnant.

Somehow, Dan and I beat all the odds. Despite my birth control and the condoms we used, something got through, and now there's a baby growing inside of me.

Our baby.

Dr. Rhodes gave me some information on early pregnancy, a prescription for some anti-nausea medication, and then, I guess my shock — and lack of immediate joy over the news — was apparent because she also gave me some brochures on other options.

Abortion and adoption.

I've never been opposed to either. I firmly believe every woman has the right to choose what is the best decision for them and their body. I also never expected to be in a position where I would be considering either one.

But Dan made it clear, he doesn't want kids right now. He needs to focus on baseball, on his career, and on securing a good contract after this season. Dr. Rhodes estimated my due date to be near the end of September but said we could confirm with an ultrasound at my next appointment. I'm approximately six weeks along, assuming this little bean was conceived that first time when the condom slipped, which makes the most sense.

Who am I kidding, none of this makes sense. The odds are a zillion to one, and yet, here I am, staring at pamphlets on babies while one's inside of me right this very second.

A little spark of life that defied the odds. A life that is a perfect blend of me and the man I love.

My hands go to my stomach, and a smile creeps across my face for the first time since finding Dan's latest love note this morning. And I know, without a doubt, I'm keeping this baby.

Even if Dan decides he can't be involved, that he has to put his career first, I don't care. I won't force him to give up baseball. But I also won't let anyone force me to give up this baby.

Picking up my phone, I go to call him but stop myself. This isn't the kind of news I can drop on him over the phone. I actually don't even know how to start the conversation.

Hey, remember the first time you had sex with me, when you lost your virginity? Guess what, your super sperm were just waiting for the chance to create new life.

Yeah, that'll go over well.

As I stare down at my phone, a notification pops up. An email about the research internship at the university.

This time when my stomach twists, it's not only from pregnancy hormones. My breath is shaky as I click to open the email.

We are pleased to offer you placement in our fall internship program...

I can't even continue reading. Tears start to fall from my eyes, landing on my phone screen, blurring the words in front of me. I wipe them off the phone and dash them away from my face, moving to lie down on my side. One hand immediately goes to my stomach. To the life growing there. To the child who has unknowingly turned everything in my world upside down.

I don't know what this means for me, for Dan, or for us.

But I do know, whatever happens, this baby will be loved.

Unconditionally.

Wholly.

Without question, or doubt, or expectation.

Chapter Thirty-Three

Monty

For three days, I've been focused on baseball. Pitchers and catchers always head south for spring training early since our dynamic is key on the field. If we aren't in sync, everything falls apart.

The Tridents like to focus on partnerships between catchers and pitchers, believing a strong dynamic and communication is key on the field.

But even though Yami and I will most often be paired together, it's important I get to know all the pitchers since I'll be catching for each of them at some point in the season. Which means my days have been long, filled with drills, sessions in the bullpen, and conditioning activities designed to help us all connect.

I like the other guys, but Yami's my boy. We're close to capturing the magic Pops and I used to have. And today, at the end of another long day under the Arizona sun, I feel like we're really clicking.

Except, Yami can't seem to get his speed up to where it needs to be. And it's starting to mess with his head.

From my position behind home plate, I flash him the signal for a slider. He lets it rip, and it hits my glove a few seconds later.

"Ninety-nine point seven. Let's go again," Coach shouts from the side. I see Yami wince and know he's not happy. Hopping up from my crouch, I jog up to the mound and wrap my hand around his neck, pulling his head to mine.

"Shake it off, bro. You know what you're capable of. One-oh-three, baby. I was there, and my hand felt the impact for days."

"Why the fuck am I going so slow?" he mutters, eyes still downcast. "It's not the fucking yips, I kept up my conditioning all winter, so what gives?"

"It doesn't matter. When the time comes, your arm will be on fucking fire. I know it, Coach knows it. Send it with a changeup next, and we'll get there."

I thump him on the back, finally seeing a smile.

"Thanks, bro. Let's do this."

I jog back to my spot behind home and drop down. Pulling my mask over my face, I give him the signal for a changeup.

This time, he lets it fucking fly.

"One-oh-one point two. Getting better. Three more, boys."

Yami's grin grows. I throw down a signal, and he lets it rip. We finish up the session, and after a quick chat with Coach, head to the locker room.

"Fuck, Arizona is hot." Warren, one of the rookie pitchers, drops down to the bench in front of his locker with a groan. "I'm from Alaska, man. We don't do heat."

I whip a towel at him with a grin. "Get used to it. We got four more weeks here."

He shoots me a half-hearted scowl. "I might melt. How am I gonna pitch if my hand is slippery with sweat?"

His complaints are nothing new. Arizona *is* hot. But it's only gonna get hotter when we play down here during the season, so new guy better toughen up.

"You'll be lucky to throw a single game if you're that much of a princess. Hey, maybe that's your nickname. Princess." A deep voice comes from across the locker room.

I glance over at Carter Jones, a second-string pitcher who joined the team the season after I did. Not gonna lie, glad he said it so I didn't have to.

"Jonesie is right," Yami says, strolling in from the showers. "Toughen up, Princess. This is the big leagues, and yeah, sometimes we play when the heat makes you want to curl up and die. At least we aren't freezing our asses off on the ice like those hockey weirdos."

I stifle a laugh. Yami's dislike of hockey is infamous.

The rookie looks suitably chastised, and I almost feel sorry for the guy. Moving over to sit next to him, I lean in. "Listen. You'll adjust. Where did you play before this?"

He looks over at me, his face belligerent. Great. This guy's gonna be fun. "Nebraska, for college. It got hot but not seventh circle of hell."

I nod, keeping my expression calm. Doesn't this guy understand that Arizona in February is nothing? Wait till it's August and we're down here, or in Nevada, or hell, in Florida. Lots of places are hotter than this, and we'll play ball in all of them.

"At least we don't play in the rain." I give him a wide grin and stand up. Some guys just want to complain, not realizing how goddamn lucky they are to be here. Not me. I'll play no matter what the weather is. Wind, rain, snow. Okay, maybe not snow. Don't wanna ruin my gear.

But I've never taken one day of my career for granted. Never complained about the fucking weather, that's for damn sure.

Once I'm dressed, I head out for the bus that'll take us back to the hotel. I'm eager to call Lark and see how the doctor visit went. Hopefully, she'll have good news and will be on the plane headed south in a couple of days.

As soon as I'm in my hotel room, I flop onto my stomach on the bed and call her up on a video chat. The call connects, and there she is. My girl.

"Hey, beautiful." I grin, unable to hold it back. "How are you feeling?"

"Fine."

My grin falters. Something's not right. She keeps glancing to the side.

"Yeah? Great. So what did the doc say?"

Her eyes dart away, and she licks her lips. *Shit.*

"Birdie? Babe, you're freaking me out." Finally, she looks at me, and fuck me, her eyes are shiny as if she's about to cry. I scramble up to sit, panic consuming me. "Lark. Talk to me."

She smiles. But it's fake, I can tell. "I'm fine, Dan. Really. It's nothing serious, and the doctor gave me some medicine to help settle my stomach. I'll be on the plane with the team."

That news should have me feeling ecstatic. But I can't seem to push past the dread.

"That's great. I can't wait to see you."

"Me neither."

We stare at each other for a few seconds. I hate this. I don't know what's wrong, just that something is. I want to push her to tell me what's going on. But as I open my mouth to do just that, she cuts me off.

"I have to go, Sadie's coming over for dinner and to help me pack. I'll see you soon, okay?"

I nod silently.

"I love you, Dan." At least this time, her smile seems a touch more genuine.

"I love you, too."

She ends the call before I can say anything else, and I'm left staring at a dark screen.

A fist pounds on my door, and I hear Jonesie's voice shout through it.

"Monty! Let's go, bro, Yami found a barbecue place we're headed to for dinner."

I'm not even hungry. But somehow, I manage to drag myself up off the bed. Grabbing a Tridents ball cap and pushing it on my head, I stuff my wallet and phone in my pocket and open the door. "Yeah, let's go."

I brush past him, striding down the hall to the elevator.

"Dude. Everything okay?" he asks as the door slides shut in front of us. I like Jonesie. But I sure as shit don't know him well enough to talk to him about Lark.

"Yeah, fine. Just tired."

That seems to be good enough for him because he nods and leaves me alone. Downstairs, we meet up with the rest of the guys, and head out for dinner. Being around everyone helps take my mind off things for the most part, and I try my best to focus on my teammates.

But later, when I'm lying in bed alone, there's no avoiding my thoughts and the mental panic spiral I'm trying to ignore.

Somewhere around 1 am, when sleep continues to evade me, I roll over and thump my pillow with a grunt. Tomorrow is gonna suck donkey balls if I don't get any sleep.

Giving in, I grab my phone and open up my texts with Lark.

> **DAN: Baby, I know something's wrong. I just hope whatever it is, I can fix it. Because I love you. Nothing's gonna change that.**

I'm not expecting her to reply, certain she's asleep even though I'm an hour ahead of her. But to my surprise, just as I'm about to set the phone down, I see the three dots that indicate she's typing. I sit upright, staring at the screen, willing her reply to appear.

> **LARK: I'm sorry, I didn't mean to worry you. There's nothing to fix, I promise. I love you too.**

It doesn't tell me anything about what's upsetting her. I debate calling her and demand she tell me what's going on. But it's the middle of the night, and we both need to try and sleep. Dragging in a deep breath, I try to convince my brain that she means what she says, and I don't have anything major to worry about.

> **DAN: There's a giant hug and even more giant kiss waiting for you when you get here.**

LARK: Oh yeah? How giant.

Finally, I crack a smile. There's my Birdie.

> **DAN: As big as a baseball field.**

LARK: Pffft that's not so big.

> **DAN: Okay, as big as the night sky.**

LARK: Wow, that's big.

> **DAN: That's what she said.**

LARK: Omg.

> **DAN: Love you, Birdie.**

LARK: Love you too.

This time, when I set my phone down and roll over, my eyes start to droop. And finally, I drift off, visions of Lark lying in the bed beside me replace the worry that's consumed me all evening.

But sleep is short-lived. When I bolt upright a short while later, the room is still dark. My heart is racing and my breath is coming fast. I feel clammy with sweat, and the sheets are tangled around me.

Fuck, I haven't had a nightmare since I was a kid, but there's no denying the unsettling feeling of waking up from one.

Reaching for the glass of water on my bedside table, I chug it down, letting the cool liquid soothe me somewhat. I try to grasp onto the threads of the dream that are fading fast but can't. All I remember is the terrifying feeling that everything I've ever wanted, everything I've worked so hard for, is slipping away from me.

And if I don't run fast enough, I'll lose it all.

Chapter Thirty-Four

Lark

The plane to Arizona is packed with boisterous baseball players. Thankfully, they mostly leave me alone. I guess word of me feeling unwell the last week or so has gotten around. I tuck myself into a window seat and stare out at the clouds, my thoughts flipping between the unbridled joy I feel, knowing I'm carrying a piece of Dan inside of me, and the sheer overwhelm that crashes over me whenever I try to think through how to handle this.

Telling him is only the first hurdle. He's got to focus on his season, and if this news distracts him to the point he doesn't perform at his best, I'll never forgive myself.

Then there's the sacrifice I'm going to have to make. I'm still struggling to accept the fact that I have to turn down the internship at the university. After all, there's no chance I can participate in that while caring for a newborn.

The voice of the players sitting behind me breaks through my thoughts. "I heard the rookie's got his nickname. Princess." They both laugh at that, and I can't help but wonder what the new player did to earn that nickname from the pitchers and catchers already on the ground in Phoenix.

"Sounds like things are good. But Jonesie said Yami's struggling with his speed, and Monty's been distracted the last couple of days. Maybe the dream team isn't gonna happen."

"Dude, shut up."

I duck my head, a blush darkening my cheeks. Obviously, one of them knows about my relationship with Dan and realized I could hear them. But being caught unintentionally eavesdropping isn't what has me biting my thumb from nervousness.

Dan's been distracted? Why? I know it's not because of having to leave me at home because the first few days he was away, he sounded confident and happy when he reported training was going well.

But then there was our conversation the day I went to the doctor. He could tell something was up, I know he could. I thought I had reassured him well enough that it could wait until I arrived, but maybe I was wrong.

And if just the idea of big news is enough to distract him, how the hell will he handle the actual news itself?

Oh God.

For the rest of the flight, I'm a nervous wreck. Thank goodness for the medication the doctor gave me, which alleviated my morning sickness symptoms quickly. If I had that on top of the anxious churning in my stomach, I'd be turning the airplane restroom into my new home for the remainder of the flight.

As it is, I pop a peppermint, roll on some lavender essential oil, and close my eyes, trying to find some calm.

It doesn't work, and two hours later when we touch down in Phoenix, I'm feeling totally drained.

But then I walk into the blessedly air-conditioned Phoenix airport and see Dan Montgomery standing there holding a huge sign with arrows pointing toward him and massive letters that spell out "GUESS WHO'S EXCITED TO SEE LARK? THIS GUY!"

It's all I can do not to burst into tears at the sight of him. But in an effort to try and hold it in, I come to a complete standstill, nowhere near close enough to feel his arms wrap around me. Someone jostles me from behind and I stumble forward. Dan's grin falters. Then he drops his sign to the ground and jogs over, and then finally, *finally*, I'm in his arms.

"Birdie. Hey, baby, it's okay. I'm here." He continues to mumble sweet things as people stream around us. They're probably staring at the crazy lady being hugged by the hot baseball player, but I don't care. I need this.

After several moments just soaking up his strong, warm, loving embrace, I sniff a few times and pull back, swiping away the tears.

"Hi," I say, my voice all wobbly. "Sorry to be such a mess."

He gives me a soft smile and tucks some hair behind my ears. "You're not a mess. You're the most beautiful woman in the world. And I'm so fucking happy you're here." After pressing a kiss to my forehead, his lips lingering for a second longer, Dan tucks me into his side and grabs my carry-on suitcase.

"Come on, we'll Uber back to the hotel."

I realize with some horror that thanks to my mini meltdown, the rest of the team has already loaded onto the bus and I'm guessing left the airport. I can only assume my luggage made it on as well.

"How did they know not to wait?" I say as we walk outside to the rideshare area.

"I told Sin I'd be picking you up. He, ah, figured we might want some time alone." Dan ducks his head and I catch his blush.

Despite my emotional roller coaster, I giggle. "Why? It's not like we're going to do anything in the back seat of an Uber."

He casts me a sidelong glance. "I mean...we could."

I slap his arm, laughing louder now. "Dream on. Besides, I'm all gross from the flight."

His lips land on my hair as he squeezes me tight. "Again, no you're not. You're beautiful."

I sigh happily, feeling a small amount of my turmoil settle. Even though the clock is ticking, and I know he's going to want to talk very soon, for now, I can just enjoy being with him again. And pretend I'm not about to turn everything upside down with my news.

My reprieve lasts only as long as the team dinner we both attend back at the hotel. With everyone now here, we've taken over one of the banquet rooms for a feast. Tomorrow, all the players will hit the field, and spring training begins in earnest. Tonight is a chance for them to connect, relax, and have some fun before the work starts.

I'm booked to share a room with another trainer at the hotel. The team policy of players sleeping alone is a bit more relaxed during spring training than it is during the actual season, but rooms were booked before Dan and I became a couple.

However, room assignments don't seem to matter to him as he bypasses my floor and leads me straight to what I assume is his. We're silent the short walk down the corridor and as he unlocks his door.

As soon as it snicks shut behind us, I expect him to reach for me and our clothes to fly off. Or at least, I think that's what I expect. It's perhaps what I should want? Or need? Truth is, I'm so mixed-up from seeing him again, being near him and soaking in his love, I can't think straight. Or maybe it's the nervous energy constantly running through me, knowing the conversation I need to have with him is coming sooner, rather than later.

He doesn't start undressing me, however. No, instead, he leads me over to his bed, sits down, and pulls me into his lap. Then, gripping my chin, he turns my head to face him, and with an uncharacteristically serious expression on his face, he says one word that seals my fate for the evening.

"Talk."

Chapter Thirty-Five

Monty

Something is definitely wrong. I've known it for days, and try as I might, it's affecting my game. I've been calling it the yips, and so far, the other players and staff seem to believe it's just a bump in the road for me.

Only Yami seems to suspect it's more than that, and I've caught him starting to ask me what's up a few times, only to stop. It's as if he knows something I don't, but for the fucking life of me, I can't bring myself to ask him.

Then today, seeing her at the airport filled me with a weird mixture of relief, elation, and absolute panic.

Because instead of laughing at my ridiculous sign or running and jumping into my arms like the reunions you see on cheesy movies, Lark just stood there, her beautiful face struggling to contain tears.

When she finally moved toward me, the ice that was rapidly gripping my heart cracked. And when I had her in my arms, I felt like I could take in a full breath once again.

Yet still, that unease remained. Something is wrong, and I need to know what it is.

"Talk to me, please," I say again, trying to make my voice firm and not sound as shaky as I feel. "I know there's something going on, Birdie. And I gotta be real with you, it's freaking me the fuck out. I can't stop worrying about you, about us." I suck in a breath. Now's the time to get fully vulnerable. "It's messing with me. I fucked up the signals the other day, let way too many balls past me, and tripped over my own goddamn feet trying to get to one. Whatever it is, I can handle it. What I can't handle is not knowing if you're okay. If we're okay."

The last three words are said in a whisper. The deepest, darkest fears of my heart. That somehow, I've done something wrong. That it's me, I'm not enough for her, she's not happy, that I'm losing her.

When tears spill from her eyes, I reach up to wipe them away with my thumb, ignoring the wetness tracking down my own face.

"Birdie. Lark. Please, talk to me."

I see her throat move in a swallow and her shoulders rise and fall in a long, slow breath. When she opens her mouth, I brace myself for the worst.

"I'm pregnant."

What the actual fuck?

In all the scenarios that played out in my mind the last few days, a baby never factored into a single one.

Pregnant?

But even as I stare at her, the pieces fall into place. I swear, I'm not an idiot, but I sure as shit feel like one. She was exhausted, nauseous, and emotional.

I may not have ever had a girlfriend, but I went to sex-ed class in high school. I've been around guys with kids. I've watched movies and heard the stories. I know what the early signs of pregnancy can be.

Yet still, somehow, I never considered this.

At some point in my mental processing, Lark has managed to move off my lap without me noticing. Until I open my mouth and say probably the stupidest thing I've ever said.

"How?"

She paces away from me, her arms wrapped around her stomach, and I hate that I'm not touching her. Especially when she chokes out a laugh.

"Well, you see, when a man and a woman —"

No. No fucking way. I stand up and close the distance between us in a second, gripping her gently by the shoulders.

"Lark. Give me a second, please. I'm handling this all wrong. I just..." Words fail me, and I know I've got to figure my shit out, and fast, or I'll lose her. "Shit, Birdie, a *baby*?"

Another forced laugh.

I drop to my knees and place my hands on her stomach. "Hi, baby bird." When I look up at her, she's staring down at me, her mouth partly open and eyes filled with tears.

"Dan?" she whispers brokenly. And there's so much weight to that one word, my name, phrased as a question.

"This is amazing," I say quietly. "I don't know the odds, but I'm guessing they were not exactly good. And yet somehow, we did this. We made a fucking baby." I grin, even through my tears that are no longer based in fear but in pure, exquisite joy. "I've got super sperm."

Lark snorts, then claps her hand over her mouth, muffling her laugh. But it's music to my ears. I lean in and kiss her stomach. Once, twice, then again just because I can't stop marveling at it.

"We need to talk about this," Lark says, her voice still a little shaky. With a decisive nod, I stand and take her hands.

"Yeah, we do."

She lets me lead her back to the bed, but this time, instead of sitting down, I stretch out on my side and pull her down with me. As much as I want to be looking into her beautiful eyes right now, I need to feel like I'm protecting her from all the craziness she's been dealing with alone for the last few days.

Wrapping my big spoon around her little spoon, my hand lands on her stomach, my fingers splayed out as wide as I can.

There's a baby in there. *My baby.*

"I know this isn't what you wanted," Lark starts. "And it wasn't exactly like this was in my plan, either. But I want to keep it. I know you need to focus on baseball, and that's fine. I'll be okay. Whatever you need to do. I don't want you to think I expect anything from you, I just...I decided I'm keeping the baby."

For the second time tonight, I'm stunned speechless. Only this time, it's not a good feeling. I remove my hand, sliding away and scrubbing my hand over my face, trying to make sense of what she just said. But once again, my lack of experience with relationships fucks me over, and I instantly know pulling away was the wrong choice.

Lark draws her knees up, pointedly staying on her side, facing away from me. And when I touch her hip, she tenses up.

"Lark."

She doesn't move.

"Lark Miller, love of my fucking life, stop being so stupid."

That makes her move. Rolling over, she glares at me. Good. I want her angry. It's better than her thinking I could possibly be anything other than thrilled right now.

"Let me make one thing crystal clear," I say, my voice firm as I stare down at her. "This baby is growing inside your body. That means, ultimately, it's your choice what happens. And I would respect your decision, no matter what it was, no matter how much it might hurt. But make no mistake. I want this baby. I want *our* baby. And I want to have it with you. This is a fucking miracle, and there's not a chance I'm ever gonna see it as anything but."

If you were to ask me four months ago how I felt about the idea of having a kid right now, I would have been horrified. A baby changes everything. But that was before. Before I knew Lark loved me. Before I knew I could have the future I never let myself even dream of. A future with her in it.

Now? Yeah, sure, it's going to change things. I'm not naive enough to think a baby won't fundamentally alter my entire life.

But none of that matters anymore. Because the second she uttered those two words, something locked into place inside of me. A part of myself I didn't even know existed. As if every priority, every goal, every dream rearranged themselves in my brain, making room for a new number one.

"You're really okay with this?" Lark whispers, and I can see hope starting to clear away the anguish that was there before.

It kills me to think she spent any time at all worrying about my reaction instead of being filled with joy and excitement.

"Yeah, I am. I'm more than okay. I'm so fucking excited, I

honestly don't know how to express it." I leap up to stand on the bed, pumping my fists in the air and hitting the goddamn ceiling, but who the hell cares? "I'm having a baby!" I shout at the top of my lungs before following it up with a loud *whoop*.

"Oh my God, stop!" Lark says, but she's laughing again as she pulls at my hand, dragging me back down beside her. I go willingly and push her onto her back so I can cover her with my body.

"Lark, I've never been this happy. Not even on the day I got my first major league contract or the day you kissed me. This beats out everything else for best moment of my entire life."

I lean down and kiss her, and finally, everything feels right. She melts underneath me, her hands raking through my hair before settling into place, looped around my neck. I move to the side, and she rolls to me as I lift one of her legs up to drape it over my hip.

"You realize one thing, I hope," I murmur against her lips.

"What?"

"You're stuck with me for life now."

"You say that like it's a bad thing."

Fuck. I want to ask her to marry me. Right here, right now. But we haven't ever talked about that. Hell, we talked about kids but not marriage. Backward, I know, but hey, maybe some weird, cosmic part of us knew what was coming.

I guess it doesn't matter whether my ring's on her finger or not. Lark Miller is mine, now and always.

Chapter Thirty-Six

Monty

"Dan," Lark whispers in between kisses. "Dan, stop. Hold on."

I can't help pouting a little when she pushes me away, but I let her, rolling onto my back and running a hand through my hair as I turn my head to look at her. "What's wrong?"

She doesn't answer. Instead, she moves off the bed and slowly starts to peel off her clothes. I lick my lips, not daring to look away as she strips until she's completely naked.

"I didn't have time to shower before dinner. Want to wash my back? Help me get all clean?"

The wicked smile she gives me says everything and I leap off the bed, shucking my clothes in record time. "Last one in has to have the first orgasm."

Her shriek of laughter makes me smile, but there's no chance of her beating me as I dart past her and into the bathroom. I fling the shower on and step in before yelping at the cold water. Lark stands outside, her tits shaking with laughter.

"I think you got that wrong," she says, testing the water before stepping in with me. "Shouldn't the last one in have to *give* the first orgasm?"

My head moves side to side slowly as I grip her hips and spin her so she's under the now-warm spray. "Nope." I emphasize the *p*, then drop to my knees in front of her, my hands running around to her ass and squeezing. "Trust me, I didn't get anything wrong. This is my reward."

My mouth covers her pussy, and she cries out my name, the sound echoing in the glass enclosure. God bless large showers. And apologies to whoever is in the room next to us. Because hearing my woman come undone? Fucking hot as hell. Not a chance I'm asking her to be quiet.

"Ohhh," she says, the one word drawn out in a long, low moan as my tongue circles her clit. I suck it into my mouth, toying with her, lapping at her. The hot water spilling down on us, the heat of her pussy under my tongue, the sound of her panting, this is heaven. I know it. Eating Lark's pussy is nirvana.

I nibble, I suck, I lick, and I suck some more. And I can sense Lark spiraling upward toward the orgasm I want her to have. But something's holding her back. I kiss her clit and look up her body.

"Lark. Tell me what you want."

"Wh-what?" she pants, tilting her head down. Water falls onto my face, and I blink it away.

"You're holding back, baby. Don't. What do you want?"

"I...God."

"Nope, just Dan."

Another choked laugh, but at least I know this time, it's not from fear.

"I don't know why I can't come." Her voice is plaintive and

stirs something in me, some primal, caveman, alpha instinct.

"You can and you will, Birdie. Ride my fucking face if you have to. Use me. I'm yours."

I dive back between her legs, plunging my tongue in and out of her heat a few times before replacing it with my fingers. I hear the slap of her hand onto the wall next to us and feel the other grip my hair tightly, so tight it almost hurts. But in the best possible way.

She starts to writhe against my mouth, and I know she's finally out of her head.

I'll keep her that way for the rest of the night if I have my way.

Her hips start to grind in circles, and I curl my middle two fingers over, pressing my heel to her clit as I press a kiss just above. "That's it. Let go."

She comes with a hoarse cry, her hips quivering, hands clenching, breath gasping. I don't stop stroking her until I feel her sag against the wall. Only then do I slowly drag my fingers out and bring them quickly to my mouth to suck off every drop before the water washes it away.

I surge up and immediately lift her in my arms. Her legs wrap around my waist as I kiss her, letting her taste herself on my tongue. She moans into my mouth, her heels digging into my ass.

"Thank you, Jesus, for catcher quads," she says, smiling at me in between kisses. I laugh, but secretly agree with her. All that time in the gym and spent in a crouch is paying off. I gently thrust my hips against hers, bumping her into the wall. We should probably get on with the actual shower portion of the evening so I can take her to bed and fuck her properly.

But that thought disappears when Lark sneaks a hand down between us, somehow wrapping it around my dick.

"Can you fuck me like this?" she asks in a low, sultry voice. "Are your legs strong enough to make me come against the wall of this shower?" She guides my dick to her entrance, dragging it back and forth as much as she can with how tightly pressed together we are.

I arch my brow, my jaw clenching with how hard it is not to plunge right into her. "Is that a challenge?"

She nods and I stop resisting, slowly pushing my way inside.

"Challenge accepted."

She buries her head in my neck and I feel her lips press into my skin as I start to move, dragging part of the way out, then in again. It's a little precarious, making sure I don't draw too far out, to say nothing of trying to keep my balance and not send us both crashing down. But the feel of being inside of her without a condom erases any sense I might have once had.

"Shit. This... You... Fuck." My words are a garbled mess as I try valiantly to steady my movements. But it's too goddamn good, her heat surrounding me, squeezing me, consuming me. "Lark," I breathe, her name a prayer on my lips. My hips stutter, and I have to adjust my grip so I can brace one hand on the wall, somehow managing to hold her up with the other arm banded around her.

I try to slow down. To make it last. But being in her bare is making me semi-feral, and there's no chance.

"Tell me if you don't want me to come inside of you," I manage to grind out. Lark's only answer is a moan and her lips smashing against mine. That pushes me over the edge and I spill inside her, jet after jet, my hips pounding her into the wall as she clenches around me like a vice. Her cries are muffled by my grunts and tangled in our kiss.

"Fuck," I breathe when my orgasm finally ends. Our foreheads are pressed together along with the rest of our bodies. And despite my strength, I can feel my legs start to shake. Slowly, I shift my hips back, sliding out of her, and set her down, making sure she's steady on her feet.

I kiss the top of her head, feeling my pulse slowly settle. Until she squirms a little and I look down.

"Are you okay?" I ask, tenderly pushing the wet hair away from her face.

"Yeah...it's just...a little messy."

"What? Oh. Fuck." My fingers find their way between her legs, and I swipe at the sticky mess that is slowly oozing out of her, only to be rinsed away by the water running down her legs. "I probably shouldn't find that so hot, but God help me, I do." I rub my fingers in slow circles, and she goes up on her toes, whispering my name.

I push inside, just one finger, and rub in a circle. Lark's teeth land on my shoulder, biting down as she whimpers.

"Can you give me another?" I don't bother waiting for her answer, ducking my head to take her nipple in my mouth. I toy with it, using my tongue and letting my teeth graze across the tip, all while slowly sliding my finger in and out of her.

"Dan. More," she whimpers and I am happy to oblige. Adding a second finger, I gently press my thumb to her clit. "Yes," she cries, her nails digging into my shoulder. "Oh God, yes!" Her head falls back against the wall as I stroke her through another orgasm. This time when she feebly pushes me away, I go, sliding my fingers free and dipping my head to kiss her.

Then I take some shampoo and slowly start washing her hair. Relishing the simple act of caring for my girl, the mother of my child.

We have a lot to figure out. But right now, there's no where else I want to be and nothing I would rather be doing.

A short while later, I'm wearing a pair of boxers with bananas on them, and she's in my T-shirt. We're wrapped in each other's arms in the middle of my king-size bed.

"I want you to focus on baseball. This season is so important." Lark's fingers trail up and down my bare chest. "Your teammates were talking about you being distracted on the flight down here." She looks at me, the worry clear in her eyes. "You can't afford to be distracted, Dan. I could never forgive myself if this ruined your season."

I move forward slightly so I can meet her lips and kiss her. "Lark, I was distracted because I was worried about you. About us. I knew you weren't feeling well, and then when we talked, you sounded so distant. I didn't know what was wrong, and I couldn't fix it from so far away. But now, knowing it's not something I did" — I pause and chuckle — "okay, well it *is*, but you know what I mean." She slaps my chest and giggles. "Now that I know what's going on, I feel great. I know we've got a lot to deal with, and it's not always going to be easy. But I'll do whatever I need to do to take care of you. You and baby bird."

I hear her sniff and I tilt her chin up, frowning when I see more tears in her eyes. "Hey, what's wrong? Don't cry again, please."

Lark gives me a watery smile, her hand coming up to brush away the tears. "Pregnancy hormones, Dan. I cry a lot these days."

"But nothing's wrong? I didn't say something I shouldn't have?"

She shakes her head. "Not at all. You're perfect. I love that you'd support me, no matter what. That you respect me enough to let this be my choice. And I love that you want this baby as much as I do. But let's get something straight. You have to kick ass this season. Which might mean putting baseball first sometimes."

I open my mouth to protest, but she covers it with her hand. My tongue darts out to lick her palm and she pulls it away with a laugh. "Dan Montgomery, stop being a child."

Giving her a mock pout, I take her hand in mine, bring it back to my mouth, and press a kiss there instead.

"Better. Now may I finish?"

I smirk and she goes on.

"We're going to do this together. Have our baby. But if there are times when you're away, and I'm home for whatever reason, I need to know you won't get distracted again. That you'll be able to focus on what you need to get your contract signed and take this team all the way."

"I'm sorry, all I heard was that we're gonna have a baby."

Lark shrieks, and throws herself over top of me, her wickedly strong fingers pinching my sides and tickling me. We wrestle for a few minutes, both of us laughing, until her knee lands in my groin.

"Oh shit." I groan, rolling to my side.

"Dan, I'm so sorry. Are you okay?" Lark's hands roam my body, and when she hits my hips, I pounce, pushing her onto her back and looming over her. I grab her hands and pin them beside her head.

"I'll be fine. Good thing we did the baby making thing already in case there's serious damage."

Her hips lift and grind against my semihard dick. "Seems fine to me."

I smirk down at her. "Listen, that's a permanent state when I'm around you."

She grins back up at me. "Well, maybe we should take care of that."

"Maybe we should. What do you have in mind?"

In answer, Lark takes me in her hand, sliding up and down a few times until I'm almost fully erect. Then she notches me at her entrance. "I think you can figure it out from here."

You bet your ass I can.

Chapter Thirty-Seven

Lark

There's no one but myself to blame for my exhaustion the next day. Not even pregnancy hormones. This is solely the result of Dan and I getting very little sleep. Next to none, actually.

He sneaks out before I'm even out of bed for a run with some of the other players. When the door to the hotel room opens an hour later, I smell the gift he's brought me even before I open my eyes.

"Coffee?" I croak, blinking against the light streaming in from the open curtains. I'm still wearing one of his T-shirts and nothing else, and as he walks over, there's no ignoring the way his eyes zero in on my boobs.

He settles beside me, handing me the cup. "Before you get too excited, you need to know it's decaf."

I pout, even as I take a sip. "I know, it sucks. No caffeine, no wine, no sushi. Women get the shit end of the deal with this whole pregnancy thing."

"To say nothing of giving birth at the end of it," he adds. That earns him a glare. "What?"

"I'm trying not to think about that part quite yet."

He has the decency to look remorseful. "Sorry, Birdie. But I tell you what. I'll suffer with you. No caffeine, alcohol, or sushi for me, either. I can't do much about the other stuff you're gonna have to deal with, but I can do this."

I pat his arm and look at his very likely caffeinated coffee. "Oh yeah? You're going to do that with me? Starting when?"

His face falls. "Oh. Shit."

I'm about to reassure him it doesn't matter and he can drink the damn coffee when he stands up and goes to the bathroom. I hear him dump the contents of his cup down the sink. When he comes back, he takes my cup from me and takes a large sip.

"You're gonna have to share."

"You didn't have to do that," I say, blinking furiously and trying not to cry.

Dan just fixes me with a strangely affectionate look. "Yeah, I did. We're in this together, I told you."

Crap. The first tear falls, followed by another. "Stop being so wonderful," I wail as he pulls me into his warm chest with a chuckle.

"Sorry, my love. No can do."

I sniffle and sip my coffee. "Fine. I guess I'll just have to get used to it."

"Guess so. Hey, did you ever hear about your internship?"

I push myself up to sit, staring down at my coffee. "I did. I got accepted."

Dan nudges me slightly. "That's awesome, Birdie. So why don't you seem excited?"

My gaze lifts to look at him. "Because it starts in the fall, Dan. And news flash, this baby is coming in the fall. Internships don't exactly mix well with newborns."

"Hmm."

His casual response annoys me a little. I bite my tongue and drink my coffee.

"Why don't you explain the situation and ask if you can start in the new year instead? You said the research study is ongoing, maybe they'll let you delay your placement."

I climb out of bed and set my coffee cup down on the dresser after draining the last few sips. "I don't want to sound all negative, but do you really think that would work? They must have tons of applicants. Why would they wait for me?"

Dan stands up and walks over to me, running his hands down my arms. "Because you're Lark Miller, and you're incredible. You're worth waiting for. Trust me."

"Now you're gonna make me cry again."

He laughs and kisses my forehead. "Oh no, what a surprise."

I drop my head down on his chest with a sigh. "Even if they did let me delay my start, we'd have to figure out childcare, and I'd still have a very young baby at home. I don't know."

"Listen, a wise woman once told me, sometimes you have to put your own needs first. Or something like that. Anyway, you're not putting your goals on hold any less than I am. We're in this together, and we'll find a way to make it work. If you start in January, I'll stay home with the baby." He cocks his head to the side with a smirk. "You gotta admit, I'll make one hell of a DILF."

I laugh, but my head's nodding in agreement. "As long as I'm the only one who gets to actually *F* you."

"Duh. Besides, I bet you anything my parents will help out,

or we'll find a nanny. Heck, doesn't the stadium have a daycare? There's options, Lark. Don't give up on your dream. Promise me you'll at least ask them if you can start later."

I let myself consider it, trying to imagine participating in the internship in the new year. It won't be easy, there's a lot to consider, including my position with the Tridents. But he's right. I won't know what's possible if I don't ask. "Okay. I'll send them an email."

"Great. Are you up for some breakfast? I've got to be at the field pretty soon. But I want to make sure you're fed."

"I can take care of myself, you go to training."

Dan steps back and looks down at me, intense love shining in his eyes. "Baby. Let me take care of you, please."

I let out a mock sigh of suffering. "Is this a new kink for you? Caring for me? First, it was the shower last night, now you want to feed me? What's next, are you going to dress me and carry me everywhere, too?"

He pretends to consider it, and I slap his chest with a laugh.

"Ouch, hey! Don't kink shame, Birdie."

"You're ridiculous." I giggle, dodging his hand that's reaching for me as I dart into the bathroom. After brushing my teeth, I open the door and see him sitting on the couch, a goofy expression on his face as he scrolls on his phone.

"What are you looking at?"

His gaze bounces up with a dash of guilt. "Nothing."

"Liar."

"Seriously. It was nothing."

I fist my hands on my hips and stare him down.

"Okay, fine, I was looking at this chart that talks about the size of a baby throughout pregnancy. Right now, it's the size of a raspberry. A raspberry! Lark, come on. That's freaking cute." He launches off the couch, pulls my shirt off, and before I can say anything, he's blowing a raspberry on my stomach.

"Dan!" I shriek, trying and failing to push him away.

When he finishes, he rocks back on his heels and gives me an unrepentant grin. "A raspberry for our raspberry."

"You. Are. Ridiculous." I try to frown, but it doesn't work; I know I'm smiling back at him. "Come on, let's go and get breakfast."

"Maybe they'll have raspberries!"

After breakfast, everyone makes their way to the field. I find the trainer's area and check in with Mattias.

"Glad you're feeling better."

"Thanks, me too." I debate telling him why I was sick, but don't. It feels too soon, not just because the experts say to wait, but because I want to keep it just between me and Dan a little while longer.

Our baby bird.

Our secret raspberry.

"So far, no new injuries. A few players need increased conditioning, which Caden is designing some plans for. If you can connect with him and make sure the conditioning plans cover the ongoing rehab for anyone that needs it, that would be great."

"On it."

After checking out the rest of the facilities and making a list of supplies we need, I head over to the gym area where Caden is working with Rhett and Ben on the mats.

"Lark!" Rhett's deep voice booms. "Y'here to save us from Caden's torture?"

"Nope," I reply cheerfully. "Quite the opposite. We need to make sure your knees are strong, especially since you, Rhett Darlington, aren't getting any younger. I'm here to see what I can add to Caden's plan."

Rhett clutches his chest. "Damn, darlin'. Way to hit a guy where it hurts."

I arch my brow. "Oh, so it wasn't you that was complaining about knee pain last fall? Hmm. I seem to recall recommending cortisone shots to someone." I tap my chin. "You sure it wasn't you?"

"I plead the fifth."

"You play for Canada, Rhett, we don't have that up there."

"Semantics. Besides, we're in the good ol' United States right now."

I chuckle and move over to Caden's side. "How's it going?"

The muscular fitness trainer looks at the two players on the mats. "Good. I think they're both fine as long as we focus on quad strength. Can you add in some fascia work on their hips?"

"Got it."

I wave goodbye to the guys and move on, at last heading out to the field. The real work for me will start soon, once the guys start needing treatments like taping and massage. For now, I can observe and help as needed.

Outside, the sun is hot, but not too uncomfortable. At least, not for me, standing in the shade of the dugout. For the players on the field, it's likely worse. One group is doing some fielding drills, while more are working on batting into a net.

Eventually, I find Dan standing with the other first-string catcher, and a couple of the second-string guys who are here to train with the team, even if they never actually play this season. They're laughing about something, and I watch him for a minute.

"Whatever yips he had are gone now that you're here."

I startle at Kai's voice as he leans on the railing next to me. "Oh?"

He nods slowly. "It was strange. He didn't want to leave Vancouver, then we got here and all was good. Then, a few days later, something changed and Monty's dropping balls and missing shit all over the place. You arrive, and our boy's back on top." His gaze shifts from the field to me. "Everything all good with you, Lark?"

Kai's normally a boisterous, outgoing, happy guy. So being under this level of scrutiny from him is unnerving.

I lick my lips. "Everything's great, Yami."

A smile covers his handsome face. "Good. That's really good." He pushes off the railing and moves to the stairs that lead to the field. He pauses, and I think he's about to say something before he changes his mind, I guess. Tapping the rail with his glove, he gives me a smile, his eyes dropping down to my stomach and back up again before he jogs onto the field.

It might be harder than I thought to keep this baby a secret.

Chapter Thirty-Eight

Monty

I let out a whoop as Yami throws yet another strike. "Three up, three down, baby!"

We jog toward each other, meeting in the middle with a chest bump. "That's what I'm talking about," he cheers. "Fuck, man, I think we found it."

"Hell yeah, we did."

We walk over to the dugout with the rest of the players that were on our team for this practice game. I jog down the stairs, setting my catcher's helmet on the bench before sinking beside it and taking a long drink of water.

"Lookin' good out there, hot stuff."

My head turns, my grin at the ready at Lark's voice. "Hey, Birdie. Did you see that? Yami was on fire."

"You both were." She bends over and kisses my upturned face. "You're sweaty."

"We can't all spend our day in the air-conditioned facility, baby. Some of us need to be out here doing the work."

Lark just snorts. "Yeah, and some of us have to deal with your stinky, sweaty bodies every time you get so much as a paper cut."

I shrug; she's got a point. When she sits down beside me, I drop a hand to her bare thigh and squeeze gently. Lowering my voice, I ask, "How are you feeling?"

"Like I told you this morning, and yesterday, and the day before, I feel great. The medication the doctor gave me works wonders."

"I'm still gonna ask."

"I know you are." She leans in and kisses me softly. "That's why I love you."

"Hey, lovebirds."

We both turn at Yami's voice. He points at us, his finger wagging between us both. "This is cute and all, but I need my boy in the bullpen."

I stand up with an exaggerated groan. "Pitchers. They're so fucking demanding."

Yami snorts. "You think I'm demanding? Just wait."

My brow furrows. It's not the first cryptic comment he's made. He walks off and I turn to Lark. "Do you think —"

"I think he —"

We both start to talk at the same time. I gesture for her to continue.

Leaning in, Lark drops her voice to a whisper. "Do you think he knows? About the raspberry?"

"I'm wondering the same thing, but how? I haven't said anything, I swear."

Lark chews on her lower lip. "Then how..."

"I'll talk to him later at taco night." She nods and I reach out my thumb to free her lip. "It wouldn't be so bad, though, if he did know. We're gonna have to tell people eventually."

"I know. I guess it's not the end of the world, but I'm still curious about how he knows."

"I'll ask." Dropping one more kiss to her forehead, I step toward the stairs of the dugout. "Better get back to work. See you later, Birdie."

Practice finishes several hours later, and after we all get back to the hotel, we regroup and head out to the Mexican restaurant we end up at every year for a team dinner. Taco night is a spring training tradition for the Tridents.

I let everyone go inside before me, grabbing Yami's arm to hold him back. "Hey, hang on a sec, would you?"

He comes to a stop and looks at me with a half smirk. "What's up?"

I swallow. I told Lark I'd ask him if he knew, but now that the time's come, I don't know how to say it.

"So, ah, me and Lark. Um. You know there was that stuff when she was sick. And, um, okay, so —"

"Dude. She's pregnant, isn't she?" His smirk grows.

"How the fuck do you know?" I ask, bewildered, but also grateful I didn't have to say it. Although, I guess I'd better practice. Soon enough, we'll be telling everyone.

"How did you *not* know?" He holds up one hand and starts counting off. "She was exhausted and nauseous. I'm guessing she got the news that day you went off the rails and she didn't tell you, making you worry. Then she shows up, you guys disappear for the evening, and the next day, you're both smiling nonstop.

She can't stop touching her stomach, and you keep staring at it."

My mouth falls open. "Damn, Yami. Are you some kind of fucking detective?"

"Nah, man, just got two older sisters that had kids not too long ago and good observation skills."

My head moves side to side. "Well, shit. Hopefully, no one else is that good. We wanted to keep it a secret for a while longer."

Yami steps forward and drops a hand to my shoulder. "I won't tell anyone. But can I say one thing?"

I nod.

"I'm really fucking happy for you, man, you two are gonna be fantastic parents." He smirks again. "And I'm gonna be the best goddamn uncle out there."

I pull him in for a back-slapping hug. "Thanks, bro."

We break apart and he turns to look inside the restaurant. "C'mon, let's go before they eat all the chips."

Inside, we join the rest of the team seated around a huge table in the back of the restaurant. For a few minutes, I let the conversation go on around me and just soak it in. This is my life? Seriously? Playing ball on a team with some of the greatest men I know, in love with the best woman in the entire goddamn world, and about to have a baby.

I don't know what I did to get this fucking lucky, but I'm grateful for it.

After everyone's done eating, Sin, who happens to be seated next to me, reaches down beside his chair and lifts up a bag before standing up and clapping his hands to get everyone's attention.

"When I came to my first Tridents' spring training camp last year and Monty pulled out a giant fucking fishbowl, I have to admit, I was confused. Then they explained the tradition, and I was skeptical. But at the end of last year, we read them out loud, and goddamn if most of them hadn't come true. We all know ballplayers are nothing if not superstitious, which means the fishbowl is back. Write down your goals and dreams for the season, boys, and let's make it our best ever."

He sits down amid the raucous applause and I lean in. "As far as speeches go, that was pretty good. You've got the job."

"What job?" he asks with a laugh.

"The keeper of the bowl," I say, keeping my face and voice dead serious.

As expected, Sin looks at me like I just grew a second head. "The what?"

I nod slowly. "You'll collect the bowl tonight and be responsible for it all year. Then at the barbecue in the fall, you have to read the messages out loud."

"Fuck that, this is your gig. I just got it started."

After holding his stare for a beat, I laugh. "Fine, fine. You're not ready yet."

I take some of the paper that is circulating around and grab a pen from the pile in the middle of the table. Most years, my goals come easily to me. Because most years, they're the same. Play to win, go to the championships, that kind of stuff.

This year, things are different. But my goal still comes to me easily.

Be the man Lark deserves and the father our baby deserves.

It's late by the time we get back to the hotel. And when I let myself into my hotel room, where Lark has essentially moved in, having spent zero time in the room the team booked for her to share with another trainer, it takes my eyes a second to adjust in the dim light.

She's curled up on her side, facing me. Her eyes are closed, her face peaceful. She's so goddamn beautiful it takes my breath away, and I have to put my hand over my heart to make sure it's still beating and hasn't jumped ship to land in her hands instead.

Because that woman has my entire heart, and I would lay my life down for her and our baby.

When I can move again, I silently and quickly strip down to my underwear, then walk as quietly as possible into the bathroom to finish getting ready for bed. When I finally lift the covers and slip in behind her, I carefully sneak my arm around her waist, wrapping my body around the curve of hers.

My hand lands on her stomach, my thumb lightly caressing the life growing inside.

It's funny. I went from a virgin to a father-to-be in a very short time. It might not be what I ever would have planned for myself, but I don't regret a single thing.

How could I when the first woman I've ever loved will also be the last woman I love?

The only woman I'll ever love.

CHAPTER THIRTY-NINE

Lark

"We should probably start looking at houses."

My hands freeze in the middle of folding a shirt at Dan's casual statement. I turn, and he's where he was a second ago, stretched out on his side in the middle of my bed, surrounded by my laundry. He just finished helping me match up my socks as I put everything away from spring training.

Despite the domestic nature of our morning, his words catch me by surprise. Which quickly makes me feel foolish. And excited.

Of course, we need to discuss our living situation, but isn't it too soon for that? I mean, we're having a baby, and we love each other, but...

But what? What more do I need?

I subtly shake my head and clear my throat. "Oh yeah?"

He looks up from his phone and turns it around to face me. "What about this one? It's close to where Sin and Willow live, has four bedrooms, and a big backyard. Oooh, we could get a dog!"

"Dan, we're going to have a baby. I'm not adding a puppy

into that chaos."

He waves his hand at me, looking back at his phone "I said dog, not puppy. We could rescue an older one."

It's moments like this that make me pause and question if he's being silly or serious. With Dan, it could be either.

"We don't have to rush on a house, you know, either one of our apartments will be fine at first."

"Well, yeah, but which one? I've got the security and the amenities, but you've got the view."

"You want to move in together. Now?"

I suppose Dan hears the question in my voice because he sets his phone down and sits up. "Well, yeah. Don't you?"

Moving to the bed, I sink down on the edge. He moves to sit beside me, drawing my legs up and over his lap.

"I don't know." I sense him tense up and grab his hand. "Not because I don't want to, but I guess..." I pause, trying to collect my thoughts into something that makes sense. "I guess I never let myself consider it. I know that sounds so stupid, we're having a child together. And I know you love me, and I love you, so moving in together should be obvious. But —"

"But you still have a hard time fully believing that nothing is going to diminish my love and that our future is clear to me."

If the way he understands me better than I understand myself isn't a sign he is the only man for me, I don't know what is.

My head moves up and down, even as moisture wells in my eyes. Dan chuckles, wiping away the tears.

"I haven't wanted to overwhelm you or rush you. I mean, you were engaged, literally the day before you kissed me for the first time. But maybe that was a mistake and I should have said it sooner. I plan on marrying you, Birdie. You're my end game. My championship. The only trophy that truly matters. I want to spend the rest of my life dedicated to you and our family. So whether we move in together now or later, I don't really care. As long as you know deep down, this is it. You and me, together forever."

I'm blinking away my tears as his words heal the cracks I hadn't even realized were still covering my heart. I don't want to be a woman who needs constant reassurance, but if there was ever a man who would be happy to provide that, it's Dan. I lean in and kiss him softly, wrapping my arms around his shoulders and climbing farther into his lap.

"I love you."

"I know." His lips quirk up in a grin.

We kiss again and again, and just as I'm ready to make a mess of my piles of clean laundry, Dan stands up, cradling me in his arms.

"Come on, Birdie. We can finish this later. Let's get a snack and go for a walk."

He carries me out to the kitchen, setting me down on the counter before going to the cabinet where I keep all of my favourite snacks.

Pulling out a package of licorice, he waves it at me, and I reach for it with grabby hands. But as soon as I open the package, I gag. "Oh my God, nope." I throw it at him, and of course, he catches it. "Get that away from me, please."

Reaching for the basket on my counter, I grab a vial of essential oils, not even caring what it is. When I open and inhale the bright scent of bergamot, I sigh in relief.

"No licorice during pregnancy. Noted."

I pout. "That's depressing. Can you get rid of it all?" I ask, hopping down from the counter and giving him a wide berth, seeing as he's still holding the offending package. I take another inhale of bergamot and move to the couch, leaning against the back of it as Dan pulls out all the licorice and puts it in a bag before tying the ends.

"Garbage?"

"No, don't waste it. Take it in for the team? Just tell them not to eat it around me." I shudder, imagining one of the guys coming in for a massage, smelling of licorice.

Dan chuckles. "You got it."

His phone starts to ring, and I move to pick it up from the table, handing it to him.

"It's my parents." He looks at me, and I know what he's about to ask.

"We should tell them."

"Really?" His eyes widen and his smile grows. "Are you sure? We haven't told anyone yet."

"I know, but your parents should know."

He answers the video call with a grin. "Hey, Mom!"

"Hi honey, just wanted to check in, see how you're settling in now that you're back."

"Great, actually." Dan moves to lean against the couch next to me. "I'm at Lark's right now."

"Oh, hi, sweetheart," Edith says cheerfully, lifting her hand to wave at me.

"Hi, Edith." I wave back. "How are you and Howard doing?"

"We're just fine. Busy as always, but very excited for the game this weekend!"

"So are we. The team is looking really strong."

Dan turns the phone back to himself and takes my hand before pushing off the couch and dragging me around to the other side so we can sit on it properly. "Hey, Mom, is Dad nearby?"

"I think so, he was at the bank to do a deposit but I heard him come back a few minutes ago. Why?"

"Can you go and get him, please?" Dan's leg is bouncing up and down with excitement, and I place my hand on it. He flashes me a grin and kisses my forehead. Right in front of his mother, who's still smiling at us.

"It's good to see you two so happy."

"We are, Mom. Very happy." Dan covers my hand on his leg with one of his own. Then his dad's face shows up on the small screen. "Hey, Dad!"

"Hi, son, Lark, how are you both doing?"

"We're good. Hey, um, we've got some news." All of a sudden, Dan's face turns bright red.

I watch his Dad's brows furrow as he peers closer at the phone. "Son? Are you alright?"

He musters up a nod, then turns to me. He's clearly choked up, and while it's sweet, I'm also freaking out at the realization that I'm going to have to be the one to say it.

"Ah, well..." I start, then take a deep breath. Ripping off the Band-Aid in three...two...one... "I'm pregnant."

There's a stunned silence, broken only by Dan's loud exhale. When I glance over at him, he's managing to hold the phone steady, and the redness is starting to recede from his cheeks, replaced by a goofy grin.

"Yeah, you're gonna be grandparents."

"What? I... Oh my goodness!" Edith covers her mouth with her hands, the phone falling to the side. Howard seems to grab it, and takes over holding it, but I can see him wiping under his glasses.

"That's quite the news, kids," he says gruffly.

"It's good news, Dad. The best. I mean, it wasn't planned, but we're incredibly happy and excited about it."

After a second, Howard nods. "That's all that matters."

"What can we do to help?" Edith chimes in, seeming less shocked and more in control. "How are you feeling, Lark?"

"I'm okay now. I had some nausea at first. Actually, we thought it was a virus. But the doctor confirmed I'm about twelve weeks along and gave me some medicine for the nausea. You're the first to hear the news, but we'll be telling the team soon."

"And thanks for the offer Mom, but we're good right now. I'm sure we'll need you later, though. How do you feel about babysitting?" Dan grins.

Edith scoffs. "Do you really think you can keep me away from my grandbaby? I'll be there as often as you'll allow me. Whatever you need, both of you."

"Thank you," I say softly, feeling a little blown away by their reaction. Their only son is having a baby with a woman he's only been dating for a few months, and they're thrilled.

I know, I just know, that my parents would *not* react this way. They would likely see it as a personal insult or attack on them. Somehow, it would be a disappointment at worst, and a nuisance at best.

I manage to push away the depressing thoughts of how different my family is from Dan's just in time to hear him agree to send his mom the ultrasound photos after our appointment this week.

"If that's okay with you, Birdie?" He squeezes my knee gently.

I nod quickly. "Of course. I'm glad you're as excited as we are." I smile, but it's a small one, and Dan gives me a questioning look.

"Hey, Mom, Dad, we better get going. We've got a team thing later on."

It's a lie, but I'm grateful for it. We say goodbye to his parents, Dan sets the phone down, and he turns to face me. "What happened there?"

I don't answer right away. Instead, I snuggle into his side, resting my hand on his chest to feel his heartbeat, calm and steady, as always. He kisses the top of my head, seeming to be willing to give me a minute.

"Your parents are so lovely, and I'm glad they're happy for us. Really. But it made me think about how my parents might react if they find out. And it definitely won't be the same."

"What do you mean, *if*?" Dan asks. "We're gonna tell them, Birdie. And if they choose to be miserable assholes about it, then I'll set them straight. But we have to give them a chance."

I sit upright and twist my hands together in my lap.

"Do we? It's not like they cared all that much for me, and I was their daughter. Why would they care about a grandchild?"

"They might not," he says somberly. "But we have to give them a chance. And at the end of the day, it doesn't matter what they think. I won't let them or anyone else hurt you or our baby bird. And I promise you, this child will always know they're loved. Unconditionally, wholly, and without end. Just like their mama."

Reaching my hand up, I cup his cheek, then pull him down to meet my kiss.

"And just like their daddy."

Chapter Forty

Lark

I give the waiter a smile of thanks as he sets the water glass down in front of me.

"Will you be wanting anything else to drink?"

Wanting, yes. Having, no.

"Water is fine for me. My friends might have something when they get here."

He nods and walks away. I run my finger through the condensation on the glass. I don't know why I'm anxious. Telling Willow and Sadie about the baby should be easy. I honestly can't imagine them not being happy for us, even if it is unexpected.

But we haven't told anyone aside from Dan's parents yet. The plan is to announce it to the team after the home opener tomorrow. Dan wants to be able to focus on the game and not have anyone be distracted by the news. Of course, we didn't account for how nervous either one of us might be about keeping it a secret until then...

"Hey, Lark!"

I look up to see Willow and Sadie weaving through the tables toward me. Standing, I hug both of them before we sit back down.

"Drinks?" Willow asks, looking at the menu. "I could go for a glass of wine."

I shake my head. "Just water for me."

"I'll join you, Willow," Sadie says in her soft voice.

"Perfect. Lark, are you sure?" Willow signals for the waiter before looking over at me. "You're not feeling sick again, are you?"

"Not exactly." I fidget with the paper wrapper that holds the cutlery and napkin together.

The waiter saves me from having to say anything more by taking their order for wine and some appetizers. But as soon as he leaves, Willow leans forward. She's got her game face on. The one I've witnessed her use to wrangle a locker room full of players and a conference room full of media.

"Lark Miller. Spill."

My mouth suddenly feels dry. I take a sip of water. "I'm pregnant."

"I knew it!"

"What? How?" I ask as Willow holds her hand out to Sadie for a high five.

"Oh, come on, Lark. You were nauseous and tired, and then miraculously better. I'm guessing your doctor confirmed the pregnancy and gave you some drugs? Just because I've never been pregnant doesn't mean I'm clueless to the signs."

"Well, I sure felt clueless because that was the shock of my life," I mumble, looking down at my glass.

"You really didn't suspect it?" Sadie asks curiously.

"Nope. I mean, I guess I should have, seeing as the first time we had sex the condom slipped. But I truly didn't worry. I was on the pill, making the chances so slim."

Willow winces. "Yikes about the condom, though. Hopefully, Monty was a good boy and had a clean bill of health at his last physical."

I only just manage to stop myself from saying that wasn't a concern, what with it being his first time and all.

"Yeah, everything was fine. Well, except for the baby thing, but that's fine, too." I feel a small smile break free. "More than fine, actually."

"I would imagine it's pretty overwhelming," Sadie says gently. "But it is very exciting, too. As long as you and Monty are both happy."

"We are." Happy is an understatement...

Our appetizers arrive, and now that I'm not feeling the pressure to tell them, I can relax and enjoy lunch with my friends. They have a hundred questions, and I answer what I can. We laugh about crazy name ideas, and nursery themes, and Willow insists she's throwing me a baby shower in a few months during the All-Star break.

A while later, as we're leaving the restaurant, Willow pulls me into her arms. "Ahh, I still can't believe you're having a baby. This is just so freaking exciting!"

"What did you just say?"

At the sound of a familiar, shrill voice, my good mood dissipates in an instant. Willow draws back and mouths *sorry* to me. Standing close to us is none other than Cordelia Hazelwood. I hadn't noticed her approaching, and I'm guessing neither did Willow, who has moved to my side, tucking my arm in hers.

Poor Sadie is hovering next to us. She hasn't had the pleasure of meeting my former almost-mother-in-law. But the tension is obvious to anyone.

"Cordelia. Nice to see you. I trust you're well?" I ask, my voice stiff. There's no chance we can get away without a confrontation, especially if she heard what Willow said.

"Did your friend truly just say you're with child, Lark?" Cordelia's voice is cold. I suppose any remotely positive feelings she held toward me ended the second Baron and I broke off the engagement.

"Yes." I force my spine to straighten and look her in the eye. "I am. And if you'll excuse us, we need to be going. Have a nice day."

I move past her, dragging Willow with me and hoping Sadie follows. As soon as we round the corner, however, I stumble to a stop, leaning on Willow.

"Oh God. Tell me that didn't happen and it was just some bizarre pregnancy hallucination."

"Um, sorry, babe, but you definitely just told your ex's mom that you're pregnant," Willow says, her voice laced with sympathy.

"Hopefully, she doesn't think the baby's father is your ex," Sadie says, and I look at her in horror.

"Oh shit, I didn't even consider that." I remove my arm from Willow's and cover my face in my hands. "What am I going to do?"

"Nothing," Willow says firmly, pulling my hands down. "You're going to do nothing. You don't owe that witch or her family anything. If Baron, for some crazy reason, thinks the baby is his, he can reach out. But didn't you tell me you two hadn't had sex in months? He's not an idiot, he can do the math. Don't let her ruin your vibe, girlfriend."

I pull her in for a hug. "Thank you for having my back and being amazing friends. This baby is going to have the best aunties ever."

"You'll have a built-in babysitter in a few years when Peyton's older." Willow smiles. "On that note, I better get back to the office. When will you two be announcing this to the team officially?"

"After the home opener."

Willow flashes me a thumbs-up. "Got it. My lips are sealed until then. Girl code."

"I won't tell Maverick anything, either." Sadie hugs me. "But I'm also really happy for you. Monty will be a wonderful dad, he's got such a good heart."

We say our goodbyes and I make my way home. It's difficult to say where feels more like that nowadays. Half of my things are at my apartment and half at Dan's. We do need to sort out our living situation. But now, with the season starting, who knows when we'll have time for house hunting if we decide to buy somewhere new. The easiest thing would be to just get rid of one of our apartments and move into the other. But which one?

I ponder that question the entire drive back to my apartment. When I open the door and let myself in, I look around with fresh eyes, trying to envision both of us living here, and maybe even a baby.

It's smaller than Dan's place, yet filled with light, and the view of the city is wonderful. As I stand in the living room, looking around, I reflect back on when Baron and I got engaged. I didn't want to leave my apartment and move into his. I hated his apartment; it felt cold and sterile.

But when I think about moving into Dan's, I'm filled with happiness. His spare bedroom would make a good nursery, and being so close to the stadium would be convenient. It all clicks in that moment. I want to move into his place until we decide on a long-term plan. Now I just have to wait for him to get back from the stadium so I can tell him.

To occupy my time, I start searching for moving companies. Even though I'm sure the guys would help, they're going to be a little busy starting tomorrow. So am I, for that matter, with today being a rare day off for me.

In the middle of reading reviews for one company, my phone rings. I suppose I shouldn't be surprised to see Baron's name, but I am a little disappointed. Obviously, Cordelia wasted no time in contacting her son about my news.

"Hello," I say coolly. It might not be fair to be mad at him when his mother is the overbearing cunt.

"Hey Lark, how are you?" He doesn't sound freaked out or worried, giving me hope that he's using some common sense.

"I'm fine, thank you. I'm guessing your mother called you." I jump straight to the point, not wanting to be on the phone with my ex-fiancé any longer than necessary.

Baron clears his throat. "Ah, yeah, she did. I tried to tell her I was certain it wasn't mine, but you know how she is."

Yeah. A freaking steamroller.

"Mm-hmm. Well, it's not yours."

"Cool. Yeah. I figured, seeing as we..."

Good grief, he sounds uncomfortable. And weirdly, it makes me happy. For a man who always seemed unruffled, it's gratifying to hear him squirm a little.

"Seeing as we didn't have sex for, oh, what, six or seven months before we broke up? Not even the night we got engaged. Yeah, it would be tricky for you to be the father of this baby."

"Right."

There's a pause, and I wonder if he's going to ask me who *is* the father. Assuming he even wants to know. I don't care either way, but I do want him to know one thing.

"I never cheated on you, Baron. The baby was conceived on New Year's Eve."

"I see. Thank you for telling me," he says stiffly. I hear him exhale. "I feel like an idiot even asking this, but is it him? That baseball player?"

This time, the pause is mine.

"Yes."

Another sigh. "How long have you loved him?"

"Honestly? I don't know. I never thought about him that way because I was with you. But he…"

"He's better for you than I ever was," Baron finishes my thought.

"Yeah."

"Well, I'm happy for you, Lark. I wish you nothing but the best."

Even though he can't see me, I smile. "Thank you. Same to you."

"Right, well, I guess it's goodbye —"

"Wait!" I interrupt. "Will you please try to get your mother to hear the truth? I don't want her thinking the worst of me."

Baron laughs, but there's no warmth to it. "Not sure she deserves that, but yeah, I'll tell her. Goodbye, Lark."

We hang up and I stare at my phone. Why do I care what Baron's mother believes of me? I wish I knew, but I don't. Honestly, her opinion matters less than almost anyone else's. Still, I don't want people thinking I would disrespect Baron like that.

Just because we were wrong for each other doesn't make him a bad guy.

But I certainly am glad this baby is Dan's and not his.

CHAPTER FORTY-ONE

Monty

There's something magical about opening day. The sounds, the smells, the sun. It's a perfect symphony for the senses. The feeling of a fresh start and another chance to go all the way.

I'm feeling damn good about our team. Spring training was exactly what it should have been. A chance for us to come together as a team, figure out our dynamic, and hone our skills. And it all led up to this: Yami's on the mound, I'm behind the plate, and the Toronto Wolverines have their first player walking up to bat.

I take a deep breath and shut out everything but my focus on Yami. I give him the signal. A curveball.

He nods, then takes a step and winds up. The ball is in my glove seconds later, and the umpire calls a strike.

That's how it's done, boys. Even though no one can see it, I'm grinning behind my mask. The rest of the inning goes much the same with three up, three down.

Guess the Wolverines didn't have as good a time at spring training.

We jog off the field, everyone clapping Yami on the back and celebrating his incredible start. I peel off my gear before finding him, knocking our heads together.

"There you go, brother. Unstoppable."

He claps me on the back. "Hell, yeah. Dynamic duo. We should get matching tattoos."

"Dude. Seriously?" I look at him, my mouth stretching in a maniacal grin. "I'm *so* in. Hey, Mav!" I shout for our teammate who has more tattoos than anyone. "Got a good tattoo artist? Me and Yami are gonna be twins."

He fixes us with an inscrutable look. The guy has loosened up a lot over the last several months, but he still doesn't laugh quite as easily as everyone else chuckling over my announcement.

"Unicorns shitting baseballs or mermaids?" I turn back to Yami. "Personally, I'm a fan of the unicorns."

He just shakes his head. "Way to ruin my idea, Monty." His smile betrays his griping.

Together, we turn to the field where Sin is stepping up to the plate against his former teammate. I lean against the railing, resting one foot on the lower bar. The pitcher sends the ball flying, but Sin's a statue, familiar with the pitcher from when he played for the Wolverines.

Sure enough, the ump calls it a ball. He gets one more that's too low, then a slider comes straight at him. The entire dugout holds their breath as Sin takes a swing.

CRACK.

"There it is!" I shout, clapping my hands as Sin takes off for first. He makes it with time to spare.

"You boys are off to a great start."

I spin around at Lark's voice. "Hey, Birdie." I drop a kiss to her head and try to subtly touch her stomach as I lean in to whisper, "How's baby bird doing?"

Her hand grazes over mine as she tips her head up, a wide grin on her face. "Just fine. Ready to watch Daddy hit a home run."

"You got it. And we're still planning to tell the bosses?"

"Yup."

I kiss her nose. "Okay."

Someone calls her name, and Lark turns and nods in acknowledgment.

"Get back to work," I say with a wink. My eyes stay trained on her as she walks away, over to one of the coaches.

"Everythin' good?"

I turn to look at Darling. "Everything's fucking awesome. Let's win this."

He bumps my held-up fist and we focus on the game. Sin's on third now, and Jonesie is up to bat. Unfortunately, he strikes out and stomps off the field with his jaw clenched.

"It's all good, man, next time. You went down swingin'," Darling calls out, but Jonesie just gives him a sharp nod, his eyes staring straight out at the field.

It never feels good to strike out. Especially not in your first at bat, in the first goddamn game.

Good thing I hit the homer my baby wanted when it's my turn.

The game is over all too soon with Yami getting another shutout inning, securing our four-run lead.

The press is demanding of him and me, wanting to talk about our partnership, the Tridents' strategy of letting one catcher and one pitcher work together as much as reasonably possible, and asking about our predictions for the coming season. It's annoying when all I want to do is shower and find Lark. But this is part of the gig. And at the end of the day, I wouldn't change it for anything.

Eventually, we're done, and we can jog down into the locker room. Yami looks over at me as I rush to get changed. "You got somewhere to be?"

"Yeah," I say, yanking a hoodie on. "Lark and I have a meeting with management."

"Oh." His eyes widen. "Oh!"

I pause and grin as I lower my voice and say, "We're gonna tell the team at morning practice tomorrow."

He walks over, one hand on his towel. With the other, he pulls me in for a hug. "That's fantastic. Everyone is gonna be thrilled."

"Thanks, man. I appreciate you keeping it quiet."

A strange look crosses his face. "All good. Everyone's allowed to have a secret or two."

I don't get a chance to ask him what he means before he turns and walks over to his locker, keeping his back turned as he gets dressed.

As much as I want to check on him, I've got somewhere to be.

Grabbing my bag, I head out of the locker room and turn right, making my way to the trainer's area. Lark is coming out of the gym, and we meet with a kiss.

"Ready for this?" she asks, taking my hand.

"So ready."

We head upstairs to the executive level where we asked Mike Cartwright, the team's owner, to meet us along with the head trainer and head coach. Not gonna lie, I'm scared shitless. I need them to be happy for us so we go into this season with them still thinking I'm worth keeping around for another five years.

My parents are excited about the baby, which is awesome. But they're stretched thin enough managing the store. If I don't land a good contract at the end of this season, I don't have a hope in hell of convincing them to retire.

And I don't want them killing themselves, trying to be there for Lark and the baby, as well as running the store. I want them to be able to relax and enjoy being grandparents. Enjoy the rest of their lives and let me pay them back however I can, for everything they've done for me.

Mike, Coach Stirling, and Mattias are already waiting for us in one of the conference rooms, and we walk in hand in hand. I pull out Lark's chair and then sit beside her.

"Great game, Monty. You looked good out there," Mike says, leaning back in his chair. "You must know we're already aware of your relationship with Lark, so what's the reason for this meeting?"

I look at Lark, who gives me a nervous smile. Then I turn back to the other side of the table. "Thank you, Mike. The team pulled off an excellent start to the season. We wanted to meet with the three of you because we have some news that may impact how things go this fall."

Crap, that was the wrong thing to say, judging by the frowns and raised eyebrows.

"Not in terms of my ability to play," I hurry to clarify, then wince, because that's not exactly true. If Lark goes into labour, I sure as shit don't want to miss it because of a game. But that might be out of my hands, which is something we've already discussed.

"Sorry. I'm saying this all wrong."

"I'm pregnant," Lark blurts out. "That's what Dan is trying to say. We're having a baby, due near the end of September. Dan will play the entire season, of course. But I may need to slow down come September and will, unfortunately, likely be on maternity leave for the end of the season."

The room falls silent, the three men across from us absorbing the news. Mike reacts first, leaning forward with a smile creasing his face. "Well, first of all, congratulations. I take it this is happy news?"

My head bobs up and down. "Very happy. The happiest."

He nods and turns to Lark. "Are you doing okay? Need anything?"

Her mouth falls open in surprise. I guess that's warranted. I mean, it's not every day the owner of the company you work for asks if you need anything because you're pregnant.

"N-no thank you, Mr. Cartwright. I'm doing fine. We're...we're all doing fine."

"Good. I suggest you get your names on the day care list soon. From what I hear, spaces don't come available often." He turns to Coach. "And we'll make sure all the catchers are ready to go, in case Dan needs to miss anything. Family first."

Now it's my turn for my jaw to drop. "Thank you, Mike,

but really, I don't plan on missing any games unless it's an emergency."

Lark squeezes my hand in agreement. But I can't fight the rising fear. Will they use the baby as a reason not to give me a good contract next year? If I have to miss games, will that work against me?

Mike turns back to me and his tone leaves no room for discussion. "Monty, I've always believed baseball is a family sport. This team has been my family for years. We take care of our own, first and foremost. Which means if you need to be there for Lark and your little one, you will be supported as much as possible. I know you've got one of the best work ethics on the team and your dedication does not go unnoticed." His face softens. "But priorities shift, son. And now, you need to turn that dedication to your future family. The Tridents are here for you both, we're not going anywhere. If the time comes that you need to be with Lark, that's where we all want you to be."

Well, shit. It's not often I'm stunned silent. But I am right now. How did I get so lucky to end up on a major league team with someone like Mike Cartwright as the owner?

"Thank you, sir," I choke out, my throat thick with emotion. I look over at Lark to see her eyes glistening with tears.

Mike gives us both a smile, then leans back in his chair once more. "Now, when are we announcing this news to everyone?"

That time comes the next morning when Lark walks out onto the field with me as the guys are all getting warmed up for a quick practice before we play again tonight.

I put my fingers in my mouth and blow a short, sharp whistle to get their attention. "Hey! Get your asses over here, I've got news!"

Everyone makes their way over, including a few of the training staff and coaches that were in the dugout. When they're all loosely gathered around, I pull Lark in front of me, and drop my hands to her stomach, cradling it protectively.

"Everyone, meet the newest Tridents team member. They'll be hitting the field this fall. And if we're lucky, in twenty years, they'll be taking my place behind home plate."

There's a split second of silence as everyone figures out what I'm saying, and then the group erupts into cheers. Next thing we know, Lark and I are surrounded, passed around for hug after hug.

Mike was right. Baseball is a family sport. And this team is my family.

But none so much as the beautiful woman smiling at me.

Chapter Forty-Two

Lark

"Are you going to answer that?" Willow asks from across her desk. We're having lunch together, but any appetite I had has disappeared.

"It's my mom."

"Oh."

My phone stops ringing, and I look up at my friend. "Why is she calling me? We haven't spoken in weeks."

Willow gets up and comes around to crouch down beside me, placing her hand on my knee. "You don't have to talk to her if you don't want to. But…" Her voice trails off with a hint of sorrow. Having lost her adoptive father when she was younger, Willow knows the pain of losing a parent.

Except mine aren't dead.

They're just not talking to me.

Which isn't all that different from how it's been my entire life, I suppose. But that doesn't change the fact that deep down, I've always longed to have some sort of a relationship with them. One that doesn't feel like I'm an afterthought. Or like I somehow owe them for simply being alive.

My hand drops to my stomach, feeling the slight rounding that popped out this week. I'm just under seventeen weeks along, so the nausea has fully subsided and I finally have some energy. Just in time, seeing as the season is in full swing, and both Dan and I are going nonstop. I'm anxious to feel the baby move, even though my midwife has cautioned me it's normal not to have felt it yet.

I just hope Dan and I are together when it happens so he can experience it as well.

I can't help but wonder how my mother felt when she was pregnant with me. Did she get excited to feel me kick? Or was it just another annoyance? Something to be endured, not cherished.

"I guess I should see what she wants," I finally say.

"Only if you actually want to," Willow says firmly. "You don't owe her anything, Lark. Not a goddamn thing."

"She's my mom," I whisper, my voice cracking at the end, and Willow pulls me into her arms.

"I know she is, but even so, if she doesn't treat you right, then she doesn't deserve your energy or time."

I pull back and pick up my phone. "You're right. I'll see what she wants and then decide."

Willow stands. "Do you want some privacy?"

My head moves side to side. "No, stay. Please?"

She moves to the chair next to me and sits down. I take a deep breath and call my mom back.

"Hello, Lark."

"Hi, Mom. Sorry, I couldn't answer when you called. What's up?"

There's a long pause. I start to fidget in my seat, and Willow raises her eyebrows.

"I was hoping you would meet me for lunch later this week. I checked the Tridents' schedule, and it seems the team is in town. Would that mean you're available?"

My mouth falls open in complete shock. It's not the meeting for lunch part that has me flabbergasted. It's the fact that she took the time to check the team's schedule instead of demanding I make time and then being annoyed when I try to say I'm away or working. I can't recall a time she has ever been this considerate of my schedule and responsibilities.

It feels a little like I've somehow landed in the twilight zone, to be honest.

"I...I." I stumble over my words, clear my throat, and try again. "Yes, I can meet for lunch. Tomorrow or Thursday?"

"Wonderful. I'll make a reservation for us, say, noon tomorrow at Pescados?"

Of course, she names a fancy seafood restaurant, even though I have never liked fish. But I'll get a salad or something, I guess.

"Sounds good, see you then."

"Goodbye, Lark."

We hang up and I again stare at my phone in disbelief.

"I guess I'm on my own for lunch tomorrow?" Willow asks lightly, breaking the tension. I look up at her and nod.

"Guess so."

The next day, I smooth my hand down the front of the dark

green sweater I chose to wear. It sort of hides my small baby bump, which is key since I don't know how today is going to go. I want desperately to be able to share the news with my mother. But not if she's going to twist it around somehow.

That's also why I wanted to show up early. So I can be seated when she arrives, letting the table conceal the rounding of my stomach.

But my plan is foiled when I walk inside to see her already handing her coat to one of the hosts. She turns and spots me, and a small yet surprisingly genuine-looking smile creases her face.

"Hello, Lark." She leans in to press an air-kiss in the vicinity of my cheek.

"Hi, Mom."

Her gaze doesn't drop to my stomach, which I count as a small mercy, as we're led to our table. We sit down and the waiter asks for our drink order.

"I'll have a glass of the Chablis, please," Mom says.

"Just water for me." I give him a small smile. "I have to go back to work."

He nods and is gone. For a long moment, neither one of us speaks. Personally, I have no idea what to say. This lunch was her idea, but if it's going to be nothing more than awkward silence, I might feign an emergency and leave.

"I spoke to Cordelia yesterday morning."

Oh. Crap.

I rub my hands along the tops of my thighs to try and stop them from bouncing. So that's what this is all about. She already knows.

"It's not Baron's."

Why *that* is the first thing that comes out of my mouth, I don't know. But it is, and now I have to move on.

"I'm in love with someone from the team. We've been friends for a long time, and when I ended things with Baron, I realized our friendship was something more. We didn't plan on getting pregnant, but it happened and we're very happy about it."

I finish speaking and can feel my pulse thundering in my veins. I'm certain my cheeks are flushed, and I might very well be leaving bruises on my thighs from gripping them so hard.

But then, instead of the condemning lecture I'm expecting, my mother just looks at me, her expression a mix of emotions I don't know how to make sense of

"Oh, Lark," she murmurs softly. "Congratulations. Are you feeling well?"

It takes me a second to adjust, to lower my defenses enough to nod.

"That's good. I was so sick the first few weeks with you. Couldn't keep anything down except for crackers and peppermint tea."

I clear my throat. "Yeah, I was sick at first. That's what made me go to the doctor, and they gave me a pregnancy test. It was quite the shock."

Her hand reaches out over the table, but when I don't move to take it, she slowly draws it back. I watch carefully as she straightens her spine, lacing her fingers together on the table in front of her.

"Lark, I owe you an apology."

I blink slowly.

"I know we've never been close. And when you announced your engagement to Baron was over, that your relationship was over, well, your father and I did not handle that well. I acknowledge that. But once I was over the shock of it, I realized just how disconnected I was from my own daughter. To not realize how trapped you felt? How we made you feel pressured into staying with him?" She shakes her head in dismay, and I'm instantly transported back in time to the day I told my parents it was over with Baron.

Somehow, I had found the courage to tell them the truth. That the only reason I stayed with Baron was because I thought it was what they wanted me to do. Not because I loved him. At the time, my father waved his hand at me and dismissed my feelings with a scoff. My mother, however, was silent. I guess she was dealing with the emotions she's describing now.

"Your father and I argued about it for a long time. He thought you were being dramatic and your decision to end things with Baron was impulsive. Something you'd regret. I tried to tell him I believed you and we should support your choice." Regret colours her tone. "I'm sorry I didn't reach out sooner to tell you that."

This time, I'm the one to place my hand on the table, covering one of hers. "Mom, it's okay."

"No, Lark, it's not." She raises her head and looks me straight in the eyes. "It's not alright that my own daughter felt she needed to marry a man to make her parents happy. And it's not alright that you didn't feel you could tell me that you started seeing someone who made *you* happy. And it's certainly far from alright that I had to find out you were pregnant from Cordelia bloody Hazelwood!"

"I'm sorry," I start to say, but she shakes her head.

"Please, do not apologize. I understand why you made the choices you did. I'm not trying to make you feel guilty, not when I know your father and I are the only ones to blame for our relationship being this way." She glances down, then back up again. "And for what it's worth, the Hazelwoods are pompous, self-righteous snobs. I've never liked them, and I'm glad you're not marrying into that family. When Cordelia called to tell me she saw my 'harlot daughter' parading around town, I told her exactly what I thought of her and her opinions."

A broken part of my heart heals in that moment, hearing my mother defend me.

"I thought you were friends?" I blurt out.

Mom lets out a small sigh. "Much like you and Baron ended up together because of our families' connection, I found myself spending time with Cordelia simply because of your father's partnership. I didn't feel I had much of a choice except to spend time with her, no matter how boring I found her topics of conversation, or how grating her voice would be at times."

I choke back a laugh. Have I ever heard my mother speak so candidly? I don't think I'll ever truly move on from how toxic our relationship was my entire life until now, but this conversation is going a long way toward me being able to forgive her and hopefully, start anew.

Apparently, my mother feels the same way.

"I know I haven't been a very good mother to you. Truthfully, I was unprepared for having a child. I didn't know how to handle the emotions and responsibility that came along with it all, and I fear I chose avoidance and denial instead of embracing it." She shakes her head, and I can see her eyes glistening. "You'll never know just how much I regret that."

I watch her brush away a tear, and when she reaches for me, I let Mom take my hand again and squeeze it gently. She gives me a cautious smile. "Do you think we could...I could...have a chance to do better? Could we try to have a relationship? I'd like to get to know your new gentleman and possibly be a part of your baby's life." Another tear tracks down her cheek.

I'm already nodding, feeling matching tears build in my eyes. I don't know what the future looks like for my mother and me, but I'm willing to find out.

"I'd like that."

Chapter Forty-Three

Monty

"Should we change your nickname? Papa Bear instead of Monty? Oooh, or we could just call you Daddy." Yami smirks at me as he struts past, a towel wrapped around his waist. We've just won our game against the Boston Revs, and we're all feeling pretty fucking good about how the season is going. And because today's was an early afternoon game, I'm looking forward to a quiet evening with my girl.

I pretend to consider his suggestions. "If only I was older, I would make a hot Zaddy."

"Too young for that," Orson calls out. It's good to hear him joking around again. He went through a shitty time last fall when his wife abruptly filed for divorce.

I shrug and give them all a grin. "Call me what you want. But you best believe I'm gonna be killing it with the dad jokes."

"Boys, cover up. Ladies coming in." Willow's loud voice carries from outside the locker room.

Everyone scrambles to make sure their bits are covered as Sin glowers at anyone who's taking too long. Willow struts in, followed by a couple of other women from the marketing department. Clapping her hands, she fixes us with a sharp stare.

"Alright. None of you here right now are rookies, so I expect you all to know the drill. We've had a good start to the season and no one has made any messes I needed to clean up. Let's keep it that way, okay? Don't do any stupid shit that I'm gonna have to deal with. If you find yourself tempted by stupid shit, stop and think WWWD."

"What would Willow do?" Yami says, scratching his head. "But Wills. You'll do just about anything!"

Sin slaps him upside the head, but it's Willow he should be scared of. Her eyes are glinting. "That's right, Yami. I will. Don't mess with me this season."

You can sense everyone's balls shriveling. Willow Lawson is a powerful woman, and now, as head of the media relations team, she's even more intense. I respect the hell out of her and we get along great. Probably helps that I've never done anything to cause an issue with the press.

"Moving on." She raises her voice. "Sheena and Gurdeep are here to shoot some B-roll for socials and some short-form content. We're stepping up our game in connecting with the fans, which means you all need to put on your best smiles and get ready to charm the camera."

There are nods and sounds of acknowledgment as she looks around the room. Once satisfied, Willow saunters over to Sin and presses a kiss to his cheek before leaving the locker room. Her two colleagues stay behind and make their way over to certain players to get to work while the rest of us try to get dressed without flashing them.

When it looks like I'm getting out of here without having

to do any media shit, I make a hasty exit and head through the building to find Lark.

She moved into my place this past weekend. Despite our having a game that evening, most of the team showed up to help, and we were done in record time. Having her officially living with me is fucking awesome. Seeing her toothbrush next to mine, our laundry mixed together in the hamper, hell, even her long blond hairs clogging the shower drain makes me smile.

I find her attempting to reach something on a high shelf in her treatment room, her adorable grumble of frustration causing a grin to spread across my face.

"Need some help, Birdie?" I ask, walking over and nuzzling her neck.

"Yes, I do," she gripes. "Your darn baby is getting in my way."

I wrap my arms around her, cradling the growing bump. I still marvel at the miracle every time I see her. "My baby, huh? It's half yours, you know. You have to take some accountability for this."

Turning in my arms, Lark tries hard to hide her smile under a glare. "Right now, it's all yours. This belly is getting in the way of everything. How am I going to work when I'm the size of a house?"

"We'll figure it out." I press a kiss to her lips, waiting until I feel her soften under me. Even now, months later, it amazes me that I get to do this. I get to touch her, kiss her, and have her whenever I want. She's mine. The only woman I've ever wanted.

"Now, will you let me help so we can go home and I can rub your feet while you eat that disgusting olive crap?" I tease, hoping that mentioning her latest bizarre pregnancy craving will make her smile. She's halfway through her pregnancy, just shy of twenty-one weeks, and the belly is definitely growing on her small frame. I only made the mistake of asking if it could be twins once, and I know better than to mention that possibility again, thanks to the death glare it earned me.

"Tapenade is not crap. It's delicious," she replies. "But yes. Please help me get this put away. I'm exhausted." She emphasizes this with a yawn.

I take the boxes of supplies and get them up on the shelf easily while she grabs her things. Then, taking her hand, we head down the hall to the parking lot. The drive home is quiet, with Lark dozing in the passenger seat. The midwife said it's normal to fatigue quickly, especially with a physically demanding job like Lark's.

We've talked about her cutting back on travel and possibly even working reduced hours as we get further on in the pregnancy, but right now, my stubborn Birdie is determined to do as much as possible. She did, at least, agree for Mattias to hire someone early for her maternity leave so they can work together for a while, hopefully lightening Lark's load. Personally, I can't wait for that person to start. As much as I want Lark with me, traveling to the away games and at the stadium every day, it's hard seeing the toll it's taking on her pregnant body.

When we get home, I drop a kiss to her head. "Go take a shower. I'll order some Thai for dinner."

She nods and pads off down the hallway to the bedroom. I hear the water turn on and pick up my phone to sort out dinner. Once that's done, I scroll through my messages and emails.

There's a voicemail from my mom, asking me to call her back

when I have time. The food won't be here for another half hour, so I dial my parents' house phone.

"Hello?" my dad's deep voice answers. "Dan? Great game tonight, son."

"Thanks, Dad. I'm just returning Mom's call."

"Oh right. Hang on, let me get her."

I hear the clatter of him setting the phone down, the creak of his recliner chair being moved upright, and then his distant voice calling for Mom.

"Honey? Dan?" I hear her pick up the phone, probably the one in the kitchen, then Dad's back on the other one.

"Hey, Mom." I grin, picturing the two of them on separate phones. The way we used to talk before video calls were a thing.

"Hi, good job tonight. How are you doing? How's Lark and the baby?" she rattles off the questions at me, and I know perfectly well she wants me to answer the second one first.

"They're good. Lark's tired, but that's normal right now. She's in the shower, but if we're still talking when she's done, I know she'll come say hi." The relationship Lark and my mom are building is freaking adorable. Don't get me wrong, I'm glad she's mending fences with her own mother, but I have no doubt that no matter what happens there, Lark has a mom in Edith Montgomery.

"Of course, she's tired. She's growing a human. You sucked the life out of me for nine months, Daniel Montgomery. Make sure you're taking care of her properly. Water, healthy food, and plenty of rest."

"Yes, Mom," I reply dutifully. I hear the water shut off and know Lark will join me soon. "So, you wanted to talk about something?"

"Oh, yes. Howard? Do you want to tell him or should I?" Mom sounds weirdly excited.

Dad clears his throat. "I'll let you do it, honey."

"Well, I hope you and Lark are prepared to see a lot more of us." She pauses, I guess for dramatic effect? At that moment, Lark wanders out of the bedroom, toweling off her hair. She sits beside me, and I mouth *my parents* to her before putting the call on speaker.

"Mom? Dad? Sorry to interrupt the announcement, but Lark's here now. I put you on speaker."

"Hi," she says into the phone. "What announcement?"

"I was just about to tell Dan. But this is perfect, you can both hear at the same time." Mom clears her throat. "We sold the store."

I leap off the couch, tugging at my hair. "What? How? Why? When?"

"Would you like to add in *where*?" My dad chuckles. "Take a breath, son. Is he pacing, Lark? He sounds like he's pacing."

She glances up at me, a worried expression on her face before she answers. "Um, not yet, Howard, but he is pulling at his hair."

"Daniel Dawson Montgomery, sit down and listen," Mom says sharply. "You've been on us to retire for years. I thought you'd be thrilled with this news."

"I am, Mom, but I'm allowed to be surprised. I thought you couldn't retire because the shop wouldn't go for enough money with the current market?"

"Turns out, we were wrong," Dad interjects, then laughs.

"We got double what we were told it was valued at two years ago. Don't worry about us, son, we've got more money than we know what to do with. We've already put a down payment on an apartment closer to the city."

"And I finally convinced your dad to buy one of those fancy camper vans so we can tour the continent," Mom pipes in. "See you play in all those cities we've never been to. Oh, we could even come south for spring training next year, so Lark and the baby have somewhere to stay."

"That's a lovely idea, Edith," Lark says, raising her eyebrows at me. I finally sink down onto the couch and she takes my hand, giving it a squeeze. "We're both thrilled for you. It's just a bit of a shock, I think. But a good one, truly."

I clear my throat. "Yeah, it's great news. Sorry, you just took me by surprise, you know? I had this whole plan to convince you to retire next year once I secured my contract."

"Oh, Daniel," Mom murmurs. "Honey, it was never your job to take care of us like that."

"I know, but I wanted to. I wanted you to know you were taken care of, and that you didn't have to work so hard all the time."

There's a beat of silence before my Dad's voice, gruff and emotional, comes down the line. "You're a good man, Dan. I'm proud of you. And thank you. But now you can focus on your family and let us be the doting grandparents."

Lark leans against my arm, and I sigh into the top of her head. A weight lifts from my shoulders. A weight I expected to carry for many more months.

We finish up the conversation with my parents when my

phone beeps with the notification that our food has arrived. After saying goodbye, I pop downstairs to get it while Lark sets up for dinner.

When I get back to the apartment, she meets me at the door, taking the bag to set it down, then wrapping her arms around my neck.

"You're still going to get an amazing contract at the end of the season. Because you are an amazing player and an even more amazing man. I love you, you know."

I let my head rest on hers, breathing in the sweet smell of her shampoo. There's nowhere on this earth that makes me happier or feel more at peace than right here in her arms.

She moves, tilting her head up to look at me. Love and mischief dance in her eyes. "We could always reheat dinner."

I raise my eyebrows quizzically. "Reheat? Why would we reheat?"

In response, her hands travel down my body to my belt buckle, which she slowly slides open. "Because I'd like an appetizer."

My grin tells her I knew exactly what she was getting at as I scoop her into my arms and walk to the bedroom.

"Only if I get to eat first."

Chapter Forty-Four

Lark

"Yes!" The dugout erupts in cheers as Kai throws another perfect strike into Dan's glove. My cheeks hurt from smiling so much, watching the two of them dominate the field. As our opponent switches batters, I turn back to the player who is currently on the bench, icing his shoulder.

"How's it feeling, Ben?"

He grimaces, then slowly rotates it. "Better. Now it's just my pride that's injured."

"You're allowed to fumble a catch now and then." I give him a sympathetic smile, hoping he doesn't get too down on himself. He's got a long career ahead, and there will be plenty of catches to make — and miss.

"Thanks, Lark." He stands up, handing me the ice pack. "I'm gonna get warmed up." He pauses and then frowns. "If I'm cleared?"

I nod and his frown turns into an expression of relief.

"Great."

"We'll keep an eye on him," Mattias says, coming up beside me. "But I'm betting it's just a bruise."

"Agreed. He had full range, just point tenderness. I think he'll be fine."

Together we watch the game play, wincing when the batter hits a beauty of a line drive off Kai's pitch. But our fielders are on it, with Rhett snatching up the ball and tossing it to Ronan at first for an easy out.

"It's not going to be the same around here without you," Mattias says casually, turning to lean his back against the railing. "But I'm glad the research team was willing to let you start late."

"Me too." And I am, happy that is, that I can start my internship in January. But I'll miss working with the team for those six months. By the time I'm finished, the season will be in full swing.

The top of the sixth inning ends with the other team scoring two runs, and our guys jog off the field with fierce determination to take back the lead with their at bats. Dan comes straight over to me, dropping a kiss to my forehead as his glove taps my protruding belly.

"Hey, babe. How's Wilson?"

"He'll be fine." I lift my head for a proper kiss. "You and Kai are doing great. How's your knee feeling?"

He gives me a grin. "Just fine, thanks to you."

For the last two weeks, his left knee had been aching slightly, but with a few targeted strength exercises and some acupuncture done by one of our other trainers, he's been feeling much better.

"All I did was nag you about doing the exercises," I tease, not bothering to hide my stare as he strips off his catching gear in preparation for being up to bat this inning. As he bends over to remove his leg pads, he peers back and catches my eyes trained on his butt. He gives it a wiggle, and I instantly blush.

"Go ahead and look all you want, Birdie." His voice catches the attention of a couple of the other guys.

It's Maverick who walks past and slaps Dan's butt, making me giggle.

"Stop shaking that ass and get your bat, Monty."

"Told you, we're calling him Daddy from now on," Kai chimes in, making my eyebrows raise.

Dan straightens and looks at me with a blush on his cheeks.

"Daddy?" I ask, folding my arms over my stomach.

His shoulders lift in a shrug. "I mean, I couldn't be Pops, that one's taken."

My smile softens at the mention of our retired pitcher, Rafe. He and Dan were always close.

Taking a step closer, I lift onto my toes so only he can hear me. "You make one hot DILF."

His groan is quiet, but it's what he whispers in my ear that has me clenching my thighs together.

"Do you have any idea how painful it is to have a hard-on inside a jock?"

I turn my head to whisper back, "Poor baby. I'll take care of you later, okay?"

He leans back with a grin. "Promise?"

I nod, licking my lips. "Promise."

Just then, the crowd erupts in cheers, and I realize we've missed the start of the inning. Mav must've had a great hit, seeing as he's racing for second by the time we reach the railing. He slides in with one arm outstretched, and the trainer side of me winces, hoping his recently healed clavicle didn't take the brunt of it. He seems to be fine as he stands up, but I'll check in with him when he makes it to home.

"Okay, I'm on deck. Love you." Dan kisses me again before putting on his helmet and jogging up the steps to the field. I watch him take his practice swings, only glancing away when our batter hits a ground ball and takes off, sprinting for first. He makes it just in time, and Maverick manages to make it home, having stolen third on a previous pitch.

I wait for him to come off the field before going over, watching closely for any signs of discomfort. Mav is one of the worst when it comes to admitting he's in pain.

"That was quite the slide," I say when he's finally close by. He glances at me, peeling off his helmet and replacing it with his cap.

"Yeah, shoulder's fine, though."

"Okay, good to hear. Mind if I still put you through a few moves once Dan's finished batting?"

All I get is a grunt of acknowledgment, but it's enough. I turn my attention to home plate, where Dan is in his batting stance, watching the pitcher. I hold my breath as he winds up. The ball goes flying and he doesn't move. The ump calls it a strike, and I curse quietly.

The next pitch comes and this time he swings, making contact. Unfortunately, it's a pop fly, easily caught by the second baseman, and Dan turns to jog into the dugout.

"Sorry, babe," I say when he reaches me.

His grimace tells me he's frustrated. "It happens."

Shifting back to Maverick, I raise my eyebrows and that's all it takes. He knows the drill, and we work through a couple quick checks of his shoulder. It doesn't take long before I'm satisfied he didn't do any damage with his slide.

"Oof," I say, grimacing myself when the baby decides to give a strong kick to my ribs. "Settle down, baby bird." I rub my stomach as Dan comes over, having heard my grunt.

"Everything okay?" he asks, running his hands over mine.

"Yeah, just your daughter waking up."

His face softens into a grin as he drops into a crouch to press his lips to my belly. "Hi, baby bird. Love you, kiddo."

Finding out we were having a little girl made Dan even more excited. That week, he showed me the Pinterest board he started for a nursery, filled with all kinds of baseball-themed items in nothing but purple and teal colours.

He stands up as there's another cheer, and we look to see our batter making it to second, bringing the previous one home.

"We're tied," I exhale. It's been a close game, which is always nerve-racking for everyone.

"Their pitcher is on fire," Dan admits, wrapping an arm around my shoulders as we watch the game. "His curveball is deadly."

Sure enough, that curveball strikes out our next player, ending the first half of the seventh inning. Which means...

En masse, every Tridents player and staff in the dugout comes over and crowds around me.

The voice on the loudspeakers announces the seventh inning stretch, and then music starts to play. Everyone who can reach my stomach places a hand or even a finger on it. And right on cue, our little girl starts to go crazy, flipping around, punching and kicking.

It doesn't feel great, but it is special the way everyone gets excited, wanting their chance to feel the baby enjoying the cherished tradition of "Take Me Out to the Ballgame." It just proves the idea that family isn't always about blood. It's about the people who love you, respect you, and support you.

It can look like many things, and for Dan and me, it's an entire baseball team and staff celebrating our daughter.

The players all raise their voices near the end of the song, something that started a few weeks ago when the team had the strongest second half of an inning ever after singing along to the final few words.

"For it's one, two, three strikes, you're out, at the old ball game!"

Chapter Forty-Five

Monty

"You realize you have to give her back to me eventually, right?"

I tuck my teeny-tiny daughter into my chest and turn away from Lark's hospital bed with a glare. "Not unless she's hungry. I can do everything else."

She chuckles, then winces, and I immediately feel guilty. Turning back, I gingerly sit on the edge of the bed.

"Fine, fine. I guess you need the oxytocin boost this little one is giving more than me."

She looks at me dryly as I transfer Stella into her mama's arms. "Gee, you think?"

Once my girls are settled, I lean back on the cramped hospital bed, resting my hand on Stella's back.

"You're amazing, you know that? I knew you were strong, powerful, and brave, but holy shit, Birdie. Watching you give birth, watching you bring our daughter into this world, I..." I choke up again.

Lark leans her head forward and kisses Stella's downy head before turning to look at me. "I couldn't have done it without you."

I give her a watery smile. "Yeah, you could have, because you can do anything. But I'm so happy and honoured I got to be here by your side."

"You did cut it a little close," she remarks, and this time, I'm the one wincing.

"Yeah, sorry 'bout that. You didn't exactly give me a lot of warning."

"Kind of hard to predict how fast these things will go."

"Still, waiting till the fifth inning to say anything?"

Stella lets out a little sound, and both of us immediately look down. I'm not sure if it's normal to be so laser-focused on such a tiny human being, but I swear, every time she moves or grunts or anything, the rest of the world falls away.

As if she's been a mom for a lot longer than less than twenty-four hours, Lark maneuvers our little girl into a nursing position. It takes a few tries, but soon, she latches on, and it's the most beautiful sight in the entire goddamn universe.

Lark leans her head back with a tired sigh. And she's got every right to be exhausted. I might have been in the middle of the last game of a three-game stretch when Mattias pulled me off the field and said Lark and my mom were headed to the hospital, but she's the one who went through a day and a half of labour pains at home before things ramped up to that point. Thank fuck we weren't traveling. I should have listened to my gut when it told me not to go to the game tonight. But she insisted, and with my mom promising to get in touch if anything happened, I reluctantly went.

I'll never forget the drive from the Tridents' stadium to the hospital. Willow drove me because there wasn't a chance in hell I'd be able to do it safely myself. Not with how nervous, excited, and terrified I was.

I got here just in time to hear Lark moaning her way through a fucking *intense* contraction, and from there, things moved at warp speed.

Our little one, Stella Marie Montgomery, was born just forty minutes after I arrived. Six pounds of squalling, scrunched-up beauty.

It was love at first sight.

"You made it and that's all that matters."

I kiss Lark's forehead, letting my lips linger against her skin. I never thought I could have this. A love so deep, so strong, and so consuming. But here I am, loving my girls with every fiber of my being.

"I'll always be here for you, Birdie. You and little bird. You're my whole life, you know that."

Lark tilts her chin up and we kiss. It's sweet, soft, and gentle. Mindful of the tiny human currently sucking on my girl's boob, I don't press in any deeper. No matter how much I crave feeling her in my arms.

A gentle knock on the door has us breaking apart. It slowly opens and my mom peers around the side. "Hi kids, are you up for some visitors?"

I look to Lark and she nods. "Sure, Mom," I say, getting up from the bed and taking a once again sleeping Stella so Lark can cover herself back up.

Mom and Dad are the first ones in. They've already met Stella, but Mom still coos over her while Dad gives Lark a gentle hug.

"Room for any more?"

Willow and Sin enter next, holding a teddy bear and a piece of paper. After quietly closing the door, Sin heads over to Lark while Willow makes grabby hands for the baby.

"Gimme that sweet girl."

I gingerly hand over my daughter, and Willow's face beams with happiness. "Oh Lark, she's gorgeous."

I glance over to the bed, just in time to see Sin hand Lark the piece of paper. "Peyton drew this for you. She says it's your family."

Lark bursts out in laughter, then instantly winces. "Dang it, I love it, but I don't want to laugh right now."

Well, now I want to know what's so funny. Moving to the bed, I look down at the paper and clap my hand over my mouth to muffle my snort of amusement.

"Uh, hey, Sin, does your daughter know what people look like?"

My teammate rolls his eyes. "Yeah. Apparently they all look like dicks."

Sure enough, Peyton has drawn three stick people. Except, instead of sticks for bodies, the shape is much more...twig and berries looking.

"Please thank her for us," Lark says, her eyes twinkling.

Another knock lands on the door, and Lark looks to it with her eyebrows raised. "Did someone put out a welcome sign or something?"

Willow immediately looks guilty. "Yeah, that might be my fault. When I got back from dropping Monty off earlier, I told the guys what time we were coming to visit. I think they want to meet our newest Tridents team member."

I walk over and open the door, and sure enough, Yami, Mav, and Darling are all standing there with hopeful grins.

"Sorry, I tried to tell them too many visitors would be a bad thing but they didn't listen."

Craning my neck around, I see Sadie walking up with two coffee cups. I reach for them, simultaneously glaring at the guys. "You are welcome, bringer of lifeblood. The rest of these yahoos can wait outside."

"C'mon, Monty, we wanna meet our girl."

Yami's whining isn't convincing me of shit. I let Sadie slip past me, but then my dad opens the door wider.

"We're heading out, son. Lark said your friends can come in. Your mom and I will go to your apartment and tidy up. Let us know if you need anything."

I pull him in for a hug. "Thanks, Dad."

After hugging my mom as well, I turn to the guys, folding my arms across my chest. "You will be quiet. You will not swear. You will not make Lark laugh. And I swear to God, if one of you wakes up my daughter, I will beat your ass."

They each nod, and I let them in. Lark is now sitting up, cradling her coffee in her hands. "Hey, guys," she says as one by one, they make their way over to give her a hug. Don't get me wrong, I love that my teammates all adore my girl and want to meet my daughter. But all I want right now is to go back to being alone with Lark and Stella in our own little bubble. Because when I see Willow hand my baby girl off to Yami, I have to clench my fists to prevent myself from taking her back.

"It's scary shit, isn't it? Seeing your kid, your flesh and blood, out there in the world."

I turn at Sin's quiet voice.

"Even when they're with people you know and trust, some instinct kicks in. *Must protect what's mine.* Makes you feel kinda caveman. But it gets easier when you remind yourself that the more people loving your kid, the better."

I exhale slowly, letting his words sink in. "So you mean that feeling like I want to rip her out of Yami's arms and kick everyone out is normal?"

Sin chuckles. "Yeah. Totally normal. And if you really want everyone out, I'll make it happen. But everyone here loves you, loves Lark, and loves your little girl. Just remember that."

I look at Lark, at the smile beaming across her face, as she talks with Sadie and Willow. Then at the guys who are all peering down at Stella, now cradled in Darling's arms. They've got the goofiest grins on their faces.

And something settles in me. Sin's right. More love is never a bad thing. Moving over to the bed, I sit down next to Lark again, lifting my arm so she can snuggle in.

I set my coffee down on the table next to the bed and use that hand to tilt her chin up to my face. "Thank you for making my dreams come true, Birdie. Even ones I didn't know I had."

Her hand comes up to cup my cheek. "I love you."

I smile and press a kiss to her lips, feeling hers turn up in response.

"I know."

EPILOGUE

Monty

3 years later

After I smile for the hundreds of cameras pointed my way, I hand off the trophy to Yami, who has just as many tears coming down his cheeks as I do.

"We did it, brother," he says, hoisting it over his head. "Woo!"

Damn right, we did.

With three years left in my career, I finally made it. The Vancouver Tridents are the league champions. And everyone I love is here to celebrate. Well, almost everyone.

Unfortunately, our daughter Stella, who I still call baby bird, has the flu and had to miss the game. But I know Lark's mom will have it on the TV.

Speaking of my wife, I finally get my eyes on her, winding her way through the crowd, a wide smile on her face. She was kept busy the entire game, as not a single one of us stubborn assholes wanted to sit out even a second of play, no matter how tired, sore, and bruised we were.

Closing the last few steps at a run, Lark leaps into my arms, wrapping her legs around my waist. "You did it!" she yells, only sort of into my ear. I spin her around before setting her down, grabbing her face in my hands and kissing her deeply.

We break apart when the voice of Sin and Willow's daughter Peyton reaches us.

"Congrats, Uncle Monty!" We turn as one and pull her in for a hug.

"Thanks, kiddo. Your dad was the real star."

Peyton rolls her eyes the way only a nine-year-old can. "He did okay, but it was Darling that got the winning run."

"It's a team sport," I chide gently, knowing the girl has a bit of a crush on our southern boy.

"I know," she admits before turning at her name being called by her grandmother.

As much as I love the kid, I'm glad to have her attention elsewhere so I can focus back on my girl. My wife. My love.

We were made for each other from day one. She just needed some time to catch up to me in realizing that.

But once she did, there was no stopping us from free-falling into love and happily ever after. There's nothing better than waking up every morning with her in my arms.

The life we've made, it's more than I ever thought I'd have. It's more than I could ever dream of.

"Hey, earth to Dan."

I blink at Lark's hand waving in my face. "Sorry, Birdie. Did you say something?"

"No," she replies with a soft smile. "You just looked lost in thought."

I lean down and squeeze her tightly. "Just thinking about

how damn lucky I am."

"It's not luck when you play a good game." She laughs.

I kiss her deeply before replying, "I'm not talking about the game. I'm talking about you."

The look of love she gives me is better than any championship. "I'm the lucky one. Lucky you never gave up on me and never stopped loving me." She kisses me this time, and for a few seconds, the noise and the crowd disappears. It's just us.

Until two hands are on my shoulders and Darling's southern accent is in my ear. "How 'bout that, Monty! Champions!"

I turn to see him grinning at us. He moves to drape his arms over our shoulders, making his way between us.

"That last run, Darling, that was amazing," Lark says, leaning into his side affectionately. Darling's face lights up as he steps forward, his arms dropping from our shoulders.

"Yeah, thanks, Lark." We're quickly forgotten as he walks toward the woman coming our way with a wide smile.

I pull Lark in front of me and drop a kiss to her head as we watch the two of them kiss. Now that was an interesting time, watching Darling fumble around as they tried to figure their shit out.

The crowd has started to thin as players and staff clear from the field. I don't want to go. I don't want this night to ever end, even though a part of me is anxious to get back and check on Stella.

"Hey, Birdie." I lean down, squeezing her even tighter into my chest. "Wanna go make out in a storage closet with me?"

She slaps my arm and laughs. "No! You're nuts."

"Nuts for you, maybe."

"Oh my God, stop." She turns in my arms, looping hers around my neck. "No storage closets." She slaps my stomach, pushing me away with a laugh.

I step back, running my hands down my body. "What, you don't want all this delicious dad bod goodness?"

It's a good thing most of the press has left so they don't hear Lark's snort of amusement.

"You don't have a dad bod, Dan. Far from it."

I nod sagely and take her hand to lead her off the field. "You're right, it's far more of a father figure." I bend over and kiss the side of her head. "Something I never imagined I'd be until you finally admitted your love for me."

"You mean until the condom slipped," she replies dryly, but her eyes are full of love.

"That, too," I agree as we reach the dugout. I jog down the steps first and turn to face her, placing my hands on her hips. "Hey, I love you."

She leans into my hands, letting me lift her down the stairs as she kisses the tip of my nose.

"I know."

You know you want a sneak peek into Monty and Lark's future... Kids, babies, puppies oh my! Grab it by scanning this QR code.

Acknowledgements

This was probably the book I have been the most nervous and excited to publish. Writing a story with a controversial plot point like an unplanned pregnancy is risky, but I'm glad I took the chance and I hope I did it justice. Thank you to Katie D for sparking the idea for it!

Monty and Lark would not be who they are without the incredible plotting help from my coach Nancy, always helpful feedback from Kelly, Carolina and Jess, and the editing prowess of Chris and Andrea. I owe you all for making my work shine.

Alex, Theresa, Chelle, thank you for keeping me sane and somewhat on task... I don't think I can write a book without you.

And to the husband and kiddos. Your love and patience keeps me going.

XOXO Julia

About Julia Jarrett

Julia Jarrett is a busy mother of two boys, a happy wife to her real-life book boyfriend and the owner of two rescue dogs, one from Guatemala and another one from Taiwan. She lives on the West Coast of Canada and when she isn't writing contemporary romance novels full of relatable heroines and swoon-worthy heroes, she's probably drinking tea (or wine) and reading.

For a complete listing of Julia Jarrett books please visit www.authorjuliajarrett.com/books

Follow Julia:
Instagram @juliajarrettauthor
Facebook Reader Group: Julia Jarrett's Nutty Muffins
TikTok @julia.jarrett.author

Printed in Great Britain
by Amazon